CATHOLIC
SUNDAY AND DAILY MASS REA
2025

CATHOLIC SUNDAY AND DAILY MASS READINGS FOR 2025 WITH
THE PRINCIPAL CELEBRATIONS OF THE LITURGICAL YEAR C, 2025

Compiled by

Catholic Lectionary Publishers

© *2025 Catholic Lectionary Publishers.*
Published with the authority of the Committee on Divine Worship, United States Conference of Catholic Bishops.
Excerpts from the *New American Bible for Use in the Dioceses in the United States of America.* Used with permission. All rights reserved. No part of this text may be reproduced by any means without permission in writing from the copyright owner.

Excerpts from the *Lectionary for Mass for Use in the Dioceses of the United States of America, second typical edition* © 2001, 1998, 1997, 1986, 1970 Confraternity of Christian Doctrine, Inc., Washington, DC. Used with permission. All rights reserved. No portion of this text may be reproduced by any means without permission in writing from the copyright owner.

The English translation of some Psalm responses, some Alleluia and Gospel verses, and the Lenten Gospel Acclamations, some Summaries, and the Titles and Conclusion of the Readings, from the Lectionary for Mass © 1968, 1981, 1997, International Committee on English in the Liturgy, Inc., Washington, D.C. All rights reserved.

The poetic English translation of the sequences of the Roman Missal are taken from the Roman Missal approved by the National Conference of Catholic Bishops of the United States © 1964 by the National Catholic Welfare Conference, Inc. All rights reserved.

CONTENTS

Section A

PRINCIPAL CELEBRATIONS OF THE LITURGICAL YEAR C, 2025 - - - - 4

Section B

SUNDAY AND DAILY MASS READINGS FOR 2025 - - - - - - - - 5

- JANUARY - - - - - - - - - - - - - - - - - - 5 - 53
- FEBRUARY - - - - - - - - - - - - - - - - - 53 - 101
- MARCH - - - - - - - - - - - - - - - - - - 102 - 155
- APRIL - - - - - - - - - - - - - - - - - - 155 - 233
- MAY - - - - - - - - - - - - - - - - - - - 234 - 280
- JUNE - - - - - - - - - - - - - - - - - - - 280 - 334
- JULY - - - - - - - - - - - - - - - - - - - 334 - 384
- AUGUST - - - - - - - - - - - - - - - - - - 385 - 435
- SEPTEMBER - - - - - - - - - - - - - - - - - 435 - 480
- OCTOBER - - - - - - - - - - - - - - - - - - 481 - 525
- NOVEMBER - - - - - - - - - - - - - - - - - 525 - 577
- DECEMBER - - - - - - - - - - - - - - - - - 577 - 640

SECTION A
PRINCIPAL CELEBRATIONS OF THE LITURGICAL YEAR C, 2025

CELEBRATIONS	DATE
First Sunday of Advent, Year C	December 1, 2024
Ash Wednesday	March 5, 2025
Easter Sunday	April 20, 2025
The Ascension of the Lord	June 1, 2025
Pentecost Sunday	June 8, 2025
The Most Holy Body and Blood of Christ (*Corpus Christi*)	June 22, 2025
First Sunday of Advent, Year A	November 30, 2025

SECTION B
SUNDAY AND DAILY MASS READINGS 2025
JANUARY 2025
Wednesday January 1, 2025
Solemnity of Blessed Virgin Mary, Mother of God

First Reading: Numbers 6:22-27
22 The LORD said to Moses: 23 "Speak to Aaron and his sons and tell them: This is how you shall bless the Israelites. Say to them:
24 The LORD bless you and keep you!
25 The LORD let his face shine upon you, and be gracious to you!
26 The LORD look upon you kindly and give you peace!
27 So shall they invoke my name upon the Israelites, and I will bless them."

Responsorial Psalm: Psalms 67:2-3, 5, 6, 8.
R. (2a) May God bless us in his mercy.
2 May God have pity on us and bless us;
    may he let his face shine upon us.
3 So may your way be known upon earth;
    among all nations, your salvation.
R. May God bless us in his mercy.
5 May the nations be glad and exult
    because you rule the peoples in equity;
    the nations on the earth you guide.
R. May God bless us in his mercy.
6 May the peoples praise you, O God;
    may all the peoples praise you!
8 May God bless us,
    and may all the ends of the earth fear him!
R. May God bless us in his mercy.

Second Reading: Galatians 4:4-7
Brothers and sisters: 4 When the fullness of time had come, God sent his Son, born of a woman, born under the law, 5 to ransom those under the law, so that we might receive adoption as sons. 6 As proof that you are sons, God sent the Spirit of his Son into our hearts, crying out, "Abba, Father!" 7 So you are no longer a slave but a son, and if a son then also an heir, through God.

Alleluia: Hebrews 1:1-2
R. Alleluia, alleluia.
1 In the past God spoke to our ancestors
    through the prophets;
2 in these last days, he has spoken to us

through the Son.
R. Alleluia, alleluia.

Gospel: Luke 2:16-21

[16] The shepherds went in haste to Bethlehem and found Mary and Joseph, and the infant lying in the manger. [17] When they saw this, they made known the message that had been told them about this child. [18] All who heard it were amazed by what had been told them by the shepherds. [19] And Mary kept all these things, reflecting on them in her heart. [20] Then the shepherds returned, glorifying and praising God for all they had heard and seen, just as it had been told to them.

[21] When eight days were completed for his circumcision, he was named Jesus, the name given him by the angel before he was conceived in the womb.

Thursday January 2, 2025

Memorial of Saints Basil the Great and Gregory Nazianzen, Bishops and Doctors

First Reading: 1 John 2:22-28

Beloved: [22] Who is the liar? Whoever denies that Jesus is the Christ. Whoever denies the Father and the Son, this is the antichrist. [23] Anyone who denies the Son does not have the Father, but whoever confesses the Son has the Father as well.

[24] Let what you heard from the beginning remain in you. If what you heard from the beginning remains in you, then you will remain in the Son and in the Father. [25] And this is the promise that he made us: eternal life. [26] I write you these things about those who would deceive you. [27] As for you, the anointing that you received from him remains in you, so that you do not need anyone to teach you. But his anointing teaches you about everything and is true and not false; just as it taught you, remain in him.

[28] And now, children, remain in him, so that when he appears we may have confidence and not be put to shame by him at his coming.

Responsorial Psalm: Psalms 98:1, 2-3AB, 3CD-4

R. *(3cd)* **All the ends of the earth have seen the
saving power of God.**

[1] Sing to the LORD a new song,
for he has done wondrous deeds;
His right hand has won victory for him,
his holy arm.

**R. All the ends of the earth have seen the saving
power of God.**

[2] The LORD has made his salvation known:
in the sight of the nations he has revealed
his justice.
[3AB] He has remembered his kindness and his
faithfulness
toward the house of Israel.

R. All the ends of the earth have seen the saving power of God.

³ᶜᴰAll the ends of the earth have seen
    the salvation by our God.
⁴ Sing joyfully to the LORD, all you lands;
    break into song; sing praise.

R. All the ends of the earth have seen the saving power of God.

Alleluia: Hebrews 1:1-2
R. Alleluia, alleluia.
¹ In times past, God spoke to our ancestors
    through the prophets:
² in these last days, he has spoken to us
    through the Son.
R. Alleluia, alleluia.

Gospel: John 1:19-28

¹⁹This is the testimony of John. When the Jews from Jerusalem sent priests and Levites to him to ask him, "Who are you?" ²⁰ he admitted and did not deny it, but admitted, "I am not the Christ." ²¹So they asked him, "What are you then? Are you Elijah?" And he said, "I am not." "Are you the Prophet?" He answered, "No." ²²So they said to him, "Who are you, so we can give an answer to those who sent us? What do you have to say for yourself?" ²³He said: "I am *the voice of one crying out in the desert, 'Make straight the way of the Lord,'* as Isaiah the prophet said." ²⁴Some Pharisees were also sent. ²⁵They asked him, "Why then do you baptize if you are not the Christ or Elijah or the Prophet?" ²⁶John answered them, "I baptize with water; but there is one among you whom you do not recognize, ²⁷the one who is coming after me, whose sandal strap I am not worthy to untie." ²⁸This happened in Bethany across the Jordan, where John was baptizing.

Friday January 3, 2025
Friday of the Christmas Weekday
First Reading: 1 John 2:29-3:6

²⁹If you consider that God is righteous, you also know that everyone who acts in righteousness is begotten by him.

¹See what love the Father has bestowed on us that we may be called the children of God. Yet so we are. The reason the world does not know us is that it did not know him. ²Beloved, we are God's children now; what we shall be has not yet been revealed. We do know that when it is revealed we shall be like him, for we shall see him as he is. ³Everyone who has this hope based on him makes himself pure, as he is pure.

⁴Everyone who commits sin commits lawlessness, for sin is lawlessness. ⁵You know that he was revealed to take away sins, and in him there is no sin. ⁶No one who remains in him sins; no one who sins has seen him or known him.

Responsorial Psalm: Psalms 98:1, 3CD-4,5-6

R. *(3cd)* *All the ends of the earth have seen the saving power of God.*

¹ Sing to the LORD a new song,
    for he has done wondrous deeds;
His right hand has won victory for him,
    his holy arm.

R. *All the ends of the earth have seen the saving power of God.*

³ᶜᴰ All the ends of the earth have seen
    the salvation by our God.
⁴ Sing joyfully to the LORD, all you lands;
    break into song; sing praise.

R. *All the ends of the earth have seen the saving power of God.*

⁵ Sing praise to the LORD with the harp,
    with the harp and melodious song.
⁶ With trumpets and the sound of the horn
    sing joyfully before the King, the LORD.

R. *All the ends of the earth have seen the saving power of God.*

Alleluia: John 1:14A, 12A

R. Alleluia, alleluia.

¹⁴ᴬ The Word of God became flesh and dwelt
    among us.
¹²ᴬ To those who accepted him
he gave power to become the children of
    God.

R. Alleluia, alleluia.

Gospel: John 1:29-34

²⁹John the Baptist saw Jesus coming toward him and said, "Behold, the Lamb of God, who takes away the sin of the world. ³⁰He is the one of whom I said, 'A man is coming after me who ranks ahead of me because he existed before me.' ³¹I did not know him, but the reason why I came baptizing with water was that he might be made known to Israel." ³²John testified further, saying, "I saw the Spirit come down like a dove from the sky and remain upon him. ³³I did not know him, but the one who sent me to baptize with water told me, 'On whomever you see the Spirit come down and remain, he is the one who will baptize with the Holy Spirit.' ³⁴Now I have seen and testified that he is the Son of God."

Saturday January 4, 2025
Memorial of Saint Elizabeth Ann Seton, Religious

First Reading: 1 John 3:7-10

7Children, let no one deceive you. The person who acts in righteousness is righteous, just as he is righteous. 8Whoever sins belongs to the Devil, because the Devil has sinned from the beginning. Indeed, the Son of God was revealed to destroy the works of the Devil. 9No one who is begotten by God commits sin, because God's seed remains in him; he cannot sin because he is begotten by God. 10In this way, the children of God and the children of the Devil are made plain; no one who fails to act in righteousness belongs to God, nor anyone who does not love his brother.

Responsorial Psalm: Psalms 98:1, 7-8, 9

R. *(3cd)* **All the ends of the earth have seen the saving power of God.**

1 Sing to the LORD a new song,
   for he has done wondrous deeds;
His right hand has won victory for him,
   his holy arm.

R. **All the ends of the earth have seen the saving power of God.**

7 Let the sea and what fills it resound,
   the world and those who dwell in it;
8 Let the rivers clap their hands,
   the mountains shout with them for joy
      before the LORD.

R. **All the ends of the earth have seen the saving power of God.**

9 The LORD comes;
   he comes to rule the earth;
He will rule the world with justice
   and the peoples with equity.

R. **All the ends of the earth have seen the saving power of God.**

Alleluia: Hebrews 1:1-2

R. Alleluia, alleluia.
1 In the past God spoke to our ancestors
      through the prophets:
2 in these last days, he has spoken to us
      through the Son.
R. Alleluia, alleluia.

Gospel: John 1:35-42

³⁵John was standing with two of his disciples, ³⁶and as he watched Jesus walk by, he said, "Behold, the Lamb of God." ³⁷The two disciples heard what he said and followed Jesus. ³⁸Jesus turned and saw them following him and said to them, "What are you looking for?" They said to him, "Rabbi" (which translated means Teacher), "where are you staying?" ³⁹He said to them, "Come, and you will see." So they went and saw where he was staying, and they stayed with him that day. It was about four in the afternoon. ⁴⁰Andrew, the brother of Simon Peter, was one of the two who heard John and followed Jesus. ⁴¹He first found his own brother Simon and told him, "We have found the Messiah," which is translated Christ. ⁴²Then he brought him to Jesus. Jesus looked at him and said, "You are Simon the son of John; you will be called Cephas," which is translated Peter.

Sunday January 5, 2025
Solemnity of the Epiphany of the Lord

First Reading: Isaiah 60:1-6

¹Rise up in splendor, Jerusalem! Your light
    has come,
  the glory of the Lord shines upon you.
²See, darkness covers the earth,
  and thick clouds cover the peoples;
but upon you the LORD shines,
  and over you appears his glory.
³ Nations shall walk by your light,
  and kings by your shining radiance.
⁴Raise your eyes and look about;
  they all gather and come to you:
your sons come from afar,
  and your daughters in the arms of their
    nurses.

⁵ Then you shall be radiant at what you see,
  your heart shall throb and overflow,
for the riches of the sea shall be emptied out
    before you,
  the wealth of nations shall be brought to
    you.
⁶Caravans of camels shall fill you,
  dromedaries from Midian and Ephah;
all from Sheba shall come
  bearing gold and frankincense,
  and proclaiming the praises of the LORD.

Responsorial Psalm: Psalms 72:1-2, 7-8, 10-11, 12-13.
R. (cf. 11) Lord, every nation on earth will adore you.
¹ O God, with your judgment endow the king,

and with your justice, the king's son;
² He shall govern your people with justice
and your afflicted ones with judgment.
R. Lord, every nation on earth will adore you.
⁷ Justice shall flower in his days,
and profound peace, till the moon be no more.
⁸ May he rule from sea to sea,
and from the River to the ends of the earth.
R. Lord, every nation on earth will adore you.
¹⁰ The kings of Tarshish and the Isles shall offer gifts;
the kings of Arabia and Seba shall bring tribute.
¹¹ All kings shall pay him homage,
all nations shall serve him.
R. Lord, every nation on earth will adore you.
¹² For he shall rescue the poor when he cries out,
and the afflicted when he has no one to help him.
¹³ He shall have pity for the lowly and the poor;
the lives of the poor he shall save.
R. Lord, every nation on earth will adore you.

Second Reading: Ephesians 3:2-3A, 5-6

Brothers and sisters: ²You have heard of the stewardship of God's grace that was given to me for your benefit, ³ᴬnamely, that the mystery was made known to me by revelation. ⁵It was not made known to people in other generations as it has now been revealed to his holy apostles and prophets by the Spirit: ⁶that the Gentiles are coheirs, members of the same body, and copartners in the promise in Christ Jesus through the gospel.

Alleluia: Matthew 2:2
R. Alleluia, alleluia.
² We saw his star at its rising
and have come to do him homage.
R. Alleluia, alleluia.

Gospel: Matthew 2:1-12

¹When Jesus was born in Bethlehem of Judea, in the days of King Herod, behold, magi from the east arrived in Jerusalem, ²saying, "Where is the newborn king of the Jews? We saw his star at its rising and have come to do him homage." ³When King Herod heard this, he was greatly troubled, and all Jerusalem with him. ⁴Assembling all the chief priests and the scribes of the people, He inquired of them where the Christ was to be born. ⁵They said to him, "In Bethlehem of Judea, for thus it has been written through the prophet:
⁶*And you, Bethlehem, land of Judah,*
are by no means least among the rulers of
Judah;
since from you shall come a ruler,
who is to shepherd my people Israel."

⁷Then Herod called the magi secretly and ascertained from them the time of the star's appearance. ⁸He sent them to Bethlehem and said, "Go and search diligently for the child. When you have found him, bring me word, that I too may go and do him homage." ⁹After their audience with the king they set out. And behold, the star that they had seen at its rising preceded them, until it came and stopped over the place where the child was. ¹⁰They were overjoyed at seeing the star, ¹¹and on entering the house they saw the child with Mary his mother. They prostrated themselves and did him homage. Then they opened their treasures and offered him gifts of gold, frankincense, and myrrh. ¹²And having been warned in a dream not to return to Herod, they departed for their country by another way.

Monday January 6, 2025
Memorial of Saint Andre Bessette

First Reading: 1 John 3:22-4:6

Beloved: ²² We receive from him whatever we ask, because we keep his commandments and do what pleases him. ²³ And his commandment is this: we should believe in the name of his Son, Jesus Christ, and love one another just as he commanded us. ²⁴ Those who keep his commandments remain in him, and he in them, and the way we know that he remains in us is from the Spirit whom he gave us.

¹ Beloved, do not trust every spirit but test the spirits to see whether they belong to God, because many false prophets have gone out into the world. ²This is how you can know the Spirit of God: every spirit that acknowledges Jesus Christ come in the flesh belongs to God, ³and every spirit that does not acknowledge Jesus does not belong to God. This is the spirit of the antichrist who, as you heard, is to come, but in fact is already in the world. ⁴You belong to God, children, and you have conquered them, for the one who is in you is greater than the one who is in the world. ⁵ They belong to the world; accordingly, their teaching belongs to the world, and the world listens to them. ⁶We belong to God, and anyone who knows God listens to us, while anyone who does not belong to God refuses to hear us. This is how we know the spirit of truth and the spirit of deceit.

Responsorial Psalm: Psalms 2:7BC-8, 10-12A

R. (8ab) *I will give you all the nations for an inheritance.*

7BC The LORD said to me, "You are my Son;
　　 this day I have begotten you.
8 Ask of me and I will give you
　　 the nations for an inheritance
　　 and the ends of the earth for your possession."

R. *I will give you all the nations for an inheritance.*

10 And now, O kings, give heed;
take warning, you rulers of the earth.
11 Serve the LORD with fear, and rejoice before him;
with trembling rejoice.

R. *I will give you all the nations for an inheritance.*

Alleluia: see. Matthew 4:23

R. Alleluia, alleluia.
23 Jesus proclaimed the Gospel of the Kingdom
and cured every disease among the people.
R. Alleluia, alleluia.

Gospel: Matthew 4:12-17, 23-25

12 When Jesus heard that John had been arrested, he withdrew to Galilee. 13 He left Nazareth and went to live in Capernaum by the sea, in the region of Zebulun and Naphtali, 14 that what had been said through Isaiah the prophet might be fulfilled:

15 *Land of Zebulun and land of Naphtali,
　　 the way to the sea, beyond the Jordan,
　　 Galilee of the Gentiles,
16 the people who sit in darkness have seen a
　　 great light,
on those dwelling in a land overshadowed by
　　 death
　　　 light has arisen.*

17 From that time on, Jesus began to preach and say, "Repent, for the Kingdom of heaven is at hand."

23 He went around all of Galilee, teaching in their synagogues, proclaiming the Gospel of the Kingdom, and curing every disease and illness among the people. 24 His fame spread to all of Syria, and they brought to him all who were sick with various diseases and racked with pain, those who were possessed, lunatics,

and paralytics, and he cured them. ²⁵And great crowds from Galilee, the Decapolis, Jerusalem, and Judea, and from beyond the Jordan followed him.

Tuesday January 7, 2025
Memorial of Saint Raymond of Penyafort, Priest

First Reading: 1 John 4:7-10

⁷Beloved, let us love one another, because love is of God; everyone who loves is begotten by God and knows God. ⁸Whoever is without love does not know God, for God is love. ⁹In this way the love of God was revealed to us: God sent his only-begotten Son into the world so that we might have life through him. ¹⁰In this is love: not that we have loved God, but that he loved us and sent his Son as expiation for our sins.

Responsorial Psalm: Psalms 72:1-2, 3-4, 7-8

R. (see 11) **Lord, every nation on earth will adore you.**
¹ O God, with your judgment endow the king,
    and with your justice, the king's son;
² He shall govern your people with justice
    and your afflicted ones with judgment.
R. Lord, every nation on earth will adore you.
³ The mountains shall yield peace for the people,
    and the hills justice.
⁴ He shall defend the afflicted among the people,
    save the children of the poor.
R. Lord, every nation on earth will adore you.
⁷ Justice shall flower in his days,
    and profound peace, till the moon be no more.
⁸ May he rule from sea to sea,
    and from the River to the ends of the earth.
R. Lord, every nation on earth will adore you.

Alleluia: Luke 4:18

R. Alleluia, alleluia.
¹⁸ The Lord has sent me to bring glad tidings to the poor
and to proclaim liberty to captives.
R. Alleluia, alleluia.

Gospel: Mark 6:34-44

[34] When Jesus saw the vast crowd, his heart was moved with pity for them, for they were like sheep without a shepherd; and he began to teach them many things. [35] By now it was already late and his disciples approached him and said, "This is a deserted place and it is already very late. [36] Dismiss them so that they can go to the surrounding farms and villages and buy themselves something to eat." [37] He said to them in reply, "Give them some food yourselves." But they said to him, "Are we to buy two hundred days' wages worth of food and give it to them to eat?" [38] He asked them, "How many loaves do you have? Go and see." And when they had found out they said, "Five loaves and two fish." [39] So he gave orders to have them sit down in groups on the green grass. [40] The people took their places in rows by hundreds and by fifties. [41] Then, taking the five loaves and the two fish and looking up to heaven, he said the blessing, broke the loaves, and gave them to his disciples to set before the people; he also divided the two fish among them all. [42] They all ate and were satisfied. [43] And they picked up twelve wicker baskets full of fragments and what was left of the fish. [44] Those who ate of the loaves were five thousand men.

Wednesday January 8, 2025
Wednesday after Epiphany Sunday

First Reading: 1 John 4:11-18

[11] Beloved, if God so loved us, we also must love one another. [12] No one has ever seen God. Yet, if we love one another, God remains in us, and his love is brought to perfection in us.

[13] This is how we know that we remain in him and he in us, that he has given us of his Spirit. [14] Moreover, we have seen and testify that the Father sent his Son as savior of the world. [15] Whoever acknowledges that Jesus is the Son of God, God remains in him and he in God. [16] We have come to know and to believe in the love God has for us.

God is love, and whoever remains in love remains in God and God in him. [17] In this is love brought to perfection among us, that we have confidence on the day of judgment because as he is, so are we in this world. [18] There is no fear in love, but perfect love drives out fear because fear has to do with punishment, and so one who fears is not yet perfect in love.

Responsorial Psalm: Psalms 72:1-2, 10, 12-13

R. (see 11) **Lord, every nation on earth will adore you.**

[1] O God, with your judgment endow the king,
   and with your justice, the king's son;
[2] He shall govern your people with justice
   and your afflicted ones with judgment.

R. Lord, every nation on earth will adore you.

[10] The kings of Tarshish and the Isles shall
      offer gifts;
   the kings of Arabia and Seba shall bring
      tribute.

R. Lord, every nation on earth will adore you.

[12] For he shall rescue the poor when he cries

>out,
>>and the afflicted when he has no one to
>>>help him.
¹³ He shall have pity for the lowly and the
>poor;
>>the lives of the poor he shall save.

R. Lord, every nation on earth will adore you.

Alleluia: see 1 Timothy 3:16
R. Alleluia, alleluia.
¹⁶ Glory to you, O Christ, proclaimed to the
>Gentiles.
Glory to you, O Christ, believed in
>throughout the world.
R. Alleluia, alleluia.

Gospel: Mark 6:45-52
⁴⁵After the five thousand had eaten and were satisfied, Jesus made his disciples get into the boat and precede him to the other side toward Bethsaida, while he dismissed the crowd. ⁴⁶And when he had taken leave of them, he went off to the mountain to pray. ⁴⁷When it was evening, the boat was far out on the sea and he was alone on shore. ⁴⁸Then he saw that they were tossed about while rowing, for the wind was against them. About the fourth watch of the night, he came toward them walking on the sea. He meant to pass by them. ⁴⁹But when they saw him walking on the sea, they thought it was a ghost and cried out. ⁵⁰They had all seen him and were terrified. But at once he spoke with them, "Take courage, it is I, do not be afraid!" ⁵¹He got into the boat with them and the wind died down. They were completely astounded. ⁵²They had not understood the incident of the loaves. On the contrary, their hearts were hardened.

Thursday January 9, 2025
Thursday after Epiphany Sunday
First Reading: 1 John 4:19-5:4
¹⁹Beloved, we love God because he first loved us. ²⁰If anyone says, "I love God," but hates his brother, he is a liar; for whoever does not love a brother whom he has seen cannot love God whom he has not seen. ²¹This is the commandment we have from him: Whoever loves God must also love his brother.

¹Everyone who believes that Jesus is the Christ is begotten by God, and everyone who loves the Father loves also the one begotten by him. ²In this way we know that we love the children of God when we love God and obey his commandments. ³For the love of God is this, that we keep his commandments. And his commandments are not burdensome, ⁴for whoever is begotten by God conquers the world. And the victory that conquers the world is our faith.

Responsorial Psalm: Psalms 72:1-2, 14 AND 15BC, 17

R. (see 11) Lord, every nation on earth will adore you.
[1] O God, with your judgment endow the king,
    and with your justice, the king's son;
[2] He shall govern your people with justice
    and your afflicted ones with judgment.
R. Lord, every nation on earth will adore you.
[14] From fraud and violence he shall redeem
    them,
    and precious shall their blood be in his sight.
[15BC] May they be prayed for continually;
    day by day shall they bless him.
R. Lord, every nation on earth will adore you.
[17] May his name be blessed forever;
    as long as the sun his name shall remain.
In him shall all the tribes of the earth be
    blessed;
    all the nations shall proclaim his
    happiness.
R. Lord, every nation on earth will adore you.

Alleluia: Luke 4:18

R. Alleluia, alleluia.
[18] The Lord has sent me to bring glad tidings to
    the poor
and to proclaim liberty to captives.
R. Alleluia, alleluia.

Gospel: Luke 4:14-22

[14] Jesus returned to Galilee in the power of the Spirit, and news of him spread throughout the whole region. [15] He taught in their synagogues and was praised by all.

    [16] He came to Nazareth, where he had grown up, and went according to his custom into the synagogue on the sabbath day. He stood up to read [17] and was handed a scroll of the prophet Isaiah. He unrolled the scroll and found the passage where it was written:

[18] *The Spirit of the Lord is upon me,*
    because he has anointed me
    to bring glad tidings to the poor.
He has sent me to proclaim liberty to captives
    and recovery of sight to the blind,
    to let the oppressed go free,
    [19] *and to proclaim a year acceptable to the*
    Lord.

[20]Rolling up the scroll, he handed it back to the attendant and sat down, and the eyes of all in the synagogue looked intently at him. [21]He said to them, "Today this Scripture passage is fulfilled in your hearing." [22]And all spoke highly of him and were amazed at the gracious words that came from his mouth.

Friday January 10, 2025
Friday after Epiphany Sunday

First Reading: 1 John 5:5-13

Beloved: [5]Who indeed is the victor over the world but the one who believes that Jesus is the Son of God?

[6]This is the one who came through water and Blood, Jesus Christ, not by water alone, but by water and Blood. The Spirit is the one who testifies, and the Spirit is truth. [7]So there are three who testify, [8]the Spirit, the water, and the Blood, and the three are of one accord. [9]If we accept human testimony, the testimony of God is surely greater. Now the testimony of God is this, that he has testified on behalf of his Son. [10]Whoever believes in the Son of God has this testimony within himself. Whoever does not believe God has made him a liar by not believing the testimony God has given about his Son. [11]And this is the testimony: God gave us eternal life, and this life is in his Son. [12]Whoever possesses the Son has life; whoever does not possess the Son of God does not have life.

[13]I write these things to you so that you may know that you have eternal life, you who believe in the name of the Son of God.

Responsorial Psalm: Psalms 147:12-13, 14-15, 19-20

R. [12a] Praise the Lord, Jerusalem. or: *R. Alleluia.*

[12] Glorify the LORD, O Jerusalem;
   praise your God, O Zion.
[13] For he has strengthened the bars of your
      gates;
   he has blessed your children within you.

R. Praise the Lord, Jerusalem. or: *R. Alleluia.*

[14] He has granted peace in your borders;
   with the best of wheat he fills you.
[15] He sends forth his command to the earth;
   swiftly runs his word!

R. Praise the Lord, Jerusalem. or: *R. Alleluia.*

[19] He has proclaimed his word to Jacob,
   his statutes and his ordinances to Israel.
[20] He has not done thus for any other nation;
   his ordinances he has not made known to
      them. Alleluia.

R. Praise the Lord, Jerusalem. or: *R. Alleluia.*

Alleluia: see Matthew 4:23

R. Alleluia, alleluia.
[23]Jesus proclaimed the Gospel of the Kingdom

and cured every disease among the people.
R. Alleluia, alleluia.

Gospel: Luke 5:12-16

¹²It happened that there was a man full of leprosy in one of the towns where Jesus was; and when he saw Jesus, he fell prostrate, pleaded with him, and said, "Lord, if you wish, you can make me clean." ¹³Jesus stretched out his hand, touched him, and said, "I do will it. Be made clean." And the leprosy left him immediately. ¹⁴Then he ordered him not to tell anyone, but "Go, show yourself to the priest and offer for your cleansing what Moses prescribed; that will be proof for them." ¹⁵The report about him spread all the more, and great crowds assembled to listen to him and to be cured of their ailments, ¹⁶but he would withdraw to deserted places to pray.

Friday January 11, 2025
Saturday after Epiphany Sunday

First Reading: 1 John 5:14-21

Beloved: ¹⁴We have this confidence in him that if we ask anything according to his will, he hears us. ¹⁵And if we know that he hears us in regard to whatever we ask, we know that what we have asked him for is ours. ¹⁶If anyone sees his brother sinning, if the sin is not deadly, he should pray to God and he will give him life. This is only for those whose sin is not deadly. There is such a thing as deadly sin, about which I do not say that you should pray. ¹⁷All wrongdoing is sin, but there is sin that is not deadly.

¹⁸We know that anyone begotten by God does not sin; but the one begotten by God he protects, and the Evil One cannot touch him. ¹⁹We know that we belong to God, and the whole world is under the power of the Evil One. ²⁰We also know that the Son of God has come and has given us discernment to know the one who is true. And we are in the one who is true, in his Son Jesus Christ. He is the true God and eternal life. ²¹Children, be on your guard against idols.

Responsorial Psalm: Psalms 149:1-2, 3-4, 5-6A AND 9B

*R. (see 4a) **The Lord takes delight in his people.** or: **R. Alleluia.***

¹ Sing to the LORD a new song
    of praise in the assembly of the faithful.
² Let Israel be glad in their maker,
    let the children of Zion rejoice in their
      king.

R. The Lord takes delight in his people.** or: **R. Alleluia.

³ Let them praise his name in the festive
    dance,
    let them sing praise to him with timbrel
      and harp.
⁴ For the LORD loves his people,
    and he adorns the lowly with victory.

R. The Lord takes delight in his people.** or: **R. Alleluia.

⁵ Let the faithful exult in glory;

        let them sing for joy upon their couches;
⁶ᴬ Let the high praises of God be in their
        throats.
   ⁹ᴮ This is the glory of all his faithful.
        Alleluia.
R. The Lord takes delight in his people. or: **R. Alleluia.**

Alleluia: Matthew 4:16
R. Alleluia, alleluia.
¹⁶ The people who sit in darkness have seen a
        great light,
on those dwelling in a land overshadowed
        by death
light has arisen.
R. Alleluia, alleluia.

Gospel: John 3:22-30
²²Jesus and his disciples went into the region of Judea, where he spent some time with them baptizing. ²³John was also baptizing in Aenon near Salim, because there was an abundance of water there, and people came to be baptized, ²⁴ for John had not yet been imprisoned. ²⁵Now a dispute arose between the disciples of John and a Jew about ceremonial washings. ²⁶So they came to John and said to him, "Rabbi, the one who was with you across the Jordan, to whom you testified, here he is baptizing and everyone is coming to him." ²⁷John answered and said, "No one can receive anything except what has been given from heaven. ²⁸You yourselves can testify that I said that I am not the Christ, but that I was sent before him. ²⁹The one who has the bride is the bridegroom; the best man, who stands and listens for him, rejoices greatly at the bridegroom's voice. So this joy of mine has been made complete. ³⁰He must increase; I must decrease."

Sunday January 12, 2025
Feast of the Baptism of the Lord

First Reading: Isaiah 42:1-4, 6-7
Thus says the LORD:

¹Here is my servant whom I uphold,
   my chosen one with whom I am
      pleased,
upon whom I have put my spirit;
   he shall bring forth justice to the
      nations,
²not crying out, not shouting,
   not making his voice heard in the
      street.
³A bruised reed he shall not break,
   and a smoldering wick he shall not

quench,
⁴until he establishes justice on the earth;
   the coastlands will wait for his
      teaching.

⁶I, the LORD, have called you for the
      victory of justice,
   I have grasped you by the hand;
I formed you, and set you
   as a covenant of the people,
   a light for the nations,
⁷to open the eyes of the blind,
   to bring out prisoners from
      confinement,
     and from the dungeon, those who
      live in darkness.

Or Isaiah 40:1-5, 9-11
¹Comfort, give comfort to my people,
   says your God.
²Speak tenderly to Jerusalem, and
      proclaim to her
   that her service is at an end,
   her guilt is expiated;
indeed, she has received from the hand
      of the LORD
   double for all her sins.

³A voice cries out:
In the desert prepare the way of the
      LORD!
   Make straight in the wasteland a
      highway for our God!
⁴Every valley shall be filled in,
   every mountain and hill shall be
      made low;
the rugged land shall be made a plain,
   the rough country, a broad valley.
⁵Then the glory of the LORD shall be
      revealed,
   and all people shall see it together;
   for the mouth of the LORD has spoken.

⁹Go up on to a high mountain,
   Zion, herald of glad tidings;

cry out at the top of your voice,
>   Jerusalem, herald of good news!
Fear not to cry out
>   and say to the cities of Judah:
>   Here is your God!

¹⁰Here comes with power
>   the Lord GOD,
>   who rules by a strong arm;
here is his reward with him,
>   his recompense before him.

¹¹Like a shepherd he feeds his flock;
>   in his arms he gathers the lambs,
carrying them in his bosom,
>   and leading the ewes with care.

Responsorial Psalm: Psalms 104:1B-2, 3-4, 24-25, 27-28, 29-30

R. ⁽¹⁾ O bless the Lord, my soul.

¹ᴮ O LORD, my God, you are great indeed!
>   You are clothed with majesty and glory,

² robed in light as with a cloak.
>   You have spread out the heavens like a tent-cloth;

R. O bless the Lord, my soul.

³You have constructed your palace upon the waters.
>   You make the clouds your chariot;
you travel on the wings of the wind.
>   ⁴You make the winds your messengers,
and flaming fire your ministers.

R. O bless the Lord, my soul.

²⁴ How manifold are your works, O LORD!
>   In wisdom you have wrought them all—
>   the earth is full of your creatures;

²⁵ the sea also, great and wide,
>   in which are schools without number
>   of living things both small and great.

R. O bless the Lord, my soul.

²⁷ They look to you to give them food in due time.
>   ²⁸When you give it to them, they gather it;
>   when you open your hand, they are filled with good things.

R. O bless the Lord, my soul.

²⁹If you take away their breath, they perish
>   and return to the dust.

³⁰When you send forth your spirit, they are
   created,
and you renew the face of the earth.
R. O bless the Lord, my soul.

Second Reading: Acts 10:34-38
³⁴Peter proceeded to speak to those gathered in the house of Cornelius, saying: "In truth, I see that God shows no partiality. ³⁵Rather, in every nation whoever fears him and acts uprightly is acceptable to him. ³⁶You know the word that he sent to the Israelites as he proclaimed peace through Jesus Christ, who is Lord of all, ³⁷what has happened all over Judea, beginning in Galilee after the baptism that John preached, ³⁸how God anointed Jesus of Nazareth with the Holy Spirit and power. He went about doing good and healing all those oppressed by the devil, for God was with him."

Or Titus 2:11-14; 3:4-7
Beloved: ¹¹The grace of God has appeared, saving all ¹²and training us to reject godless ways and worldly desires and to live temperately, justly, and devoutly in this age, ¹³as we await the blessed hope, the appearance of the glory of our great God and savior Jesus Christ, ¹⁴who gave himself for us to deliver us from all lawlessness and to cleanse for himself a people as his own, eager to do what is good.

⁴When the kindness and generous love of God our savior appeared, ⁵not because of any righteous deeds we had done but because of his mercy, He saved us through the bath of rebirth and renewal by the Holy Spirit, ⁶whom he richly poured out on us through Jesus Christ our savior, ⁷so that we might be justified by his grace and become heirs in hope of eternal life.

Alleluia: see Luke 3:16
R. Alleluia, alleluia.
¹⁶ John said: One mightier than I is coming;
he will baptize you with the Holy Spirit and
   with fire.
R. Alleluia, alleluia.

Gospel: Luke 3:15-16, 21-22
¹⁵The people were filled with expectation, and all were asking in their hearts whether John might be the Christ. ¹⁶John answered them all, saying, "I am baptizing you with water, but one mightier than I is coming. I am not worthy to loosen the thongs of his sandals. He will baptize you with the Holy Spirit and fire."

²¹After all the people had been baptized and Jesus also had been baptized and was praying, heaven was opened ²²and the Holy Spirit descended upon him in bodily form like a dove. And a voice came from heaven, "You are my beloved Son; with you I am well pleased."

Monday January 13, 2025
Monday of the First Week in Ordinary Time

First Reading: Hebrews 1:1-6

Brothers and sisters: [1]In times past, God spoke in partial and various ways to our ancestors through the prophets; [2]in these last days, he spoke to us through the Son, whom he made heir of all things and through whom he created the universe,

[3]*who is the refulgence of his glory,*
the very imprint of his being,
and who sustains all things by his mighty word.
When he had accomplished purification from sins,
he took his seat at the right hand of the Majesty on high,
[4]*as far superior to the angels*
as the name he has inherited is more excellent than theirs.

[5] For to which of the angels did God ever say:

You are my Son; this day I have begotten you?

Or again:
I will be a father to him, and he shall be a Son to me?

[6] And again, when he leads the first born into the world, he says:

Let all the angels of God worship him.

Responsorial Psalm: Psalms 97:1 AND 2B, 6 AND 7C, 9

R. (see 7c) **Let all his angels worship him.**
[1]The LORD is king; let the earth rejoice;
  let the many isles be glad.
  [2B]Justice and judgment are the foundation
    of his throne.
R. Let all his angels worship him.
[6]The heavens proclaim his justice,
  and all peoples see his glory.
[7C]Let all his angels worship him.
R. Let all his angels worship him.
[9]Because you, O LORD, are the Most High over
  all the earth,

exalted far above all gods.
R. Let all his angels worship him.

Alleluia: Mark 1:15
R. Alleluia, alleluia.
¹⁵ The Kingdom of God is at hand;
repent and believe in the Gospel.
R. Alleluia, alleluia.

Gospel: Mark 1:14-20
¹⁴After John had been arrested, Jesus came to Galilee proclaiming the Gospel of God: ¹⁵"This is the time of fulfillment. The Kingdom of God is at hand. Repent, and believe in the Gospel."

¹⁶As he passed by the Sea of Galilee, he saw Simon and his brother Andrew casting their nets into the sea; they were fishermen. ¹⁷Jesus said to them, "Come after me, and I will make you fishers of men." ¹⁸Then they left their nets and followed him. ¹⁹He walked along a little farther and saw James, the son of Zebedee, and his brother John. They too were in a boat mending their nets. ²⁰Then he called them. So they left their father Zebedee in the boat along with the hired men and followed him.

Tuesday January 14, 2025
Tuesday of the First Week in Ordinary Time
First Reading: Hebrews 2:5-12
⁵It was not to angels that God subjected the world to come, of which we are speaking. ⁶Instead, someone has testified somewhere:

What is man that you are mindful of him,
   or the son of man that you care for him?
⁷*You made him for a little while lower than the*
      angels;
   you crowned him with glory and honor,
⁸*subjecting all things under his feet.*

In "subjecting" all things to him, he left nothing not "subject to him." Yet at present we do not see "all things subject to him," ⁹but we do see Jesus "crowned with glory and honor" because he suffered death, he who "for a little while" was made "lower than the angels," that by the grace of God he might taste death for everyone.

¹⁰For it was fitting that he, for whom and through whom all things exist, in bringing many children to glory, should make the leader to their salvation perfect through suffering. ¹¹He who consecrates and those who are being consecrated all have one origin. Therefore, he is not ashamed to call them "brothers" ¹² saying:

I will proclaim your name to my brethren,
   in the midst of the assembly I will praise
      you.

Responsorial Psalm: Psalms 8:2AB AND 5, 6-7, 8-9

R. (see 7) **You have given your Son rule over the works of your hands.**

²ᴬᴮ O LORD, our Lord,
>how glorious is your name over all the earth!

⁵ What is man that you should be mindful of him,
>or the son of man that you should care for him?

R. You have given your Son rule over the works of your hands.

⁶ You have made him little less than the angels,
>and crowned him with glory and honor.

⁷ You have given him rule over the works of your hands,
>putting all things under his feet.

R. You have given your Son rule over the works of your hands.

⁸ All sheep and oxen,
>yes, and the beasts of the field,

⁹ The birds of the air, the fishes of the sea,
>and whatever swims the paths of the seas.

R. You have given your Son rule over the works of your hands.

Alleluia: see 1 Thessalonians 2:13

R. Alleluia, alleluia.
¹³ Receive the word of God, not as the word of men,
but as it truly is, the word of God.
R. Alleluia, alleluia.

Gospel: Mark 1:21-28

²¹Jesus came to Capernaum with his followers, and on the sabbath he entered the synagogue and taught. ²²The people were astonished at his teaching, for he taught them as one having authority and not as the scribes. ²³In their synagogue was a man with an unclean spirit; ²⁴he cried out, "What have you to do with us, Jesus of Nazareth? Have you come to destroy us? I know who you are–the Holy One of God!" ²⁵Jesus rebuked him and said, "Quiet! Come out of him!" ²⁶The unclean spirit convulsed him and with a loud cry came out of him. ²⁷All were amazed and asked one another, "What is this? A new teaching with authority. He commands even the

unclean spirits and they obey him." ²⁸His fame spread everywhere throughout the whole region of Galilee.

Wednesday January 15, 2025
Wednesday of First Week in Ordinary Time

First Reading: Hebrews 2:14-18

¹⁴Since the children share in blood and Flesh, Jesus likewise shared in them, that through death he might destroy the one who has the power of death, that is, the Devil, ¹⁵and free those who through fear of death had been subject to slavery all their life. ¹⁶Surely he did not help angels but rather the descendants of Abraham; ¹⁷therefore, he had to become like his brothers and sisters in every way, that he might be a merciful and faithful high priest before God to expiate the sins of the people. ¹⁸Because he himself was tested through what he suffered, he is able to help those who are being tested.

Responsorial Psalm: Psalms 105:1-2, 3-4, 6-7, 8-9

R. ⁽⁸ᵃ⁾ *The Lord remembers his covenant for ever.* or: *R. Alleluia.*

¹ Give thanks to the LORD, invoke his name;
   make known among the nations his
      deeds.
² Sing to him, sing his praise,
   proclaim all his wondrous deeds.

R. The Lord remembers his covenant for ever. or: *R. Alleluia.*

³ Glory in his holy name;
   rejoice, O hearts that seek the LORD!
⁴ Look to the LORD in his strength;
   seek to serve him constantly.

R. The Lord remembers his covenant for ever. or: *R. Alleluia.*

⁶ You descendants of Abraham, his servants,
   sons of Jacob, his chosen ones!
⁷ He, the LORD, is our God;
   throughout the earth his judgments
      prevail.

R. The Lord remembers his covenant for ever. or: *R. Alleluia.*

⁸ He remembers forever his covenant
   which he made binding for a thousand
      generations—
⁹ Which he entered into with Abraham
   and by his oath to Isaac.

R. The Lord remembers his covenant for ever. or: *R. Alleluia.*

Alleluia: John 10:27

R. Alleluia, alleluia.
²⁷ My sheep hear my voice, says the Lord.
I know them, and they follow me.
R. Alleluia, alleluia.

Gospel: Mark 1:29-39

²⁹On leaving the synagogue Jesus entered the house of Simon and Andrew with James and John. ³⁰Simon's mother-in-law lay sick with a fever. They immediately told him about her. ³¹He approached, grasped her hand, and helped her up. Then the fever left her and she waited on them.

³²When it was evening, after sunset, they brought to him all who were ill or possessed by demons. ³³The whole town was gathered at the door. ³⁴He cured many who were sick with various diseases, and he drove out many demons, not permitting them to speak because they knew him.

³⁵Rising very early before dawn, he left and went off to a deserted place, where he prayed. ³⁶Simon and those who were with him pursued him ³⁷and on finding him said, "Everyone is looking for you." ³⁸He told them, "Let us go on to the nearby villages that I may preach there also. For this purpose have I come." ³⁹So he went into their synagogues, preaching and driving out demons throughout the whole of Galilee.

Thursday January 16, 2025
Thursday of the First Week in Ordinary Time

First Reading: Hebrews 3:7-14

⁷The Holy Spirit says: *Oh, that today you would hear his voice,* ⁸*"Harden not your hearts as at the rebellion in the day of testing in the desert,* ⁹*where your ancestors tested and tried me and saw my works* ¹⁰*for forty years. Because of this I was provoked with that generation and I said, 'They have always been of erring heart, and they do not know my ways.'* ¹¹*As I swore in my wrath, 'They shall not enter into my rest.'"* ¹²Take care, brothers and sisters, that none of you may have an evil and unfaithful heart, so as to forsake the living God. ¹³Encourage yourselves daily while it is still "today," so that none of you may grow hardened by the deceit of sin. ¹⁴We have become partners of Christ if only we hold the beginning of the reality firm until the end.

Responsorial Psalm: Psalms 95:6-7C, 8-9, 10-11

R. ⁽⁸⁾ If today you hear his voice, harden not your hearts.

⁶ Come, let us bow down in worship;
   let us kneel before the LORD who made us.
⁷ᴬᴮᶜ For he is our God,
   and we are the people he shepherds, the
      flock he guides.

R. If today you hear his voice, harden not your hearts.

⁸ Oh, that today you would hear his voice:
   "Harden not your hearts as at Meribah,
   as in the day of Massah in the desert,
⁹ Where your fathers tempted me;
   they tested me though they had seen my
      works."

R. If today you hear his voice, harden not your

> *hearts.*

¹⁰ Forty years I was wearied of that generation;
   I said: "This people's heart goes astray,
   they do not know my ways."
¹¹ Therefore I swore in my anger:
   "They shall never enter my rest."

R. If today you hear his voice, harden not your hearts.

Alleluia: see Matthew 4:23
R. Alleluia, alleluia.
²³Jesus preached the Gospel of the Kingdom
and cured every disease among the people.
R. Alleluia, alleluia.

Gospel: Mark 1:40-45
⁴⁰A leper came to him and kneeling down begged him and said, "If you wish, you can make me clean." ⁴¹Moved with pity, he stretched out his hand, touched the leper, and said to him, "I do will it. Be made clean." ⁴²The leprosy left him immediately, and he was made clean. ⁴³Then, warning him sternly, he dismissed him at once. ⁴⁴Then he said to him, "See that you tell no one anything, but go, show yourself to the priest and offer for your cleansing what Moses prescribed; that will be proof for them." ⁴⁵The man went away and began to publicize the whole matter. He spread the report abroad so that it was impossible for Jesus to enter a town openly. He remained outside in deserted places, and people kept coming to him from everywhere.

Friday January 17, 2025
Memorial of Saint Anthony, Abbot

First Reading: Hebrews 4:1-5, 11
¹Let us be on our guard while the promise of entering into his rest remains, that none of you seem to have failed. ²For in fact we have received the Good News just as our ancestors did. But the word that they heard did not profit them, for they were not united in faith with those who listened. ³For we who believed enter into that rest, just as he has said:

As I swore in my wrath,
   "They shall not enter into my rest,"

and yet his works were accomplished at the foundation of the world. ⁴For he has spoken somewhere about the seventh day in this manner,

And God rested on the seventh day from all
   his works;

⁵and again, in the previously mentioned place,

They shall not enter into my rest.

¹¹ Therefore, let us strive to enter into that rest, so that no one may fall after the same example of disobedience.

Responsorial Psalm: Psalms 78:3 AND 4BC, 6C-7, 8
R. *(see 7b)* **Do not forget the works of the Lord!**
³ What we have heard and know,
    and what our fathers have declared to us,
       ⁴ᴮᶜ we will declare to the generation to come
The glorious deeds of the LORD and his
    strength.
R. Do not forget the works of the Lord!
⁶ᶜ That they too may rise and declare to their
    sons
    ⁷that they should put their hope in God,
And not forget the deeds of God
    but keep his commands.
R. Do not forget the works of the Lord!
⁸ And not be like their fathers,
    a generation wayward and rebellious,
A generation that kept not its heart steadfast
    nor its spirit faithful toward God.
R. Do not forget the works of the Lord!

Alleluia: Luke 7:16
R. Alleluia, alleluia.
¹⁶A great prophet has arisen in our midst
and God has visited his people.
R. Alleluia, alleluia.

Gospel: Mark 2:1-12
¹When Jesus returned to Capernaum after some days, it became known that he was at home. ²Many gathered together so that there was no longer room for them, not even around the door, and he preached the word to them. ³They came bringing to him a paralytic carried by four men. ⁴Unable to get near Jesus because of the crowd, they opened up the roof above him. After they had broken through, they let down the mat on which the paralytic was lying. ⁵When Jesus saw their faith, he said to him, "Child, your sins are forgiven." ⁶Now some of the scribes were sitting there asking themselves, ⁷"Why does this man speak that way? He is blaspheming. Who but God alone can forgive sins?" ⁸Jesus immediately knew in his mind what they were thinking to themselves, so he said, "Why are you thinking such things in your hearts? ⁹Which is easier, to say to the paralytic, 'Your sins are forgiven,' or to say, 'Rise, pick up your mat and walk'? ¹⁰But that you may know

that the Son of Man has authority to forgive sins on earth" [11]—he said to the paralytic, "I say to you, rise, pick up your mat, and go home." [12]He rose, picked up his mat at once, and went away in the sight of everyone. They were all astounded and glorified God, saying, "We have never seen anything like this."

Saturday January 18, 2025
Saturday of the First Week in Ordinary Time

First Reading: Hebrews 4:12-16

[12]The word of God is living and effective, sharper than any two-edged sword, penetrating even between soul and spirit, joints and marrow, and able to discern reflections and thoughts of the heart. [13]No creature is concealed from him, but everything is naked and exposed to the eyes of him to whom we must render an account.

[14]Since we have a great high priest who has passed through the heavens, Jesus, the Son of God, let us hold fast to our confession. [15]For we do not have a high priest who is unable to sympathize with our weaknesses, but one who has similarly been tested in every way, yet without sin. [16]So let us confidently approach the throne of grace to receive mercy and to find grace for timely help.

Responsorial Psalm: Psalms 19:8, 9, 10, 15

R. (see John 6:63c) *Your words, Lord, are Spirit and life.*

[8]The law of the LORD is perfect,
　　refreshing the soul;
The decree of the LORD is trustworthy,
　　giving wisdom to the simple.

R. Your words, Lord, are Spirit and life.

[9] The precepts of the LORD are right,
　　rejoicing the heart;
The command of the LORD is clear,
　　enlightening the eye.

R. Your words, Lord, are Spirit and life.

[10] The fear of the LORD is pure,
　　enduring forever;
The ordinances of the LORD are true,
　　all of them just.

R. Your words, Lord, are Spirit and life.

[15] Let the words of my mouth and the thought
　　　of my heart
　　find favor before you,
　　O LORD, my rock and my redeemer.

R. Your words, Lord, are Spirit and life.

Alleluia: Luke 4:18

R. Alleluia, alleluia.

[18] The Lord sent me to bring glad tidings to the
　　　poor,

and to proclaim liberty to captives.
R. Alleluia, alleluia.

Gospel: Mark 2:13-17

[13]Jesus went out along the sea. All the crowd came to him and he taught them. [14]As he passed by, he saw Levi, son of Alphaeus, sitting at the customs post. Jesus said to him, "Follow me." And he got up and followed Jesus. [15]While he was at table in his house, many tax collectors and sinners sat with Jesus and his disciples; for there were many who followed him. [16]Some scribes who were Pharisees saw that Jesus was eating with sinners and tax collectors and said to his disciples, "Why does he eat with tax collectors and sinners?" [17]Jesus heard this and said to them, "Those who are well do not need a physician, but the sick do. I did not come to call the righteous but sinners."

Sunday January 19, 2025
Second Sunday in Ordinary Time Year C

First Reading: Isaiah 62:1-5

[1]For Zion's sake I will not be silent,
  for Jerusalem's sake I will not be quiet,
until her vindication shines forth like the
    dawn
  and her victory like a burning torch.

[2]Nations shall behold your vindication,
  and all the kings your glory;
you shall be called by a new name
  pronounced by the mouth of the LORD.
[3]You shall be a glorious crown in the hand of
    the LORD,
  a royal diadem held by your God.
[4]No more shall people call you "Forsaken,"
  or your land "Desolate,"
but you shall be called "My Delight,"
  and your land "Espoused."
For the LORD delights in you
  and makes your land his spouse.
[5]As a young man marries a virgin,
  your Builder shall marry you;
and as a bridegroom rejoices in his bride
  so shall your God rejoice in you.

Responsorial Psalm: Psalms 96:1-2, 2-3, 7-8, 9-10

R. *(3) Proclaim his marvelous deeds to all the
    nations.*
[1] Sing to the LORD a new song;
    sing to the LORD, all you lands.

²ᴬ Sing to the LORD; bless his name.
R. Proclaim his marvelous deeds to all the nations.
²ᴮ Announce his salvation, day after day.
³Tell his glory among the nations;
among all peoples, his wondrous deeds.
R. Proclaim his marvelous deeds to all the nations.
⁷ Give to the LORD, you families of nations,
give to the LORD glory and praise;
⁸ᴬ give to the LORD the glory due his name!
R. Proclaim his marvelous deeds to all the nations.
⁹ Worship the LORD in holy attire.
Tremble before him, all the earth;
¹⁰ Say among the nations: The LORD is king.
He governs the peoples with equity.
R. Proclaim his marvelous deeds to all the nations.

Second Reading: 1 Corinthians 12:4-11

Brothers and sisters: ⁴There are different kinds of spiritual gifts but the same Spirit; ⁵there are different forms of service but the same Lord; ⁶there are different workings but the same God who produces all of them in everyone. ⁷To each individual the manifestation of the Spirit is given for some benefit. ⁸To one is given through the Spirit the expression of wisdom; to another, the expression of knowledge according to the same Spirit; ⁹to another, faith by the same Spirit; to another, gifts of healing by the one Spirit; ¹⁰to another, mighty deeds; to another, prophecy; to another, discernment of spirits; to another, varieties of tongues; to another, interpretation of tongues. ¹¹But one and the same Spirit produces all of these, distributing them individually to each person as he wishes.

Alleluia: see 2 Thessalonians 2:14
R. Alleluia, alleluia.
¹⁴ God has called us through the Gospel
to possess the glory of our Lord Jesus Christ.
R. Alleluia, alleluia.

Gospel: John 2:1-11

¹There was a wedding at Cana in Galilee, and the mother of Jesus was there. ²Jesus and his disciples were also invited to the wedding. ³When the wine ran short, the mother of Jesus said to him, "They have no wine." ⁴And Jesus said to her, "Woman, how does your concern affect me? My hour has not yet come." ⁵His mother said to the servers, "Do whatever he tells you." ⁶Now there were six stone water jars there for Jewish ceremonial washings, each holding twenty to thirty

gallons. ⁷Jesus told the them, "Fill the jars with water." So they filled them to the brim. ⁸Then he told them, "Draw some out now and take it to the headwaiter." So they took it. ⁹And when the headwaiter tasted the water that had become wine, without knowing where it came from —although the servers who had drawn the water knew,— the headwaiter called the bridegroom ¹⁰and said to him, "Everyone serves good wine first, and then when people have drunk freely, an inferior one; but you have kept the good wine until now." ¹¹Jesus did this as the beginning of his signs at Cana in Galilee and so revealed his glory, and his disciples began to believe in him.

Monday January 20, 2025
Monday of Second Week in Ordinary Time
First Reading: Hebrews 5:1-10

Brothers and sisters: ¹Every high priest is taken from among men and made their representative before God, to offer gifts and sacrifices for sins. ²He is able to deal patiently with the ignorant and erring, for he himself is beset by weakness ³and so, for this reason, must make sin offerings for himself as well as for the people. ⁴No one takes this honor upon himself but only when called by God, just as Aaron was. ⁵In the same way, it was not Christ who glorified himself in becoming high priest, but rather the one who said to him:

You are my Son:
   this day I have begotten you;

⁶just as he says in another place,

You are a priest forever
   according to the order of Melchizedek.

⁷In the days when he was in the Flesh, he offered prayers and supplications with loud cries and tears to the one who was able to save him from death, and he was heard because of his reverence. ⁸Son though he was, he learned obedience from what he suffered; ⁹and when he was made perfect, he became the source of eternal salvation for all who obey him.

Responsorial Psalm: Psalms 110:1, 2, 3, 4
R. ⁽⁴ᵇ⁾ **You are a priest for ever, in the line of Melchizedek.**
¹ The LORD said to my Lord: "Sit at my right
      hand
   till I make your enemies your footstool."
R. **You are a priest for ever, in the line of Melchizedek.**
² The scepter of your power the LORD will
      stretch forth from Zion:

"Rule in the midst of your enemies."
R. You are a priest for ever, in the line of Melchizedek.
³ "Yours is princely power in the day of your birth, in holy splendor;
before the daystar, like the dew, I have begotten you."
R. You are a priest for ever, in the line of Melchizedek.
⁴ The LORD has sworn, and he will not repent:
"You are a priest forever, according to the order of Melchizedek."
R. You are a priest for ever, in the line of Melchizedek.

Alleluia: Hebrews 4:12
R. Alleluia, alleluia.
¹² The word of God is living and effective,
able to discern reflections and thoughts of the heart.
R. Alleluia, alleluia.

Gospel: Mark 2:18-22
¹⁸The disciples of John and of the Pharisees were accustomed to fast. People came to Jesus and objected, "Why do the disciples of John and the disciples of the Pharisees fast, but your disciples do not fast?" ¹⁹Jesus answered them, "Can the wedding guests fast while the bridegroom is with them? As long as they have the bridegroom with them they cannot fast. ²⁰But the days will come when the bridegroom is taken away from them, and then they will fast on that day. ²¹No one sews a piece of unshrunken cloth on an old cloak. If he does, its fullness pulls away, the new from the old, and the tear gets worse. ²²Likewise, no one pours new wine into old wineskins. Otherwise, the wine will burst the skins, and both the wine and the skins are ruined. Rather, new wine is poured into fresh wineskins."

Tuesday January 21, 2025
Memorial of Saint Agnes, Virgin & Martyr
First Reading: Hebrews 6:10-20
Brothers and sisters: ¹⁰God is not unjust so as to overlook your work and the love you have demonstrated for his name by having served and continuing to serve the holy ones. ¹¹We earnestly desire each of you to demonstrate the same eagerness for the fulfillment of hope until the end, ¹²so that you may not become sluggish, but imitators of those who, through faith and patience, are inheriting the promises.

¹³When God made the promise to Abraham, since he had no one greater by whom to swear, *he swore by himself,* ¹⁴and said, *I will indeed bless you and multiply you.* ¹⁵And so, after patient waiting, Abraham obtained the promise. ¹⁶Now, men swear by someone greater than themselves; for them an oath serves as a guarantee and puts an end to all argument. ¹⁷So when God wanted to give the

heirs of his promise an even clearer demonstration of the immutability of his purpose, he intervened with an oath, [18]so that by two immutable things, in which it was impossible for God to lie, we who have taken refuge might be strongly encouraged to hold fast to the hope that lies before us. [19]This we have as an anchor of the soul, sure and firm, which reaches into the interior behind the veil, [20]where Jesus has entered on our behalf as forerunner, becoming high priest forever according to the order of Melchizedek.

Responsorial Psalm: Psalms 111:1-2, 4-5, 9 AND 10C
R. [(5)] The Lord will remember his covenant for ever. or: *R. Alleluia.*

[1] I will give thanks to the LORD with all my
 heart
 in the company and assembly of the just.
[2] Great are the works of the LORD,
 exquisite in all their delights.
R. The Lord will remember his covenant for ever. or: ***R. Alleluia.***

[4] He has won renown for his wondrous deeds;
 gracious and merciful is the LORD.
[5] He has given food to those who fear him;
 he will forever be mindful of his
 covenant.
R. The Lord will remember his covenant for ever. or: ***R. Alleluia.***

[9] He has sent deliverance to his people;
 he has ratified his covenant forever;
 holy and awesome is his name.
 [10C] His praise endures forever.
R. The Lord will remember his covenant for ever. or: ***R. Alleluia.***

Alleluia: see Ephesians 1:17-18
R. Alleluia, alleluia.
[17] May the Father of our Lord Jesus Christ
enlighten the eyes of our hearts,
[18] that we may know what is the hope
that belongs to our call.
R. Alleluia, alleluia.

Gospel: Mark 2:23-28
[23]As Jesus was passing through a field of grain on the sabbath, his disciples began to make a path while picking the heads of grain. [24]At this the Pharisees said to him, "Look, why are they doing what is unlawful on the sabbath?" [25]He said to them, "Have you never read what David did when he was in need and he and his companions were hungry? [26]How he went into the house of God when Abiathar was high priest and ate the bread of offering that only the priests could lawfully eat, and shared it with his companions?" [27]Then he said to them, "The sabbath was

made for man, not man for the sabbath. ²⁸That is why the Son of Man is lord even of the sabbath."

Wednesday January 22, 2025
Wednesday of Second Week in Ordinary Time
First Reading: Hebrews 7:1-3, 15-17

¹*Melchizedek, king of Salem and priest of God Most High, met Abraham as he returned from his defeat of the kings* and *blessed him.* ²And Abraham apportioned to him *a tenth of everything.* His name first means righteous king, and he was also "king of Salem," that is, king of peace. ³Without father, mother, or ancestry, without beginning of days or end of life, thus made to resemble the Son of God, he remains a priest forever.

¹⁵It is even more obvious if another priest is raised up after the likeness of Melchizedek, ¹⁶who has become so, not by a law expressed in a commandment concerning physical descent but by the power of a life that cannot be destroyed. ¹⁷For it is testified:

*You are a priest forever according to the
 order of Melchizedek.*

Responsorial Psalm: Psalms 110:1, 2, 3, 4

R. ⁽⁴ᵇ⁾ **You are a priest for ever, in the line of
 Melchizedek.**

¹ The LORD said to my Lord: "Sit at my right
 hand
 till I make your enemies your footstool."

**R. You are a priest for ever, in the line of
 Melchizedek.**

² The scepter of your power the LORD will
 stretch forth from Zion:
 "Rule in the midst of your enemies."

**R. You are a priest for ever, in the line of
 Melchizedek.**

³ "Yours is princely power in the day of your
 birth, in holy splendor;
 before the daystar, like the dew, I have
 begotten you."

**R. You are a priest for ever, in the line of
 Melchizedek.**

⁴ The LORD has sworn, and he will not repent:
 "You are a priest forever, according to the
 order of Melchizedek."

**R. You are a priest for ever, in the line of
 Melchizedek.**

Alleluia: Matthew 4:23
R. Alleluia, alleluia.
[23] Jesus preached the Gospel of the Kingdom and cured every disease among the people.
R. Alleluia, alleluia.

Gospel: Mark 3:1-6
[1] Jesus entered the synagogue. There was a man there who had a withered hand. [2] They watched Jesus closely to see if he would cure him on the sabbath so that they might accuse him. [3] He said to the man with the withered hand, "Come up here before us." [4] Then he said to the Pharisees, "Is it lawful to do good on the sabbath rather than to do evil, to save life rather than to destroy it?" But they remained silent. [5] Looking around at them with anger and grieved at their hardness of heart, Jesus said to the man, "Stretch out your hand." He stretched it out and his hand was restored. [6] The Pharisees went out and immediately took counsel with the Herodians against him to put him to death.

Thursday January 23, 2025
Thursday of Second Week in Ordinary Time

First Reading: Hebrews 7:25-8:6
[25] Jesus is always able to save those who approach God through him, since he lives forever to make intercession for them.

[26] It was fitting that we should have such a high priest: holy, innocent, undefiled, separated from sinners, higher than the heavens. [27] He has no need, as did the high priests, to offer sacrifice day after day, first for his own sins and then for those of the people; he did that once for all when he offered himself. [28] For the law appoints men subject to weakness to be high priests, but the word of the oath, which was taken after the law, appoints a son, who has been made perfect forever.

[1] The main point of what has been said is this: we have such a high priest, who has taken his seat at the right hand of the throne of the Majesty in heaven, [2] a minister of the sanctuary and of the true tabernacle that the Lord, not man, set up. [3] Now every high priest is appointed to offer gifts and sacrifices; thus the necessity for this one also to have something to offer. [4] If then he were on earth, he would not be a priest, since there are those who offer gifts according to the law. [5] They worship in a copy and shadow of the heavenly sanctuary, as Moses was warned when he was about to erect the tabernacle. For God says, "See that you make everything according to the pattern shown you on the mountain." [6] Now he has obtained so much more excellent a ministry as he is mediator of a better covenant, enacted on better promises.

Responsorial Psalm: Psalms 40:7-8A, 8B-9, 10, 17
R. (8a and 9a) *Here am I, Lord; I come to do your will.*
[7] Sacrifice or oblation you wished not,
    but ears open to obedience you gave me.
[8A] Burnt offerings or sin-offerings you sought not;
    then said I, "Behold I come."

R. Here am I, Lord; I come to do your will.
⁸ᴮ "In the written scroll it is prescribed for me,
⁹ To do your will, O my God, is my delight,
    and your law is within my heart!"
R. Here am I, Lord; I come to do your will.
¹⁰ I announced your justice in the vast
      assembly;
   I did not restrain my lips, as you, O LORD,
     know.
R. Here am I, Lord; I come to do your will.
¹⁷ May all who seek you
    exult and be glad in you,
And may those who love your salvation
     say ever, "The LORD be glorified."
R. Here am I, Lord; I come to do your will.

Alleluia: 2 Timothy 1:10
R. Alleluia, alleluia.
¹⁰Our Savior Jesus Christ has destroyed death and brought life to light through the Gospel.
R. Alleluia, alleluia.

Gospel: Mark 3:7-12
⁷Jesus withdrew toward the sea with his disciples. A large number of people followed from Galilee and from Judea. ⁸Hearing what he was doing, a large number of people came to him also from Jerusalem, from Idumea, from beyond the Jordan, and from the neighborhood of Tyre and Sidon. ⁹He told his disciples to have a boat ready for him because of the crowd, so that they would not crush him. ¹⁰He had cured many and, as a result, those who had diseases were pressing upon him to touch him. ¹¹And whenever unclean spirits saw him they would fall down before him and shout, "You are the Son of God." ¹²He warned them sternly not to make him known.

Friday January 24, 2025
Memorial of Saint Francis de Sales, Bp & Doc
First Reading: Hebrews 8:6-13
Brothers and sisters: ⁶Now our high priest has obtained so much more excellent a ministry as he is mediator of a better covenant, enacted on better promises.
    ⁷For if that first covenant had been faultless, no place would have been sought for a second one. ⁸But he finds fault with them and says:

Behold, the days are coming, says the Lord,
    when I will conclude a new covenant with
      the house of
  Israel and the house of Judah.
⁹*It will not be like the covenant I made with*
    their fathers

> the day I took them by the hand to lead
> > them forth from the land of Egypt;
> for they did not stand by my covenant
> > and I ignored them, says the Lord.
> ¹⁰But this is the covenant I will establish with
> > the house of Israel
> after those days, says the Lord:
> I will put my laws in their minds
> > and I will write them upon their hearts.
> I will be their God,
> > and they shall be my people.
> ¹¹And they shall not teach, each one his fellow
> > citizen and kin, saying,
> > "Know the Lord,"
> for all shall know me, from least to
> > greatest.
> ¹²For I will forgive their evildoing
> > and remember their sins no more.

¹³When he speaks of a "new" covenant, he declares the first one obsolete. And what has become obsolete and has grown old is close to disappearing.

Responsorial Psalm: Psalms 85:8 AND 10, 11-12, 13-14
R. ^(11a) Kindness and truth shall meet.
⁸ Show us, O LORD, your mercy,
> and grant us your salvation.
¹⁰ Near indeed is his salvation to those who
> fear him,
> glory dwelling in our land.
R. Kindness and truth shall meet.
¹¹ Kindness and truth shall meet;
> justice and peace shall kiss.
¹² Truth shall spring out of the earth,
> and justice shall look down from heaven.
R. Kindness and truth shall meet.
¹³ The LORD himself will give his benefits;
> our land shall yield its increase.
¹⁴ Justice shall walk before him,
> and salvation, along the way of his steps.
R. Kindness and truth shall meet.

Alleluia: 2 Corinthians 5:19
R. Alleluia, alleluia.
¹⁹God was reconciling the world to himself in

Christ,
and entrusting to us the message of
    reconciliation.
R. Alleluia, alleluia.

Gospel: Mark 3:13-19

¹³Jesus went up the mountain and summoned those whom he wanted and they came to him. ¹⁴He appointed Twelve, whom he also named Apostles, that they might be with him and he might send them forth to preach ¹⁵and to have authority to drive out demons: ¹⁶He appointed the Twelve: Simon, whom he named Peter; ¹⁷James, son of Zebedee, and John the brother of James, whom he named Boanerges, that is, sons of thunder; ¹⁸Andrew, Philip, Bartholomew, Matthew, Thomas, James the son of Alphaeus; Thaddeus, Simon the Cananean, ¹⁹and Judas Iscariot who betrayed him.

Saturday January 25, 2025
Feast of Conversion of Saint Paul, Apostle

First Reading: Acts 22:3-16

³Paul addressed the people in these words: "I am a Jew, born in Tarsus in Cilicia, but brought up in this city. At the feet of Gamaliel I was educated strictly in our ancestral law and was zealous for God, just as all of you are today. ⁴I persecuted this Way to death, binding both men and women and delivering them to prison. ⁵Even the high priest and the whole council of elders can testify on my behalf. For from them I even received letters to the brothers and set out for Damascus to bring back to Jerusalem in chains for punishment those there as well.

⁶"On that journey as I drew near to Damascus, about noon a great light from the sky suddenly shone around me. ⁷I fell to the ground and heard a voice saying to me, 'Saul, Saul, why are you persecuting me?' ⁸I replied, 'Who are you, sir?' And he said to me, 'I am Jesus the Nazorean whom you are persecuting.' ⁹My companions saw the light but did not hear the voice of the one who spoke to me. ¹⁰I asked, 'What shall I do, sir?' The Lord answered me, 'Get up and go into Damascus, and there you will be told about everything appointed for you to do.' ¹¹Since I could see nothing because of the brightness of that light, I was led by hand by my companions and entered Damascus.

¹²"A certain Ananias, a devout observer of the law, and highly spoken of by all the Jews who lived there, ¹³came to me and stood there and said, 'Saul, my brother, regain your sight.' And at that very moment I regained my sight and saw him. ¹⁴Then he said, 'The God of our ancestors designated you to know his will, to see the Righteous One, and to hear the sound of his voice; ¹⁵for you will be his witness before all to what you have seen and heard. ¹⁶Now, why delay? Get up and have yourself baptized and your sins washed away, calling upon his name.'"

Or Acts 9:1-22

¹Saul, still breathing murderous threats against the disciples of the Lord, went to the high priest ²and asked him for letters to the synagogues in Damascus, that, if he should find any men or women who belonged to the Way, he might bring them back to Jerusalem in chains. ³On his journey, as he was nearing Damascus, a light

from the sky suddenly flashed around him. ⁴He fell to the ground and heard a voice saying to him, "Saul, Saul, why are you persecuting me?" ⁵He said, "Who are you, sir?" The reply came, "I am Jesus, whom you are persecuting. ⁶Now get up and go into the city and you will be told what you must do." ⁷The men who were traveling with him stood speechless, for they heard the voice but could see no one. ⁸Saul got up from the ground, but when he opened his eyes he could see nothing; so they led him by the hand and brought him to Damascus. ⁹For three days he was unable to see, and he neither ate nor drank.

¹⁰There was a disciple in Damascus named Ananias, and the Lord said to him in a vision, "Ananias." He answered, "Here I am, Lord." ¹¹The Lord said to him, "Get up and go to the street called Straight and ask at the house of Judas for a man from Tarsus named Saul. He is there praying, ¹²and in a vision he has seen a man named Ananias come in and lay his hands on him, that he may regain his sight." ¹³But Ananias replied, "Lord, I have heard from many sources about this man, what evil things he has done to your holy ones in Jerusalem. ¹⁴And here he has authority from the chief priests to imprison all who call upon your name." ¹⁵But the Lord said to him, "Go, for this man is a chosen instrument of mine to carry my name before Gentiles, kings, and children of Israel, ¹⁶and I will show him what he will have to suffer for my name." ¹⁷So Ananias went and entered the house; laying his hands on him, he said, "Saul, my brother, the Lord has sent me, Jesus who appeared to you on the way by which you came, that you may regain your sight and be filled with the Holy Spirit." ¹⁸Immediately things like scales fell from his eyes and he regained his sight. He got up and was baptized, ¹⁹and when he had eaten, he recovered his strength.

He stayed some days with the disciples in Damascus, ²⁰and he began at once to proclaim Jesus in the synagogues, that he is the Son of God. ²¹All who heard him were astounded and said, "Is not this the man who in Jerusalem ravaged those who call upon this name, and came here expressly to take them back in chains to the chief priests?" ²²But Saul grew all the stronger and confounded the Jews who lived in Damascus, proving that this is the Christ.

Responsorial Psalm: Psalms 117:1BC, 2
R. *(Mark 16:15)* **Go out to all the world and tell the Good News. Or R. Alleluia, alleluia.**
¹ᴮᶜPraise the LORD, all you nations;
    glorify him, all you peoples!
R. Go out to all the world, and tell the Good News. Or R. Alleluia, alleluia.
² For steadfast is his kindness toward us,
    and the fidelity of the LORD endures
        forever.
R. Go out to all the world, and tell the Good News. Or R. Alleluia, alleluia.

Alleluia: cf. John 15:16
R. Alleluia, alleluia.
[16]I chose you from the world,
to go and bear fruit that will last, says the
 Lord.
R. Alleluia, alleluia.

Gospel: Mark 16:15-18
[15]Jesus appeared to the Eleven and said to them: "Go into the whole world and proclaim the Gospel to every creature. [16]Whoever believes and is baptized will be saved; whoever does not believe will be condemned. [17]These signs will accompany those who believe: in my name they will drive out demons, they will speak new languages. [18]They will pick up serpents with their hands, and if they drink any deadly thing, it will not harm them. They will lay hands on the sick, and they will recover."

Sunday January 26, 2025
Third Sunday in Ordinary Time, Year C

First Reading: Nehemiah 8:2-4A, 5-6, 8-10
[2]Ezra the priest brought the law before the assembly, which consisted of men, women, and those children old enough to understand. [3]Standing at one end of the open place that was before the Water Gate, he read out of the book from daybreak till midday, in the presence of the men, the women, and those children old enough to understand; and all the people listened attentively to the book of the law. [4A]Ezra the scribe stood on a wooden platform that had been made for the occasion. [5]He opened the scroll so that all the people might see it —for he was standing higher up than any of the people—; and, as he opened it, all the people rose. [6]Ezra blessed the LORD, the great God, and all the people, their hands raised high, answered, "Amen, amen!" Then they bowed down and prostrated themselves before the LORD, their faces to the ground. [8]Ezra read plainly from the book of the law of God, interpreting it so that all could understand what was read. [9]Then Nehemiah, that is, His Excellency, and Ezra the priest-scribe and the Levites who were instructing the people said to all the people: "Today is holy to the LORD your God. Do not be sad, and do not weep"— for all the people were weeping as they heard the words of the law. [10]He said further: "Go, eat rich foods and drink sweet drinks, and allot portions to those who had nothing prepared; for today is holy to our LORD. Do not be saddened this day, for rejoicing in the LORD must be your strength!"

Responsorial Psalm: Psalms 19:8, 9, 10, 15
R. *(cf John 6:63c)* **Your words, Lord, are Spirit and life.**
[8] The law of the LORD is perfect,
 refreshing the soul;
The decree of the LORD is trustworthy,
 giving wisdom to the simple.
R. Your words, Lord, are Spirit and life.
[9] The precepts of the LORD are right,

  rejoicing the heart;
The command of the LORD is clear,
  enlightening the eye.
R. Your words, Lord, are Spirit and life.
¹⁰ The fear of the LORD is pure,
  enduring forever;
The ordinances of the LORD are true,
  all of them just.
R. Your words, Lord, are Spirit and life.
¹⁵ Let the words of my mouth and the thought
   of my heart
  find favor before you,
O LORD, my rock and my redeemer.
R. Your words, Lord, are Spirit and life.

Second Reading: 1 Corinthians 12:12-30

Brothers and sisters: ¹²As a body is one though it has many parts, and all the parts of the body, though many, are one body, so also Christ. ¹³For in one Spirit we were all baptized into one body, whether Jews or Greeks, slaves or free persons, and we were all given to drink of one Spirit.

 ¹⁴Now the body is not a single part, but many. ¹⁵If a foot should say, "Because I am not a hand I do not belong to the body," it does not for this reason belong any less to the body. ¹⁶Or if an ear should say, "Because I am not an eye I do not belong to the body," it does not for this reason belong any less to the body. ¹⁷If the whole body were an eye, where would the hearing be? If the whole body were hearing, where would the sense of smell be? ¹⁸But as it is, God placed the parts, each one of them, in the body as he intended. ¹⁹If they were all one part, where would the body be? ²⁰But as it is, there are many parts, yet one body. ²¹The eye cannot say to the hand, "I do not need you," nor again the head to the feet, "I do not need you." ²²Indeed, the parts of the body that seem to be weaker are all the more necessary, ²³and those parts of the body that we consider less honorable we surround with greater honor, and our less presentable parts are treated with greater propriety, ²⁴whereas our more presentable parts do not need this. But God has so constructed the body as to give greater honor to a part that is without it, ²⁵so that there may be no division in the body, but that the parts may have the same concern for one another. ²⁶If one part suffers, all the parts suffer with it; if one part is honored, all the parts share its joy.

 ²⁷Now you are Christ's body, and individually parts of it. ²⁸Some people God has designated in the church to be, first, apostles; second, prophets; third, teachers; then, mighty deeds; then gifts of healing, assistance, administration, and varieties of tongues. ²⁹Are all apostles? Are all prophets? Are all teachers? Do all work mighty deeds? ³⁰Do all have gifts of healing? Do all speak in tongues? Do all interpret?

Or 1 Corinthians 12:12-14, 27
Brothers and sisters: [12]As a body is one though it has many parts, and all the parts of the body, though many, are one body, so also Christ. [13]For in one Spirit we were all baptized into one body, whether Jews or Greeks, slaves or free persons, and we were all given to drink of one Spirit. [14]Now the body is not a single part, but many. [27]Now you are Christ's body, and individually parts of it.

Alleluia: Luke 4:18
R. Alleluia, alleluia.
[18] The Lord sent me to bring glad tidings to the
        poor,
and to proclaim liberty to captives.
R. Alleluia, alleluia.

Gospel: Luke 1:1-4; 4:14-21
[1]Since many have undertaken to compile a narrative of the events that have been fulfilled among us, [2]just as those who were eyewitnesses from the beginning and ministers of the word have handed them down to us, [3]I too have decided, after investigating everything accurately anew, to write it down in an orderly sequence for you, most excellent Theophilus, [4]so that you may realize the certainty of the teachings you have received.

    [14]Jesus returned to Galilee in the power of the Spirit, and news of him spread throughout the whole region. [15]He taught in their synagogues and was praised by all.

    [16]He came to Nazareth, where he had grown up, and went according to his custom into the synagogue on the sabbath day. He stood up to read [17]and was handed a scroll of the prophet Isaiah. He unrolled the scroll and found the passage where it was written:

[18]*The Spirit of the Lord is upon me,*
    because he has anointed me
    to bring glad tidings to the poor.
He has sent me to proclaim liberty to captives
    and recovery of sight to the blind,
    to let the oppressed go free,
        [19]*and to proclaim a year acceptable to the*
            Lord.

[20]Rolling up the scroll, he handed it back to the attendant and sat down, and the eyes of all in the synagogue looked intently at him. [21]He said to them, "Today this Scripture passage is fulfilled in your hearing."

Monday January 27, 2025
Monday of Third Week in Ordinary Time
First Reading: Hebrews 9:15, 24-28

[15]Christ is mediator of a new covenant: since a death has taken place for deliverance from transgressions under the first covenant, those who are called may receive the promised eternal inheritance.

[24]For Christ did not enter into a sanctuary made by hands, a copy of the true one, but heaven itself, that he might now appear before God on our behalf. [25]Not that he might offer himself repeatedly, as the high priest enters each year into the sanctuary with blood that is not his own; [26]if that were so, he would have had to suffer repeatedly from the foundation of the world. But now once for all he has appeared at the end of the ages to take away sin by his sacrifice. [27]Just as it is appointed that human beings die once, and after this the judgment, [28]so also Christ, offered once to take away the sins of many, will appear a second time, not to take away sin but to bring salvation to those who eagerly await him.

Responsorial Psalm: Psalms 98:1, 2-3AB, 3CD-4, 5-6

R. [1a] Sing to the Lord a new song, for he has done marvelous deeds.

[1] Sing to the LORD a new song,
> for he has done wondrous deeds;
His right hand has won victory for him,
> his holy arm.

R. Sing to the Lord a new song, for he has done marvelous deeds.

[2] The LORD has made his salvation known:
> in the sight of the nations he has revealed
> > his justice.
[3AB] He has remembered his kindness and his
> faithfulness
toward the house of Israel.

R. Sing to the Lord a new song, for he has done marvelous deeds.

[3CD] All the ends of the earth have seen
> the salvation by our God.
[4] Sing joyfully to the LORD, all you lands;
> break into song; sing praise.

R. Sing to the Lord a new song, for he has done marvelous deeds.

[5] Sing praise to the LORD with the harp,
> with the harp and melodious song.
[6] With trumpets and the sound of the horn
> sing joyfully before the King, the LORD.

R. Sing to the Lord a new song, for he has done

marvelous deeds.

Alleluia: 2 Timothy 1:10
R. Alleluia, alleluia.
¹⁰Our Savior Jesus Christ has destroyed death and brought life to light through the Gospel.
R. Alleluia, alleluia.

Gospel: Mark 3:22-30
²²The scribes who had come from Jerusalem said of Jesus, "He is possessed by Beelzebul," and "By the prince of demons he drives out demons." ²³Summoning them, he began to speak to them in parables, "How can Satan drive out Satan? ²⁴If a kingdom is divided against itself, that kingdom cannot stand. ²⁵And if a house is divided against itself, that house will not be able to stand. ²⁶And if Satan has risen up against himself and is divided, he cannot stand; that is the end of him. ²⁷But no one can enter a strong man's house to plunder his property unless he first ties up the strong man. Then he can plunder his house. ²⁸Amen, I say to you, all sins and all blasphemies that people utter will be forgiven them. ²⁹But whoever blasphemes against the Holy Spirit will never have forgiveness, but is guilty of an everlasting sin." ³⁰For they had said, "He has an unclean spirit."

Tuesday January 28, 2025
Memorial of Saint Thomas Aquinas, Priest & Doc

First Reading: Hebrews 10:1-10
Brothers and sisters: ¹Since the law has only a shadow of the good things to come, and not the very image of them, it can never make perfect those who come to worship by the same sacrifices that they offer continually each year. ²Otherwise, would not the sacrifices have ceased to be offered, since the worshipers, once cleansed, would no longer have had any consciousness of sins? ³But in those sacrifices there is only a yearly remembrance of sins, ⁴for it is impossible that the blood of bulls and goats take away sins. ⁵For this reason, when he came into the world, he said:

Sacrifice and offering you did not desire,
   but a body you prepared for me;
⁶in burnt offerings and sin offerings you took
   no delight.
⁷Then I said, As is written of me in the scroll,
   behold, I come to do your will, O God.

⁸First he says, *Sacrifices and offerings, burnt offerings and sin offerings, you neither desired nor delighted in*. These are offered according to the law. ⁹Then he says, *Behold, I come to do your will*. He takes away the first to establish the second. ¹⁰By this "will," we have been consecrated through the offering of the Body of Jesus Christ once for all.

Responsorial Psalm: Psalms 40:2 AND 4AB, 7-8A, 10, 11
R. *(8a and 9a)* **Here am I Lord; I come to do your will.**

²I have waited, waited for the LORD,
    and he stooped toward me.
⁴ᴬᴮAnd he put a new song into my mouth,
    a hymn to our God.
R. Here am I Lord; I come to do your will.
⁷Sacrifice or oblation you wished not,
    but ears open to obedience you gave me.
Burnt offerings or sin-offerings you sought
       not;
    ⁸ᴬthen said I, "Behold I come."
R. Here am I Lord; I come to do your will.
¹⁰I announced your justice in the vast
    assembly;
    I did not restrain my lips, as you, O LORD,
       know.
R. Here am I Lord; I come to do your will.
¹¹Your justice I kept not hid within my heart;
    your faithfulness and your salvation I
       have spoken of;
I have made no secret of your kindness and
    your truth
    in the vast assembly.
R. Here am I Lord; I come to do your will.

Alleluia: Matthew 11:25
R. Alleluia, alleluia.
²⁵ Blessed are you, Father, Lord of heaven and
    earth;
you have revealed to little ones the
    mysteries of the Kingdom.
R. Alleluia, alleluia.

Gospel: Mark 3:31-35
³¹The mother of Jesus and his brothers arrived at the house. Standing outside, they sent word to Jesus and called him. ³²A crowd seated around him told him, "Your mother and your brothers and your sisters are outside asking for you." ³³But he said to them in reply, "Who are my mother and my brothers?" ³⁴And looking around at those seated in the circle he said, "Here are my mother and my brothers.³⁵For whoever does the will of God is my brother and sister and mother."

Wednesday January 29, 2025
Wednesday of Third Week in Ordinary Time
First Reading: Hebrews 10:11-18
¹¹Every priest stands daily at his ministry, offering frequently those same sacrifices that can never take away sins. ¹²But this one offered one sacrifice for sins, and

took his seat forever at the right hand of God; ¹³now he waits until his enemies are made his footstool. ¹⁴For by one offering he has made perfect forever those who are being consecrated. ¹⁵The Holy Spirit also testifies to us, for after saying:

¹⁶*This is the covenant I will establish with them*
  after those days, says the Lord:
"I will put my laws in their hearts,
  and I will write them upon their minds,"

¹⁷he also says:

Their sins and their evildoing
  I will remember no more.

¹⁸Where there is forgiveness of these, there is no longer offering for sin.

Responsorial Psalm: Psalms 110:1, 2, 3, 4

R. *(4b)* **You are a priest for ever, in the line of Melchizedek.**
¹ The LORD said to my Lord: "Sit at my right hand
  till I make your enemies your footstool."
R. **You are a priest for ever, in the line of Melchizedek.**
² The scepter of your power the LORD will stretch forth from Zion:
  "Rule in the midst of your enemies."
R. **You are a priest for ever, in the line of Melchizedek.**
³ "Yours is princely power in the day of your birth, in holy splendor;
  before the daystar, like the dew, I have begotten you."
R. **You are a priest for ever, in the line of Melchizedek.**
⁴ The LORD has sworn, and he will not repent:
  "You are a priest forever, according to the order of Melchizedek."
R. **You are a priest for ever, in the line of Melchizedek.**

Alleluia: John 6:68

R. **Alleluia, alleluia.**
The seed is the word of God, Christ is the

sower;
all who come to him will live for ever.
R. Alleluia, alleluia.

Gospel: Mark 4:1-20

¹On another occasion, Jesus began to teach by the sea. A very large crowd gathered around him so that he got into a boat on the sea and sat down. And the whole crowd was beside the sea on land. ²And he taught them at length in parables, and in the course of his instruction he said to them, ³"Hear this! A sower went out to sow. ⁴And as he sowed, some seed fell on the path, and the birds came and ate it up. ⁵Other seed fell on rocky ground where it had little soil. It sprang up at once because the soil was not deep. ⁶And when the sun rose, it was scorched and it withered for lack of roots. ⁷Some seed fell among thorns, and the thorns grew up and choked it and it produced no grain. ⁸And some seed fell on rich soil and produced fruit. It came up and grew and yielded thirty, sixty, and a hundredfold." ⁹He added, "Whoever has ears to hear ought to hear."

¹⁰And when he was alone, those present along with the Twelve questioned him about the parables. ¹¹He answered them, "The mystery of the Kingdom of God has been granted to you. But to those outside everything comes in parables, ¹²so that

they may look and see but not perceive,
 and hear and listen but not understand,
in order that they may not be converted and
 be forgiven."

¹³Jesus said to them, "Do you not understand this parable? Then how will you understand any of the parables? ¹⁴The sower sows the word. ¹⁵These are the ones on the path where the word is sown. As soon as they hear, Satan comes at once and takes away the word sown in them. ¹⁶And these are the ones sown on rocky ground who, when they hear the word, receive it at once with joy. ¹⁷But they have no roots; they last only for a time. Then when tribulation or persecution comes because of the word, they quickly fall away. ¹⁸Those sown among thorns are another sort. They are the people who hear the word, ¹⁹but worldly anxiety, the lure of riches, and the craving for other things intrude and choke the word, and it bears no fruit. ²⁰But those sown on rich soil are the ones who hear the word and accept it and bear fruit thirty and sixty and a hundredfold."

Thursday January 30, 2025
Thursday of the Third Week in Ordinary Time
First Reading: Hebrews 10:19-25

Brothers and sisters: ¹⁹Since through the Blood of Jesus we have confidence of entrance into the sanctuary ²⁰by the new and living way he opened for us through the veil, that is, his flesh, ²¹and since we have "a great priest over the house of God," ²²let us approach with a sincere heart and in absolute trust, with our hearts sprinkled clean from an evil conscience and our bodies washed in pure water. ²³Let us hold unwaveringly to our confession that gives us hope, for he who made the promise is trustworthy. ²⁴We must consider how to rouse one another to love and good works. ²⁵We should not stay away from our assembly, as is the custom of some, but encourage one another, and this all the more as you see the day drawing near.

Responsorial Psalm: Psalms 24:1-2, 3-4AB, 5-6
R. (see 6) Lord, this is the people that longs to see your face.
¹ The LORD's are the earth and its fullness;
   the world and those who dwell in it.
² For he founded it upon the seas
   and established it upon the rivers.
R. Lord, this is the people that longs to see your face.
³ Who can ascend the mountain of the LORD?
   or who may stand in his holy place?
⁴ᴬᴮ He whose hands are sinless, whose heart is clean,
   who desires not what is vain.
R. Lord, this is the people that longs to see your face.
⁵ He shall receive a blessing from the LORD,
   a reward from God his savior.
⁶ Such is the race that seeks for him,
   that seeks the face of the God of Jacob.
R. Lord, this is the people that longs to see your face.

Alleluia: Psalms 119:105
R. Alleluia, alleluia.
¹⁰⁵ A lamp to my feet is your word,
a light to my path.
R. Alleluia, alleluia.

Gospel: Mark 4:21-25
²¹Jesus said to his disciples, "Is a lamp brought in to be placed under a bushel basket or under a bed, and not to be placed on a lampstand? ²²For there is nothing hidden except to be made visible; nothing is secret except to come to light. ²³Anyone who has ears to hear ought to hear." ²⁴He also told them, "Take care what you hear. The measure with which you measure will be measured out to you, and still more will be given to you. ²⁵To the one who has, more will be given; from the one who has not, even what he has will be taken away."

Friday January 31, 2025
Memorial of Saint John Bosco, Priest

First Reading: Hebrews 10:32-39

³²Remember the days past when, after you had been enlightened, you endured a great contest of suffering. ³³At times you were publicly exposed to abuse and affliction; at other times you associated yourselves with those so treated. ³⁴You even joined in the sufferings of those in prison and joyfully accepted the confiscation of your property, knowing that you had a better and lasting possession. ³⁵Therefore, do not throw away your confidence; it will have great recompense. ³⁶You need endurance to do the will of God and receive what he has promised.

³⁷For, after just a brief moment,
he who is to come shall come;
he shall not delay.
³⁸But my just one shall live by faith,
and if he draws back I take no pleasure in him.

³⁹We are not among those who draw back and perish, but among those who have faith and will possess life.

Responsorial Psalm: Psalms 37:3-4, 5-6, 23-24, 39-40

R. ^(39a) **The salvation of the just comes from the Lord.**

³ Trust in the LORD and do good,
    that you may dwell in the land and be fed
        in security.
⁴ Take delight in the LORD,
    and he will grant you your heart's
        requests.

R. The salvation of the just comes from the Lord.

⁵ Commit to the LORD your way;
    trust in him, and he will act.
⁶ He will make justice dawn for you like the
        light;
    bright as the noonday shall be your
        vindication.

R. The salvation of the just comes from the Lord.

²³ By the LORD are the steps of a man made
        firm,
    and he approves his way.
²⁴ Though he fall, he does not lie prostrate,
    for the hand of the LORD sustains him.

R. The salvation of the just comes from the Lord.

³⁹ The salvation of the just is from the LORD;
    he is their refuge in time of distress.

⁴⁰ And the LORD helps them and delivers them;
>   he delivers them from the wicked and
>   saves them,
>   because they take refuge in him.

R. The salvation of the just comes from the Lord.

Alleluia: Matthew 11:25
R. Alleluia, alleluia.
²⁵Blessed are you, Father, Lord of heaven and
    earth;
you have revealed to little ones the
    mysteries of the Kingdom.
R. Alleluia, alleluia.

Gospel: Mark 4:26-34
²⁶Jesus said to the crowds: "This is how it is with the Kingdom of God; it is as if a man were to scatter seed on the land ²⁷and would sleep and rise night and day and the seed would sprout and grow, he knows not how. ²⁸Of its own accord the land yields fruit, first the blade, then the ear, then the full grain in the ear. ²⁹And when the grain is ripe, he wields the sickle at once, for the harvest has come."

³⁰He said, "To what shall we compare the Kingdom of God, or what parable can we use for it? ³¹It is like a mustard seed that, when it is sown in the ground, is the smallest of all the seeds on the earth. ³²But once it is sown, it springs up and becomes the largest of plants and puts forth large branches, so that the birds of the sky can dwell in its shade." ³³With many such parables he spoke the word to them as they were able to understand it. ³⁴Without parables he did not speak to them, but to his own disciples he explained everything in private.

FEBRUARY 2025
Saturday February 1, 2025
Saturday of the Third Week in Ordinary Time
First Reading: Hebrews 11:1-2, 8-19
Brothers and sisters: ¹Faith is the realization of what is hoped for and evidence of things not seen. ²Because of it the ancients were well attested.

⁸By faith Abraham obeyed when he was called to go out to a place that he was to receive as an inheritance; he went out, not knowing where he was to go. ⁹By faith he sojourned in the promised land as in a foreign country, dwelling in tents with Isaac and Jacob, heirs of the same promise; ¹⁰for he was looking forward to the city with foundations, whose architect and maker is God. ¹¹By faith he received power to generate, even though he was past the normal age and Sarah herself was sterile for he thought that the one who had made the promise was trustworthy. ¹²So it was that there came forth from one man, himself as good as dead,
descendants as numerous as the stars in the sky and as countless as the sands on the seashore.

¹³All these died in faith. They did not receive what had been promised but saw it and greeted it from afar and acknowledged themselves to be strangers and aliens on earth, ¹⁴for those who speak thus show that they are seeking a homeland. ¹⁵If they had been thinking of the land from which they had come, they would have had opportunity to return. ¹⁶But now they desire a better homeland, a heavenly one. Therefore, God is not ashamed to be called their God, for he has prepared a city for them.

¹⁷By faith Abraham, when put to the test, offered up Isaac, and he who had received the promises was ready to offer his only son, ¹⁸of whom it was said, *Through Isaac descendants shall bear your name*. ¹⁹He reasoned that God was able to raise even from the dead, and he received Isaac back as a symbol.

Responsorial Psalm: Luke 1:69-70, 71-72, 73-75
R. *(see 68)* ***Blessed be the Lord the God of Israel;***
    he has come to his people.
⁶⁹ He has raised up for us a mighty savior,
    born of the house of his servant David.
R. *Blessed be the Lord the God of Israel; he has*
    come to his people.
⁷⁰ Through his holy prophets he promised of
        old.
    ⁷¹that he would save us from our sins
    from the hands of all who hate us.
⁷² He promised to show mercy to our fathers
    and to remember his holy covenant.
R. *Blessed be the Lord the God of Israel; he has*
    come to his people.
⁷³ This was the oath he swore to our father
        Abraham:
    ⁷⁴to set us free from the bonds of our
        enemies,
    free to worship him without fear,
    ⁷⁵holy and righteous in his sight
    all the days of our life.
R. *Blessed be the Lord the God of Israel; he has*
    come to his people.

Alleluia: John 3:16
R. Alleluia, alleluia.
¹⁶God so loved the world that he gave his only-
        begotten Son,
so that everyone who believes in him might
        have eternal life.
R. Alleluia, alleluia.

Gospel: Mark 4:35-41

³⁵On that day, as evening drew on, Jesus said to his disciples: "Let us cross to the other side." ³⁶Leaving the crowd, they took Jesus with them in the boat just as he was. And other boats were with him. ³⁷A violent squall came up and waves were breaking over the boat, so that it was already filling up. ³⁸Jesus was in the stern, asleep on a cushion. They woke him and said to him, "Teacher, do you not care that we are perishing?" ³⁹He woke up, rebuked the wind, and said to the sea, "Quiet! Be still!" The wind ceased and there was great calm. ⁴⁰Then he asked them, "Why are you terrified? Do you not yet have faith?" ⁴¹They were filled with great awe and said to one another, "Who then is this whom even wind and sea obey?"

Sunday February 2, 2025
Feast of the Presentation of the Lord

First Reading: Malachi 3:1-4

¹ Thus says the Lord GOD:
Lo, I am sending my messenger
    to prepare the way before me;
And suddenly there will come to the temple
    the LORD whom you seek,
And the messenger of the covenant whom
      you desire.
    Yes, he is coming, says the LORD of hosts.
² But who will endure the day of his coming?
    And who can stand when he appears?
For he is like the refiner's fire,
    or like the fuller's lye.
³ He will sit refining and purifying silver,
    and he will purify the sons of Levi,
Refining them like gold or like silver
    that they may offer due sacrifice to the
      LORD.
⁴ Then the sacrifice of Judah and Jerusalem
    will please the LORD,
      as in the days of old, as in years gone by.

Responsorial Psalm: Psalms 24:7, 8, 9, 10

R. ⁽⁸⁾ Who is this king of glory? It is the Lord!
⁷ Lift up, O gates, your lintels;
    reach up, you ancient portals,
    that the king of glory may come in!
R. Who is this king of glory? It is the Lord!
⁸ Who is this king of glory?
    The LORD, strong and mighty,
    the LORD, mighty in battle.
R. Who is this king of glory? It is the Lord!

⁹ Lift up, O gates, your lintels;
    reach up, you ancient portals,
    that the king of glory may come in!
R. Who is this king of glory? It is the Lord!
¹⁰ Who is this king of glory?
    The LORD of hosts; he is the king of glory.
R. Who is this king of glory? It is the Lord!

Second Reading: Hebrews 2:14-18

¹⁴ Since the children share in blood and flesh, Jesus likewise shared in them, that through death he might destroy the one who has the power of death, that is, the Devil, ¹⁵ and free those who through fear of death had been subject to slavery all their life. ¹⁶Surely he did not help angels but rather the descendants of Abraham; ¹⁷ therefore, he had to become like his brothers and sisters in every way, that he might be a merciful and faithful high priest before God to expiate the sins of the people. ¹⁸Because he himself was tested through what he suffered, he is able to help those who are being tested.

Alleluia: Luke 2:32
R. Alleluia, alleluia.
³² A light of revelation to the Gentiles,
and glory for your people Israel.
R. Alleluia, alleluia.

Gospel: Luke 2:22-40

²² When the days were completed for their purification according to the law of Moses, Mary and Joseph took Jesus up to Jerusalem to present him to the Lord, ²³ just as it is written in the law of the Lord, *Every male that opens the womb shall be consecrated to the Lord*, ²⁴ and to offer the sacrifice of *a pair of turtledoves or two young pigeons*, in accordance with the dictate in the law of the Lord.

    ²⁵ Now there was a man in Jerusalem whose name was Simeon. This man was righteous and devout, awaiting the consolation of Israel, and the Holy Spirit was upon him. ²⁶ It had been revealed to him by the Holy Spirit that he should not see death before he had seen the Christ of the Lord. ²⁷ He came in the Spirit into the temple; and when the parents brought in the child Jesus to perform the custom of the law in regard to him, ²⁸ he took him into his arms and blessed God, saying:

²⁹ "Now, Master, you may let your servant
    go
  in peace, according to your word,
³⁰ for my eyes have seen your salvation,
    ³¹ which you prepared in the sight of all
      the peoples:
³² a light for revelation to the Gentiles,
  and glory for your people Israel."

³³ The child's father and mother were amazed at what was said about him; ³⁴ and Simeon blessed them and said to Mary his mother, "Behold, this child is destined for the fall and rise of many in Israel, and to be a sign that will be contradicted ³⁵ —and you yourself a sword will pierce— so that the thoughts of many hearts may be revealed." ³⁶ There was also a prophetess, Anna, the daughter of Phanuel, of the tribe of Asher. She was advanced in years, having lived seven years with her husband after her marriage, ³⁷ and then as a widow until she was eighty-four. She never left the temple, but worshiped night and day with fasting and prayer. ³⁸And coming forward at that very time, she gave thanks to God and spoke about the child to all who were awaiting the redemption of Jerusalem.

³⁹ When they had fulfilled all the prescriptions of the law of the Lord, they returned to Galilee, to their own town of Nazareth. ⁴⁰ The child grew and became strong, filled with wisdom; and the favor of God was upon him.

Or Luke 2:22-32

²² When the days were completed for their purification according to the law of Moses, Mary and Joseph took Jesus up to Jerusalem to present him to the Lord, ²³ just as it is written in the law of the Lord, *Every male that opens the womb shall be consecrated to the Lord,* ²⁴ and to offer the sacrifice of *a pair of turtledoves or two young pigeons*, in accordance with the dictate in the law of the Lord.

²⁵ Now there was a man in Jerusalem whose name was Simeon. This man was righteous and devout, awaiting the consolation of Israel, and the Holy Spirit was upon him. ²⁶It had been revealed to him by the Holy Spirit that he should not see death before he had seen the Christ of the Lord. ²⁷He came in the Spirit into the temple; and when the parents brought in the child Jesus to perform the custom of the law in regard to him, ²⁸he took him into his arms and blessed God, saying:

²⁹ "Now, Master, you may let your servant
> go
in peace, according to your word,
³⁰ for my eyes have seen your salvation,
³¹ which you prepared in the sight of all
the peoples:
³² a light for revelation to the Gentiles,
and glory for your people Israel."

Monday February 3, 2025
Monday of Fourth Week in Ordinary Time
First Reading: Hebrews 11:32-40

Brothers and sisters: ³²What more shall I say? I have not time to tell of Gideon, Barak, Samson, Jephthah, of David and Samuel and the prophets, ³³who by faith conquered kingdoms, did what was righteous, obtained the promises; they closed the mouths of lions, ³⁴put out raging fires, escaped the devouring sword; out of weakness they were made powerful, became strong in battle, and turned back foreign invaders. ³⁵Women received back their dead through resurrection. Some were tortured and would not accept deliverance, in order to obtain a better resurrection. ³⁶Others endured mockery, scourging, even chains and imprisonment. ³⁷They were stoned, sawed in two, put to death at sword's point; they went about in skins of sheep or goats, needy, afflicted, tormented. ³⁸The world was not worthy of them. They wandered about in deserts and on mountains, in caves and in crevices in the earth.

³⁹Yet all these, though approved because of their faith, did not receive what had been promised. ⁴⁰God had foreseen something better for us, so that without us they should not be made perfect.

Responsorial Psalm: Psalms 31:20, 21, 22, 23, 24

R. ⁽²⁵⁾ *Let your hearts take comfort, all who hope in the Lord.*

²⁰ How great is the goodness, O LORD,
  which you have in store for those who
    fear you,
And which, toward those who take refuge in
    you,
  you show in the sight of the children of
    men.

R. *Let your hearts take comfort, all who hope in the Lord.**

²¹ You hide them in the shelter of your
    presence
  from the plottings of men;
You screen them within your abode
  from the strife of tongues.

R. *Let your hearts take comfort, all who hope in the Lord.**

²² Blessed be the LORD whose wondrous mercy
  he has shown me in a fortified city.

R. *Let your hearts take comfort, all who hope in the Lord.**

²³ Once I said in my anguish,
  "I am cut off from your sight";
Yet you heard the sound of my pleading
  when I cried out to you.

R. *Let your hearts take comfort, all who hope in the Lord.**

²⁴ Love the LORD, all you his faithful ones!
  The LORD keeps those who are constant,
    but more than requites those who act
      proudly.

R. *Let your hearts take comfort, all who hope in the Lord.**

Alleluia: Luke 7:16
R. Alleluia, alleluia.
[16] A great prophet has arisen in our midst and God has visited his people.
R. Alleluia, alleluia.

Gospel: Mark 5:1-20
[1] Jesus and his disciples came to the other side of the sea, to the territory of the Gerasenes. [2] When he got out of the boat, at once a man from the tombs who had an unclean spirit met him. [3] The man had been dwelling among the tombs, and no one could restrain him any longer, even with a chain. [4] In fact, he had frequently been bound with shackles and chains, but the chains had been pulled apart by him and the shackles smashed, and no one was strong enough to subdue him. [5] Night and day among the tombs and on the hillsides he was always crying out and bruising himself with stones. [6] Catching sight of Jesus from a distance, he ran up and prostrated himself before him, [7] crying out in a loud voice, "What have you to do with me, Jesus, Son of the Most High God? I adjure you by God, do not torment me!" [8] (He had been saying to him, "Unclean spirit, come out of the man!") [9] He asked him, "What is your name?" He replied, "Legion is my name. There are many of us." [10] And he pleaded earnestly with him not to drive them away from that territory.

[11] Now a large herd of swine was feeding there on the hillside. [12] And they pleaded with him, "Send us into the swine. Let us enter them." [13] And he let them, and the unclean spirits came out and entered the swine. The herd of about two thousand rushed down a steep bank into the sea, where they were drowned. [14] The swineherds ran away and reported the incident in the town and throughout the countryside. And people came out to see what had happened. [15] As they approached Jesus, they caught sight of the man who had been possessed by Legion, sitting there clothed and in his right mind. And they were seized with fear. [16] Those who witnessed the incident explained to them what had happened to the possessed man and to the swine. [17] Then they began to beg him to leave their district. [18] As he was getting into the boat, the man who had been possessed pleaded to remain with him. [19] But Jesus would not permit him but told him instead, "Go home to your family and announce to them all that the Lord in his pity has done for you." [20] Then the man went off and began to proclaim in the Decapolis what Jesus had done for him; and all were amazed.

Tuesday February 4, 2025
Tuesday of Fourth Week in Ordinary Time
First Reading: Hebrews 12:1-4
Brothers and sisters: [1] Since we are surrounded by so great a cloud of witnesses, let us rid ourselves of every burden and sin that clings to us and persevere in running the race that lies before us [2] while keeping our eyes fixed on Jesus, the leader and perfecter of faith. For the sake of the joy that lay before him Jesus endured the cross, despising its shame, and has taken his seat at the right of the throne of God. [3] Consider how he endured such opposition from sinners, in order that you may not grow weary and lose heart. [4] In your struggle against sin you have not yet resisted to the point of shedding blood.

Responsorial Psalm: Psalms 22:26B-27, 28 AND 30, 31-32

R. (see 27b) They will praise you, Lord, who long for you.

26B I will fulfill my vows before those who fear
    him.
27 The lowly shall eat their fill;
    they who seek the LORD shall praise him:
    "May your hearts be ever merry!"

R. They will praise you, Lord, who long for you.

28 All the ends of the earth
    shall remember and turn to the LORD;
All the families of the nations
    shall bow down before him.
30 To him alone shall bow down
    all who sleep in the earth;
Before him shall bend
    all who go down into the dust.

R. They will praise you, Lord, who long for you.

31 And to him my soul shall live;
    my descendants shall serve him.
32 Let the coming generation be told of the LORD
    that they may proclaim to a people yet to
        be born
    the justice he has shown.

R. They will praise you, Lord, who long for you.

Alleluia: Matthew 8:17

R. Alleluia, alleluia.
17 Christ took away our infirmities
and bore our diseases.
R. Alleluia, alleluia.

Gospel: Mark 5:21-43

21 When Jesus had crossed again in the boat to the other side, a large crowd gathered around him, and he stayed close to the sea. 22 One of the synagogue officials, named Jairus, came forward. Seeing him he fell at his feet 23 and pleaded earnestly with him, saying, "My daughter is at the point of death. Please, come lay your hands on her that she may get well and live." 24 He went off with him and a large crowd followed him.

    25 There was a woman afflicted with hemorrhages for twelve years. 26 She had suffered greatly at the hands of many doctors and had spent all that she had. Yet she was not helped but only grew worse. 27 She had heard about Jesus and came up behind him in the crowd and touched his cloak. 28 She said, "If I but touch his clothes, I shall be cured." 29 Immediately her flow of blood dried up. She felt in her body that she was healed of her affliction. 30 Jesus, aware at once that power

had gone out from him, turned around in the crowd and asked, "Who has touched my clothes?" ³¹But his disciples said to him, "You see how the crowd is pressing upon you, and yet you ask, Who touched me?" ³²And he looked around to see who had done it. ³³The woman, realizing what had happened to her, approached in fear and trembling. She fell down before Jesus and told him the whole truth. ³⁴He said to her, "Daughter, your faith has saved you. Go in peace and be cured of your affliction."

³⁵While he was still speaking, people from the synagogue official's house arrived and said, "Your daughter has died; why trouble the teacher any longer?" ³⁶Disregarding the message that was reported, Jesus said to the synagogue official, "Do not be afraid; just have faith." ³⁷He did not allow anyone to accompany him inside except Peter, James, and John, the brother of James. ³⁸When they arrived at the house of the synagogue official, he caught sight of a commotion, people weeping and wailing loudly. ³⁹So he went in and said to them, "Why this commotion and weeping? The child is not dead but asleep." ⁴⁰And they ridiculed him. Then he put them all out. He took along the child's father and mother and those who were with him and entered the room where the child was. ⁴¹He took the child by the hand and said to her, *"Talitha koum,"* which means, "Little girl, I say to you, arise!" ⁴²The girl, a child of twelve, arose immediately and walked around. At that they were utterly astounded. ⁴³He gave strict orders that no one should know this and said that she should be given something to eat.

Wednesday February 5, 2025
Memorial of Saint Agatha, Virgin & Martyr
First Reading: Hebrew 12:4-7, 11-15

Brothers and sisters: ⁴In your struggle against sin you have not yet resisted to the point of shedding blood. ⁵You have also forgotten the exhortation addressed to you as children:

"My son, do not disdain the discipline of the
　　Lord
　or lose heart when reproved by him;
⁶for whom the Lord loves, he disciplines;
　he scourges every son he acknowledges."

⁷Endure your trials as "discipline"; God treats you as his sons. For what "son" is there whom his father does not discipline? ¹¹At the time, all discipline seems a cause not for joy but for pain, yet later it brings the peaceful fruit of righteousness to those who are trained by it.

¹²So strengthen your drooping hands and your weak knees. ¹³Make straight paths for your feet, that what is lame may not be dislocated but healed.

¹⁴Strive for peace with everyone, and for that holiness without which no one will see the Lord. ¹⁵See to it that no one be deprived of the grace of God, that no bitter root spring up and cause trouble, through which many may become defiled.

Responsorial Psalm: Psalms 103:1-2, 13-14, 17-18A

R. *(see 17)* ***The Lord's kindness is everlasting to those who fear him.***

¹ Bless the LORD, O my soul;
   and all my being, bless his holy name.
² Bless the LORD, O my soul,
   and forget not all his benefits.

R. *The Lord's kindness is everlasting to those who fear him.*

¹³ As a father has compassion on his children,
   so the LORD has compassion on those who fear him,
¹⁴ For he knows how we are formed;
   he remembers that we are dust.

R. *The Lord's kindness is everlasting to those who fear him.*

¹⁷ But the kindness of the LORD is from eternity
   to eternity toward those who fear him,
¹⁸ᴬ And his justice toward children's children
   among those who keep his covenant.

R. *The Lord's kindness is everlasting to those who fear him.*

Alleluia: John 10:27
R. Alleluia, alleluia.
²⁷My sheep hear my voice, says the Lord;
I know them, and they follow me.
R. Alleluia, alleluia.

Gospel: Mark 6:1-6

¹Jesus departed from there and came to his native place, accompanied by his disciples. ²When the sabbath came he began to teach in the synagogue, and many who heard him were astonished. They said, "Where did this man get all this? What kind of wisdom has been given him? What mighty deeds are wrought by his hands! ³Is he not the carpenter, the son of Mary, and the brother of James and Joseph and Judas and Simon? And are not his sisters here with us?" And they took offense at him. ⁴Jesus said to them, "A prophet is not without honor except in his native place and among his own kin and in his own house." ⁵So he was not able to perform any mighty deed there, apart from curing a few sick people by laying his hands on them. ⁶ He was amazed at their lack of faith.

Thursday February 6, 2025
Memorial of Saint Paul Miki and his Companions, Martyrs
First Reading: Hebrews 12:18-19, 21-24

Brothers and sisters: ¹⁸You have not approached that which could be touched and a blazing fire and gloomy darkness and storm ¹⁹and a trumpet blast and a voice speaking words such that those who heard begged that no message be further addressed to them. ²¹Indeed, so fearful was the spectacle that Moses said, "I am terrified and trembling." ²²No, you have approached Mount Zion and the city of the living God, the heavenly Jerusalem, and countless angels in festal gathering, ²³and the assembly of the firstborn enrolled in heaven, and God the judge of all, and the spirits of the just made perfect, ²⁴and Jesus, the mediator of a new covenant, and the sprinkled Blood that speaks more eloquently than that of Abel.

Responsorial Psalm: Psalms 48:2-3AB, 3CD-4, 9, 10-11

R. (see 10) ***O God, we ponder your mercy within your temple.***

² Great is the LORD and wholly to be praised
    in the city of our God. His holy mountain,
³ᴬᴮ fairest of heights,
    is the joy of all the earth.

R. ***O God, we ponder your mercy within your temple.***

³ᶜᴰ Mount Zion, "the recesses of the North,"
    the city of the great King.
⁴ God is with her castles;
    renowned is he as a stronghold.

R. ***O God, we ponder your mercy within your temple.***

⁹ As we had heard, so have we seen
    in the city of the LORD of hosts,
In the city of our God;
    God makes it firm forever.

R. ***O God, we ponder your mercy within your temple.***

¹⁰ O God, we ponder your mercy
    within your temple.
¹¹ As your name, O God, so also your praise
    reaches to the ends of the earth.
Of justice your right hand is full.

R. ***O God, we ponder your mercy within your temple.***

Alleluia: Mark 1:15
R. Alleluia, alleluia.
¹⁵ The Kingdom of God is at hand;
repent and believe in the Gospel.
R. Alleluia, alleluia.

Gospel: Mark 6:7-13
⁷Jesus summoned the Twelve and began to send them out two by two and gave them authority over unclean spirits. ⁸ He instructed them to take nothing for the journey but a walking stick –no food, no sack, no money in their belts. ⁹ They were, however, to wear sandals but not a second tunic. ¹⁰ He said to them, "Wherever you enter a house, stay there until you leave from there. ¹¹ Whatever place does not welcome you or listen to you, leave there and shake the dust off your feet in testimony against them." ¹²So they went off and preached repentance. ¹³ The Twelve drove out many demons, and they anointed with oil many who were sick and cured them.

Friday February 7, 2025
Friday of Fourth Week in Ordinary Time
First Reading: Hebrews 13:1-8
¹Let brotherly love continue. ²Do not neglect hospitality, for through it some have unknowingly entertained angels. ³Be mindful of prisoners as if sharing their imprisonment, and of the ill-treated as of yourselves, for you also are in the body. ⁴Let marriage be honored among all and the marriage bed be kept undefiled, for God will judge the immoral and adulterers. ⁵Let your life be free from love of money but be content with what you have, for he has said, *I will never forsake you or abandon you.* ⁶Thus we may say with confidence:

The Lord is my helper,
     and I will not be afraid.
What can anyone do to me?

⁷Remember your leaders who spoke the word of God to you. Consider the outcome of their way of life and imitate their faith. ⁸Jesus Christ is the same yesterday, today, and forever.

Responsorial Psalm: Psalms 27:1, 3, 5, 8B-9ABC
R. ⁽¹ᵃ⁾ *The Lord is my light and my salvation.*
¹The LORD is my light and my salvation;
     whom should I fear?
The LORD is my life's refuge;
     of whom should I be afraid?
R. *The Lord is my light and my salvation.*
³ Though an army encamp against me,
     my heart will not fear;

Though war be waged upon me,
>even then will I trust.

R. The Lord is my light and my salvation.

⁵ For he will hide me in his abode
>in the day of trouble;

He will conceal me in the shelter of his tent,
>he will set me high upon a rock.

R. The Lord is my light and my salvation.

⁸ᴮ Your presence, O LORD, I seek.

⁹ᴬᴮᶜ Hide not your face from me;
>do not in anger repel your servant.

You are my helper: cast me not off.

R. The Lord is my light and my salvation.

Alleluia: Luke 8:15
R. Alleluia, alleluia.
¹⁵Blessed are they who have kept the word
>with a generous heart,

and yield a harvest through perseverance.

R. Alleluia, alleluia.

Gospel: Mark 6:14-29

¹⁴King Herod heard about Jesus, for his fame had become widespread, and people were saying, "John the Baptist has been raised from the dead; That is why mighty powers are at work in him." ¹⁵Others were saying, "He is Elijah"; still others, "He is a prophet like any of the prophets." ¹⁶But when Herod learned of it, he said, "It is John whom I beheaded. He has been raised up."

¹⁷Herod was the one who had John arrested and bound in prison on account of Herodias, the wife of his brother Philip, whom he had married. ¹⁸John had said to Herod, "It is not lawful for you to have your brother's wife." ¹⁹Herodias harbored a grudge against him and wanted to kill him but was unable to do so. ²⁰Herod feared John, knowing him to be a righteous and holy man, and kept him in custody. When he heard him speak he was very much perplexed, yet he liked to listen to him. ²¹Herodias had an opportunity one day when Herod, on his birthday, gave a banquet for his courtiers, his military officers, and the leading men of Galilee. ²²His own daughter came in and performed a dance that delighted Herod and his guests. The king said to the girl, "Ask of me whatever you wish and I will grant it to you." ²³He even swore many things to her, "I will grant you whatever you ask of me, even to half of my kingdom." ²⁴She went out and said to her mother, "What shall I ask for?" Her mother replied, "The head of John the Baptist." ²⁵The girl hurried back to the king's presence and made her request, "I want you to give me at once on a platter the head of John the Baptist." ²⁶The king was deeply distressed, but because of his oaths and the guests he did not wish to break his word to her. ²⁷So he promptly dispatched an executioner with orders to bring back

his head. He went off and beheaded him in the prison. [28]He brought in the head on a platter and gave it to the girl. The girl in turn gave it to her mother. [29]When his disciples heard about it, they came and took his body and laid it in a tomb.

Saturday February 8, 2025
Saturday of Fourth Week in Ordinary Time

First Reading: Hebrew 13:15-17, 20-21

Brothers and sisters: [15]Through Jesus, let us continually offer God a sacrifice of praise, that is, the fruit of lips that confess his name. [16]Do not neglect to do good and to share what you have; God is pleased by sacrifices of that kind.

[17]Obey your leaders and defer to them, for they keep watch over you and will have to give an account, that they may fulfill their task with joy and not with sorrow, for that would be of no advantage to you.

[20]May the God of peace, who brought up from the dead the great shepherd of the sheep by the Blood of the eternal covenant, [21]furnish you with all that is good, that you may do his will. May he carry out in you what is pleasing to him through Jesus Christ, to whom be glory forever and ever. Amen.

Responsorial Psalm: Psalms 23:1-3A, 3B-4, 5, 6

R. [(1)] The Lord is my shepherd; there is nothing I shall want.

[1] The LORD is my shepherd; I shall not want.
   In verdant pastures he gives me repose.
Beside restful waters he leads me;
   [3A] he refreshes my soul.

R. The Lord is my shepherd; there is nothing I shall want.

[3B] He guides me in right paths
   for his name's sake.
[4] Even though I walk in the dark valley
   I fear no evil; for you are at my side
With your rod and your staff
   that give me courage.

R. The Lord is my shepherd; there is nothing I shall want.

[5] You spread the table before me
   in the sight of my foes;
You anoint my head with oil;
   my cup overflows.

R. The Lord is my shepherd; there is nothing I shall want.

[6] Only goodness and kindness follow me
   all the days of my life;
And I shall dwell in the house of the LORD
   for years to come.

R. *The Lord is my shepherd; there is nothing I shall want.*

Alleluia: John 10:27
R. **Alleluia, alleluia.**
²⁷ My sheep hear my voice, says the Lord;
I know them, and they follow me.
R. **Alleluia, alleluia.**

Gospel: Mark 6:30-34
³⁰The Apostles gathered together with Jesus and reported all they had done and taught. ³¹He said to them, "Come away by yourselves to a deserted place and rest a while." People were coming and going in great numbers, and they had no opportunity even to eat. ³²So they went off in the boat by themselves to a deserted place. ³³People saw them leaving and many came to know about it. They hastened there on foot from all the towns and arrived at the place before them.

³⁴When Jesus disembarked and saw the vast crowd, his heart was moved with pity for them, for they were like sheep without a shepherd; and he began to teach them many things.

Sunday February 9, 2025
Fifth Sunday in Ordinary Time Year C

First Reading: Isaiah 6:1-2A, 3-8
¹In the year King Uzziah died, I saw the Lord seated on a high and lofty throne, with the train of his garment filling the temple. ²ᴬSeraphim were stationed above.

³They cried one to the other, "Holy, holy, holy is the LORD of hosts! All the earth is filled with his glory!" ⁴At the sound of that cry, the frame of the door shook and the house was filled with smoke.

⁵Then I said, "Woe is me, I am doomed! For I am a man of unclean lips, living among a people of unclean lips; yet my eyes have seen the King, the LORD of hosts!" ⁶Then one of the seraphim flew to me, holding an ember that he had taken with tongs from the altar.

⁷He touched my mouth with it, and said, "See, now that this has touched your lips, your wickedness is removed, your sin purged."

⁸Then I heard the voice of the Lord saying, "Whom shall I send? Who will go for us?" "Here I am," I said; "send me!"

Responsorial Psalm: Psalms 138:1-2, 2-3, 4-5, 7-8
R. ⁽¹ᶜ⁾ *In the sight of the angels I will sing your praises, Lord.*
¹I will give thanks to you, O LORD, with all my
    heart,
    for you have heard the words of my
        mouth;
    in the presence of the angels I will sing

    your praise;
²ᴬᴮ I will worship at your holy temple
    and give thanks to your name.

R. In the sight of the angels I will sing your praises, Lord.

²ᴮᶜ Because of your kindness and your truth;
    for you have made great above all things
    your name and your promise.
³ When I called, you answered me;
    you built up strength within me.

R. In the sight of the angels I will sing your praises, Lord.

⁴All the kings of the earth shall give thanks to you, O LORD,
    when they hear the words of your mouth;
⁵ and they shall sing of the ways of the LORD:
    "Great is the glory of the LORD."

R. In the sight of the angels I will sing your praises, Lord.

⁷ᴰYour right hand saves me.
    ⁸The LORD will complete what he has done for me;
your kindness, O LORD, endures forever;
    forsake not the work of your hands.

R. In the sight of the angels I will sing your praises, Lord.

Second Reading: 1 Corinthians 15:1-11

¹I am reminding you, brothers and sisters, of the gospel I preached to you, which you indeed received and in which you also stand. ²Through it you are also being saved, if you hold fast to the word I preached to you, unless you believed in vain. ³For I handed on to you as of first importance what I also received: that Christ died for our sins in accordance with the Scriptures; ⁴that he was buried; that he was raised on the third day in accordance with the Scriptures; ⁵that he appeared to Cephas, then to the Twelve. ⁶After that, Christ appeared to more than five hundred brothers at once, most of whom are still living, though some have fallen asleep. ⁷After that he appeared to James, then to all the apostles. ⁸Last of all, as to one born abnormally, he appeared to me. ⁹For I am the least of the apostles, not fit to be called an apostle, because I persecuted the church of God. ¹⁰But by the grace of God I am what I am, and his grace to me has not been ineffective. Indeed, I have toiled harder than all of them; not I, however, but the grace of God that is with me. ¹¹Therefore, whether it be I or they, so we preach and so you believed.

Or 1 Corinthians 15:3-8, 11

Brothers and sisters, ³For I handed on to you as of first importance what I also received: that Christ died for our sins in accordance with the Scriptures; ⁴that he was buried; that he was raised on the third day in accordance with the Scriptures; ⁵that he appeared to Cephas, then to the Twelve. ⁶After that, he appeared to more than five hundred brothers at once, most of whom are still living, though some have fallen asleep. ⁷After that he appeared to James, then to all the apostles. ⁸Last of all, as to one abnormally born, he appeared to me. ¹¹Therefore, whether it be I or they, so we preach and so you believed.

Alleluia: Matthew 4:19

R. Alleluia, alleluia.
¹⁹ Come after me
and I will make you fishers of men.
R. Alleluia, alleluia.

Gospel: Luke 5:1-11

¹While the crowd was pressing in on Jesus and listening to the word of God, he was standing by the Lake of Gennesaret. ²He saw two boats there alongside the lake; the fishermen had disembarked and were washing their nets. ³Getting into one of the boats, the one belonging to Simon, he asked him to put out a short distance from the shore. Then he sat down and taught the crowds from the boat. ⁴After he had finished speaking, he said to Simon, "Put out into deep water and lower your nets for a catch." ⁵Simon said in reply, "Master, we have worked hard all night and have caught nothing, but at your command I will lower the nets." ⁶When they had done this, they caught a great number of fish and their nets were tearing. ⁷They signaled to their partners in the other boat to come to help them. They came and filled both boats so that the boats were in danger of sinking. ⁸When Simon Peter saw this, he fell at the knees of Jesus and said, "Depart from me, Lord, for I am a sinful man." ⁹For astonishment at the catch of fish they had made seized him and all those with him,¹⁰and likewise James and John, the sons of Zebedee, who were partners of Simon. Jesus said to Simon, "Do not be afraid; from now on you will be catching men." ¹¹When they brought their boats to the shore, they left everything and followed him.

Monday February 10, 2025
Memorial of Saint Scholastica, Virgin

First Reading: Genesis 1:1-19

¹In the beginning, when God created the heavens and the earth, ²the earth was a formless wasteland, and darkness covered the abyss, while a mighty wind swept over the waters.

³Then God said, "Let there be light," and there was light. ⁴God saw how good the light was. God then separated the light from the darkness. ⁵God called the light "day," and the darkness he called "night." Thus evening came, and morning followed–the first day.

⁶Then God said, "Let there be a dome in the middle of the waters, to separate one body of water from the other." And so it happened: ⁷God made the dome, and it separated the water above the dome from the water below it. ⁸God called the dome "the sky." Evening came, and morning followed— the second day.

⁹Then God said, "Let the water under the sky be gathered into a single basin, so that the dry land may appear." And so it happened: the water under the sky was gathered into its basin, and the dry land appeared. ¹⁰God called the dry land "the earth," and the basin of the water he called "the sea." God saw how good it was. ¹¹Then God said, "Let the earth bring forth vegetation: every kind of plant that bears seed and every kind of fruit tree on earth that bears fruit with its seed in it." And so it happened: ¹²the earth brought forth every kind of plant that bears seed and every kind of fruit tree on earth that bears fruit with its seed in it. God saw how good it was. ¹³Evening came, and morning followed– the third day.

¹⁴Then God said: "Let there be lights in the dome of the sky, to separate day from night. Let them mark the fixed times, the days and the years, ¹⁵and serve as luminaries in the dome of the sky, to shed light upon the earth." And so it happened: ¹⁶God made the two great lights, the greater one to govern the day, and the lesser one to govern the night; and he made the stars. ¹⁷God set them in the dome of the sky, to shed light upon the earth, ¹⁸to govern the day and the night, and to separate the light from the darkness. God saw how good it was. ¹⁹Evening came, and morning followed–the fourth day.

Responsorial Psalm: Psalms 104:1-2A, 5-6, 10 AND 12, 24 AND 35C
R. [31b] **May the Lord be glad in his works.**
¹Bless the LORD, O my soul!
    O LORD, my God, you are great indeed!
You are clothed with majesty and glory,
    ²ᴬ robed in light as with a cloak.
R. May the Lord be glad in his works.
⁵ You fixed the earth upon its foundation,
    not to be moved forever;
⁶ With the ocean, as with a garment, you
      covered it;
    above the mountains the waters stood.
R. May the Lord be glad in his works.
¹⁰ You send forth springs into the watercourses
    that wind among the mountains.
¹² Beside them the birds of heaven dwell;
    from among the branches they send forth
      their song.
R. May the Lord be glad in his works.
²⁴ How manifold are your works, O LORD!
    In wisdom you have wrought them all—
    the earth is full of your creatures;
³⁵ᶜ Bless the LORD, O my soul! Alleluia.
R. May the Lord be glad in his works.

Alleluia: Matthew 4:23
R. Alleluia, alleluia.
[23] Jesus preached the Gospel of the Kingdom and cured every disease among the people.
R. Alleluia, alleluia.

Gospel: Mark 6:53-56
[53] After making the crossing to the other side of the sea, Jesus and his disciples came to land at Gennesaret and tied up there. [54] As they were leaving the boat, people immediately recognized him. [55] They scurried about the surrounding country and began to bring in the sick on mats to wherever they heard he was. [56] Whatever villages or towns or countryside he entered, they laid the sick in the marketplaces and begged him that they might touch only the tassel on his cloak; and as many as touched it were healed.

Tuesday February 11, 2025
Tuesday of Fifth Week in Ordinary Time
First Reading: Genesis 1:20-2:4A
[20] God said, "Let the water teem with an abundance of living creatures, and on the earth let birds fly beneath the dome of the sky." And so it happened: [21] God created the great sea monsters and all kinds of swimming creatures with which the water teems, and all kinds of winged birds. God saw how good it was, [22] and God blessed them, saying, "Be fertile, multiply, and fill the water of the seas; and let the birds multiply on the earth." [23] Evening came, and morning followed— the fifth day.

[24] Then God said, "Let the earth bring forth all kinds of living creatures: cattle, creeping things, and wild animals of all kinds." And so it happened: [25] God made all kinds of wild animals, all kinds of cattle, and all kinds of creeping things of the earth. God saw how good it was. [26] Then God said: "Let us make man in our image, after our likeness. Let them have dominion over the fish of the sea, the birds of the air, and the cattle, and over all the wild animals and all the creatures that crawl on the ground."

[27] God created man in his image;
   in the divine image he created him;
   male and female he created them.

[28] God blessed them, saying: "Be fertile and multiply; fill the earth and subdue it. Have dominion over the fish of the sea, the birds of the air, and all the living things that move on the earth." [29] God also said: "See, I give you every seed-bearing plant all over the earth and every tree that has seed-bearing fruit on it to be your food; [30] and to all the animals of the land, all the birds of the air, and all the living creatures that crawl on the ground, I give all the green plants for food." And so it happened. [31] God looked at everything he had made, and he found it very good. Evening came, and morning followed— the sixth day.

[1] Thus the heavens and the earth and all their array were completed. [2] Since on the seventh day God was finished with the work he had been doing, he rested on the seventh day from all the work he had undertaken. [3] So God blessed the seventh day and made it holy, because on it he rested from all the work he had done in creation.

[4A] Such is the story of the heavens and the earth at their creation.

Responsorial Psalm: Psalms 8:4-5, 6-7, 8-9
R. (2ab) O Lord, our God, how wonderful your name in all the earth!

⁴When I behold your heavens, the work of your fingers,
> the moon and the stars which you set in place—

⁵ What is man that you should be mindful of him,
> or the son of man that you should care for him?

R. O Lord, our God, how wonderful your name in all the earth!

⁶ You have made him little less than the angels,
> and crowned him with glory and honor.

⁷ You have given him rule over the works of your hands,
> putting all things under his feet.

R. O Lord, our God, how wonderful your name in all the earth!

⁸All sheep and oxen,
> yes, and the beasts of the field,

⁹ The birds of the air, the fishes of the sea,
> and whatever swims the paths of the seas.

R. O Lord, our God, how wonderful your name in all the earth!

Alleluia: Psalms 119:36, 29B
R. Alleluia, alleluia.
³⁶ Incline my heart, O God, to your decrees;
²⁹ᴮ and favor me with your law.
R. Alleluia, alleluia.

Gospel: Mark 7:1-13
¹ When the Pharisees with some scribes who had come from Jerusalem gathered around Jesus, ² they observed that some of his disciples ate their meals with unclean, that is, unwashed, hands. ³ (For the Pharisees and, in fact, all Jews, do not eat without carefully washing their hands, keeping the tradition of the elders. ⁴And on coming from the marketplace they do not eat without purifying themselves. And there are many other things that they have traditionally observed, the purification of cups and jugs and kettles and beds.) ⁵ So the Pharisees and scribes questioned him, "Why do your disciples not follow the tradition of the elders but

instead eat a meal with unclean hands?" ⁶ He responded, "Well did Isaiah prophesy about you hypocrites, as it is written:

This people honors me with their lips,
but their hearts are far from me;
⁷ *in vain do they worship me,*
teaching as doctrines human precepts.

⁸ You disregard God's commandment but cling to human tradition." ⁹ He went on to say, "How well you have set aside the commandment of God in order to uphold your tradition! ¹⁰ For Moses said, *Honor your father and your mother,* and *Whoever curses father or mother shall die.* ¹¹ Yet you say, 'If someone says to father or mother, "Any support you might have had from me is *qorban*"' (meaning, dedicated to God), ¹² you allow him to do nothing more for his father or mother. ¹³ You nullify the word of God in favor of your tradition that you have handed on. And you do many such things."

Wednesday February 12, 2025
Wednesday of Fifth Week in Ordinary Time
First Reading: Genesis 2:4B-9, 15-17

⁴ᴮAt the time when the LORD God made the earth and the heavens, ⁵—while as yet there was no field shrub on earth and no grass of the field had sprouted, for the LORD God had sent no rain upon the earth and there was no man to till the soil, ⁶but a stream was welling up out of the earth and was watering all the surface of the ground— ⁷the LORD God formed man out of the clay of the ground and blew into his nostrils the breath of life, and so man became a living being.

⁸Then the LORD God planted a garden in Eden, in the east, and he placed there the man whom he had formed. ⁹Out of the ground the LORD God made various trees grow that were delightful to look at and good for food, with the tree of life in the middle of the garden and the tree of the knowledge of good and evil.

¹⁵The LORD God then took the man and settled him in the garden of Eden, to cultivate and care for it. ¹⁶The LORD God gave man this order: "You are free to eat from any of the trees of the garden ¹⁷except the tree of knowledge of good and evil. From that tree you shall not eat; the moment you eat from it you are surely doomed to die."

Responsorial Psalm: Psalms 104:1-2A, 27-28, 29BC-30
R. ⁽¹ᵃ⁾ *O bless the Lord, my soul!*
¹Bless the LORD, O my soul!
O LORD, my God, you are great indeed!
You are clothed with majesty and glory,
²ᴬ robed in light as with a cloak.
R. *O bless the Lord, my soul!*
²⁷All creatures look to you
to give them food in due time.
²⁸ When you give it to them, they gather it;
when you open your hand, they are filled

with good things.
R. O bless the Lord, my soul!
²⁹ᴮᶜ If you take away their breath, they perish
    and return to their dust.
³⁰ When you send forth your spirit, they are created,
    and you renew the face of the earth.
R. O bless the Lord, my soul!

Alleluia: John 17:17B, 17A
R. Alleluia, alleluia.
¹⁷ᴮYour word, O Lord, is truth:
¹⁷ᴬ consecrate us in the truth.
R. Alleluia, alleluia.

Gospel: Mark 7:14-23
¹⁴Jesus summoned the crowd again and said to them, "Hear me, all of you, and understand. ¹⁵Nothing that enters one from outside can defile that person; but the things that come out from within are what defile."
¹⁷ When he got home away from the crowd his disciples questioned him about the parable. ¹⁸He said to them, "Are even you likewise without understanding? Do you not realize that everything that goes into a person from outside cannot defile, ¹⁹since it enters not the heart but the stomach and passes out into the latrine?" (Thus he declared all foods clean.) ²⁰"But what comes out of the man, that is what defiles him. ²¹From within the man, from his heart, come evil thoughts, unchastity, theft, murder, ²²adultery, greed, malice, deceit, licentiousness, envy, blasphemy, arrogance, folly. ²³All these evils come from within and they defile."

Thursday February 13, 2025
Thursday of Fifth Week in Ordinary Time
First Reading: Genesis 2:18-25
¹⁸The LORD God said: "It is not good for the man to be alone. I will make a suitable partner for him." ¹⁹So the LORD God formed out of the ground various wild animals and various birds of the air, and he brought them to the man to see what he would call them; whatever the man called each of them would be its name. ²⁰The man gave names to all the cattle, all the birds of the air, and all the wild animals; but none proved to be the suitable partner for the man.
²¹So the LORD God cast a deep sleep on the man, and while he was asleep, he took out one of his ribs and closed up its place with flesh. ²²The LORD God then built up into a woman the rib that he had taken from the man. When he brought her to the man, ²³the man said:

"This one, at last, is bone of my bones
    and flesh of my flesh;
this one shall be called 'woman,'

> for out of 'her man' this one has been
> taken."

²⁴That is why a man leaves his father and mother and clings to his wife, and the two of them become one flesh.
> ²⁵The man and his wife were both naked, yet they felt no shame.

Responsorial Psalm: Psalms 128:1-2, 3, 4-5
R. *(see 1a)* ***Blessed are those who fear the Lord.***
¹Blessed are you who fear the LORD,
> who walk in his ways!

² For you shall eat the fruit of your
> handiwork;
> blessed shall you be, and favored.

R. Blessed are those who fear the Lord.
³Your wife shall be like a fruitful vine
> in the recesses of your home;

Your children like olive plants
> around your table.

R. Blessed are those who fear the Lord.
⁴ Behold, thus is the man blessed
> who fears the LORD.

⁵ The LORD bless you from Zion:
> may you see the prosperity of Jerusalem
> all the days of your life.

R. Blessed are those who fear the Lord.

Alleluia: James 1:21BC
R. Alleluia, alleluia.
²¹ᴮᶜ Humbly welcome the word that has been
> planted in you

and is able to save your souls.
R. Alleluia, alleluia.

Gospel: Mark 7:24-30
²⁴Jesus went to the district of Tyre. He entered a house and wanted no one to know about it, but he could not escape notice. ²⁵ Soon a woman whose daughter had an unclean spirit heard about him. She came and fell at his feet. ²⁶ The woman was a Greek, a Syrophoenician by birth, and she begged him to drive the demon out of her daughter. ²⁷He said to her, "Let the children be fed first. For it is not right to take the food of the children and throw it to the dogs." ²⁸ She replied and said to him, "Lord, even the dogs under the table eat the children's scraps." ²⁹ Then he said to her, "For saying this, you may go. The demon has gone out of your daughter." ³⁰ When the woman went home, she found the child lying in bed and the demon gone.

Friday February 14, 2025
Memorial of Saints Cyril, monk, and Methodius, Bishop
First Reading: Genesis 3:1-8

¹Now the serpent was the most cunning of all the animals that the LORD God had made. The serpent asked the woman, "Did God really tell you not to eat from any of the trees in the garden?" ²The woman answered the serpent: "We may eat of the fruit of the trees in the garden; ³it is only about the fruit of the tree in the middle of the garden that God said, 'You shall not eat it or even touch it, lest you die.'" ⁴But the serpent said to the woman: "You certainly will not die! ⁵No, God knows well that the moment you eat of it your eyes will be opened and you will be like gods who know what is good and what is evil." ⁶The woman saw that the tree was good for food, pleasing to the eyes, and desirable for gaining wisdom. So she took some of its fruit and ate it; and she also gave some to her husband, who was with her, and he ate it. ⁷Then the eyes of both of them were opened, and they realized that they were naked; so they sewed fig leaves together and made loincloths for themselves.

⁸When they heard the sound of the LORD God moving about in the garden at the breezy time of the day, the man and his wife hid themselves from the LORD God among the trees of the garden.

Responsorial Psalm: Psalms 32:1-2, 5, 6, 7
R. (1a) **Blessed are those whose sins are forgiven.**
¹Blessed is he whose fault is taken away,
   whose sin is covered.
² Blessed the man to whom the LORD imputes
      not guilt,
   in whose spirit there is no guile.
R. Blessed are those whose sins are forgiven.
⁵Then I acknowledged my sin to you,
   my guilt I covered not.
I said, "I confess my faults to the LORD,"
   and you took away the guilt of my sin.
R. Blessed are those whose sins are forgiven.
⁶ For this shall every faithful man pray to you
   in time of stress.
Though deep waters overflow,
   they shall not reach him.
R. Blessed are those whose sins are forgiven.
⁷ You are my shelter; from distress you will
      preserve me;
   with glad cries of freedom you will ring
      me round.
R. Blessed are those whose sins are forgiven.

Alleluia: Acts 16:14B
R. Alleluia, alleluia.
14B Open our hearts, O Lord,
to listen to the words of your Son.
R. Alleluia, alleluia.

Gospel: Mark 7:31-37
31 Jesus left the district of Tyre and went by way of Sidon to the Sea of Galilee, into the district of the Decapolis. 32 And people brought to him a deaf man who had a speech impediment and begged him to lay his hand on him. 33 He took him off by himself away from the crowd. He put his finger into the man's ears and, spitting, touched his tongue; 34 then he looked up to heaven and groaned, and said to him, "*Ephphatha!*" (that is, "Be opened!") 35 And immediately the man's ears were opened, his speech impediment was removed, and he spoke plainly. 36 He ordered them not to tell anyone. But the more he ordered them not to, the more they proclaimed it. 37 They were exceedingly astonished and they said, "He has done all things well. He makes the deaf hear and the mute speak."

Saturday February 15, 2025
Saturday of Fifth Week in Ordinary Time

First Reading: Genesis 3:9-24
9The LORD God called to Adam and asked him, "Where are you?" 10He answered, "I heard you in the garden; but I was afraid, because I was naked, so I hid myself." 11Then he asked, "Who told you that you were naked? You have eaten, then, from the tree of which I had forbidden you to eat!" 12The man replied, "The woman whom you put here with me she gave me fruit from the tree, and so I ate it." 13The LORD God then asked the woman, "Why did you do such a thing?" The woman answered, "The serpent tricked me into it, so I ate it."

14Then the LORD God said to the serpent:
"Because you have done this, you shall be
   banned
      from all the animals
      and from all the wild creatures;
On your belly shall you crawl,
      and dirt shall you eat
      all the days of your life.
15I will put enmity between you and the
      woman,
      and between your offspring and hers;
He will strike at your head,
      while you strike at his heel."

16To the woman he said:

"I will intensify the pangs of your
      childbearing;
      in pain shall you bring forth children.

Yet your urge shall be for your husband,
    and he shall be your master."

¹⁷To the man he said: "Because you listened to your wife and ate from the tree of which I had forbidden you to eat,

"Cursed be the ground because of you!
    In toil shall you eat its yield
    all the days of your life.
¹⁸Thorns and thistles shall it bring forth to you,
    as you eat of the plants of the field.
¹⁹By the sweat of your face
    shall you get bread to eat,
Until you return to the ground,
    from which you were taken;
For you are dirt,
    and to dirt you shall return."

²⁰The man called his wife Eve, because she became the mother of all the living.
    ²¹For the man and his wife the LORD God made leather garments, with which he clothed them. ²²Then the LORD God said: "See! The man has become like one of us, knowing what is good and what is evil! Therefore, he must not be allowed to put out his hand to take fruit from the tree of life also, and thus eat of it and live forever." ²³The LORD God therefore banished him from the garden of Eden, to till the ground from which he had been taken. ²⁴When he expelled the man, he settled him east of the garden of Eden; and he stationed the cherubim and the fiery revolving sword, to guard the way to the tree of life.

Responsorial Psalm: Psalms 90:2, 3-4ABC, 5-6, 12-13
R. ⁽¹⁾ *In every age, O Lord, you have been our*
    refuge.
² Before the mountains were begotten
    and the earth and the world were
        brought forth,
    from everlasting to everlasting you are
        God.
R. In every age, O Lord, you have been our
    refuge.
³ You turn man back to dust,
    saying, "Return, O children of men."
⁴ᴬᴮᶜ For a thousand years in your sight
    are as yesterday, now that it is past,
    or as a watch of the night.
R. In every age, O Lord, you have been our

refuge.

⁵ You make an end of them in their sleep;
    the next morning they are like the
        changing grass,
⁶ Which at dawn springs up anew,
    but by evening wilts and fades.

R. In every age, O Lord, you have been our refuge.

¹² Teach us to number our days aright,
    that we may gain wisdom of heart.
¹³ Return, O LORD! How long?
    Have pity on your servants!

R. In every age, O Lord, you have been our refuge.

Alleluia: Matthew 4:4B
R. Alleluia, alleluia.
⁴ᴮ One does not live on bread alone,
but on every word that comes forth from the
        mouth of God.
R. Alleluia, alleluia.

Gospel: Mark 8:1-10
¹ In those days when there again was a great crowd without anything to eat, Jesus summoned the disciples and said, ² "My heart is moved with pity for the crowd, because they have been with me now for three days and have nothing to eat. ³ If I send them away hungry to their homes, they will collapse on the way, and some of them have come a great distance." ⁴ His disciples answered him, "Where can anyone get enough bread to satisfy them here in this deserted place?" ⁵ Still he asked them, "How many loaves do you have?" They replied, "Seven." ⁶ He ordered the crowd to sit down on the ground. Then, taking the seven loaves he gave thanks, broke them, and gave them to his disciples to distribute, and they distributed them to the crowd. ⁷ They also had a few fish. He said the blessing over them and ordered them distributed also. ⁸ They ate and were satisfied. They picked up the fragments left over—seven baskets. ⁹ There were about four thousand people.

He dismissed the crowd ¹⁰ and got into the boat with his disciples and came to the region of Dalmanutha.

Sunday February 16, 2025
Sixth Sunday in Ordinary Time Year C
First Reading: Jeremiah 17:5-8
⁵Thus says the LORD:

Cursed is the one who trusts in human
    beings,
    who seeks his strength in flesh,

whose heart turns away from the LORD.
⁶He is like a barren bush in the desert
    that enjoys no change of season,
but stands in a lava waste,
    a salt and empty earth.
⁷Blessed is the one who trusts in the LORD,
    whose hope is the LORD.
⁸He is like a tree planted beside the waters
    that stretches out its roots to the stream:
It fears not the heat when it comes;
    its leaves stay green;
in the year of drought it shows no distress,
    but still bears fruit.

Responsorial Psalm: Psalms 1:1-2, 3, 4 AND 6
R. *(40:5a)* **Blessed are they who hope in the Lord.**
¹Blessed the man who follows not
    the counsel of the wicked,
nor walks in the way of sinners,
    nor sits in the company of the insolent,
² but delights in the law of the LORD
    and meditates on his law day and night.
R. Blessed are they who hope in the Lord.
³He is like a tree
    planted near running water,
that yields its fruit in due season,
    and whose leaves never fade.
    Whatever he does, prospers.
R. Blessed are they who hope in the Lord.
⁴ Not so the wicked, not so;
    they are like chaff which the wind drives
        away.
⁶ For the LORD watches over the way of the
      just,
    but the way of the wicked vanishes.
R. Blessed are they who hope in the Lord.

Second Reading: 1 Corinthians 15:12, 16-20
Brothers and sisters: ¹²If Christ is preached as raised from the dead, how can some among you say there is no resurrection of the dead? ¹⁶If the dead are not raised, neither has Christ been raised, ¹⁷and if Christ has not been raised, your faith is vain; you are still in your sins. ¹⁸Then those who have fallen asleep in Christ have perished. ¹⁹If for this life only we have hoped in Christ, we are the most pitiable people of all.

[20]But now Christ has been raised from the dead, the firstfruits of those who have fallen asleep.

Alleluia: Luke 6:23AB
R. Alleluia, alleluia.
[23AB] Rejoice and be glad;
your reward will be great in heaven.
R. Alleluia, alleluia.

Gospel: Luke 6:17, 20-26
[17]Jesus came down with the Twelve and stood on a stretch of level ground with a great crowd of his disciples and a large number of the people from all Judea and Jerusalem and the coastal region of Tyre and Sidon. [20]And raising his eyes toward his disciples he said:

"Blessed are you who are poor,
    for the kingdom of God is yours.
[21] Blessed are you who are now hungry,
    for you will be satisfied.
Blessed are you who are now weeping,
    for you will laugh.
[22] Blessed are you when people hate you,
    and when they exclude and insult you,
    and denounce your name as evil
    on account of the Son of Man.

[23] Rejoice and leap for joy on that day! Behold, your reward will be great in heaven. For their ancestors treated the prophets in the same way.

[24]But woe to you who are rich,
    for you have received your consolation.
[25] Woe to you who are filled now,
    for you will be hungry.
Woe to you who laugh now,
    for you will grieve and weep.
[26]Woe to you when all speak well of you,
    for their ancestors treated the false
        prophets in this way."

Monday February 17, 2025
Monday of Sixth Week in Ordinary Time
First Reading: Genesis 4:1-15, 25
[1]The man had relations with his wife Eve, and she conceived and bore Cain, saying, "I have produced a man with the help of the LORD." [2]Next she bore his brother Abel. Abel became a keeper of flocks, and Cain a tiller of the soil. [3]In the course of time Cain brought an offering to the LORD from the fruit of the soil,

⁴while Abel, for his part, brought one of the best firstlings of his flock. The LORD looked with favor on Abel and his offering, ⁵but on Cain and his offering he did not. Cain greatly resented this and was crestfallen. ⁶So the LORD said to Cain: "Why are you so resentful and crestfallen? ⁷If you do well, you can hold up your head; but if not, sin is a demon lurking at the door: his urge is toward you, yet you can be his master."

⁸Cain said to his brother Abel, "Let us go out in the field." When they were in the field, Cain attacked his brother Abel and killed him. ⁹Then the LORD asked Cain, "Where is your brother Abel?" He answered, "I do not know. Am I my brother's keeper?" ¹⁰The LORD then said: "What have you done! Listen: your brother's blood cries out to me from the soil! ¹¹Therefore you shall be banned from the soil that opened its mouth to receive your brother's blood from your hand. ¹²If you till the soil, it shall no longer give you its produce. You shall become a restless wanderer on the earth." ¹³Cain said to the LORD: "My punishment is too great to bear. ¹⁴Since you have now banished me from the soil, and I must avoid your presence and become a restless wanderer on the earth, anyone may kill me at sight." ¹⁵"Not so!" the LORD said to him. "If anyone kills Cain, Cain shall be avenged sevenfold." So the LORD put a mark on Cain, lest anyone should kill him at sight.

²⁵Adam again had relations with his wife, and she gave birth to a son whom she called Seth. "God has granted me more offspring in place of Abel," she said, "because Cain slew him."

Responsorial Psalm: Psalms 50:1 AND 8, 16BC-17, 20-21

R. ⁽¹⁴ᵃ⁾ Offer to God a sacrifice of praise.
¹God the LORD has spoken and summoned the
     earth,
   from the rising of the sun to its setting.
⁸ "Not for your sacrifices do I rebuke you,
   for your burnt offerings are before me
     always."
R. Offer to God a sacrifice of praise.
¹⁶ᴮᶜ "Why do you recite my statutes,
   and profess my covenant with your
     mouth
¹⁷ Though you hate discipline
   and cast my words behind you?"
R. Offer to God a sacrifice of praise.
²⁰ "You sit speaking against your brother;
   against your mother's son you spread
     rumors.
²¹ When you do these things, shall I be deaf to
     it?
   Or do you think that I am like yourself?
   I will correct you by drawing them up

before your eyes."
R. *Offer to God a sacrifice of praise.*

Alleluia: John 14:6
R. Alleluia, alleluia.
⁶ I am the way and the truth and the life, says
>   the Lord;
no one comes to the Father except through
>   me.
R. Alleluia, alleluia.

Gospel: Mark 8:11-13
¹¹ The Pharisees came forward and began to argue with Jesus, seeking from him a sign from heaven to test him. ¹² He sighed from the depth of his spirit and said, "Why does this generation seek a sign? Amen, I say to you, no sign will be given to this generation." ¹³ Then he left them, got into the boat again, and went off to the other shore.

Tuesday February 18, 2025
Tuesday of Sixth Week in Ordinary Time
First Reading: Genesis 6:5-8; 7:1-5, 10

⁵When the LORD saw how great was man's wickedness on earth, and how no desire that his heart conceived was ever anything but evil, ⁶he regretted that he had made man on the earth, and his heart was grieved.

⁷So the LORD said: "I will wipe out from the earth the men whom I have created, and not only the men, but also the beasts and the creeping things and the birds of the air, for I am sorry that I made them." ⁸But Noah found favor with the LORD.

¹Then the LORD said to Noah: "Go into the ark, you and all your household, for you alone in this age have I found to be truly just. ²Of every clean animal, take with you seven pairs, a male and its mate; and of the unclean animals, one pair, a male and its mate; ³likewise, of every clean bird of the air, seven pairs, a male and a female, and of all the unclean birds, one pair, a male and a female. Thus you will keep their issue alive over all the earth. ⁴Seven days from now I will bring rain down on the earth for forty days and forty nights, and so I will wipe out from the surface of the earth every moving creature that I have made." ⁵Noah did just as the LORD had commanded him.

¹⁰As soon as the seven days were over, the waters of the flood came upon the earth.

Responsorial Psalm: Psalms 29:1A AND 2, 3AC-4, 3B AND 9C-10
R. ⁽¹¹ᵇ⁾ *The Lord will bless his people with peace.*
¹ᴬ Give to the LORD, you sons of God,
>   give to the LORD glory and praise,
² Give to the LORD the glory due his name;
>   adore the LORD in holy attire.
R. *The Lord will bless his people with peace.*
³ᴬᶜ The voice of the LORD is over the waters,

the LORD, over vast waters.
⁴ The voice of the LORD is mighty;
 the voice of the LORD is majestic.
R. The Lord will bless his people with peace.
³ᴮ The God of glory thunders,
 ⁹ᶜ and in his temple all say, "Glory!"
¹⁰ The LORD is enthroned above the flood;
 the LORD is enthroned as king forever.
R. The Lord will bless his people with peace.

Alleluia: John 14:23
R. Alleluia, alleluia.
²³ Whoever loves me will keep my word, says
 the Lord;
and my Father will love him
and we will come to him.
R. Alleluia, alleluia.

Gospel: Mark 8:14-21
¹⁴ The disciples had forgotten to bring bread, and they had only one loaf with them in the boat. ¹⁵ Jesus enjoined them, "Watch out, guard against the leaven of the Pharisees and the leaven of Herod." ¹⁶ They concluded among themselves that it was because they had no bread. ¹⁷ When he became aware of this he said to them, "Why do you conclude that it is because you have no bread? Do you not yet understand or comprehend? Are your hearts hardened? ¹⁸ Do you have eyes and not see, ears and not hear? And do you not remember, ¹⁹ when I broke the five loaves for the five thousand, how many wicker baskets full of fragments you picked up?" They answered him, "Twelve." ²⁰ "When I broke the seven loaves for the four thousand, how many full baskets of fragments did you pick up?" They answered him, "Seven." ²¹ He said to them, "Do you still not understand?"

Wednesday February 19, 2025
Wednesday of Sixth Week in Ordinary Time
First Reading: Genesis 8:6-13, 20-22
⁶At the end of forty days Noah opened the hatch he had made in the ark, ⁷and he sent out a raven, to see if the waters had lessened on the earth. It flew back and forth until the waters dried off from the earth. ⁸Then he sent out a dove, to see if the waters had lessened on the earth. ⁹But the dove could find no place to alight and perch, and it returned to him in the ark, for there was water all over the earth. Putting out his hand, he caught the dove and drew it back to him inside the ark. ¹⁰He waited seven days more and again sent the dove out from the ark. ¹¹In the evening the dove came back to him, and there in its bill was a plucked-off olive leaf! So Noah knew that the waters had lessened on the earth. ¹²He waited still another seven days and then released the dove once more; and this time it did not come back.

¹³In the six hundred and first year of Noah's life, in the first month, on the first day of the month, the water began to dry up on the earth. Noah then removed the covering of the ark and saw that the surface of the ground was drying up.
²⁰Noah built an altar to the LORD, and choosing from every clean animal and every clean bird, he offered burnt offerings on the altar. ²¹When the LORD smelled the sweet odor, he said to himself: "Never again will I doom the earth because of man since the desires of man's heart are evil from the start; nor will I ever again strike down all living beings, as I have done.

²²As long as the earth lasts,
    seedtime and harvest,
    cold and heat,
Summer and winter,
    and day and night
    shall not cease."

Responsorial Psalm: Psalms 116:12-13, 14-15, 18-19
R. *(17a)* *To you, Lord, I will offer a sacrifice of praise.* or: *R. Alleluia.*
¹² How shall I make a return to the LORD
    for all the good he has done for me?
¹³ The cup of salvation I will take up,
    and I will call upon the name of the LORD.
R. To you, Lord, I will offer a sacrifice of praise. or: *R. Alleluia.*
¹⁴ My vows to the LORD I will pay
    in the presence of all his people.
¹⁵ Precious in the eyes of the LORD
    is the death of his faithful ones.
R. To you, Lord, I will offer a sacrifice of praise. or: *R. Alleluia.*
¹⁸ My vows to the LORD I will pay
    in the presence of all his people,
¹⁹ In the courts of the house of the LORD,
    in your midst, O Jerusalem.
R. To you, Lord, I will offer a sacrifice of praise. or: *R. Alleluia.*

Alleluia: Ephesians 1:17-18
R. Alleluia, alleluia.
¹⁷May the Father of our Lord Jesus Christ
enlighten the eyes of our hearts,
¹⁸ that we may know what is the hope
that belongs to his call.
R. Alleluia, alleluia.

Gospel: Mark 8:22-26

[22] When Jesus and his disciples arrived at Bethsaida, people brought to him a blind man and begged Jesus to touch him. [23] He took the blind man by the hand and led him outside the village. Putting spittle on his eyes he laid his hands on the man and asked, "Do you see anything?" [24] Looking up the man replied, "I see people looking like trees and walking." [25] Then he laid hands on the man's eyes a second time and he saw clearly; his sight was restored and he could see everything distinctly. [26] Then he sent him home and said, "Do not even go into the village."

Thursday February 20, 2025
Thursday of Sixth Week in Ordinary Time

First Reading: Genesis 9:1-13

[1] God blessed Noah and his sons and said to them: "Be fertile and multiply and fill the earth. [2] Dread fear of you shall come upon all the animals of the earth and all the birds of the air, upon all the creatures that move about on the ground and all the fishes of the sea; into your power they are delivered. [3] Every creature that is alive shall be yours to eat; I give them all to you as I did the green plants. [4] Only flesh with its lifeblood still in it you shall not eat. [5] For your own lifeblood, too, I will demand an accounting: from every animal I will demand it, and from one man in regard to his fellow man I will demand an accounting for human life.

[6] If anyone sheds the blood of man,
    by man shall his blood be shed;
For in the image of God
    has man been made.

[7] Be fertile, then, and multiply; abound on earth and subdue it."

[8] God said to Noah and to his sons with him: [9] "See, I am now establishing my covenant with you and your descendants after you [10] and with every living creature that was with you: all the birds, and the various tame and wild animals that were with you and came out of the ark. [11] I will establish my covenant with you, that never again shall all bodily creatures be destroyed by the waters of a flood; there shall not be another flood to devastate the earth." [12] God added: "This is the sign that I am giving for all ages to come, of the covenant between me and you and every living creature with you: [13] I set my bow in the clouds to serve as a sign of the covenant between me and the earth."

Responsorial Psalm: Psalms 102:16-18, 19-21, 29 AND 22-23

R. (20b) *From heaven the Lord looks down on the earth.*

[16] The nations shall revere your name, O LORD,
    and all the kings of the earth your glory,
[17] When the LORD has rebuilt Zion
    and appeared in his glory;
[18] When he has regarded the prayer of the destitute,

and not despised their prayer.
R. From heaven the Lord looks down on the earth.

¹⁸ Let this be written for the generation to come,
and let his future creatures praise the LORD:
²⁰ "The LORD looked down from his holy height,
from heaven he beheld the earth,
²¹ To hear the groaning of the prisoners,
to release those doomed to die."
R. From heaven the Lord looks down on the earth.

²⁹ The children of your servants shall abide,
and their posterity shall continue in your presence,
²² That the name of the LORD may be declared in Zion,
and his praise, in Jerusalem,
²³ When the peoples gather together,
and the kingdoms, to serve the LORD.
R. From heaven the Lord looks down on the earth.

Alleluia: John 6:63C, 68C
R. Alleluia, alleluia.
⁶³ᶜ Your words, Lord, are Spirit and life;
⁶⁸ᶜ you have the words of everlasting life.
R. Alleluia, alleluia.

Gospel: Mark 8:27-33
²⁷Jesus and his disciples set out for the villages of Caesarea Philippi. Along the way he asked his disciples, "Who do people say that I am?" ²⁸They said in reply, "John the Baptist, others Elijah, still others one of the prophets." ²⁹And he asked them, "But who do you say that I am?" Peter said to him in reply, "You are the Christ." ³⁰Then he warned them not to tell anyone about him.

³¹He began to teach them that the Son of Man must suffer greatly and be rejected by the elders, the chief priests, and the scribes, and be killed, and rise after three days. ³²He spoke this openly. Then Peter took him aside and began to rebuke him. ³³At this he turned around and, looking at his disciples, rebuked Peter and said, "Get behind me, Satan. You are thinking not as God does, but as human beings do."

Friday February 21, 2025
Friday of Sixth Week in Ordinary Time

First Reading: Genesis 11:1-9

¹The whole world spoke the same language, using the same words. ²While the people were migrating in the east, they came upon a valley in the land of Shinar and settled there. ³They said to one another, "Come, let us mold bricks and harden them with fire." They used bricks for stone, and bitumen for mortar. ⁴Then they said, "Come, let us build ourselves a city and a tower with its top in the sky, and so make a name for ourselves; otherwise we shall be scattered all over the earth."

⁵The LORD came down to see the city and the tower that they had built. ⁶Then the LORD said: "If now, while they are one people, all speaking the same language, they have started to do this, nothing will later stop them from doing whatever they presume to do. ⁷Let us then go down and there confuse their language, so that one will not understand what another says." ⁸Thus the LORD scattered them from there all over the earth, and they stopped building the city. ⁹That is why it was called Babel, because there the LORD confused the speech of all the world. It was from that place that he scattered them all over the earth.

Responsorial Psalm: Psalms 33:10-11, 12-13, 14-15

R. (12) *Blessed the people the Lord has chosen to be his own.*

¹⁰ The LORD brings to nought the plans of nations;
  he foils the designs of peoples.
¹¹ But the plan of the LORD stands forever;
  the design of his heart, through all generations.

R. *Blessed the people the Lord has chosen to be his own.*

¹² Blessed the nation whose God is the LORD,
  the people he has chosen for his own inheritance.
¹³ From heaven the LORD looks down;
  he sees all mankind.

R. *Blessed the people the Lord has chosen to be his own.*

¹⁴ From his fixed throne he beholds
  all who dwell on the earth,
¹⁵ He who fashioned the heart of each,
  he who knows all their works.

R. *Blessed the people the Lord has chosen to be his own.*

Alleluia: John 15:15B
R. Alleluia, alleluia.
15B I call you my friends, says the Lord,
for I have made known to you all that the
> Father has told me.
R. Alleluia, alleluia.

Gospel: Mark 8:34-9:1
34 Jesus summoned the crowd with his disciples and said to them, "Whoever wishes to come after me must deny himself, take up his cross, and follow me. 35 For whoever wishes to save his life will lose it, but whoever loses his life for my sake and that of the Gospel will save it. 36 What profit is there for one to gain the whole world and forfeit his life? 37 What could one give in exchange for his life? 38 Whoever is ashamed of me and of my words in this faithless and sinful generation, the Son of Man will be ashamed of when he comes in his Father's glory with the holy angels."

1 He also said to them, "Amen, I say to you, there are some standing here who will not taste death until they see that the Kingdom of God has come in power."

Saturday February 22, 2025
Feast of the Chair of Saint Peter, Apostle

First Reading: 1 Peter 5:1-4
Beloved: 1 I exhort the presbyters among you, as a fellow presbyter and witness to the sufferings of Christ and one who has a share in the glory to be revealed. 2 Tend the flock of God in your midst, overseeing not by constraint but willingly, as God would have it, not for shameful profit but eagerly. 3 Do not lord it over those assigned to you, but be examples to the flock. 4 And when the chief Shepherd is revealed, you will receive the unfading crown of glory.

Responsorial Psalm: Psalms 23:1-3A, 4, 5, 6
**R. (1) The Lord is my shepherd; there is nothing I
> shall want.**
1 The LORD is my shepherd; I shall not want.
> 2 In verdant pastures he gives me repose;
Beside restful waters he leads me;
> 3A he refreshes my soul.
**R. The Lord is my shepherd; there is nothing I
> shall want.**
4 Even though I walk in the dark valley
> I fear no evil; for you are at my side
With your rod and your staff
> that give me courage.
**R. The Lord is my shepherd; there is nothing I
> shall want.**
5 You spread the table before me
> in the sight of my foes;

You anoint my head with oil;
> my cup overflows.

**R. The Lord is my shepherd; there is nothing I
> shall want.**

⁶ Only goodness and kindness follow me
> all the days of my life;
And I shall dwell in the house of the LORD
> for years to come.

**R. The Lord is my shepherd; there is nothing I
> shall want.**

Alleluia: Matthew 16:18
R. Alleluia, alleluia.
¹⁸ You are Peter, and upon this rock I will build
> my Church;
the gates of the netherworld shall not prevail
> against it.
R. Alleluia, alleluia.

Gospel: Matthew 16:13-19
¹³ When Jesus went into the region of Caesarea Philippi he asked his disciples, "Who do people say that the Son of Man is?" ¹⁴ They replied, "Some say John the Baptist, others Elijah, still others Jeremiah or one of the prophets." ¹⁵ He said to them, "But who do you say that I am?" ¹⁶ Simon Peter said in reply, "You are the Christ, the Son of the living God." ¹⁷ Jesus said to him in reply, "Blessed are you, Simon son of Jonah. For flesh and blood has not revealed this to you, but my heavenly Father. ¹⁸ And so I say to you, you are Peter, and upon this rock I will build my Church, and the gates of the netherworld shall not prevail against it. ¹⁹ I will give you the keys to the Kingdom of heaven. Whatever you bind on earth shall be bound in heaven; and whatever you loose on earth shall be loosed in heaven."

Sunday February 23, 2025
Seventh Sunday in Ordinary Time, Year C
First Reading: 1 Samuel 26:2,7-9,12-13, 22-23
²In those days, Saul went down to the desert of Ziph with three thousand picked men of Israel, to search for David in the desert of Ziph. ⁷So David and Abishai went among Saul's soldiers by night and found Saul lying asleep within the barricade, with his spear thrust into the ground at his head and Abner and his men sleeping around him.
⁸Abishai whispered to David: "God has delivered your enemy into your grasp this day. Let me nail him to the ground with one thrust of the spear; I will not need a second thrust!" ⁹But David said to Abishai, "Do not harm him, for who can lay hands on the LORD's anointed and remain unpunished?" ¹²So David took the spear and the water jug from their place at Saul's head, and they got away without anyone's seeing or knowing or awakening. All remained asleep, because the LORD had put them into a deep slumber.

¹³Going across to an opposite slope, David stood on a remote hilltop at a great distance from Abner, son of Ner, and the troops. ²²He said: "Here is the king's spear. Let an attendant come over to get it. ²³The LORD will reward each man for his justice and faithfulness. Today, though the LORD delivered you into my grasp, I would not harm the LORD's anointed."

Responsorial Psalm: Psalms 103:1-2, 3-4, 8, 10, 12-13

R. *(8a)* **The Lord is kind and merciful.**
¹ Bless the LORD, O my soul;
    and all my being, bless his holy name.
² Bless the LORD, O my soul,
    and forget not all his benefits.
R. The Lord is kind and merciful.
² He pardons all your iniquities,
    heals all your ills.
⁴ He redeems your life from destruction,
    crowns you with kindness and
        compassion.
R. The Lord is kind and merciful.
⁸ Merciful and gracious is the LORD,
    slow to anger and abounding in
        kindness.
¹⁰ Not according to our sins does he deal with
    us,
    nor does he requite us according to our
        crimes.
R. The Lord is kind and merciful.
¹² As far as the east is from the west,
    so far has he put our transgressions from
        us.
¹³ As a father has compassion on his children,
    so the LORD has compassion on those who
        fear him.
R. The Lord is kind and merciful.

Second Reading: 1 Corinthians 15:45-49

Brothers and sisters: ⁴⁵It is written, *The first man, Adam, became a living being,* the last Adam a life-giving spirit. ⁴⁶But the spiritual was not first; rather the natural and then the spiritual. ⁴⁷The first man was from the earth, earthly; the second man, from heaven. ⁴⁸As was the earthly one, so also are the earthly, and as is the heavenly one, so also are the heavenly. ⁴⁹Just as we have borne the image of the earthly one, we shall also bear the image of the heavenly one.

Alleluia: John 13:34
R. Alleluia, alleluia.
34 I give you a new commandment, says the
> Lord:
Love one another as I have loved you.
R. Alleluia, alleluia.

Gospel: Luke 6:27-38
Jesus said to his disciples: 27"To you who hear I say, love your enemies, do good to those who hate you, 28bless those who curse you, pray for those who mistreat you. 29To the person who strikes you on one cheek, offer the other one as well,
and from the person who takes your cloak, do not withhold even your tunic. 30Give to everyone who asks of you, and from the one who takes what is yours do not demand it back. 31Do to others as you would have them do to you. 32For if you love those who love you, what credit is that to you? Even sinners love those who love them. 33And if you do good to those who do good to you, what credit is that to you? Even sinners do the same. 34If you lend money to those from whom you expect repayment, what credit is that to you? Even sinners lend to sinners, and get back the same amount. 35But rather, love your enemies and do good to them, and lend expecting nothing back; then your reward will be great and you will be children of the Most High, for he himself is kind to the ungrateful and the wicked. 36Be merciful, just as your Father is merciful.
37"Stop judging and you will not be judged. Stop condemning and you will not be condemned. Forgive and you will be forgiven. 38Give, and gifts will be given to you; a good measure, packed together, shaken down, and overflowing, will be poured into your lap. For the measure with which you measure will in return be measured out to you."

Monday February 24, 2025
Monday of Seventh Week in Ordinary Time
First Reading: Sirach 1:1-10
1All wisdom comes from the LORD
> and with him it remains forever, and is
>> before all time
2The sand of the seashore, the drops of rain,
> the days of eternity: who can number
>> these?
3 Heaven's height, earth's breadth,
> the depths of the abyss: who can explore
>> these?
4 Before all things else wisdom was created;
> and prudent understanding, from
>> eternity.
5 The word of God on high is the fountain of
>> wisdom
> and her ways are everlasting.
6 To whom has wisdom's root been revealed?

Who knows her subtleties?
⁷ To whom has the discipline of wisdom been revealed?
And who has understood the multiplicity of her ways?
⁸ There is but one, Most High
all-powerful creator-king and truly awe-inspiring one,
seated upon his throne and he is the God of dominion.
⁹ It is the LORD; he created her through the Holy Spirit,
has seen her and taken note of her.
He has poured her forth upon all his works,
¹⁰upon every living thing according to his bounty;
he has lavished her upon his friends.

Responsorial Psalm: Psalms 93:1AB, 1CD-2, 5
R.^(1a) The Lord is king; he is robed in majesty.
^{1AB} The LORD is king, in splendor robed;
robed is the LORD and girt about with strength.
R. The Lord is king; he is robed in majesty.
^{1CD} And he has made the world firm,
not to be moved.
² Your throne stands firm from of old;
from everlasting you are, O LORD.
R. The Lord is king; he is robed in majesty.
⁵ Your decrees are worthy of trust indeed:
holiness befits your house,
O LORD, for length of days.
R. The Lord is king; he is robed in majesty.

Alleluia: 2 Timothy 1:10
R. Alleluia, alleluia.
¹⁰ Our Savior Jesus Christ has destroyed death and brought life to light through the Gospel.
R. Alleluia, alleluia.

Gospel: Mark 9:14-29

[14] As Jesus came down from the mountain with Peter, James, John and approached the other disciples, they saw a large crowd around them and scribes arguing with them. [15] Immediately on seeing him, the whole crowd was utterly amazed. They ran up to him and greeted him. [16] He asked them, "What are you arguing about with them?" [17] Someone from the crowd answered him, "Teacher, I have brought to you my son possessed by a mute spirit. [18] Wherever it seizes him, it throws him down; he foams at the mouth, grinds his teeth, and becomes rigid. I asked your disciples to drive it out, but they were unable to do so." [19] He said to them in reply, "O faithless generation, how long will I be with you? How long will I endure you? Bring him to me." [20] They brought the boy to him. And when he saw him, the spirit immediately threw the boy into convulsions. As he fell to the ground, he began to roll around and foam at the mouth. [21] Then he questioned his father, "How long has this been happening to him?" He replied, "Since childhood. [22] It has often thrown him into fire and into water to kill him. But if you can do anything, have compassion on us and help us." [23] Jesus said to him, "'If you can!' Everything is possible to one who has faith." [24] Then the boy's father cried out, "I do believe, help my unbelief!" [25] Jesus, on seeing a crowd rapidly gathering, rebuked the unclean spirit and said to it, "Mute and deaf spirit, I command you: come out of him and never enter him again!" [26] Shouting and throwing the boy into convulsions, it came out. He became like a corpse, which caused many to say, "He is dead!" [27] But Jesus took him by the hand, raised him, and he stood up. [28] When he entered the house, his disciples asked him in private, "Why could we not drive the spirit out?" [29] He said to them, "This kind can only come out through prayer."

Tuesday February 25, 2025
Tuesday of Seventh Week in Ordinary Time
First Reading: Sirach 2:1-11

[1] My son, when you come to serve the LORD,
  stand in justice and fear,
  prepare yourself for trials.
[2] Be sincere of heart and steadfast,
  incline your ear and receive the word of
    understanding,
  undisturbed in time of adversity.
[3] Wait on God, with patience, cling to him,
    forsake him not;
  thus will you be wise in all your ways.
[4] Accept whatever befalls you,
  when sorrowful, be steadfast,
  and in crushing misfortune be patient;
[5] For in fire gold and silver are tested,
  and worthy people in the crucible of
    humiliation.
[6] Trust God and God will help you;
trust in him, and he will direct your way;

keep his fear and grow old therein.

⁷ You who fear the LORD, wait for his mercy,
turn not away lest you fall.
⁸ You who fear the LORD, trust him,
and your reward will not be lost.

⁹ You who fear the LORD, hope for good things,
for lasting joy and mercy.
You who fear the LORD, love him,
and your hearts will be enlightened.
¹⁰ Study the generations long past and
    understand;
has anyone hoped in the LORD and been
    disappointed?
Has anyone persevered in his
    commandments and been forsaken?
has anyone called upon him and been
    rebuffed?
¹¹ Compassionate and merciful is the LORD;
he forgives sins, he saves in time of trouble and he is a protector to all who seek him in truth.

Responsorial Psalm: Psalms 37:3-4, 18-19, 27-28, 39-40

**R. (see 5) Commit your life to the Lord, and he will
    help you.**
³ Trust in the LORD and do good,
    that you may dwell in the land and be fed
        in security.
⁴ Take delight in the LORD,
    and he will grant you your heart's
        requests.
**R. Commit your life to the Lord, and he will help
    you.**
¹⁸ The LORD watches over the lives of the
    wholehearted;
    their inheritance lasts forever.
¹⁹ They are not put to shame in an evil time;
    in days of famine they have plenty.
**R. Commit your life to the Lord, and he will help
    you.**
²⁷ Turn from evil and do good,
    that you may abide forever;
²⁸ For the LORD loves what is right,
    and forsakes not his faithful ones.

R. Commit your life to the Lord, and he will help you.

³⁹ The salvation of the just is from the LORD;
   he is their refuge in time of distress.
⁴⁰ And the LORD helps them and delivers them;
   he delivers them from the wicked and
      saves them,
   because they take refuge in him.

R. Commit your life to the Lord, and he will help you.

Alleluia: Galatians 6:14
R. Alleluia, alleluia.
¹⁴ May I never boast except in the Cross of our
      Lord Jesus Christ,
through which the world has been crucified
      to me and I to the world.
R. Alleluia, alleluia.

Gospel: Mark 9:30-37

³⁰ Jesus and his disciples left from there and began a journey through Galilee, but he did not wish anyone to know about it. ³¹ He was teaching his disciples and telling them, "The Son of Man is to be handed over to men and they will kill him, and three days after his death the Son of Man will rise." ³² But they did not understand the saying, and they were afraid to question him.

³³ They came to Capernaum and, once inside the house, he began to ask them, "What were you arguing about on the way?" ³⁴ But they remained silent. For they had been discussing among themselves on the way who was the greatest. ³⁵ Then he sat down, called the Twelve, and said to them, "If anyone wishes to be first, he shall be the last of all and the servant of all." ³⁶ Taking a child, he placed it in their midst, and putting his arms around it, he said to them, ³⁷ "Whoever receives one child such as this in my name, receives me; and whoever receives me, receives not me but the One who sent me."

Wednesday February 26, 2025
Wednesday of Seventh Week in Ordinary Time

First Reading: Sirach 4:11-19

¹¹ Wisdom breathes life into her children
      and admonishes those who seek her.
¹² He who loves her loves life;
      those who seek her will be embraced by
         the Lord.
¹³ He who holds her fast inherits glory;
      wherever he dwells, the LORD bestows
         blessings.

¹⁴ Those who serve her serve the Holy One;
    those who love her the LORD loves.
¹⁵ He who obeys her judges nations;
he who hearkens to her dwells in her
    inmost chambers.
¹⁶ If one trusts her, he will possess her;
    his descendants too will inherit her.
¹⁷ She walks with him as a stranger
    and at first she puts him to the test;
Fear and dread she brings upon him
    and tries him with her discipline
    until she try him by her laws and trust
    his soul.
¹⁸ Then she comes back to bring him happiness
    and reveal her secrets to them
    and she will heap upon him
    treasures of knowledge and an
    understanding of justice.
¹⁹ But if he fails her, she will abandon him
    and deliver him into the hands of
    despoilers.

Responsorial Psalm: Psalms 119:165, 168, 171, 172, 174, 175

R. [165a] *O Lord, great peace have they who love your law.*

¹⁶⁵ Those who love your law have great peace,
    and for them there is no stumbling block.

R. *O Lord, great peace have they who love your law.*

¹⁶⁸ I keep your precepts and your decrees,
    for all my ways are before you.

R. *O Lord, great peace have they who love your law.*

¹⁷¹ My lips pour forth your praise,
    because you teach me your statutes.

R. *O Lord, great peace have they who love your law.*

¹⁷² May my tongue sing of your promise,
    for all your commands are just.

R. *O Lord, great peace have they who love your law.*

¹⁷⁴ I long for your salvation, O LORD,
    and your law is my delight.

R. *O Lord, great peace have they who love your law.*

[175] Let my soul live to praise you,
> and may your ordinances help me.

R. O Lord, great peace have they who love your law.

Alleluia: John 14:6
R. Alleluia, alleluia.
[6] I am the way and the truth and the life, says the Lord;
no one comes to the Father except through me.
R. Alleluia, alleluia.

Gospel: Mark 9:38-40
[38] John said to Jesus, "Teacher, we saw someone driving out demons in your name, and we tried to prevent him because he does not follow us." [39] Jesus replied, "Do not prevent him. There is no one who performs a mighty deed in my name who can at the same time speak ill of me. [40] For whoever is not against us is for us."

Thursday February 27, 2025
Thursday of Seventh Week in Ordinary Time
First Reading: Sirach 5:1-8
[1] Rely not on your wealth;
> say not: "I have the power."

[2] Rely not on your strength
> in following the desires of your heart.

[3] Say not: "Who can prevail against me?"
> or, "Who will subdue me for my deeds?"
> for God will surely exact the punishment.

[4] Say not: "I have sinned, yet what has befallen me?"
> for the Most High bides his time.

[5] Of forgiveness be not overconfident,
> adding sin upon sin.

[6] Say not: "Great is his mercy;
> my many sins he will forgive."

For mercy and anger alike are with him;
> upon the wicked alights his wrath.

[7] Delay not your conversion to the LORD,
> put it not off from day to day.

For suddenly his wrath flames forth;
> at the time of vengeance, you will be destroyed.

[8] Rely not upon deceitful wealth,
> for it will be no help on the day of wrath.

Responsorial Psalm: Psalms 1:1-2, 3, 4 AND 6
R. (40:5a) Blessed are they who hope in the Lord.
1 Blessed the man who follows not
    the counsel of the wicked
Nor walks in the way of sinners,
    nor sits in the company of the insolent,
2 But delights in the law of the LORD
    and meditates on his law day and night.
R. Blessed are they who hope in the Lord.
3 He is like a tree
    planted near running water,
That yields its fruit in due season,
    and whose leaves never fade.
    Whatever he does, prospers.
R. Blessed are they who hope in the Lord.
4 Not so the wicked, not so;
    they are like chaff which the wind drives
        away.
6 For the LORD watches over the way of the
        just,
    but the way of the wicked vanishes.
R. Blessed are they who hope in the Lord.

Alleluia: cf.1 Thessalonians 2:13
R. Alleluia, alleluia.
13 Receive the word of God, not as the word of
        men,
but as it truly is, the word of God.
R. Alleluia, alleluia.

Gospel: Mark 9:41-50
41 Jesus said to his disciples: "Anyone who gives you a cup of water to drink because you belong to Christ, amen, I say to you, will surely not lose his reward.

42 "Whoever causes one of these little ones who believe in me to sin, it would be better for him if a great millstone were put around his neck and he were thrown into the sea. 43 If your hand causes you to sin, cut it off. It is better for you to enter into life maimed than with two hands to go into Gehenna, into the unquenchable fire. 45 And if your foot causes you to sin, cut if off. It is better for you to enter into life crippled than with two feet to be thrown into Gehenna. 47 And if your eye causes you to sin, pluck it out. Better for you to enter into the Kingdom of God with one eye than with two eyes to be thrown into Gehenna, 48 where *their worm does not die, and the fire is not quenched.*

49 "Everyone will be salted with fire. 50 Salt is good, but if salt becomes insipid, with what will you restore its flavor? Keep salt in yourselves and you will have peace with one another."

Friday February 28, 2025
Friday of Seventh Week in Ordinary Time

First Reading: Sirach 6:5-17

[5] A kind mouth multiplies friends and
    appeases enemies,
  and gracious lips prompt friendly
    greetings.
[6] Let your acquaintances be many,
  but one in a thousand your confidant.
[7] When you gain a friend, first test him,
  and be not too ready to trust him.
[8] For one sort is a friend when it suits him,
  but he will not be with you in time of
    distress.
[9] Another is a friend who becomes an enemy,
and tells of the quarrel to your shame.
[10] Another is a friend, a boon companion,
    who will not be with you when sorrow
      comes.
[11] When things go well, he is your other self,
  and lords it over your servants;
[12] But if you are brought low, he turns against
    you
  and avoids meeting you.
[13] Keep away from your enemies;
  be on your guard with your friends.
[14] A faithful friend is a sturdy shelter;
  he who finds one finds a treasure.
[15] A faithful friend is beyond price,
  no sum can balance his worth.
[16] A faithful friend is a life-saving remedy,
  such as he who fears God finds;
[17] For he who fears God behaves accordingly,
  and his friend will be like himself.

Responsorial Psalm: Psalms 119:12, 16, 18, 27, 34, 35

**R. [35a] Guide me, Lord, in the way of your
    commands.**

[12] Blessed are you, O LORD;
  teach me your statutes.

**R. Guide me, Lord, in the way of your
    commands.**

[16] In your statutes I will delight;
  I will not forget your words.

R. Guide me, Lord, in the way of your commands.

[18] Open my eyes, that I may consider
the wonders of your law.
R. Guide me, Lord, in the way of your commands.

[27] Make me understand the way of your precepts,
and I will meditate on your wondrous deeds.
R. Guide me, Lord, in the way of your commands.

[34] Give me discernment, that I may observe your law
and keep it with all my heart.
R. Guide me, Lord, in the way of your commands.

[35] Lead me in the path of your commands,
for in it I delight.
R. Guide me, Lord, in the way of your commands.

Alleluia: cf. John 17:17B, 17A
R. Alleluia, alleluia.
[17B] Your word, O Lord, is truth;
[17A] consecrate us in the truth.
R. Alleluia, alleluia.

Gospel: Mark 10:1-12

[1] Jesus came into the district of Judea and across the Jordan. Again crowds gathered around him and, as was his custom, he again taught them. [2] The Pharisees approached him and asked, "Is it lawful for a husband to divorce his wife?" They were testing him. [3] He said to them in reply, "What did Moses command you?" [4] They replied, "Moses permitted a husband to write a bill of divorce and dismiss her." [5] But Jesus told them, "Because of the hardness of your hearts he wrote you this commandment. [6] But from the beginning of creation, *God made them male and female.* [7] *For this reason a man shall leave his father and mother and be joined to his wife,* [8] *and the two shall become one flesh.* So they are no longer two but one flesh. [9] Therefore what God has joined together, no human being must separate." [10] In the house the disciples again questioned Jesus about this. [11] He said to them, "Whoever divorces his wife and marries another commits adultery against her; [12] and if she divorces her husband and marries another, she commits adultery."

MARCH 2025
Saturday March 1, 2025
Saturday of Seventh Week in Ordinary Time

First Reading: Sirach 17:1-15

¹God from the earth created man,
    and in his own image he made him.
He makes man return to earth again,
    ³and endows him with a strength of his own.
² Limited days of life he gives him,
    with power over all things else on earth.
⁴ He puts the fear of him in all flesh,
    and gives him rule over beasts and birds.
⁶ He created for them counsel, and a tongue and eyes and ears,
    and an inventive heart,
    ⁷and filled them with the discipline of understanding.
He created in them knowledge of the spirit;
With wisdom he fills their heart;
    good and evil he shows them.
⁸ He put the fear of himself upon their hearts,
    and showed them his mighty works,
⁹ That they might glory in the wonder of his deeds
    ¹⁰ and praise his holy name.
¹¹ He has set before them knowledge,
    a law of life as their inheritance;
¹² An everlasting covenant he has made with them,
    his justice and his judgments he has revealed to them.
¹³ His majestic glory their eyes beheld,
    his glorious voice their ears heard.
¹⁴ He says to them, "Avoid all evil";
    each of them he gives precepts about his fellow men.
¹⁵ Their ways are ever known to him,
    they cannot be hidden from his eyes.
¹⁷ Over every nation, he places a ruler,
    but God's own portion is Israel.
¹⁹ All their actions are clear as the sun to him,
    his eyes are ever upon their ways.

Responsorial Psalm: Psalms 103:13-14, 15-16, 17-18

R. (see 17) *The Lord's kindness is everlasting to those who fear him.*

¹³ As a father has compassion on his children,
    so the LORD has compassion on those who fear him,
¹⁴ For he knows how we are formed;
    he remembers that we are dust.

R. *The Lord's kindness is everlasting to those who fear him.*

¹⁵ Man's days are like those of grass;
    like a flower of the field he blooms;
¹⁶ The wind sweeps over him and he is gone,
    and his place knows him no more.

R. *The Lord's kindness is everlasting to those who fear him.*

¹⁷ But the kindness of the LORD is from eternity
    to eternity toward those who fear him,
¹⁸ And his justice toward children's children
    among those who keep his covenant.

R. *The Lord's kindness is everlasting to those who fear him.*

Alleluia: cf. Matthew 11:25

R. Alleluia, alleluia.
²⁵ Blessed are you, Father, Lord of heaven and earth;
you have revealed to little ones the
    mysteries of the Kingdom.
R. Alleluia, alleluia.

Gospel: Mark 10:13-16

¹³ People were bringing children to Jesus that he might touch them, but the disciples rebuked them. ¹⁴ When Jesus saw this he became indignant and said to them, "Let the children come to me; do not prevent them, for the Kingdom of God belongs to such as these. ¹⁵ Amen, I say to you, whoever does not accept the Kingdom of God like a child will not enter it." ¹⁶ Then he embraced the children and blessed them, placing his hands on them.

Sunday March 2, 2025
Eighth Sunday in Ordinary Time, Year C

First Reading: Sirach 27:4-7

⁴When a sieve is shaken, the husks appear;
    so do one's faults when one speaks.

⁵ As the test of what the potter molds is in the furnace,
  so in tribulation is the test of the just.
⁶ The fruit of a tree shows the care it has had;
  so too does one's speech disclose the bent of one's mind.
⁷ Praise no one before he speaks,
  for it is then that people are tested.

Responsorial Psalm: Psalms 92:2-3, 13-14, 15-16
R. (cf. 2a) *Lord, it is good to give thanks to you.*
² It is good to give thanks to the LORD,
  to sing praise to your name, Most High,
³ To proclaim your kindness at dawn
  and your faithfulness throughout the night.
R. Lord, it is good to give thanks to you.
¹³ The just one shall flourish like the palm tree,
  like a cedar of Lebanon shall he grow.
¹⁴ They that are planted in the house of the LORD
  shall flourish in the courts of our God.
R. Lord, it is good to give thanks to you.
¹⁵ They shall bear fruit even in old age;
  vigorous and sturdy shall they be,
¹⁶ Declaring how just is the LORD,
  my rock, in whom there is no wrong.
R. Lord, it is good to give thanks to you.

Second Reading: 1 Corinthians 15:54-58
Brothers and sisters: ⁵⁴When this which is corruptible clothes itself with incorruptibility and this which is mortal clothes itself with immortality, then the word that is written shall come about:

Death is swallowed up in victory.
⁵⁵Where, O death, is your victory?
Where, O death, is your sting?

⁵⁶The sting of death is sin, and the power of sin is the law. ⁵⁷But thanks be to God who gives us the victory through our Lord Jesus Christ.
  ⁵⁸Therefore, my beloved brothers and sisters, be firm, steadfast, always fully devoted to the work of the Lord, knowing that in the Lord your labor is not in vain.

Alleluia: Philippians 2:15D, 16A
R. Alleluia, alleluia.
15D Shine like lights in the world
16A as you hold on to the word of life.
R. Alleluia, alleluia.

Gospel: Luke 6:39-45
39 Jesus told his disciples a parable, "Can a blind person guide a blind person? Will not both fall into a pit? 40 No disciple is superior to the teacher; but when fully trained, every disciple will be like his teacher. 41 Why do you notice the splinter in your brother's eye, but do not perceive the wooden beam in your own? 42 How can you say to your brother, 'Brother, let me remove that splinter in your eye,' when you do not even notice the wooden beam in your own eye? You hypocrite! Remove the wooden beam from your eye first; then you will see clearly to remove the splinter in your brother's eye.

43 "A good tree does not bear rotten fruit, nor does a rotten tree bear good fruit. 44 For every tree is known by its own fruit. For people do not pick figs from thornbushes, nor do they gather grapes from brambles. 45 A good person out of the store of goodness in his heart produces good, but an evil person out of a store of evil produces evil; for from the fullness of the heart the mouth speaks."

Monday March 3, 2025
Monday of Eighth Week in ordinary Time

First Reading: Sirach 17:20-24
24 To the penitent God provides a way back,
    he encourages those who are losing hope
    and has chosen for them the lot of truth.
25 Return to him and give up sin,
    pray to the LORD and make your offences
        few.
26 Turn again to the Most High and away from
       your sin,
    hate intensely what he loathes,
    and know the justice and judgments of
        God,
Stand firm in the way set before you,
    in prayer to the Most High God.

27 Who in the nether world can glorify the
       Most High
    in place of the living who offer their
        praise?
Dwell no longer in the error of the ungodly,
    but offer your praise before death.
28 No more can the dead give praise
    than those who have never lived;

You who are alive and well
> shall praise and glorify God in his mercies.

²⁹How great the mercy of the LORD,
> his forgiveness of those who return to him!

Responsorial Psalm: Psalms 32:1-2, 5, 6, 7
R. ⁽¹¹ᵃ⁾ Let the just exult and rejoice in the Lord.
¹ Blessed is he whose fault is taken away,
> whose sin is covered.

² Blessed the man to whom the LORD imputes not guilt,
> in whose spirit there is no guile.

R. Let the just exult and rejoice in the Lord.

⁵ Then I acknowledged my sin to you,
> my guilt I covered not.

I said, "I confess my faults to the LORD,"
> and you took away the guilt of my sin.

R. Let the just exult and rejoice in the Lord.

⁶ For this shall every faithful man pray to you
> in time of stress.

Though deep waters overflow,
> they shall not reach him.

R. Let the just exult and rejoice in the Lord.

⁷ You are my shelter; from distress you will preserve me;
> with glad cries of freedom you will ring me round.

R. Let the just exult and rejoice in the Lord.

Alleluia: 2 Corinthians 8:9
R. Alleluia, alleluia.
⁹ Jesus Christ became poor although he was rich,
so that by his poverty you might become rich.
R. Alleluia, alleluia.

Gospel: Mark 10:17-27

[17] As Jesus was setting out on a journey, a man ran up, knelt down before him, and asked him, "Good teacher, what must I do to inherit eternal life?" [18] Jesus answered him, "Why do you call me good? No one is good but God alone. [19] You know the commandments: *You shall not kill; you shall not commit adultery; you shall not steal; you shall not bear false witness; you shall not defraud; honor your father and your mother."* [20] He replied and said to him, "Teacher, all of these I have observed from my youth." [21] Jesus, looking at him, loved him and said to him, "You are lacking in one thing. Go, sell what you have, and give to the poor and you will have treasure in heaven; then come, follow me." [22] At that statement, his face fell, and he went away sad, for he had many possessions.

[23] Jesus looked around and said to his disciples, "How hard it is for those who have wealth to enter the Kingdom of God!" [24] The disciples were amazed at his words. So Jesus again said to them in reply, "Children, how hard it is to enter the Kingdom of God! [25] It is easier for a camel to pass through the eye of a needle than for one who is rich to enter the Kingdom of God." [26] They were exceedingly astonished and said among themselves, "Then who can be saved?" [27] Jesus looked at them and said, "For men it is impossible, but not for God. All things are possible for God."

Tuesday March 4, 2025
Tuesday of Eighth Week in Ordinary Time
First Reading: Sirach 35:1-12

[1] To keep the law is a great oblation,
    [2] and he who observes the commandments
        sacrifices a peace offering.
[3] In works of charity one offers fine flour,
    [4] and when he gives alms he presents his
        sacrifice of praise.
[5] To refrain from evil pleases the LORD,
    and to avoid injustice is an atonement.
[6] Appear not before the LORD empty-handed,
    [7] for all that you offer is in fulfillment of
        the precepts.
[8] The just one's offering enriches the altar
    and rises as a sweet odor before the Most
        High.
[9] The just one's sacrifice is most pleasing,
    nor will it ever be forgotten.
[10] In a generous spirit pay homage to the LORD,
    be not sparing of freewill gifts.
[11] With each contribution show a cheerful
        countenance,
    and pay your tithes in a spirit of joy.
[12] Give to the Most High as he has given to you,
    generously, according to your means.

¹³ For the LORD is one who always repays,
    and he will give back to you sevenfold.
¹⁴ But offer no bribes, these he does not accept!
    ¹⁵Trust not in sacrifice of the fruits of
        extortion.
For he is a God of justice,
    who knows no favorites.

Responsorial Psalm: Psalms 50:5-6, 7-8, 14 and 23
R. ⁽²³ᵇ⁾ To the upright I will show the saving power of God.

⁵ "Gather my faithful ones before me,
    those who have made a covenant with
        me by sacrifice."
⁶ And the heavens proclaim his justice;
    for God himself is the judge.

R. To the upright I will show the saving power of God.

⁷ "Hear, my people, and I will speak;
    Israel, I will testify against you;
    God, your God, am I.
⁸ Not for your sacrifices do I rebuke you,
    for your burnt offerings are before me
        always."

R. To the upright I will show the saving power of God.

¹⁴ "Offer to God praise as your sacrifice
    and fulfil your vows to the Most High.
²³ He that offers praise as a sacrifice glorifies
    me;
    and to him that goes the right way I will
        show the salvation of God."

R. To the upright I will show the saving power of God.

Alleluia: cf. Matthew 11:25
R. Alleluia, alleluia.
²⁵ Blessed are you, Father, Lord of heaven and
    earth;
you have revealed to little ones the
    mysteries of the Kingdom.
R. Alleluia, alleluia.

Gospel: Mark 10:28-31

[28] Peter began to say to Jesus, "We have given up everything and followed you." [29] Jesus said, "Amen, I say to you, there is no one who has given up house or brothers or sisters or mother or father or children or lands for my sake and for the sake of the Gospel [30] who will not receive a hundred times more now in this present age: houses and brothers and sisters and mothers and children and lands, with persecutions, and eternal life in the age to come. [31] But many that are first will be last, and the last will be first."

Wednesday March 5, 2025
Ash Wednesday

First Reading: Joel 2:12-18

[12] Even now, says the LORD,
> return to me with your whole heart,
> with fasting, and weeping, and mourning;

[13] Rend your hearts, not your garments,
> and return to the LORD, your God.

For gracious and merciful is he,
> slow to anger, rich in kindness,
> and relenting in punishment.

[14] Perhaps he will again relent
> and leave behind him a blessing,

Offerings and libations
> for the LORD, your God.

[15] Blow the trumpet in Zion!
> proclaim a fast,
> call an assembly;

[16] Gather the people,
> notify the congregation;

Assemble the elders,
> gather the children
> and the infants at the breast;

Let the bridegroom quit his room
> and the bride her chamber.

[17] Between the porch and the altar
> let the priests, the ministers of the LORD,
>> weep,

And say, "Spare, O LORD, your people,
> and make not your heritage a reproach,
> with the nations ruling over them!

Why should they say among the peoples,
> 'Where is their God?'"

[18] Then the LORD was stirred to concern for his
> land

and took pity on his people.

Responsorial Psalm: Psalms 51:3-4, 5-6AB, 12-13, 14 AND 17
R. (see 3a) **Be merciful, O Lord, for we have sinned.**
³ Have mercy on me, O God, in your goodness;
>   in the greatness of your compassion wipe
>   > out my offense.

⁴ Thoroughly wash me from my guilt
>   and of my sin cleanse me.

R. Be merciful, O Lord, for we have sinned.
⁵ For I acknowledge my offense,
>   and my sin is before me always:

⁶ᴬᴮ "Against you only have I sinned,
>   and done what is evil in your sight."

R. Be merciful, O Lord, for we have sinned.
¹² A clean heart create for me, O God,
>   and a steadfast spirit renew within me.

¹³ Cast me not out from your presence,
>   and your Holy Spirit take not from me.

R. Be merciful, O Lord, for we have sinned.
¹⁴ Give me back the joy of your salvation,
>   and a willing spirit sustain in me.

¹⁷ O Lord, open my lips,
>   and my mouth shall proclaim your
>   > praise.

R. Be merciful, O Lord, for we have sinned.

Second Reading: 2 Corinthians 5:20-6:2
²⁰ Brothers and sisters: We are ambassadors for Christ, as if God were appealing through us. We implore you on behalf of Christ, be reconciled to God. ²¹ For our sake he made him to be sin who did not know sin, so that we might become the righteousness of God in him.

¹ Working together, then, we appeal to you not to receive the grace of God in vain. ² For he says:
In an acceptable time I heard you,
>   *and on the day of salvation I helped you.*

Behold, now is a very acceptable time; behold, now is the day of salvation.

Verse Before the Gospel: cf. Psalms 95:8
⁸ If today you hear his voice,
harden not your hearts.

Gospel: Matthew 6:1-6, 16-18

Jesus said to his disciples: [1] "Take care not to perform righteous deeds in order that people may see them; otherwise, you will have no recompense from your heavenly Father. [2] When you give alms, do not blow a trumpet before you, as the hypocrites do in the synagogues and in the streets to win the praise of others. Amen, I say to you, they have received their reward. [3] But when you give alms, do not let your left hand know what your right is doing, [4] so that your almsgiving may be secret. And your Father who sees in secret will repay you.

[5] "When you pray, do not be like the hypocrites, who love to stand and pray in the synagogues and on street corners so that others may see them. Amen, I say to you, they have received their reward. [6] But when you pray, go to your inner room, close the door, and pray to your Father in secret. And your Father who sees in secret will repay you.

[16] "When you fast, do not look gloomy like the hypocrites. They neglect their appearance, so that they may appear to others to be fasting. Amen, I say to you, they have received their reward. [17] But when you fast, anoint your head and wash your face, [18] so that you may not appear to be fasting, except to your Father who is hidden. And your Father who sees what is hidden will repay you."

Thursday March 6, 2025
Thursday after Ash Wednesday

First Reading: Deuteronomy 30:15-20

[15] Moses said to the people: "Today I have set before you life and prosperity, death and doom. [16] If you obey the commandments of the LORD, your God, which I enjoin on you today, loving him, and walking in his ways, and keeping his commandments, statutes and decrees, you will live and grow numerous, and the LORD, your God, will bless you in the land you are entering to occupy. [17] If, however, you turn away your hearts and will not listen, but are led astray and adore and serve other gods, [18] I tell you now that you will certainly perish; you will not have a long life on the land that you are crossing the Jordan to enter and occupy. [19] I call heaven and earth today to witness against you: I have set before you life and death, the blessing and the curse. Choose life, then, that you and your descendants may live, [20] by loving the LORD, your God, heeding his voice, and holding fast to him. For that will mean life for you, a long life for you to live on the land that the LORD swore he would give to your fathers Abraham, Isaac and Jacob."

Responsorial Psalm: Psalms 1:1-2,3,4AND 6

R. (40:5a) *Blessed are they who hope in the Lord.*

[1] Blessed the man who follows not
    the counsel of the wicked
Nor walks in the way of sinners,
    nor sits in the company of the insolent,
[2] But delights in the law of the LORD
    and meditates on his law day and night.

R. Blessed are they who hope in the Lord.

[3] He is like a tree
    planted near running water,
That yields its fruit in due season,

    and whose leaves never fade.
        Whatever he does, prospers.
R. Blessed are they who hope in the Lord.
⁴ Not so the wicked, not so;
    they are like chaff which the wind drives away.
⁶ For the LORD watches over the way of the just,
    but the way of the wicked vanishes.
R. Blessed are they who hope in the Lord.

Verse Before The Gospel: Matthew 4:17
¹⁷ Repent, says the Lord;
the Kingdom of heaven is at hand.

Gospel: Luke 9:22-25
²² Jesus said to his disciples: "The Son of Man must suffer greatly and be rejected by the elders, the chief priests, and the scribes, and be killed and on the third day be raised." ²³ Then he said to all, "If anyone wishes to come after me, he must deny himself and take up his cross daily and follow me. ²⁴ For whoever wishes to save his life will lose it, but whoever loses his life for my sake will save it. ²⁵ What profit is there for one to gain the whole world yet lose or forfeit himself?"

Friday March 7, 2025
Friday after Ash Wednesday

First Reading: Isaiah 58:1-9A
¹ Thus says the Lord GOD:
Cry out full-throated and unsparingly,
    lift up your voice like a trumpet blast;
Tell my people their wickedness,
    and the house of Jacob their sins.
² They seek me day after day,
    and desire to know my ways,
Like a nation that has done what is just
    and not abandoned the law of their God;
They ask me to declare what is due them,
    pleased to gain access to God.
³ "Why do we fast, and you do not see it?
    afflict ourselves, and you take no note of it?"

Lo, on your fast day you carry out your own pursuits,
    and drive all your laborers.
⁴ Yes, your fast ends in quarreling and

fighting,
   striking with wicked claw.
Would that today you might fast
   so as to make your voice heard on high!
⁵ Is this the manner of fasting I wish,
   of keeping a day of penance:
That a man bow his head like a reed
   and lie in sackcloth and ashes?
Do you call this a fast,
   a day acceptable to the LORD?
⁶ This, rather, is the fasting that I wish:
   releasing those bound unjustly,
   untying the thongs of the yoke;
Setting free the oppressed,
   breaking every yoke;
⁷ Sharing your bread with the hungry,
   sheltering the oppressed and the
      homeless;
Clothing the naked when you see them,
   and not turning your back on your own.
⁸ Then your light shall break forth like the
      dawn,
   and your wound shall quickly be healed;
Your vindication shall go before you,
   and the glory of the LORD shall be your
      rear guard.
⁹ᴬ Then you shall call, and the LORD will answer,
   you shall cry for help, and he will say:
      Here I am!

Responsorial Psalm: Psalms 51:3-4, 5-6AB, 18-19
R. ⁽¹⁹ᵇ⁾ A heart contrite and humbled, O God, you will not spurn.
³ Have mercy on me, O God, in your goodness;
   in the greatness of your compassion wipe
      out my offense.
⁴ Thoroughly wash me from my guilt
   and of my sin cleanse me.
R. A heart contrite and humbled, O God, you will not spurn.
⁵ For I acknowledge my offense,
   and my sin is before me always:
⁶ᴬᴮ "Against you only have I sinned,
   and done what is evil in your sight."
R. A heart contrite and humbled, O God, you will

113

not spurn.
¹⁸ For you are not pleased with sacrifices;
> should I offer a burnt offering, you would not accept it.

¹⁹ My sacrifice, O God, is a contrite spirit;
> a heart contrite and humbled, O God, you will not spurn.

R. A heart contrite and humbled, O God, you will not spurn.

Verse Before the Gospel: cf. Amos 5:14
¹⁴ Seek good and not evil so that you may live,
and the Lord will be with you.

Gospel: Matthew 9:14-15
¹⁴ The disciples of John approached Jesus and said, "Why do we and the Pharisees fast much, but your disciples do not fast?" ¹⁵ Jesus answered them, "Can the wedding guests mourn as long as the bridegroom is with them? The days will come when the bridegroom is taken away from them, and then they will fast."

Saturday March 8, 2025
Saturday after Ash Wednesday

First Reading: Isaiah 58:9B-14
⁹ᴮ Thus says the LORD:
If you remove from your midst oppression,
> false accusation and malicious speech;

¹⁰ If you bestow your bread on the hungry
> and satisfy the afflicted;

Then light shall rise for you in the darkness,
> and the gloom shall become for you like midday;

¹¹ Then the LORD will guide you always
> and give you plenty even on the parched land.

He will renew your strength,
> and you shall be like a watered garden,
> like a spring whose water never fails.

¹² The ancient ruins shall be rebuilt for your sake,
> and the foundations from ages past you shall raise up;

"Repairer of the breach," they shall call you,
> "Restorer of ruined homesteads."

¹³ If you hold back your foot on the sabbath

from following your own pursuits on my
>holy day;
If you call the sabbath a delight,
>and the LORD's holy day honorable;
If you honor it by not following your ways,
>seeking your own interests, or speaking
>>with malice—
¹⁴ Then you shall delight in the LORD,
>and I will make you ride on the heights of
>>the earth;
I will nourish you with the heritage of Jacob,
>your father,
>>for the mouth of the LORD has spoken.

Responsorial Psalm: Psalms 86:1-2, 3-4, 5-6
R. ^(11ab) **Teach me your way, O Lord, that I may walk in your truth.**
¹ Incline your ear, O LORD; answer me,
>for I am afflicted and poor.
² Keep my life, for I am devoted to you;
>save your servant who trusts in you.
>You are my God.
R. Teach me your way, O Lord, that I may walk in your truth.
³ Have mercy on me, O Lord,
>for to you I call all the day.
⁴ Gladden the soul of your servant,
>for to you, O Lord, I lift up my soul.
R. Teach me your way, O Lord, that I may walk in your truth.
⁵ For you, O Lord, are good and forgiving,
>abounding in kindness to all who call
>>upon you.
⁶ Hearken, O LORD, to my prayer
>and attend to the sound of my pleading.
R. Teach me your way, O Lord, that I may walk in your truth.

Verse Before the Gospel: Ezekiel 33:11
¹¹ I take no pleasure in the death of the wicked
>man, says the Lord,
but rather in his conversion, that he may
>live.

Gospel: Luke 5:27-32

27 Jesus saw a tax collector named Levi sitting at the customs post. He said to him, "Follow me." 28 And leaving everything behind, he got up and followed him. 29 Then Levi gave a great banquet for him in his house, and a large crowd of tax collectors and others were at table with them. 30 The Pharisees and their scribes complained to his disciples, saying, "Why do you eat and drink with tax collectors and sinners?" 31 Jesus said to them in reply, "Those who are healthy do not need a physician, but the sick do. 32 I have not come to call the righteous to repentance but sinners."

Sunday March 9, 2025
First Sunday of Lent, Year C

First Reading: Deuteronomy 26:4-10

Moses spoke to the people, saying: 4"The priest shall receive the basket from you and shall set it in front of the altar of the LORD, your God. 5Then you shall declare before the LORD, your God, 'My father was a wandering Aramean who went down to Egypt with a small household and lived there as an alien. But there he became a nation great, strong, and numerous. 6When the Egyptians maltreated and oppressed us, imposing hard labor upon us, 7we cried to the LORD, the God of our fathers, and he heard our cry and saw our affliction, our toil, and our oppression. 8He brought us out of Egypt with his strong hand and outstretched arm, with terrifying power, with signs and wonders; 9and bringing us into this country, he gave us this land flowing with milk and honey. 10Therefore, I have now brought you the firstfruits of the products of the soil which you, O LORD, have given me.' And having set them before the LORD, your God, you shall bow down in his presence."

Responsorial Psalm: Psalms 91:1-2, 10-11, 12-13, 14-15.

R. (cf. 15b) Be with me, Lord, when I am in trouble.

1 You who dwell in the shelter of the Most High,
 who abide in the shadow of the Almighty,
2 say to the LORD, "My refuge and fortress,
 my God in whom I trust."
R. Be with me, Lord, when I am in trouble.
10 No evil shall befall you,
 nor shall affliction come near your tent,
11 For to his angels he has given command about you,
 that they guard you in all your ways.
R. Be with me, Lord, when I am in trouble.
12 Upon their hands they shall bear you up,
 lest you dash your foot against a stone.
13 You shall tread upon the asp and the viper;
 you shall trample down the lion and the dragon.
R. Be with me, Lord, when I am in trouble.

¹⁴ Because he clings to me, I will deliver him;
　I will set him on high because he
　　acknowledges my name.
¹⁵ He shall call upon me, and I will answer
　　him;
　I will be with him in distress;
I will deliver him and glorify him.
R. Be with me, Lord, when I am in trouble.

Second Reading: Romans 10:8-13
Brothers and sisters: ⁸What does Scripture say?

*The word is near you,
　in your mouth and in your heart*

—that is, the word of faith that we preach—, ⁹for, if you confess with your mouth that Jesus is Lord and believe in your heart that God raised him from the dead, you will be saved. ¹⁰For one believes with the heart and so is justified, and one confesses with the mouth and so is saved. ¹¹For the Scripture says,

*No one who believes in him will be put to
　shame.*

¹²For there is no distinction between Jew and Greek; the same Lord is Lord of all, enriching all who call upon him. ¹³For "everyone who calls on the name of the Lord will be saved."

Verse before the Gospel: Matthew 4:4B
⁴ᴮ One does not live on bread alone,
but on every word that comes forth from the
　　mouth of God.

Gospel: Luke 4:1-13
¹Filled with the Holy Spirit, Jesus returned from the Jordan and was led by the Spirit into the desert ²for forty days, to be tempted by the devil. He ate nothing during those days and when they were over he was hungry. ³The devil said to him, "If you are the Son of God, command this stone to become bread." ⁴Jesus answered him, "It is written, *One does not live on bread alone.*" ⁵Then he took him up and showed him all the kingdoms of the world in a single instant. ⁶The devil said to him, "I shall give to you all this power and glory; for it has been handed over to me, and I may give it to whomever I wish. ⁷All this will be yours, if you worship me." ⁸Jesus said to him in reply, "It is written:

*You shall worship the Lord, your God,
　and him alone shall you serve."*

⁹ Then he led him to Jerusalem, made him stand on the parapet of the temple, and said to him, "If you are the Son of God, throw yourself down from here, ¹⁰for it is written:

He will command his angels concerning you,
  to guard you,

¹¹and:

With their hands they will support you,
  lest you dash your foot against a stone."

¹² Jesus said to him in reply, "It also says,

You shall not put the Lord, your God, to the test."

¹³ When the devil had finished every temptation, he departed from him for a time.

Monday March 10, 2025
Monday of the First Week of Lent
First Reading: Leviticus 19:1-2, 11-18

¹ The LORD said to Moses, ² "Speak to the whole assembly of the children of Israel and tell them: Be holy, for I, the LORD, your God, am holy.

¹¹ "You shall not steal. You shall not lie or speak falsely to one another. ¹² You shall not swear falsely by my name, thus profaning the name of your God. I am the LORD.

¹³ "You shall not defraud or rob your neighbor. You shall not withhold overnight the wages of your day laborer. ¹⁴ You shall not curse the deaf, or put a stumbling block in front of the blind, but you shall fear your God. I am the LORD.

¹⁵ "You shall not act dishonestly in rendering judgment. Show neither partiality to the weak nor deference to the mighty, but judge your fellow men justly. ¹⁶ You shall not go about spreading slander among your kin; nor shall you stand by idly when your neighbor's life is at stake. I am the LORD.

¹⁷ "You shall not bear hatred for your brother in your heart. Though you may have to reprove him, do not incur sin because of him. ¹⁸ Take no revenge and cherish no grudge against your fellow countrymen. You shall love your neighbor as yourself. I am the LORD."

Responsorial Psalm: Psalms 19:8, 9, 10, 15
R. *(John 6:63b)* **Your words, Lord, are Spirit and life.**
⁸ The law of the LORD is perfect,
  refreshing the soul.
The decree of the LORD is trustworthy,
  giving wisdom to the simple.
R. Your words, Lord, are Spirit and life.
⁹ The precepts of the LORD are right,

rejoicing the heart.
The command of the LORD is clear,
    enlightening the eye.
R. Your words, Lord, are Spirit and life.
[10] The fear of the LORD is pure,
    enduring forever;
The ordinances of the LORD are true,
    all of them just.
R. Your words, Lord, are Spirit and life.
[15] Let the words of my mouth and the thought
      of my heart
    find favor before you,
    O LORD, my rock and my redeemer.
R. Your words, Lord, are Spirit and life.

Verse Before the Gospel: 2 Corinthians 6:2B
[2B] Behold, now is a very acceptable time;
behold, now is the day of salvation.

Gospel: Matthew 25:31-46
Jesus said to his disciples: [31] "When the Son of Man comes in his glory, and all the angels with him, he will sit upon his glorious throne, [32] and all the nations will be assembled before him. And he will separate them one from another, as a shepherd separates the sheep from the goats. [33] He will place the sheep on his right and the goats on his left. [34] Then the king will say to those on his right, 'Come, you who are blessed by my Father. Inherit the kingdom prepared for you from the foundation of the world. [35] For I was hungry and you gave me food, I was thirsty and you gave me drink, a stranger and you welcomed me, [36] naked and you clothed me, ill and you cared for me, in prison and you visited me.' [37] Then the righteous will answer him and say, 'Lord, when did we see you hungry and feed you, or thirsty and give you drink? [38] When did we see you a stranger and welcome you, or naked and clothe you? [39] When did we see you ill or in prison, and visit you?' [40] And the king will say to them in reply, 'Amen, I say to you, whatever you did for one of these least brothers of mine, you did for me.' [41] Then he will say to those on his left, 'Depart from me, you accursed, into the eternal fire prepared for the Devil and his angels. [42] For I was hungry and you gave me no food, I was thirsty and you gave me no drink, [43] a stranger and you gave me no welcome, naked and you gave me no clothing, ill and in prison, and you did not care for me.' [44] Then they will answer and say, 'Lord, when did we see you hungry or thirsty or a stranger or naked or ill or in prison, and not minister to your needs?' [45] He will answer them, 'Amen, I say to you, what you did not do for one of these least ones, you did not do for me.' [46] And these will go off to eternal punishment, but the righteous to eternal life."

Tuesday March 11, 2025
Tuesday of the First Week of Lent

First Reading: Isaiah 55:10-11

[10] Thus says the LORD:
Just as from the heavens
    the rain and snow come down
And do not return there
    till they have watered the earth,
    making it fertile and fruitful,
Giving seed to the one who sows
    and bread to the one who eats,
[11] So shall my word be
    that goes forth from my mouth;
It shall not return to me void,
    but shall do my will,
    achieving the end for which I sent it.

Responsorial Psalm: Psalms 34:4-5, 6-7, 16-17, 18-19

R. [18b] *From all their distress God rescues the just.*
[4] Glorify the LORD with me,
    let us together extol his name.
[5] I sought the LORD, and he answered me
    and delivered me from all my fears.

R. From all their distress God rescues the just.

[6] Look to him that you may be radiant with
      joy,
    and your faces may not blush with
      shame.
[7] When the poor one called out, the LORD
      heard,
    and from all his distress he saved him.

R. From all their distress God rescues the just.

[16] The LORD has eyes for the just,
    and ears for their cry.
[17] The LORD confronts the evildoers,
    to destroy remembrance of them from
      the earth.

R. From all their distress God rescues the just.

[18] When the just cry out, the LORD hears them,
    and from all their distress he rescues
      them.
[19] The LORD is close to the brokenhearted;
    and those who are crushed in spirit he
      saves.

R. From all their distress God rescues the just.

Verse Before the Gospel: Matthew 4:4B
4B One does not live on bread alone,
but on every word that comes forth from the
      mouth of God.

Gospel: Matthew 6:7-15
Jesus said to his disciples: 7 "In praying, do not babble like the pagans, who think that they will be heard because of their many words. 8 Do not be like them. Your Father knows what you need before you ask him.
9 "This is how you are to pray:

Our Father who art in heaven,
    hallowed be thy name,
      10 thy Kingdom come,
thy will be done,
    on earth as it is in heaven.
11 Give us this day our daily bread;
    12 and forgive us our trespasses,
    as we forgive those who trespass against
        us;
    13 and lead us not into temptation,
    but deliver us from evil.

14 "If you forgive men their transgressions, your heavenly Father will forgive you. 15 But if you do not forgive men, neither will your Father forgive your transgressions."

Wednesday March 12, 2025
Wednesday of the First Week of Lent
First Reading: Jonah 3:1-10
1 The word of the LORD came to Jonah a second time: 2 "Set out for the great city of Nineveh, and announce to it the message that I will tell you." 3 So Jonah made ready and went to Nineveh, according to the LORD's bidding. Now Nineveh was an enormously large city; it took three days to go through it. 4 Jonah began his journey through the city, and had gone but a single day's walk announcing, "Forty days more and Nineveh shall be destroyed," 5 when the people of Nineveh believed God; they proclaimed a fast and all of them, great and small, put on sackcloth.

    6 When the news reached the king of Nineveh, he rose from his throne, laid aside his robe, covered himself with sackcloth, and sat in the ashes. 7 Then he had this proclaimed throughout Nineveh, by decree of the king and his nobles: "Neither man nor beast, neither cattle nor sheep, shall taste anything; they shall not eat, nor shall they drink water. 8 Man and beast shall be covered with sackcloth and call loudly to God; every man shall turn from his evil way and from the violence he has in hand. 9 Who knows, God may relent and forgive, and withhold his blazing wrath,

so that we shall not perish." ¹⁰ When God saw by their actions how they turned from their evil way, he repented of the evil that he had threatened to do to them; he did not carry it out.

Responsorial Psalm: Psalms 51:3-4, 12-13, 18-19
R. ⁽¹⁹ᵇ⁾ *A heart contrite and humbled, O God, you will not spurn.*
³ Have mercy on me, O God, in your goodness;
    in the greatness of your compassion wipe
        out my offense.
⁴ Thoroughly wash me from my guilt
    and of my sin cleanse me.
R. *A heart contrite and humbled, O God, you will not spurn.*
¹² A clean heart create for me, O God,
    and a steadfast spirit renew within me.
¹³ Cast me not out from your presence,
    and your Holy Spirit take not from me.
R. *A heart contrite and humbled, O God, you will not spurn.*
¹⁸ For you are not pleased with sacrifices;
    should I offer a burnt offering, you would
        not accept it.
¹⁹ My sacrifice, O God, is a contrite spirit;
    a heart contrite and humbled, O God, you
        will not spurn.
R. *A heart contrite and humbled, O God, you will not spurn.*

Verse Before the Gospel: Joel 2:12-13
¹² Even now, says the LORD,
¹³ return to me with your whole heart
for I am gracious and merciful.

Gospel: Luke 11:29-32
²⁹ While still more people gathered in the crowd, Jesus said to them, "This generation is an evil generation; it seeks a sign, but no sign will be given it, except the sign of Jonah. ³⁰ Just as Jonah became a sign to the Ninevites, so will the Son of Man be to this generation. ³¹ At the judgment the queen of the south will rise with the men of this generation and she will condemn them, because she came from the ends of the earth to hear the wisdom of Solomon, and there is something greater than Solomon here. ³² At the judgment the men of Nineveh will arise with this generation and condemn it, because at the preaching of Jonah they repented, and there is something greater than Jonah here."

Thursday March 13, 2025
Thursday of the First Week of Lent
First Reading: Esther C:12, 14-16, 23-25

¹²Queen Esther, seized with mortal anguish, had recourse to the LORD. ¹⁴She lay prostrate upon the ground, together with her handmaids, from morning until evening, and said: "God of Abraham, God of Isaac, and God of Jacob, blessed are you. Help me, who am alone and have no help but you, ¹⁵ for I am taking my life in my hand. ¹⁶As a child I used to hear from the books of my forefathers that you, O LORD, always free those who are pleasing to you. ²⁴Now help me, who am alone and have no one but you, O LORD, my God.

"And now, come to help me, an orphan. ²⁴Put in my mouth persuasive words in the presence of the lion and turn his heart to hatred for our enemy, so that he and those who are in league with him may perish. ²⁵Save us from the hand of our enemies; turn our mourning into gladness and our sorrows into wholeness."

Responsorial Psalm: Psalms 138:1-2AB, 2CDE-3, 7C-8
R. ⁽³ᵃ⁾ *Lord, on the day I called for help, you answered me.*

¹ I will give thanks to you, O LORD, with all my heart,
   for you have heard the words of my mouth;
   in the presence of the angels I will sing your praise;
²ᴬᴮ I will worship at your holy temple
   and give thanks to your name.

R. *Lord, on the day I called for help, you answered me.*

²ᶜᴰᴱBecause of your kindness and your truth;
   for you have made great above all things
   your name and your promise.
³ When I called, you answered me;
   you built up strength within me.

R. *Lord, on the day I called for help, you answered me.*

⁷ᶜ Your right hand saves me.
⁸ The LORD will complete what he has done for me;
   your kindness, O LORD, endures forever;
   forsake not the work of your hands.

R. *Lord, on the day I called for help, you answered me.*

Verse before the Gospel: Psalms 51:12A, 14A
¹²ᴬ A clean heart create for me, O God;

14A give me back the joy of your salvation.

Gospel: Matthew 7:7-12

7 Jesus said to his disciples: "Ask and it will be given to you; seek and you will find; knock and the door will be opened to you. 8For everyone who asks, receives; and the one who seeks, finds; and to the one who knocks, the door will be opened. 9Which one of you would hand his son a stone when he asked for a loaf of bread, 10or a snake when he asked for a fish? 11If you then, who are wicked, know how to give good gifts to your children, how much more will your heavenly Father give good things to those who ask him. 12"Do to others whatever you would have them do to you. This is the law and the prophets."

Friday March 14, 2025
Friday of the First Week of Lent

First Reading: Ezekiel 18:21-28

21 Thus says the Lord GOD: If the wicked man turns away from all the sins he committed, if he keeps all my statutes and does what is right and just, he shall surely live, he shall not die. 22 None of the crimes he committed shall be remembered against him; he shall live because of the virtue he has practiced. 23 Do I indeed derive any pleasure from the death of the wicked? says the Lord GOD. Do I not rather rejoice when he turns from his evil way that he may live?

24 And if the virtuous man turns from the path of virtue to do evil, the same kind of abominable things that the wicked man does, can he do this and still live? None of his virtuous deeds shall be remembered, because he has broken faith and committed sin; because of this, he shall die. 25 You say, "The LORD's way is not fair!" Hear now, house of Israel: Is it my way that is unfair, or rather, are not your ways unfair? 26 When someone virtuous turns away from virtue to commit iniquity, and dies, it is because of the iniquity he committed that he must die. 27 But if the wicked, turning from the wickedness he has committed, does what is right and just, he shall preserve his life; 28 since he has turned away from all the sins that he committed, he shall surely live, he shall not die.

Responsorial Psalm: Psalms 130:1-2, 3-4, 5-7A, 7BC-8

R. (3) *If you, O Lord, mark iniquities, who can stand?*
1 Out of the depths I cry to you, O LORD;
    LORD, hear my voice!
2 Let your ears be attentive
    to my voice in supplication.
R. *If you, O Lord, mark iniquities, who can stand?*
3 If you, O LORD, mark iniquities,
    LORD, who can stand?
4 But with you is forgiveness,
    that you may be revered.
R. *If you, O Lord, mark iniquities, who can*

> *stand?*

⁵ I trust in the LORD;
>   my soul trusts in his word.
⁶ My soul waits for the LORD
>   more than sentinels wait for the dawn.
>   ⁷ᴬ Let Israel wait for the LORD.

R. If you, O Lord, mark iniquities, who can stand?

⁷ᴮᶜ For with the LORD is kindness
>   and with him is plenteous redemption;
⁸ And he will redeem Israel
>   from all their iniquities.

R. If you, O Lord, mark iniquities, who can stand?

Verse Before the Gospel: Ezekiel 18:31

³¹ Cast away from you all the crimes you have
>   committed, says the Lord,
and make for yourselves a new heart and a
>   new spirit.

Gospel: Matthew 5:20-26

Jesus said to his disciples: ²⁰ "I tell you, unless your righteousness surpasses that of the scribes and Pharisees, you will not enter into the Kingdom of heaven.

²¹ "You have heard that it was said to your ancestors, *You shall not kill; and whoever kills will be liable to judgment.* ²² But I say to you, whoever is angry with his brother will be liable to judgment, and whoever says to his brother, *Raqa*, will be answerable to the Sanhedrin, and whoever says, 'You fool,' will be liable to fiery Gehenna. ²³ Therefore, if you bring your gift to the altar, and there recall that your brother has anything against you, ²⁴ leave your gift there at the altar, go first and be reconciled with your brother, and then come and offer your gift. ²⁵ Settle with your opponent quickly while on the way to court. Otherwise your opponent will hand you over to the judge, and the judge will hand you over to the guard, and you will be thrown into prison. ²⁶ Amen, I say to you, you will not be released until you have paid the last penny."

Saturday March 15, 2025
Saturday of the First Week of Lent
First Reading: Deuteronomy 26:16-19

¹⁶ Moses spoke to the people, saying: "This day the LORD, your God, commands you to observe these statutes and decrees. Be careful, then, to observe them with all your heart and with all your soul. ¹⁷ Today you are making this agreement with the LORD: he is to be your God and you are to walk in his ways and observe his statutes, commandments and decrees, and to hearken to his voice. ¹⁸ And today the LORD is making this agreement with you: you are to be a people peculiarly his

own, as he promised you; and provided you keep all his commandments,[19] he will then raise you high in praise and renown and glory above all other nations he has made, and you will be a people sacred to the LORD, your God, as he promised."

Responsorial Psalm: Psalms 119:1-2, 4-5,7-8
*R. [1b] **Blessed are they who follow the law of the Lord!***
[1] Blessed are they whose way is blameless,
  who walk in the law of the LORD.
[2] Blessed are they who observe his decrees,
  who seek him with all their heart.
R. Blessed are they who follow the law of the Lord!
[4] You have commanded that your precepts
  be diligently kept.
[5] Oh, that I might be firm in the ways
  of keeping your statutes!
R. Blessed are they who follow the law of the Lord!
[7] I will give you thanks with an upright heart,
  when I have learned your just
    ordinances.
[8] I will keep your statutes;
  do not utterly forsake me.
R. Blessed are they who follow the law of the Lord!

Verse Before the Gospel: 2 Corinthians 6:2B
[6B] Behold, now is a very acceptable time;
behold, now is the day of salvation.

Gospel: Matthew 5:43-48
Jesus said to his disciples: [43] "You have heard that it was said, *You shall love your neighbor and hate your enemy.* [44] But I say to you, love your enemies, and pray for those who persecute you, [45] that you may be children of your heavenly Father, for he makes his sun rise on the bad and the good, and causes rain to fall on the just and the unjust. [46] For if you love those who love you, what recompense will you have? Do not the tax collectors do the same? [47] And if you greet your brothers and sisters only, what is unusual about that? Do not the pagans do the same? [48] So be perfect, just as your heavenly Father is perfect."

Sunday March 16, 2025
Second Sunday of Lent, Year C

First Reading: Genesis 15:5-12, 17-18

⁵The Lord God took Abram outside and said, "Look up at the sky and count the stars, if you can. Just so," he added, "shall your descendants be." ⁶Abram put his faith in the LORD, who credited it to him as an act of righteousness.

⁷He then said to him, "I am the LORD who brought you from Ur of the Chaldeans to give you this land as a possession." ⁸"O Lord GOD," he asked, "how am I to know that I shall possess it?" ⁹He answered him, "Bring me a three-year-old heifer, a three-year-old she-goat, a three-year-old ram, a turtledove, and a young pigeon." ¹⁰Abram brought him all these, split them in two, and placed each half opposite the other; but the birds he did not cut up. ¹¹Birds of prey swooped down on the carcasses, but Abram stayed with them. ¹²As the sun was about to set, a trance fell upon Abram, and a deep, terrifying darkness enveloped him.

¹⁷When the sun had set and it was dark, there appeared a smoking fire pot and a flaming torch, which passed between those pieces. ¹⁸It was on that occasion that the LORD made a covenant with Abram, saying: "To your descendants I give this land, from the Wadi of Egypt to the Great River, the Euphrates."

Responsorial Psalm: Psalms 27:1, 7-8, 8-9, 13-14.

R. ⁽¹ᵃ⁾ *The Lord is my light and my salvation.*

¹The LORD is my light and my salvation;

> whom should I fear?

The LORD is my life's refuge;

> of whom should I be afraid?

R. *The Lord is my light and my salvation.*

⁷Hear, O LORD, the sound of my call;

> have pity on me, and answer me.

⁸ᴬ Of you my heart speaks; you my glance

> seeks.

R. *The Lord is my light and my salvation.*

⁸ᴮ Your presence, O LORD, I seek.

> ⁹Hide not your face from me;

do not in anger repel your servant.

> You are my helper: cast me not off.

R. The Lord is my light and my salvation.

[13] I believe that I shall see the bounty of the

> LORD

in the land of the living.

[14] Wait for the LORD with courage;

be stouthearted, and wait for the LORD.

R. The Lord is my light and my salvation.

Second Reading: Philippians 3:17-4:1

[17]Join with others in being imitators of me, brothers and sisters, and observe those who thus conduct themselves according to the model you have in us. [18]For many, as I have often told you and now tell you even in tears, conduct themselves as enemies of the cross of Christ. [19]Their end is destruction. Their God is their stomach; their glory is in their "shame." Their minds are occupied with earthly things. [20]But our citizenship is in heaven, and from it, we also await a savior, the Lord Jesus Christ. [21]He will change our lowly body to conform with his glorified body by the power that enables him also to bring all things into subjection to himself.

[1]Therefore, my brothers and sisters, whom I love and long for, my joy and crown, in this way stand firm in the Lord.

Or Philippians 3:20-4:1

Brothers and sisters: [20]But our citizenship is in heaven, and from it we also await a savior, the Lord Jesus Christ. [21]He will change our lowly body to conform with his glorified body by the power that enables him also to bring all things into subjection to himself.

[1]Therefore, my brothers and sisters, whom I love and long for, my joy and crown, in this way stand firm in the Lord, beloved.

Verse before the Gospel: Matthew 17:5

[5] From the shining cloud the Father's voice is

> heard:

This is my beloved Son, hear him.

Gospel: Luke 9:28B-36

[28B]Jesus took Peter, John, and James and went up the mountain to pray. [29]While he was praying his face changed in appearance and his clothing became dazzling white. [30]And behold, two men were conversing with him, Moses and Elijah,[31]who appeared in glory and spoke of his exodus that he was going to accomplish in Jerusalem. ³²Peter and his companions had been overcome by sleep, but becoming fully awake, they saw his glory and the two men standing with him. ³³As they were about to part from him, Peter said to Jesus, "Master, it is good that we are here; let us make three tents, one for you, one for Moses, and one for Elijah." But he did not know what he was saying. ³⁴While he was still speaking, a cloud came and cast a shadow over them, and they became frightened when they entered the cloud. ³⁵Then from the cloud came a voice that said, "This is my chosen Son; listen to him." ³⁶After the voice had spoken, Jesus was found alone. They fell silent and did not at that time tell anyone what they had seen.

Monday March 17, 2025
Monday of the Second Week of Lent
First Reading: Daniel 9:4B-10

⁴ᴮ "Lord, great and awesome God, you who keep your merciful covenant toward those who love you and observe your commandments! ⁵ We have sinned, been wicked and done evil; we have rebelled and departed from your commandments and your laws. ⁶ We have not obeyed your servants the prophets, who spoke in your name to our kings, our princes, our fathers, and all the people of the land. ⁷ Justice, O Lord, is on your side; we are shamefaced even to this day: we, the men of Judah, the residents of Jerusalem, and all Israel, near and far, in all the countries to which you have scattered them because of their treachery toward you. ⁸ O LORD, we are shamefaced, like our kings, our princes, and our fathers, for having sinned against you. ⁹ But yours, O Lord, our God, are compassion and forgiveness! Yet we rebelled against you ¹⁰ and paid no heed to your command, O LORD, our God, to live by the law you gave us through your servants the prophets."

Responsorial Psalm: Psalms 79:8, 9,11 AND 13

R. (see 103:10a) **Lord, do not deal with us according to our sins.**

⁸ Remember not against us the iniquities of
   the past;
      may your compassion quickly come to us,
      for we are brought very low.

R. Lord, do not deal with us according to our sins.

⁹ Help us, O God our savior,
   because of the glory of your name;
Deliver us and pardon our sins
   for your name's sake.

R. Lord, do not deal with us according to our sins.

¹¹ Let the prisoners' sighing come before you;
   with your great power free those doomed

to death.
¹³ Then we, your people and the sheep of your pasture,
   will give thanks to you forever;
   through all generations we will declare your praise.
R. Lord, do not deal with us according to our sins.

Verse Before the Gospel: cf John 6:63C, 68C
⁶³ᶜ Your words, Lord, are Spirit and life;
⁶⁸ᶜ you have the words of everlasting life.

Gospel: Luke 6:36-38
³⁶ Jesus said to his disciples: "Be merciful, just as your Father is merciful.
³⁷ "Stop judging and you will not be judged. Stop condemning and you will not be condemned. Forgive and you will be forgiven. ³⁸ Give and gifts will be given to you; a good measure, packed together, shaken down, and overflowing, will be poured into your lap. For the measure with which you measure will in return be measured out to you."

Tuesday March 18, 2025
Tuesday of the Second Week of Lent

First Reading: Isaiah 1:10, 16-20
¹⁰ Hear the word of the LORD,
   princes of Sodom!
Listen to the instruction of our God,
   people of Gomorrah!

¹⁶ Wash yourselves clean!
Put away your misdeeds from before my eyes;
   cease doing evil; ¹⁷ learn to do good.
Make justice your aim: redress the wronged,
   hear the orphan's plea, defend the widow.

¹⁸ Come now, let us set things right,
   says the LORD:
Though your sins be like scarlet,
   they may become white as snow;
Though they be crimson red,
   they may become white as wool.
¹⁹ If you are willing, and obey,
   you shall eat the good things of the land;
²⁰ But if you refuse and resist,
   the sword shall consume you:

for the mouth of the LORD has spoken!

Responsorial Psalm: Psalms 50:8-9, 16BC-17, 21 AND 23

R. *(23b)* *To the upright I will show the saving power of God.*

8 "Not for your sacrifices do I rebuke you,
for your burnt offerings are before me always.
9 I take from your house no bullock,
no goats out of your fold."

R. *To the upright I will show the saving power of God.*

16BC "Why do you recite my statutes,
and profess my covenant with your mouth,
17 Though you hate discipline
and cast my words behind you?"

R. *To the upright I will show the saving power of God.*

21 "When you do these things, shall I be deaf to it?
Or do you think that I am like yourself?
I will correct you by drawing them up before your eyes.
23 He that offers praise as a sacrifice glorifies me;
and to him that goes the right way I will show the salvation of God."

R. *To the upright I will show the saving power of God.*

Verse Before the Gospel: Ezekiel 18:31

31 Cast away from you all the crimes you have committed, says the Lord,
and make for yourselves a new heart and a new spirit.

Gospel: Matthew 23:1-12

1 Jesus spoke to the crowds and to his disciples, 2 saying, "The scribes and the Pharisees have taken their seat on the chair of Moses. 3 Therefore, do and observe all things whatsoever they tell you, but do not follow their example. For they preach but they do not practice. 4 They tie up heavy burdens hard to carry and lay them on people's shoulders, but they will not lift a finger to move them. 5 All their works are performed to be seen. They widen their phylacteries and lengthen their tassels. 6

They love places of honor at banquets, seats of honor in synagogues, ⁷ greetings in marketplaces, and the salutation 'Rabbi.' ⁸ As for you, do not be called 'Rabbi.' You have but one teacher, and you are all brothers. ⁹ Call no one on earth your father; you have but one Father in heaven. ¹⁰ Do not be called 'Master'; you have but one master, the Christ. ¹¹ The greatest among you must be your servant. ¹² Whoever exalts himself will be humbled; but whoever humbles himself will be exalted."

Wednesday March 19, 2025

Solemnity of Saint Joseph, Husband of the Blessed Virgin Mary
First Reading: 2 Samuel 7:4-5A, 12-14A, 16

⁴ The LORD spoke to Nathan and said: ⁵ᴬ "Go, tell my servant David, ¹² 'When your time comes and you rest with your ancestors, I will raise up your heir after you, sprung from your loins, and I will make his kingdom firm. ¹³ It is he who shall build a house for my name. And I will make his royal throne firm forever. ¹⁴ᴬ I will be a father to him, and he shall be a son to me. ¹⁶ Your house and your kingdom shall endure forever before me; your throne shall stand firm forever.'"

Responsorial Psalm: Psalms 89:2-3, 4-5, 27 and 29
R. ⁽³⁷⁾ *The son of David will live for ever.*

² The promises of the LORD I will sing forever;
 through all generations my mouth shall
  proclaim your faithfulness,
³ For you have said, "My kindness is
 established for ever";
 in heaven you have confirmed your
  faithfulness.

R. *The son of David will live for ever.*

⁴ "I have made a covenant with my chosen
 one,
 I have sworn to David my servant:
⁵ Forever will I confirm your posterity
 and establish your throne for all
  generations."

R. *The son of David will live for ever.*

²⁷ "He shall say of me, 'You are my father,
 my God, the Rock, my savior.'
²⁹ Forever I will maintain my kindness toward
 him,
 and my covenant with him stands firm."

R. *The son of David will live for ever.*

Second Reading: Romans 4:13, 16-18, 22

Brothers and sisters: 13 It was not through the law that the promise was made to Abraham and his descendants that he would inherit the world, but through the righteousness that comes from faith. 16 For this reason, it depends on faith, so that it may be a gift, and the promise may be guaranteed to all his descendants, not to those who only adhere to the law but to those who follow the faith of Abraham, who is the father of all of us, 17 as it is written, *I have made you father of many nations*. He is our father in the sight of God, in whom he believed, who gives life to the dead and calls into being what does not exist. 18 He believed, hoping against hope, that he would become *the father of many nations*, according to what was said, *Thus shall your descendants be.* 22 That is why *it was credited to him as righteousness*.

Verse Before the Gospel: Psalms 84:5

5 Blessed are those who dwell in your house, O
    Lord;
they never cease to praise you.

Gospel: Matthew 1:16, 18-21, 24A

16 Jacob was the father of Joseph, the husband of Mary. Of her was born Jesus who is called the Christ.

18 Now this is how the birth of Jesus Christ came about. When his mother Mary was betrothed to Joseph, but before they lived together, she was found with child through the Holy Spirit. 19 Joseph her husband, since he was a righteous man, yet unwilling to expose her to shame, decided to divorce her quietly. 20 Such was his intention when, behold, the angel of the Lord appeared to him in a dream and said, "Joseph, son of David, do not be afraid to take Mary your wife into your home. For it is through the Holy Spirit that this child has been conceived in her. 21 She will bear a son and you are to name him Jesus, because he will save his people from their sins." 24 When Joseph awoke, he did as the angel of the Lord had commanded him and took his wife into his home.

Or Luke 2:41-51A

41 Each year Jesus' parents went to Jerusalem for the feast of Passover, 42 and when he was twelve years old, they went up according to festival custom. 43 After they had completed its days, as they were returning, the boy Jesus remained behind in Jerusalem, but his parents did not know it. 44 Thinking that he was in the caravan, they journeyed for a day and looked for him among their relatives and acquaintances, 45 but not finding him, they returned to Jerusalem to look for him. 46 After three days they found him in the temple, sitting in the midst of the teachers, listening to them and asking them questions, 47 and all who heard him were astounded at his understanding and his answers. 48 When his parents saw him, they were astonished, and his mother said to him, "Son, why have you done this to us? Your father and I have been looking for you with great anxiety." 49 And he said to them, "Why were you looking for me? Did you not know that I must be in my Father's house?" 50 But they did not understand what he said to them. 51A He went down with them and came to Nazareth, and was obedient to them.

Thursday March 20, 2025
Thursday of the Second Week of Lent

First Reading: Jeremiah 17:5-10

⁵ Thus says the LORD:
Cursed is the man who trusts in human
    beings,
  who seeks his strength in flesh,
  whose heart turns away from the LORD.
⁶ He is like a barren bush in the desert
  that enjoys no change of season,
But stands in a lava waste,
  a salt and empty earth.
⁷ Blessed is the man who trusts in the LORD,
  whose hope is the LORD.
⁸ He is like a tree planted beside the waters
  that stretches out its roots to the stream:
It fears not the heat when it comes,
  its leaves stay green;
In the year of drought it shows no distress,
  but still bears fruit.
⁹ More tortuous than all else is the human
    heart,
  beyond remedy; who can understand it?
¹⁰ I, the LORD, alone probe the mind
  and test the heart,
To reward everyone according to his ways,
  according to the merit of his deeds.

Responsorial Psalm: Psalms 1:1-2, 3, 4 AND 6

R. (40:5a) Blessed are they who hope in the Lord.

¹ Blessed the man who follows not
  the counsel of the wicked
Nor walks in the way of sinners,
  nor sits in the company of the insolent,
² But delights in the law of the LORD
  and meditates on his law day and night.

R. Blessed are they who hope in the Lord.

³ He is like a tree
  planted near running water,
That yields its fruit in due season,
  and whose leaves never fade.
  Whatever he does, prospers.

R. Blessed are they who hope in the Lord.

⁴ Not so, the wicked, not so;

    they are like chaff which the wind drives
        away.
[6] For the LORD watches over the way of the
        just,
    but the way of the wicked vanishes.
R. Blessed are they who hope in the Lord.

Verse Before the Gospel: cf. Luke 8:15
[15] Blessed are they who have kept the word
        with a generous heart
and yield a harvest through perseverance.

Gospel: Luke 16:19-31
Jesus said to the Pharisees: [19] "There was a rich man who dressed in purple garments and fine linen and dined sumptuously each day. [20] And lying at his door was a poor man named Lazarus, covered with sores, [21] who would gladly have eaten his fill of the scraps that fell from the rich man's table. Dogs even used to come and lick his sores. [22] When the poor man died, he was carried away by angels to the bosom of Abraham. The rich man also died and was buried, [23] and from the netherworld, where he was in torment, he raised his eyes and saw Abraham far off and Lazarus at his side. [24] And he cried out, 'Father Abraham, have pity on me. Send Lazarus to dip the tip of his finger in water and cool my tongue, for I am suffering torment in these flames.' [25] Abraham replied, 'My child, remember that you received what was good during your lifetime while Lazarus likewise received what was bad; but now he is comforted here, whereas you are tormented. [26] Moreover, between us and you a great chasm is established to prevent anyone from crossing who might wish to go from our side to yours or from your side to ours.' [27] He said, 'Then I beg you, father, send him to my father's house, [28] for I have five brothers, so that he may warn them, lest they too come to this place of torment.' [29] But Abraham replied, 'They have Moses and the prophets. Let them listen to them.' [30] He said, 'Oh no, father Abraham, but if someone from the dead goes to them, they will repent.' [31] Then Abraham said, 'If they will not listen to Moses and the prophets, neither will they be persuaded if someone should rise from the dead.'"

Friday March 21, 2025
Friday of the Second Week of Lent
First Reading: Genesis 37:3-4, 12-13A, 17B-28A
[3] Israel loved Joseph best of all his sons, for he was the child of his old age; and he had made him a long tunic. [4] When his brothers saw that their father loved him best of all his sons, they hated him so much that they would not even greet him.

    [12] One day, when his brothers had gone to pasture their father's flocks at Shechem, [13A] Israel said to Joseph, "Your brothers, you know, are tending our flocks at Shechem. Get ready; I will send you to them."

    [17B] So Joseph went after his brothers and caught up with them in Dothan. [18] They noticed him from a distance, and before he came up to them, they plotted to kill him. [19] They said to one another: "Here comes that master dreamer! [20] Come on, let us kill him and throw him into one of the cisterns here; we could say that a wild beast devoured him. We shall then see what comes of his dreams."

[21] When Reuben heard this, he tried to save him from their hands, saying, "We must not take his life. [22] Instead of shedding blood," he continued, "just throw him into that cistern there in the desert; but do not kill him outright." His purpose was to rescue him from their hands and return him to his father. [23] So when Joseph came up to them, they stripped him of the long tunic he had on; [24] then they took him and threw him into the cistern, which was empty and dry.

[25] They then sat down to their meal. Looking up, they saw a caravan of Ishmaelites coming from Gilead, their camels laden with gum, balm and resin to be taken down to Egypt. [26] Judah said to his brothers: "What is to be gained by killing our brother and concealing his blood? [27] Rather, let us sell him to these Ishmaelites, instead of doing away with him ourselves. After all, he is our brother, our own flesh." His brothers agreed. [28B] They sold Joseph to the Ishmaelites for twenty pieces of silver.

Responsorial Psalm: Psalms 105:16-17, 18-19, 20-21
R. [5a] Remember the marvels the Lord has done.
[16] When the LORD called down a famine on the
    land
    and ruined the crop that sustained them,
[17] He sent a man before them,
    Joseph, sold as a slave.
R. Remember the marvels the Lord has done.
[18] They had weighed him down with fetters,
    and he was bound with chains,
[19] Till his prediction came to pass
    and the word of the LORD proved him
        true.
R. Remember the marvels the Lord has done.
[20] The king sent and released him,
    the ruler of the peoples set him free.
[21] He made him lord of his house
    and ruler of all his possessions.
R. Remember the marvels the Lord has done.

Verse Before the Gospel: John 3:16
[16] God so loved the world that he gave his only-
    begotten Son;
so that everyone who believes in him might
    have eternal life.

Gospel: Matthew 21:33-43, 45-46

³³ Jesus said to the chief priests and the elders of the people: "Hear another parable. There was a landowner who planted a vineyard, put a hedge around it, dug a wine press in it, and built a tower. Then he leased it to tenants and went on a journey. ³⁴ When vintage time drew near, he sent his servants to the tenants to obtain his produce. ³⁵ But the tenants seized the servants and one they beat, another they killed, and a third they stoned. ³⁶ Again he sent other servants, more numerous than the first ones, but they treated them in the same way. ³⁷ Finally, he sent his son to them, thinking, 'They will respect my son.' ³⁸ But when the tenants saw the son, they said to one another, 'This is the heir. Come, let us kill him and acquire his inheritance.' ³⁹ They seized him, threw him out of the vineyard, and killed him. ⁴⁰ What will the owner of the vineyard do to those tenants when he comes?" ⁴¹They answered him, "He will put those wretched men to a wretched death and lease his vineyard to other tenants who will give him the produce at the proper times." ⁴² Jesus said to them, "Did you never read in the Scriptures:

The stone that the builders rejected
  has become the cornerstone;
by the Lord has this been done,
  and it is wonderful in our eyes?

⁴³ Therefore, I say to you, the Kingdom of God will be taken away from you and given to a people that will produce its fruit." ⁴⁵ When the chief priests and the Pharisees heard his parables, they knew that he was speaking about them. ⁴⁶ And although they were attempting to arrest him, they feared the crowds, for they regarded him as a prophet.

Saturday March 22, 2025
Saturday of the Second Week of Lent
First Reading: Micah 7:14-15, 18-20

¹⁴ Shepherd your people with your staff,
  the flock of your inheritance,
That dwells apart in a woodland,
  in the midst of Carmel.
Let them feed in Bashan and Gilead,
  as in the days of old;
¹⁵ As in the days when you came from the land
    of Egypt,
  show us wonderful signs.

¹⁸ Who is there like you, the God who removes
      guilt
    and pardons sin for the remnant of his
      inheritance;
Who does not persist in anger forever,
  but delights rather in clemency,
¹⁹ And will again have compassion on us,

  treading underfoot our guilt?
You will cast into the depths of the sea all
  our sins;
[20] You will show faithfulness to Jacob,
  and grace to Abraham,
As you have sworn to our fathers
  from days of old.

Responsorial Psalm: Psalms 103:1-2, 3-4, 9-10, 11-12
R. [8a] The Lord is kind and merciful.
[1] Bless the LORD, O my soul;
  and all my being, bless his holy name.
[2] Bless the LORD, O my soul,
  and forget not all his benefits.
R. The Lord is kind and merciful.
[3] He pardons all your iniquities,
  he heals all your ills.
[4] He redeems your life from destruction,
  he crowns you with kindness and
   compassion.
R. The Lord is kind and merciful.
[9] He will not always chide,
  nor does he keep his wrath forever.
[10] Not according to our sins does he deal with us,
  nor does he requite us according to our
   crimes.
R. The Lord is kind and merciful.
[11] For as the heavens are high above the earth,
  so surpassing is his kindness toward
   those who fear him.
[12] As far as the east is from the west,
  so far has he put our transgressions from
   us.
R. The Lord is kind and merciful.

Verse Before the Gospel: Luke 15:18
[18] I will get up and go to my father and shall
  say to him,
Father, I have sinned against heaven and
  against you.

Gospel: Luke 15:1-3, 11-32

[1] Tax collectors and sinners were all drawing near to listen to Jesus, [2] but the Pharisees and scribes began to complain, saying, "This man welcomes sinners and eats with them." [3] So to them Jesus addressed this parable. [11] "A man had two sons, [12] and the younger son said to his father, 'Father, give me the share of your estate that should come to me.' So the father divided the property between them. [13] After a few days, the younger son collected all his belongings and set off to a distant country where he squandered his inheritance on a life of dissipation. [14] When he had freely spent everything, a severe famine struck that country, and he found himself in dire need. [15] So he hired himself out to one of the local citizens who sent him to his farm to tend the swine. [16] And he longed to eat his fill of the pods on which the swine fed, but nobody gave him any. [17] Coming to his senses he thought, 'How many of my father's hired workers have more than enough food to eat, but here am I, dying from hunger. [18] I shall get up and go to my father and I shall say to him, "Father, I have sinned against heaven and against you. [19] I no longer deserve to be called your son; treat me as you would treat one of your hired workers."' [20] So he got up and went back to his father. While he was still a long way off, his father caught sight of him, and was filled with compassion. He ran to his son, embraced him and kissed him. [21] His son said to him, 'Father, I have sinned against heaven and against you; I no longer deserve to be called your son.' [22] But his father ordered his servants, 'Quickly, bring the finest robe and put it on him; put a ring on his finger and sandals on his feet. [23] Take the fattened calf and slaughter it. Then let us celebrate with a feast, [24] because this son of mine was dead, and has come to life again; he was lost, and has been found.' Then the celebration began. [25] Now the older son had been out in the field and, on his way back, as he neared the house, he heard the sound of music and dancing. [26] He called one of the servants and asked what this might mean. [27] The servant said to him, 'Your brother has returned and your father has slaughtered the fattened calf because he has him back safe and sound.' [28] He became angry, and when he refused to enter the house, his father came out and pleaded with him. [29] He said to his father in reply, 'Look, all these years I served you and not once did I disobey your orders; yet you never gave me even a young goat to feast on with my friends. [30] But when your son returns who swallowed up your property with prostitutes, for him you slaughter the fattened calf.' [31] He said to him, 'My son, you are here with me always; everything I have is yours. [32] But now we must celebrate and rejoice, because your brother was dead and has come to life again; he was lost and has been found.'"

Sunday March 23, 2025
Third Sunday of Lent, Year C

First Reading: Exodus 3:1-8A, 13-15

[1] Moses was tending the flock of his father-in-law Jethro, the priest of Midian. Leading the flock across the desert, he came to Horeb, the mountain of God. [2] There an angel of the LORD appeared to Moses in fire flaming out of a bush. As he looked on, he was surprised to see that the bush, though on fire, was not consumed. [3] So Moses decided, "I must go over to look at this remarkable sight, and see why the bush is not burned."

⁴When the LORD saw him coming over to look at it more closely, God called out to him from the bush, "Moses! Moses!" He answered, "Here I am." ⁵God said, "Come no nearer! Remove the sandals from your feet, for the place where you stand is holy ground. ⁶I am the God of your fathers," he continued, "the God of Abraham, the God of Isaac, the God of Jacob." Moses hid his face, for he was afraid to look at God. ⁷But the LORD said, "I have witnessed the affliction of my people in Egypt

and have heard their cry of complaint against their slave drivers, so I know well what they are suffering. ⁸ᴬTherefore I have come down to rescue them from the hands of the Egyptians and lead them out of that land into a good and spacious land, a land flowing with milk and honey."

¹³Moses said to God, "But when I go to the Israelites and say to them, 'The God of your fathers has sent me to you,' if they ask me, 'What is his name?' what am I to tell them?" ¹⁴God replied, "I am who am." Then he added, "This is what you shall tell the Israelites: I AM sent me to you."

¹⁵God spoke further to Moses, "Thus shall you say to the Israelites: The LORD, the God of your fathers, the God of Abraham, the God of Isaac, the God of Jacob, has sent me to you.

"This is my name forever;
    thus am I to be remembered through all
        generations."

Responsorial Psalm: Psalms 103: 1-2, 3-4, 6-7, 8, 11.
*R. ⁽⁸ᵃ⁾ **The Lord is kind and merciful.***
¹ Bless the LORD, O my soul;
    and all my being, bless his holy name.
² Bless the LORD, O my soul,
    and forget not all his benefits.
R. The Lord is kind and merciful.
³ He pardons all your iniquities,
    heals all your ills,
⁴ He redeems your life from destruction,
    crowns you with kindness and
        compassion.
R. The Lord is kind and merciful.
⁶ The LORD secures justice
    and the rights of all the oppressed.
⁷ He has made known his ways to Moses,
    and his deeds to the children of Israel.
R. The Lord is kind and merciful.
⁸ Merciful and gracious is the LORD,
    slow to anger and abounding in kindness.
¹¹ For as the heavens are high above the earth,
    so surpassing is his kindness toward
        those who fear him.

R. The Lord is kind and merciful.

Second Reading: 1 Corinthians 10:1-6, 10-12
¹I do not want you to be unaware, brothers and sisters, that our ancestors were all under the cloud and all passed through the sea, ²and all of them were baptized into Moses in the cloud and in the sea. ³All ate the same spiritual food, ⁴and all drank the same spiritual drink, for they drank from a spiritual rock that followed them, and the rock was the Christ. ⁵Yet God was not pleased with most of them, for they were struck down in the desert.

⁶These things happened as examples for us, so that we might not desire evil things, as they did. ¹⁰Do not grumble as some of them did, and suffered death by the destroyer. ¹¹These things happened to them as an example, and they have been written down as a warning to us, upon whom the end of the ages has come. ¹²Therefore, whoever thinks he is standing secure should take care not to fall.

Verse before the Gospel: Matthew 4:17
¹⁷Repent, says the Lord;
the kingdom of heaven is at hand.

Gospel: Luke 13:1-9
¹Some people told Jesus about the Galileans whose blood Pilate had mingled with the blood of their sacrifices. ²Jesus said to them in reply, "Do you think that because these Galileans suffered in this way they were greater sinners than all other Galileans? ³By no means! But I tell you, if you do not repent, you will all perish as they did! ⁴Or those eighteen people who were killed when the tower at Siloam fell on them— do you think they were more guilty than everyone else who lived in Jerusalem? ⁵By no means! But I tell you, if you do not repent, you will all perish as they did!"

⁶And he told them this parable: "There once was a person who had a fig tree planted in his orchard, and when he came in search of fruit on it but found none, ⁷he said to the gardener, 'For three years now I have come in search of fruit on this fig tree but have found none. So cut it down. Why should it exhaust the soil?' ⁸He said to him in reply, 'Sir, leave it for this year also, and I shall cultivate the ground around it and fertilize it; ⁹it may bear fruit in the future. If not you can cut it down.'"

Monday March 24, 2025
Monday of the Third Week of Lent
First Reading: 2 Kings 5:1-15AB
¹ Naaman, the army commander of the king of Aram, was highly esteemed and respected by his master, for through him the LORD had brought victory to Aram. But valiant as he was, the man was a leper. ² Now the Arameans had captured in a raid on the land of Israel a little girl, who became the servant of Naaman's wife. "If only my master would present himself to the prophet in Samaria," ³ she said to her mistress, "he would cure him of his leprosy." ⁴ Naaman went and told his lord just what the slave girl from the land of Israel had said. ⁵ "Go," said the king of Aram. "I will send along a letter to the king of Israel." So Naaman set out, taking along ten

silver talents, six thousand gold pieces, and ten festal garments. ⁶ To the king of Israel he brought the letter, which read: "With this letter I am sending my servant Naaman to you, that you may cure him of his leprosy."

⁷ When he read the letter, the king of Israel tore his garments and exclaimed: "Am I a god with power over life and death, that this man should send someone to me to be cured of leprosy? Take note! You can see he is only looking for a quarrel with me!" ⁸ When Elisha, the man of God, heard that the king of Israel had torn his garments, he sent word to the king: "Why have you torn your garments? Let him come to me and find out that there is a prophet in Israel."

⁹ Naaman came with his horses and chariots and stopped at the door of Elisha's house. ¹⁰ The prophet sent him the message: "Go and wash seven times in the Jordan, and your flesh will heal, and you will be clean." ¹¹ But Naaman went away angry, saying, "I thought that he would surely come out and stand there to invoke the LORD his God, and would move his hand over the spot, and thus cure the leprosy. ¹² Are not the rivers of Damascus, the Abana and the Pharpar, better than all the waters of Israel? Could I not wash in them and be cleansed?" With this, he turned about in anger and left.

¹³ But his servants came up and reasoned with him. "My father," they said, "if the prophet had told you to do something extraordinary, would you not have done it? All the more now, since he said to you, 'Wash and be clean,' should you do as he said." ¹⁴ So Naaman went down and plunged into the Jordan seven times at the word of the man of God. His flesh became again like the flesh of a little child, and he was clean.

¹⁵ He returned with his whole retinue to the man of God. On his arrival he stood before him and said, "Now I know that there is no God in all the earth, except in Israel."

Responsorial Psalm: Psalms 42:2, 3; 43:3, 4

R. (see 42:3) ***Athirst is my soul for the living God.***
   When shall I go and behold the face of God?

² As the hind longs for the running waters,
   so my soul longs for you, O God.

R. Athirst is my soul for the living God. When
   shall I go and behold the face of God?

³ Athirst is my soul for God, the living God.
   When shall I go and behold the face of
      God?

R. Athirst is my soul for the living God. When
   shall I go and behold the face of God?

³ Send forth your light and your fidelity;
   they shall lead me on
And bring me to your holy mountain,
   to your dwelling-place.

R. Athirst is my soul for the living God. When
   shall I go and behold the face of God?

⁴ Then will I go in to the altar of God,
  the God of my gladness and joy;
Then will I give you thanks upon the harp,
  O God, my God!
R. Athirst is my soul for the living God. When shall I go and behold the face of God?

Verse Before the Gospel: cf. Psalms 130:5, 7
⁵ I hope in the LORD, I trust in his word;
⁷ with him there is kindness and plenteous
  redemption.

Gospel: Luke 4:24-30
²⁴ Jesus said to the people in the synagogue at Nazareth: "Amen, I say to you, no prophet is accepted in his own native place. ²⁵ Indeed, I tell you, there were many widows in Israel in the days of Elijah when the sky was closed for three and a half years and a severe famine spread over the entire land. ²⁶ It was to none of these that Elijah was sent, but only to a widow in Zarephath in the land of Sidon. ²⁷ Again, there were many lepers in Israel during the time of Elisha the prophet; yet not one of them was cleansed, but only Naaman the Syrian." ²⁸ When the people in the synagogue heard this, they were all filled with fury. ²⁹ They rose up, drove him out of the town, and led him to the brow of the hill on which their town had been built, to hurl him down headlong. ³⁰ But he passed through the midst of them and went away.

Tuesday March 25, 2025
Solemnity of the Annunciation of the Lord

First Reading: Isaiah 7:10-14; 8:10
¹⁰ The LORD spoke to Ahaz, saying: ¹¹ Ask for a sign from the LORD, your God; let it be deep as the netherworld, or high as the sky! ¹² But Ahaz answered, "I will not ask! I will not tempt the LORD!" ¹³ Then Isaiah said: Listen, O house of David! Is it not enough for you to weary people, must you also weary my God? ¹⁴ Therefore the Lord himself will give you this sign: the virgin shall be with child, and bear a son, and shall name him Emmanuel, which means "God is with us!"

Responsorial Psalm: Psalms 40:7-8A, 8B-9, 10, 11
*R. ⁽⁸ᵃ ᵃⁿᵈ ⁹ᵃ⁾ **Here I am, Lord; I come to do your will.***
⁷ Sacrifice or oblation you wished not,
  but ears open to obedience you gave me.
⁸ᴬ Holocausts or sin-offerings you sought not;
  then said I, "Behold I come."
R. Here I am, Lord; I come to do your will.
⁸ᴮ "In the written scroll it is prescribed for me,
⁹ To do your will, O my God, is my delight,
  and your law is within my heart!"

R. Here I am, Lord; I come to do your will.
¹⁰ I announced your justice in the vast
assembly;
I did not restrain my lips, as you, O LORD,
know.
R. Here I am, Lord; I come to do your will.
¹¹ Your justice I kept not hid within my heart;
your faithfulness and your salvation I
have spoken of;
I have made no secret of your kindness and
your truth
in the vast assembly.
R. Here I am, Lord; I come to do your will.

Second Reading: Hebrews 10:4-10

Brothers and sisters: ⁴It is impossible that the blood of bulls and goats take away sins. ⁵For this reason, when Christ came into the world, he said:

"Sacrifice and offering you did not desire,
but a body you prepared for me;
⁶in holocausts and sin offerings you took
no delight.
⁷Then I said, 'As is written of me in the scroll,
behold, I come to do your will, O God.'"

⁸First, he says, "Sacrifices and offerings, holocausts and sin offerings, you neither desired nor delighted in." These are offered according to the law. ⁹Then he says, "Behold, I come to do your will." He takes away the first to establish the second. ¹⁰By this "will," we have been consecrated through the offering of the Body of Jesus Christ once for all.

Verse before the Gospel: John 1:14AB

¹⁴ᴬᴮThe Word of God became flesh and made his
dwelling among us;
and we saw his glory.

Gospel: Luke 1:26-38

²⁶The angel Gabriel was sent from God to a town of Galilee called Nazareth, ²⁷to a virgin betrothed to a man named Joseph, of the house of David, and the virgin's name was Mary. ²⁸And coming to her, he said, "Hail, full of grace! The Lord is with you." ²⁹But she was greatly troubled at what was said and pondered what sort of greeting this might be. ³⁰Then the angel said to her, "Do not be afraid, Mary, for you have found favor with God. ³¹Behold, you will conceive in your womb and bear a son, and you shall name him Jesus. ³²He will be great and will be called Son of

the Most High, and the Lord God will give him the throne of David his father, ³³and he will rule over the house of Jacob forever, and of his Kingdom there will be no end." ³⁴But Mary said to the angel, "How can this be, since I have no relations with a man?" ³⁵And the angel said to her in reply, "The Holy Spirit will come upon you, and the power of the Most High will overshadow you. Therefore the child to be born will be called holy, the Son of God. ³⁶And behold, Elizabeth, your relative, has also conceived a son in her old age, and this is the sixth month for her who was called barren; ³⁷for nothing will be impossible for God." ³⁸Mary said, "Behold, I am the handmaid of the Lord. May it be done to me according to your word." Then the angel departed from her.

Wednesday March 26, 2025
Wednesday of the Third Week of Lent
First Reading: Deuteronomy 4:1, 5-9

¹ Moses spoke to the people and said: "Now, Israel, hear the statutes and decrees which I am teaching you to observe, that you may live, and may enter in and take possession of the land which the LORD, the God of your fathers, is giving you. ⁵ Therefore, I teach you the statutes and decrees as the LORD, my God, has commanded me, that you may observe them in the land you are entering to occupy. ⁶ Observe them carefully, for thus will you give evidence of your wisdom and intelligence to the nations, who will hear of all these statutes and say, 'This great nation is truly a wise and intelligent people.' ⁷ For what great nation is there that has gods so close to it as the LORD, our God, is to us whenever we call upon him? ⁸ Or what great nation has statutes and decrees that are as just as this whole law which I am setting before you today?

⁹ "However, take care and be earnestly on your guard not to forget the things which your own eyes have seen, nor let them slip from your memory as long as you live, but teach them to your children and to your children's children."

Responsorial Psalm: Psalms 147:12-13, 15-16, 19-20

R. ⁽¹²ᵃ⁾ *Praise the Lord, Jerusalem.*
¹² Glorify the LORD, O Jerusalem;
    praise your God, O Zion.
¹³ For he has strengthened the bars of your
        gates;
    he has blessed your children within you.
R. Praise the Lord, Jerusalem.
¹⁵ He sends forth his command to the earth;
    swiftly runs his word!
¹⁶ He spreads snow like wool;
    frost he strews like ashes.
R. Praise the Lord, Jerusalem.
¹⁹ He has proclaimed his word to Jacob,
    his statutes and his ordinances to Israel.
²⁰ He has not done thus for any other nation;
    his ordinances he has not made known to

them.
R. Praise the Lord, Jerusalem.

Verse Before the Gospel: John 6:63C, 68C
[63C] Your words, Lord, are Spirit and life;
[68C] you have the words of everlasting life.

Gospel: Matthew 5:17-19
Jesus said to his disciples: [17] "Do not think that I have come to abolish the law or the prophets. I have come not to abolish but to fulfill. [18] Amen, I say to you, until heaven and earth pass away, not the smallest letter or the smallest part of a letter will pass from the law, until all things have taken place. [19] Therefore, whoever breaks one of the least of these commandments and teaches others to do so will be called least in the Kingdom of heaven. But whoever obeys and teaches these commandments will be called greatest in the Kingdom of heaven."

Thursday March 27, 2025
Thursday of the Third Week of Lent
First Reading: Jeremiah 7:23-28
Thus says the LORD:

[23] This is what I commanded my people:
    Listen to my voice;
    then I will be your God and you shall be
        my people.
Walk in all the ways that I command you,
    so that you may prosper.

[24] But they obeyed not, nor did they pay heed.
They walked in the hardness of their evil
        hearts
    and turned their backs, not their faces, to
        me.
[25] From the day that your fathers left the land
        of Egypt even to this day,
    I have sent you untiringly all my servants
        the prophets.
[26] Yet they have not obeyed me nor paid heed;
    they have stiffened their necks and done
        worse than their fathers.
[27] When you speak all these words to them,
    they will not listen to you either;
    when you call to them, they will not
        answer you.
[28] Say to them:

> This is the nation that does not listen
> to the voice of the LORD, its God,
> or take correction.
Faithfulness has disappeared;
> the word itself is banished from their
> speech.

Responsorial Psalm: Psalms 95:1-2, 6-7, 8-9

R. (8) *If today you hear his voice, harden not your hearts.*

¹ Come, let us sing joyfully to the LORD;
> let us acclaim the Rock of our salvation.
² Let us come into his presence with thanksgiving;
> let us joyfully sing psalms to him.

R. *If today you hear his voice, harden not your hearts.*

⁶ Come, let us bow down in worship;
> let us kneel before the LORD who made us.
⁷ᴬᴮᶜ For he is our God,
> and we are the people he shepherds, the
> flock he guides.

R. *If today you hear his voice, harden not your hearts.*

⁷ᴰ Oh, that today you would hear his voice:
⁸ "Harden not your hearts as at Meribah,
> as in the day of Massah in the desert,
⁹ Where your fathers tempted me;
> they tested me though they had seen my
> works."

R. *If today you hear his voice, harden not your hearts.*

Verse Before the Gospel: Joel 2:12-13

¹² Even now, says the LORD,
return to me with your whole heart,
¹³ for I am gracious and merciful.

Gospel: Luke 11:14-23

¹⁴ Jesus was driving out a demon that was mute, and when the demon had gone out, the mute man spoke and the crowds were amazed. ¹⁵ Some of them said, "By the power of Beelzebul, the prince of demons, he drives out demons." ¹⁶ Others, to test him, asked him for a sign from heaven. ¹⁷ But he knew their thoughts and said to them, "Every kingdom divided against itself will be laid waste and house will fall

against house. ¹⁸ And if Satan is divided against himself, how will his kingdom stand? For you say that it is by Beelzebul that I drive out demons. ¹⁹ If I, then, drive out demons by Beelzebul, by whom do your own people drive them out? Therefore they will be your judges. ²⁰ But if it is by the finger of God that I drive out demons, then the Kingdom of God has come upon you. ²¹ When a strong man fully armed guards his palace, his possessions are safe. ²² But when one stronger than he attacks and overcomes him, he takes away the armour on which he relied and distributes the spoils. ²³ Whoever is not with me is against me, and whoever does not gather with me scatters."

Friday March 28, 2025
Friday of the Third Week of Lent
First Reading: Hosea 14:2-10

² Thus says the LORD:

Return, O Israel, to the LORD, your God;
    you have collapsed through your guilt.
³ Take with you words,
    and return to the LORD;
Say to him, "Forgive all iniquity,
    and receive what is good, that we may render
    as offerings the bullocks from our stalls.
⁴ Assyria will not save us,
    nor shall we have horses to mount;
We shall say no more, 'Our god,'
    to the work of our hands;
    for in you the orphan finds compassion."

⁵ I will heal their defection, says the LORD,
    I will love them freely;
    for my wrath is turned away from them.
⁶ I will be like the dew for Israel:
    he shall blossom like the lily;
He shall strike root like the Lebanon cedar,
    ⁷ and put forth his shoots.
His splendor shall be like the olive tree
    and his fragrance like the Lebanon cedar.
⁸ Again they shall dwell in his shade
    and raise grain;
They shall blossom like the vine,
    and his fame shall be like the wine of
        Lebanon.

⁹ Ephraim! What more has he to do with

idols?
>I have humbled him, but I will prosper him.
"I am like a verdant cypress tree" -
>Because of me you bear fruit!

[10] Let him who is wise understand these things;
>let him who is prudent know them.
Straight are the paths of the LORD,
>in them the just walk,
>but sinners stumble in them.

Responsorial Psalm: Psalms 81:6C-8A, 8BC-9, 10-11AB, 14 AND 17

R. (see 11 and 9a) I am the Lord your God: hear my voice.

[7] An unfamiliar speech I hear:
>"I relieved his shoulder of the burden;
>his hands were freed from the basket.
[8A] In distress you called, and I rescued you."

R. I am the Lord your God: hear my voice.

[8BC] "Unseen, I answered you in thunder;
>I tested you at the waters of Meribah.
[9] Hear, my people, and I will admonish you;
>O Israel, will you not hear me?"

R. I am the Lord your God: hear my voice.

[10] "There shall be no strange god among you
>nor shall you worship any alien god.
[11AB] I, the LORD, am your God
>who led you forth from the land of Egypt."

R. I am the Lord your God: hear my voice.

[14] "If only my people would hear me,
>and Israel walk in my ways,
[17] I would feed them with the best of wheat,
>and with honey from the rock I would fill them."

R. I am the Lord your God: hear my voice.

Verse Before the Gospel: Matthew 4:17

[17] Repent, says the Lord;
the Kingdom of heaven is at hand.

Gospel: Mark 12:28-34

[28] One of the scribes came to Jesus and asked him, "Which is the first of all the commandments?" [29] Jesus replied, "The first is this: *Hear, O Israel! The Lord our God is Lord alone!* [30] *You shall love the Lord your God with all your heart, with all your soul, with all your mind, and with all your strength.* [31] The second is this: *You shall love your neighbor as yourself.* There is no other commandment greater than these." [32] The scribe said to him, "Well said, teacher. You are right in saying, *He is One and there is no other than he.* [33] And *to love him with all your heart, with all your understanding, with all your strength, and to love your neighbor as yourself* is worth more than all burnt offerings and sacrifices." [34] And when Jesus saw that he answered with understanding, he said to him, "You are not far from the Kingdom of God." And no one dared to ask him any more questions.

Saturday March 29, 2025
Saturday of the Third Week of Lent

First Reading: Hosea 6:1-6

[1] "Come, let us return to the LORD,
 it is he who has rent, but he will heal us;
 he has struck us, but he will bind our
  wounds.
[2] He will revive us after two days;
 on the third day he will raise us up,
 to live in his presence.
[3] Let us know, let us strive to know the LORD;
 as certain as the dawn is his coming,
 and his judgment shines forth like the
  light of day!
He will come to us like the rain,
 like spring rain that waters the earth."

[4] What can I do with you, Ephraim?
What can I do with you, Judah?
Your piety is like a morning cloud,
 like the dew that early passes away.
[5] For this reason I smote them through the
   prophets,
 I slew them by the words of my mouth;
[6] For it is love that I desire, not sacrifice,
 and knowledge of God rather than burnt
  offerings.

Responsorial Psalm: Psalms 51:3-4, 18-19, 20-21AB

R. (see Hosea 6:6) *It is mercy I desire, and not sacrifice.*
[3] Have mercy on me, O God, in your goodness;
 in the greatness of your compassion wipe

out my offense.
⁴ Thoroughly wash me from my guilt
    and of my sin cleanse me.
R. It is mercy I desire, and not sacrifice.
¹⁸ For you are not pleased with sacrifices;
    should I offer a burnt offering, you would
        not accept it.
¹⁹ My sacrifice, O God, is a contrite spirit;
    a heart contrite and humbled, O God, you
        will not spurn.
R. It is mercy I desire, and not sacrifice.
²⁰ Be bountiful, O LORD, to Zion in your
    kindness
    by rebuilding the walls of Jerusalem;
²¹ᴬᴮ Then shall you be pleased with due
    sacrifices,
    burnt offerings and holocausts.
R. It is mercy I desire, and not sacrifice.

Verse Before the Gospel: Psalms 95:8
⁸ If today you hear his voice,
harden not your hearts.

Gospel: Luke 18:9-14
⁹ Jesus addressed this parable to those who were convinced of their own righteousness and despised everyone else. ¹⁰ "Two people went up to the temple area to pray; one was a Pharisee and the other was a tax collector. ¹¹ The Pharisee took up his position and spoke this prayer to himself, 'O God, I thank you that I am not like the rest of humanity —greedy, dishonest, adulterous— or even like this tax collector. ¹² I fast twice a week, and I pay tithes on my whole income.' ¹³ But the tax collector stood off at a distance and would not even raise his eyes to heaven but beat his breast and prayed, 'O God, be merciful to me a sinner.' ¹⁴ I tell you, the latter went home justified, not the former; for everyone who exalts himself will be humbled, and the one who humbles himself will be exalted."

Sunday March 30, 2025
Fourth Sunday of Lent, Year C
First Reading: Joshua 5:9A, 10-12
⁹The LORD said to Joshua, "Today I have removed the reproach of Egypt from you."
¹⁰While the Israelites were encamped at Gilgal on the plains of Jericho, they celebrated the Passover on the evening of the fourteenth of the month. ¹¹On the day after the Passover, they ate of the produce of the land in the form of unleavened cakes and parched grain. On that same day ¹²after the Passover, on which they ate of the produce of the land, the manna ceased. No longer was there manna for the Israelites, who that year ate of the yield of the land of Canaan.

Responsorial Psalm: Psalms 34:2-3, 4-5, 6-7.

R. (9a) Taste and see the goodness of the Lord.

2 I will bless the LORD at all times;
> his praise shall be ever in my mouth.
3 Let my soul glory in the LORD;
> the lowly will hear me and be glad.

R. Taste and see the goodness of the Lord.

4 Glorify the LORD with me,
> let us together extol his name.
5 I sought the LORD, and he answered me
> and delivered me from all my fears.

R. Taste and see the goodness of the Lord.

6 Look to him that you may be radiant with joy,
> and your faces may not blush with shame.
7 When the poor one called out, the LORD heard,
> and from all his distress he saved him.

R. Taste and see the goodness of the Lord.

Second Reading: 2 Corinthians 5:17-21

17 Brothers and sisters: Whoever is in Christ is a new creation: the old things have passed away; behold, new things have come. 18 And all this is from God, who has reconciled us to himself through Christ and given us the ministry of reconciliation, 19 namely, God was reconciling the world to himself in Christ, not counting their trespasses against them and entrusting to us the message of reconciliation. 20 So we are ambassadors for Christ, as if God were appealing through us. We implore you on behalf of Christ, be reconciled to God. 21 For our sake he made him be sin who did not know sin, so that we might become the righteousness of God in him.

Verse Before the Gospel: Luke 15:18

18 I will get up and go to my Father and shall say to him:
Father, I have sinned against heaven and against you.

Gospel: Luke 15:1-3, 11-32

1 Tax collectors and sinners were all drawing near to listen to Jesus, 2 but the Pharisees and scribes began to complain, saying, "This man welcomes sinners and eats with them." 3 So to them, Jesus addressed this parable: 11 "A man had two sons, 12 and the younger son said to his father, 'Father give me the share of your estate that should come to me.' So the father divided the property between them. 13 After a few days, the younger son collected all his belongings and set off to a

distant country where he squandered his inheritance on a life of dissipation. ¹⁴When he had freely spent everything, a severe famine struck that country, and he found himself in dire need. ¹⁵So he hired himself out to one of the local citizens who sent him to his farm to tend the swine. ¹⁶And he longed to eat his fill of the pods on which the swine fed, but nobody gave him any. ¹⁷Coming to his senses he thought, 'How many of my father's hired workers have more than enough food to eat, but here am I, dying from hunger. ¹⁸I shall get up and go to my father and I shall say to him, "Father, I have sinned against heaven and against you. ¹⁹I no longer deserve to be called your son; treat me as you would treat one of your hired workers."' ²⁰So he got up and went back to his father. While he was still a long way off, his father caught sight of him and was filled with compassion. He ran to his son, embraced him and kissed him. ²¹His son said to him, 'Father, I have sinned against heaven and against you; I no longer deserve to be called your son.' ²²But his father ordered his servants, 'Quickly bring the finest robe and put it on him; put a ring on his finger and sandals on his feet. ²³Take the fattened calf and slaughter it. Then let us celebrate with a feast, ²⁴because this son of mine was dead and has come to life again; he was lost, and has been found.' Then the celebration began. ²⁵Now the older son had been out in the field and, on his way back, as he neared the house, he heard the sound of music and dancing. ²⁶He called one of the servants and asked what this might mean. ²⁷The servant said to him, 'Your brother has returned and your father has slaughtered the fattened calf because he has him back safe and sound.' ²⁸He became angry, and when he refused to enter the house, his father came out and pleaded with him. ²⁹He said to his father in reply, 'Look, all these years I served you and not once did I disobey your orders; yet you never gave me even a young goat to feast on with my friends. ³⁰But when your son returns who swallowed up your property with prostitutes, for him, you slaughter the fattened calf.' ³¹He said to him, 'My son, you are here with me always; everything I have is yours. ³²But now we must celebrate and rejoice, because your brother was dead and has come to life again; he was lost and has been found.'"

Monday March 31, 2025
Monday of the Fourth Week of Lent
First Reading: Isaiah 65:17-21

¹⁷ Thus says the LORD:

Lo, I am about to create new heavens
    and a new earth;
The things of the past shall not be
      remembered
    or come to mind.
¹⁸ Instead, there shall always be rejoicing and
      happiness
    in what I create;
For I create Jerusalem to be a joy
    and its people to be a delight;

¹⁹ I will rejoice in Jerusalem
    and exult in my people.
²⁰ No longer shall the sound of weeping be
      heard there,
    or the sound of crying;
No longer shall there be in it
    an infant who lives but a few days,
    or an old man who does not round out
      his full lifetime;
He dies a mere youth who reaches but a
    hundred years,
    and he who fails of a hundred shall be
      thought accursed.
²¹ They shall live in the houses they build,
    and eat the fruit of the vineyards they
      plant.

Responsorial Psalm: Psalms 30:2 AND 4, 5-6, 11-12A AND 13B

R. ⁽²ᵃ⁾ *I will praise you, Lord, for you have rescued me.*
² I will extol you, O LORD, for you drew me
      clear
    and did not let my enemies rejoice over
      me.
⁴ O LORD, you brought me up from the nether
      world;
    you preserved me from among those
      going down into the pit.

R. I will praise you, Lord, for you have rescued me.

⁵ Sing praise to the LORD, you his faithful ones,
    and give thanks to his holy name.
⁶ For his anger lasts but a moment;
    a lifetime, his good will.
At nightfall, weeping enters in,
    but with the dawn, rejoicing.

R. I will praise you, Lord, for you have rescued me.

¹¹ "Hear, O LORD, and have pity on me;
    O LORD, be my helper."
¹²ᴬ You changed my mourning into dancing;
    ¹³ᴮ O LORD, my God, forever will I give you
      thanks.

R. I will praise you, Lord, for you have rescued me.

Verse Before the Gospel: Amos 5:14
[14] Seek good and not evil so that you may live,
and the LORD will be with you.

Gospel: John 4:43-54
[43] At that time Jesus left [Samaria] for Galilee. [44] For Jesus himself testified that a prophet has no honor in his native place. [45] When he came into Galilee, the Galileans welcomed him, since they had seen all he had done in Jerusalem at the feast; for they themselves had gone to the feast.

[46] Then he returned to Cana in Galilee, where he had made the water wine. Now there was a royal official whose son was ill in Capernaum. [47] When he heard that Jesus had arrived in Galilee from Judea, he went to him and asked him to come down and heal his son, who was near death. [48] Jesus said to him, "Unless you people see signs and wonders, you will not believe." [49] The royal official said to him, "Sir, come down before my child dies." [50] Jesus said to him, "You may go; your son will live." The man believed what Jesus said to him and left. [51] While the man was on his way back, his slaves met him and told him that his boy would live. [52] He asked them when he began to recover. They told him, "The fever left him yesterday, about one in the afternoon." [53] The father realized that just at that time Jesus had said to him, "Your son will live," and he and his whole household came to believe. [54] Now this was the second sign Jesus did when he came to Galilee from Judea.

APRIL 2025
Tuesday April 1, 2025
Tuesday of the Fourth Week of Lent
First Reading: Ezekiel 47:1-9, 12
[1] The angel brought me, Ezekiel, back to the entrance of the temple of the LORD, and I saw water flowing out from beneath the threshold of the temple toward the east, for the façade of the temple was toward the east; the water flowed down from the right side of the temple, south of the altar. [2] He led me outside by the north gate, and around to the outer gate facing the east, where I saw water trickling from the right side. [3] Then when he had walked off to the east with a measuring cord in his hand, he measured off a thousand cubits and had me wade through the water, which was ankle-deep. [4] He measured off another thousand and once more had me wade through the water, which was now knee-deep. Again he measured off a thousand and had me wade; the water was up to my waist. [5] Once more he measured off a thousand, but there was now a river through which I could not wade; for the water had risen so high it had become a river that could not be crossed except by swimming. [6] He asked me, "Have you seen this, son of man?" Then he brought me to the bank of the river, where he had me sit. [7] Along the bank of the river I saw very many trees on both sides. [8] He said to me, "This water flows into the eastern district down upon the Arabah, and empties into the sea, the salt waters, which it makes fresh. [9] Wherever the river flows, every sort of living creature that can multiply shall live, and there shall be abundant fish, for wherever this water comes the sea shall be made fresh. [12] Along both banks of the river, fruit trees of every kind shall grow; their leaves shall not fade, nor their fruit fail. Every month they shall bear fresh fruit, for they shall be watered by the flow from the sanctuary. Their fruit shall serve for food, and their leaves for medicine."

Responsorial Psalm: Psalms 46:2-3, 5-6, 8-9

R. *(8)* *The Lord of hosts is with us; our stronghold is the God of Jacob.*

² God is our refuge and our strength,
    an ever-present help in distress.
³ Therefore we fear not, though the earth be shaken
    and mountains plunge into the depths of the sea.

R. *The Lord of hosts is with us; our stronghold is the God of Jacob.*

⁵ There is a stream whose runlets gladden the city of God,
    the holy dwelling of the Most High.
⁶ God is in its midst; it shall not be disturbed;
    God will help it at the break of dawn.

R. *The Lord of hosts is with us; our stronghold is the God of Jacob.*

⁸ The LORD of hosts is with us;
    our stronghold is the God of Jacob.
⁹ Come! behold the deeds of the LORD,
    the astounding things he has wrought on earth.

R. *The Lord of hosts is with us; our stronghold is the God of Jacob.*

Verse before the Gospel: Psalms 51:12A, 14A

¹²ᴬ A clean heart create for me, O God;
¹⁴ᴬ give me back the joy of your salvation.

Gospel: John 5:1-16

¹ There was a feast of the Jews, and Jesus went up to Jerusalem. ² Now there is in Jerusalem at the Sheep Gate a pool called in Hebrew Bethesda, with five porticoes. ³ In these lay a large number of ill, blind, lame, and crippled. ⁵ One man was there who had been ill for thirty-eight years. ⁶ When Jesus saw him lying there and knew that he had been ill for a long time, he said to him, "Do you want to be well?" ⁷The sick man answered him, "Sir, I have no one to put me into the pool when the water is stirred up; while I am on my way, someone else gets down there before me." ⁸ Jesus said to him, "Rise, take up your mat, and walk." ⁹ Immediately the man became well, took up his mat, and walked.

    Now that day was a sabbath. ¹⁰ So the Jews said to the man who was cured, "It is the sabbath, and it is not lawful for you to carry your mat." ¹¹ He answered them, "The man who made me well told me, 'Take up your mat and walk.'" ¹² They asked him, "Who is the man who told you, 'Take it up and walk'?" ¹³

The man who was healed did not know who it was, for Jesus had slipped away, since there was a crowd there. ¹⁴ After this Jesus found him in the temple area and said to him, "Look, you are well; do not sin anymore, so that nothing worse may happen to you." ¹⁵ The man went and told the Jews that Jesus was the one who had made him well. ¹⁶ Therefore, the Jews began to persecute Jesus because he did this on a sabbath.

Wednesday April 2, 2025
Wednesday of the Fourth Week of Lent
First Reading: Isaiah 49:8-15

⁸ Thus says the LORD:
In a time of favor I answer you,
   on the day of salvation I help you;
   and I have kept you and given you as a
     covenant to the people,
To restore the land
   and allot the desolate heritages,
⁹ Saying to the prisoners: Come out!
To those in darkness: Show yourselves!
Along the ways they shall find pasture,
   on every bare height shall their pastures
     be.
¹⁰ They shall not hunger or thirst,
   nor shall the scorching wind or the sun
     strike them;
For he who pities them leads them
   and guides them beside springs of water.
¹¹ I will cut a road through all my mountains,
   and make my highways level.
¹² See, some shall come from afar,
   others from the north and the west,
   and some from the land of Syene.
¹³ Sing out, O heavens, and rejoice, O earth,
   break forth into song, you mountains.
For the LORD comforts his people
   and shows mercy to his afflicted.

¹⁴ But Zion said, "The LORD has forsaken me;
   my Lord has forgotten me."
¹⁵ Can a mother forget her infant,
   be without tenderness for the child of her
     womb?
Even should she forget,
   I will never forget you.

Responsorial Psalm: Psalms 145:8-9, 13CD-14, 17-18

R. *(8a)* *The Lord is gracious and merciful.*

8 The LORD is gracious and merciful,
    slow to anger and of great kindness.
9 The LORD is good to all
    and compassionate toward all his works.

R. The Lord is gracious and merciful.

13CD The LORD is faithful in all his words
    and holy in all his works.
14 The LORD lifts up all who are falling
    and raises up all who are bowed down.

R. The Lord is gracious and merciful.

17 The LORD is just in all his ways
    and holy in all his works.
18 The LORD is near to all who call upon him,
    to all who call upon him in truth.

R. The Lord is gracious and merciful.

Verse Before the Gospel: John 11:25A, 26

25A I am the resurrection and the life, says the
        Lord;
26 whoever believes in me will never die.

Gospel: John 5:17-30

17 Jesus answered the Jews: "My Father is at work until now, so I am at work." 18 For this reason they tried all the more to kill him, because he not only broke the sabbath but he also called God his own father, making himself equal to God.

19 Jesus answered and said to them, "Amen, amen, I say to you, the Son cannot do anything on his own, but only what he sees the Father doing; for what he does, the Son will do also. 20 For the Father loves the Son and shows him everything that he himself does, and he will show him greater works than these, so that you may be amazed. 21 For just as the Father raises the dead and gives life, so also does the Son give life to whomever he wishes. 22 Nor does the Father judge anyone, but he has given all judgment to the Son, 23 so that all may honor the Son just as they honor the Father. Whoever does not honor the Son does not honor the Father who sent him. 24 Amen, amen, I say to you, whoever hears my word and believes in the one who sent me has eternal life and will not come to condemnation, but has passed from death to life. 25 Amen, amen, I say to you, the hour is coming and is now here when the dead will hear the voice of the Son of God, and those who hear will live. 26 For just as the Father has life in himself, so also he gave to the Son the possession of life in himself. 27 And he gave him power to exercise judgment, because he is the Son of Man. 28 Do not be amazed at this, because the hour is coming in which all who are in the tombs will hear his voice 29 and will come out, those who have done good deeds to the resurrection of life, but those who have done wicked deeds to the resurrection of condemnation.

³⁰ "I cannot do anything on my own; I judge as I hear, and my judgment is just, because I do not seek my own will but the will of the one who sent me."

Thursday April 3, 2025
Thursday of the Fourth Week of Lent

First Reading: Exodus 32:7-14

⁷ The LORD said to Moses, "Go down at once to your people whom you brought out of the land of Egypt, for they have become depraved. ⁸ They have soon turned aside from the way I pointed out to them, making for themselves a molten calf and worshiping it, sacrificing to it and crying out, 'This is your God, O Israel, who brought you out of the land of Egypt!' ⁹ The LORD said to Moses, "I see how stiff-necked this people is. ¹⁰ Let me alone, then, that my wrath may blaze up against them to consume them. Then I will make of you a great nation."

¹¹ But Moses implored the LORD, his God, saying, "Why, O LORD, should your wrath blaze up against your own people, whom you brought out of the land of Egypt with such great power and with so strong a hand? ¹² Why should the Egyptians say, 'With evil intent he brought them out, that he might kill them in the mountains and exterminate them from the face of the earth'? Let your blazing wrath die down; relent in punishing your people. ¹³ Remember your servants Abraham, Isaac and Israel, and how you swore to them by your own self, saying, 'I will make your descendants as numerous as the stars in the sky; and all this land that I promised, I will give your descendants as their perpetual heritage.'" ¹⁴ So the LORD relented in the punishment he had threatened to inflict on his people.

Responsorial Psalm: Psalms 106:19-20, 21-22, 23

R. ⁽⁴ᵃ⁾ *Remember us, O Lord, as you favor your people.*

¹⁹ Our fathers made a calf in Horeb
    and adored a molten image;
²⁰ They exchanged their glory
    for the image of a grass-eating bullock.

R. *Remember us, O Lord, as you favor your people.*

²¹ They forgot the God who had saved them,
    who had done great deeds in Egypt,
²² Wondrous deeds in the land of Ham,
    terrible things at the Red Sea.

R. *Remember us, O Lord, as you favor your people.*

²³ Then he spoke of exterminating them,
    but Moses, his chosen one,
Withstood him in the breach
    to turn back his destructive wrath.

R. *Remember us, O Lord, as you favor your people.*

Verse Before the Gospel: John 3:16

¹⁶ God so loved the world that he gave his only-
begotten Son,
so that everyone who believes in him might have
eternal life.

Gospel: John 5:31-47

³¹Jesus said to the Jews: "If I testify on my own behalf, my testimony is not true. ³² But there is another who testifies on my behalf, and I know that the testimony he gives on my behalf is true. ³³ You sent emissaries to John, and he testified to the truth. ³⁴ I do not accept human testimony, but I say this so that you may be saved. ³⁵ He was a burning and shining lamp, and for a while you were content to rejoice in his light. ³⁶ But I have testimony greater than John's. The works that the Father gave me to accomplish, these works that I perform testify on my behalf that the Father has sent me. ³⁷ Moreover, the Father who sent me has testified on my behalf. But you have never heard his voice nor seen his form, ³⁸ and you do not have his word remaining in you, because you do not believe in the one whom he has sent. ³⁹ You search the Scriptures, because you think you have eternal life through them; even they testify on my behalf. ⁴⁰ But you do not want to come to me to have life.

⁴¹ "I do not accept human praise; ⁴² moreover, I know that you do not have the love of God in you. ⁴³ I came in the name of my Father, but you do not accept me; yet if another comes in his own name, you will accept him. ⁴⁴ How can you believe, when you accept praise from one another and do not seek the praise that comes from the only God? ⁴⁵ Do not think that I will accuse you before the Father: the one who will accuse you is Moses, in whom you have placed your hope. ⁴⁶ For if you had believed Moses, you would have believed me, because he wrote about me. ⁴⁷ But if you do not believe his writings, how will you believe my words?"

Friday April 4, 2025
Friday of the Fourth Week of Lent

First Reading: Wisdom 2:1A, 12-22

¹ᴬ The wicked said among themselves,
thinking not aright:
¹² "Let us beset the just one, because he is
obnoxious to us;
he sets himself against our doings,
Reproaches us for transgressions of the law
and charges us with violations of our
training.
¹³ He professes to have knowledge of God
and styles himself a child of the LORD.
¹⁴ To us he is the censure of our thoughts;
merely to see him is a hardship for us,
¹⁵ Because his life is not like that of others,
and different are his ways.

¹⁶ He judges us debased;
> he holds aloof from our paths as from
> > things impure.
He calls blest the destiny of the just
> and boasts that God is his Father.
¹⁷ Let us see whether his words be true;
> let us find out what will happen to him.
¹⁸ For if the just one be the son of God, he will
> > defend him
> and deliver him from the hand of his
> > foes.
¹⁹ With revilement and torture let us put him
> > to the test
> that we may have proof of his gentleness
> and try his patience.
²⁰ Let us condemn him to a shameful death;
> for according to his own words, God will
> > take care of him."
²¹ These were their thoughts, but they erred;
> for their wickedness blinded them,
²² and they knew not the hidden counsels of
> > God;
> neither did they count on a recompense
> > of holiness
> nor discern the innocent souls' reward.

Responsorial Psalm: Psalms 34:17-18, 19-20, 21 AND 23
R. ⁽¹⁹ᵃ⁾ The Lord is close to the brokenhearted.
¹⁷ The LORD confronts the evildoers,
> to destroy remembrance of them from
> > the earth.
¹⁸ When the just cry out, the LORD hears them,
> and from all their distress he rescues
> > them.
R. The Lord is close to the brokenhearted.
¹⁹ The LORD is close to the brokenhearted;
> and those who are crushed in spirit he
> > saves.
²⁰ Many are the troubles of the just man,
> but out of them all the LORD delivers him.
R. The Lord is close to the brokenhearted.
²¹ He watches over all his bones;
> not one of them shall be broken.
²³ The LORD redeems the lives of his servants;
> no one incurs guilt who takes refuge in

him.
R. The Lord is close to the brokenhearted.

Verse Before the Gospel: Matthew 4:4B
4B One does not live on bread alone,
but on every word that comes forth from the
    mouth of God.

Gospel: John 7:1-2, 10, 25-30
1 Jesus moved about within Galilee; he did not wish to travel in Judea, because the Jews were trying to kill him. 2 But the Jewish feast of Tabernacles was near.
10 But when his brothers had gone up to the feast, he himself also went up, not openly but as it were in secret.
25 Some of the inhabitants of Jerusalem said, "Is he not the one they are trying to kill? 26 And look, he is speaking openly and they say nothing to him. Could the authorities have realized that he is the Christ? 27 But we know where he is from. When the Christ comes, no one will know where he is from." 28 So Jesus cried out in the temple area as he was teaching and said, "You know me and also know where I am from. Yet I did not come on my own, but the one who sent me, whom you do not know, is true. 29 I know him, because I am from him, and he sent me." 30 So they tried to arrest him, but no one laid a hand upon him, because his hour had not yet come.

Saturday April 5, 2025
Saturday of the Fourth Week of Lent

First Reading: Jeremiah 11:18-20
18 I knew their plot because the LORD informed me; at that time you, O LORD, showed me their doings.
19 Yet I, like a trusting lamb led to slaughter, had not realized that they were hatching plots against me: "Let us destroy the tree in its vigor; let us cut him off from the land of the living, so that his name will be spoken no more."
20 But, you, O LORD of hosts, O just Judge,
    searcher of mind and heart,
Let me witness the vengeance you take on
    them,
    for to you I have entrusted my cause!

Responsorial Psalm: Psalms 7:2-3, 9BC-10, 11-12
R. (2a) *O Lord, my God, in you I take refuge.*
2 O LORD, my God, in you I take refuge;
    save me from all my pursuers and rescue
        me,
3 Lest I become like the lion's prey,
    to be torn to pieces, with no one to rescue
        me.

R. O Lord, my God, in you I take refuge.
⁹ᴮᶜ Do me justice, O LORD, because I am just,
    and because of the innocence that is
        mine.
¹⁰ Let the malice of the wicked come to an end,
    but sustain the just,
    O searcher of heart and soul, O just God.
R. O Lord, my God, in you I take refuge.
¹¹A shield before me is God,
    who saves the upright of heart;
¹²A just judge is God,
    a God who punishes day by day.
R. O Lord, my God, in you I take refuge.

Verse Before the Gospel: Luke 8:15
¹⁵ Blessed are they who have kept the word
    with a generous heart
and yield a harvest through perseverance.

Gospel: John 7:40-53
⁴⁰ Some in the crowd who heard these words of Jesus said, "This is truly the Prophet." ⁴¹ Others said, "This is the Christ." But others said, "The Christ will not come from Galilee, will he? ⁴² Does not Scripture say that the Christ will be of David's family and come from Bethlehem, the village where David lived?" ⁴³ So a division occurred in the crowd because of him. ⁴⁴ Some of them even wanted to arrest him, but no one laid hands on him.

    ⁴⁵ So the guards went to the chief priests and Pharisees, who asked them, "Why did you not bring him?" ⁴⁶ The guards answered, "Never before has anyone spoken like this man." ⁴⁷ So the Pharisees answered them, "Have you also been deceived? ⁴⁸ Have any of the authorities or the Pharisees believed in him? ⁴⁹ But this crowd, which does not know the law, is accursed." ⁵⁰ Nicodemus, one of their members who had come to him earlier, said to them, ⁵¹ "Does our law condemn a man before it first hears him and finds out what he is doing?" ⁵² They answered and said to him, "You are not from Galilee also, are you? Look and see that no prophet arises from Galilee."

    Then each went to his own house.

Sunday April 6, 2025
Fifth Sunday of Lent, Year C

First Reading: Isaiah 43:16-21
¹⁶ Thus says the LORD,
    who opens a way in the sea
    and a path in the mighty waters,
¹⁷ who leads out chariots and horsemen,
    a powerful army,
till they lie prostrate together, never to rise,
    snuffed out and quenched like a wick.

¹⁸ Remember not the events of the past,
> the things of long ago consider not;
¹⁹ see, I am doing something new!
> Now it springs forth, do you not perceive it?

In the desert I make a way,
> in the wasteland, rivers.

²⁰ Wild beasts honor me,
> jackals and ostriches,

for I put water in the desert
> and rivers in the wasteland
>> for my chosen people to drink,

²¹ the people whom I formed for myself,
> that they might announce my praise.

Responsorial Psalm: Psalms 126:1-2, 2-3, 4-5, 6.

R. ⁽³⁾ The Lord has done great things for us; we are filled with joy.

¹ When the LORD brought back the captives of Zion,
> we were like men dreaming.

²AB Then our mouth was filled with laughter,
> and our tongue with rejoicing.

R. The Lord has done great things for us; we are filled with joy.

²CD Then they said among the nations,
> "The LORD has done great things for them."

³ The LORD has done great things for us;
> we are glad indeed.

R. The Lord has done great things for us; we are filled with joy.

⁴ Restore our fortunes, O LORD,
> like the torrents in the southern desert.

⁵ Those that sow in tears
> shall reap rejoicing.

R. The Lord has done great things for us; we are filled with joy.

⁶ Although they go forth weeping,
> carrying the seed to be sown,

They shall come back rejoicing,
> carrying their sheaves.

R. The Lord has done great things for us; we are filled with joy.

Second Reading: Philippians 3:8-14

Brothers and sisters: [8]I consider everything as a loss because of the supreme good of knowing Christ Jesus my Lord. For his sake I have accepted the loss of all things and I consider them so much rubbish, that I may gain Christ [9]and be found in him, not having any righteousness of my own based on the law but that which comes through faith in Christ, the righteousness from God, depending on faith [10] to know him and the power of his resurrection and the sharing of his sufferings by being conformed to his death, [11]if somehow I may attain the resurrection from the dead.

[12]It is not that I have already taken hold of it or have already attained perfect maturity, but I continue my pursuit in hope that I may possess it, since I have indeed been taken possession of by Christ Jesus. [13]Brothers and sisters, I for my part do not consider myself to have taken possession. Just one thing: forgetting what lies behind but straining forward to what lies ahead, [14]I continue my pursuit toward the goal, the prize of God's upward calling, in Christ Jesus.

Verse Before the Gospel: Joel 2:12-13

[12] Even now, says the Lord,
return to me with your whole heart;
[13] for I am gracious and merciful.

Gospel: John 8:1-11

[1]Jesus went to the Mount of Olives. [2]But early in the morning he arrived again in the temple area, and all the people started coming to him, and he sat down and taught them. [3]Then the scribes and the Pharisees brought a woman who had been caught in adultery and made her stand in the middle. [4]They said to him, "Teacher, this woman was caught in the very act of committing adultery. [5]Now in the law, Moses commanded us to stone such women. So what do you say?" [6]They said this to test him, so that they could have some charge to bring against him. Jesus bent down and began to write on the ground with his finger. [7]But when they continued asking him, he straightened up and said to them, "Let the one among you who is without sin be the first to throw a stone at her." [8]Again he bent down and wrote on the ground. [9]And in response, they went away one by one, beginning with the elders. So he was left alone with the woman before him. [10]Then Jesus straightened up and said to her, "Woman, where are they? Has no one condemned you?" [11]She replied, "No one, sir." Then Jesus said, "Neither do I condemn you. Go, and from now on do not sin any more."

Monday April 7, 2025
Monday of the Fifth Week of Lent
First Reading: Daniel 13:1-9,15-17, 19-30, 33-62

[1] In Babylon there lived a man named Joakim, [2] who married a very beautiful and God-fearing woman, Susanna, the daughter of Hilkiah; [3] her pious parents had trained their daughter according to the law of Moses. [4] Joakim was very rich; he had a garden near his house, and the Jews had recourse to him often because he was the most respected of them all.

⁵ That year, two elders of the people were appointed judges, of whom the Lord said, "Wickedness has come out of Babylon: from the elders who were to govern the people as judges." ⁶ These men, to whom all brought their cases, frequented the house of Joakim. ⁷When the people left at noon, Susanna used to enter her husband's garden for a walk. ⁸ When the old men saw her enter every day for her walk, they began to lust for her. ⁹ They suppressed their consciences; they would not allow their eyes to look to heaven, and did not keep in mind just judgments.

¹⁵ One day, while they were waiting for the right moment, she entered the garden as usual, with two maids only. She decided to bathe, for the weather was warm. ¹⁶ Nobody else was there except the two elders, who had hidden themselves and were watching her. ¹⁷ "Bring me oil and soap," she said to the maids, "and shut the garden doors while I bathe."

¹⁹ As soon as the maids had left, the two old men got up and hurried to her. ²⁰ "Look," they said, "the garden doors are shut, and no one can see us; give in to our desire, and lie with us. ²¹ If you refuse, we will testify against you that you dismissed your maids because a young man was here with you."

²² "I am completely trapped," Susanna groaned. "If I yield, it will be my death; if I refuse, I cannot escape your power. ²³ Yet it is better for me to fall into your power without guilt than to sin before the Lord." ²⁴ Then Susanna shrieked, and the old men also shouted at her, ²⁵ as one of them ran to open the garden doors. ²⁶ When the people in the house heard the cries from the garden, they rushed in by the side gate to see what had happened to her. ²⁷ At the accusations by the old men, the servants felt very much ashamed, for never had any such thing been said about Susanna.

²⁸ When the people came to her husband Joakim the next day, the two wicked elders also came, fully determined to put Susanna to death. ²⁹ Before all the people they ordered: "Send for Susanna, the daughter of Hilkiah, the wife of Joakim." When she was sent for, ³⁰ she came with her parents, children and all her relatives. ³³ All her relatives and the onlookers were weeping.

³⁴ In the midst of the people the two elders rose up and laid their hands on her head. ³⁵ Through tears she looked up to heaven, for she trusted in the Lord wholeheartedly. ³⁶ The elders made this accusation: "As we were walking in the garden alone, this woman entered with two girls and shut the doors of the garden, dismissing the girls. ³⁷ A young man, who was hidden there, came and lay with her. ³⁸ When we, in a corner of the garden, saw this crime, we ran toward them. ³⁹ We saw them lying together, but the man we could not hold, because he was stronger than we; he opened the doors and ran off. ⁴⁰ Then we seized her and asked who the young man was, ⁴¹ but she refused to tell us. We testify to this." The assembly believed them, since they were elders and judges of the people, and they condemned her to death.

⁴² But Susanna cried aloud: "O eternal God, you know what is hidden and are aware of all things before they come to be: ⁴³ you know that they have testified falsely against me. Here I am about to die, though I have done none of the things with which these wicked men have charged me."

⁴⁴ The Lord heard her prayer. ⁴⁵ As she was being led to execution, God stirred up the holy spirit of a young boy named Daniel, ⁴⁶ and he cried aloud: "I will have no part in the death of this woman." ⁴⁷ All the people turned and asked him, "What is this you are saying?" ⁴⁸ He stood in their midst and continued, "Are you such fools, O children of Israel! To condemn a woman of Israel without examination and without clear evidence? ⁴⁹ Return to court, for they have testified falsely against her."

⁵⁰ Then all the people returned in haste. To Daniel the elders said, "Come, sit with us and inform us, since God has given you the prestige of old age." ⁵¹ But he replied, "Separate these two far from each other that I may examine them."

⁵² After they were separated one from the other, he called one of them and said: "How you have grown evil with age! Now have your past sins come to term: ⁵³ passing unjust sentences, condemning the innocent, and freeing the guilty, although the Lord says, 'The innocent and the just you shall not put to death.' ⁵⁴ Now, then, if you were a witness, tell me under what tree you saw them together." ⁵⁵ "Under a mastic tree," he answered. Daniel replied, "Your fine lie has cost you your head, for the angel of God shall receive the sentence from him and split you in two." ⁵⁶ Putting him to one side, he ordered the other one to be brought. Daniel said to him, "Offspring of Canaan, not of Judah, beauty has seduced you, lust has subverted your conscience. ⁵⁷ This is how you acted with the daughters of Israel, and in their fear they yielded to you; but a daughter of Judah did not tolerate your wickedness. ⁵⁸ Now, then, tell me under what tree you surprised them together." ⁵⁹ "Under an oak," he said. Daniel replied, "Your fine lie has cost you also your head, for the angel of God waits with a sword to cut you in two so as to make an end of you both."

⁶⁰ The whole assembly cried aloud, blessing God who saves those who hope in him. ⁶¹ They rose up against the two elders, for by their own words Daniel had convicted them of perjury. ⁶² According to the law of Moses, they inflicted on them the penalty they had plotted to impose on their neighbor: they put them to death. Thus was innocent blood spared that day.

or Daniel 13:41c-62

⁴¹ᶜ The assembly condemned Susanna to death.

⁴² But Susanna cried aloud: "O eternal God, you know what is hidden and are aware of all things before they come to be: ⁴³ you know that they have testified falsely against me. Here I am about to die, though I have done none of the things for which these men have charged me."

⁴⁴ The Lord heard her prayer. ⁴⁵ As she was being led to execution, God stirred up the holy spirit of a young boy named Daniel, ⁴⁶ and he cried aloud: "I will have no part in the death of this woman." ⁴⁷ All the people turned and asked him, "What are you saying?" ⁴⁸ He stood in their midst and said, "Are you such fools, O children of Israel! To condemn a woman of Israel without investigation and without clear evidence? ⁴⁹ Return to court, for they have testified falsely against her."

⁵⁰ Then all the people returned in haste. To Daniel the elders said, "Come, sit with us and inform us, since God has given you the prestige of old age." ⁵¹ But he replied, "Separate these two far from each other that I may examine them."

⁵² After they were separated from each other, he called one of them and said: "How you have grown evil with age! Now have your past sins come to term: ⁵³ passing unjust sentences, condemning the innocent, and freeing the guilty, although the Lord says, 'The innocent and the just you shall not put to death.' ⁵⁴ Now, then, if you were a witness, tell me under what tree you saw them together." ⁵⁵ "Under a mastic tree," he answered. Daniel replied, "Your fine lie has cost you your head, for the angel of God shall receive the sentence from him and split you into two." ⁵⁶ Putting him to one side, he ordered the other one to be brought. Daniel said to him, "Offspring of Canaan, not of Judah, beauty has seduced you, lust has subverted your conscience. ⁵⁷ This is how you acted with the daughters of Israel, and in their fear they yielded to you; but a daughter of Judah did not tolerate your wickedness. ⁵⁸ Now, then, tell me under what tree you surprised them together." ⁵⁹ "Under an oak," he said. Daniel replied, "Your fine lie has cost you also your head, for the angel of God waits with a sword to cut you in two so as to make an end of you both."

⁶⁰ The whole assembly cried aloud, blessing God who saves those who hope in him. ⁶¹ They rose up against the two elders, for by their own words Daniel had convicted them of perjury. According to the law of Moses, they inflicted on them the penalty they had plotted to impose on their neighbor: ⁶² they put them to death. Thus was innocent blood spared that day.

Responsorial Psalm: Psalms 23:1-3A, 3B-4, 5, 6

R. ⁽⁴ᵃᵇ⁾ *Even though I walk in the dark valley I fear*
no evil; for you are at my side.

¹ The LORD is my shepherd; I shall not want.
² In verdant pastures he gives me repose;
Beside restful waters he leads me;
³ᴬ he refreshes my soul.

R. *Even though I walk in the dark valley I fear no*
evil; for you are at my side.

³ᴮᶜ He guides me in right paths
for his name's sake.
⁴ Even though I walk in the dark valley
I fear no evil; for you are at my side
With your rod and your staff
that give me courage.

R. *Even though I walk in the dark valley I fear no*
evil; for you are at my side.

⁵ You spread the table before me
in the sight of my foes;
You anoint my head with oil;
my cup overflows.

R. *Even though I walk in the dark valley I fear no*
evil; for you are at my side.

⁶ Only goodness and kindness follow me
all the days of my life;

And I shall dwell in the house of the LORD
>   for years to come.
**R. Even though I walk in the dark valley I fear no
>   evil; for you are at my side.**

Verse Before the Gospel: Ezekiel 33:11
[11] I take no pleasure in the death of the wicked
>   man, says the Lord,
but rather in his conversion, that he may
>   live.

Gospel: John 8:1-11
[1] Jesus went to the Mount of Olives. [2] But early in the morning he arrived again in the temple area, and all the people started coming to him, and he sat down and taught them. [3] Then the scribes and the Pharisees brought a woman who had been caught in adultery and made her stand in the middle. [4] They said to him, "Teacher, this woman was caught in the very act of committing adultery. [5] Now in the law, Moses commanded us to stone such women. So what do you say?" [6] They said this to test him, so that they could have some charge to bring against him. Jesus bent down and began to write on the ground with his finger. [7] But when they continued asking him, he straightened up and said to them, "Let the one among you who is without sin be the first to throw a stone at her." [8] Again he bent down and wrote on the ground. [9] And in response, they went away one by one, beginning with the elders. So he was left alone with the woman before him. [10] Then Jesus straightened up and said to her, "Woman, where are they? Has no one condemned you?" [11] She replied, "No one, sir." Then Jesus said, "Neither do I condemn you. Go, and from now on do not sin anymore."

Tuesday April 8, 2025
Tuesday of the Fifth Week of Lent
First Reading: Numbers 21:4-9
[4]From Mount Hor the children of Israel set out on the Red Sea road, to bypass the land of Edom. But with their patience worn out by the journey, [5]the people complained against God and Moses, "Why have you brought us up from Egypt to die in this desert, where there is no food or water? We are disgusted with this wretched food!"

[6]In punishment the LORD sent among the people saraph serpents, which bit the people so that many of them died. [7]Then the people came to Moses and said, "We have sinned in complaining against the LORD and you. Pray the LORD to take the serpents away from us." So Moses prayed for the people, [8]and the LORD said to Moses, "Make a saraph and mount it on a pole, and whoever looks at it after being bitten will live." [9]Moses accordingly made a bronze serpent and mounted it on a pole, and whenever anyone who had been bitten by a serpent looked at the bronze serpent, he lived.

Responsorial Psalm: Psalms 102:2-3, 16-18, 19-21

R. (2) O Lord, hear my prayer, and let my cry come to you.

2 O LORD, hear my prayer,
  and let my cry come to you.
3 Hide not your face from me
  in the day of my distress.
Incline your ear to me;
  in the day when I call, answer me
    speedily.

R. O Lord, hear my prayer, and let my cry come to you.

16 The nations shall revere your name, O LORD,
  and all the kings of the earth your glory,
17 When the LORD has rebuilt Zion
  and appeared in his glory;
18 When he has regarded the prayer of the destitute,
  and not despised their prayer.

R. O Lord, hear my prayer, and let my cry come to you.

19 Let this be written for the generation to come,
  and let his future creatures praise the LORD:
20 "The LORD looked down from his holy height,
  from heaven he beheld the earth,
21 To hear the groaning of the prisoners,
  to release those doomed to die."

R. O Lord, hear my prayer, and let my cry come to you.

Verse Before the Gospel
The seed is the word of God, Christ is the sower;
all who come to him will live for ever.

Gospel: John 8:21-30

21 Jesus said to the Pharisees: "I am going away and you will look for me, but you will die in your sin. Where I am going you cannot come." 22 So the Jews said, "He is not going to kill himself, is he, because he said, 'Where I am going you cannot come'?" 23 He said to them, "You belong to what is below, I belong to what is above. You belong to this world, but I do not belong to this world. 24 That is why I told you that you will die in your sins. For if you do not believe that I AM, you will

die in your sins." ²⁵ So they said to him, "Who are you?" Jesus said to them, "What I told you from the beginning. ²⁶ I have much to say about you in condemnation. But the one who sent me is true, and what I heard from him I tell the world." ²⁷ They did not realize that he was speaking to them of the Father. ²⁸ So Jesus said to them, "When you lift up the Son of Man, then you will realize that I AM, and that I do nothing on my own, but I say only what the Father taught me. ²⁹ The one who sent me is with me. He has not left me alone, because I always do what is pleasing to him." ³⁰ Because he spoke this way, many came to believe in him.

Wednesday April 9, 2025
Wednesday of the Fifth Week of Lent
First Reading: Daniel 3:14-20, 91-92, 95

¹⁴ King Nebuchadnezzar said: "Is it true, Shadrach, Meshach, and Abednego, that you will not serve my god, or worship the golden statue that I set up? ¹⁵ Be ready now to fall down and worship the statue I had made, whenever you hear the sound of the trumpet, flute, lyre, harp, psaltery, bagpipe, and all the other musical instruments; otherwise, you shall be instantly cast into the white-hot furnace; and who is the God who can deliver you out of my hands?" ¹⁶ Shadrach, Meshach, and Abednego answered King Nebuchadnezzar, "There is no need for us to defend ourselves before you in this matter. ¹⁷ If our God, whom we serve, can save us from the white-hot furnace and from your hands, O king, may he save us! ¹⁸ But even if he will not, know, O king, that we will not serve your god or worship the golden statue that you set up."

¹⁹ King Nebuchadnezzar's face became livid with utter rage against Shadrach, Meshach, and Abednego. He ordered the furnace to be heated seven times more than usual ²⁰ and had some of the strongest men in his army bind Shadrach, Meshach, and Abednego and cast them into the white-hot furnace.

⁹¹ Nebuchadnezzar rose in haste and asked his nobles, "Did we not cast three men bound into the fire?" "Assuredly, O king," they answered. ⁹² "But," he replied, "I see four men unfettered and unhurt, walking in the fire, and the fourth looks like a son of God." ⁹⁵ Nebuchadnezzar exclaimed, "Blessed be the God of Shadrach, Meshach, and Abednego, who sent his angel to deliver the servants who trusted in him; they disobeyed the royal command and yielded their bodies rather than serve or worship any god except their own God."

Responsorial Psalm: Daniel 3:52, 53, 54, 55, 56
R. ⁽⁵²ᵇ⁾ *Glory and praise for ever!*

⁵² "Blessed are you, O Lord, the God of our
    fathers,
  praiseworthy and exalted above all
    forever;
And blessed is your holy and glorious name,
  praiseworthy and exalted above all for all
    ages."

R. *Glory and praise for ever!*
⁵³ "Blessed are you in the temple of your holy

> glory,
>> praiseworthy and exalted above all
>>> forever."

R. *Glory and praise for ever!*

⁵⁴ "Blessed are you on the throne of your
> Kingdom,
>> praiseworthy and exalted above all
>>> forever."

R. *Glory and praise for ever!*

⁵⁵ "Blessed are you who look into the depths
> from your throne upon the cherubim;
>> praiseworthy and exalted above all
>>> forever."

R. *Glory and praise for ever!*

⁵⁶ "Blessed are you in the firmament of heaven,
> praiseworthy and glorious forever."

R. *Glory and praise for ever!*

Verse Before the Gospel: Luke 8:15

¹⁵ Blessed are they who have kept the word
> with a generous heart
and yield a harvest through perseverance.

Gospel: John 8:31-42

Jesus said to those Jews who believed in him, ³¹ "If you remain in my word, you will truly be my disciples, ³² and you will know the truth, and the truth will set you free." ³³ They answered him, "We are descendants of Abraham and have never been enslaved to anyone. How can you say, 'You will become free'?" ³⁴ Jesus answered them, "Amen, amen, I say to you, everyone who commits sin is a slave of sin. ³⁵ A slave does not remain in a household forever, but a son always remains. ³⁶ So if the Son frees you, then you will truly be free. ³⁷ I know that you are descendants of Abraham. But you are trying to kill me, because my word has no room among you. ³⁸ I tell you what I have seen in the Father's presence; then do what you have heard from the Father."

³⁹ They answered and said to him, "Our father is Abraham." Jesus said to them, "If you were Abraham's children, you would be doing the works of Abraham. ⁴⁰ But now you are trying to kill me, a man who has told you the truth that I heard from God; Abraham did not do this. ⁴¹ You are doing the works of your father!" So they said to him, "We were not born of fornication. We have one Father, God." ⁴² Jesus said to them, "If God were your Father, you would love me, for I came from God and am here; I did not come on my own, but he sent me."

Thursday April 10, 2025
Thursday of the Fifth Week of Lent

First Reading: Genesis 17:3-9

3 When Abram prostrated himself, God spoke to him: 4 "My covenant with you is this: you are to become the father of a host of nations. 5 No longer shall you be called Abram; your name shall be Abraham, for I am making you the father of a host of nations. 6 I will render you exceedingly fertile; I will make nations of you; kings shall stem from you. 7 I will maintain my covenant with you and your descendants after you throughout the ages as an everlasting pact, to be your God and the God of your descendants after you. 8 I will give to you and to your descendants after you the land in which you are now staying, the whole land of Canaan, as a permanent possession; and I will be their God."

9 God also said to Abraham: "On your part, you and your descendants after you must keep my covenant throughout the ages."

Responsorial Psalm: Psalms 105:4-5, 6-7, 8-9

R. (8a) *The Lord remembers his covenant for ever.*

4 Look to the LORD in his strength;
    seek to serve him constantly.
5 Recall the wondrous deeds that he has
        wrought,
    his portents, and the judgments he has
        uttered.

R. *The Lord remembers his covenant for ever.*

6 You descendants of Abraham, his servants,
    sons of Jacob, his chosen ones!
7 He, the LORD, is our God;
    throughout the earth his judgments
        prevail.

R. *The Lord remembers his covenant for ever.*

8 He remembers forever his covenant
    which he made binding for a thousand
        generations–
9 Which he entered into with Abraham
    and by his oath to Isaac.

R. *The Lord remembers his covenant for ever.*

Verse Before the Gospel: Psalms 95:8

8 If today you hear his voice,
harden not your hearts.

Gospel: John 8:51-59

⁵¹ Jesus said to the Jews: "Amen, amen, I say to you, whoever keeps my word will never see death." ⁵² So the Jews said to him, "Now we are sure that you are possessed. Abraham died, as did the prophets, yet you say, 'Whoever keeps my word will never taste death.' ⁵³ Are you greater than our father Abraham, who died? Or the prophets, who died? Who do you make yourself out to be?" ⁵⁴ Jesus answered, "If I glorify myself, my glory is worth nothing; but it is my Father who glorifies me, of whom you say, 'He is our God.' ⁵⁵ You do not know him, but I know him. And if I should say that I do not know him, I would be like you a liar. But I do know him and I keep his word. ⁵⁶ Abraham your father rejoiced to see my day; he saw it and was glad." ⁵⁷ So the Jews said to him, "You are not yet fifty years old and you have seen Abraham?" ⁵⁸ Jesus said to them, "Amen, amen, I say to you, before Abraham came to be, I AM." ⁵⁹ So they picked up stones to throw at him; but Jesus hid and went out of the temple area.

Friday April 11, 2025
Friday of the Fifth Week of Lent

First Reading: Jeremiah 20:10-13

¹⁰ I hear the whisperings of many:
    "Terror on every side!
    Denounce! let us denounce him!"
All those who were my friends
    are on the watch for any misstep of mine.
"Perhaps he will be trapped; then we can
       prevail,
    and take our vengeance on him."
¹¹ But the LORD is with me, like a mighty
       champion:
    my persecutors will stumble, they will
       not triumph.
In their failure they will be put to utter
       shame,
    to lasting, unforgettable confusion.
¹² O LORD of hosts, you who test the just,
    who probe mind and heart,
Let me witness the vengeance you take on
       them,
    for to you I have entrusted my cause.
¹³ Sing to the LORD,
    praise the LORD,
For he has rescued the life of the poor
    from the power of the wicked!

Responsorial Psalm: Psalms 18:2-3A, 3BC-4, 5-6, 7

R. (see 7) **In my distress I called upon the Lord, and he heard my voice.**

² I love you, O LORD, my strength,
> ³ᴬ O LORD, my rock, my fortress, my deliverer.

R. In my distress I called upon the Lord, and he heard my voice.

³ᴮᶜ My God, my rock of refuge,
> my shield, the horn of my salvation, my stronghold!

⁴ Praised be the LORD, I exclaim,
> and I am safe from my enemies.

R. In my distress I called upon the Lord, and he heard my voice.

⁵ The breakers of death surged round about me,
> the destroying floods overwhelmed me;

⁶ The cords of the nether world enmeshed me,
> the snares of death overtook me.

R. In my distress I called upon the Lord, and he heard my voice.

⁷ In my distress I called upon the LORD
> and cried out to my God;

From his temple he heard my voice,
> and my cry to him reached his ears.

R. In my distress I called upon the Lord, and he heard my voice.

Verse Before the Gospel: John 6:63C, 68C

⁶³ᶜ Your words, Lord, are Spirit and life;
⁶⁸ᶜ you have the words of everlasting life.

Gospel: John 10:31-42

³¹ The Jews picked up rocks to stone Jesus. ³² Jesus answered them, "I have shown you many good works from my Father. For which of these are you trying to stone me?" ³³ The Jews answered him, "We are not stoning you for a good work but for blasphemy. You, a man, are making yourself God." ³⁴ Jesus answered them, "Is it not written in your law, 'I said, 'You are gods'"? ³⁵ If it calls them gods to whom the word of God came, and Scripture cannot be set aside, ³⁶ can you say that the one whom the Father has consecrated and sent into the world blasphemes because I said, 'I am the Son of God'? ³⁷ If I do not perform my Father's works, do not believe me; ³⁸ but if I perform them, even if you do not believe me, believe the works, so that you may realize and understand that the Father is in me and I am in the Father." ³⁹ Then they tried again to arrest him; but he escaped from their power.

⁴⁰ He went back across the Jordan to the place where John first baptized, and there he remained. ⁴¹ Many came to him and said, "John performed no sign, but everything John said about this man was true." ⁴² And many there began to believe in him.

Saturday April 12, 2025
Saturday of the Fifth Week of Lent
First Reading: Ezekiel 37:21-28

21 Thus says the Lord GOD: I will take the children of Israel from among the nations to which they have come, and gather them from all sides to bring them back to their land. 22 I will make them one nation upon the land, in the mountains of Israel, and there shall be one prince for them all. Never again shall they be two nations, and never again shall they be divided into two kingdoms.

23 No longer shall they defile themselves with their idols, their abominations, and all their transgressions. I will deliver them from all their sins of apostasy, and cleanse them so that they may be my people and I may be their God. 24 My servant David shall be prince over them, and there shall be one shepherd for them all; they shall live by my statutes and carefully observe my decrees. 25 They shall live on the land that I gave to my servant Jacob, the land where their fathers lived; they shall live on it forever, they, and their children, and their children's children, with my servant David their prince forever. 26 I will make with them a covenant of peace; it shall be an everlasting covenant with them, and I will multiply them, and put my sanctuary among them forever. 27 My dwelling shall be with them; I will be their God, and they shall be my people. 28 Thus the nations shall know that it is I, the LORD, who make Israel holy, when my sanctuary shall be set up among them forever.

Responsorial Psalm: Jeremiah 31:10, 11-12ABCD, 13

R. (see 10d) **The Lord will guard us, as a shepherd guards his flock.**

10 Hear the word of the LORD, O nations,
    proclaim it on distant isles, and say:
He who scattered Israel, now gathers them together,
    he guards them as a shepherd his flock.

R. The Lord will guard us, as a shepherd guards his flock.

11 The LORD shall ransom Jacob,
    he shall redeem him from the hand of his conqueror.
12 Shouting, they shall mount the heights of Zion,
    they shall come streaming to the LORD's blessings:
The grain, the wine, and the oil,
    the sheep and the oxen.

R. The Lord will guard us, as a shepherd guards his flock.

13 Then the virgins shall make merry and dance,

and young men and old as well.
I will turn their mourning into joy,
> I will console and gladden them after
>> their sorrows.

R. The Lord will guard us, as a shepherd guards his flock.

Verse Before the Gospel: Ezekiel 18:31

[31] Cast away from you all the crimes you have committed, says the Lord, and make for yourselves a new heart and a new spirit.

Gospel: John 11:45-56

[45] Many of the Jews who had come to Mary and seen what Jesus had done began to believe in him. [46] But some of them went to the Pharisees and told them what Jesus had done. [47] So the chief priests and the Pharisees convened the Sanhedrin and said, "What are we going to do? This man is performing many signs. [48] If we leave him alone, all will believe in him, and the Romans will come and take away both our land and our nation." [49] But one of them, Caiaphas, who was high priest that year, said to them, "You know nothing, [50] nor do you consider that it is better for you that one man should die instead of the people, so that the whole nation may not perish." [51] He did not say this on his own, but since he was high priest for that year, he prophesied that Jesus was going to die for the nation, [52] and not only for the nation, but also to gather into one the dispersed children of God. [53] So from that day on they planned to kill him.

[54] So Jesus no longer walked about in public among the Jews, but he left for the region near the desert, to a town called Ephraim, and there he remained with his disciples.

[55] Now the Passover of the Jews was near, and many went up from the country to Jerusalem before Passover to purify themselves. [56] They looked for Jesus and said to one another as they were in the temple area, "What do you think? That he will not come to the feast?"

Sunday April 13, 2025
Palm Sunday, Year C

At The Procession with Palms – Gospel – Luke 19:28-40

[28] Jesus proceeded on his journey up to Jerusalem. [29] As he drew near to Bethphage and Bethany at the place called the Mount of Olives, he sent two of his disciples. [30] He said, "Go into the village opposite you, and as you enter it you will find a colt tethered on which no one has ever sat. Untie it and bring it here. [31] And if anyone should ask you, 'Why are you untying it?' you will answer, 'The Master has need of it.'" [32] So those who had been sent went off and found everything just as he had told them. [33] And as they were untying the colt, its owners said to them, "Why are you untying this colt?" [34] They answered, "The Master has need of it." [35] So they brought it to Jesus, threw their cloaks over the colt, and helped Jesus to mount.

[36] As he rode along, the people were spreading their cloaks on the road; [37] and now as he was approaching the slope of the Mount of Olives, the whole multitude of his disciples began to praise God aloud with joy for all the mighty deeds they had seen. [38] They proclaimed:

"Blessed is the king who comes
    in the name of the Lord.
Peace in heaven
    and glory in the highest."

[39] Some of the Pharisees in the crowd said to him, "Teacher, rebuke your disciples." [31] He said in reply, "I tell you, if they keep silent, the stones will cry out!"

At The Mass – First Reading - Isaiah 50:4-7

[4] The Lord GOD has given me
    a well-trained tongue,
that I might know how to speak to the weary
    a word that will rouse them.
Morning after morning
    he opens my ear that I may hear;
[5] and I have not rebelled,
    have not turned back.
    [6] I gave my back to those who beat me,
    my cheeks to those who plucked my
        beard;
my face I did not shield
    from buffets and spitting.

[7] The Lord GOD is my help,
    therefore I am not disgraced;
I have set my face like flint,
    knowing that I shall not be put to shame.

Responsorial Psalm: Psalms 22:8-9, 17-18, 19-20, 23-24

R. [2a] **My God, my God, why have you abandoned me?**
[8] All who see me scoff at me;
    they mock me with parted lips, they wag
        their heads:
[9] "He relied on the LORD; let him deliver him,
    let him rescue him, if he loves him."
R. My God, my God, why have you abandoned me?
[17] Indeed, many dogs surround me,

a pack of evildoers closes in upon me;
¹⁸They have pierced my hands and my feet;
   I can count all my bones.
R. My God, my God, why have you abandoned me?
¹⁹They divide my garments among them,
   and for my vesture they cast lots.
²⁰But you, O LORD, be not far from me;
   O my help, hasten to aid me.
R. My God, my God, why have you abandoned me?
²³I will proclaim your name to my brethren;
   in the midst of the assembly I will praise you:
²⁴"You who fear the LORD, praise him;
   all you descendants of Jacob, give glory to him;
   revere him, all you descendants of Israel!"
R. My God, my God, why have you abandoned me?

Second Reading: Philippians 2:6-11
⁶Christ Jesus, though he was in the form of God,
   did not regard equality with God
   something to be grasped.
⁷Rather, he emptied himself,
   taking the form of a slave,
   coming in human likeness;
   and found human in appearance,
⁸he humbled himself,
   becoming obedient to the point of death,
   even death on a cross.
⁹Because of this, God greatly exalted him
   and bestowed on him the name
   which is above every name,
¹⁰that at the name of Jesus
   every knee should bend,
   of those in heaven and on earth and
      under the earth,
¹¹and every tongue confess that
   Jesus Christ is Lord,
   to the glory of God the Father.

Verse Before the Gospel: Philippians 2:8-9

⁸Christ became obedient to the point of death,
even death on a cross.
⁹Because of this, God greatly exalted him
and bestowed on him the name which is
    above every name.

Gospel: Luke 22:14-23:56

¹⁴When the hour came, Jesus took his place at table with the apostles. ¹⁵He said to them, "I have eagerly desired to eat this Passover with you before I suffer, ¹⁶for, I tell you, I shall not eat it again until there is fulfillment in the kingdom of God." ¹⁷Then he took a cup, gave thanks, and said, "Take this and share it among yourselves; ¹⁸for I tell you that from this time on I shall not drink of the fruit of the vine until the kingdom of God comes." ¹⁹Then he took the bread, said the blessing, broke it, and gave it to them, saying, "This is my body, which will be given for you; do this in memory of me." ²⁰And likewise the cup after they had eaten, saying, "This cup is the new covenant in my blood, which will be shed for you.

²¹"And yet behold, the hand of the one who is to betray me is with me on the table; ²²for the Son of Man indeed goes as it has been determined; but woe to that man by whom he is betrayed." ²³And they began to debate among themselves who among them would do such a deed.

²⁴Then an argument broke out among them about which of them should be regarded as the greatest. ²⁵He said to them, "The kings of the Gentiles lord it over them and those in authority over them are addressed as 'Benefactors'; ²⁶but among you it shall not be so. Rather, let the greatest among you be as the youngest, and the leader as the servant. ²⁷For who is greater: the one seated at table or the one who serves? Is it not the one seated at table? I am among you as the one who serves. ²⁸It is you who have stood by me in my trials; ²⁹and I confer a kingdom on you, just as my Father has conferred one on me, ³⁰that you may eat and drink at my table in my kingdom; and you will sit on thrones judging the twelve tribes of Israel.

³¹"Simon, Simon, behold Satan has demanded to sift all of you like wheat, ³²but I have prayed that your own faith may not fail; and once you have turned back, you must strengthen your brothers." ³³He said to him, "Lord, I am prepared to go to prison and to die with you." ³⁴But he replied, "I tell you, Peter, before the cock crows this day, you will deny three times that you know me."

³⁵He said to them, "When I sent you forth without a money bag or a sack or sandals, were you in need of anything?" "No, nothing, " they replied. ³⁶He said to them, "But now one who has a money bag should take it, and likewise a sack, and one who does not have a sword should sell his cloak and buy one. ³⁷For I tell you that this Scripture must be fulfilled in me, namely, *He was counted among the wicked*; and indeed what is written about me is coming to fulfillment." ³⁸Then they said, "Lord, look, there are two swords here." But he replied, "It is enough!"

³⁹Then going out, he went, as was his custom, to the Mount of Olives, and the disciples followed him. ⁴⁰When he arrived at the place he said to them, "Pray that you may not undergo the test." ⁴¹After withdrawing about a stone's throw from them and kneeling, he prayed, ⁴²saying, "Father, if you are willing, take this cup away from me; still, not my will but yours be done." ⁴³And to strengthen him an angel from heaven appeared to him. ⁴⁴He was in such agony and he prayed so fervently that his sweat became like drops of blood falling on the ground. ⁴⁵When he rose from prayer and returned to his disciples, he found them sleeping from grief. ⁴⁶He said to them, "Why are you sleeping? Get up and pray that you may not undergo the test."

⁴⁷While he was still speaking, a crowd approached and in front was one of the Twelve, a man named Judas. He went up to Jesus to kiss him. ⁴⁸Jesus said to him, "Judas, are you betraying the Son of Man with a kiss?" ⁴⁹His disciples realized what was about to happen, and they asked, "Lord, shall we strike with a sword?" ⁵⁰And one of them struck the high priest's servant and cut off his right ear. ⁵¹But Jesus said in reply, "Stop, no more of this!" Then he touched the servant's ear and healed him. ⁵²And Jesus said to the chief priests and temple guards and elders who had come for him, "Have you come out as against a robber, with swords and clubs? ⁵³Day after day I was with you in the temple area, and you did not seize me; but this is your hour, the time for the power of darkness."

⁵⁴After arresting him they led him away and took him into the house of the high priest; Peter was following at a distance. ⁵⁵They lit a fire in the middle of the courtyard and sat around it, and Peter sat down with them. ⁵⁶When a maid saw him seated in the light, she looked intently at him and said, "This man too was with him." ⁵⁷But he denied it saying, "Woman, I do not know him." ⁵⁸A short while later someone else saw him and said, "You too are one of them"; but Peter answered, "My friend, I am not." ⁵⁹About an hour later, still another insisted, "Assuredly, this man too was with him, for he also is a Galilean." ⁶⁰But Peter said, "My friend, I do not know what you are talking about." Just as he was saying this, the cock crowed, ⁶¹and the Lord turned and looked at Peter; and Peter remembered the word of the Lord, how he had said to him, "Before the cock crows today, you will deny me three times." ⁶²He went out and began to weep bitterly. ⁶³The men who held Jesus in custody were ridiculing and beating him. ⁶⁴They blindfolded him and questioned him, saying, "Prophesy! Who is it that struck you?" ⁶⁵And they reviled him in saying many other things against him.

⁶⁶When day came the council of elders of the people met, both chief priests and scribes, and they brought him before their Sanhedrin. ⁶⁷They said, "If you are the Christ, tell us, " but he replied to them, "If I tell you, you will not believe, ⁶⁸and if I question, you will not respond. ⁶⁹But from this time on the Son of Man will be seated at the right hand of the power of God." ⁷⁰They all asked, "Are you then the Son of God?" He replied to them, "You say that I am." ⁷¹Then they said, "What further need have we for testimony? We have heard it from his own mouth."

¹Then the whole assembly of them arose and brought him before Pilate. ²They brought charges against him, saying, "We found this man misleading our people; he opposes the payment of taxes to Caesar and maintains that he is the Christ, a king." ³Pilate asked him, "Are you the king of the Jews?" He said to him in reply, "You say so." ⁴Pilate then addressed the chief priests and the crowds, "I find this man not guilty." ⁵But they were adamant and said, "He is inciting the people with his teaching throughout all Judea, from Galilee where he began even to here."

⁶On hearing this Pilate asked if the man was a Galilean; ⁷and upon learning that he was under Herod's jurisdiction, he sent him to Herod who was in Jerusalem at that time. ⁸Herod was very glad to see Jesus; he had been wanting to see him for a long time, for he had heard about him and had been hoping to see him perform some sign. ⁹He questioned him at length, but he gave him no answer. ¹⁰The chief priests and scribes, meanwhile, stood by accusing him harshly. ¹¹Herod and his soldiers treated him contemptuously and mocked him, and after clothing him in resplendent garb, he sent him back to Pilate. ¹²Herod and Pilate became friends that very day, even though they had been enemies formerly. ¹³Pilate then summoned the chief priests, the rulers, and the people ¹⁴and said to them, "You brought this man to me and accused him of inciting the people to revolt. I have conducted my investigation in your presence and have not found this man guilty of the charges you have brought against him, ¹⁵nor did Herod, for he sent him back to us. So no capital crime has been committed by him. ¹⁶Therefore I shall have him flogged and then release him."

¹⁸ But all together they shouted out, "Away with this man! Release Barabbas to us." ¹⁹—Now Barabbas had been imprisoned for a rebellion that had taken place in the city and for murder.— ²⁰Again Pilate addressed them, still wishing to release Jesus, ²¹but they continued their shouting, "Crucify him! Crucify him!" ²² Pilate addressed them a third time, "What evil has this man done? I found him guilty of no capital crime. Therefore I shall have him flogged and then release him." ²³With loud shouts, however, they persisted in calling for his crucifixion, and their voices prevailed. ²⁴ The verdict of Pilate was that their demand should be granted. ²⁵So he released the man who had been imprisoned for rebellion and murder, for whom they asked, and he handed Jesus over to them to deal with as they wished.

²⁶As they led him away they took hold of a certain Simon, a Cyrenian, who was coming in from the country; and after laying the cross on him, they made him carry it behind Jesus. ²⁷ A large crowd of people followed Jesus, including many women who mourned and lamented him. ²⁸ Jesus turned to them and said, "Daughters of Jerusalem, do not weep for me; weep instead for yourselves and for your children ²⁹for indeed, the days are coming when people will say, 'Blessed are the barren, the wombs that never bore and the breasts that never nursed.' ³⁰At that time people will say to the mountains, 'Fall upon us!' and to the hills, 'Cover us!' ³¹for if these things are done when the wood is green what will happen when it is dry?" ³²Now two others, both criminals, were led away with him to be executed.

⁳³When they came to the place called the Skull, they crucified him and the criminals there, one on his right, the other on his left. ³⁴Then Jesus said, "Father, forgive them, they know not what they do." They divided his garments by casting lots. ³⁵The people stood by and watched; the rulers, meanwhile, sneered at him and said, "He saved others, let him save himself if he is the chosen one, the Christ of God." ³⁶Even the soldiers jeered at him. As they approached to offer him wine ³⁷they called out, "If you are King of the Jews, save yourself." ³⁸Above him there was an inscription that read, "This is the King of the Jews."

³⁹Now one of the criminals hanging there reviled Jesus, saying, "Are you not the Christ? Save yourself and us." ⁴⁰The other, however, rebuking him, said in reply, "Have you no fear of God, for you are subject to the same condemnation? ⁴¹And indeed, we have been condemned justly, for the sentence we received corresponds to our crimes, but this man has done nothing criminal." ⁴²Then he said, "Jesus, remember me when you come into your kingdom." ⁴³He replied to him, "Amen, I say to you, today you will be with me in Paradise."

⁴⁴It was now about noon and darkness came over the whole land until three in the afternoon ⁴⁵because of an eclipse of the sun. Then the veil of the temple was torn down the middle. ⁴⁶Jesus cried out in a loud voice, "Father, into your hands I commend my spirit"; and when he had said this he breathed his last.

(Here all kneel and pause for a short time)

⁴⁷The centurion who witnessed what had happened glorified God and said, "This man was innocent beyond doubt." ⁴⁸When all the people who had gathered for this spectacle saw what had happened, they returned home beating their breasts; ⁴⁹but all his acquaintances stood at a distance, including the women who had followed him from Galilee and saw these events.

⁵⁰Now there was a virtuous and righteous man named Joseph who, though he was a member of the council, ⁵¹had not consented to their plan of action. He came from the Jewish town of Arimathea and was awaiting the kingdom of God. ⁵²He went to Pilate and asked for the body of Jesus. ⁵³After he had taken the body down, he wrapped it in a linen cloth and laid him in a rock-hewn tomb in which no one had yet been buried. ⁵⁴It was the day of preparation, and the Sabbath was about to begin. ⁵⁵The women who had come from Galilee with him followed behind, and when they had seen the tomb and the way in which his body was laid in it, ⁵⁶they returned and prepared spices and perfumed oils. Then they rested on the Sabbath according to the commandment.

Or Luke 23:1-49

¹The elders of the people, chief priests and scribes, arose and brought him before Pilate. ² They brought charges against him, saying, "We found this man misleading our people; he opposes the payment of taxes to Caesar and maintains that he is the Christ, a king." ³ Pilate asked him, "Are you the king of the Jews?" He said to him in reply, "You say so." ⁴ Pilate then addressed the chief priests and the crowds, "I find this man not guilty." ⁵ But they were adamant and said, "He is inciting the people with his teaching throughout all Judea, from Galilee where he began even to here."

⁶On hearing this Pilate asked if the man was a Galilean; ⁷and upon learning that he was under Herod's jurisdiction, he sent him to Herod who was in Jerusalem at that time. ⁸Herod was very glad to see Jesus; he had been wanting to see him for a long time, for he had heard about him and had been hoping to see him perform some sign. ⁹He questioned him at length, but he gave him no answer. ¹⁰The chief priests and scribes, meanwhile, stood by accusing him harshly. ¹¹Herod and his soldiers treated him contemptuously and mocked him, and after clothing him in resplendent garb, he sent him back to Pilate. ¹²Herod and Pilate became friends that very day, even though they had been enemies formerly. ¹³Pilate then summoned the chief priests, the rulers, and the people ¹⁴and said to them, "You brought this man to me and accused him of inciting the people to revolt. I have conducted my investigation in your presence and have not found this man guilty of the charges you have brought against him, ¹⁵nor did Herod, for he sent him back to us. So no capital crime has been committed by him. ¹⁶Therefore I shall have him flogged and then release him."

¹⁸But all together they shouted out, "Away with this man! Release Barabbas to us." ¹⁹—Now Barabbas had been imprisoned for a rebellion that had taken place in the city and for murder.— ²⁰Again Pilate addressed them, still wishing to release Jesus, ²¹but they continued their shouting, "Crucify him! Crucify him!" ²²Pilate addressed them a third time, "What evil has this man done? I found him guilty of no capital crime. Therefore I shall have him flogged and then release him." ²³With loud shouts, however, they persisted in calling for his crucifixion, and their voices prevailed. ²⁴The verdict of Pilate was that their demand should be granted. ²⁵So he released the man who had been imprisoned for rebellion and murder, for whom they asked, and he handed Jesus over to them to deal with as they wished.

²⁶As they led him away they took hold of a certain Simon, a Cyrenian, who was coming in from the country; and after laying the cross on him, they made him carry it behind Jesus. ²⁷A large crowd of people followed Jesus, including many women who mourned and lamented him. ²⁸Jesus turned to them and said, "Daughters of Jerusalem, do not weep for me; weep instead for yourselves and for your children ²⁹for indeed, the days are coming when people will say, 'Blessed are the barren, the wombs that never bore and the breasts that never nursed.' ³⁰At that time people will say to the mountains, 'Fall upon us!' and to the hills, 'Cover us!' ³¹for if these things are done when the wood is green what will happen when it is dry?" ³²Now two others, both criminals, were led away with him to be executed.

³³When they came to the place called the Skull, they crucified him and the criminals there, one on his right, the other on his left. ³⁴Then Jesus said, "Father, forgive them, they know not what they do." They divided his garments by casting lots. ³⁵The people stood by and watched; the rulers, meanwhile, sneered at him and said, "He saved others, let him save himself if he is the chosen one, the Christ of God." ³⁶Even the soldiers jeered at him. As they approached to offer him wine ³⁷they called out, "If you are King of the Jews, save yourself." ³⁸Above him there was an inscription that read, "This is the King of the Jews."

³⁹Now one of the criminals hanging there reviled Jesus, saying, "Are you not the Christ? Save yourself and us." ⁴⁰The other, however, rebuking him, said in reply, "Have you no fear of God, for you are subject to the same condemnation? ⁴¹And indeed, we have been condemned justly, for the sentence we received corresponds to our crimes, but this man has done nothing criminal." ⁴²Then he said, "Jesus, remember me when you come into your kingdom." ⁴³He replied to him, "Amen, I say to you, today you will be with me in Paradise." ⁴⁴It was now about noon and darkness came over the whole land until three in the afternoon ⁴⁵because of an eclipse of the sun. Then the veil of the temple was torn down the middle. ⁴⁶Jesus cried out in a loud voice, "Father, into your hands I commend my spirit"; and when he had said this he breathed his last.

(Here all kneel and pause for a short time)

⁴⁷The centurion who witnessed what had happened glorified God and said, "This man was innocent beyond doubt." ⁴⁸When all the people who had gathered for this spectacle saw what had happened, they returned home beating their breasts; ⁴⁹but all his acquaintances stood at a distance, including the women who had followed him from Galilee and saw these events.

Monday April 14, 2025
Monday of Holy Week

First Reading: Isaiah 42:1-7

¹ Here is my servant whom I uphold,
   my chosen one with whom I am pleased,
Upon whom I have put my Spirit;
   he shall bring forth justice to the nations,
² Not crying out, not shouting,
   not making his voice heard in the street.
³ A bruised reed he shall not break,
   and a smoldering wick he shall not
      quench,
⁴ Until he establishes justice on the earth;
   the coastlands will wait for his teaching.

⁵ Thus says God, the LORD,
   who created the heavens and stretched
      them out,
   who spreads out the earth with its crops,
Who gives breath to its people
   and spirit to those who walk on it:
⁶ I, the LORD, have called you for the victory of
      justice,
   I have grasped you by the hand;
I formed you, and set you
   as a covenant of the people,
   a light for the nations,
⁷ To open the eyes of the blind,

to bring out prisoners from confinement,
and from the dungeon, those who live in darkness.

Responsorial Psalm: Psalms 27:1, 2, 3, 13-14
R. (1a) *The Lord is my light and my salvation.*
[1] The LORD is my light and my salvation;
whom should I fear?
The LORD is my life's refuge;
of whom should I be afraid?
R. The Lord is my light and my salvation.
[2] When evildoers come at me
to devour my flesh,
My foes and my enemies
themselves stumble and fall.
R. The Lord is my light and my salvation.
[3] Though an army encamp against me,
my heart will not fear;
Though war be waged upon me,
even then will I trust.
R. The Lord is my light and my salvation.
[13] I believe that I shall see the bounty of the LORD
in the land of the living.
[14] Wait for the LORD with courage;
be stouthearted, and wait for the LORD.
R. The Lord is my light and my salvation.

Verse Before the Gospel
Hail to you, our King;
you alone are compassionate with our faults.

Gospel: John 12:1-11
[1] Six days before Passover Jesus came to Bethany, where Lazarus was, whom Jesus had raised from the dead. [2] They gave a dinner for him there, and Martha served, while Lazarus was one of those reclining at table with him. [3] Mary took a liter of costly perfumed oil made from genuine aromatic nard and anointed the feet of Jesus and dried them with her hair; the house was filled with the fragrance of the oil. [4] Then Judas the Iscariot, one of his disciples, and the one who would betray him, said, [5] "Why was this oil not sold for three hundred days' wages and given to the poor?" [6] He said this not because he cared about the poor but because he was a thief and held the money bag and used to steal the contributions. [7] So Jesus said, "Leave her alone. Let her keep this for the day of my burial. [8] You always have the poor with you, but you do not always have me."

⁹ The large crowd of the Jews found out that he was there and came, not only because of him, but also to see Lazarus, whom he had raised from the dead. ¹⁰ And the chief priests plotted to kill Lazarus too, ¹¹ because many of the Jews were turning away and believing in Jesus because of him.

Tuesday April 15, 2025
Tuesday of Holy Week

First Reading: Isaiah 49:1-6

¹ Hear me, O islands,
    listen, O distant peoples.
The LORD called me from birth,
    from my mother's womb he gave me my name.
² He made of me a sharp-edged sword
    and concealed me in the shadow of his arm.
He made me a polished arrow,
    in his quiver he hid me.
³ You are my servant, he said to me,
    Israel, through whom I show my glory.

⁴ Though I thought I had toiled in vain,
    and for nothing, uselessly, spent my strength,
Yet my reward is with the LORD,
    my recompense is with my God.
⁵ For now the LORD has spoken
    who formed me as his servant from the womb,
That Jacob may be brought back to him
    and Israel gathered to him;
And I am made glorious in the sight of the LORD,
    and my God is now my strength!
⁶ It is too little, he says, for you to be my servant,
    to raise up the tribes of Jacob,
    and restore the survivors of Israel;
I will make you a light to the nations,
    that my salvation may reach to the ends of the earth.

Responsorial Psalm: Psalms 71:1-2, 3-4A,5AB-6AB,15and 17

R. *(see 15ab)* ***I will sing of your salvation.***
¹ In you, O LORD, I take refuge;

let me never be put to shame.
² In your justice rescue me, and deliver me;
  incline your ear to me, and save me.
R. I will sing of your salvation.
³ Be my rock of refuge,
  a stronghold to give me safety,
  for you are my rock and my fortress.
⁴ᴬ O my God, rescue me from the hand of the wicked.
R. I will sing of your salvation.
⁵ᴬᴮ For you are my hope, O Lord;
  my trust, O God, from my youth.
⁶ᴬᴮ On you I depend from birth;
  from my mother's womb you are my strength.
R. I will sing of your salvation.
¹⁵ My mouth shall declare your justice,
  day by day your salvation.
¹⁷ O God, you have taught me from my youth,
  and till the present I proclaim your wondrous deeds.
R. I will sing of your salvation.

Verse Before the Gospel
Hail to you, our King, obedient to the Father;
you were led to your crucifixion like a gentle
  lamb to the slaughter.

Gospel: John 13:21-33, 36-38

²¹ Reclining at table with his disciples, Jesus was deeply troubled and testified, "Amen, amen, I say to you, one of you will betray me." ²² The disciples looked at one another, at a loss as to whom he meant. ²³ One of his disciples, the one whom Jesus loved, was reclining at Jesus' side. ²⁴ So Simon Peter nodded to him to find out whom he meant. ²⁵ He leaned back against Jesus' chest and said to him, "Master, who is it?" ²⁶ Jesus answered, "It is the one to whom I hand the morsel after I have dipped it." So he dipped the morsel and took it and handed it to Judas, son of Simon the Iscariot. ²⁷ After Judas took the morsel, Satan entered him. So Jesus said to him, "What you are going to do, do quickly." ²⁸ Now none of those reclining at table realized why he said this to him. ²⁹ Some thought that since Judas kept the money bag, Jesus had told him, "Buy what we need for the feast," or to give something to the poor. ³⁰ So Judas took the morsel and left at once. And it was night.

³¹ When he had left, Jesus said, "Now is the Son of Man glorified, and God is glorified in him. ³² If God is glorified in him, God will also glorify him in himself, and he will glorify him at once. ³³ My children, I will be with you only a little while longer. You will look for me, and as I told the Jews, 'Where I go you cannot come,' so now I say it to you."

³⁶ Simon Peter said to him, "Master, where are you going?" Jesus answered him, "Where I am going, you cannot follow me now, though you will follow later." ³⁷ Peter said to him, "Master, why can I not follow you now? I will lay down my life for you." ³⁸ Jesus answered, "Will you lay down your life for me? Amen, amen, I say to you, the cock will not crow before you deny me three times."

Wednesday April 16, 2025
Wednesday of Holy Week

First Reading: Isaiah 50:4-9A
⁴ The Lord GOD has given me
    a well-trained tongue,
That I might know how to speak to the
      weary
    a word that will rouse them.
Morning after morning
    he opens my ear that I may hear;
⁵ And I have not rebelled,
    have not turned back.
⁶ I gave my back to those who beat me,
    my cheeks to those who plucked my
      beard;
My face I did not shield
    from buffets and spitting.

⁷ The Lord GOD is my help,
    therefore I am not disgraced;
I have set my face like flint,
    knowing that I shall not be put to shame.
⁸ He is near who upholds my right;
    if anyone wishes to oppose me,
    let us appear together.
Who disputes my right?
    Let him confront me.
⁹ See, the Lord GOD is my help;
    who will prove me wrong?

Responsorial Psalm: Psalms 69:8-10, 21-22, 31 and 33-34
R. ⁽¹⁴ᶜ⁾ *Lord, in your great love, answer me.*
⁸ For your sake I bear insult,
    and shame covers my face.
⁹ I have become an outcast to my brothers,
    a stranger to my mother's sons,
¹⁰ because zeal for your house consumes me,
    and the insults of those who blaspheme
      you fall upon me.

R. Lord, in your great love, answer me.
²¹ Insult has broken my heart, and I am weak,
> I looked for sympathy, but there was none;
> for consolers, not one could I find.

²² Rather they put gall in my food,
> and in my thirst they gave me vinegar to drink.

R. Lord, in your great love, answer me.
³¹ I will praise the name of God in song,
> and I will glorify him with thanksgiving:

³³ "See, you lowly ones, and be glad;
> you who seek God, may your hearts revive!

³⁴ For the LORD hears the poor,
> and his own who are in bonds he spurns not."

R. Lord, in your great love, answer me.

Verse Before the Gospel
Hail to you, our King;
you alone are compassionate with our
> errors.

Or
Hail to you, our King, obedient to the Father;
you were led to your crucifixion like a gentle
> lamb to the slaughter.

Gospel: Matthew 26:14-25

¹⁴ One of the Twelve, who was called Judas Iscariot, went to the chief priests ¹⁵ and said, "What are you willing to give me if I hand him over to you?" They paid him thirty pieces of silver, ¹⁶ and from that time on he looked for an opportunity to hand him over.

¹⁷ On the first day of the Feast of Unleavened Bread, the disciples approached Jesus and said, "Where do you want us to prepare for you to eat the Passover?" ¹⁸ He said, "Go into the city to a certain man and tell him, 'The teacher says, "My appointed time draws near; in your house I shall celebrate the Passover with my disciples."'" ¹⁹ The disciples then did as Jesus had ordered, and prepared the Passover.

²⁰ When it was evening, he reclined at table with the Twelve. ²¹ And while they were eating, he said, "Amen, I say to you, one of you will betray me." ²² Deeply distressed at this, they began to say to him one after another, "Surely it is not I, Lord?" ²³ He said in reply, "He who has dipped his hand into the dish with me is the one who will betray me. ²⁴ The Son of Man indeed goes, as it is written of him, but woe to that man by whom the Son of Man is betrayed. It would be better for that man if he had never been born." ²⁵ Then Judas, his betrayer, said in reply, "Surely it is not I, Rabbi?" He answered, "You have said so."

Thursday April 17, 2025
Holy Thursday of the Lord's Supper
First Reading: Exodus 12:1-8, 11-14

¹ The LORD said to Moses and Aaron in the land of Egypt, ² "This month shall stand at the head of your calendar; you shall reckon it the first month of the year. ³ Tell the whole community of Israel: On the tenth of this month every one of your families must procure for itself a lamb, one apiece for each household. ⁴ If a family is too small for a whole lamb, it shall join the nearest household in procuring one and shall share in the lamb in proportion to the number of persons who partake of it. ⁵ The lamb must be a year-old male and without blemish. You may take it from either the sheep or the goats. ⁶ You shall keep it until the fourteenth day of this month, and then, with the whole assembly of Israel present, it shall be slaughtered during the evening twilight. ⁷ They shall take some of its blood and apply it to the two doorposts and the lintel of every house in which they partake of the lamb. ⁸ That same night they shall eat its roasted flesh with unleavened bread and bitter herbs.

¹¹ "This is how you are to eat it: with your loins girt, sandals on your feet and your staff in hand, you shall eat like those who are in flight. It is the Passover of the LORD. ¹² For on this same night I will go through Egypt, striking down every firstborn of the land, both man and beast, and executing judgment on all the gods of Egypt—I, the LORD! ¹³ But the blood will mark the houses where you are. Seeing the blood, I will pass over you; thus, when I strike the land of Egypt, no destructive blow will come upon you.

¹⁴ "This day shall be a memorial feast for you, which all your generations shall celebrate with pilgrimage to the LORD, as a perpetual institution."

Responsorial Psalm: Psalms 116:12-13, 15-16BC, 17-18

R. (cf. 1 Cor 10:16) *Our blessing-cup is a communion with the Blood of Christ.*

¹² How shall I make a return to the LORD
   for all the good he has done for me?
¹³ The cup of salvation I will take up,
   and I will call upon the name of the LORD.

R. *Our blessing-cup is a communion with the Blood of Christ.*

¹⁵ Precious in the eyes of the LORD
   is the death of his faithful ones.
¹⁶BC I am your servant, the son of your handmaid;
   you have loosed my bonds.

R. *Our blessing-cup is a communion with the Blood of Christ.*

¹⁷ To you will I offer sacrifice of thanksgiving,
   and I will call upon the name of the LORD.
¹⁸ My vows to the LORD I will pay
   in the presence of all his people.

R. *Our blessing-cup is a communion with the*

Blood of Christ.

Second Reading: 1 Corinthians 11:23-26
Brothers and sisters: [23] I received from the Lord what I also handed on to you, that the Lord Jesus, on the night he was handed over, took bread, [24] and, after he had given thanks, broke it and said, "This is my body that is for you. Do this in remembrance of me." [25] In the same way also the cup, after supper, saying, "This cup is the new covenant in my blood. Do this, as often as you drink it, in remembrance of me." [26] For as often as you eat this bread and drink the cup, you proclaim the death of the Lord until he comes.

Verse Before the Gospel: John 13:34
[34] I give you a new commandment, says the Lord:
love one another as I have loved you.

Gospel: John 13:1-15
[1] Before the feast of Passover, Jesus knew that his hour had come to pass from this world to the Father. He loved his own in the world and he loved them to the end. [2] The devil had already induced Judas, son of Simon the Iscariot, to hand him over. So, during supper, [3] fully aware that the Father had put everything into his power and that he had come from God and was returning to God, [4] he rose from supper and took off his outer garments. He took a towel and tied it around his waist. [5] Then he poured water into a basin and began to wash the disciples' feet and dry them with the towel around his waist. [6] He came to Simon Peter, who said to him, "Master, are you going to wash my feet?" [7] Jesus answered and said to him, "What I am doing, you do not understand now, but you will understand later." [8] Peter said to him, "You will never wash my feet." Jesus answered him, "Unless I wash you, you will have no inheritance with me." [9] Simon Peter said to him, "Master, then not only my feet, but my hands and head as well." [10] Jesus said to him, "Whoever has bathed has no need except to have his feet washed, for he is clean all over; so you are clean, but not all." [11] For he knew who would betray him; for this reason, he said, "Not all of you are clean."

[12] So when he had washed their feet and put his garments back on and reclined at table again, he said to them, "Do you realize what I have done for you? [13] You call me 'teacher' and 'master,' and rightly so, for indeed I am. [14] If I, therefore, the master and teacher, have washed your feet, you ought to wash one another's feet. [15] I have given you a model to follow, so that as I have done for you, you should also do."

Friday April 18, 2025
Good Friday of the Lord's Passion
First Reading: Isaiah 52:13-53:12
[13] See, my servant shall prosper,
  he shall be raised high and greatly
    exalted.
[14] Even as many were amazed at him—
  so marred was his look beyond human

semblance
and his appearance beyond that of the
sons of man—
¹⁵ so shall he startle many nations,
because of him kings shall stand
speechless;
for those who have not been told shall see,
those who have not heard shall ponder it.

¹ Who would believe what we have heard?
To whom has the arm of the LORD been
revealed?
² He grew up like a sapling before him,
like a shoot from the parched earth;
there was in him no stately bearing to make
us look at him,
nor appearance that would attract us to
him.
³ He was spurned and avoided by people,
a man of suffering, accustomed to
infirmity,
one of those from whom people hide their
faces,
spurned, and we held him in no esteem.

⁴ Yet it was our infirmities that he bore,
our sufferings that he endured,
while we thought of him as stricken,
as one smitten by God and afflicted.
⁵ But he was pierced for our offenses,
crushed for our sins;
upon him was the chastisement that makes
us whole,
by his stripes we were healed.
⁶ We had all gone astray like sheep,
each following his own way;
but the LORD laid upon him
the guilt of us all.

⁷ Though he was harshly treated, he
submitted
and opened not his mouth;
like a lamb led to the slaughter
or a sheep before the shearers,
he was silent and opened not his mouth.

⁸ Oppressed and condemned, he was taken
    away,
   and who would have thought any more of
       his destiny?
When he was cut off from the land of the
       living,
   and smitten for the sin of his people,
⁹ a grave was assigned him among the wicked
   and a burial place with evildoers,
though he had done no wrong
   nor spoken any falsehood.
¹⁰ But the LORD was pleased
   to crush him in infirmity.

If he gives his life as an offering for sin,
   he shall see his descendants in a long life,
   and the will of the LORD shall be
       accomplished through him.

¹¹ Because of his affliction
   he shall see the light
   in fullness of days;
through his suffering, my servant shall
       justify many,
   and their guilt he shall bear.
¹² Therefore I will give him his portion
       among the great,
and he shall divide the spoils with the
       mighty,
because he surrendered himself to death
   and was counted among the wicked;
and he shall take away the sins of many,
   and win pardon for their offenses.

Responsorial Psalm: Psalms 31:2, 6, 12-13, 15-16, 17, 25

R. (Luke 23:46) Father, into your hands I commend my spirit.
² In you, O LORD, I take refuge;
   let me never be put to shame.
In your justice rescue me.
   ⁶ Into your hands I commend my spirit;
you will redeem me, O LORD, O faithful God.
R. Father, into your hands I commend my spirit.
¹² For all my foes I am an object of reproach,
   a laughingstock to my neighbors, and a dread
       to my friends;

    they who see me abroad flee from me.
[13] I am forgotten like the unremembered dead;
    I am like a dish that is broken.
R. Father, into your hands I commend my spirit.
[15] But my trust is in you, O LORD;
    I say, "You are my God.
[16] In your hands is my destiny; rescue me
    from the clutches of my enemies and my persecutors."
R. Father, into your hands I commend my spirit.
[17] Let your face shine upon your servant;
    save me in your kindness.
[25] Take courage and be stouthearted,
    all you who hope in the LORD.
R. Father, into your hands I commend my spirit.

Second Reading: Hebrews 4:14-16; 5:7-9

[14] Brothers and sisters: Since we have a great high priest who has passed through the heavens, Jesus, the Son of God, let us hold fast to our confession. [15] For we do not have a high priest who is unable to sympathize with our weaknesses, but one who has similarly been tested in every way, yet without sin. [16] So let us confidently approach the throne of grace to receive mercy and to find grace for timely help.

    [7] In the days when Christ was in the flesh, he offered prayers and supplications with loud cries and tears to the one who was able to save him from death, and he was heard because of his reverence. [8] Son though he was, he learned obedience from what he suffered; [9] and when he was made perfect, he became the source of eternal salvation for all who obey him.

Verse Before the Gospel: Philippians 2:8-9

[8] Christ became obedient to the point of death,
even death on a cross.
[9] Because of this, God greatly exalted him
and bestowed on him the name which is
    above every other name.

(**Please Note:** The passion narratives are proclaimed in full so that all see vividly the love of Christ for each person. In light of this, the crimes during the Passion of Christ cannot be attributed, in either preaching or catechesis, indiscriminately to all Jews of that time, nor to Jews today. The Jewish people should not be referred to as though rejected or cursed, as if this view followed from Scripture. The Church ever keeps in mind that Jesus, his mother Mary, and the apostles all were Jewish. As the Church has always held, Christ freely suffered his passion and death because of the sins of all, that all might be saved).

Gospel: John 18:1-19:42

¹ Jesus went out with his disciples across the Kidron valley to where there was a garden, into which he and his disciples entered. ² Judas his betrayer also knew the place, because Jesus had often met there with his disciples. ³ So Judas got a band of soldiers and guards from the chief priests and the Pharisees and went there with lanterns, torches, and weapons. ⁴ Jesus, knowing everything that was going to happen to him, went out and said to them, "Whom are you looking for?" ⁵ They answered him, "Jesus the Nazorean." He said to them, "I AM." Judas his betrayer was also with them. ⁶ When he said to them, "I AM," they turned away and fell to the ground. ⁷ So he again asked them, "Whom are you looking for?" They said, "Jesus the Nazorean." ⁸ Jesus answered, "I told you that I AM. So if you are looking for me, let these men go." ⁹ This was to fulfill what he had said, "I have not lost any of those you gave me." ¹⁰ Then Simon Peter, who had a sword, drew it, struck the high priest's slave, and cut off his right ear. The slave's name was Malchus. ¹¹ Jesus said to Peter, "Put your sword into its scabbard. Shall I not drink the cup that the Father gave me?"

¹² So the band of soldiers, the tribune, and the Jewish guards seized Jesus, bound him, ¹³ and brought him to Annas first. He was the father-in-law of Caiaphas, who was high priest that year. ¹⁴ It was Caiaphas who had counseled the Jews that it was better that one man should die rather than the people.

¹⁵ Simon Peter and another disciple followed Jesus. Now the other disciple was known to the high priest, and he entered the courtyard of the high priest with Jesus. ¹⁶ But Peter stood at the gate outside. So the other disciple, the acquaintance of the high priest, went out and spoke to the gatekeeper and brought Peter in. ¹⁷ Then the maid who was the gatekeeper said to Peter, "You are not one of this man's disciples, are you?" He said, "I am not." ¹⁸ Now the slaves and the guards were standing around a charcoal fire that they had made, because it was cold, and were warming themselves. Peter was also standing there keeping warm.

¹⁹ The high priest questioned Jesus about his disciples and about his doctrine. ²⁰ Jesus answered him, "I have spoken publicly to the world. I have always taught in a synagogue or in the temple area where all the Jews gather, and in secret I have said nothing. ²¹ Why ask me? Ask those who heard me what I said to them. They know what I said." ²² When he had said this, one of the temple guards standing there struck Jesus and said, "Is this the way you answer the high priest?" ²³ Jesus answered him, "If I have spoken wrongly, testify to the wrong; but if I have spoken rightly, why do you strike me?" ²⁴ Then Annas sent him bound to Caiaphas the high priest.

²⁵ Now Simon Peter was standing there keeping warm. And they said to him, "You are not one of his disciples, are you?" He denied it and said, "I am not." ²⁶ One of the slaves of the high priest, a relative of the one whose ear Peter had cut off, said, "Didn't I see you in the garden with him?" ²⁷ Again Peter denied it. And immediately the cock crowed.

⁲⁸ Then they brought Jesus from Caiaphas to the praetorium. It was morning. And they themselves did not enter the praetorium, in order not to be defiled so that they could eat the Passover. ²⁹ So Pilate came out to them and said, "What charge do you bring against this man?" ³⁰ They answered and said to him, "If he were not a criminal, we would not have handed him over to you." ³¹ At this, Pilate said to them, "Take him yourselves, and judge him according to your law." The Jews answered him, "We do not have the right to execute anyone, " ³² in order that the word of Jesus might be fulfilled that he said indicating the kind of death he would die. ³³ So Pilate went back into the praetorium and summoned Jesus and said to him, "Are you the King of the Jews?" ³⁴ Jesus answered, "Do you say this on your own or have others told you about me?" ³⁵ Pilate answered, "I am not a Jew, am I? Your own nation and the chief priests handed you over to me. What have you done?" ³⁶ Jesus answered, "My kingdom does not belong to this world. If my kingdom did belong to this world, my attendants would be fighting to keep me from being handed over to the Jews. But as it is, my kingdom is not here." ³⁷ So Pilate said to him, "Then you are a king?" Jesus answered, "You say I am a king. For this I was born and for this I came into the world, to testify to the truth. Everyone who belongs to the truth listens to my voice." ³⁸ Pilate said to him, "What is truth?"

When he had said this, he again went out to the Jews and said to them, "I find no guilt in him. ³⁹ But you have a custom that I release one prisoner to you at Passover. Do you want me to release to you the King of the Jews?" ⁴⁰ They cried out again, "Not this one but Barabbas!" Now Barabbas was a revolutionary.

¹ Then Pilate took Jesus and had him scourged. ² And the soldiers wove a crown out of thorns and placed it on his head, and clothed him in a purple cloak, ³ and they came to him and said, "Hail, King of the Jews!" And they struck him repeatedly. ⁴ Once more Pilate went out and said to them, "Look, I am bringing him out to you, so that you may know that I find no guilt in him." ⁵ So Jesus came out, wearing the crown of thorns and the purple cloak. And he said to them, "Behold, the man!" ⁶ When the chief priests and the guards saw him they cried out, "Crucify him, crucify him!" Pilate said to them, "Take him yourselves and crucify him. I find no guilt in him." ⁷ The Jews answered, "We have a law, and according to that law he ought to die, because he made himself the Son of God." ⁸ Now when Pilate heard this statement, he became even more afraid, ⁹ and went back into the praetorium and said to Jesus, "Where are you from?" Jesus did not answer him. ¹⁰ So Pilate said to him, "Do you not speak to me? Do you not know that I have power to release you and I have power to crucify you?" ¹¹ Jesus answered him, "You would have no power over me if it had not been given to you from above. For this reason the one who handed me over to you has the greater sin." ¹² Consequently, Pilate tried to release him; but the Jews cried out, "If you release him, you are not a Friend of Caesar. Everyone who makes himself a king opposes Caesar."

¹³ When Pilate heard these words he brought Jesus out and seated him on the judge's bench in the place called Stone Pavement, in Hebrew, Gabbatha. ¹⁴It was preparation day for Passover, and it was about noon. And he said to the Jews, "Behold, your king!" ¹⁵ They cried out, "Take him away, take him away! Crucify him!" Pilate said to them, "Shall I crucify your king?" The chief priests answered, "We have no king but Caesar." ¹⁶ Then he handed him over to them to be crucified.

So they took Jesus, ²⁷ and, carrying the cross himself, he went out to what is called the Place of the Skull, in Hebrew, Golgotha. ¹⁸ There they crucified him, and with him two others, one on either side, with Jesus in the middle. ¹⁹ Pilate also had an inscription written and put on the cross. It read, "Jesus the Nazorean, the King of the Jews." ²⁰ Now many of the Jews read this inscription, because the place where Jesus was crucified was near the city; and it was written in Hebrew, Latin, and Greek. ²¹ So the chief priests of the Jews said to Pilate, "Do not write 'The King of the Jews,' but that he said, 'I am the King of the Jews'." ²² Pilate answered, "What I have written, I have written."

²³ When the soldiers had crucified Jesus, they took his clothes and divided them into four shares, a share for each soldier. They also took his tunic, but the tunic was seamless, woven in one piece from the top down. ²⁴ So they said to one another, "Let's not tear it, but cast lots for it to see whose it will be, " in order that the passage of Scripture might be fulfilled that says:

They divided my garments among them,
 and for my vesture they cast lots.

This is what the soldiers did. ²⁵ Standing by the cross of Jesus were his mother and his mother's sister, Mary the wife of Clopas, and Mary of Magdala. ²⁶ When Jesus saw his mother and the disciple there whom he loved he said to his mother, "Woman, behold, your son." ²⁷ Then he said to the disciple, "Behold, your mother." And from that hour the disciple took her into his home.

²⁸ After this, aware that everything was now finished, in order that the Scripture might be fulfilled, Jesus said, "I thirst." ²⁹ There was a vessel filled with common wine. So they put a sponge soaked in wine on a sprig of hyssop and put it up to his mouth. ³⁰ When Jesus had taken the wine, he said, "It is finished." And bowing his head, he handed over the spirit.

(Here all kneel and pause for a short time)

³¹ Now since it was preparation day, in order that the bodies might not remain on the cross on the sabbath, for the sabbath day of that week was a solemn one, the Jews asked Pilate that their legs be broken and that they be taken down. ³² So the soldiers came and broke the legs of the first and then of the other one who was crucified with Jesus. ³³ But when they came to Jesus and saw that he was already dead, they did not break his legs, ³⁴ but one soldier thrust his lance into his side, and immediately blood and water flowed out. ³⁵ An eyewitness has testified, and his testimony is true; he knows that he is speaking the truth, so that you also may come to believe. ³⁶ For this happened so that the Scripture passage might be fulfilled:

Not a bone of it will be broken.

³⁷ And again another passage says:

They will look upon him whom they have
 pierced.

38 After this, Joseph of Arimathea, secretly a disciple of Jesus for fear of the Jews, asked Pilate if he could remove the body of Jesus. And Pilate permitted it. So he came and took his body. 39 Nicodemus, the one who had first come to him at night, also came bringing a mixture of myrrh and aloes weighing about one hundred pounds. 40 They took the body of Jesus and bound it with burial cloths along with the spices, according to the Jewish burial custom. 41 Now in the place where he had been crucified there was a garden, and in the garden a new tomb, in which no one had yet been buried. 42 So they laid Jesus there because of the Jewish preparation day; for the tomb was close by.

Saturday April 19, 2025
Holy Saturday Night of Easter – Easter Vigil
First Reading: Genesis 1:1-2:2

1 In the beginning, when God created the heavens and the earth, 2 the earth was a formless wasteland, and darkness covered the abyss, while a mighty wind swept over the waters.

3 Then God said, "Let there be light," and there was light. 4 God saw how good the light was. God then separated the light from the darkness. 5 God called the light "day," and the darkness he called "night." Thus evening came, and morning followed—the first day.

6 Then God said, "Let there be a dome in the middle of the waters, to separate one body of water from the other." And so it happened: 7 God made the dome, and it separated the water above the dome from the water below it. 8 God called the dome "the sky." Evening came, and morning followed—the second day.

9 Then God said, "Let the water under the sky be gathered into a single basin, so that the dry land may appear." And so it happened: the water under the sky was gathered into its basin, and the dry land appeared. 10 God called the dry land "the earth, " and the basin of the water he called "the sea." God saw how good it was. 11 Then God said, "Let the earth bring forth vegetation: every kind of plant that bears seed and every kind of fruit tree on earth that bears fruit with its seed in it." And so it happened: 12 the earth brought forth every kind of plant that bears seed and every kind of fruit tree on earth that bears fruit with its seed in it. God saw how good it was. 13 Evening came, and morning followed—the third day.

14 Then God said: "Let there be lights in the dome of the sky, to separate day from night. Let them mark the fixed times, the days and the years, 15 and serve as luminaries in the dome of the sky, to shed light upon the earth." And so it happened: 16 God made the two great lights, the greater one to govern the day, and the lesser one to govern the night; and he made the stars. 17 God set them in the dome of the sky, to shed light upon the earth, 18 to govern the day and the night, and to separate the light from the darkness. God saw how good it was. 19 Evening came, and morning followed—the fourth day.

20 Then God said, "Let the water teem with an abundance of living creatures, and on the earth let birds fly beneath the dome of the sky." And so it happened: 21 God created the great sea monsters and all kinds of swimming creatures with which the water teems, and all kinds of winged birds. God saw how good it was, 22 and God blessed them, saying, "Be fertile, multiply, and fill the water of the seas; and let the birds multiply on the earth." 23 Evening came, and morning followed—the fifth day.

24 Then God said, "Let the earth bring forth all kinds of living creatures: cattle, creeping things, and wild animals of all kinds." And so it happened: 25 God made all kinds of wild animals, all kinds of cattle, and all kinds of creeping things of the earth. God saw how good it was. 26 Then God said: "Let us make man in our image, after our likeness. Let them have dominion over the fish of the sea, the birds of the air, and the cattle, and over all the wild animals and all the creatures that crawl on the ground."
27 God created man in his image;
> in the image of God he created him;
> male and female he created them.

28 God blessed them, saying: "Be fertile and multiply; fill the earth and subdue it. Have dominion over the fish of the sea, the birds of the air, and all the living things that move on the earth." 29 God also said: "See, I give you every seed-bearing plant all over the earth and every tree that has seed-bearing fruit on it to be your food; 30 and to all the animals of the land, all the birds of the air, and all the living creatures that crawl on the ground, I give all the green plants for food." And so it happened. 31 God looked at everything he had made, and he found it very good. Evening came, and morning followed—the sixth day.
1 Thus the heavens and the earth and all their array were completed. 2 Since on the seventh day God was finished with the work he had been doing, he rested on the seventh day from all the work he had undertaken.

Or Genesis 1:1, 26-31A
1 In the beginning, when God created the heavens and the earth, 26 God said: "Let us make man in our image, after our likeness. Let them have dominion over the fish of the sea, the birds of the air, and the cattle, and over all the wild animals and all the creatures that crawl on the ground."
27 God created man in his image;
> in the image of God he created him;
> male and female he created them.

28 God blessed them, saying: "Be fertile and multiply; fill the earth and subdue it. Have dominion over the fish of the sea, the birds of the air, and all the living things that move on the earth." 29 God also said: "See, I give you every seed-bearing plant all over the earth and every tree that has seed-bearing fruit on it to be your food; 30 and to all the animals of the land, all the birds of the air, and all the living creatures that crawl on the ground, I give all the green plants for food." And so it happened. 31 God looked at everything he had made, and he found it very good.

Responsorial Psalm: Psalms 104:1-2, 5-6, 10,12,13-14, 24, 35
R. (30) **Lord, send out your Spirit, and renew the
> face of the earth.**
1 Bless the LORD, O my soul!
> O LORD, my God, you are great indeed!
2 You are clothed with majesty and glory,

robed in light as with a cloak.
R. Lord, send out your Spirit, and renew the face of the earth.
⁵ You fixed the earth upon its foundation,
 not to be moved forever;
⁶ with the ocean, as with a garment, you covered it;
 above the mountains the waters stood.
R. Lord, send out your Spirit, and renew the face of the earth.
¹⁰ You send forth springs into the watercourses
 that wind among the mountains.
¹² Beside them the birds of heaven dwell;
 from among the branches they send forth their song.
R. Lord, send out your Spirit, and renew the face of the earth.
¹³ You water the mountains from your palace;
 the earth is replete with the fruit of your works.
¹⁴ You raise grass for the cattle,
 and vegetation for man's use,
producing bread from the earth.
R. Lord, send out your Spirit, and renew the face of the earth.
²⁴ How manifold are your works, O LORD!
 In wisdom you have wrought them all—
the earth is full of your creatures.
 ³⁵ Bless the LORD, O my soul!
R. Lord, send out your Spirit, and renew the face of the earth.

Or Psalms 33:4-5, 6-7, 12-13, 20 and 22
R. ⁽⁵ᵇ⁾ The earth is full of the goodness of the Lord.
⁴ Upright is the word of the LORD,
 and all his works are trustworthy.
⁵ He loves justice and right;
 of the kindness of the LORD the earth is full.
R. The earth is full of the goodness of the

> ***Lord.***

⁶ By the word of the LORD the heavens were made;
　by the breath of his mouth all their host.
⁷ He gathers the waters of the sea as in a flask;
　in cellars he confines the deep.

R. *The earth is full of the goodness of the Lord.*

¹² Blessed the nation whose God is the LORD,
　the people he has chosen for his own inheritance.
¹³ From heaven the LORD looks down;
　he sees all mankind.

R. *The earth is full of the goodness of the Lord.*

²⁰ Our soul waits for the LORD,
　who is our help and our shield.
²² May your kindness, O LORD, be upon us
　who have put our hope in you.

R. *The earth is full of the goodness of the Lord.*

Second Reading: Genesis 22:1-18

¹ God put Abraham to the test. He called to him, "Abraham!" "Here I am, " he replied. ² Then God said: "Take your son Isaac, your only one, whom you love, and go to the land of Moriah. There you shall offer him up as a holocaust on a height that I will point out to you." ³ Early the next morning Abraham saddled his donkey, took with him his son Isaac and two of his servants as well, and with the wood that he had cut for the holocaust, set out for the place of which God had told him.

⁴ On the third day Abraham got sight of the place from afar. ⁵ Then he said to his servants: "Both of you stay here with the donkey, while the boy and I go on over yonder. We will worship and then come back to you." ⁶ Thereupon Abraham took the wood for the holocaust and laid it on his son Isaac's shoulders, while he himself carried the fire and the knife. As the two walked on together, ⁷Isaac spoke to his father Abraham: "Father!" Isaac said. "Yes, son," he replied. Isaac continued, "Here are the fire and the wood, but where is the sheep for the holocaust?" ⁸ "Son," Abraham answered, "God himself will provide the sheep for the holocaust." Then the two continued going forward.

⁹ When they came to the place of which God had told him, Abraham built an altar there and arranged the wood on it. Next he tied up his son Isaac, and put him on top of the wood on the altar. ¹⁰ Then he reached out and took the knife to slaughter his son. ¹¹ But the LORD's messenger called to him from heaven, "Abraham, Abraham!" "Here I am!" he answered. ¹² "Do not lay your hand on the boy," said the messenger. "Do not do the least thing to him. I know now how devoted you are to God, since you did not withhold from me your own beloved son." ¹³ As Abraham looked about, he spied a ram caught by its horns in the thicket. So he went and took the ram and offered it up as a holocaust in place of his son. ¹⁴ Abraham named the site Yahweh-yireh; hence people now say, "On the mountain the LORD will see."

¹⁵ Again the LORD's messenger called to Abraham from heaven ¹⁶ and said: "I swear by myself, declares the LORD, that because you acted as you did in not withholding from me your beloved son, ¹⁷ I will bless you abundantly and make your descendants as countless as the stars of the sky and the sands of the seashore; ¹⁸ your descendants shall take possession of the gates of their enemies, and in your descendants all the nations of the earth shall find blessings— all this because you obeyed my command."

Or Genesis 22:1-2, 9A, 10-13, 15-18

¹ God put Abraham to the test. He called to him, "Abraham!" "Here I am, " he replied. ² Then God said: "Take your son Isaac, your only one, whom you love, and go to the land of Moriah. There you shall offer him up as a holocaust on a height that I will point out to you."

⁹ᴬ When they came to the place of which God had told him, Abraham built an altar there and arranged the wood on it. ¹⁰ Then he reached out and took the knife to slaughter his son. ¹¹ But the LORD's messenger called to him from heaven, "Abraham, Abraham!" "Here I am," he answered. ¹² "Do not lay your hand on the boy, " said the messenger. "Do not do the least thing to him. I know now how devoted you are to God, since you did not withhold from me your own beloved son." ¹³ As Abraham looked about, he spied a ram caught by its horns in the thicket. So he went and took the ram and offered it up as a holocaust in place of his son.

¹⁵ Again the LORD's messenger called to Abraham from heaven ¹⁶ and said: "I swear by myself, declares the LORD, that because you acted as you did in not withholding from me your beloved son, ¹⁷ I will bless you abundantly and make your descendants as countless as the stars of the sky and the sands of the seashore; ¹⁸ your descendants shall take possession of the gates of their enemies, and in your descendants all the nations of the earth shall find blessing— all this because you obeyed my command."

Responsorial Psalm: Psalms 16:5, 8, 9-10, 11
R. ⁽¹⁾ *You are my inheritance, O Lord.*
⁵ O LORD, my allotted portion and my cup,
    you it is who hold fast my lot.
⁸ I set the LORD ever before me;
        with him at my right hand I shall not be
            disturbed.
R. *You are my inheritance, O Lord.*

⁹ Therefore my heart is glad and my soul
> rejoices,
> my body, too, abides in confidence;
¹⁰ because you will not abandon my soul to the
> netherworld,
> nor will you suffer your faithful one to
> undergo corruption.
R. You are my inheritance, O Lord.
¹¹ You will show me the path to life,
> fullness of joys in your presence,
> the delights at your right hand forever.
R. You are my inheritance, O Lord.

Third Reading: Exodus 14:15-15:1

¹⁵ The LORD said to Moses, "Why are you crying out to me? Tell the Israelites to go forward. ¹⁶ And you, lift up your staff and, with hand outstretched over the sea, split the sea in two, that the Israelites may pass through it on dry land. ¹⁷ But I will make the Egyptians so obstinate that they will go in after them. Then I will receive glory through Pharaoh and all his army, his chariots and charioteers. ¹⁸ The Egyptians shall know that I am the LORD, when I receive glory through Pharaoh and his chariots and charioteers."

¹⁹ The angel of God, who had been leading Israel's camp, now moved and went around behind them. The column of cloud also, leaving the front, took up its place behind them, ²⁰ so that it came between the camp of the Egyptians and that of Israel. But the cloud now became dark, and thus the night passed without the rival camps coming any closer together all night long. ²¹ Then Moses stretched out his hand over the sea, and the LORD swept the sea with a strong east wind throughout the night and so turned it into dry land. ²² When the water was thus divided, the Israelites marched into the midst of the sea on dry land, with the water like a wall to their right and to their left.

²³ The Egyptians followed in pursuit; all Pharaoh's horses and chariots and charioteers went after them right into the midst of the sea. ²⁴ In the night watch just before dawn the LORD cast through the column of the fiery cloud upon the Egyptian force a glance that threw it into a panic; ²⁵ and he so clogged their chariot wheels that they could hardly drive. With that the Egyptians sounded the retreat before Israel, because the LORD was fighting for them against the Egyptians.

²⁶ Then the LORD told Moses, stretch out your hand over the sea, that the water may flow back upon the Egyptians, upon their chariots and their charioteers." ²⁷ So Moses stretched out his hand over the sea, and at dawn the sea flowed back to its normal depth. The Egyptians were fleeing head on toward the sea, when the LORD hurled them into its midst. ²⁸ As the water flowed back, it covered the chariots and the charioteers of Pharaoh's whole army which had followed the Israelites into the sea. Not a single one of them escaped. ²⁹ But the Israelites had marched on dry land through the midst of the sea, with the water like a wall to their right and to their left. ³⁰ Thus the LORD saved Israel on that day from the power of the Egyptians. When Israel saw the Egyptians lying dead on the seashore ³¹ and beheld the great power that the LORD had shown against the Egyptians, they feared the LORD and believed in him and in his servant Moses.

[1] Then Moses and the Israelites sang this song to the LORD:

I will sing to the LORD, for he is gloriously
> triumphant;
>> horse and chariot he has cast into the sea.

Responsorial Psalm: Exodus 15:1-2, 3-4, 5-6, 17-18

R. (1b) Let us sing to the Lord; he has covered himself in glory.

[1] I will sing to the LORD, for he is gloriously
> triumphant;
>> horse and chariot he has cast into the sea.

[2] My strength and my courage is the LORD,
> and he has been my savior.

He is my God, I praise him;
> the God of my father, I extol him.

R. Let us sing to the Lord; he has covered himself in glory.

[3] The LORD is a warrior,
> LORD is his name!

[4] Pharaoh's chariots and army he hurled into
> the sea;

the elite of his officers were submerged in
> the Red Sea.

R. Let us sing to the Lord; he has covered himself in glory.

[5] The flood waters covered them,
> they sank into the depths like a stone.

[6] Your right hand, O LORD, magnificent in
> power,
>> your right hand, O LORD, has shattered the
>> enemy.

R. Let us sing to the Lord; he has covered himself in glory.

[17] You brought in the people you redeemed
> and planted them on the mountain of
>> your inheritance—

the place where you made your seat, O LORD,
> the sanctuary, LORD, which your hands
>> established.

[18] The LORD shall reign forever and ever.

R. Let us sing to the Lord; he has covered himself in glory.

Fourth Reading: Isaiah 54:5-14

⁵ The One who has become your husband is
> your Maker;
>> his name is the LORD of hosts;
> your redeemer is the Holy One of Israel,
>> called God of all the earth.

⁶ The LORD calls you back,
> like a wife forsaken and grieved in spirit,
> a wife married in youth and then cast off,
> says your God.

⁷ For a brief moment I abandoned you,
> but with great tenderness I will take you back.

⁸ In an outburst of wrath, for a moment
> I hid my face from you;
> but with enduring love I take pity on you,
> says the LORD, your redeemer.

⁹ This is for me like the days of Noah,
> when I swore that the waters of Noah
> should never again deluge the earth;
> so I have sworn not to be angry with you,
> or to rebuke you.

¹⁰ Though the mountains leave their place
> and the hills be shaken,
> my love shall never leave you
> nor my covenant of peace be shaken,
> says the LORD, who has mercy on you.

¹¹ O afflicted one, storm-battered and unconsoled,
> I lay your pavements in carnelians,
> and your foundations in sapphires;

¹² I will make your battlements of rubies,
> your gates of carbuncles,
> and all your walls of precious stones.

¹³ All your children shall be taught by the LORD,
> and great shall be the peace of your children.

¹⁴ In justice shall you be established,
> far from the fear of oppression,
> where destruction cannot come near you.

Responsorial Psalm: Psalms 30:2, 4, 5-6, 11-12, 13

R. (2a) *I will praise you, Lord, for you have rescued me.*

² I will extol you, O LORD, for you drew me
        clear
    and did not let my enemies rejoice over
        me.
⁴ O LORD, you brought me up from the
        netherworld;
    you preserved me from among those
        going down into the pit.
**R. I will praise you, Lord, for you have rescued
        me.**
⁵ Sing praise to the LORD, you his faithful ones,
    and give thanks to his holy name.
⁶ For his anger lasts but a moment;
    a lifetime, his good will.
At nightfall, weeping enters in,
    but with the dawn, rejoicing.
**R. I will praise you, Lord, for you have rescued
        me.**
¹¹ Hear, O LORD, and have pity on me;
    O LORD, be my helper.
¹² You changed my mourning into dancing;
        ¹³ O LORD, my God, forever will I give you
            thanks.
**R. I will praise you, Lord, for you have rescued
        me.**

Fifth Reading: Isaiah 55:1-11
¹ Thus says the LORD:

All you who are thirsty,
    come to the water!
You who have no money,
    come, receive grain and eat;
come, without paying and without cost,
    drink wine and milk!
² Why spend your money for what is not
        bread,
    your wages for what fails to satisfy?
Heed me, and you shall eat well,
    you shall delight in rich fare.
³ Come to me heedfully,
    listen, that you may have life.
I will renew with you the everlasting
        covenant,
    the benefits assured to David.

⁴ As I made him a witness to the peoples,
>   a leader and commander of nations,
⁵ so shall you summon a nation you knew not,
>   and nations that knew you not shall run
>   to you,
because of the LORD, your God,
>   the Holy One of Israel, who has glorified
>   you.

⁶ Seek the LORD while he may be found,
>   call him while he is near.
⁷ Let the scoundrel forsake his way,
>   and the wicked man his thoughts;
let him turn to the LORD for mercy;
>   to our God, who is generous in forgiving.
⁸ For my thoughts are not your thoughts,
>   nor are your ways my ways, says the
>   LORD.
⁹ As high as the heavens are above the earth,
>   so high are my ways above your ways
>   and my thoughts above your thoughts.

¹⁰ For just as from the heavens
>   the rain and snow come down
and do not return there
>   till they have watered the earth,
>   making it fertile and fruitful,
giving seed to the one who sows
>   and bread to the one who eats,
¹¹ so shall my word be
>   that goes forth from my mouth;
my word shall not return to me void,
>   but shall do my will,
>   achieving the end for which I sent it.

Responsorial Psalm: Isaiah 12:2-3, 4, 5-6
*R. ⁽³⁾ **You will draw water joyfully from the springs of salvation.***
² God indeed is my savior;
>   I am confident and unafraid.
My strength and my courage is the LORD,
>   and he has been my savior.
³ With joy you will draw water
>   at the fountain of salvation.
R. You will draw water joyfully from the springs

> *of salvation.*

⁴ Give thanks to the LORD, acclaim his name;
> among the nations make known his deeds,
> proclaim how exalted is his name.

R. *You will draw water joyfully from the springs of salvation.*

⁵ Sing praise to the LORD for his glorious achievement;
> let this be known throughout all the earth.

⁶ Shout with exultation, O city of Zion,
> for great in your midst
> is the Holy One of Israel!

R. *You will draw water joyfully from the springs of salvation.*

Sixth Reading: Baruch 3:9-15, 32C4:4

⁹ Hear, O Israel, the commandments of life:
> listen, and know prudence!

¹⁰ How is it, Israel,
> that you are in the land of your foes,
> grown old in a foreign land,

¹¹ defiled with the dead,
> accounted with those destined for the netherworld?

¹² You have forsaken the fountain of wisdom!

¹³ Had you walked in the way of God,
> you would have dwelt in enduring peace.

¹⁴ Learn where prudence is,
> where strength, where understanding;
that you may know also
> where are length of days, and life,
> where light of the eyes, and peace.

¹⁵ Who has found the place of wisdom,
> who has entered into her treasuries?

³² The One who knows all things knows her;
> he has probed her by his knowledge—
the One who established the earth for all time,
> and filled it with four-footed beasts;

³³ he who dismisses the light, and it departs,
> calls it, and it obeys him trembling;

³⁴ before whom the stars at their posts

shine and rejoice;
³⁵ when he calls them, they answer, "Here we
    are!"
  shining with joy for their Maker.
³⁶ Such is our God;
  no other is to be compared to him:
³⁷ he has traced out the whole way of
    understanding,
  and has given her to Jacob, his servant,
  to Israel, his beloved son.

³⁸ Since then she has appeared on earth,
  and moved among people.
¹ She is the book of the precepts of God,
  the law that endures forever;
all who cling to her will live,
  but those will die who forsake her.
² Turn, O Jacob, and receive her:
  walk by her light toward splendor.
³ Give not your glory to another,
  your privileges to an alien race.
⁴ Blessed are we, O Israel;
  for what pleases God is known to us!

Responsorial Psalm: Psalms 19:8, 9, 10, 11
R. *(John 6:68c)* **Lord, you have the words of everlasting life.**
⁸ The law of the LORD is perfect,
  refreshing the soul;
the decree of the LORD is trustworthy,
  giving wisdom to the simple.
R. Lord, you have the words of everlasting life.
⁹ The precepts of the LORD are right,
  rejoicing the heart;
the command of the LORD is clear,
  enlightening the eye.
R. Lord, you have the words of everlasting life.
¹⁰ The fear of the LORD is pure,
  enduring forever;
the ordinances of the LORD are true,
  all of them just.
R. Lord, you have the words of everlasting life.
¹¹ They are more precious than gold,
  than a heap of purest gold;
sweeter also than syrup
  or honey from the comb.

R. Lord, you have the words of everlasting life.

Seventh Reading: Ezekiel 36:16-17A, 18-28

16 The word of the LORD came to me, saying: 17Son of man, when the house of Israel lived in their land, they defiled it by their conduct and deeds. 18 Therefore I poured out my fury upon them because of the blood that they poured out on the ground, and because they defiled it with idols. 19 I scattered them among the nations, dispersing them over foreign lands; according to their conduct and deeds I judged them. 20 But when they came among the nations wherever they came, they served to profane my holy name, because it was said of them: "These are the people of the LORD, yet they had to leave their land." 21 So I have relented because of my holy name which the house of Israel profaned among the nations where they came. 22 Therefore say to the house of Israel: Thus says the Lord GOD: Not for your sakes do I act, house of Israel, but for the sake of my holy name, which you profaned among the nations to which you came. 23 I will prove the holiness of my great name, profaned among the nations, in whose midst you have profaned it. Thus the nations shall know that I am the LORD, says the Lord GOD, when in their sight I prove my holiness through you. 24 For I will take you away from among the nations, gather you from all the foreign lands, and bring you back to your own land. 25 I will sprinkle clean water upon you to cleanse you from all your impurities, and from all your idols I will cleanse you. 26 I will give you a new heart and place a new spirit within you, taking from your bodies your stony hearts and giving you natural hearts. 27 I will put my spirit within you and make you live by my statutes, careful to observe my decrees. 28 You shall live in the land I gave your fathers; you shall be my people, and I will be your God.

Responsorial Psalm: Psalms 42:3, 5; 43:3, 4

When baptism is celebrated on Easter Vigil
R. (42:2) ***Like a deer that longs for running streams, my soul longs for you, my God.***

3 Athirst is my soul for God, the living God.
When shall I go and behold the face of God?
R. *Like a deer that longs for running streams, my soul longs for you, my God.*

5 I went with the throng
and led them in procession to the house of God,
Amid loud cries of joy and thanksgiving, with the multitude keeping festival.
R. *Like a deer that longs for running streams, my soul longs for you, my God.*

³ Send forth your light and your fidelity;
    they shall lead me on
And bring me to your holy mountain,
    to your dwelling-place.
R. Like a deer that longs for running streams, my soul longs for you, my God.
⁴ Then will I go in to the altar of God,
    the God of my gladness and joy;
then will I give you thanks upon the harp,
    O God, my God!
R. Like a deer that longs for running streams, my soul longs for you, my God.

Or Psalms 51:12-13, 14-15, 18-19
When baptism is not celebrated During Easter Vigil
R. (12a) Create a clean heart in me, O God.
¹² A clean heart create for me, O God,
    and a steadfast spirit renew within me.
¹³ Cast me not out from your presence,
    and your Holy Spirit take not from me.
R. Create a clean heart in me, O God.

¹⁴ Give me back the joy of your salvation,
    and a willing spirit sustain in me.
¹⁵ I will teach transgressors your ways,
    and sinners shall return to you.
R. Create a clean heart in me, O God.

¹⁸ For you are not pleased with sacrifices;
    should I offer a holocaust, you would not accept it.
¹⁹ My sacrifice, O God, is a contrite spirit;
    a heart contrite and humbled, O God,
        you will not spurn.
R. Create a clean heart in me, O God.

Epistle: Romans 6:3-11

Brothers and sisters: ³ Are you unaware that we who were baptized into Christ Jesus were baptized into his death? ⁴ We were indeed buried with him through baptism into death, so that, just as Christ was raised from the dead by the glory of the Father, we too might live in newness of life.

⁵ For if we have grown into union with him through a death like his, we shall also be united with him in the resurrection. ⁶ We know that our old self was crucified with him, so that our sinful body might be done away with, that we might no longer be in slavery to sin. ⁷ For a dead person has been absolved from sin. ⁸ If, then, we have died with Christ, we believe that we shall also live with him. ⁹ We know that Christ, raised from the dead, dies no more; death no longer has power over him. ¹⁰ As to his death, he died to sin once and for all; as to his life, he lives for God. ¹¹ Consequently, you too must think of yourselves as being dead to sin and living for God in Christ Jesus.

Responsorial Psalm: Psalms 118:1-2, 16-17, 22-23

R. Alleluia, alleluia, alleluia.
¹ Give thanks to the LORD, for he is good,
    for his mercy endures forever.
² Let the house of Israel say,
    "His mercy endures forever."
R. Alleluia, alleluia, alleluia.
¹⁶ The right hand of the LORD has struck with
    power;
    the right hand of the LORD is exalted.
¹⁷ I shall not die, but live,
    and declare the works of the LORD.
R. Alleluia, alleluia, alleluia.
²² The stone the builders rejected
    has become the cornerstone.
²³ By the LORD has this been done;
    it is wonderful in our eyes.
R. Alleluia, alleluia, alleluia.

Gospel: Luke 24:1-12

¹At daybreak on the first day of the week the women who had come from Galilee with Jesus took the spices they had prepared and went to the tomb. ²They found the stone rolled away from the tomb; ³but when they entered, they did not find the body of the Lord Jesus. ⁴While they were puzzling over this, behold, two men in dazzling garments appeared to them. ⁵They were terrified and bowed their faces to the ground. They said to them, "Why do you seek the living one among the dead? ⁶He is not here, but he has been raised. Remember what he said to you while he was still in Galilee, ⁷that the Son of Man must be handed over to sinners and be crucified, and rise on the third day." ⁸And they remembered his words. ⁹Then they returned from the tomb and announced all these things to the eleven and to all the

others. ¹⁰The women were Mary Magdalene, Joanna, and Mary the mother of James; the others who accompanied them also told this to the apostles, ¹¹but their story seemed like nonsense and they did not believe them. ¹²But Peter got up and ran to the tomb, bent down, and saw the burial cloths alone; then he went home amazed at what had happened.

Sunday April 20, 2025
Easter Sunday

First Reading: Acts 10:34A, 37-43

³⁴ᴬ Peter proceeded to speak and said: ³⁷ "You know what has happened all over Judea, beginning in Galilee after the baptism that John preached, ³⁸ how God anointed Jesus of Nazareth with the Holy Spirit and power. He went about doing good and healing all those oppressed by the devil, for God was with him. ³⁹ We are witnesses of all that he did both in the country of the Jews and in Jerusalem. They put him to death by hanging him on a tree. ⁴⁰ This man God raised on the third day and granted that he be visible, ⁴¹ not to all the people, but to us, the witnesses chosen by God in advance, who ate and drank with him after he rose from the dead. ⁴² He commissioned us to preach to the people and testify that he is the one appointed by God as judge of the living and the dead. ⁴³ To him all the prophets bear witness, that everyone who believes in him will receive forgiveness of sins through his name."

Responsorial Psalm: Psalms 118:1-2, 16-17, 22-23.

R. ⁽²⁴⁾ This is the day the Lord has made; let us rejoice and be glad. or: *R. Alleluia.*

¹ Give thanks to the LORD, for he is good,
    for his mercy endures forever.
² Let the house of Israel say,
    "His mercy endures forever."

R. This is the day the Lord has made; let us rejoice and be glad. or: *R. Alleluia.*

¹⁶ The right hand of the LORD has struck with
       power;
    the right hand of the LORD is exalted.
¹⁷ I shall not die, but live,
    and declare the works of the LORD.

R. This is the day the Lord has made; let us rejoice and be glad. or: *R. Alleluia.*

²² The stone which the builders rejected
    has become the cornerstone.
²³ By the LORD has this been done;
    it is wonderful in our eyes.

R. This is the day the Lord has made; let us rejoice and be glad. or: *R. Alleluia.*

Second Reading: Colossians 3:1-4

Brothers and sisters: ¹ If then you were raised with Christ, seek what is above, where Christ is seated at the right hand of God. ² Think of what is above, not of what is on earth. ³ For you have died, and your life is hidden with Christ in God. ⁴ When Christ your life appears, then you too will appear with him in glory.

Or 1 Corinthians 5:6B-8

Brothers and sisters: ⁶ᴮ Do you not know that a little yeast leavens all the dough? ⁷ Clear out the old yeast, so that you may become a fresh batch of dough, inasmuch as you are unleavened. For our paschal lamb, Christ, has been sacrificed. ⁸ Therefore, let us celebrate the feast, not with the old yeast, the yeast of malice and wickedness, but with the unleavened bread of sincerity and truth.

Sequence - *Victimae Paschali Laudes*

Christians, to the Paschal Victim
Offer your thankful praises!
A Lamb the sheep redeems;
Christ, who only is sinless,
Reconciles sinners to the Father.
Death and life have contended in that combat stupendous:
The Prince of life, who died, reigns immortal.
Speak, Mary, declaring
What you saw, wayfaring.
"The tomb of Christ, who is living,
The glory of Jesus' resurrection;
Bright angels attesting,
The shroud and napkin resting.
Yes, Christ my hope is arisen;
To Galilee he goes before you."
Christ indeed from death is risen, our new life obtaining.
Have mercy, victor King, ever reigning!
Amen. Alleluia.

Alleluia: cf. 1 Corinthians 5:7B-8A

R. Alleluia, alleluia.
⁷ᴮ Christ, our paschal lamb, has been
    sacrificed;
⁸ᴬ let us then feast with joy in the Lord.
R. Alleluia, alleluia.

Gospel: John 20:1-9

¹ On the first day of the week, Mary of Magdala came to the tomb early in the morning, while it was still dark, and saw the stone removed from the tomb. ² So she ran and went to Simon Peter and to the other disciple whom Jesus loved, and told

them, "They have taken the Lord from the tomb, and we don't know where they put him." ³ So Peter and the other disciple went out and came to the tomb. ⁴ They both ran, but the other disciple ran faster than Peter and arrived at the tomb first; ⁵ he bent down and saw the burial cloths there, but did not go in. ⁶ When Simon Peter arrived after him, he went into the tomb and saw the burial cloths there, ⁷ and the cloth that had covered his head, not with the burial cloths but rolled up in a separate place. ⁸ Then the other disciple also went in, the one who had arrived at the tomb first, and he saw and believed. ⁹ For they did not yet understand the Scripture that he had to rise from the dead.

Or Luke 24:1-12

¹At daybreak on the first day of the week the women who had come from Galilee with Jesus took the spices they had prepared and went to the tomb. ²They found the stone rolled away from the tomb; ³but when they entered, they did not find the body of the Lord Jesus. ⁴While they were puzzling over this, behold, two men in dazzling garments appeared to them. ⁵They were terrified and bowed their faces to the ground. They said to them, "Why do you seek the living one among the dead? ⁶He is not here, but he has been raised. Remember what he said to you while he was still in Galilee, ⁷that the Son of Man must be handed over to sinners and be crucified, and rise on the third day." ⁸And they remembered his words. ⁹Then they returned from the tomb and announced all these things to the eleven and to all the others. ¹⁰The women were Mary Magdalene, Joanna, and Mary the mother of James; the others who accompanied them also told this to the apostles, ¹¹but their story seemed like nonsense and they did not believe them. ¹²But Peter got up and ran to the tomb, bent down, and saw the burial cloths alone; then he went home amazed at what had happened.

Or Luke: 24:13-35
At an afternoon or evening Mass.

¹³ That very day, the first day of the week, two of Jesus' disciples were going to a village seven miles from Jerusalem called Emmaus, ¹⁴ and they were conversing about all the things that had occurred. ¹⁵ And it happened that while they were conversing and debating, Jesus himself drew near and walked with them, ¹⁶ but their eyes were prevented from recognizing him. ¹⁷ He asked them, "What are you discussing as you walk along?" They stopped, looking downcast. ¹⁸ One of them, named Cleopas, said to him in reply, "Are you the only visitor to Jerusalem who does not know of the things that have taken place there in these days?" ¹⁹ And he replied to them, "What sort of things?" They said to him, "The things that happened to Jesus the Nazarene, who was a prophet mighty in deed and word before God and all the people, ²⁰ how our chief priests and rulers both handed him over to a sentence of death and crucified him. ²¹ But we were hoping that he would be the one to redeem Israel; and besides all this, it is now the third day since this took place. ²² Some women from our group, however, have astounded us: they were at the tomb early in the morning ²³ and did not find his body; they came back and

reported that they had indeed seen a vision of angels who announced that he was alive. ²⁴ Then some of those with us went to the tomb and found things just as the women had described, but him they did not see." ²⁵ And he said to them, "Oh, how foolish you are! How slow of heart to believe all that the prophets spoke! ²⁶ Was it not necessary that the Christ should suffer these things and enter into his glory?" ²⁷ Then beginning with Moses and all the prophets, he interpreted to them what referred to him in all the Scriptures. ²⁸ As they approached the village to which they were going, he gave the impression that he was going on farther. ²⁹ But they urged him, "Stay with us, for it is nearly evening and the day is almost over." So he went in to stay with them. ³⁰ And it happened that, while he was with them at table, he took bread, said the blessing, broke it, and gave it to them. ³¹ With that their eyes were opened and they recognized him, but he vanished from their sight.

³² Then they said to each other, "Were not our hearts burning within us while he spoke to us on the way and opened the Scriptures to us?" ³³ So they set out at once and returned to Jerusalem where they found gathered together the eleven and those with them ³⁴ who were saying, "The Lord has truly been raised and has appeared to Simon!" ³⁵ Then the two recounted what had taken place on the way and how he was made known to them in the breaking of bread.

Monday April 21, 2025
Monday in the Octave of Easter
First Reading: Acts 2:14, 22-33

¹⁴ On the day of Pentecost, Peter stood up with the Eleven, raised his voice, and proclaimed: "You who are Jews, indeed all of you staying in Jerusalem. Let this be known to you, and listen to my words.

²² "You who are children of Israel, hear these words. Jesus the Nazorean was a man commended to you by God with mighty deeds, wonders, and signs, which God worked through him in your midst, as you yourselves know. ²³ This man, delivered up by the set plan and foreknowledge of God, you killed, using lawless men to crucify him. ²⁴ But God raised him up, releasing him from the throes of death, because it was impossible for him to be held by it. ²⁵ For David says of him:

I saw the Lord ever before me,
 with him at my right hand I shall not be
  disturbed.
²⁶ *Therefore my heart has been glad and my*
  tongue has exulted;
 my flesh, too, will dwell in hope,
²⁷ *because you will not abandon my soul to the*
  nether world,
 nor will you suffer your holy one to see
  corruption.
²⁸ *You have made known to me the paths of life;*
 you will fill me with joy in your presence.

²⁹ My brothers, one can confidently say to you about the patriarch David that he died and was buried, and his tomb is in our midst to this day. ³⁰ But since he was a prophet and knew that God had sworn an oath to him that he would set one of his descendants upon his throne, ³¹ he foresaw and spoke of the resurrection of the Christ, that neither was he abandoned to the netherworld nor did his flesh see corruption. ³² God raised this Jesus; of this we are all witnesses. ³³ Exalted at the right hand of God, he poured forth the promise of the Holy Spirit that he received from the Father, as you both see and hear."

Responsorial Psalm: Psalms 16:1-2A AND 5, 7-8, 9-10, 11
R. ⁽¹⁾ Keep me safe, O God; you are my hope. or: Alleluia.
¹ Keep me, O God, for in you I take refuge;
    ²ᴬ I say to the LORD, "My Lord are you."
⁵ O LORD, my allotted portion and my cup,
    you it is who hold fast my lot.
R. Keep me safe, O God; you are my hope. or: Alleluia.
⁷ I bless the LORD who counsels me;
    even in the night my heart exhorts me.
⁸ I set the LORD ever before me;
    with him at my right hand I shall not be
        disturbed.
R. Keep me safe, O God; you are my hope. or: Alleluia.
⁹ Therefore my heart is glad and my soul
        rejoices,
    my body, too, abides in confidence;
¹⁰ Because you will not abandon my soul to the
        nether world,
    nor will you suffer your faithful one to
        undergo corruption.
R. Keep me safe, O God; you are my hope. or: Alleluia.
¹¹ You will show me the path to life,
    fullness of joys in your presence,
    the delights at your right hand forever.
R. Keep me safe, O God; you are my hope. or: Alleluia.

Alleluia: Psalms 118:24
R. Alleluia, alleluia.
²⁴ This is the day the LORD has made;
let us be glad and rejoice in it.
R. Alleluia, alleluia.

Gospel: Matthew 28:8-15
⁸ Mary Magdalene and the other Mary went away quickly from the tomb, fearful yet overjoyed, and ran to announce the news to his disciples. ⁹ And behold, Jesus met

them on their way and greeted them. They approached, embraced his feet, and did him homage. ¹⁰ Then Jesus said to them, "Do not be afraid. Go tell my brothers to go to Galilee, and there they will see me."

¹¹ While they were going, some of the guard went into the city and told the chief priests all that had happened. ¹² The chief priests assembled with the elders and took counsel; then they gave a large sum of money to the soldiers, ¹³ telling them, "You are to say, 'His disciples came by night and stole him while we were asleep.' ¹⁴ And if this gets to the ears of the governor, we will satisfy him and keep you out of trouble." ¹⁵ The soldiers took the money and did as they were instructed. And this story has circulated among the Jews to the present day.

Tuesday April 22, 2025
Tuesday in the Octave of Easter
First Reading: Acts 2:36-41

³⁶ On the day of Pentecost, Peter said to the Jewish people, "Let the whole house of Israel know for certain that God has made him both Lord and Christ, this Jesus whom you crucified."

³⁷ Now when they heard this, they were cut to the heart, and they asked Peter and the other Apostles, "What are we to do, my brothers?" ³⁸ Peter said to them, "Repent and be baptized, every one of you, in the name of Jesus Christ, for the forgiveness of your sins; and you will receive the gift of the Holy Spirit. ³⁹ For the promise is made to you and to your children and to all those far off, whomever the Lord our God will call." ⁴⁰ He testified with many other arguments, and was exhorting them, "Save yourselves from this corrupt generation." ⁴¹ Those who accepted his message were baptized, and about three thousand persons were added that day.

Responsorial Psalm: Psalms 33:4-5, 18-19, 20 AND 22
R. ⁽⁵ᵇ⁾ The earth is full of the goodness of the Lord. or: Alleluia.
⁴ Upright is the word of the LORD,
    and all his works are trustworthy.
⁵ He loves justice and right;
    of the kindness of the LORD the earth is
        full.
R. The earth is full of the goodness of the Lord. or: Alleluia.
¹⁸ See, the eyes of the LORD are upon those who
        fear him,
    upon those who hope for his kindness,
¹⁹ To deliver them from death
    and preserve them in spite of famine.
R. The earth is full of the goodness of the Lord. or: Alleluia.
²⁰ Our soul waits for the LORD,
    who is our help and our shield.
²² May your kindness, O LORD, be upon us
    who have put our hope in you.
R. The earth is full of the goodness of the Lord. or: Alleluia.

Alleluia: Psalms 118:24
R. Alleluia, alleluia.
[24] This is the day the LORD has made;
let us be glad and rejoice in it.
R. Alleluia, alleluia.

Gospel: John 20:11-18
[11] Mary Magdalene stayed outside the tomb weeping. And as she wept, she bent over into the tomb [12] and saw two angels in white sitting there, one at the head and one at the feet where the Body of Jesus had been. [13] And they said to her, "Woman, why are you weeping?" She said to them, "They have taken my Lord, and I don't know where they laid him." [14] When she had said this, she turned around and saw Jesus there, but did not know it was Jesus. [15] Jesus said to her, "Woman, why are you weeping? Whom are you looking for?" She thought it was the gardener and said to him, "Sir, if you carried him away, tell me where you laid him, and I will take him." [16] Jesus said to her, "Mary!" She turned and said to him in Hebrew, "Rabbouni," which means Teacher. [17] Jesus said to her, "Stop holding on to me, for I have not yet ascended to the Father. But go to my brothers and tell them, 'I am going to my Father and your Father, to my God and your God.'" [18] Mary went and announced to the disciples, "I have seen the Lord," and then reported what he had told her.

Wednesday April 23, 2025
Wednesday in the Octave of Easter

First Reading: Acts 3:1-10
[1] Peter and John were going up to the temple area for the three o'clock hour of prayer. [2] And a man crippled from birth was carried and placed at the gate of the temple called "the Beautiful Gate" every day to beg for alms from the people who entered the temple. [3] When he saw Peter and John about to go into the temple, he asked for alms. [4] But Peter looked intently at him, as did John, and said, "Look at us." [5] He paid attention to them, expecting to receive something from them. [6] Peter said, "I have neither silver nor gold, but what I do have I give you: in the name of Jesus Christ the Nazorean, rise and walk." [7] Then Peter took him by the right hand and raised him up, and immediately his feet and ankles grew strong. [8] He leaped up, stood, and walked around, and went into the temple with them, walking and jumping and praising God. [9] When all the people saw him walking and praising God, [10] they recognized him as the one who used to sit begging at the Beautiful Gate of the temple, and they were filled with amazement and astonishment at what had happened to him.

Responsorial Psalm: Psalms 105:1-2, 3-4, 6-7, 8-9
R. [3b] *Rejoice, O hearts that seek the Lord. or: Alleluia.*
[1] Give thanks to the LORD, invoke his name;
> make known among the nations his
>> deeds.
[2] Sing to him, sing his praise,
> proclaim all his wondrous deeds.

R. Rejoice, O hearts that seek the Lord. or: **Alleluia.**
³ Glory in his holy name;
>rejoice, O hearts that seek the LORD!
⁴ Look to the LORD in his strength;
>seek to serve him constantly.

R. Rejoice, O hearts that seek the Lord. or: **Alleluia.**
⁶ You descendants of Abraham, his servants,
>sons of Jacob, his chosen ones!
⁷ He, the LORD, is our God;
>throughout the earth his judgments
>>prevail.

R. Rejoice, O hearts that seek the Lord. or: **Alleluia.**
⁸ He remembers forever his covenant
>which he made binding for a thousand
>>generations—
⁹ Which he entered into with Abraham
>and by his oath to Isaac.

R. Rejoice, O hearts that seek the Lord. or: **Alleluia.**

Alleluia: Psalms 118:24
R. Alleluia, alleluia.
²⁴ This is the day the LORD has made;
let us be glad and rejoice in it.
R. Alleluia, alleluia.

Gospel: Luke 24:13-35

¹³ That very day, the first day of the week, two of Jesus' disciples were going to a village seven miles from Jerusalem called Emmaus, ¹⁴ and they were conversing about all the things that had occurred. ¹⁵ And it happened that while they were conversing and debating, Jesus himself drew near and walked with them, ¹⁶ but their eyes were prevented from recognizing him. ¹⁷ He asked them, "What are you discussing as you walk along?" They stopped, looking downcast. ¹⁸ One of them, named Cleopas, said to him in reply, "Are you the only visitor to Jerusalem who does not know of the things that have taken place there in these days?" ¹⁹ And he replied to them, "What sort of things?" They said to him, "The things that happened to Jesus the Nazarene, who was a prophet mighty in deed and word before God and all the people, ²⁰ how our chief priests and rulers both handed him over to a sentence of death and crucified him. ²¹ But we were hoping that he would be the one to redeem Israel; and besides all this, it is now the third day since this took place. ²² Some women from our group, however, have astounded us: they were at the tomb early in the morning ²³ and did not find his Body; they came back and reported that they had indeed seen a vision of angels who announced that he was alive. ²⁴ Then some of those with us went to the tomb and found things just as the women had described, but him they did not see." ²⁵ And he said to them, "Oh, how

foolish you are! How slow of heart to believe all that the prophets spoke! ²⁶ Was it not necessary that the Christ should suffer these things and enter into his glory?" ²⁷ Then beginning with Moses and all the prophets, he interpreted to them what referred to him in all the Scriptures. ²⁸ As they approached the village to which they were going, he gave the impression that he was going on farther. ²⁹ But they urged him, "Stay with us, for it is nearly evening and the day is almost over." So he went in to stay with them. ³⁰ And it happened that, while he was with them at table, he took bread, said the blessing, broke it, and gave it to them. ³¹ With that their eyes were opened and they recognized him, but he vanished from their sight. ³² Then they said to each other, "Were not our hearts burning within us while he spoke to us on the way and opened the Scriptures to us?" ³³ So they set out at once and returned to Jerusalem where they found gathered together the Eleven and those with them ³⁴ who were saying, "The Lord has truly been raised and has appeared to Simon!" ³⁵ Then the two recounted what had taken place on the way and how he was made known to them in the breaking of the bread.

Thursday April 24, 2025
Thursday in the Octave of Easter
First Reading: Acts 3:11-26

¹¹As the crippled man who had been cured clung to Peter and John, all the people hurried in amazement toward them in the portico called "Solomon's Portico." ¹² When Peter saw this, he addressed the people, "You children of Israel, why are you amazed at this, and why do you look so intently at us as if we had made him walk by our own power or piety? ¹³ The God of Abraham, the God of Isaac, and the God of Jacob, the God of our fathers, has glorified his servant Jesus whom you handed over and denied in Pilate's presence, when he had decided to release him. ¹⁴ You denied the Holy and Righteous One and asked that a murderer be released to you. ¹⁵ The author of life you put to death, but God raised him from the dead; of this we are witnesses. ¹⁶ And by faith in his name, this man, whom you see and know, his name has made strong, and the faith that comes through it has given him this perfect health, in the presence of all of you. ¹⁷ Now I know, brothers and sisters, that you acted out of ignorance, just as your leaders did; ¹⁸ but God has thus brought to fulfillment what he had announced beforehand through the mouth of all the prophets, that his Christ would suffer. ¹⁹ Repent, therefore, and be converted, that your sins may be wiped away, ²⁰ and that the Lord may grant you times of refreshment and send you the Christ already appointed for you, Jesus, ²¹ whom heaven must receive until the times of universal restoration of which God spoke through the mouth of his holy prophets from of old. ²² For Moses said:

A prophet like me will the Lord, your God,
*   raise up for you*
* from among your own kin;*
* to him you shall listen in all that he may*
*   say to you.*
²³ *Everyone who does not listen to that prophet*

will be cut off from the people.

²⁴ "Moreover, all the prophets who spoke, from Samuel and those afterwards, also announced these days. ²⁵ You are the children of the prophets and of the covenant that God made with your ancestors when he said to Abraham,

*In your offspring all the families of the earth
    shall be blessed.*

²⁶ For you first, God raised up his servant and sent him to bless you by turning each of you from your evil ways."

Responsorial Psalm: Psalms 8:2AB and 5, 6-7, 8-9
**R. *(2ab)* O Lord, our God, how wonderful your
    name in all the earth!** or: ***Alleluia.***

²ᴬᴮ O LORD, our Lord,
    how glorious is your name over all the
        earth!
⁵ What is man that you should be mindful of
    him,
    or the son of man that you should care
        for him?
***R. O Lord, our God, how wonderful your name in
    all the earth!* or: *Alleluia.***
⁶ You have made him little less than the
    angels,
    and crowned him with glory and honor.
⁷ You have given him rule over the works of
    your hands,
    putting all things under his feet.
***R. O Lord, our God, how wonderful your name in
    all the earth!* or: *Alleluia.***
⁸ All sheep and oxen,
    yes, and the beasts of the field,
⁹ The birds of the air, the fishes of the sea,
    and whatever swims the paths of the
        seas.
***R. O Lord, our God, how wonderful your name in
    all the earth!* or: *Alleluia.***

Alleluia: Psalms 118:24
R. Alleluia, alleluia.
²⁴ This is the day the LORD has made;
let us be glad and rejoice in it.

R. Alleluia, alleluia.

Gospel: Luke 24:35-48

[35] The disciples of Jesus recounted what had taken place along the way, and how they had come to recognize him in the breaking of bread.

[36] While they were still speaking about this, he stood in their midst and said to them, "Peace be with you." [37] But they were startled and terrified and thought that they were seeing a ghost. [38] Then he said to them, "Why are you troubled? And why do questions arise in your hearts? [39] Look at my hands and my feet, that it is I myself. Touch me and see, because a ghost does not have flesh and bones as you can see I have." [40] And as he said this, he showed them his hands and his feet. [41] While they were still incredulous for joy and were amazed, he asked them, "Have you anything here to eat?" [42] They gave him a piece of baked fish; [43] he took it and ate it in front of them.

[44] He said to them, "These are my words that I spoke to you while I was still with you, that everything written about me in the law of Moses and in the prophets and psalms must be fulfilled." [45] Then he opened their minds to understand the Scriptures. [46] And he said to them, "Thus it is written that the Christ would suffer and rise from the dead on the third day [47] and that repentance, for the forgiveness of sins, would be preached in his name to all the nations, beginning from Jerusalem. [48] You are witnesses of these things."

Friday April 25, 2025
Friday in the Octave of Easter

First Reading: Acts 4:1-12

[1] After the crippled man had been cured, while Peter and John were still speaking to the people, the priests, the captain of the temple guard, and the Sadducees confronted them, [2] disturbed that they were teaching the people and proclaiming in Jesus the resurrection of the dead. [3] They laid hands on Peter and John and put them in custody until the next day, since it was already evening. [4] But many of those who heard the word came to believe and the number of men grew to about five thousand.

[5] On the next day, their leaders, elders, and scribes were assembled in Jerusalem, [6] with Annas the high priest, Caiaphas, John, Alexander, and all who were of the high-priestly class. [7] They brought them into their presence and questioned them, "By what power or by what name have you done this?" [8] Then Peter, filled with the Holy Spirit, answered them, "Leaders of the people and elders: [9] If we are being examined today about a good deed done to a cripple, namely, by what means he was saved, [10] then all of you and all the people of Israel should know that it was in the name of Jesus Christ the Nazorean whom you crucified, whom God raised from the dead; in his name this man stands before you healed. [11] He is *the stone rejected by you, the builders, which has become the cornerstone*. [12] There is no salvation through anyone else, nor is there any other name under heaven given to the human race by which we are to be saved."

Responsorial Psalm: Psalms 118:1-2 and 4, 22-24, 25-27A

R. [22] **The stone rejected by the builders has become the cornerstone.** or: **Alleluia.**

[1] Give thanks to the LORD, for he is good,

for his mercy endures forever.
² Let the house of Israel say,
"His mercy endures forever."
⁴ Let those who fear the LORD say,
"His mercy endures forever."
R. The stone rejected by the builders has become the cornerstone. or: Alleluia.
²² The stone which the builders rejected
has become the cornerstone.
²³ By the LORD has this been done;
it is wonderful in our eyes.
²⁴ This is the day the LORD has made;
let us be glad and rejoice in it.
R. The stone rejected by the builders has become the cornerstone. or: Alleluia.
²⁵ O LORD, grant salvation!
O LORD, grant prosperity!
²⁶ Blessed is he who comes in the name of the LORD;
we bless you from the house of the LORD.
²⁷ᴬ The LORD is God, and he has given us light.
R. The stone rejected by the builders has become the cornerstone. or: Alleluia.

Alleluia: Psalms 118:24
R. Alleluia, alleluia.
²⁴ This is the day the LORD has made;
let us be glad and rejoice in it.
R. Alleluia, alleluia.

Gospel: John 21:1-14
¹ Jesus revealed himself again to his disciples at the Sea of Tiberias. He revealed himself in this way. ² Together were Simon Peter, Thomas called Didymus, Nathanael from Cana in Galilee, Zebedee's sons, and two others of his disciples. ³ Simon Peter said to them, "I am going fishing." They said to him, "We also will come with you." So they went out and got into the boat, but that night they caught nothing. ⁴ When it was already dawn, Jesus was standing on the shore; but the disciples did not realize that it was Jesus. ⁵ Jesus said to them, "Children, have you caught anything to eat?" They answered him, "No." ⁶ So he said to them, "Cast the net over the right side of the boat and you will find something." So they cast it, and were not able to pull it in because of the number of fish. ⁷ So the disciple whom Jesus loved said to Peter, "It is the Lord." When Simon Peter heard that it was the Lord, he tucked in his garment, for he was lightly clad, and jumped into the sea. ⁸ The other disciples came in the boat, for they were not far from shore, only about a

hundred yards, dragging the net with the fish. ⁹ When they climbed out on shore, they saw a charcoal fire with fish on it and bread. ¹⁰ Jesus said to them, "Bring some of the fish you just caught." ¹¹ So Simon Peter went over and dragged the net ashore full of one hundred fifty-three large fish. Even though there were so many, the net was not torn. ¹² Jesus said to them, "Come, have breakfast." And none of the disciples dared to ask him, "Who are you?" because they realized it was the Lord. ¹³ Jesus came over and took the bread and gave it to them, and in like manner the fish. ¹⁴ This was now the third time Jesus was revealed to his disciples after being raised from the dead.

Saturday April 26, 2025
Saturday in the Octave of Easter
First Reading: Acts 4:13-21

¹³ Observing the boldness of Peter and John and perceiving them to be uneducated, ordinary men, the leaders, elders, and scribes were amazed, and they recognized them as the companions of Jesus. ¹⁴ Then when they saw the man who had been cured standing there with them, they could say nothing in reply. ¹⁵ So they ordered them to leave the Sanhedrin, and conferred with one another, saying, ¹⁶ "What are we to do with these men? Everyone living in Jerusalem knows that a remarkable sign was done through them, and we cannot deny it. ¹⁷ But so that it may not be spread any further among the people, let us give them a stern warning never again to speak to anyone in this name."

¹⁸ So they called them back and ordered them not to speak or teach at all in the name of Jesus. ¹⁹ Peter and John, however, said to them in reply, "Whether it is right in the sight of God for us to obey you rather than God, you be the judges. ²⁰It is impossible for us not to speak about what we have seen and heard." ²¹ After threatening them further, they released them, finding no way to punish them, on account of the people who were all praising God for what had happened.

Responsorial Psalm: Psalms 118:1 and 14-15AB,16-18,19-21

R. ⁽²¹ᵃ⁾ *I will give thanks to you, for you have answered me.* or: ***Alleluia.***

¹ Give thanks to the LORD, for he is good,
    for his mercy endures forever.
¹⁴ My strength and my courage is the LORD,
    and he has been my savior.
¹⁵ᴬᴮ The joyful shout of victory
    in the tents of the just.

R. *I will give thanks to you, for you have answered me.* or: ***Alleluia.***

¹⁶ "The right hand of the LORD is exalted;
    the right hand of the LORD has struck with power."
¹⁷ I shall not die, but live,
    and declare the works of the LORD.

¹⁸ Though the LORD has indeed chastised me,
    yet he has not delivered me to death.
R. I will give thanks to you, for you have answered me. or: **Alleluia.**
¹⁹ Open to me the gates of justice;
    I will enter them and give thanks to the LORD.
²⁰ This is the gate of the LORD;
    the just shall enter it.
²¹ I will give thanks to you, for you have answered me
    and have been my savior.
R. I will give thanks to you, for you have answered me. or: **Alleluia.**

Alleluia: Psalms 118:24
R. Alleluia, alleluia.
²⁴ This is the day the LORD has made;
let us be glad and rejoice in it.
R. Alleluia, alleluia.

Gospel: Mark 16:9-15
⁹ When Jesus had risen, early on the first day of the week, he appeared first to Mary Magdalene, out of whom he had driven seven demons. ¹⁰ She went and told his companions who were mourning and weeping. ¹¹ When they heard that he was alive and had been seen by her, they did not believe.

¹² After this he appeared in another form to two of them walking along on their way to the country. ¹³ They returned and told the others; but they did not believe them either.

¹⁴ But later, as the Eleven were at table, he appeared to them and rebuked them for their unbelief and hardness of heart because they had not believed those who saw him after he had been raised. ¹⁵ He said to them, "Go into the whole world and proclaim the Gospel to every creature."

Sunday April 27, 2025
Second Sunday of Easter – Divine Mercy Sunday Year C
First Reading: Acts 5:12-16
¹²Many signs and wonders were done among the people at the hands of the apostles. They were all together in Solomon's portico. ¹³None of the others dared to join them, but the people esteemed them. ¹⁴Yet more than ever, believers in the Lord, great numbers of men and women, were added to them. ¹⁵Thus they even carried the sick out into the streets and laid them on cots and mats so that when Peter came by, at least his shadow might fall on one or another of them. ¹⁶A large number of people from the towns in the vicinity of Jerusalem also gathered, bringing the sick and those disturbed by unclean spirits, and they were all cured.

Responsorial Psalm: Psalms 118:2-4, 13-15, 22-24

**R. (1) Give thanks to the Lord for he is good,
   his love is everlasting.** or: **R. Alleluia.**

² Let the house of Israel say,
   "His mercy endures forever."
³ Let the house of Aaron say,
   "His mercy endures forever."
⁴ Let those who fear the LORD say,
   "His mercy endures forever."

**R. Give thanks to the Lord for he is good, his
   love is everlasting.** or: **R. Alleluia.**

¹³ I was hard pressed and was falling,
   but the LORD helped me.
¹⁴ My strength and my courage is the LORD,
   and he has been my savior.
¹⁵ The joyful shout of victory
   in the tents of the just:

**R. Give thanks to the Lord for he is good, his
   love is everlasting.** or: **R. Alleluia.**

²² The stone which the builders rejected
   has become the cornerstone.
²³ By the LORD has this been done;
   it is wonderful in our eyes.
²⁴ This is the day the LORD has made;
   let us be glad and rejoice in it.

**R. Give thanks to the Lord for he is good, his
   love is everlasting.** or: **R. Alleluia.**

Second Reading: Revelation 1:9-11A, 12-13, 17-19

⁹ I, John, your brother, who share with you the distress, the kingdom, and the endurance we have in Jesus, found myself on the island called Patmos because I proclaimed God's word and gave testimony to Jesus. ¹⁰ I was caught up in spirit on the Lord's day and heard behind me a voice as loud as a trumpet, ¹¹ᴬ which said, "Write on a scroll what you see." ¹²Then I turned to see whose voice it was that spoke to me, and when I turned, I saw seven gold lampstands ¹³and in the midst of the lampstands one like a son of man, wearing an ankle-length robe, with a gold sash around his chest.

¹⁷When I caught sight of him, I fell down at his feet as though dead. He touched me with his right hand and said, "Do not be afraid. I am the first and the last, ¹⁸the one who lives. Once I was dead, but now I am alive forever and ever. I hold the keys to death and the netherworld. ¹⁹Write down, therefore, what you have seen, and what is happening, and what will happen afterwards."

Alleluia: John 20:29
R. Alleluia, alleluia.
²⁹You believe in me, Thomas, because you
      have seen me, says the Lord;
Blessed are those who have not seen me, but
      still believe!
R. Alleluia, alleluia.

Gospel: John 20:19-31
¹⁹On the evening of that first day of the week, when the doors were locked, where the disciples were, for fear of the Jews, Jesus came and stood in their midst and said to them, "Peace be with you." ²⁰When he had said this, he showed them his hands and his side. The disciples rejoiced when they saw the Lord. ²¹Jesus said to them again, "Peace be with you. As the Father has sent me, so I send you." ²²And when he had said this, he breathed on them and said to them, "Receive the Holy Spirit. ²³Whose sins you forgive are forgiven them, and whose sins you retain are retained."

²⁴Thomas, called Didymus, one of the Twelve, was not with them when Jesus came. ²⁵So the other disciples said to him, "We have seen the Lord." But he said to them, "Unless I see the mark of the nails in his hands and put my finger into the nailmarks and put my hand into his side, I will not believe."

²⁶Now a week later his disciples were again inside and Thomas was with them. Jesus came, although the doors were locked, and stood in their midst and said, "Peace be with you." ²⁷Then he said to Thomas, "Put your finger here and see my hands, and bring your hand and put it into my side, and do not be unbelieving, but believe." ²⁸Thomas answered and said to him, "My Lord and my God!" ²⁹Jesus said to him, "Have you come to believe because you have seen me? Blessed are those who have not seen and have believed."

³⁰Now Jesus did many other signs in the presence of his disciples that are not written in this book. ³¹But these are written that you may come to believe that Jesus is the Christ, the Son of God, and that through this belief you may have life in his name.

Monday April 28, 2025
Monday of the Second Week of Easter
First Reading: Acts 4:23-31
²³After their release Peter and John went back to their own people and reported what the chief priests and elders had told them. ²⁴And when they heard it, they raised their voices to God with one accord and said, "Sovereign Lord, maker of heaven and earth and the sea and all that is in them, ²⁵you said by the Holy Spirit through the mouth of our father David, your servant:

Why did the Gentiles rage
    and the peoples entertain folly?
²⁶*The kings of the earth took their stand*
    and the princes gathered together
    against the Lord and against his anointed.

[27]Indeed they gathered in this city against your holy servant Jesus whom you anointed, Herod and Pontius Pilate, together with the Gentiles and the peoples of Israel, [28]to do what your hand and your will had long ago planned to take place. [29]And now, Lord, take note of their threats, and enable your servants to speak your word with all boldness, [30]as you stretch forth your hand to heal, and signs and wonders are done through the name of your holy servant Jesus." [31]As they prayed, the place where they were gathered shook, and they were all filled with the Holy Spirit and continued to speak the word of God with boldness.

Responsorial Psalm: Psalms 2:1-3,4-7A, 7B-9
R. (see 11d) Blessed are all who take refuge in the Lord. or: R. Alleluia.
[1] Why do the nations rage
   and the peoples utter folly?
[2] The kings of the earth rise up,
   and the princes conspire together
   against the LORD and against his anointed:
[3] "Let us break their fetters
   and cast their bonds from us!"
R. Blessed are all who take refuge in the Lord. or: R. Alleluia.
[4] He who is throned in heaven laughs;
   the LORD derides them.
[5] Then in anger he speaks to them;
   he terrifies them in his wrath:
[6] "I myself have set up my king
   on Zion, my holy mountain."
[7A] I will proclaim the decree of the LORD.
R. Blessed are all who take refuge in the Lord. or: R. Alleluia.
[7B] The LORD said to me, "You are my Son;
   this day I have begotten you.
[8] Ask of me and I will give you
   the nations for an inheritance
   and the ends of the earth for your
      possession.
[9] You shall rule them with an iron rod;
   you shall shatter them like an earthen
      dish."
R. Blessed are all who take refuge in the Lord. or: R. Alleluia.

Alleluia: Colossians 3:1
R. Alleluia, alleluia.
[1]If then you were raised with Christ,
seek what is above,
where Christ is seated at the right hand of
   God.

R. Alleluia, alleluia.

Gospel: John 3:1-8

¹There was a Pharisee named Nicodemus, a ruler of the Jews. ²He came to Jesus at night and said to him, "Rabbi, we know that you are a teacher who has come from God, for no one can do these signs that you are doing unless God is with him." ³Jesus answered and said to him, "Amen, amen, I say to you, unless one is born from above, he cannot see the Kingdom of God." ⁴Nicodemus said to him, "How can a man once grown old be born again? Surely he cannot reenter his mother's womb and be born again, can he?" ⁵Jesus answered, "Amen, amen, I say to you, unless one is born of water and Spirit he cannot enter the Kingdom of God. ⁶What is born of flesh is flesh and what is born of spirit is spirit. ⁷Do not be amazed that I told you, 'You must be born from above.' ⁸The wind blows where it wills, and you can hear the sound it makes, but you do not know where it comes from or where it goes; so it is with everyone who is born of the Spirit."

Tuesday April 29, 2025
Memorial of Saint Catherine of Siena, Virgin and Doctor

First Reading: Acts 4:32-37

³² The community of believers was of one heart and mind, and no one claimed that any of his possessions was his own, but they had everything in common. ³³ With great power the Apostles bore witness to the resurrection of the Lord Jesus, and great favor was accorded them all. ³⁴ There was no needy person among them, for those who owned property or houses would sell them, bring the proceeds of the sale, ³⁵ and put them at the feet of the Apostles, and they were distributed to each according to need.

³⁶ Thus Joseph, also named by the Apostles Barnabas (which is translated "son of encouragement"), a Levite, a Cypriot by birth, ³⁷sold a piece of property that he owned, then brought the money and put it at the feet of the Apostles.

Responsorial Psalm: Psalms 93:1AB, 1CD-2, 5

R. ⁽¹ᵃ⁾ *The Lord is king; he is robed in majesty.* or: *Alleluia.*

¹ᴬᴮ The LORD is king, in splendor robed;
    robed is the LORD and girt about with
        strength.

R. *The Lord is king; he is robed in majesty.* or: *Alleluia.*

¹ᶜᴰ And he has made the world firm,
    not to be moved.
² Your throne stands firm from of old;
    from everlasting you are, O LORD.

R. *The Lord is king; he is robed in majesty.* or: *Alleluia.*

⁵ Your decrees are worthy of trust indeed:
    holiness befits your house,
        O LORD, for length of days.

R. *The Lord is king; he is robed in majesty.* or: *Alleluia.*

Alleluia: John 3:14-15
R. Alleluia, alleluia.
[14] The Son of Man must be lifted up,
[15] so that everyone who believes in him
may have eternal life.
R. Alleluia, alleluia.

Gospel: John 3:7B-15
[7B] Jesus said to Nicodemus: "'You must be born from above.' [8] The wind blows where it wills, and you can hear the sound it makes, but you do not know where it comes from or where it goes; so it is with everyone who is born of the Spirit." [9] Nicodemus answered and said to him, 'How can this happen?" [10] Jesus answered and said to him, "You are the teacher of Israel and you do not understand this? [11] Amen, amen, I say to you, we speak of what we know and we testify to what we have seen, but you people do not accept our testimony. [12] If I tell you about earthly things and you do not believe, how will you believe if I tell you about heavenly things? [13] No one has gone up to heaven except the one who has come down from heaven, the Son of Man. [14] And just as Moses lifted up the serpent in the desert, so must the Son of Man be lifted up, so that everyone who believes in him may have eternal life."

Wednesday April 30, 2025
Wednesday of the Second Week of Easter

First Reading: Acts 5:17-26
[17] The high priest rose up and all his companions, that is, the party of the Sadducees, and, filled with jealousy, [18] laid hands upon the Apostles and put them in the public jail. [19] But during the night, the angel of the Lord opened the doors of the prison, led them out, and said, [20] "Go and take your place in the temple area, and tell the people everything about this life." [21] When they heard this, they went to the temple early in the morning and taught. When the high priest and his companions arrived, they convened the Sanhedrin, the full senate of the children of Israel, and sent to the jail to have them brought in. [22] But the court officers who went did not find them in the prison, so they came back and reported, [23] "We found the jail securely locked and the guards stationed outside the doors, but when we opened them, we found no one inside." [24] When the captain of the temple guard and the chief priests heard this report, they were at a loss about them, as to what this would come to. [25] Then someone came in and reported to them, "The men whom you put in prison are in the temple area and are teaching the people." [26] Then the captain and the court officers went and brought them, but without force, because they were afraid of being stoned by the people.

Responsorial Psalm: Psalms 34:2-3, 4-5, 6-7, 8-9
R. [7a] ***The Lord hears the cry of the poor.*** Or: ***Alleluia.***
[2] I will bless the LORD at all times;
   his praise shall be ever in my mouth.
[3] Let my soul glory in the LORD;

the lowly will hear me and be glad.
R. The Lord hears the cry of the poor. or: ***Alleluia.***
⁴ Glorify the LORD with me,
  let us together extol his name.
⁵ I sought the LORD, and he answered me
  and delivered me from all my fears.
R. The Lord hears the cry of the poor. or: ***Alleluia.***
⁶ Look to him that you may be radiant with
    joy,
  and your faces may not blush with
      shame.
⁷ When the poor one called out, the LORD
      heard,
  and from all his distress he saved him.
R. The Lord hears the cry of the poor. or: ***Alleluia.***
⁸ The angel of the LORD encamps
  around those who fear him, and delivers
      them.
⁹ Taste and see how good the LORD is;
  blessed the man who takes refuge in him.
R. The Lord hears the cry of the poor. or: ***Alleluia.***

Alleluia: John 3:16
R. Alleluia, alleluia.
¹⁶ God so love the world that he gave his only-
    begotten Son,
so that everyone who believes in him might
    have eternal life.
R. Alleluia, alleluia.

Gospel: John 3:16-21
¹⁶ God so loved the world that he gave his only-begotten Son, so that everyone who believes in him might not perish but might have eternal life. ¹⁷ For God did not send his Son into the world to condemn the world, but that the world might be saved through him. ¹⁸ Whoever believes in him will not be condemned, but whoever does not believe has already been condemned, because he has not believed in the name of the only-begotten Son of God. ¹⁹ And this is the verdict, that the light came into the world, but people preferred darkness to light, because their works were evil. ²⁰ For everyone who does wicked things hates the light and does not come toward the light, so that his works might not be exposed. ²¹ But whoever lives the truth comes to the light, so that his works may be clearly seen as done in God.

MAY 2025
Thursday May 1, 2025
Thursday of the Second Week of Easter

First Reading: Acts 5:27-33

[27] When the court officers had brought the Apostles in and made them stand before the Sanhedrin, the high priest questioned them, [28] "We gave you strict orders did we not, to stop teaching in that name. Yet you have filled Jerusalem with your teaching and want to bring this man's blood upon us." [29] But Peter and the Apostles said in reply, "We must obey God rather than men. [30] The God of our ancestors raised Jesus, though you had him killed by hanging him on a tree. [31] God exalted him at his right hand as leader and savior to grant Israel repentance and forgiveness of sins. [32] We are witnesses of these things, as is the Holy Spirit whom God has given to those who obey him."

[33] When they heard this, they became infuriated and wanted to put them to death.

Responsorial Psalm: Psalms 34:2 and 9, 17-18, 19-20

R. [7a] *The Lord hears the cry of the poor.* or: *Alleluia.*

[2] I will bless the LORD at all times;
> his praise shall be ever in my mouth.

[9] Taste and see how good the LORD is;
> blessed the man who takes refuge in him.

R. The Lord hears the cry of the poor. or: Alleluia.

[17] The LORD confronts the evildoers,
> to destroy remembrance of them from
>> the earth.

[18] When the just cry out, the LORD hears them,
> and from all their distress he rescues
>> them.

R. The Lord hears the cry of the poor. or: Alleluia.

[19] The LORD is close to the brokenhearted;
> and those who are crushed in spirit he
>> saves.

[20] Many are the troubles of the just man,
> but out of them all the LORD delivers him.

R. The Lord hears the cry of the poor. or: Alleluia.

Alleluia: John 20:29

R. Alleluia, alleluia.
[29] You believe in me, Thomas, because you
> have seen me, says the Lord;
blessed are those who have not seen, but still
> believe!
R. Alleluia, alleluia.

Gospel: John 3:31-36

³¹ The one who comes from above is above all. The one who is of the earth is earthly and speaks of earthly things. But the one who comes from heaven is above all. ³² He testifies to what he has seen and heard, but no one accepts his testimony. ³³ Whoever does accept his testimony certifies that God is trustworthy. ³⁴ For the one whom God sent speaks the words of God. He does not ration his gift of the Spirit. ³⁵ The Father loves the Son and has given everything over to him. ³⁶ Whoever believes in the Son has eternal life, but whoever disobeys the Son will not see life, but the wrath of God remains upon him.

Friday May 2, 2025
Memorial of Saint Athanasius, Bp & Doc

First Reading: Acts 5:34-42

³⁴ A Pharisee in the Sanhedrin named Gamaliel, a teacher of the law, respected by all the people, stood up, ordered the Apostles to be put outside for a short time, ³⁵ and said to the Sanhedrin, "Fellow children of Israel, be careful what you are about to do to these men. ³⁶ Some time ago, Theudas appeared, claiming to be someone important, and about four hundred men joined him, but he was killed, and all those who were loyal to him were disbanded and came to nothing. ³⁷ After him came Judas the Galilean at the time of the census. He also drew people after him, but he too perished and all who were loyal to him were scattered. ³⁸ So now I tell you, have nothing to do with these men, and let them go. For if this endeavor or this activity is of human origin, it will destroy itself. ³⁹ But if it comes from God, you will not be able to destroy them; you may even find yourselves fighting against God." They were persuaded by him. ⁴⁰ After recalling the Apostles, they had them flogged, ordered them to stop speaking in the name of Jesus, and dismissed them. ⁴¹ So they left the presence of the Sanhedrin, rejoicing that they had been found worthy to suffer dishonor for the sake of the name. ⁴² And all day long, both at the temple and in their homes, they did not stop teaching and proclaiming the Christ, Jesus.

Responsorial Psalm: Psalms 27:1, 4, 13-14

R. (see 4abc) **One thing I seek: to dwell in the house of the Lord.** or: *Alleluia.*

¹ The LORD is my light and my salvation;
   whom should I fear?
The LORD is my life's refuge;
   of whom should I be afraid?

R. One thing I seek: to dwell in the house of the Lord. Or: Alleluia.

⁴ One thing I ask of the LORD;
   this I seek:
To dwell in the house of the LORD
   all the days of my life,
That I may gaze on the loveliness of the LORD
   and contemplate his temple.

R. One thing I seek: to dwell in the house of the Lord. Or: Alleluia.

¹³ I believe that I shall see the bounty of the
        LORD
    in the land of the living.
¹⁴ Wait for the LORD with courage;
    be stouthearted, and wait for the LORD.
**R. One thing I seek: to dwell in the house of the
        Lord.** Or: **Alleluia.**

Alleluia: Matthew 4:4B
R. Alleluia, alleluia.
⁴ᴮ One does not live on bread alone,
but on every word that comes forth from the
        mouth of God.
R. Alleluia, alleluia.

Gospel: John 6:1-15
¹ Jesus went across the Sea of Galilee. ² A large crowd followed him, because they saw the signs he was performing on the sick. ³ Jesus went up on the mountain, and there he sat down with his disciples. ⁴ The Jewish feast of Passover was near. ⁵ When Jesus raised his eyes and saw that a large crowd was coming to him, he said to Philip, "Where can we buy enough food for them to eat?" ⁶ He said this to test him, because he himself knew what he was going to do. Philip answered him, ⁷ "Two hundred days' wages worth of food would not be enough for each of them to have a little." ⁸ One of his disciples, Andrew, the brother of Simon Peter, said to him, ⁹ "There is a boy here who has five barley loaves and two fish; but what good are these for so many?" ¹⁰ Jesus said, "Have the people recline." Now there was a great deal of grass in that place. So the men reclined, about five thousand in number. ¹¹ Then Jesus took the loaves, gave thanks, and distributed them to those who were reclining, and also as much of the fish as they wanted. ¹² When they had had their fill, he said to his disciples, "Gather the fragments left over, so that nothing will be wasted." ¹³ So they collected them, and filled twelve wicker baskets with fragments from the five barley loaves that had been more than they could eat. ¹⁴ When the people saw the sign he had done, they said, "This is truly the Prophet, the one who is to come into the world." ¹⁵ Since Jesus knew that they were going to come and carry him off to make him king, he withdrew again to the mountain alone.

Saturday May 3, 2025
Feast of Saints Philip and James, Apostles
First Reading: 1 Corinthians 15:1-8
¹ I am reminding you, brothers and sisters, of the Gospel I preached to you, which you indeed received and in which you also stand. ² Through it you are also being saved, if you hold fast to the word I preached to you, unless you believed in vain. ³ For I handed on to you as of first importance what I also received: that Christ died for our sins in accordance with the Scriptures; ⁴ that he was buried; that he was

raised on the third day in accordance with the Scriptures; ⁵ that he appeared to Cephas, then to the Twelve. ⁶ After that, he appeared to more than five hundred brothers and sisters at once, most of whom are still living, though some have fallen asleep. ⁷ After that he appeared to James, then to all the Apostles. ⁸ Last of all, as to one born abnormally, he appeared to me.

Responsorial Psalm: Psalms 19:2-3, 4-5
R. ⁽⁵⁾ Their message goes out through all the earth. or: Alleluia.
² The heavens declare the glory of God;
 and the firmament proclaims his handiwork.
³ Day pours out the word to day,
 and night to night imparts knowledge.
R. Their message goes out through all the earth. or: Alleluia.
⁴ Not a word nor a discourse
 whose voice is not heard;
⁵ Through all the earth their voice resounds,
 and to the ends of the world, their message.
R. Their message goes out through all the earth. or: Alleluia.

Alleluia: John 14:6B, 9C
R. Alleluia, alleluia.
⁶ᴮ I am the way, the truth, and the life, says the Lord;
⁹ᶜ Philip, whoever has seen me has seen the Father.
R. Alleluia, alleluia.

Gospel: John 14:6-14
⁶ Jesus said to Thomas, "I am the way and the truth and the life. No one comes to the Father except through me. ⁷ If you know me, then you will also know my Father. From now on you do know him and have seen him." ⁸ Philip said to him, "Master, show us the Father, and that will be enough for us." ⁹ Jesus said to him, "Have I been with you for so long a time and you still do not know me, Philip? Whoever has seen me has seen the Father. How can you say, 'Show us the Father'? ¹⁰ Do you not believe that I am in the Father and the Father is in me? The words that I speak to you I do not speak on my own. The Father who dwells in me is doing his works. ¹¹ Believe me that I am in the Father and the Father is in me, or else, believe because of the works themselves. ¹² Amen, amen, I say to you, whoever believes in me will do the works that I do, and will do greater ones than these, because I am going to the Father. ¹³ And whatever you ask in my name, I will do, so that the Father may be glorified in the Son. ¹⁴ If you ask anything of me in my name, I will do it."

Sunday May 4, 2025
Third Sunday of Easter Year C

First Reading: Acts 5:27-32, 40B-41

[27]When the captain and the court officers had brought the apostles in and made them stand before the Sanhedrin, the high priest questioned them, [28]"We gave you strict orders, did we not, to stop teaching in that name? Yet you have filled Jerusalem with your teaching and want to bring this man's blood upon us." [29]But Peter and the apostles said in reply, "We must obey God rather than men. [30]The God of our ancestors raised Jesus, though you had him killed by hanging him on a tree. [31]God exalted him at his right hand as leader and savior to grant Israel repentance and forgiveness of sins. [32]We are witnesses of these things, as is the Holy Spirit whom God has given to those who obey him."

[40B]The Sanhedrin ordered the apostles to stop speaking in the name of Jesus, and dismissed them. [41]So they left the presence of the Sanhedrin, rejoicing that they had been found worthy to suffer dishonor for the sake of the name.

Responsorial Psalm: Psalms 30:2, 4, 5-6, 11-12, 13

R. [2a] *I will praise you, Lord, for you have rescued me.* or: **R.** *Alleluia.*

[2] I will extol you, O LORD, for you drew me clear
   and did not let my enemies rejoice over me.
[4] O LORD, you brought me up from the netherworld;
   you preserved me from among those going down into the pit.

R. *I will praise you, Lord, for you have rescued me.* or: **R.** *Alleluia.*

[5] Sing praise to the LORD, you his faithful ones,
   and give thanks to his holy name.
[6] For his anger lasts but a moment;
   a lifetime, his good will.
At nightfall, weeping enters in,
   but with the dawn, rejoicing.

R. *I will praise you, Lord, for you have rescued me.* or: **R.** *Alleluia.*

[11] Hear, O LORD, and have pity on me;
   O LORD, be my helper.
[12A] You changed my mourning into dancing;
   [13C] O LORD, my God, forever will I give you thanks.

R. *I will praise you, Lord, for you have rescued*

me. or: **R. Alleluia**.

Second Reading: Revelation 5:11-14

[11] I, John, looked and heard the voices of many angels who surrounded the throne and the living creatures and the elders. They were countless in number, [12] and they cried out in a loud voice:

"Worthy is the Lamb that was slain
    to receive power and riches, wisdom and
        strength,
    honor and glory and blessing."

[13] Then I heard every creature in heaven and on earth and under the earth and in the sea, everything in the universe, cry out:

"To the one who sits on the throne and to the
    Lamb
    be blessing and honor, glory and might,
    forever and ever."

[14] The four living creatures answered, "Amen," and the elders fell down and worshiped.

Alleluia: Luke 24:32
R. Alleluia, alleluia.
Christ is risen, creator of all;
he has shown pity on all people.
R. Alleluia, alleluia.

Gospel: John 21:1-19

[1] At that time, Jesus revealed himself again to his disciples at the Sea of Tiberias. He revealed himself in this way. [2] Together were Simon Peter, Thomas called Didymus, Nathanael from Cana in Galilee, Zebedee's sons, and two others of his disciples. [3] Simon Peter said to them, "I am going fishing." They said to him, "We also will come with you." So they went out and got into the boat, but that night they caught nothing. [4] When it was already dawn, Jesus was standing on the shore; but the disciples did not realize that it was Jesus. [5] Jesus said to them, "Children, have you caught anything to eat?" They answered him, "No." [6] So he said to them, "Cast the net over the right side of the boat and you will find something." So they cast it, and were not able to pull it in because of the number of fish. [7] So the disciple whom Jesus loved said to Peter, "It is the Lord." When Simon Peter heard that it was the Lord, he tucked in his garment, for he was lightly clad, and jumped into the sea. [8] The other disciples came in the boat, for they were not far from shore, only about a hundred yards, dragging the net with the fish. [9] When they climbed out on shore, they saw a charcoal fire with fish on it and bread. [10] Jesus said to them, "Bring some of the fish you just caught."

¹¹ So Simon Peter went over and dragged the net ashore full of one hundred fifty-three large fish. Even though there were so many, the net was not torn. ¹² Jesus said to them, "Come, have breakfast." And none of the disciples dared to ask him, "Who are you?" because they realized it was the Lord. ¹³ Jesus came over and took the bread and gave it to them, and in like manner the fish. ¹⁴This was now the third time Jesus was revealed to his disciples after being raised from the dead.

¹⁵When they had finished breakfast, Jesus said to Simon Peter, "Simon, son of John, do you love me more than these?" Simon Peter answered him, "Yes, Lord, you know that I love you." Jesus said to him, "Feed my lambs." ¹⁶He then said to Simon Peter a second time, "Simon, son of John, do you love me?" Simon Peter answered him, "Yes, Lord, you know that I love you." Jesus said to him, "Tend my sheep." ¹⁷Jesus said to him the third time, "Simon, son of John, do you love me?" Peter was distressed that Jesus had said to him a third time, "Do you love me?" and he said to him, "Lord, you know everything; you know that I love you." Jesus said to him, "Feed my sheep. ¹⁸Amen, amen, I say to you, when you were younger, you used to dress yourself and go where you wanted; but when you grow old, you will stretch out your hands, and someone else will dress you and lead you where you do not want to go." ¹⁹He said this signifying by what kind of death he would glorify God. And when he had said this, he said to him, "Follow me."

Or John 21:1-14

¹At that time, Jesus revealed himself again to his disciples at the Sea of Tiberias. He revealed himself in this way. ²Together were Simon Peter, Thomas called Didymus, Nathanael from Cana in Galilee, Zebedee's sons, and two others of his disciples. ³ Simon Peter said to them, "I am going fishing." They said to him, "We also will come with you." So they went out and got into the boat, but that night they caught nothing. ⁴ When it was already dawn, Jesus was standing on the shore; but the disciples did not realize that it was Jesus. ⁵Jesus said to them, "Children, have you caught anything to eat?" They answered him, "No." ⁶ So he said to them, "Cast the net over the right side of the boat and you will find something." So they cast it, and were not able to pull it in because of the number of fish. ⁷ So the disciple whom Jesus loved said to Peter, "It is the Lord." When Simon Peter heard that it was the Lord, he tucked in his garment, for he was lightly clad, and jumped into the sea. ⁸ The other disciples came in the boat, for they were not far from shore, only about a hundred yards, dragging the net with the fish. ⁹When they climbed out on shore, they saw a charcoal fire with fish on it and bread. ¹⁰Jesus said to them, "Bring some of the fish you just caught." ¹¹So Simon Peter went over and dragged the net ashore full of one hundred fifty-three large fish. Even though there were so many, the net was not torn. ¹²Jesus said to them, "Come, have breakfast." And none of the disciples dared to ask him, "Who are you?" because they realized it was the Lord. ¹³Jesus came over and took the bread and gave it to them, and in like manner the fish. ¹⁴This was now the third time Jesus was revealed to his disciples after being raised from the dead.

Monday May 5, 2025
Monday of the Third Week of Easter

First Reading: Acts 6:8-15

8 Stephen, filled with grace and power, was working great wonders and signs among the people. 9 Certain members of the so-called Synagogue of Freedmen, Cyreneans, and Alexandrians, and people from Cilicia and Asia, came forward and debated with Stephen, 10 but they could not withstand the wisdom and the Spirit with which he spoke. 11 Then they instigated some men to say, "We have heard him speaking blasphemous words against Moses and God." 12 They stirred up the people, the elders, and the scribes, accosted him, seized him, and brought him before the Sanhedrin. 13 They presented false witnesses who testified, "This man never stops saying things against this holy place and the law. 14 For we have heard him claim that this Jesus the Nazorean will destroy this place and change the customs that Moses handed down to us." 15 All those who sat in the Sanhedrin looked intently at him and saw that his face was like the face of an angel.

Responsorial Psalm: Psalms 119:23-24, 26-27, 29-30

R. (1ab) *Blessed are they who follow the law of the Lord!* or: *Alleluia.*

23 Though princes meet and talk against me,
   your servant meditates on your statutes.
24 Yes, your decrees are my delight;
   they are my counselors.

R. *Blessed are they who follow the law of the Lord!* or: *Alleluia.*

26 I declared my ways, and you answered me;
   teach me your statutes.
27 Make me understand the way of your precepts,
   and I will meditate on your wondrous deeds.

R. *Blessed are they who follow the law of the Lord!* or: *Alleluia.*

29 Remove from me the way of falsehood,
   and favor me with your law.
30 The way of truth I have chosen;
   I have set your ordinances before me.

R. *Blessed are they who follow the law of the Lord!* or: *Alleluia.*

Alleluia: Matthew 4:4B

R. Alleluia, alleluia.
4B One does not live on bread alone
but on every word that comes forth from the
   mouth of God.

R. Alleluia, alleluia.

Gospel: John 6:22-29

[After Jesus had fed the five thousand men, his disciples saw him walking on the sea.] 22 The next day, the crowd that remained across the sea saw that there had been only one boat there, and that Jesus had not gone along with his disciples in the boat, but only his disciples had left. 23 Other boats came from Tiberias near the place where they had eaten the bread when the Lord gave thanks. 24 When the crowd saw that neither Jesus nor his disciples were there, they themselves got into boats and came to Capernaum looking for Jesus. 25 And when they found him across the sea they said to him, "Rabbi, when did you get here?" 26 Jesus answered them and said, "Amen, amen, I say to you, you are looking for me not because you saw signs but because you ate the loaves and were filled. 27 Do not work for food that perishes but for the food that endures for eternal life, which the Son of Man will give you. For on him the Father, God, has set his seal." 28 So they said to him, "What can we do to accomplish the works of God?" 29 Jesus answered and said to them, "This is the work of God, that you believe in the one he sent."

Tuesday May 6, 2025
Tuesday of the Third Week of Easter

First Reading: Acts 7:51-8:1A

51 Stephen said to the people, the elders, and the scribes: "You stiff-necked people, uncircumcised in heart and ears, you always oppose the Holy Spirit; you are just like your ancestors. 52 Which of the prophets did your ancestors not persecute? They put to death those who foretold the coming of the righteous one, whose betrayers and murderers you have now become. 53 You received the law as transmitted by angels, but you did not observe it."

54 When they heard this, they were infuriated, and they ground their teeth at him. 55 But Stephen, filled with the Holy Spirit, looked up intently to heaven and saw the glory of God and Jesus standing at the right hand of God, 56 and Stephen said, "Behold, I see the heavens opened and the Son of Man standing at the right hand of God." 57 But they cried out in a loud voice, covered their ears, and rushed upon him together. 58 They threw him out of the city, and began to stone him. The witnesses laid down their cloaks at the feet of a young man named Saul. 59 As they were stoning Stephen, he called out, "Lord Jesus, receive my spirit." 60 Then he fell to his knees and cried out in a loud voice, "Lord, do not hold this sin against them"; and when he said this, he fell asleep.

1A Now Saul was consenting to his execution.

Responsorial Psalm: Psalms 31:3CD-4, 6 AND 7B AND 8A, 17 AND 21AB

R. (6a) *Into your hands, O Lord, I commend my spirit.* or: *Alleluia.*

3CD Be my rock of refuge,
    a stronghold to give me safety.
4 You are my rock and my fortress;

for your name's sake you will lead and
> guide me.
***R. Into your hands, O Lord, I commend my
> spirit.* or: *Alleluia.***
⁶ Into your hands I commend my spirit;
> you will redeem me, O LORD, O faithful
> God.
⁷ᴮ My trust is in the LORD;
> ⁸ᴬ I will rejoice and be glad of your mercy.
***R. Into your hands, O Lord, I commend my
> spirit.* or: *Alleluia.***
¹⁷ Let your face shine upon your servant;
> save me in your kindness.
²¹ᴬᴮ You hide them in the shelter of your
> presence
> from the plottings of men.
***R. Into your hands, O Lord, I commend my
> spirit.* or: *Alleluia.***

Alleluia: John 6:35AB
R. Alleluia, alleluia.
³⁵ᴬᴮ I am the bread of life, says the Lord;
whoever comes to me will never hunger.
R. Alleluia, alleluia.

Gospel: John 6:30-35
³⁰ The crowd said to Jesus: "What sign can you do, that we may see and believe in you? What can you do? ³¹ Our ancestors ate manna in the desert, as it is written:
> *He gave them bread from heaven to eat."*

³²So Jesus said to them, "Amen, amen, I say to you, it was not Moses who gave the bread from heaven; my Father gives you the true bread from heaven. ³³ For the bread of God is that which comes down from heaven and gives life to the world."

³⁴ So they said to Jesus, "Sir, give us this bread always." ³⁵ Jesus said to them, "I am the bread of life; whoever comes to me will never hunger, and whoever believes in me will never thirst."

Wednesday May 7, 2025
Wednesday of the Third Week of Easter
First Reading: Acts 8:1B-8
¹ᴮ There broke out a severe persecution of the Church in Jerusalem, and all were scattered throughout the countryside of Judea and Samaria, except the Apostles. ² Devout men buried Stephen and made a loud lament over him. ³ Saul, meanwhile, was trying to destroy the Church; entering house after house and dragging out men and women, he handed them over for imprisonment.

⁴ Now those who had been scattered went about preaching the word. ⁵ Thus Philip went down to the city of Samaria and proclaimed the Christ to them. ⁶ With one accord, the crowds paid attention to what was said by Philip when they heard it and saw the signs he was doing. ⁷ For unclean spirits, crying out in a loud voice, came out of many possessed people, and many paralyzed and crippled people were cured. ⁸ There was great joy in that city.

Responsorial Psalm: Psalms 66:1-3A, 4-5, 6-7A
R. (1) Let all the earth cry out to God with joy. or: *Alleluia.*
² Shout joyfully to God, all the earth,
>sing praise to the glory of his name;
>proclaim his glorious praise.

³ᴬ Say to God, "How tremendous are your
>deeds!"

R. Let all the earth cry out to God with joy. or: *Alleluia.*
⁴ "Let all on earth worship and sing praise to
>you,
>sing praise to your name!"

⁵ Come and see the works of God,
>his tremendous deeds among the
>children of Adam.

R. Let all the earth cry out to God with joy. or: *Alleluia.*
⁶ He has changed the sea into dry land;
>through the river they passed on foot;
>therefore let us rejoice in him.

⁷ᴬ He rules by his might forever.
R. Let all the earth cry out to God with joy. or: *Alleluia.*

Alleluia: cf. John 6:40
R. Alleluia, alleluia.
⁴⁰ Everyone who believes in the Son has
>eternal life,
and I shall raise him on the last day, says the
>Lord.
R. Alleluia, alleluia.

Gospel: John 6:35-40
³⁵ Jesus said to the crowds, "I am the bread of life; whoever comes to me will never hunger, and whoever believes in me will never thirst. ³⁶ But I told you that although you have seen me, you do not believe. ³⁷ Everything that the Father gives me will come to me, and I will not reject anyone who comes to me, ³⁸ because I came down from heaven not to do my own will but the will of the one who sent me. ³⁹ And this is the will of the one who sent me, that I should not lose anything of what he gave me, but that I should raise it on the last day. ⁴⁰ For this is the will of my Father, that everyone who sees the Son and believes in him may have eternal life, and I shall raise him on the last day."

Thursday May 8, 2025
Thursday of the Third Week of Easter
First Reading: Acts 8:26-40

²⁶ The angel of the Lord spoke to Philip, "Get up and head south on the road that goes down from Jerusalem to Gaza, the desert route." ²⁷ So he got up and set out. Now there was an Ethiopian eunuch, a court official of the Candace, that is, the queen of the Ethiopians, in charge of her entire treasury, who had come to Jerusalem to worship, ²⁸ and was returning home. Seated in his chariot, he was reading the prophet Isaiah. ²⁹ The Spirit said to Philip, "Go and join up with that chariot." ³⁰ Philip ran up and heard him reading Isaiah the prophet and said, "Do you understand what you are reading?" ³¹ He replied, "How can I, unless someone instructs me?" So he invited Philip to get in and sit with him. ³² This was the Scripture passage he was reading:

Like a sheep he was led to the slaughter,
 and as a lamb before its shearer is silent,
 so he opened not his mouth.
³³ In his humiliation justice was denied him.
 Who will tell of his posterity?
 For his life is taken from the earth.

³⁴ Then the eunuch said to Philip in reply, "I beg you, about whom is the prophet saying this? About himself, or about someone else?" ³⁵ Then Philip opened his mouth and, beginning with this Scripture passage, he proclaimed Jesus to him. ³⁶ As they traveled along the road they came to some water, and the eunuch said, "Look, there is water. What is to prevent my being baptized?" ³⁸ Then he ordered the chariot to stop, and Philip and the eunuch both went down into the water, and he baptized him. ³⁹ When they came out of the water, the Spirit of the Lord snatched Philip away, and the eunuch saw him no more, but continued on his way rejoicing. ⁴⁰ Philip came to Azotus, and went about proclaiming the good news to all the towns until he reached Caesarea.

Responsorial Psalm: Psalms 66:8-9, 16-17, 20

R. ⁽¹⁾ Let all the earth cry out to God with joy. or: ***Alleluia.***
⁸ Bless our God, you peoples,
 loudly sound his praise;
⁹ He has given life to our souls,
 and has not let our feet slip.
R. Let all the earth cry out to God with joy. or: ***Alleluia.***
¹⁶ Hear now, all you who fear God, while I
  declare
 what he has done for me.
¹⁷ When I appealed to him in words,
 praise was on the tip of my tongue.
R. Let all the earth cry out to God with joy. or: ***Alleluia.***
²⁰ Blessed be God who refused me not

my prayer or his kindness!
R. Let all the earth cry out to God with joy. or: *Alleluia.*

Alleluia: John 6:51
R. Alleluia, alleluia.
⁵¹ I am the living bread that came down from
     heaven,
says the Lord;
whoever eats this bread will live forever.
R. Alleluia, alleluia.

Gospel: John 6:44-51
⁴⁴ Jesus said to the crowds: "No one can come to me unless the Father who sent me draw him, and I will raise him on the last day. ⁴⁵ It is written in the prophets:

They shall all be taught by God.
Everyone who listens to my Father and learns from him comes to me. ⁴⁶ Not that anyone has seen the Father except the one who is from God; he has seen the Father. ⁴⁷ Amen, amen, I say to you, whoever believes has eternal life. ⁴⁸ I am the bread of life. ⁴⁹ Your ancestors ate the manna in the desert, but they died; ⁵⁰ this is the bread that comes down from heaven so that one may eat it and not die. ⁵¹ I am the living bread that came down from heaven; whoever eats this bread will live forever; and the bread that I will give is my Flesh for the life of the world."

Friday May 9, 2025
Friday of the Third Week of Easter
First Reading: Acts 9:1-20
¹ Saul, still breathing murderous threats against the disciples of the Lord, went to the high priest ² and asked him for letters to the synagogues in Damascus, that, if he should find any men or women who belonged to the Way, he might bring them back to Jerusalem in chains. ³ On his journey, as he was nearing Damascus, a light from the sky suddenly flashed around him. ⁴ He fell to the ground and heard a voice saying to him, "Saul, Saul, why are you persecuting me?" ⁵ He said, "Who are you, sir?" The reply came, "I am Jesus, whom you are persecuting. ⁶ Now get up and go into the city and you will be told what you must do." ⁷ The men who were traveling with him stood speechless, for they heard the voice but could see no one. ⁸ Saul got up from the ground, but when he opened his eyes he could see nothing; so they led him by the hand and brought him to Damascus. ⁹ For three days he was unable to see, and he neither ate nor drank.

¹⁰ There was a disciple in Damascus named Ananias, and the Lord said to him in a vision, "Ananias." He answered, "Here I am, Lord." ¹¹ The Lord said to him, "Get up and go to the street called Straight and ask at the house of Judas for a man from Tarsus named Saul. He is there praying, ¹² and in a vision he has seen a man named Ananias come in and lay his hands on him, that he may regain his sight." ¹³ But Ananias replied, "Lord, I have heard from many sources about this

man, what evil things he has done to your holy ones in Jerusalem. ¹⁴ And here he has authority from the chief priests to imprison all who call upon your name." ¹⁵ But the Lord said to him, "Go, for this man is a chosen instrument of mine to carry my name before Gentiles, kings, and children of Israel, ¹⁶ and I will show him what he will have to suffer for my name." ¹⁷ So Ananias went and entered the house; laying his hands on him, he said, "Saul, my brother, the Lord has sent me, Jesus who appeared to you on the way by which you came, that you may regain your sight and be filled with the Holy Spirit." ¹⁸ Immediately things like scales fell from his eyes and he regained his sight. He got up and was baptized, ¹⁹ and when he had eaten, he recovered his strength.

He stayed some days with the disciples in Damascus, ²⁰ and he began at once to proclaim Jesus in the synagogues, that he is the Son of God.

Responsorial Psalm: Psalms 117:1BC, 2
R. *(Mark 16:15)* **Go out to all the world and tell the Good News.** or: *Alleluia.*
¹ᴮᶜ Praise the LORD, all you nations;
  glorify him, all you peoples!
R. Go out to all the world and tell the Good News. or: *Alleluia.*
² For steadfast is his kindness toward us,
  and the fidelity of the LORD endures forever.
R. Go out to all the world and tell the Good News. or: *Alleluia.*

Alleluia: John 6:56
R. Alleluia, alleluia.
⁵⁶ Whoever eats my Flesh and drinks my
  Blood,
remains in me and I in him, says the Lord.
R. Alleluia, alleluia.

Gospel: John 6:52-59
⁵² The Jews quarreled among themselves, saying, "How can this man give us his Flesh to eat?" ⁵³ Jesus said to them, "Amen, amen, I say to you, unless you eat the Flesh of the Son of Man and drink his Blood, you do not have life within you. ⁵⁴ Whoever eats my Flesh and drinks my Blood has eternal life, and I will raise him on the last day. ⁵⁵ For my Flesh is true food, and my Blood is true drink. ⁵⁶ Whoever eats my Flesh and drinks my Blood remains in me and I in him. ⁵⁷ Just as the living Father sent me and I have life because of the Father, so also the one who feeds on me will have life because of me. ⁵⁸ This is the bread that came down from heaven. Unlike your ancestors who ate and still died, whoever eats this bread will live forever." ⁵⁹ These things he said while teaching in the synagogue in Capernaum.

Saturday May 10, 2025
Saturday of the Third Week of Easter

First Reading: Acts 9:31-42

[31] The Church throughout all Judea, Galilee, and Samaria was at peace. She was being built up and walked in the fear of the Lord, and with the consolation of the Holy Spirit she grew in numbers.

[32] As Peter was passing through every region, he went down to the holy ones living in Lydda. [33] There he found a man named Aeneas, who had been confined to bed for eight years, for he was paralyzed. [34] Peter said to him, "Aeneas, Jesus Christ heals you. Get up and make your bed." He got up at once. [35] And all the inhabitants of Lydda and Sharon saw him, and they turned to the Lord.

[36] Now in Joppa there was a disciple named Tabitha (which translated is Dorcas). She was completely occupied with good deeds and almsgiving. [37] Now during those days she fell sick and died, so after washing her, they laid her out in a room upstairs. [38] Since Lydda was near Joppa, the disciples, hearing that Peter was there, sent two men to him with the request, "Please come to us without delay." [39] So Peter got up and went with them. When he arrived, they took him to the room upstairs where all the widows came to him weeping and showing him the tunics and cloaks that Dorcas had made while she was with them. [40] Peter sent them all out and knelt down and prayed. Then he turned to her body and said, "Tabitha, rise up." She opened her eyes, saw Peter, and sat up. [41] He gave her his hand and raised her up, and when he had called the holy ones and the widows, he presented her alive. [42] This became known all over Joppa, and many came to believe in the Lord.

Responsorial Psalm: Psalms 116:12-13, 14-15, 16-17

R. (12) *How shall I make a return to the Lord for all the good he has done for me?* or: *Alleluia.*

[12] How shall I make a return to the LORD
    for all the good he has done for me?
[13] The cup of salvation I will take up,
    and I will call upon the name of the LORD.

R. *How shall I make a return to the Lord for all the good he has done for me?* or: *Alleluia.*

[14] My vows to the LORD I will pay
    in the presence of all his people.
[15] Precious in the eyes of the LORD
    is the death of his faithful ones.

R. *How shall I make a return to the Lord for all the good he has done for me?* or: *Alleluia.*

[16] O LORD, I am your servant;
    I am your servant, the son of your handmaid;
    you have loosed my bonds.
[17] To you will I offer sacrifice of thanksgiving,

and I will call upon the name of the LORD.
**R. How shall I make a return to the Lord for all
    the good he has done for me?** or: *Alleluia.*

Alleluia: cf. John 6:63C, 68C
R. Alleluia, alleluia.
63C Your words, Lord, are Spirit and life;
68C you have the words of everlasting life.
R. Alleluia, alleluia.

Gospel: John 6:60-69
60 Many of the disciples of Jesus who were listening said, "This saying is hard; who can accept it?" 61 Since Jesus knew that his disciples were murmuring about this, he said to them, "Does this shock you? 62 What if you were to see the Son of Man ascending to where he was before? 63 It is the Spirit that gives life, while the flesh is of no avail. The words I have spoken to you are Spirit and life. 64 But there are some of you who do not believe." Jesus knew from the beginning the ones who would not believe and the one who would betray him. 65 And he said, "For this reason I have told you that no one can come to me unless it is granted him by my Father."

66 As a result of this, many of his disciples returned to their former way of life and no longer walked with him. 67 Jesus then said to the Twelve, "Do you also want to leave?" 68 Simon Peter answered him, "Master, to whom shall we go? You have the words of eternal life. 69 We have come to believe and are convinced that you are the Holy One of God."

Sunday May 11, 2025
Fourth Sunday of Easter, Year C
First Reading: Acts 13:14, 43-52
14 Paul and Barnabas continued on from Perga and reached Antioch in Pisidia. On the sabbath they entered the synagogue and took their seats. 43 Many Jews and worshipers who were converts to Judaism followed Paul and Barnabas, who spoke to them and urged them to remain faithful to the grace of God.

44 On the following sabbath almost the whole city gathered to hear the word of the Lord. 45 When the Jews saw the crowds, they were filled with jealousy and with violent abuse contradicted what Paul said. 46 Both Paul and Barnabas spoke out boldly and said, "It was necessary that the word of God be spoken to you first, but since you reject it and condemn yourselves as unworthy of eternal life, we now turn to the Gentiles. 47 For so the Lord has commanded us, *I have made you a light to the Gentiles, that you may be an instrument of salvation to the ends of the earth.*"

48 The Gentiles were delighted when they heard this and glorified the word of the Lord. All who were destined for eternal life came to believe, 49 and the word of the Lord continued to spread through the whole region. 50 The Jews, however, incited the women of prominence who were worshipers and the leading men of the city, stirred up a persecution against Paul and Barnabas, and expelled them from their territory. 51 So they shook the dust from their feet in protest against them, and went to Iconium. 52 The disciples were filled with joy and the Holy Spirit.

Responsorial Psalm: Psalms 100:1-2, 3, 5
R. (3c) We are his people, the sheep of his flock. or: R. Alleluia.
[1] Sing joyfully to the LORD, all you lands;
> [2] serve the LORD with gladness;
> come before him with joyful song.

R. We are his people, the sheep of his flock. or: R. Alleluia.
[3] Know that the LORD is God;
> he made us, his we are;
> his people, the flock he tends.

R. We are his people, the sheep of his flock. or: R. Alleluia.
[5] The LORD is good:
> his kindness endures forever,
> and his faithfulness, to all generations.

R. We are his people, the sheep of his flock. or: R. Alleluia.

Second Reading: Revelation 7:9, 14B-17
[9] I, John, had a vision of a great multitude, which no one could count, from every nation, race, people, and tongue. They stood before the throne and before the Lamb, wearing white robes and holding palm branches in their hands.

[14B] Then one of the elders said to me, "These are the ones who have survived the time of great distress; they have washed their robes and made them white in the blood of the Lamb.

[15] "For this reason they stand before God's throne and worship him day and night in his temple. The one who sits on the throne will shelter them. [16] They will not hunger or thirst anymore, nor will the sun or any heat strike them. [17] For the Lamb who is in the center of the throne will shepherd them and lead them to springs of life-giving water, and God will wipe away every tear from their eyes."

Alleluia: John 10:14
R. Alleluia, alleluia.
[14] I am the good shepherd, says the Lord;
I know my sheep, and mine know me.
R. Alleluia, alleluia.

Gospel: John 10:27-30
Jesus said: [27] "My sheep hear my voice; I know them, and they follow me. [28] I give them eternal life, and they shall never perish. No one can take them out of my hand. [29] My Father, who has given them to me, is greater than all, and no one can take them out of the Father's hand. [30] The Father and I are one."

Monday May 12, 2025
Monday of the Fourth Week of Easter

First Reading: Acts 11:1-18

1 The Apostles and the brothers who were in Judea heard that the Gentiles too had accepted the word of God. 2 So when Peter went up to Jerusalem the circumcised believers confronted him, 3 saying, "You entered the house of uncircumcised people and ate with them." 4 Peter began and explained it to them step by step, saying, 5 "I was at prayer in the city of Joppa when in a trance I had a vision, something resembling a large sheet coming down, lowered from the sky by its four corners, and it came to me. 6 Looking intently into it, I observed and saw the four-legged animals of the earth, the wild beasts, the reptiles, and the birds of the sky. 7 I also heard a voice say to me, 'Get up, Peter. Slaughter and eat.' 8 But I said, 'Certainly not, sir, because nothing profane or unclean has ever entered my mouth.' 9 But a second time a voice from heaven answered, 'What God has made clean, you are not to call profane.' 10 This happened three times, and then everything was drawn up again into the sky. 11 Just then three men appeared at the house where we were, who had been sent to me from Caesarea. 12 The Spirit told me to accompany them without discriminating. These six brothers also went with me, and we entered the man's house. 13 He related to us how he had seen the angel standing in his house, saying, 'Send someone to Joppa and summon Simon, who is called Peter, 14 who will speak words to you by which you and all your household will be saved.' 15 As I began to speak, the Holy Spirit fell upon them as it had upon us at the beginning, 16 and I remembered the word of the Lord, how he had said, 'John baptized with water but you will be baptized with the Holy Spirit.' 17 If then God gave them the same gift he gave to us when we came to believe in the Lord Jesus Christ, who was I to be able to hinder God?" 18 When they heard this, they stopped objecting and glorified God, saying, "God has then granted life-giving repentance to the Gentiles too."

Responsorial Psalm: Psalms 42:2-3; 43:3, 4

R. (see 3a) *Athirst is my soul for the living God.* or: *Alleluia.*

2 As the hind longs for the running waters,
    so my soul longs for you, O God.
3 Athirst is my soul for God, the living God.
    When shall I go and behold the face of
        God?

R. *Athirst is my soul for the living God.* or: *Alleluia.*

3 Send forth your light and your fidelity;
    they shall lead me on
And bring me to your holy mountain,
    to your dwelling-place.

R. *Athirst is my soul for the living God.* or: *Alleluia.*

4 Then will I go in to the altar of God,
    the God of my gladness and joy;
Then will I give you thanks upon the harp,
    O God, my God!

R. *Athirst is my soul for the living God.* or: *Alleluia.*

Alleluia: John 10:14
R. Alleluia, alleluia.
[14] I am the good shepherd, says the Lord;
I know my sheep, and mine know me.
R. Alleluia, alleluia.

Gospel: John 10:1-10
[1] Jesus said: "Amen, amen, I say to you, whoever does not enter a sheepfold through the gate but climbs over elsewhere is a thief and a robber. [2] But whoever enters through the gate is the shepherd of the sheep. [3] The gatekeeper opens it for him, and the sheep hear his voice, as the shepherd calls his own sheep by name and leads them out. [4] When he has driven out all his own, he walks ahead of them, and the sheep follow him, because they recognize his voice. [5] But they will not follow a stranger; they will run away from him, because they do not recognize the voice of strangers." [6] Although Jesus used this figure of speech, they did not realize what he was trying to tell them.

[7] So Jesus said again, "Amen, amen, I say to you, I am the gate for the sheep. [8] All who came before me are thieves and robbers, but the sheep did not listen to them. [9] I am the gate. Whoever enters through me will be saved, and will come in and go out and find pasture. [10] A thief comes only to steal and slaughter and destroy; I came so that they might have life and have it more abundantly."

Tuesday May 13, 2025
Tuesday of the Fourth Week of Easter

First Reading: Acts 11:19-26
[19] Those who had been scattered by the persecution that arose because of Stephen went as far as Phoenicia, Cyprus, and Antioch, preaching the word to no one but Jews. [20] There were some Cypriots and Cyrenians among them, however, who came to Antioch and began to speak to the Greeks as well, proclaiming the Lord Jesus. [21] The hand of the Lord was with them and a great number who believed turned to the Lord. [22] The news about them reached the ears of the Church in Jerusalem, and they sent Barnabas to go to Antioch. [24] When he arrived and saw the grace of God, he rejoiced and encouraged them all to remain faithful to the Lord in firmness of heart, for he was a good man, filled with the Holy Spirit and faith. And a large number of people was added to the Lord. [25] Then he went to Tarsus to look for Saul, [26] and when he had found him he brought him to Antioch. For a whole year they met with the Church and taught a large number of people, and it was in Antioch that the disciples were first called Christians.

Responsorial Psalm: Psalms 87:1B-3,4-5,6-7
R. [117:1a] *All you nations, praise the Lord.* or: *Alleluia.*
[1B] His foundation upon the holy mountains
 the LORD loves:
[2] The gates of Zion,

more than any dwelling of Jacob.
³ Glorious things are said of you,
 O city of God!
R. All you nations, praise the Lord. or: ***Alleluia.***
⁴ I tell of Egypt and Babylon
 among those who know the LORD;
Of Philistia, Tyre, Ethiopia:
 "This man was born there."
⁵ And of Zion they shall say:
 "One and all were born in her;
And he who has established her
 is the Most High LORD."
R. All you nations, praise the Lord. or: ***Alleluia.***
⁶ They shall note, when the peoples are
  enrolled:
 "This man was born there."
⁷ And all shall sing, in their festive dance:
 "My home is within you."
R. All you nations, praise the Lord. or: ***Alleluia.***

Alleluia: John 10:27
R. Alleluia, alleluia.
²⁷ My sheep hear my voice, says the Lord;
I know them, and they follow me.
R. Alleluia, alleluia.

Gospel: John 10:22-30
²² The feast of the Dedication was taking place in Jerusalem. It was winter. ²³ And Jesus walked about in the temple area on the Portico of Solomon. ²⁴ So the Jews gathered around him and said to him, "How long are you going to keep us in suspense? If you are the Christ, tell us plainly." ²⁵ Jesus answered them, "I told you and you do not believe. The works I do in my Father's name testify to me. ²⁶ But you do not believe, because you are not among my sheep. ²⁷ My sheep hear my voice; I know them, and they follow me. ²⁸ I give them eternal life, and they shall never perish. No one can take them out of my hand. ²⁹ My Father, who has given them to me, is greater than all, and no one can take them out of the Father's hand. ³⁰ The Father and I are one."

Wednesday May 14, 2025
Feast of Saint Matthias, Apostle
First Reading: Acts 1:15-17, 20-26
¹⁵ Peter stood up in the midst of the brothers and sisters (there was a group of about one hundred and twenty persons in the one place). ¹⁶ He said, "My brothers and sisters, the Scripture had to be fulfilled which the Holy Spirit spoke beforehand through the mouth of David, concerning Judas, who was the guide for those who

arrested Jesus. ⁱ⁷ Judas was numbered among us and was allotted a share in this ministry. ²⁰ For it is written in the Book of Psalms:

Let his encampment become desolate,
  and may no one dwell in it.
and:
May another take his office.

²¹ Therefore, it is necessary that one of the men who accompanied us the whole time the Lord Jesus came and went among us, ²² beginning from the baptism of John until the day on which he was taken up from us, become with us a witness to his resurrection." ²³ So they proposed two, Joseph called Barsabbas, who was also known as Justus, and Matthias. ²⁴ Then they prayed, "You, Lord, who know the hearts of all, show which one of these two you have chosen ²⁵ to take the place in this apostolic ministry from which Judas turned away to go to his own place." ²⁶ Then they gave lots to them, and the lot fell upon Matthias, and he was counted with the Eleven Apostles.

Responsorial Psalm: Psalms 113:1-2, 3-4, 5-6, 7-8
R. ⁽⁸⁾ *The Lord will give him a seat with the leaders of his people.* or: *Alleluia.*

¹ Praise, you servants of the LORD,
  praise the name of the LORD.
² Blessed be the name of the LORD
  both now and forever.
R. *The Lord will give him a seat with the leaders of his people.* or: *Alleluia.*
³ From the rising to the setting of the sun
  is the name of the LORD to be praised.
⁴ High above all nations is the LORD;
  above the heavens is his glory.
R. *The Lord will give him a seat with the leaders of his people.* or: *Alleluia.*
⁵ Who is like the LORD, our God, who is
    enthroned on high
  ⁶ and looks upon the heavens and the earth
    below?
R. *The Lord will give him a seat with the leaders of his people.* or: *Alleluia.*
⁷ He raises up the lowly from the dust;
  from the dunghill he lifts up the poor
⁸ To seat them with princes,
  with the princes of his own people.
R. *The Lord will give him a seat with the leaders of his people.* or: *Alleluia.*

Alleluia: cf. John 15:16
R. Alleluia, alleluia.
¹⁶ I chose you from the world,
to go and bear fruit that will last, says the Lord.
R. Alleluia, alleluia.

Gospel: John 15:9-17
⁹ Jesus said to his disciples: "As the Father loves me, so I also love you. Remain in my love. ¹⁰ If you keep my commandments, you will remain in my love, just as I have kept my Father's commandments and remain in his love.

¹¹ "I have told you this so that my joy might be in you and your joy might be complete. ¹² This is my commandment: love one another as I love you. ¹³ No one has greater love than this, to lay down one's life for one's friends. ¹⁴ You are my friends if you do what I command you. ¹⁵ I no longer call you slaves, because a slave does not know what his master is doing. I have called you friends, because I have told you everything I have heard from my Father. ¹⁶ It was not you who chose me, but I who chose you and appointed you to go and bear fruit that will remain, so that whatever you ask the Father in my name he may give you. ¹⁷ This I command you: love one another."

Thursday May 15, 2025
Thursday of the Fourth Week of Easter

First Reading: Acts 13:13-25
¹³From Paphos, Paul and his companions set sail and arrived at Perga in Pamphylia. But John left them and returned to Jerusalem. ¹⁴They continued on from Perga and reached Antioch in Pisidia. On the Sabbath they entered into the synagogue and took their seats. ¹⁵After the reading of the law and the prophets, the synagogue officials sent word to them, "My brothers, if one of you has a word of exhortation for the people, please speak."

¹⁶So Paul got up, motioned with his hand, and said, "Fellow children of Israel and you others who are God-fearing, listen. ¹⁷The God of this people Israel chose our ancestors and exalted the people during their sojourn in the land of Egypt. With uplifted arm he led them out, ¹⁸and for about forty years he put up with them in the desert. ¹⁹When he had destroyed seven nations in the land of Canaan, he gave them their land as an inheritance ²⁰at the end of about four hundred and fifty years. After these things he provided judges up to Samuel the prophet. ²¹Then they asked for a king. God gave them Saul, son of Kish, a man from the tribe of Benjamin, for forty years. ²²Then he removed him and raised up David as their king; of him he testified, *I have found David, son of Jesse, a man after my own heart; he will carry out my every wish*.

²³ From this man's descendants God, according to his promise, has brought to Israel a savior, Jesus. ²⁴John heralded his coming by proclaiming a baptism of repentance to all the people of Israel; ²⁵ and as John was completing his course, he would say, 'What do you suppose that I am? I am not he. Behold, one is coming after me; I am not worthy to unfasten the sandals of his feet.'"

Responsorial Psalm: Psalms 89:2-3, 21-22, 25 AND 27
R. (2) For ever I will sing the goodness of the Lord. or: *R. Alleluia.*

² The favors of the LORD I will sing forever;
> through all generations my mouth shall
>> proclaim your faithfulness.

³ For you have said, "My kindness is
> established forever";
> in heaven you have confirmed your
>> faithfulness.

R. For ever I will sing the goodness of the Lord. or: *R. Alleluia.*

²¹ "I have found David, my servant;
> with my holy oil I have anointed him,

²² That my hand may be always with him,
> and that my arm may make him strong."

R. For ever I will sing the goodness of the Lord. or: *R. Alleluia.*

²⁵ "My faithfulness and my mercy shall be with
>> him,
> and through my name shall his horn be
>> exalted.

²⁷ He shall say of me, 'You are my father,
> my God, the Rock, my savior.'"

R. For ever I will sing the goodness of the Lord. or: *R. Alleluia.*

Alleluia: cf. Revelation 1:5AB
R. Alleluia, alleluia.
⁵ᴬᴮ Jesus Christ, you are the faithful witness,
the firstborn of the dead,
you have loved us and freed us from our sins
> by your Blood.

R. Alleluia, alleluia.

Gospel: John 13:16-20
¹⁶When Jesus had washed the disciples' feet, he said to them: "Amen, amen, I say to you, no slave is greater than his master nor any messenger greater than the one who sent him. ¹⁷If you understand this, blessed are you if you do it. ¹⁸I am not speaking of all of you. I know those whom I have chosen. But so that the Scripture might be fulfilled,

The one who ate my food has raised his heel
> *against me.*

¹⁹From now on I am telling you before it happens, so that when it happens you may believe that I AM. ²⁰Amen, amen, I say to you, whoever receives the one I send receives me, and whoever receives me receives the one who sent me."

Friday May 16, 2025
Friday of the Fourth Week of Easter

First Reading: Acts 13:26-33

²⁶ When Paul came to Antioch in Pisidia, he said in the synagogue: "My brothers, children of the family of Abraham, and those others among you who are God-fearing, to us this word of salvation has been sent. ²⁷ The inhabitants of Jerusalem and their leaders failed to recognize him, and by condemning him they fulfilled the oracles of the prophets that are read sabbath after sabbath. ²⁸ For even though they found no grounds for a death sentence, they asked Pilate to have him put to death, ²⁹ and when they had accomplished all that was written about him, they took him down from the tree and placed him in a tomb. ³⁰ But God raised him from the dead, ³¹ and for many days he appeared to those who had come up with him from Galilee to Jerusalem. These are now his witnesses before the people. ³² We ourselves are proclaiming this good news to you that what God promised our fathers ³³ he has brought to fulfillment for us, their children, by raising up Jesus, as it is written in the second psalm, *You are my Son; this day I have begotten you.*"

Responsorial Psalm: Psalms 2:6-7, 8-9, 10-11AB

R. (7bc) *You are my Son; this day I have begotten you*. or: *Alleluia*.

⁶ "I myself have set up my king
> on Zion, my holy mountain."
⁷ I will proclaim the decree of the LORD:
> The LORD said to me, "You are my Son;
> this day I have begotten you."

R. *You are my Son; this day I have begotten you*. or: *Alleluia*.

⁸ "Ask of me and I will give you
> the nations for an inheritance
> and the ends of the earth for your
>> possession.
⁹ You shall rule them with an iron rod;
> you shall shatter them like an earthen
>> dish."

R. *You are my Son; this day I have begotten you*. or: *Alleluia*.

¹⁰ And now, O kings, give heed;
> take warning, you rulers of the earth.
¹¹ᴬᴮ Serve the LORD with fear, and rejoice before
>> him;
> with trembling rejoice.

R. *You are my Son; this day I have begotten you*. or: *Alleluia*.

Alleluia: John 14:6

R. Alleluia, alleluia.
⁶ I am the way and the truth and the life, says
> the Lord;
no one comes to the Father except through

me.
R. Alleluia, alleluia.

Gospel: John 14:1-6
¹ Jesus said to his disciples: "Do not let your hearts be troubled. You have faith in God; have faith also in me. ² In my Father's house there are many dwelling places. If there were not, would I have told you that I am going to prepare a place for you? ³ And if I go and prepare a place for you, I will come back again and take you to myself, so that where I am you also may be. ⁴ Where I am going you know the way." ⁵ Thomas said to him, "Master, we do not know where you are going; how can we know the way?" ⁶ Jesus said to him, "I am the way and the truth and the life. No one comes to the Father except through me."

Saturday May 17, 2025
Saturday of the Fourth Week of Easter

First Reading: Acts 13:44-52
⁴⁴ On the following sabbath almost the whole city gathered to hear the word of the Lord. ⁴⁵ When the Jews saw the crowds, they were filled with jealousy and with violent abuse contradicted what Paul said. ⁴⁶ Both Paul and Barnabas spoke out boldly and said, "It was necessary that the word of God be spoken to you first, but since you reject it and condemn yourselves as unworthy of eternal life, we now turn to the Gentiles. ⁴⁷ For so the Lord has commanded us, *I have made you a light to the Gentiles, that you may be an instrument of salvation to the ends of the earth.*"

⁴⁸ The Gentiles were delighted when they heard this and glorified the word of the Lord. All who were destined for eternal life came to believe, ⁴⁹ and the word of the Lord continued to spread through the whole region. ⁵⁰ The Jews, however, incited the women of prominence who were worshipers and the leading men of the city, stirred up a persecution against Paul and Barnabas, and expelled them from their territory. ⁵¹ So they shook the dust from their feet in protest against them and went to Iconium. ⁵² The disciples were filled with joy and the Holy Spirit.

Responsorial Psalm: Psalms 98:1, 2-3AB, 3CD-4
R. (3cd) All the ends of the earth have seen the saving power of God. or: *Alleluia.*

¹ Sing to the LORD a new song,
 for he has done wondrous deeds;
His right hand has won victory for him,
 his holy arm.

R. All the ends of the earth have seen the saving power of God. or: ***Alleluia.***

² The LORD has made his salvation known:
 in the sight of the nations he has revealed
  his justice.
³ᴬᴮ He has remembered his kindness and his
  faithfulness
 toward the house of Israel.

R. All the ends of the earth have seen the saving power of God. or: ***Alleluia.***

³ᶜᴰ All the ends of the earth have seen
   the salvation by our God.
⁴ Sing joyfully to the LORD, all you lands;
   break into song; sing praise.
R. All the ends of the earth have seen the saving power of God. or: **Alleluia.**

Alleluia: John 8:31B-32
R. Alleluia, alleluia.
³¹ᴮ If you remain in my word, you will truly be
      my disciples,
³² and you will know the truth, says the Lord.
R. Alleluia, alleluia.

Gospel: John 14:7-14
⁷ Jesus said to his disciples: "If you know me, then you will also know my Father. From now on you do know him and have seen him." ⁸ Philip said to Jesus, "Master, show us the Father, and that will be enough for us." ⁹ Jesus said to him, "Have I been with you for so long a time and you still do not know me, Philip? Whoever has seen me has seen the Father. How can you say, 'Show us the Father'? ¹⁰ Do you not believe that I am in the Father and the Father is in me? The words that I speak to you I do not speak on my own. The Father who dwells in me is doing his works. ¹¹ Believe me that I am in the Father and the Father is in me, or else, believe because of the works themselves. ¹² Amen, amen, I say to you, whoever believes in me will do the works that I do, and will do greater ones than these, because I am going to the Father. ¹³ And whatever you ask in my name, I will do, so that the Father may be glorified in the Son. ¹⁴ If you ask anything of me in my name, I will do it."

Sunday May 18, 2025
Fifth Sunday of Easter, Year C

First Reading: Acts 14:21-27
²¹ After Paul and Barnabas had proclaimed the good news to that city and made a considerable number of disciples, they returned to Lystra and to Iconium and to Antioch. ²²They strengthened the spirits of the disciples and exhorted them to persevere in the faith, saying, "It is necessary for us to undergo many hardships to enter the kingdom of God." ²³They appointed elders for them in each church and, with prayer and fasting, commended them to the Lord in whom they had put their faith. ²⁴Then they traveled through Pisidia and reached Pamphylia. ²⁵After proclaiming the word at Perga they went down to Attalia. ²⁶From there they sailed to Antioch, where they had been commended to the grace of God for the work they had now accomplished. ²⁷And when they arrived, they called the church together and reported what God had done with them and how he had opened the door of faith to the Gentiles.

Responsorial Psalm: Psalms 145:8-9, 10-11, 12-13
R. ⁽ᶜᶠ· ¹⁾ *I will praise your name for ever, my king*

and my God. or: **R. Alleluia.**
⁸ The LORD is gracious and merciful,
　　slow to anger and of great kindness.
⁹ The LORD is good to all
　　and compassionate toward all his works.
R. I will praise your name for ever, my king and my God. or: **R. Alleluia.**
¹⁰ Let all your works give you thanks, O LORD,
　　and let your faithful ones bless you.
¹¹ Let them discourse of the glory of your kingdom
　　and speak of your might.
R. I will praise your name for ever, my king and my God. or: **R. Alleluia.**
¹² Let them make known your might to the children of Adam,
　　and the glorious splendor of your kingdom.
¹³ Your kingdom is a kingdom for all ages,
　　and your dominion endures through all generations.
R. I will praise your name for ever, my king and my God. or: **R. Alleluia.**

Second Reading: Revelation 21:1-5A

¹ Then I, John, saw a new heaven and a new earth. The former heaven and the former earth had passed away, and the sea was no more. ² I also saw the holy city, a new Jerusalem, coming down out of heaven from God, prepared as a bride adorned for her husband. ³ I heard a loud voice from the throne saying, "Behold, God's dwelling is with the human race. He will dwell with them and they will be his people and God himself will always be with them as their God. ⁴ He will wipe every tear from their eyes, and there shall be no more death or mourning, wailing or pain, for the old order has passed away."
　　⁵The One who sat on the throne said, "Behold, I make all things new."

Alleluia: John 13:34
R. Alleluia, alleluia.
³⁴ I give you a new commandment, says the
　　Lord:
love one another as I have loved you.
R. Alleluia, alleluia.

Gospel: John 13:31-33A, 34-35

³¹ When Judas had left them, Jesus said, "Now is the Son of Man glorified, and God is glorified in him. ³² If God is glorified in him, God will also glorify him in himself, and God will glorify him at once. ³³ᴬ My children, I will be with you only a

little while longer. ³⁴ I give you a new commandment: love one another. As I have loved you, so you also should love one another. ³⁵ This is how all will know that you are my disciples, if you have love for one another."

Monday May 19, 2025
Monday of the Fifth Week of Easter

First Reading: Acts 14:5-18

⁵ There was an attempt in Iconium by both the Gentiles and the Jews, together with their leaders, to attack and stone Paul and Barnabas. ⁶ They realized it, and fled to the Lycaonian cities of Lystra and Derbe and to the surrounding countryside, ⁷ where they continued to proclaim the Good News.

⁸ At Lystra there was a crippled man, lame from birth, who had never walked. ⁹ He listened to Paul speaking, who looked intently at him, saw that he had the faith to be healed, ¹⁰ and called out in a loud voice, "Stand up straight on your feet." He jumped up and began to walk about. ¹¹ When the crowds saw what Paul had done, they cried out in Lycaonian, "The gods have come down to us in human form." ¹² They called Barnabas "Zeus" and Paul "Hermes," because he was the chief speaker. ¹³ And the priest of Zeus, whose temple was at the entrance to the city, brought oxen and garlands to the gates, for he together with the people intended to offer sacrifice.

¹⁴ The Apostles Barnabas and Paul tore their garments when they heard this and rushed out into the crowd, shouting, ¹⁵ "Men, why are you doing this? We are of the same nature as you, human beings. We proclaim to you good news that you should turn from these idols to the living God, *who made heaven and earth and sea and all that is in them*. ¹⁶ In past generations he allowed all Gentiles to go their own ways; ¹⁷ yet, in bestowing his goodness, he did not leave himself without witness, for he gave you rains from heaven and fruitful seasons, and filled you with nourishment and gladness for your hearts." ¹⁸ Even with these words, they scarcely restrained the crowds from offering sacrifice to them.

Responsorial Psalm: Psalms 115:1-2, 3-4, 15-16

R. ⁽¹ᵃᵇ⁾ ***Not to us, O Lord, but to your name give the glory.*** or: ***Alleluia.***

¹ Not to us, O LORD, not to us
　but to your name give glory
　because of your mercy, because of your
　　truth.
² Why should the pagans say,
　"Where is their God?"

R. Not to us, O Lord, but to your name give the glory. or: **Alleluia.**

³ Our God is in heaven;
　whatever he wills, he does.
⁴ Their idols are silver and gold,
　the handiwork of men.

R. Not to us, O Lord, but to your name give the glory. or: **Alleluia.**

¹⁵ May you be blessed by the LORD,
 who made heaven and earth.
¹⁶ Heaven is the heaven of the LORD,
 but the earth he has given to the children
  of men.
R. Not to us, O Lord, but to your name give the glory. or: ***Alleluia.***

Alleluia: John 14:26
R. Alleluia, alleluia.
²⁶ The Holy Spirit will teach you everything and remind you of all I told you.
R. Alleluia, alleluia.

Gospel: John 14:21-26
²¹ Jesus said to his disciples: "Whoever has my commandments and observes them is the one who loves me. Whoever loves me will be loved by my Father, and I will love him and reveal myself to him." ²² Judas, not the Iscariot, said to him, "Master, then what happened that you will reveal yourself to us and not to the world?" ²³ Jesus answered and said to him, "Whoever loves me will keep my word, and my Father will love him, and we will come to him and make our dwelling with him. ²⁴ Whoever does not love me does not keep my words; yet the word you hear is not mine but that of the Father who sent me.

²⁵ "I have told you this while I am with you. ²⁶ The Advocate, the Holy Spirit whom the Father will send in my name— he will teach you everything and remind you of all that I told you."

Tuesday May 20, 2025
Tuesday of the Fifth Week of Easter
First Reading: Acts 14:19-28
¹⁹ In those days, some Jews from Antioch and Iconium arrived and won over the crowds. They stoned Paul and dragged him out of the city, supposing that he was dead. ²⁰ But when the disciples gathered around him, he got up and entered the city. On the following day he left with Barnabas for Derbe.

²¹ After they had proclaimed the good news to that city and made a considerable number of disciples, they returned to Lystra and to Iconium and to Antioch. ²² They strengthened the spirits of the disciples and exhorted them to persevere in the faith, saying, "It is necessary for us to undergo many hardships to enter the Kingdom of God." ²³ They appointed presbyters for them in each Church and, with prayer and fasting, commended them to the Lord in whom they had put their faith. ²⁴ Then they traveled through Pisidia and reached Pamphylia. ²⁵ After proclaiming the word at Perga they went down to Attalia. ²⁶ From there they sailed to Antioch, where they had been commended to the grace of God for the work they had now accomplished. ²⁷ And when they arrived, they called the Church together and reported what God had done with them and how he had opened the door of faith to the Gentiles. ²⁸ Then they spent no little time with the disciples.

Responsorial Psalm: Psalms 145:10-11, 12-13AB, 21

R. *(see 12)* *Your friends make known, O Lord, the glorious splendor of your kingdom.*
or: *Alleluia.*

¹⁰ Let all your works give you thanks, O LORD,
    and let your faithful ones bless you.
¹¹ Let them discourse of the glory of your kingdom
    and speak of your might.

R. *Your friends make known, O Lord, the glorious splendor of your kingdom.*
or: *Alleluia.*

¹² Making known to men your might
    and the glorious splendor of your kingdom.
¹³ᴬᴮ Your kingdom is a kingdom for all ages,
    and your dominion endures through all generations.

R. *Your friends make known, O Lord, the glorious splendor of your kingdom.*
or: *Alleluia.*

²¹ May my mouth speak the praise of the LORD,
    and may all flesh bless his holy name
    forever and ever.

R. *Your friends make known, O Lord, the glorious splendor of your kingdom.*
or: *Alleluia.*

Alleluia: cf. Luke 24:46, 26
R. Alleluia, alleluia.
⁴⁶ Christ had to suffer and to rise from the dead,
²⁶ and so enter into his glory.
R. Alleluia, alleluia.

Gospel: John 14:27-31A

²⁷ Jesus said to his disciples: "Peace I leave with you; my peace I give to you. Not as the world gives do I give it to you. Do not let your hearts be troubled or afraid. ²⁸ You heard me tell you, 'I am going away and I will come back to you.' If you loved me, you would rejoice that I am going to the Father; for the Father is greater than I. ²⁹ And now I have told you this before it happens, so that when it happens you may believe. ³⁰ I will no longer speak much with you, for the ruler of the world is coming. He has no power over me, ³¹ᴬ but the world must know that I love the Father and that I do just as the Father has commanded me."

Wednesday May 21, 2025
Wednesday of the Fifth Week of Easter

First Reading: Acts 15:1-6

[1] Some who had come down from Judea were instructing the brothers, "Unless you are circumcised according to the Mosaic practice, you cannot be saved." [2] Because there arose no little dissension and debate by Paul and Barnabas with them, it was decided that Paul, Barnabas, and some of the others should go up to Jerusalem to the Apostles and presbyters about this question. [3] They were sent on their journey by the Church, and passed through Phoenicia and Samaria telling of the conversion of the Gentiles, and brought great joy to all the brethren. [4] When they arrived in Jerusalem, they were welcomed by the Church, as well as by the Apostles and the presbyters, and they reported what God had done with them. [5] But some from the party of the Pharisees who had become believers stood up and said, "It is necessary to circumcise them and direct them to observe the Mosaic law."

[6] The Apostles and the presbyters met together to see about this matter.

Responsorial Psalm: Psalms 122:1-2, 3-4AB, 4CD-5

R. [see 1] *Let us go rejoicing to the house of the Lord.* or: *Alleluia.*

[1] I rejoiced because they said to me,
"We will go up to the house of the LORD."
[2] And now we have set foot
within your gates, O Jerusalem.

R. *Let us go rejoicing to the house of the Lord.* or: *Alleluia.*

[3] Jerusalem, built as a city
with compact unity.
[4AB] To it the tribes go up,
the tribes of the LORD.

R. *Let us go rejoicing to the house of the Lord.* or: *Alleluia.*

[4CD] According to the decree for Israel,
to give thanks to the name of the LORD.
[5] In it are set up judgment seats,
seats for the house of David.

R. *Let us go rejoicing to the house of the Lord.* or: *Alleluia.*

Alleluia: John 15:4A, 5B

R. Alleluia, alleluia.
[4A] Remain in me, as I remain in you, says the Lord;
[5B] whoever remains in me will bear much fruit.
R. Alleluia, alleluia.

Gospel: John 15:1-8

[1] Jesus said to his disciples: "I am the true vine, and my Father is the vine grower. [2] He takes away every branch in me that does not bear fruit, and everyone that does he prunes so that it bears more fruit. [3] You are already pruned because of the word that I spoke to you. [4] Remain in me, as I remain in you. Just as a branch cannot bear fruit on its own unless it remains on the vine, so neither can you unless you remain in me. [5] I am the vine, you are the branches. Whoever remains in me and I in him will bear much fruit, because without me you can do nothing. [6] Anyone who does not remain in me will be thrown out like a branch and wither; people will gather them and throw them into a fire and they will be burned. [7] If you remain in me and my words remain in you, ask for whatever you want and it will be done for you. [8] By this is my Father glorified, that you bear much fruit and become my disciples."

Thursday May 22, 2025
Thursday of the Fifth Week of Easter
First Reading: Acts 15:7-21

[7] After much debate had taken place, Peter got up and said to the Apostles and the presbyters, "My brothers, you are well aware that from early days God made his choice among you that through my mouth the Gentiles would hear the word of the Gospel and believe. [8] And God, who knows the heart, bore witness by granting them the Holy Spirit just as he did us. [9] He made no distinction between us and them, for by faith he purified their hearts. [10] Why, then, are you now putting God to the test by placing on the shoulders of the disciples a yoke that neither our ancestors nor we have been able to bear? [11] On the contrary, we believe that we are saved through the grace of the Lord Jesus, in the same way as they." [12] The whole assembly fell silent, and they listened while Paul and Barnabas described the signs and wonders God had worked among the Gentiles through them.

[13] After they had fallen silent, James responded, "My brothers, listen to me. [14] Symeon has described how God first concerned himself with acquiring from among the Gentiles a people for his name. [15] The words of the prophets agree with this, as is written:

[16] *After this I shall return*
and rebuild the fallen hut of David;
from its ruins I shall rebuild it
and raise it up again,
[17] *so that the rest of humanity may seek out the*
Lord,
even all the Gentiles on whom my name is
invoked.
Thus says the Lord who accomplishes these
things,
[18] *known from of old.*

[19] It is my judgment, therefore, that we ought to stop troubling the Gentiles who turn to God, [20] but tell them by letter to avoid pollution from idols, unlawful marriage, the meat of strangled animals, and blood. [21] For Moses, for generations now, has had

those who proclaim him in every town, as he has been read in the synagogues every sabbath."

Responsorial Psalm: Psalms 96:1-2A,2B-3,10
R. (3) *Proclaim God's marvelous deeds to all the nations.* or: *Alleluia.*
¹ Sing to the LORD a new song;
  sing to the LORD, all you lands.
²ᴬ Sing to the LORD; bless his name.
R. *Proclaim God's marvelous deeds to all the nations.* or: *Alleluia.*
²ᴮ Announce his salvation, day after day.
³Tell his glory among the nations;
  among all peoples, his wondrous deeds.
R. *Proclaim God's marvelous deeds to all the nations.* or: *Alleluia.*
¹⁰Say among the nations: The LORD is king.
He has made the world firm, not to be
  moved;
  he governs the peoples with equity.
R. *Proclaim God's marvelous deeds to all the nations.* or: *Alleluia.*

Alleluia: John 10:27
R. Alleluia, alleluia.
²⁷ My sheep hear my voice, says the Lord;
I know them, and they follow me.
R. Alleluia, alleluia.

Gospel: John 15:9-11
⁹ Jesus said to his disciples: "As the Father loves me, so I also love you. Remain in my love. ¹⁰ If you keep my commandments, you will remain in my love, just as I have kept my Father's commandments and remain in his love.

¹¹ "I have told you this so that my joy might be in you and your joy might be complete."

Friday May 23, 2025
Friday of the Fifth Week of Easter
First Reading: Acts 15:22-31
²²The Apostles and presbyters, in agreement with the whole Church, decided to choose representatives and to send them to Antioch with Paul and Barnabas. The ones chosen were Judas, who was called Barsabbas, and Silas, leaders among the brothers. ²³This is the letter delivered by them: "The Apostles and the presbyters, your brothers, to the brothers in Antioch, Syria, and Cilicia of Gentile

origin: greetings. ²⁴Since we have heard that some of our number who went out without any mandate from us have upset you with their teachings and disturbed your peace of mind, ²⁵we have with one accord decided to choose representatives and to send them to you along with our beloved Barnabas and Paul, ²⁶who have dedicated their lives to the name of our Lord Jesus Christ. ²⁷So we are sending Judas and Silas who will also convey this same message by word of mouth: ²⁸'It is the decision of the Holy Spirit and of us not to place on you any burden beyond these necessities, ²⁹namely, to abstain from meat sacrificed to idols, from blood, from meats of strangled animals, and from unlawful marriage. If you keep free of these, you will be doing what is right. Farewell.'"

³⁰And so they were sent on their journey. Upon their arrival in Antioch they called the assembly together and delivered the letter. ³¹When the people read it, they were delighted with the exhortation.

Responsorial Psalm: Psalms 57:8-9, 10-12

R. ⁽¹⁰ᵃ⁾ *I will give you thanks among the peoples, O Lord.* or: R. *Alleluia.*

⁸My heart is steadfast, O God; my heart is
    steadfast;
  I will sing and chant praise.
⁹ Awake, O my soul; awake, lyre and harp!
  I will wake the dawn.

R. *I will give you thanks among the peoples, O Lord.* or: R. *Alleluia.*

¹⁰ I will give thanks to you among the peoples,
    O LORD,
  I will chant your praise among the nations.
¹¹ For your mercy towers to the heavens,
  and your faithfulness to the skies.
¹² Be exalted above the heavens, O God;
  above all the earth be your glory!

R. *I will give you thanks among the peoples, O Lord.* or: R. *Alleluia.*

Alleluia: John 15:15B

R. Alleluia, alleluia.
¹⁵ᴮ I call you my friends, says the Lord,
For I have made known to you all that the
    Father has told me.
R. Alleluia, alleluia.

Gospel: John 15:12-17

¹²Jesus said to his disciples: "This is my commandment: love one another as I love you. ¹³No one has greater love than this, to lay down one's life for one's friends.

[14]You are my friends if you do what I command you. [15] I no longer call you slaves, because a slave does not know what his master is doing. I have called you friends, because I have told you everything I have heard from my Father. [16]It was not you who chose me, but I who chose you and appointed you to go and bear fruit that will remain, so that whatever you ask the Father in my name he may give you. [17]This I command you: love one another."

Saturday May 24, 2025
Saturday of the Fifth Week of Easter

First Reading: Acts 16:1-10

[1] Paul reached also Derbe and Lystra where there was a disciple named Timothy, the son of a Jewish woman who was a believer, but his father was a Greek. [2] The brothers in Lystra and Iconium spoke highly of him, [3] and Paul wanted him to come along with him. On account of the Jews of that region, Paul had him circumcised, for they all knew that his father was a Greek. [4] As they traveled from city to city, they handed on to the people for observance the decisions reached by the Apostles and presbyters in Jerusalem. [5] Day after day the churches grew stronger in faith and increased in number.

[6] They travelled through the Phrygian and Galatian territory because they had been prevented by the Holy Spirit from preaching the message in the province of Asia. [7] When they came to Mysia, they tried to go on into Bithynia, but the Spirit of Jesus did not allow them, [8] so they crossed through Mysia and came down to Troas. [9] During the night Paul had a vision. A Macedonian stood before him and implored him with these words, "Come over to Macedonia and help us." [10] When he had seen the vision, we sought passage to Macedonia at once, concluding that God had called us to proclaim the Good News to them.

Responsorial Psalm: Psalms 100:1B-2, 3, 5

R. [(2a)] *Let all the earth cry out to God with joy.* or: *Alleluia.*
[1B] Sing joyfully to the LORD, all you lands;
    [2] serve the LORD with gladness;
    come before him with joyful song.
R. Let all the earth cry out to God with joy. or: *Alleluia.*
[3] Know that the LORD is God;
    he made us, his we are;
    his people, the flock he tends.
R. Let all the earth cry out to God with joy. or: *Alleluia.*
[5] The LORD is good:
    his kindness endures forever,
    and his faithfulness, to all generations.
R. Let all the earth cry out to God with joy. or: *Alleluia.*

Alleluia: Colossians 3:1
R. Alleluia, alleluia.
[1] If then you were raised with Christ,

seek what is above,
where Christ is seated at the right hand of
>God.
R. Alleluia, alleluia.

Gospel: John 15:18-21

¹⁸ Jesus said to his disciples: "If the world hates you, realize that it hated me first. ¹⁹ If you belonged to the world, the world would love its own; but because you do not belong to the world, and I have chosen you out of the world, the world hates you. ²⁰ Remember the word I spoke to you, 'No slave is greater than his master.' If they persecuted me, they will also persecute you. If they kept my word, they will also keep yours. ²¹ And they will do all these things to you on account of my name, because they do not know the one who sent me."

Sunday May 25, 2025
Sixth Sunday of Easter, Year C

First Reading: Acts 15:1-2, 22-29

¹Some who had come down from Judea were instructing the brothers, "Unless you are circumcised according to the Mosaic practice, you cannot be saved." ² Because there arose no little dissension and debate by Paul and Barnabas with them, it was decided that Paul, Barnabas, and some of the others should go up to Jerusalem to the apostles and elders about this question.

²²The apostles and elders, in agreement with the whole church, decided to choose representatives and to send them to Antioch with Paul and Barnabas. The ones chosen were Judas, who was called Barsabbas, and Silas, leaders among the brothers. ²³This is the letter delivered by them:

"The apostles and the elders, your brothers, to the brothers in Antioch, Syria, and Cilicia of Gentile origin: greetings. ²⁴Since we have heard that some of our number who went out without any mandate from us have upset you with their teachings and disturbed your peace of mind, ²⁵we have with one accord decided to choose representatives and to send them to you along with our beloved Barnabas and Paul, ²⁶who have dedicated their lives to the name of our Lord Jesus Christ. ²⁷So we are sending Judas and Silas who will also convey this same message by word of mouth: ²⁸'It is the decision of the Holy Spirit and of us not to place on you any burden beyond these necessities, ²⁹namely, to abstain from meat sacrificed to idols, from blood, from meats of strangled animals, and from unlawful marriage. If you keep free of these, you will be doing what is right. Farewell.'"

Responsorial Psalm: Psalms 67:2-3, 5, 6, 8

R. ⁽⁴⁾ O God, let all the nations praise you! or: *R. Alleluia.*
² May God have pity on us and bless us;
>may he let his face shine upon us.
³ So may your way be known upon earth;
>among all nations, your salvation.
R. O God, let all the nations praise you! or: *R. Alleluia.*
⁵ May the nations be glad and exult
>because you rule the peoples in equity;

the nations on the earth you guide.
R. *O God, let all the nations praise you!* or: **R. *Alleluia.***
⁶ May the peoples praise you, O God;
> may all the peoples praise you!
⁸ May God bless us,
> and may all the ends of the earth fear
>> him!

R. *O God, let all the nations praise you!* or: **R. *Alleluia.***

Second Reading: Revelation 21:10-14, 22-23

¹⁰The angel took me in spirit to a great, high mountain and showed me the holy city Jerusalem coming down out of heaven from God. ¹¹ It gleamed with the splendor of God. Its radiance was like that of a precious stone, like a jasper, clear as crystal. ¹² It had a massive, high wall, with twelve gates where twelve angels were stationed and on which names were inscribed, the names of the twelve tribes of the Israelites. ¹³There were three gates facing east, three north, three south, and three west. ¹⁴The wall of the city had twelve courses of stones as its foundation, on which were inscribed the twelve names of the twelve apostles of the Lamb.

²²I saw no temple in the city for its temple is the Lord God Almighty and the Lamb. ²³The city had no need of sun or moon to shine on it, for the glory of God gave it light, and its lamp was the Lamb.

Alleluia: John 14:23

R. Alleluia, alleluia.
²³ Whoever loves me will keep my word,
> says the Lord,
and my Father will love him and we will
> come to him.

R. Alleluia, alleluia.

Gospel: John 14:23-29

²³Jesus said to his disciples: "Whoever loves me will keep my word, and my Father will love him, and we will come to him and make our dwelling with him. ²⁴Whoever does not love me does not keep my words, yet the word you hear is not mine but that of the Father who sent me.

²⁵ "I have told you this while I am with you. ²⁶The Advocate, the Holy Spirit, whom the Father will send in my name, will teach you everything and remind you of all that I told you. ²⁷Peace I leave with you; my peace I give to you. Not as the world gives do I give it to you. Do not let your hearts be troubled or afraid. ²⁸You heard me tell you, 'I am going away and I will come back to you.' If you loved me, you would rejoice that I am going to the Father; for the Father is greater than I. ²⁹And now I have told you this before it happens, so that when it happens you may believe."

Monday May 26, 2025
Memorial of Saint Philip Neri, Priest

First Reading: Acts 16:11-15

¹¹ We set sail from Troas, making a straight run for Samothrace, and on the next day to Neapolis, ¹² and from there to Philippi, a leading city in that district of Macedonia and a Roman colony. We spent some time in that city. ¹³ On the sabbath we went outside the city gate along the river where we thought there would be a place of prayer. We sat and spoke with the women who had gathered there. ¹⁴ One of them, a woman named Lydia, a dealer in purple cloth, from the city of Thyatira, a worshiper of God, listened, and the Lord opened her heart to pay attention to what Paul was saying. ¹⁵ After she and her household had been baptized, she offered us an invitation, "If you consider me a believer in the Lord, come and stay at my home," and she prevailed on us.

Responsorial Psalm: Psalms 149:1B-2, 3-4, 5-6A AND 9B

R. (see 4a) *The Lord takes delight in his people.* or: *Alleluia.*

¹ᴮ Sing to the LORD a new song
> of praise in the assembly of the faithful.

² Let Israel be glad in their maker,
> let the children of Zion rejoice in their
>> king.

R. *The Lord takes delight in his people.* or: *Alleluia.*

³ Let them praise his name in the festive
> dance,
> let them sing praise to him with timbrel
>> and harp.

⁴ For the LORD loves his people,
> and he adorns the lowly with victory.

R. *The Lord takes delight in his people.* or: *Alleluia.*

⁵ Let the faithful exult in glory;
> let them sing for joy upon their couches.

⁶ᴬ Let the high praises of God be in their
> throats.

⁹ᴮ This is the glory of all his faithful.
> Alleluia.

R. *The Lord takes delight in his people.* or: *Alleluia.*

Alleluia: John 15:26B, 27A

R. Alleluia, alleluia.

²⁶ᴮ The Spirit of truth will testify to me, says the
> Lord,

²⁷ᴬ and you also will testify.

R. Alleluia, alleluia.

Gospel: John 15:26-16:4A

26 Jesus said to his disciples: "When the Advocate comes whom I will send you from the Father, the Spirit of truth who proceeds from the Father, he will testify to me. 27 And you also testify, because you have been with me from the beginning.

1 "I have told you this so that you may not fall away. 2 They will expel you from the synagogues; in fact, the hour is coming when everyone who kills you will think he is offering worship to God. 3 They will do this because they have not known either the Father or me. 4A I have told you this so that when their hour comes you may remember that I told you."

Tuesday May 27, 2025
Tuesday of the Sixth Week of Easter

First Reading: Acts 16:22-34

22 The crowd in Philippi joined in the attack on Paul and Silas, and the magistrates had them stripped and ordered them to be beaten with rods. 23 After inflicting many blows on them, they threw them into prison and instructed the jailer to guard them securely. 24 When he received these instructions, he put them in the innermost cell and secured their feet to a stake.

25 About midnight, while Paul and Silas were praying and singing hymns to God as the prisoners listened, 26 there was suddenly such a severe earthquake that the foundations of the jail shook; all the doors flew open, and the chains of all were pulled loose. 27 When the jailer woke up and saw the prison doors wide open, he drew his sword and was about to kill himself, thinking that the prisoners had escaped. 28 But Paul shouted out in a loud voice, "Do no harm to yourself; we are all here." 29 He asked for a light and rushed in and, trembling with fear, he fell down before Paul and Silas. 30 Then he brought them out and said, "Sirs, what must I do to be saved?" 31 And they said, "Believe in the Lord Jesus and you and your household will be saved." 32 So they spoke the word of the Lord to him and to everyone in his house. 33 He took them in at that hour of the night and bathed their wounds; then he and all his family were baptized at once. 34 He brought them up into his house and provided a meal and with his household rejoiced at having come to faith in God.

Responsorial Psalm: Psalms 138:1-2AB, 2CDE-3, 7C-8

R. (7c) *Your right hand saves me, O Lord.* or: *Alleluia.*

1 I will give thanks to you, O LORD, with all my
    heart,
  for you have heard the words of my
    mouth;
  in the presence of the angels I will sing
    your praise;
2AB I will worship at your holy temple,
  and give thanks to your name.

R. *Your right hand saves me, O Lord.* or: *Alleluia.*

2CDE Because of your kindness and your truth,
  you have made great above all things

your name and your promise.
³ When I called, you answered me;
   you built up strength within me.
R. Your right hand saves me, O Lord. or: ***Alleluia.***
⁷ᶜ Your right hand saves me.
⁸ The LORD will complete what he has done for
      me;
   your kindness, O LORD, endures forever;
   forsake not the work of your hands.
R. Your right hand saves me, O Lord. or: ***Alleluia.***

Alleluia: cf. John 16:7, 13
R. Alleluia, alleluia.
⁷ I will send to you the Spirit of truth, says the
         Lord;
¹³ he will guide you to all truth.
R. Alleluia, alleluia.

Gospel: John 16:5-11
⁵ Jesus said to his disciples: "Now I am going to the one who sent me, and not one of you asks me, 'Where are you going?' ⁶ But because I told you this, grief has filled your hearts. ⁷ But I tell you the truth, it is better for you that I go. For if I do not go, the Advocate will not come to you. But if I go, I will send him to you. ⁸ And when he comes he will convict the world in regard to sin and righteousness and condemnation: ⁹ sin, because they do not believe in me; ¹⁰ righteousness, because I am going to the Father and you will no longer see me; ¹¹ condemnation, because the ruler of this world has been condemned."

Wednesday May 28, 2025
Wednesday of the Sixth Week of Easter

First Reading: Acts 17:15, 22-18:1
¹⁵ After Paul's escorts had taken him to Athens, they came away with instructions for Silas and Timothy to join him as soon as possible.

²² Then Paul stood up at the Areopagus and said: "You Athenians, I see that in every respect you are very religious. ²³ For as I walked around looking carefully at your shrines, I even discovered an altar inscribed, 'To an Unknown God.' What therefore you unknowingly worship, I proclaim to you. ²⁴ The God who made the world and all that is in it, the Lord of heaven and earth, does not dwell in sanctuaries made by human hands, ²⁵ nor is he served by human hands because he needs anything. Rather it is he who gives to everyone life and breath and everything. ²⁶ He made from one the whole human race to dwell on the entire surface of the earth, and he fixed the ordered seasons and the boundaries of their regions, ²⁷ so that people might seek God, even perhaps grope for him and find him, though indeed he is not far from any one of us. ²⁸ For 'In him, we live and move and have our being,' as even some of your poets have said, 'For we too are his

offspring.' [29] Since therefore we are the offspring of God, we ought not to think that the divinity is like an image fashioned from gold, silver, or stone by human art and imagination. [30] God has overlooked the times of ignorance, but now he demands that all people everywhere repent [31] because he has established a day on which he will 'judge the world with justice' through a man, he has appointed, and he has provided confirmation for all by raising him from the dead."

[32] When they heard about resurrection of the dead, some began to scoff, but others said, "We should like to hear you on this some other time." [33] And so Paul left them. [34] But some did join him, and became believers. Among them were Dionysius, a member of the Court of the Areopagus, a woman named Damaris, and others with them.

[1] After this he left Athens and went to Corinth.

Responsorial Psalm: Psalms 148:1-2, 11-12, 13, 14
R. Heaven and earth are full of your glory. or: *Alleluia.*
[1] Praise the LORD from the heavens;
>praise him in the heights.

[2] Praise him, all you his angels;
>praise him, all you his hosts.

R. Heaven and earth are full of your glory. or: *Alleluia.*
[11] Let the kings of the earth and all peoples,
>the princes and all the judges of the
>>earth,

[12] Young men too, and maidens,
>old men and boys.

R. Heaven and earth are full of your glory. or: *Alleluia.*
[13] Praise the name of the LORD,
>for his name alone is exalted;

His majesty is above earth and heaven.

R. Heaven and earth are full of your glory. or: *Alleluia.*
[14] He has lifted up the horn of his people;
Be this his praise from all his faithful ones,
>from the children of Israel, the people
>>close to him.

Alleluia.
R. Heaven and earth are full of your glory. or: *Alleluia.*

Alleluia: John 14:16
R. Alleluia, alleluia.
[16] I will ask the Father
and he will give you another Advocate
to be with you always.
R. Alleluia, alleluia.

Gospel: John 16:12-15

Jesus said to his disciples: [12] "I have much more to tell you, but you cannot bear it now. [13] But when he comes, the Spirit of truth, he will guide you to all truth. He will not speak on his own, but he will speak what he hears, and will declare to you the things that are coming. [14] He will glorify me, because he will take from what is mine and declare it to you. [15] Everything that the Father has is mine; for this reason I told you that he will take from what is mine and declare it to you."

Thursday May 29, 2025
Thursday before Ascension Sunday

First Reading: Acts 18:1-8

[1] Paul left Athens and went to Corinth. [2] There he met a Jew named Aquila, a native of Pontus, who had recently come from Italy with his wife Priscilla because Claudius had ordered all the Jews to leave Rome. He went to visit them [3] and, because he practised the same trade, stayed with them and worked, for they were tentmakers by trade. [4] Every sabbath, he entered into discussions in the synagogue, attempting to convince both Jews and Greeks.

[5] When Silas and Timothy came down from Macedonia, Paul began to occupy himself totally with preaching the word, testifying to the Jews that the Christ was Jesus. [6] When they opposed him and reviled him, he shook out his garments and said to them, "Your blood be on your heads! I am clear of responsibility. From now on I will go to the Gentiles." [7] So he left there and went to a house belonging to a man named Titus Justus, a worshiper of God; his house was next to a synagogue. [8] Crispus, the synagogue official, came to believe in the Lord along with his entire household, and many of the Corinthians who heard believed and were baptized.

Responsorial Psalm: Psalms 98:1, 2-3AB, 3CD-4

R. (see 2b) **The Lord has revealed to the nations his saving power.** or: **Alleluia.**

[1] Sing to the LORD a new song,
    for he has done wondrous deeds;
His right hand has won victory for him,
    his holy arm.

R. The Lord has revealed to the nations his saving power. or: **Alleluia.**

[2] The LORD has made his salvation known:
    in the sight of the nations he has revealed
        his justice.
3AB He has remembered his kindness and his
        faithfulness
    toward the house of Israel.

R. The Lord has revealed to the nations his saving power. or: **Alleluia.**

3CD All the ends of the earth have seen
    the salvation by our God.

⁴ Sing joyfully to the LORD, all you lands;
　　break into song; sing praise.
**R. The Lord has revealed to the nations his
　　saving power.** or: **Alleluia.**

Alleluia: John 14:18
R. Alleluia, alleluia.
¹⁵ I will not leave you orphans, says the Lord;
I will come back to you, and your hearts will
　　rejoice.
R. Alleluia, alleluia.

Gospel: John 16:16-20
¹⁶ Jesus said to his disciples: "A little while and you will no longer see me, and again a little while later and you will see me." ¹⁷ So some of his disciples said to one another, "What does this mean that he is saying to us, 'A little while and you will not see me, and again a little while and you will see me,' and 'Because I am going to the Father'?" ¹⁸ So they said, "What is this 'little while' of which he speaks? We do not know what he means." ¹⁹ Jesus knew that they wanted to ask him, so he said to them, "Are you discussing with one another what I said, 'A little while and you will not see me, and again a little while and you will see me'? ²⁰ Amen, amen, I say to you, you will weep and mourn, while the world rejoices; you will grieve, but your grief will become joy."

Friday May 30, 2025
Friday before Ascension Sunday
First Reading: Acts 18:9-18
⁹ One night while Paul was in Corinth, the Lord said to him in a vision, "Do not be afraid. Go on speaking, and do not be silent, ¹⁰ for I am with you. No one will attack and harm you, for I have many people in this city." ¹¹He settled there for a year and a half and taught the word of God among them.
　¹² But when Gallio was proconsul of Achaia, the Jews rose up together against Paul and brought him to the tribunal, ¹³ saying, "This man is inducing people to worship God contrary to the law." ¹⁴ When Paul was about to reply, Gallio spoke to the Jews, "If it were a matter of some crime or malicious fraud, I should with reason hear the complaint of you Jews; ¹⁵ but since it is a question of arguments over doctrine and titles and your own law, see to it yourselves. I do not wish to be a judge of such matters." ¹⁶ And he drove them away from the tribunal. ¹⁷ They all seized Sosthenes, the synagogue official, and beat him in full view of the tribunal. But none of this was of concern to Gallio.
　¹⁸ Paul remained for quite some time, and after saying farewell to the brothers he sailed for Syria, together with Priscilla and Aquila. At Cenchreae he had shaved his head because he had taken a vow.

Responsorial Psalm: Psalms 47:2-3, 4-5, 6-7
R. *(8a) God is king of all the earth.* or: *Alleluia.*
2 All you peoples, clap your hands,
   shout to God with cries of gladness,
3 For the LORD, the Most High, the awesome,
   is the great king over all the earth.
R. God is king of all the earth. or: *Alleluia.*
4 He brings people under us;
   nations under our feet.
5 He chooses for us our inheritance,
   the glory of Jacob, whom he loves.
R. God is king of all the earth. or: *Alleluia.*
6 God mounts his throne amid shouts of joy;
   the LORD, amid trumpet blasts.
7 Sing praise to God, sing praise;
   sing praise to our king, sing praise.
R. God is king of all the earth. or: *Alleluia.*

Alleluia: cf. Luke 24:46, 26
R. Alleluia, alleluia.
46 Christ had to suffer and to rise from the dead,
26 and so enter into his glory.
R. Alleluia, alleluia.

Gospel: John 16:20-23
20 Jesus said to his disciples: "Amen, amen, I say to you, you will weep and mourn, while the world rejoices; you will grieve, but your grief will become joy. 21 When a woman is in labor, she is in anguish because her hour has arrived; but when she has given birth to a child, she no longer remembers the pain because of her joy that a child has been born into the world. 22 So you also are now in anguish. But I will see you again, and your hearts will rejoice, and no one will take your joy away from you. 23 On that day you will not question me about anything. Amen, amen, I say to you, whatever you ask the Father in my name he will give you."

Saturday May 31, 2025
Feast of Visitation of the Blessed Virgin Mary

First Reading: Zephaniah 3:14-18A
14 Shout for joy, O daughter Zion!
   Sing joyfully, O Israel!
Be glad and exult with all your heart,
   O daughter Jerusalem!
15 The LORD has removed the judgment
      against you,
   he has turned away your enemies;
The King of Israel, the LORD, is in your

midst,
you have no further misfortune to fear.

ⁱ⁶ On that day, it shall be said to Jerusalem:
Fear not, O Zion, be not discouraged!
¹⁷ The LORD, your God, is in your midst,
a mighty savior;
He will rejoice over you with gladness,
and renew you in his love,
He will sing joyfully because of you,
¹⁸ᴬ as one sings at festivals.

Or Romans 12:9-16

⁹ Brothers and sisters: Let love be sincere; hate what is evil, hold on to what is good; ¹⁰ love one another with mutual affection; anticipate one another in showing honor. ¹¹Do not grow slack in zeal, be fervent in spirit, serve the Lord. ¹² Rejoice in hope, endure in affliction, persevere in prayer. ¹³Contribute to the needs of the holy ones, exercise hospitality. ¹⁴ Bless those who persecute you, bless and do not curse them. ¹⁵ Rejoice with those who rejoice, weep with those who weep. ¹⁶ Have the same regard for one another; do not be haughty but associate with the lowly; do not be wise in your own estimation.

Responsorial Psalm: Isaiah 12:2-3, 4BCD, 5-6

R.⁽⁶⁾ Among you is the great and Holy One of Israel.

² God indeed is my savior;
I am confident and unafraid.
My strength and my courage is the LORD,
and he has been my savior.
³ With joy you will draw water
at the fountain of salvation.

R. Among you is the great and Holy One of Israel.

⁴ᴮᶜᴰ Give thanks to the LORD, acclaim his name;
among the nations make known his deeds,
proclaim how exalted is his name.

R. Among you is the great and Holy One of Israel.

⁵Sing praise to the LORD for his glorious achievement;
let this be known throughout all the earth.
⁶ Shout with exultation, O city of Zion,

for great in your midst
is the Holy One of Israel!
R. Among you is the great and Holy One of Israel.

Alleluia: cf. Luke 1:45
R. Alleluia, alleluia.
45 Blessed are you, O Virgin Mary, who believed
that what was spoken to you by the Lord would be fulfilled.
R. Alleluia, alleluia.

Gospel: Luke 1:39-56
39 Mary set out and travelled to the hill country in haste to a town of Judah, 40 where she entered the house of Zechariah and greeted Elizabeth. 41 When Elizabeth heard Mary's greeting, the infant leaped in her womb, and Elizabeth, filled with the Holy Spirit, 42 cried out in a loud voice and said, "Most blessed are you among women, and blessed is the fruit of your womb. 43 And how does this happen to me, that the mother of my Lord should come to me? 44 For at the moment the sound of your greeting reached my ears, the infant in my womb leaped for joy. 45 Blessed are you who believed that what was spoken to you by the Lord would be fulfilled."

46 And Mary said:

"My soul proclaims the greatness of the Lord;
47 my spirit rejoices in God my Savior,
48 for he has looked with favor on his lowly servant.
From this day all generations will call me blessed:
49 the Almighty has done great things for me,
and holy is his Name.
50 He has mercy on those who fear him
in every generation.
51 He has shown the strength of his arm,
he has scattered the proud in their conceit.
52 He has cast down the mighty from their thrones,
and has lifted up the lowly.
53 He has filled the hungry with good things,
and the rich he has sent away empty.
54 He has come to the help of his servant Israel

for he has remembered his promise of
> mercy,
⁵⁵the promise he made to our fathers,
to Abraham and his children for ever."

⁵⁶ Mary remained with her about three months and then returned to her home.

JUNE 2025
Sunday June 1, 2025
Solemnity of the Ascension of the Lord

First Reading: Acts 1:1-11

¹ In the first book, Theophilus, I dealt with all that Jesus did and taught ² until the day he was taken up, after giving instructions through the Holy Spirit to the apostles whom he had chosen. ³ He presented himself alive to them by many proofs after he had suffered, appearing to them during forty days and speaking about the kingdom of God. ⁴ While meeting with them, he enjoined them not to depart from Jerusalem, but to wait for "the promise of the Father about which you have heard me speak; ⁵ for John baptized with water, but in a few days you will be baptized with the Holy Spirit."

⁶ When they had gathered together they asked him, "Lord, are you at this time going to restore the kingdom to Israel?" ⁷ He answered them, "It is not for you to know the times or seasons that the Father has established by his own authority. ⁸ But you will receive power when the Holy Spirit comes upon you, and you will be my witnesses in Jerusalem, throughout Judea and Samaria, and to the ends of the earth." ⁹ When he had said this, as they were looking on, he was lifted up, and a cloud took him from their sight. ¹⁰ While they were looking intently at the sky as he was going, suddenly two men dressed in white garments stood beside them. ¹¹ They said, "Men of Galilee, why are you standing there looking at the sky? This Jesus who has been taken up from you into heaven will return in the same way as you have seen him going into heaven."

Responsorial Psalm: Psalms 47:2-3, 6-7, 8-9

R. ⁽⁶⁾ **God mounts his throne to shouts of joy: a blare of trumpets for the Lord.**
or: **Alleluia.**

² All you peoples, clap your hands,
> shout to God with cries of gladness,
³ For the LORD, the Most High, the awesome,
> is the great king over all the earth.

R. **God mounts his throne to shouts of joy: a blare of trumpets for the Lord.**
or: **Alleluia.**

⁶ God mounts his throne amid shouts of joy;
> the LORD, amid trumpet blasts.
⁷ Sing praise to God, sing praise;

sing praise to our king, sing praise.
***R. God mounts his throne to shouts of joy: a
    blare of trumpets for the Lord.***
or: ***Alleluia.***
[8] For king of all the earth is God;
    sing hymns of praise.
[9] God reigns over the nations,
    God sits upon his holy throne.
***R. God mounts his throne to shouts of joy: a
    blare of trumpets for the Lord.***
or: ***Alleluia.***

Second Reading: Ephesians 1:17-23

Brothers and sisters: [17] May the God of our Lord Jesus Christ, the Father of glory, give you a Spirit of wisdom and revelation resulting in knowledge of him. [18] May the eyes of your hearts be enlightened, that you may know what is the hope that belongs to his call, what are the riches of glory in his inheritance among the holy ones, [19] and what is the surpassing greatness of his power for us who believe, in accord with the exercise of his great might, [20] which he worked in Christ, raising him from the dead and seating him at his right hand in the heavens, [21] far above every principality, authority, power, and dominion, and every name that is named not only in this age but also in the one to come. [22] And he put all things beneath his feet and gave him as head over all things to the church, which is his body, the fullness of the one who fills all things in every way.

Hebrews 9:24-28; 10:19-23

[24] For Christ did not enter into a sanctuary made by hands, a copy of the true one, but heaven itself, that he might now appear before God on our behalf. [25] Not that he might offer himself repeatedly, as the high priest enters each year into the sanctuary with blood that is not his own; [26] if that were so, he would have had to suffer repeatedly from the foundation of the world. But now once for all he has appeared at the end of the ages to take away sin by his sacrifice. [27] Just as it is appointed that human beings die once, and after this the judgment, [28] so also Christ, offered once to take away the sins of many, will appear a second time, not to take away sin but to bring salvation to those who eagerly await him. [19] Therefore, brothers, since through the blood of Jesus we have confidence of entrance into the sanctuary [20] by the new and living way he opened for us through the veil, that is, his flesh, [21] and since we have "a great priest over the house of God," [22] let us approach with a sincere heart and in absolute trust, with our hearts sprinkled clean from an evil conscience and our bodies washed in pure water. [23] Let us hold unwaveringly to our confession that gives us hope, for he who made the promise is trustworthy.

Alleluia: Matthew 28:19A, 20B
R. Alleluia, alleluia.
[19A] Go and teach all nations, says the Lord;
[20B] I am with you always, until the end of the

world.
R. Alleluia, alleluia.

Gospel: Luke 24:46-53
⁴⁶Jesus said to his disciples: "Thus it is written that the Christ would suffer and rise from the dead on the third day ⁴⁷and that repentance, for the forgiveness of sins, would be preached in his name to all the nations, beginning from Jerusalem. ⁴⁸You are witnesses of these things. ⁴⁹And behold I am sending the promise of my Father upon you; but stay in the city until you are clothed with power from on high."
⁵⁰Then he led them out as far as Bethany, raised his hands, and blessed them. ⁵¹As he blessed them he parted from them and was taken up to heaven. ⁵²They did him homage and then returned to Jerusalem with great joy, ⁵³ and they were continually in the temple praising God.

Monday June 2, 2025
Monday of the Seventh Week of Easter

First Reading: Acts 19:1-8
¹ While Apollos was in Corinth, Paul traveled through the interior of the country and down to Ephesus where he found some disciples. ² He said to them, "Did you receive the Holy Spirit when you became believers?" They answered him, "We have never even heard that there is a Holy Spirit." ³ He said, "How were you baptized?" They replied, "With the baptism of John." ⁴ Paul then said, "John baptized with a baptism of repentance, telling the people to believe in the one who was to come after him, that is, in Jesus." ⁵ When they heard this, they were baptized in the name of the Lord Jesus. ⁶ And when Paul laid his hands on them, the Holy Spirit came upon them, and they spoke in tongues and prophesied. ⁷ Altogether there were about twelve men.
⁸ He entered the synagogue, and for three months debated boldly with persuasive arguments about the Kingdom of God.

Responsorial Psalm: Psalms 68:2-3AB, 4-5ACD, 6-7AB
R.⁽³³ᵃ⁾ ***Sing to God, O kingdoms of the earth.*** or: ***Alleluia.***
² God arises; his enemies are scattered,
    and those who hate him flee before him.
³ᴬᴮ As smoke is driven away, so are they driven;
    as wax melts before the fire.
R. *Sing to God, O kingdoms of the earth.* or: ***Alleluia.***
⁴ But the just rejoice and exult before God;
    they are glad and rejoice.
⁵ᴬᶜᴰ Sing to God, chant praise to his name;
    whose name is the LORD.
R. *Sing to God, O kingdoms of the earth.* or: ***Alleluia.***
⁶ The father of orphans and the defender of
    widows
    is God in his holy dwelling.
⁷ᴬᴮ God gives a home to the forsaken;

he leads forth prisoners to prosperity.
R. Sing to God, O kingdoms of the earth. or: **Alleluia.**

Alleluia: Colossians 3:1
R. Alleluia, alleluia.
¹ If then you were raised with Christ,
seek what is above,
where Christ is seated at the right hand of
    God.
R. Alleluia, alleluia.

Gospel: John 16:29-33
²⁹ The disciples said to Jesus, "Now you are talking plainly, and not in any figure of speech. ³⁰ Now we realize that you know everything and that you do not need to have anyone question you. Because of this, we believe that you came from God." ³¹ Jesus answered them, "Do you believe now? ³² Behold, the hour is coming and has arrived when each of you will be scattered to his own home and you will leave me alone. But I am not alone, because the Father is with me. ³³ I have told you this so that you might have peace in me. In the world you will have trouble, but take courage, I have conquered the world."

Tuesday June 3, 2025
Memorial of Saints Charles Lwanga and his Companions, Martyrs
First Reading: Acts 20:17-27
¹⁷From Miletus Paul had the presbyters of the Church at Ephesus summoned. ¹⁸When they came to him, he addressed them, "You know how I lived among you the whole time from the day I first came to the province of Asia. ¹⁹I served the Lord with all humility and with the tears and trials that came to me because of the plots of the Jews, ²⁰and I did not at all shrink from telling you what was for your benefit, or from teaching you in public or in your homes. ²¹I earnestly bore witness for both Jews and Greeks to repentance before God and to faith in our Lord Jesus. ²²But now, compelled by the Spirit, I am going to Jerusalem. What will happen to me there I do not know, ²³except that in one city after another the Holy Spirit has been warning me that imprisonment and hardships await me. ²⁴Yet I consider life of no importance to me, if only I may finish my course and the ministry that I received from the Lord Jesus, to bear witness to the Gospel of God's grace.

    ²⁵"But now I know that none of you to whom I preached the kingdom during my travels will ever see my face again. ²⁶And so I solemnly declare to you this day that I am not responsible for the blood of any of you, ²⁷for I did not shrink from proclaiming to you the entire plan of God."

Responsorial Psalm: Psalms 68:10-11, 20-21
R. ⁽³³ᵃ⁾ **Sing to God, O kingdoms of the earth.** or: **R. Alleluia.**
¹⁰ A bountiful rain you showered down, O God,
    upon your inheritance;
    you restored the land when it languished;

[11] Your flock settled in it;
>in your goodness, O God, you provided it
>>for the needy.

R. Sing to God, O kingdoms of the earth. or: R. Alleluia.

[20] Blessed day by day be the Lord,
>who bears our burdens; God, who is our
>>salvation.

[21] God is a saving God for us;
>the LORD, my Lord, controls the
>>passageways of death.

R. Sing to God, O kingdoms of the earth. or: R. Alleluia.

Alleluia: John 14:16
R. Alleluia, alleluia.
[16] I will ask the Father
and he will give you another Advocate
to be with you always.
R. Alleluia, alleluia.

Gospel: John 17:1-11A

[1] Jesus raised his eyes to heaven and said, "Father, the hour has come. Give glory to your son, so that your son may glorify you, [2] just as you gave him authority over all people, so that your son may give eternal life to all you gave him. [3] Now, this is eternal life, that they should know you, the only true God, and the one whom you sent, Jesus Christ. [4] I glorified you on earth by accomplishing the work that you gave me to do. [5] Now glorify me, Father, with you, with the glory that I had with you before the world began.

[6] "I revealed your name to those whom you gave me out of the world. They belonged to you, and you gave them to me, and they have kept your word. [7] Now they know that everything you gave me is from you, [8] because the words you gave to me I have given to them, and they accepted them and truly understood that I came from you, and they have believed that you sent me. [9] I pray for them. I do not pray for the world but for the ones you have given me, because they are yours, and everything of mine is yours [10] and everything of yours is mine, and I have been glorified in them. [11A] And now I will no longer be in the world, but they are in the world, while I am coming to you."

Wednesday June 4, 2025
Wednesday of the Seventh Week of Easter
First Reading: Acts 20:28-38

[28] At Miletus, Paul spoke to the presbyters of the Church of Ephesus: "Keep watch over yourselves and over the whole flock of which the Holy Spirit has appointed you overseers, in which you tend the Church of God that he acquired with his own Blood. [29] I know that after my departure savage wolves will come among you, and they will not spare the flock. [30] And from your own group, men will come forward

perverting the truth to draw the disciples away after them. [31] So be vigilant and remember that for three years, night and day, I unceasingly admonished each of you with tears. [32] And now I commend you to God and to that gracious word of his that can build you up and give you the inheritance among all who are consecrated. [33] I have never wanted anyone's silver or gold or clothing. [34] You know well that these very hands have served my needs and my companions. [35] In every way I have shown you that by hard work of that sort we must help the weak, and keep in mind the words of the Lord Jesus who himself said, 'It is more blessed to give than to receive.'"

[36] When he had finished speaking he knelt down and prayed with them all. [37] They were all weeping loudly as they threw their arms around Paul and kissed him, [38] for they were deeply distressed that he had said that they would never see his face again. Then they escorted him to the ship.

Responsorial Psalm: Psalms 68:29-30, 33-35A, 35BC-36AB
R.[33a] *Sing to God, O kingdoms of the earth.* or: *Alleluia.*
[29] Show forth, O God, your power,
    the power, O God, with which you took
        our part;
[30] For your temple in Jerusalem
    let the kings bring you gifts.
R. Sing to God, O Kingdoms of the earth.* or: *Alleluia.
[33] You kingdoms of the earth, sing to God,
    chant praise to the Lord
        [34] who rides on the heights of the ancient
    heavens.
Behold, his voice resounds, the voice of
    power:
    [35A] "Confess the power of God!"
R. Sing to God, O Kingdoms of the earth.* or: *Alleluia.
[35BC] Over Israel is his majesty;
    his power is in the skies.
[36AB] Awesome in his sanctuary is God, the God of
    Israel;
    he gives power and strength to his
        people.
R. Sing to God, O Kingdoms of the earth.* or: *Alleluia.

Alleluia: cf. John 17:17B, 17A
R. Alleluia, alleluia.
Your word, O Lord, is truth;
consecrate us in the truth.
R. Alleluia, alleluia.

Gospel: John 17:11B-19

Lifting up his eyes to heaven, Jesus prayed, saying: [11B] "Holy Father, keep them in your name that you have given me, so that they may be one just as we are one. [12] When I was with them I protected them in your name that you gave me, and I guarded them, and none of them was lost except the son of destruction, in order that the Scripture might be fulfilled. [13] But now I am coming to you. I speak this in the world so that they may share my joy completely. [14] I gave them your word, and the world hated them because they do not belong to the world any more than I belong to the world. [15] I do not ask that you take them out of the world but that you keep them from the Evil One. [16] They do not belong to the world any more than I belong to the world. [17] Consecrate them in the truth. Your word is truth. [18] As you sent me into the world, so I sent them into the world. [19] And I consecrate myself for them, so that they also may be consecrated in truth."

Thursday June 5, 2025
Memorial of Saint Boniface, Bishop & Martyr

First Reading: Acts 22:30; 23:6-11

[30] Wishing to determine the truth about why Paul was being accused by the Jews, the commander freed him and ordered the chief priests and the whole Sanhedrin to convene. Then he brought Paul down and made him stand before them.

[6] Paul was aware that some were Sadducees and some Pharisees, so he called out before the Sanhedrin, "My brothers, I am a Pharisee, the son of Pharisees; I am on trial for hope in the resurrection of the dead." [7] When he said this, a dispute broke out between the Pharisees and Sadducees, and the group became divided. [8] For the Sadducees say that there is no resurrection or angels or spirits, while the Pharisees acknowledge all three. [9] A great uproar occurred, and some scribes belonging to the Pharisee party stood up and sharply argued, "We find nothing wrong with this man. Suppose a spirit or an angel has spoken to him?" [10] The dispute was so serious that the commander, afraid that Paul would be torn to pieces by them, ordered his troops to go down and rescue Paul from their midst and take him into the compound. [11] The following night the Lord stood by him and said, "Take courage. For just as you have borne witness to my cause in Jerusalem, so you must also bear witness in Rome."

Responsorial Psalm: Psalms 16:1-2A AND 5, 7-8, 9-10, 11

R. [(1)] *Keep me safe, O God; you are my hope.* or: *Alleluia.*
[1] Keep me, O God, for in you I take refuge;
    [2A] I say to the LORD, "My Lord are you."
[5] O LORD, my allotted portion and my cup,
    you it is who hold fast my lot.
R. *Keep me safe, O God; you are my hope.* or: *Alleluia.*
[7] I bless the LORD who counsels me;
    even in the night my heart exhorts me.
[8] I set the LORD ever before me;
    with him at my right hand I shall not be
        disturbed.
R. *Keep me safe, O God; you are my hope.* or: *Alleluia.*

⁹ Therefore my heart is glad and my soul
> rejoices,
>> my body, too, abides in confidence;
¹⁰ Because you will not abandon my soul to the
> nether world,
>> nor will you suffer your faithful one to
>> undergo corruption.

R. Keep me safe, O God; you are my hope. or: *Alleluia.*

¹¹ You will show me the path to life,
> fullness of joys in your presence,
> the delights at your right hand forever.

R. Keep me safe, O God; you are my hope. or: *Alleluia.*

Alleluia: John 17:21
R. Alleluia, alleluia.
²¹ May they all be one as you, Father, are in me
> and I in you,
that the world may believe that you sent me,
> says the Lord.

R. Alleluia, alleluia.

Gospel: John 17:20-26
Lifting up his eyes to heaven, Jesus prayed saying: ²⁰ "I pray not only for these but also for those who will believe in me through their word, ²¹ so that they may all be one, as you, Father, are in me and I in you, that they also may be in us, that the world may believe that you sent me. ²² And I have given them the glory you gave me, so that they may be one, as we are one, ²³ I in them and you in me, that they may be brought to perfection as one, that the world may know that you sent me, and that you loved them even as you loved me. ²⁴ Father, they are your gift to me. I wish that where I am they also may be with me, that they may see my glory that you gave me because you loved me before the foundation of the world. ²⁵ Righteous Father, the world also does not know you, but I know you, and they know that you sent me. ²⁶ I made known to them your name and I will make it known, that the love with which you loved me may be in them and I in them."

Friday June 6, 2025
Friday of the Seventh Week of Easter
First Reading: Acts 25:13B-21
¹³ᴮ King Agrippa and Bernice arrived in Caesarea on a visit to Festus. ¹⁴ Since they spent several days there, Festus referred Paul's case to the king, saying, "There is a man here left in custody by Felix. ¹⁵ When I was in Jerusalem the chief priests and the elders of the Jews brought charges against him and demanded his condemnation. ¹⁶ I answered them that it was not Roman practice to hand over an accused person before he has faced his accusers and had the opportunity to defend himself against their charge. ¹⁷ So when they came together here, I made

no delay; the next day I took my seat on the tribunal and ordered the man to be brought in. ¹⁸ His accusers stood around him, but did not charge him with any of the crimes I suspected. ¹⁹ Instead they had some issues with him about their own religion and about a certain Jesus who had died but who Paul claimed was alive. ²⁰ Since I was at a loss on how to investigate this controversy, I asked if he were willing to go to Jerusalem and there stand trial on these charges. ²¹ And when Paul appealed that he be held in custody for the Emperor's decision, I ordered him held until I could send him to Caesar."

Responsorial Psalm: Psalms 103:1-2, 11-12, 19-20AB
R. [19a] ***The Lord has established his throne in heaven.*** or: ***Alleluia.***
¹ Bless the LORD, O my soul;
    and all my being, bless his holy name.
² Bless the LORD, O my soul,
    and forget not all his benefits.
R. *The Lord has established his throne in heaven.* or: ***Alleluia.***
¹¹ For as the heavens are high above the earth,
    so surpassing is his kindness toward
        those who fear him.
¹² As far as the east is from the west,
    so far has he put our transgressions from
        us.
R. *The Lord has established his throne in heaven.* or: ***Alleluia.***
¹⁹ The LORD has established his throne in
    heaven,
    and his kingdom rules over all.
²⁰ᴬᴮ Bless the LORD, all you his angels,
    you mighty in strength, who do his
        bidding.
R. *The Lord has established his throne in heaven.* or: ***Alleluia.***

Alleluia: John 14:26
R. Alleluia, alleluia.
²⁶ The Holy Spirit will teach you everything and remind you of all I told you.
R. Alleluia, alleluia.

Gospel: John 21:15-19
¹⁵ After Jesus had revealed himself to his disciples and eaten breakfast with them, he said to Simon Peter, "Simon, son of John, do you love me more than these?" Simon Peter answered him, "Yes, Lord, you know that I love you." Jesus said to

him, "Feed my lambs." ¹⁶ He then said to Simon Peter a second time, "Simon, son of John, do you love me?" Simon Peter answered him, "Yes, Lord, you know that I love you." He said to him, "Tend my sheep." ¹⁷ He said to him the third time, "Simon, son of John, do you love me?" Peter was distressed that he had said to him a third time, "Do you love me?" and he said to him, "Lord, you know everything; you know that I love you." Jesus said to him, "Feed my sheep. ¹⁸ Amen, amen, I say to you, when you were younger, you used to dress yourself and go where you wanted; but when you grow old, you will stretch out your hands, and someone else will dress you and lead you where you do not want to go." ¹⁹ He said this signifying by what kind of death he would glorify God. And when he had said this, he said to him, "Follow me."

Saturday June 7, 2025
Saturday of the Seventh Week of Easter
First Reading: Acts 28:16-20, 30-31

¹⁶ When he entered Rome, Paul was allowed to live by himself, with the soldier who was guarding him.

¹⁷ Three days later he called together the leaders of the Jews. When they had gathered he said to them, "My brothers, although I had done nothing against our people or our ancestral customs, I was handed over to the Romans as a prisoner from Jerusalem. ¹⁸ After trying my case the Romans wanted to release me, because they found nothing against me deserving the death penalty. ¹⁹ But when the Jews objected, I was obliged to appeal to Caesar, even though I had no accusation to make against my own nation. ²⁰ This is the reason, then, I have requested to see you and to speak with you, for it is on account of the hope of Israel that I wear these chains."

³⁰ He remained for two full years in his lodgings. He received all who came to him, ³¹ and with complete assurance and without hindrance he proclaimed the Kingdom of God and taught about the Lord Jesus Christ.

Responsorial Psalm: Psalms 11:4, 5 AND 7
R. *(see 7b)* ***The just will gaze on your face, O Lord.*** or: ***Alleluia.***
⁴ The LORD is in his holy temple;
    the LORD's throne is in heaven.
His eyes behold,
    his searching glance is on mankind.
R. ***The just will gaze on your face, O Lord.*** or: ***Alleluia.***
⁵ The LORD searches the just and the wicked;
    the lover of violence he hates.
⁷ For the LORD is just, he loves just deeds;
    the upright shall see his face.
R. ***The just will gaze on your face, O Lord.*** or: ***Alleluia.***

Alleluia: John 16:7, 13
R. Alleluia, alleluia.
⁷ I will send to you the Spirit of truth, says the

Lord;
[13] he will guide you to all truth.
R. Alleluia, alleluia.

Gospel: John 21:20-25

[20] Peter turned and saw the disciple following whom Jesus loved, the one who had also reclined upon his chest during the supper and had said, "Master, who is the one who will betray you?" [21] When Peter saw him, he said to Jesus, "Lord, what about him?" [22] Jesus said to him, "What if I want him to remain until I come? What concern is it of yours? You follow me." [23] So the word spread among the brothers that that disciple would not die. But Jesus had not told him that he would not die, just "What if I want him to remain until I come? What concern is it of yours?"

[24] It is this disciple who testifies to these things and has written them, and we know that his testimony is true. [25] There are also many other things that Jesus did, but if these were to be described individually, I do not think the whole world would contain the books that would be written.

Saturday June 7, 2025
Pentecost Vigil

First Reading: Genesis 11:1-9

[1] The whole world spoke the same language, using the same words. [2] While the people were migrating in the east, they came upon a valley in the land of Shinar and settled there. [3] They said to one another, "Come, let us mold bricks and harden them with fire." They used bricks for stone, and bitumen for mortar. [4] Then they said, "Come, let us build ourselves a city and a tower with its top in the sky, and so make a name for ourselves; otherwise we shall be scattered all over the earth."

[5] The LORD came down to see the city and the tower that the people had built. [6] Then the LORD said: "If now, while they are one people, all speaking the same language, they have started to do this, nothing will later stop them from doing whatever they presume to do. [7] Let us then go down there and confuse their language, so that one will not understand what another says." [8] Thus the LORD scattered them from there all over the earth, and they stopped building the city. [9] That is why it was called Babel, because there the LORD confused the speech of all the world. It was from that place that he scattered them all over the earth.

OR Exodus 19:3-8A, 16-20B

[3] Moses went up the mountain to God. Then the LORD called to him and said, "Thus shall you say to the house of Jacob; tell the Israelites: [4] You have seen for yourselves how I treated the Egyptians and how I bore you up on eagle wings and brought you here to myself. [5] Therefore, if you hearken to my voice and keep my covenant, you shall be my special possession, dearer to me than all other people, though all the earth is mine. [6] You shall be to me a kingdom of priests, a holy nation. That is what you must tell the Israelites." [7] So Moses went and summoned the elders of the people. When he set before them all that the LORD had ordered him to tell them, [8A] the people all answered together, "Everything the LORD has said, we will do."

¹⁶ On the morning of the third day there were peals of thunder and lightning, and a heavy cloud over the mountain, and a very loud trumpet blast, so that all the people in the camp trembled. ¹⁷ But Moses led the people out of the camp to meet God, and they stationed themselves at the foot of the mountain. ¹⁸ Mount Sinai was all wrapped in smoke, for the LORD came down upon it in fire. The smoke rose from it as though from a furnace, and the whole mountain trembled violently. ¹⁹ The trumpet blast grew louder and louder, while Moses was speaking, and God answering him with thunder.

²⁰ When the LORD came down to the top of Mount Sinai, he summoned Moses to the top of the mountain.

OR Ezekiel 37:1-14

¹ The hand of the LORD came upon me, and he led me out in the spirit of the LORD and set me in the center of the plain, which was now filled with bones. ² He made me walk among the bones in every direction so that I saw how many they were on the surface of the plain. How dry they were! ³ He asked me: Son of man, can these bones come to life? I answered, "Lord GOD, you alone know that." ⁴ Then he said to me: Prophesy over these bones, and say to them: Dry bones, hear the word of the LORD! ⁵ Thus says the Lord GOD to these bones: See! I will bring spirit into you, that you may come to life. ⁶ I will put sinews upon you, make flesh grow over you, cover you with skin, and put spirit in you so that you may come to life and know that I am the LORD. ⁷ I, Ezekiel, prophesied as I had been told, and even as I was prophesying I heard a noise; it was a rattling as the bones came together, bone joining bone. ⁸ I saw the sinews and the flesh come upon them, and the skin cover them, but there was no spirit in them. ⁹ Then the LORD said to me: Prophesy to the spirit, prophesy, son of man, and say to the spirit: Thus says the Lord GOD: From the four winds come, O spirit, and breathe into these slain that they may come to life. ¹⁰ I prophesied as he told me, and the spirit came into them; they came alive and stood upright, a vast army.¹¹ Then he said to me: Son of man, these bones are the whole house of Israel. They have been saying, "Our bones are dried up, our hope is lost, and we are cut off." ¹² Therefore, prophesy and say to them: Thus says the Lord GOD: O my people, I will open your graves and have you rise from them, and bring you back to the land of Israel. ¹³ Then you shall know that I am the LORD, when I open your graves and have you rise from them, O my people! ¹⁴ I will put my spirit in you that you may live, and I will settle you upon your land; thus you shall know that I am the LORD. I have promised, and I will do it, says the LORD.

OR Joel 3:1-5

¹ Thus says the LORD:

I will pour out my spirit upon all flesh.
Your sons and daughters shall prophesy,
    your old men shall dream dreams,
    your young men shall see visions;
² even upon the servants and the
       handmaids,

in those days, I will pour out my
> spirit.
³ And I will work wonders in the heavens
> and on the earth,
blood, fire, and columns of smoke;
⁴ the sun will be turned to darkness,
> and the moon to blood,
at the coming of the day of the LORD,
> the great and terrible day.
⁵ Then everyone shall be rescued
> who calls on the name of the LORD;
for on Mount Zion there shall be a
> remnant,
> as the LORD has said,
and in Jerusalem survivors
> whom the LORD shall call.

Responsorial Psalm: Psalms 104:1-2,24 AND 35,27-28, 29-30

R. (cf. 30) **Lord, send out your Spirit, and renew the face of the earth.** or: ***Alleluia.***

¹ Bless the LORD, O my soul!
> O LORD, my God, you are great indeed!
² You are clothed with majesty and glory,
> robed in light as with a cloak.

R. Lord, send out your Spirit, and renew the face of the earth. or: ***Alleluia.***

²⁴ How manifold are your works, O LORD!
> In wisdom you have wrought them all—
the earth is full of your creatures;
> ³⁵ᶜ bless the LORD, O my soul! Alleluia.

R. Lord, send out your Spirit, and renew the face of the earth. or: ***Alleluia.***

²⁷ Creatures all look to you
> to give them food in due time.
²⁸ When you give it to them, they gather it;
> when you open your hand, they are filled
> > with good things.

R. Lord, send out your Spirit, and renew the face of the earth. or: ***Alleluia.***

²⁹ If you take away their breath, they perish
> and return to their dust.
³⁰ When you send forth your spirit, they are
> created,
> and you renew the face of the earth.

R. Lord, send out your Spirit, and renew the face of the earth. or: *Alleluia.*

Second Reading: Romans 8:22-27

Brothers and sisters: 22 We know that all creation is groaning in labor pains even until now; 23 and not only that, but we ourselves, who have the first fruits of the Spirit, we also groan within ourselves as we wait for adoption, the redemption of our bodies. 24 For in hope we were saved. Now hope that sees is not hope. For who hopes for what one sees? 25 But if we hope for what we do not see, we wait with endurance.

26 In the same way, the Spirit too comes to the aid of our weakness; for we do not know how to pray as we ought, but the Spirit himself intercedes with inexpressible groanings. 27 And the one who searches hearts knows what is the intention of the Spirit, because he intercedes for the holy ones according to God's will.

Alleluia

R. Alleluia, alleluia.
Come, Holy Spirit, fill the hearts of your
    faithful
and kindle in them the fire of your love.
R. Alleluia, alleluia.

Gospel: John 7:37-39

On the last and greatest day of the feast, 37 Jesus stood up and exclaimed, "Let anyone who thirsts come to me and drink. 38 As Scripture says: *Rivers of living water will flow from within him* who believes in me." 39 He said this in reference to the Spirit that those who came to believe in him were to receive. There was, of course, no Spirit yet, because Jesus had not yet been glorified.

Sunday June 8, 2025
Pentecost Sunday

First Reading: Acts 2:1-11

1 When the time for Pentecost was fulfilled, they were all in one place together. 2 And suddenly there came from the sky a noise like a strong driving wind, and it filled the entire house in which they were. 3 Then there appeared to them tongues as of fire, which parted and came to rest on each one of them. 4 And they were all filled with the Holy Spirit and began to speak in different tongues, as the Spirit enabled them to proclaim.

5 Now there were devout Jews from every nation under heaven staying in Jerusalem. 6 At this sound, they gathered in a large crowd, but they were confused because each one heard them speaking in his own language. 7 They were astounded, and in amazement, they asked, "Are not all these people who are speaking Galileans? 8 Then how does each of us hear them in his native language? 9 We are Parthians, Medes, and Elamites, inhabitants of Mesopotamia, Judea and Cappadocia, Pontus and Asia, 10 Phrygia and Pamphylia, Egypt and the districts of Libya near Cyrene, as well as travelers from Rome, 11 both Jews and converts to Judaism, Cretans and Arabs, yet we hear them speaking in our own tongues of the mighty acts of God."

Responsorial Psalm: Psalms 104:1, 24, 29-30, 31, 34

*R. (cf. 30) **Lord, send out your Spirit, and renew the face of the earth.** or: **Alleluia.***

¹ Bless the LORD, O my soul!
   O LORD, my God, you are great indeed!
²⁴ How manifold are your works, O LORD!
   The earth is full of your creatures;

*R. **Lord, send out your Spirit, and renew the face of the earth.** or: **Alleluia.***

²⁹ If you take away their breath, they perish
   and return to their dust.
³⁰ When you send forth your spirit, they are created,
   and you renew the face of the earth.

*R. **Lord, send out your Spirit, and renew the face of the earth.** or: **Alleluia.***

³¹ May the glory of the LORD endure forever;
   may the LORD be glad in his works!
³⁴ Pleasing to him be my theme;
   I will be glad in the LORD.

*R. **Lord, send out your Spirit, and renew the face of the earth.** or: **Alleluia.***

Second Reading: 1 Corinthians 12:3B-7, 12-13

Brothers and sisters: ³ᴮ No one can say, "Jesus is Lord," except by the Holy Spirit. ⁴ There are different kinds of spiritual gifts but the same Spirit; ⁵ there are different forms of service but the same Lord; ⁶ there are different workings but the same God who produces all of them in everyone. ⁷ To each individual the manifestation of the Spirit is given for some benefit.

¹² As a body is one though it has many parts, and all the parts of the body, though many, are one body, so also Christ. ¹³ For in one Spirit we were all baptized into one body, whether Jews or Greeks, slaves or free persons, and we were all given to drink of one Spirit.

Or Romans 8:8-17

Brothers and sisters: ⁸Those who are in the flesh cannot please God. ⁹But you are not in the flesh; on the contrary, you are in the spirit, if only the Spirit of God dwells in you. Whoever does not have the Spirit of Christ does not belong to him. ¹⁰But if Christ is in you, although the body is dead because of sin, the spirit is alive because of righteousness. ¹¹If the Spirit of the one who raised Jesus from the dead dwells in you, the one who raised Christ from the dead will give life to your mortal bodies also, through his Spirit that dwells in you. ¹²Consequently, brothers and sisters, we are not debtors to the flesh, to live according to the flesh. ¹³For if you live according to the flesh, you will die, but if by the Spirit you put to death the deeds of the body, you will live.

¹⁴For those who are led by the Spirit of God are sons of God. ¹⁵For you did not receive a spirit of slavery to fall back into fear, but you received a Spirit of adoption, through whom we cry, "Abba, Father!" ¹⁶The Spirit himself bears witness with our spirit that we are children of God, ¹⁷and if children, then heirs, heirs of God and joint heirs with Christ, if only we suffer with him so that we may also be glorified with him.

Sequence - *Veni, Sancte Spiritus*
Come, Holy Spirit, come!
And from your celestial home
Shed a ray of light divine!
Come, Father of the poor!
Come, source of all our store!
Come, within our bosoms shine.
You, of comforters the best;
You, the soul's most welcome guest;
Sweet refreshment here below;
In our labor, rest most sweet;
Grateful coolness in the heat;
Solace in the midst of woe.
O most blessed Light divine,
Shine within these hearts of yours,
And our inmost being fill!
Where you are not, we have naught,
Nothing good in deed or thought,
Nothing free from taint of ill.
Heal our wounds, our strength renew;
On our dryness pour your dew;
Wash the stains of guilt away:
Bend the stubborn heart and will;
Melt the frozen, warm the chill;
Guide the steps that go astray.
On the faithful, who adore
And confess you, evermore
In your sevenfold gift descend;
Give them virtue's sure reward;
Give them your salvation, Lord;
Give them joys that never end. Amen.
Alleluia.

Alleluia
R. Alleluia, alleluia.
Come, Holy Spirit, fill the hearts of your

faithful
and kindle in them the fire of your love.
R. Alleluia, alleluia.

Gospel: John 20:19-23
[19] On the evening of that first day of the week, when the doors were locked, where the disciples were, for fear of the Jews, Jesus came and stood in their midst and said to them, "Peace be with you." [20] When he had said this, he showed them his hands and his side. The disciples rejoiced when they saw the Lord. [21] Jesus said to them again, "Peace be with you. As the Father has sent me, so I send you." [22] And when he had said this, he breathed on them and said to them, "Receive the Holy Spirit. [23] Whose sins you forgive are forgiven them, and whose sins you retain are retained."

Or John 14:15-16, 23B-26
Jesus said to his disciples: [15]"If you love me, you will keep my commandments. [16]And I will ask the Father, and he will give you another Advocate to be with you always.

[23B]"Whoever loves me will keep my word, and my Father will love him, and we will come to him and make our dwelling with him. [24]Those who do not love me do not keep my words; yet the word you hear is not mine but that of the Father who sent me.

[25]"I have told you this while I am with you. [26]The Advocate, the Holy Spirit whom the Father will send in my name, will teach you everything and remind you of all that I told you."

Monday June 9, 2025
Memorial of the Blessed Virgin Mary, Mother of the Church
First Reading: Genesis 3:9-15, 20
[9] After Adam had eaten of the tree,
the LORD God called to him and asked him, "Where are you?"
[10]He answered, "I heard you in the garden;
but I was afraid, because I was naked,
so I hid myself."
[11]Then he asked, "Who told you that you were naked?
You have eaten, then,
from the tree of which I had forbidden you to eat!"
[12]The man replied, "The woman whom you put here with me—
she gave me fruit from the tree, and so I ate it."
[13]The LORD God then asked the woman,
"Why did you do such a thing?"
The woman answered, "The serpent tricked me into it, so I ate it."

[14]Then the LORD God said to the serpent:
"Because you have done this, you shall be banned
from all the animals
and from all the wild creatures;
On your belly shall you crawl,

and dirt shall you ate
all the days of your life.
[15]I will put enmity between you and the woman,
and between your offspring and hers;
He will strike at your head,
while you strike at his heel."
[20] The man called his wife Eve,
because she became the mother of all the living.

Or Acts 1:12-14
After Jesus had been taken up to heaven,
[12]the Apostles returned to Jerusalem
from the mount called Olivet, which is near Jerusalem,
a sabbath day's journey away.

[13]When they entered the city
they went to the upper room where they were staying,
Peter and John and James and Andrew,
Philip and Thomas, Bartholomew and Matthew,
James son of Alphaeus, Simon the Zealot,
and Judas son of James.
[14]All these devoted themselves with one accord to prayer,
together with some women,
and Mary the mother of Jesus, and his brothers.

Responsorial Psalm: Psalms 87:1-2, 3 AND 5, 6-7
R. [3] Glorious things are told of you, O city of God!
[1] His foundation upon the holy mountains
the LORD loves:
[2]The gates of Zion,
more than any dwelling of Jacob.
R. Glorious things are told of you, O city of God!
[3]Glorious things are said of you,
O city of God!
[5] And of Zion they shall say:
"One and all were born in her;
And he who has established her
is the Most High LORD."
R. Glorious things are told of you, O city of God!
[6] They shall note, when the peoples are enrolled:
"This man was born there."
[7] And all shall sing, in their festive dance:
"My home is within you."
R. Glorious things are told of you, O city of God!

Alleluia
R. Alleluia, alleluia.
O happy Virgin, you gave birth to the Lord;
O blessed mother of the Church,
you warm our hearts with the Spirit of your Son Jesus Christ.
R. Alleluia, alleluia.

Gospel: John 19:25-34
25 Standing by the cross of Jesus were his mother
and his mother's sister, Mary the wife of Clopas,
and Mary of Magdala.
26 When Jesus saw his mother and the disciple there whom he loved,
he said to his mother, "Woman, behold, your son."
27 Then he said to the disciple,
"Behold, your mother."
And from that hour the disciple took her into his home.
28 After this, aware that everything was now finished,
in order that the scripture might be fulfilled,
Jesus said, "I thirst."
29 There was a vessel filled with common wine.
So they put a sponge soaked in wine on a sprig of hyssop
and put it up to his mouth.
30 When Jesus had taken the wine, he said,
"It is finished."
And bowing his head, he handed over the spirit.

31 Now since it was preparation day,
in order that the bodies might not remain on the cross on the sabbath,
for the sabbath day of that week was a solemn one,
the Jews asked Pilate that their legs be broken
and they be taken down.
32 So the soldiers came and broke the legs of the first
and then of the other one who was crucified with Jesus.
33 But when they came to Jesus and saw that he was already dead,
they did not break his legs,
34 but one soldier thrust his lance into his side,
and immediately blood and water flowed out.

Tuesday June 10, 2025
Tuesday of the Tenth Week in Ordinary Time
First Reading: 2 Corinthians 1:18-22
Brothers and sisters: 18 As God is faithful, our word to you is not "yes" and "no." 19 For the Son of God, Jesus Christ, who was proclaimed to you by us, Silvanus and Timothy and me, was not "yes" and "no," but "yes" has been in him. 20 For however many are the promises of God, their Yes is in him; therefore, the Amen from us

also goes through him to God for glory. [21] But the one who gives us security with you in Christ and who anointed us is God; [22] he has also put his seal upon us and given the Spirit in our hearts as a first installment.

Responsorial Psalm: Psalms 119:129, 130, 131, 132, 133, 135
R. [135a] Lord, let your face shine on me.
[129] Wonderful are your decrees;
    therefore I observe them.
R. Lord, let your face shine on me.
[130] The revelation of your words sheds light,
    gives understanding to the simple.
R. Lord, let your face shine on me.
[131] I gasp with open mouth
    in my yearning for your commands.
R. Lord, let your face shine on me.
[132] Turn to me in pity
    as you turn to those who love your name.
R. Lord, let your face shine on me.
[133] Steady my footsteps according to your promise,
    and let no iniquity rule over me.
R. Lord, let your face shine on me.
[135] Let your countenance shine upon your servant,
    and teach me your statutes.
R. Lord, let your face shine on me.

Alleluia: Matthew 5:16
R. Alleluia, alleluia.
[16] Let your light shine before others
that they may see your good deeds and
    glorify your heavenly Father.
R. Alleluia, alleluia.

Gospel: Matthew 5:13-16
Jesus said to his disciples: [13] "You are the salt of the earth. But if salt loses its taste, with what can it be seasoned? It is no longer good for anything but to be thrown out and trampled underfoot. [14] You are the light of the world. A city set on a mountain cannot be hidden. [15] Nor do they light a lamp and then put it under a bushel basket; it is set on a lampstand, where it gives light to all in the house. [16] Just so, your light must shine before others, that they may see your good deeds and glorify your heavenly Father."

Wednesday June 11, 2025
Feast of Saint Barnabas, Apostle

First Reading: Acts 11:21B-26; 13:1-3

²¹ᴮ In those days a great number who believed turned to the Lord. ²² The news about them reached the ears of the Church in Jerusalem, and they sent Barnabas to go to Antioch. ²³ When he arrived and saw the grace of God, he rejoiced and encouraged them all to remain faithful to the Lord in firmness of heart, ²⁴ for he was a good man, filled with the Holy Spirit and faith. And a large number of people was added to the Lord. ²⁵ Then he went to Tarsus to look for Saul, ²⁶ and when he had found him he brought him to Antioch. For a whole year they met with the Church and taught a large number of people, and it was in Antioch that the disciples were first called Christians.

¹ Now there were in the Church at Antioch prophets and teachers: Barnabas, Symeon who was called Niger, Lucius of Cyrene, Manaen who was a close friend of Herod the tetrarch, and Saul. ² While they were worshiping the Lord and fasting, the Holy Spirit said, "Set apart for me Barnabas and Saul for the work to which I have called them." ³ Then, completing their fasting and prayer, they laid hands on them and sent them off.

Responsorial Psalm: Psalms 98:1, 2-3AB, 3CD-4, 5-6

R. (see 2b) **The Lord has revealed to the nations his saving power.**

¹ Sing to the LORD a new song,
  for he has done wondrous deeds;
His right hand has won victory for him,
  his holy arm.

R. The Lord has revealed to the nations his saving power.

² The LORD has made his salvation known:
  in the sight of the nations he has revealed
    his justice.
³ᴬᴮ He has remembered his kindness and his
    faithfulness
  toward the house of Israel.

R. The Lord has revealed to the nations his saving power.

³ᶜᴰ All the ends of the earth have seen
  the salvation by our God.
⁴ Sing joyfully to the LORD, all you lands;
  break into song; sing praise.

R. The Lord has revealed to the nations his saving power.

⁵ Sing praise to the LORD with the harp,
  with the harp and melodious song.
⁶ With trumpets and the sound of the horn
  sing joyfully before the King, the LORD.

R. *The Lord has revealed to the nations his saving power.*

Alleluia: Psalm 25:4B, 5A
R. Alleluia, alleluia.
⁴ᴮTeach me your paths, my God,
⁵ᴬand guide me in your truth.
R. Alleluia, alleluia.

Gospel: Matthew 5:17-19
Jesus said to his disciples: ¹⁷"Do not think that I have come to abolish the law or the prophets. I have come not to abolish but to fulfill. ¹⁸ Amen, I say to you, until heaven and earth pass away, not the smallest letter or the smallest part of a letter will pass from the law, until all things have taken place. ¹⁹ Therefore, whoever breaks one of the least of these commandments and teaches others to do so will be called least in the kingdom of heaven. But whoever obeys and teaches these commandments will be called greatest in the kingdom of heaven."

Thursday June 12, 2025
Thursday of Tenth Week in Ordinary Time
First Reading: 2 Corinthians 3:15-4:1, 3-6
Brothers and sisters: ¹⁵ To this day, whenever Moses is read, a veil lies over the hearts of the children of Israel, ¹⁶ but whenever a person turns to the Lord the veil is removed. ¹⁷ Now the Lord is the Spirit and where the Spirit of the Lord is, there is freedom. ¹⁸ All of us, gazing with unveiled face on the glory of the Lord, are being transformed into the same image from glory to glory, as from the Lord who is the Spirit.
¹ Therefore, since we have this ministry through the mercy shown us, we are not discouraged. ³ And even though our Gospel is veiled, it is veiled for those who are perishing, ⁴ in whose case the god of this age has blinded the minds of the unbelievers, so that they may not see the light of the Gospel of the glory of Christ, who is the image of God. ⁵ For we do not preach ourselves but Jesus Christ as Lord, and ourselves as your slaves for the sake of Jesus. ⁶ For God who said, *Let light shine out of darkness*, has shone in our hearts to bring to light the knowledge of the glory of God on the face of Jesus Christ.

Responsorial Psalm: Psalms 85:9AB and 10, 11-12, 13-14
R. *(see 10b)* **The glory of the Lord will dwell in our land.**
⁹ᴬᴮ I will hear what God proclaims;
    the LORD–for he proclaims peace to his
        people.
¹⁰ Near indeed is his salvation to those who
        fear him,
    glory dwelling in our land.
R. **The glory of the Lord will dwell in our land.**
¹¹ Kindness and truth shall meet;

>justice and peace shall kiss.
> 12 Truth shall spring out of the earth,
>>and justice shall look down from heaven.

R. The glory of the Lord will dwell in our land.
> 13 The LORD himself will give his benefits;
>>our land shall yield its increase.
> 14 Justice shall walk before him,
>>and salvation, along the way of his steps.

R. The glory of the Lord will dwell in our land.

Alleluia: John 13:34
R. Alleluia, alleluia.
34 I give you a new commandment:
love one another as I have loved you.
R. Alleluia, alleluia.

Gospel: Matthew 5:20-26
20 Jesus said to his disciples: "I tell you, unless your righteousness surpasses that of the scribes and Pharisees, you will not enter into the Kingdom of heaven.
21 "You have heard that it was said to your ancestors, *You shall not kill; and whoever kills will be liable to judgment.* 22 But I say to you, whoever is angry with his brother will be liable to judgment, and whoever says to his brother, *Raqa*, will be answerable to the Sanhedrin, and whoever says, 'You fool,' will be liable to fiery Gehenna. 23 Therefore, if you bring your gift to the altar, and there recall that your brother has anything against you, 24 leave your gift there at the altar, go first and be reconciled with your brother, and then come and offer your gift. 25 Settle with your opponent quickly while on the way to court with him. Otherwise your opponent will hand you over to the judge, and the judge will hand you over to the guard, and you will be thrown into prison. 26 Amen, I say to you, you will not be released until you have paid the last penny."

Friday June 13, 2025
Memorial of Saint Anthony of Padua, Priest & Doctor
First Reading: 2 Corinthians 4:7-15
Brothers and sisters: 7We hold this treasure in earthen vessels, that the surpassing power may be of God and not from us. 8We are afflicted in every way, but not constrained; perplexed, but not driven to despair; 9persecuted, but not abandoned; struck down, but not destroyed; 10always carrying about in the Body the dying of Jesus, so that the life of Jesus may also be manifested in our body. 11For we who live are constantly being given up to death for the sake of Jesus, so that the life of Jesus may be manifested in our mortal flesh.
12So death is at work in us, but life in you. 13Since, then, we have the same spirit of faith, according to what is written, "I believed, therefore I spoke," we too believe and therefore speak, 14knowing that the one who raised the Lord Jesus will raise us also with Jesus and place us with you in his presence. 15Everything

indeed is for you, so that the grace bestowed in abundance on more and more people may cause the thanksgiving to overflow for the glory of God.

Responsorial Psalm: Psalms 116:10-11, 15-16, 17-18
R. (17a) To you, Lord, I will offer a sacrifice of praise. or: *R. Alleluia.*
10 I believed, even when I said,
    "I am greatly afflicted";
11 I said in my alarm,
    "No man is dependable."
R. To you, Lord, I will offer a sacrifice of praise. or: *R. Alleluia.*
15 Precious in the eyes of the LORD
    is the death of his faithful ones.
16 O LORD, I am your servant;
    I am your servant, the son of your
        handmaid;
    you have loosed my bonds.
R. To you, Lord, I will offer a sacrifice of praise. or: *R. Alleluia.*
17 To you will I offer sacrifice of thanksgiving,
    and I will call upon the name of the LORD.
18 My vows to the LORD I will pay
    in the presence of all his people.
R. To you, Lord, I will offer a sacrifice of praise. or: *R. Alleluia.*

Alleluia: Philippians 2:15D, 16A
R. Alleluia, alleluia.
15D Shine like lights in the world,
16A as you hold on to the word of life.
R. Alleluia, alleluia.

Gospel: Matthew 5:27-32
Jesus said to his disciples: 27"You have heard that it was said, *You shall not commit adultery.* 28 But I say to you, everyone who looks at a woman with lust has already committed adultery with her in his heart. 29 If your right eye causes you to sin, tear it out and throw it away. It is better for you to lose one of your members than to have your whole body thrown into Gehenna. 30And if your right hand causes you to sin, cut it off and throw it away. It is better for you to lose one of your members than to have your whole body go into Gehenna.
   31"It was also said, *Whoever divorces his wife must give her a bill of divorce.* 32But I say to you, whoever divorces his wife (unless the marriage is unlawful) causes her to commit adultery, and whoever marries a divorced woman commits adultery."

Saturday June 14, 2025
Saturday of Tenth Week in Ordinary Time
First Reading: 2 Corinthians 5:14-21

Brothers and sisters: [14]The love of Christ impels us, once we have come to the conviction that one died for all; therefore, all have died. [15]He indeed died for all, so that those who live might no longer live for themselves but for him who for their sake died and was raised.

[16]Consequently, from now on we regard no one according to the flesh; even if we once knew Christ according to the flesh, yet now we know him so no longer. [17]So whoever is in Christ is a new creation: the old things have passed away; behold, new things have come. [18]And all this is from God, who has reconciled us to himself through Christ and given us the ministry of reconciliation, [19]namely, God was reconciling the world to himself in Christ, not counting their trespasses against them and entrusting to us the message of reconciliation. [20]So we are ambassadors for Christ, as if God were appealing through us. We implore you on behalf of Christ, be reconciled to God. [21]For our sake he made him to be sin who did not know sin, so that we might become the righteousness of God in him.

Responsorial Psalm: Psalms 103:1-2, 3-4, 9-10, 11-12

R. [8a] The Lord is kind and merciful.
[1] Bless the LORD, O my soul;
    and all my being, bless his holy name.
[2] Bless the LORD, O my soul,
    and forget not all his benefits.
R. The Lord is kind and merciful.
[3] He pardons all your iniquities,
    he heals all your ills.
[4] He redeems your life from destruction,
    he crowns you with kindness and compassion.
R. The Lord is kind and merciful.
[9] He will not always chide,
    nor does he keep his wrath forever.
[10] Not according to our sins does he deal with us,
    nor does he requite us according to our crimes.
R. The Lord is kind and merciful.
[11] For as the heavens are high above the earth,
    so surpassing is his kindness toward
        those who fear him.
[12] As far as the east is from the west,
    so far has he put our transgressions from us.
R. The Lord is kind and merciful.

Alleluia: Psalms 119:36A, 29B
R. Alleluia, alleluia.
36A Incline my heart, O God, to your decrees;
29B and favor me with your law.
R. Alleluia, alleluia.

Gospel: Matthew 5:33-37
33 Jesus said to his disciples: "You have heard that it was said to your ancestors, *Do not take a false oath, but make good to the Lord all that you vow.* 34 But I say to you, do not swear at all; not by heaven, for it is God's throne; 35 nor by the earth, for it is his footstool; nor by Jerusalem, for it is the city of the great King. 36 Do not swear by your head, for you cannot make a single hair white or black. 37 Let your 'Yes' mean 'Yes,' and your 'No' mean 'No.' Anything more is from the Evil One."

Sunday June 15, 2025
The Solemnity of the Most Holy Trinity, Year C

First Reading: Proverbs 8:22-31
Thus says the wisdom of God:

22 "The LORD possessed me, the beginning of his ways,
　the forerunner of his prodigies of long ago;
23 from of old I was poured forth,
　at the first, before the earth.
24 When there were no depths I was brought forth,
　when there were no fountains or springs of water;
25 before the mountains were settled into place,
　before the hills, I was brought forth;
26 while as yet the earth and fields were not made,
　nor the first clods of the world.

27 "When the Lord established the heavens I was there,
　when he marked out the vault over the face of the deep;
28 when he made firm the skies above,
　when he fixed fast the foundations of the earth;
29 when he set for the sea its limit,
　so that the waters should not transgress

his command;
³⁰ then was I beside him as his craftsman,
    and I was his delight day by day,
playing before him all the while,
    ³¹playing on the surface of his earth;
    and I found delight in the human race."

Responsorial Psalm: Psalms 8:4-5, 6-7, 8-9

R. ⁽²ᵃ⁾ O Lord, our God, how wonderful your name in all the earth!

⁴When I behold your heavens, the work of your fingers,
    the moon and the stars which you set in place—
⁵ What is man that you should be mindful of him,
    or the son of man that you should care for him?

R. O Lord, our God, how wonderful your name in all the earth!

⁶ You have made him little less than the angels,
    and crowned him with glory and honor.
⁷ You have given him rule over the works of your hands,
    putting all things under his feet:

R. O Lord, our God, how wonderful your name in all the earth!

⁸ All sheep and oxen,
    yes, and the beasts of the field,
⁹ The birds of the air, the fishes of the sea,
    and whatever swims the paths of the seas.

R. O Lord, our God, how wonderful your name in all the earth!

Second Reading: Romans 5:1-5

Brothers and sisters: ¹Therefore, since we have been justified by faith, we have peace with God through our Lord Jesus Christ, ²through whom we have gained access by faith to this grace in which we stand, and we boast in hope of the glory of God. ³Not only that, but we even boast of our afflictions, knowing that affliction produces endurance, ⁴and endurance, proven character, and proven character, hope, ⁵and hope does not disappoint, because the love of God has been poured out into our hearts through the Holy Spirit that has been given to us.

Alleluia: cf. Revelation 1:8
R. Alleluia, alleluia.
8 Glory to the Father, the Son, and the Holy
    Spirit;
to God who is, who was, and who is to come.
R. Alleluia, alleluia.

Gospel: John 16:12-15
Jesus said to his disciples: 12"I have much more to tell you, but you cannot bear it now. 13But when he comes, the Spirit of truth, he will guide you to all truth. He will not speak on his own, but he will speak what he hears, and will declare to you the things that are coming. 14He will glorify me because he will take from what is mine and declare it to you. 15Everything that the Father has is mine; for this reason I told you that he will take from what is mine and declare it to you."

Monday June 16, 2025
Monday of Eleventh Week in Ordinary Time

First Reading: 2 Corinthians 6:1-10
Brothers and sisters: 1As your fellow workers, we appeal to you not to receive the grace of God in vain. 2 For he says:

In an acceptable time I heard you,
    and on the day of salvation I helped you.

Behold, now is a very acceptable time; behold, now is the day of salvation. 3 We cause no one to stumble in anything, in order that no fault may be found with our ministry; 4on the contrary, in everything we commend ourselves as ministers of God, through much endurance, in afflictions, hardships, constraints, 5 beatings, imprisonments, riots, labors, vigils, fasts; 6 by purity, knowledge, patience, kindness, in the Holy Spirit, in unfeigned love, 7 in truthful speech, in the power of God; with weapons of righteousness at the right and at the left; 8 through glory and dishonor, insult and praise. We are treated as deceivers and yet are truthful; 9 as unrecognized and yet acknowledged; as dying and behold we live; as chastised and yet not put to death; 10 as sorrowful yet always rejoicing; as poor yet enriching many; as having nothing and yet possessing all things.

Responsorial Psalm: Psalms 98:1, 2B-3AB, 3CD-4
R. (2a) *The Lord has made known his salvation.*
1 Sing to the LORD a new song,
    for he has done wondrous deeds;
His right hand has won victory for him,
    his holy arm.
R. *The Lord has made known his salvation.*
2B In the sight of the nations he has revealed
        his justice.

³ᴬᴮ He has remembered his kindness and his
faithfulness
toward the house of Israel.
R. The Lord has made known his salvation.
³ᶜᴰ All the ends of the earth have seen
the salvation by our God.
⁴ Sing joyfully to the LORD, all you lands;
break into song; sing praise.
R. The Lord has made known his salvation.

Alleluia: Psalms 119:105
R. Alleluia, alleluia.
¹⁰⁵A lamp to my feet is your word,
a light to my path.
R. Alleluia, alleluia.

Gospel: Matthew 5:38-42
³⁸ Jesus said to his disciples: "You have heard that it was said, *An eye for an eye and a tooth for a tooth*. ³⁹ But I say to you, offer no resistance to one who is evil. When someone strikes you on your right cheek, turn the other one to him as well. ⁴⁰ If anyone wants to go to law with you over your tunic, hand him your cloak as well. ⁴¹ Should anyone press you into service for one mile, go with him for two miles. ⁴² Give to the one who asks of you, and do not turn your back on one who wants to borrow."

Tuesday June 17, 2025
Tuesday of Eleventh Week in Ordinary Time
First Reading: 2 Corinthians 8:1-9
¹ We want you to know, brothers and sisters, of the grace of God that has been given to the churches of Macedonia, ² for in a severe test of affliction, the abundance of their joy and their profound poverty overflowed in a wealth of generosity on their part. ³ For according to their means, I can testify, and beyond their means, spontaneously, ⁴ they begged us insistently for the favor of taking part in the service to the holy ones, ⁵ and this, not as we expected, but they gave themselves first to the Lord and to us through the will of God, ⁶ so that we urged Titus that, as he had already begun, he should also complete for you this gracious act also. ⁷ Now as you excel in every respect, in faith, discourse, knowledge, all earnestness, and in the love we have for you, may you excel in this gracious act also.
⁸ I say this not by way of command, but to test the genuineness of your love by your concern for others. ⁹ For you know the gracious act of our Lord Jesus Christ, that for your sake he became poor although he was rich, so that by his poverty you might become rich.

Responsorial Psalm: Psalms 146:2, 5-6AB, 6C- 7, 8-9A
R. ⁽¹ᵇ⁾ *Praise the Lord, my soul!* or: *R. Alleluia*.
² Praise the LORD, my soul!

I will praise the LORD all my life;
> I will sing praise to my God while I live.

R. Praise the Lord, my soul! or: ***R. Alleluia.***

⁵ Blessed he whose help is the God of Jacob,
> whose hope is in the LORD, his God,

⁶ᴬᴮ Who made heaven and earth,
> the sea and all that is in them.

R. Praise the Lord, my soul! or: ***R. Alleluia.***

⁶ᶜ Who keeps faith forever,
> ⁷ secures justice for the oppressed,
> gives food to the hungry.

The LORD sets captives free.

R. Praise the Lord, my soul! or: ***R. Alleluia.***

⁸ The LORD gives sight to the blind.
The LORD raises up those who were bowed down;
> the LORD loves the just.

⁹ᴬ The LORD protects strangers.

R. Praise the Lord, my soul! or: ***R. Alleluia.***

Alleluia: John 13:34
R. Alleluia, alleluia.
³⁴ I give you a new commandment:
love one another as I have loved you.
R. Alleluia, alleluia.

Gospel: Matthew 5:43-48

⁴³ Jesus said to his disciples: "You have heard that it was said, *You shall love your neighbor and hate your enemy.* ⁴⁴ But I say to you, love your enemies and pray for those who persecute you, ⁴⁵ that you may be children of your heavenly Father, for he makes his sun rise on the bad and the good, and causes rain to fall on the just and the unjust. ⁴⁶ For if you love those who love you, what recompense will you have? Do not the tax collectors do the same? ⁴⁷ And if you greet your brothers only, what is unusual about that? Do not the pagans do the same? ⁴⁸ So be perfect, just as your heavenly Father is perfect."

Wednesday June 18, 2025
Wednesday of the Eleventh Week in Ordinary Time
First Reading: 2 Corinthians 9:6-11

⁶ Brothers and sisters, consider this: whoever sows sparingly will also reap sparingly, and whoever sows bountifully will also reap bountifully. ⁷ Each must do as already determined, without sadness or compulsion, for God loves a cheerful giver. ⁸ Moreover, God is able to make every grace abundant for you, so that in all things, always having all you need, you may have an abundance for every good work. ⁹ As it is written:

He scatters abroad, he gives to the poor;

his righteousness endures forever.

¹⁰The one who supplies seed to the sower and bread for food will supply and multiply your seed and increase the harvest of your righteousness.
　　¹¹You are being enriched in every way for all generosity, which through us produces thanksgiving to God.

Responsorial Psalm: Psalms 112:1BC-2, 3-4, 9
*R. ⁽¹ᵇ⁾ **Blessed the man who fears the Lord.** or: R. **Alleluia.***
¹ᴮᶜ Blessed the man who fears the LORD,
　　who greatly delights in his commands.
² His posterity shall be mighty upon the earth;
　　the upright generation shall be blessed.
R. Blessed the man who fears the Lord. or: R. Alleluia.
³ Wealth and riches shall be in his house;
　　his generosity shall endure forever.
⁴ Light shines through the darkness for the
　　　upright;
　　he is gracious and merciful and just.
R. Blessed the man who fears the Lord. or: R. Alleluia.
⁹ Lavishly he gives to the poor;
　　his generosity shall endure forever;
　　his horn shall be exalted in glory.
R. Blessed the man who fears the Lord. or: R. Alleluia.

Alleluia: John 14:23
R. Alleluia, alleluia.
²³ Whoever loves me will keep my word,
and my Father will love him
and we will come to him.
R. Alleluia, alleluia.

Gospel: Matthew 6:1-6, 16-18
¹ Jesus said to his disciples: "Take care not to perform righteous deeds in order that people may see them; otherwise, you will have no recompense from your heavenly Father. ² When you give alms, do not blow a trumpet before you, as the hypocrites do in the synagogues and in the streets to win the praise of others. Amen, I say to you, they have received their reward. ³ But when you give alms, do not let your left hand know what your right is doing, ⁴ so that your almsgiving may be secret. And your Father who sees in secret will repay you.
　　⁵ "When you pray, do not be like the hypocrites, who love to stand and pray in the synagogues and on street corners so that others may see them. Amen, I say to you, they have received their reward. ⁶ But when you pray, go to your inner room, close the door, and pray to your Father in secret. And your Father who sees in secret will repay you.

[16] "When you fast, do not look gloomy like the hypocrites. They neglect their appearance, so that they may appear to others to be fasting. Amen, I say to you, they have received their reward. [17] But when you fast, anoint your head and wash your face, [18] so that you may not appear to others to be fasting, except to your Father who is hidden. And your Father who sees what is hidden will repay you."

Thursday June 19, 2025
Thursday of the Eleventh Week in Ordinary Time

First Reading: 2 Corinthians 11:1-11

Brothers and sisters: [1] If only you would put up with a little foolishness from me! Please put up with me. [2] For I am jealous of you with the jealousy of God, since I betrothed you to one husband to present you as a chaste virgin to Christ. [3] But I am afraid that, as the serpent deceived Eve by his cunning, your thoughts may be corrupted from a sincere and pure commitment to Christ. [4] For if someone comes and preaches another Jesus than the one we preached, or if you receive a different spirit from the one you received or a different gospel from the one you accepted, you put up with it well enough. [5] For I think that I am not in any way inferior to these "superapostles." [6] Even if I am untrained in speaking, I am not so in knowledge; in every way we have made this plain to you in all things.

[7] Did I make a mistake when I humbled myself so that you might be exalted because I preached the Gospel of God to you without charge? [8] I plundered other churches by accepting from them in order to minister to you. [9] And when I was with you and in need, I did not burden anyone, for the brothers who came from Macedonia supplied my needs. So I refrained and will refrain from burdening you in any way. [10] By the truth of Christ in me, this boast of mine shall not be silenced in the regions of Achaia. [11] And why? Because I do not love you? God knows I do!

Responsorial Psalm: Psalms 111:1B-2, 3-4, 7-8

R. [7a] *Your works, O Lord, are justice and truth.* or: R. *Alleluia.*

[1B] I will give thanks to the LORD with all my
   heart
   in the company and assembly of the just.
[2] Great are the works of the LORD,
   exquisite in all their delights.

R. Your works, O Lord, are justice and truth. or: R. Alleluia.

[3] Majesty and glory are his work,
   and his justice endures forever.
[4] He has won renown for his wondrous deeds;
   gracious and merciful is the LORD.

R. Your works, O Lord, are justice and truth. or: R. Alleluia.

[7] The works of his hands are faithful and just;
   sure are all his precepts,
[8] Reliable forever and ever,
   wrought in truth and equity.

R. Your works, O Lord, are justice and truth. or: R. Alleluia.

Alleluia: Romans 8:15BC
R. Alleluia, alleluia.
¹⁵ᴮᶜ You have received a spirit of adoption as
        sons
through which we cry: Abba! Father!
R. Alleluia, alleluia.

Gospel: Matthew 6:7-15
⁷ Jesus said to his disciples: "In praying, do not babble like the pagans, who think that they will be heard because of their many words. ⁸ Do not be like them. Your Father knows what you need before you ask him.
⁹ "This is how you are to pray:

'Our Father who art in heaven,
    hallowed be thy name,
   ¹⁰ thy Kingdom come,
thy will be done,
    on earth as it is in heaven.
¹¹ Give us this day our daily bread;
   ¹² and forgive us our trespasses,
    as we forgive those who trespass against
        us;
   ¹³ and lead us not into temptation,
    but deliver us from evil.'

¹⁴ "If you forgive others their transgressions, your heavenly Father will forgive you. ¹⁵ But if you do not forgive others, neither will your Father forgive your transgressions."

Friday June 20, 2025
Friday of the Eleventh Week in Ordinary Time
First Reading: 2 Corinthians 11:18, 21-30
Brothers and sisters: ¹⁸Since many boast according to the flesh, I too will boast. ²¹ To my shame I say that we were too weak!
    But what anyone dares to boast of (I am speaking in foolishness) I also dare. ²²Are they Hebrews? So am I. Are they children of Israel? So am I. Are they descendants of Abraham? So am I. ²³Are they ministers of Christ? (I am talking like an insane person). I am still more, with far greater labors, far more imprisonments, far worse beatings, and numerous brushes with death. ²⁴Five times at the hands of the Jews I received forty lashes minus one. ²⁵Three times I was beaten with rods, once I was stoned, three times I was shipwrecked, I passed a night and a day on the deep; ²⁶on frequent journeys, in dangers from rivers, dangers from robbers, dangers from my own race, dangers from Gentiles, dangers in the city, dangers in the wilderness, dangers at sea, dangers among false brothers; ²⁷in toil and hardship, through many sleepless nights, through hunger and

thirst, through frequent fastings, through cold and exposure. ²⁸And apart from these things, there is the daily pressure upon me of my anxiety for all the churches. ²⁹Who is weak, and I am not weak? Who is led to sin, and I am not indignant?

³⁰If I must boast, I will boast of the things that show my weakness.

Responsorial Psalm: Psalms 34:2-3, 4-5, 6-7
R. (see 18b) From all their distress God rescues the just.
² I will bless the LORD at all times;
   his praise shall be ever in my mouth.
³ Let my soul glory in the LORD;
   the lowly will hear me and be glad.
R. From all their distress God rescues the just.
⁴ Glorify the LORD with me,
   let us together extol his name.
⁵ I sought the LORD, and he answered me
   and delivered me from all my fears.
R. From all their distress God rescues the just.
⁶ Look to him that you may be radiant with
      joy,
   and your faces may not blush with
      shame.
⁷ When the poor one called out, the LORD
      heard,
   and from all his distress he saved him.
R. From all their distress God rescues the just.

Alleluia: Matthew 5:3
R. Alleluia, alleluia.
³ Blessed are the poor in spirit;
for theirs is the Kingdom of heaven.
R. Alleluia, alleluia.

Gospel: Matthew 6:19-23
¹⁹ Jesus said to his disciples: "Do not store up for yourselves treasures on earth, where moth and decay destroy, and thieves break in and steal. ²⁰ But store up treasures in heaven, where neither moth nor decay destroys, nor thieves break in and steal. ²¹ For where your treasure is, there also will your heart be.

²² "The lamp of the body is the eye. If your eye is sound, your whole body will be filled with light; ²³ but if your eye is bad, your whole body will be in darkness. And if the light in you is darkness, how great will the darkness be."

Saturday June 21, 2025
Memorial of Saint Aloysius Gonzaga, Religious

First Reading: 2 Corinthians 12:1-10

Brothers and sisters: [1] I must boast; not that it is profitable, but I will go on to visions and revelations of the Lord. [2] I know a man in Christ who, fourteen years ago (whether in the body or out of the body I do not know, God knows), was caught up to the third heaven. [3] And I know that this man (whether in the body or out of the body I do not know, God knows) [4] was caught up into Paradise and heard ineffable things, which no one may utter. [5] About this man I will boast, but about myself I will not boast, except about my weaknesses. [6] Although if I should wish to boast, I would not be foolish, for I would be telling the truth. But I refrain, so that no one may think more of me than what he sees in me or hears from me [7] because of the abundance of the revelations. Therefore, that I might not become too elated, a thorn in the flesh was given to me, an angel of Satan, to beat me, to keep me from being too elated. [8] Three times I begged the Lord about this, that it might leave me, [9] but he said to me, "My grace is sufficient for you, for power is made perfect in weakness." I will rather boast most gladly of my weaknesses, in order that the power of Christ may dwell with me. [10] Therefore, I am content with weaknesses, insults, hardships, persecutions, and constraints, for the sake of Christ; for when I am weak, then I am strong.

Responsorial Psalm: Psalms 34:8-9, 10-11, 12-13

R. (9a) *Taste and see the goodness of the Lord.*

[8] The angel of the LORD encamps
   around those who fear him, and delivers them.
[9] Taste and see how good the LORD is;
   blessed the man who takes refuge in him.

R. *Taste and see the goodness of the Lord.*

[10] Fear the LORD, you his holy ones,
   for nought is lacking to those who fear him.
[11] The great grow poor and hungry;
   but those who seek the LORD want for no good thing.

R. *Taste and see the goodness of the Lord.*

[12] Come, children, hear me;
   I will teach you the fear of the LORD.
[13] Which of you desires life,
   and takes delight in prosperous days?

R. *Taste and see the goodness of the Lord.*

Alleluia: 2 Corinthians 8:9

R. Alleluia, alleluia.
[9] Jesus Christ became poor although he was

rich,
so that by his poverty you might become
    rich.
R. Alleluia, alleluia.

Gospel: Matthew 6:24-34
Jesus said to his disciples: [24]"No one can serve two masters. He will either hate one and love the other, or be devoted to one and despise the other. You cannot serve God and mammon.

[25]"Therefore I tell you, do not worry about your life, what you will eat or drink, or about your body, what you will wear. Is not life more than food and the body more than clothing? [26]Look at the birds in the sky; they do not sow or reap, they gather nothing into barns, yet your heavenly Father feeds them. Are not you more important than they? [27]Can any of you by worrying add a single moment to your life-span? [28]Why are you anxious about clothes? Learn from the way the wild flowers grow. They do not work or spin. [29]But I tell you that not even Solomon in all his splendor was clothed like one of them. [30]If God so clothes the grass of the field, which grows today and is thrown into the oven tomorrow, will he not much more provide for you, O you of little faith? [31]So do not worry and say, 'What are we to eat?' or 'What are we to drink?' or 'What are we to wear?' [32]All these things the pagans seek. Your heavenly Father knows that you need them all. [33]But seek first the Kingdom of God and his righteousness, and all these things will be given you besides. [34]Do not worry about tomorrow; tomorrow will take care of itself. Sufficient for a day is its own evil."

Sunday June 22, 2025
Solemnity of Body and Blood of Christ (*Corpus Christi*)
First Reading: Genesis 14:18-20
[18] In those days, Melchizedek, king of Salem, brought out bread and wine, and being a priest of God Most High, [19]he blessed Abram with these words:

"Blessed be Abram by God Most High,
    the creator of heaven and earth;
[20]and blessed be God Most High,
    who delivered your foes into your hand."

Then Abram gave him a tenth of everything.

Responsorial Psalm: Psalms 110:1, 2, 3, 4
R. [4b] ***You are a priest for ever, in the line of
        Melchizedek.***
[1] The LORD said to my Lord: "Sit at my right
        hand
    till I make your enemies your footstool."
**R. *You are a priest for ever, in the line of
        Melchizedek.***

² The sceptre of your power the LORD will
        stretch forth from Zion:
    "Rule in the midst of your enemies."
**R. You are a priest for ever, in the line of
    Melchizedek.**

³ "Yours is princely power in the day of your
        birth, in holy splendor;
    before the daystar, like the dew, I have
        begotten you."
**R. You are a priest for ever, in the line of
    Melchizedek.**

⁴ The LORD has sworn, and he will not repent:
    "You are a priest forever, according to the
        order of Melchizedek."
**R. You are a priest for ever, in the line of
    Melchizedek.**

Second Reading: 1 Corinthians 11:23-26

Brothers and sisters: ²³ I received from the Lord what I also handed on to you that the Lord Jesus, on the night he was handed over, took bread, ²⁴ and, after he had given thanks, broke it and said, "This is my body that is for you. Do this in remembrance of me." ²⁵ In the same way also the cup, after supper, saying, "This cup is the new covenant in my blood. Do this, as often as you drink it, in remembrance of me." ²⁶ For as often as you eat this bread and drink the cup, you proclaim the death of the Lord until he comes.

Sequence - *Lauda Sion*

Laud, O Zion, your salvation,
Laud with hymns of exultation,
Christ, your king and shepherd true:

Bring him all the praise you know,
He is more than you bestow.
Never can you reach his due.

Special theme for glad thanksgiving
Is the quick'ning and the living
Bread today before you set:

From his hands of old partaken,
As we know, by faith unshaken,
Where the Twelve at supper met.

Full and clear ring out your chanting,
Joy nor sweetest grace be wanting,

From your heart let praises burst:

For today the feast is holden,
When the institution olden
Of that supper was rehearsed.

Here the new law's new oblation,
By the new king's revelation,
Ends the form of ancient rite:

Now the new the old effaces,
Truth away the shadow chases,
Light dispels the gloom of night.

What he did at supper seated,
Christ ordained to be repeated,
His memorial ne'er to cease:

And his rule for guidance taking,
Bread and wine we hallow, making
Thus our sacrifice of peace.

This the truth each Christian learns,
Bread into his flesh he turns,
To his precious blood the wine:

Sight has fail'd, nor thought conceives,
But a dauntless faith believes,
Resting on a pow'r divine.

Here beneath these signs are hidden
Priceless things to sense forbidden;
Sign, not things are all we see:

Blood is poured and flesh is broken,
Yet in either wondrous token
Christ entire we know to be.

Whoso of this food partakes,
Does not rend the Lord nor breaks;
Christ is whole to all that tastes:

Thousands are, as one, receivers,
One, as thousands of believers,
Eats of him who cannot waste.

Bad and good the feast are sharing,
Of what divers dooms preparing,
Endless death, or endless life.

Life to these, to those damnation,
See how like participation
Is with unlike issues rife.

When the sacrament is broken,
Doubt not, but believe 'tis spoken,
That each sever'd outward token
doth the very whole contain.

Nought the precious gift divides,
Breaking but the sign betides
Jesus still the same abides,
still unbroken does remain.

The shorter form of the sequence begins here.

Lo! the angel's food is given
To the pilgrim who has striven;
See the children's bread from heaven,
which on dogs may not be spent.

Truth the ancient types fulfilling,
Isaac bound, a victim willing,
Paschal lamb, its lifeblood spilling,
manna to the fathers sent.

Very bread, good shepherd, tend us,
Jesu, of your love befriend us,
You refresh us, you defend us,
Your eternal goodness send us
In the land of life to see.

You who all things can and know,
Who on earth such food bestow,
Grant us with your saints, though lowest,
Where the heav'nly feast you show,
Fellow heirs and guests to be. Amen.
 Alleluia.

Alleluia: John 6:51
R. Alleluia, alleluia.
⁵¹ I am the living bread that came down from
　　heaven, says the Lord;
whoever eats this bread will live forever.
R. Alleluia, alleluia.

Gospel: Luke 9:11B-17
¹¹ᴮ Jesus spoke to the crowds about the kingdom of God, and he healed those who needed to be cured. ¹² As the day was drawing to a close, the Twelve approached him and said, "Dismiss the crowd so that they can go to the surrounding villages and farms and find lodging and provisions; for we are in a deserted place here." ¹³ He said to them, "Give them some food yourselves." They replied, "Five loaves and two fish are all we have, unless we ourselves go and buy food for all these people." ¹⁴ Now the men there numbered about five thousand. Then he said to his disciples, "Have them sit down in groups of about fifty." ¹⁵ They did so and made them all sit down. ¹⁶ Then taking the five loaves and the two fish, and looking up to heaven, he said the blessing over them, broke them, and gave them to the disciples to set before the crowd. ¹⁷They all ate and were satisfied. And when the leftover fragments were picked up, they filled twelve wicker baskets.

Monday June 23, 2025
Monday of Twelfth Week in Ordinary Time

First Reading: Genesis 12:1-9
¹The LORD said to Abram: "Go forth from the land of your kinsfolk and from your father's house to a land that I will show you.

²"I will make of you a great nation,
　　and I will bless you;
I will make your name great,
　　so that you will be a blessing.
³I will bless those who bless you
　　and curse those who curse you.
All the communities of the earth
　　shall find blessing in you."

⁴Abram went as the LORD directed him, and Lot went with him. Abram was seventy-five years old when he left Haran. ⁵Abram took his wife, Sarai, his brother's son Lot, all the possessions that they had accumulated, and the persons they had acquired in Haran, and they set out for the land of Canaan. When they came to the land of Canaan, ⁶Abram passed through the land as far as the sacred place at Shechem, by the terebinth of Moreh. (The Canaanites were then in the land.)

⁷The LORD appeared to Abram and said, "To your descendants I will give this land." So Abram built an altar there to the LORD who had appeared to him. ⁸From there he moved on to the hill country east of Bethel, pitching his tent with

Bethel to the west and Ai to the east. He built an altar there to the LORD and invoked the LORD by name. ⁹Then Abram journeyed on by stages to the Negeb.

Responsorial Psalm: Psalms 33:12-13, 18-19, 20 AND 22
R. ⁽¹²⁾ **Blessed the people the Lord has chosen to be his own.**
¹² Blessed the nation whose God is the LORD,
   the people he has chosen for his own inheritance.
¹³ From heaven the LORD looks down;
   he sees all mankind.
R. **Blessed the people the Lord has chosen to be his own**.
¹⁸ See, the eyes of the LORD are upon those who fear him,
   upon those who hope for his kindness,
¹⁹ To deliver them from death
   and preserve them in spite of famine.
R. **Blessed the people the Lord has chosen to be his own**.
²⁰ Our soul waits for the LORD,
   who is our help and our shield.
²² May your kindness, O LORD, be upon us
   who have put our hope in you.
R. **Blessed the people the Lord has chosen to be his own**.

Alleluia: Hebrews 4:12
R. **Alleluia, alleluia.**
¹² The word of God is living and effective,
able to discern reflections and thoughts of
   the heart.
R. **Alleluia, alleluia.**

Gospel: Matthew 7:1-5
Jesus said to his disciples: ¹"Stop judging, that you may not be judged. ²For as you judge, so will you be judged, and the measure with which you measure will be measured out to you. ³Why do you notice the splinter in your brother's eye, but do not perceive the wooden beam in your own eye? ⁴How can you say to your brother, 'Let me remove that splinter from your eye,' while the wooden beam is in your eye? ⁵You hypocrite, remove the wooden beam from your eye first; then you will see clearly to remove the splinter from your brother's eye."

Tuesday June 24, 2025
Solemnity of the Birthday of Saint John the Baptist

First Reading: Isaiah 49:1-6

¹ Hear me, O coastlands,
    listen, O distant peoples.
The LORD called me from birth,
    from my mother's womb he gave me my name.
² He made of me a sharp-edged sword
    and concealed me in the shadow of his arm.
He made me a polished arrow,
    in his quiver he hid me.
³ You are my servant, he said to me,
    Israel, through whom I show my glory.

⁴ Though I thought I had toiled in vain,
    and for nothing, uselessly, spent my strength,
yet my reward is with the LORD,
    my recompense is with my God.
⁵ For now the LORD has spoken
    who formed me as his servant from the womb,
that Jacob may be brought back to him
    and Israel gathered to him;
and I am made glorious in the sight of the LORD,
    and my God is now my strength!
⁶ It is too little, he says, for you to be my servant,
    to raise up the tribes of Jacob,
    and restore the survivors of Israel;
I will make you a light to the nations,
    that my salvation may reach to the ends of the earth.

Responsorial Psalm: Psalms 139:1B-3, 13-14AB, 14C-15

R. ⁽¹⁴⁾ *I praise you, for I am wonderfully made.*

¹ᴮ O LORD, you have probed me, you know me:
    ² you know when I sit and when I stand;
    you understand my thoughts from afar.
³ My journeys and my rest you scrutinize,
    with all my ways you are familiar.

R. I praise you for I am wonderfully made.
[13] Truly you have formed my inmost being;
> you knit me in my mother's womb.

[14AB] I give you thanks that I am fearfully, wonderfully made;
> wonderful are your works.

R. I praise you, for I am wonderfully made.
[14C] My soul also you knew full well;
> [15] nor was my frame unknown to you

When I was made in secret,
> when I was fashioned in the depths of the earth.

R. I praise you, for I am wonderfully made.

Second Reading: Acts 13:22-26

In those days, Paul said: [22] "God raised up David as king; of him God testified, *I have found David, son of Jesse, a man after my own heart; he will carry out my every wish.* [23] From this man's descendants God, according to his promise, has brought to Israel a savior, Jesus. [24] John heralded his coming by proclaiming a baptism of repentance to all the people of Israel; [25] and as John was completing his course, he would say, 'What do you suppose that I am? I am not he. Behold, one is coming after me; I am not worthy to unfasten the sandals of his feet.'

[26] "My brothers, sons of the family of Abraham, and those others among you who are God-fearing, to us this word of salvation has been sent."

Alleluia: Luke 1:76
R. Alleluia, alleluia.
[76] You, child, will be called prophet of the Most High,
for you will go before the Lord to prepare his way.
R. Alleluia, alleluia.

Gospel: Luke 1:57-66, 80

[57] When the time arrived for Elizabeth to have her child she gave birth to a son. [58] Her neighbors and relatives heard that the Lord had shown his great mercy toward her, and they rejoiced with her. [59] When they came on the eighth day to circumcise the child, they were going to call him Zechariah after his father, [60] but his mother said in reply, "No. He will be called John." [61] But they answered her, "There is no one among your relatives who has this name." [62] So they made signs, asking his father what he wished him to be called. [63] He asked for a tablet and wrote, "John is his name," and all were amazed. [64] Immediately his mouth was opened, his tongue freed, and he spoke blessing God. [65] Then fear came upon all their neighbours, and all these matters were discussed throughout the hill country of Judea. [66] All

who heard these things took them to heart, saying, "What, then, will this child be?" For surely the hand of the Lord was with him.

⁸⁰ The child grew and became strong in spirit, and he was in the desert until the day of his manifestation to Israel.

Wednesday June 25, 2025
Wednesday of Twelfth Week in Ordinary Time
First Reading: Genesis 15:1-12, 17-18

¹The word of the LORD came to Abram in a vision:

"Fear not, Abram!
 I am your shield;
 I will make your reward very great."

²But Abram said, "O Lord GOD, what good will your gifts be, if I keep on being childless and have as my heir the steward of my house, Eliezer?" ³Abram continued, "See, you have given me no offspring, and so one of my servants will be my heir." ⁴Then the word of the LORD came to him: "No, that one shall not be your heir; your own issue shall be your heir." ⁵He took him outside and said: "Look up at the sky and count the stars, if you can. Just so," he added, "shall your descendants be." ⁶Abram put his faith in the LORD, who credited it to him as an act of righteousness.

⁷He then said to him, "I am the LORD who brought you from Ur of the Chaldeans to give you this land as a possession." ⁸"O Lord GOD," he asked, "how am I to know that I shall possess it?" ⁹He answered him, "Bring me a three-year-old heifer, a three-year-old she-goat, a three-year-old ram, a turtledove, and a young pigeon." ¹⁰Abram brought him all these, split them in two, and placed each half opposite the other; but the birds he did not cut up. ¹¹Birds of prey swooped down on the carcasses, but Abram stayed with them. ¹²As the sun was about to set, a trance fell upon Abram, and a deep, terrifying darkness enveloped him.

¹⁷When the sun had set and it was dark, there appeared a smoking fire pot and a flaming torch, which passed between those pieces. ¹⁸It was on that occasion that the LORD made a covenant with Abram, saying: "To your descendants I give this land, from the Wadi of Egypt to the Great River the Euphrates."

Responsorial Psalm: Psalms 105:1-2, 3-4, 6-7, 8-9

R. *⁽⁸ᵃ⁾ The Lord remembers his covenant for ever.* or: **R. Alleluia.**

¹ Give thanks to the LORD, invoke his name;
   make known among the nations his
      deeds.
² Sing to him, sing his praise,
   proclaim all his wondrous deeds.

R. *The Lord remembers his covenant for ever.* or: **R. Alleluia.**

³ Glory in his holy name;
   rejoice, O hearts that seek the LORD!
⁴ Look to the LORD in his strength;

seek to serve him constantly.
***R. The Lord remembers his covenant for ever.* or: *R. Alleluia*.**
⁶ You descendants of Abraham, his servants,
   sons of Jacob, his chosen ones!
⁷ He, the LORD, is our God;
   throughout the earth his judgments
      prevail.
***R. The Lord remembers his covenant for ever.* or: *R. Alleluia*.**
⁸ He remembers forever his covenant
   which he made binding for a thousand
      generations—
⁹ Which he entered into with Abraham
   and by his oath to Isaac.
***R. The Lord remembers his covenant for ever.* or: *R. Alleluia*.**

Alleluia: John 15:4A, 5B
R. Alleluia, alleluia.
⁴ᴬ Remain in me, as I remain in you, says the
      Lord;
⁵ᴮ whoever remains in me will bear much fruit.
R. Alleluia, alleluia.

Gospel: Matthew 7:15-20
¹⁵ Jesus said to his disciples: "Beware of false prophets, who come to you in sheep's clothing, but underneath are ravenous wolves. ¹⁶ By their fruits you will know them. Do people pick grapes from thornbushes, or figs from thistles? ¹⁷ Just so, every good tree bears good fruit, and a rotten tree bears bad fruit. ¹⁸ A good tree cannot bear bad fruit, nor can a rotten tree bear good fruit. ¹⁹ Every tree that does not bear good fruit will be cut down and thrown into the fire. ²⁰ So by their fruits you will know them."

Thursday June 26, 2025
Thursday of Twelfth Week in Ordinary Time
First Reading: Genesis 16:1-12, 15-16
¹Abram's wife Sarai had borne him no children. She had, however, an Egyptian maidservant named Hagar. ² Sarai said to Abram: "The LORD has kept me from bearing children. Have intercourse, then, with my maid; perhaps I shall have sons through her." Abram heeded Sarai's request. ³ Thus, after Abram had lived ten years in the land of Canaan, his wife Sarai took her maid, Hagar the Egyptian, and gave her to her husband Abram to be his concubine. ⁴He had intercourse with her, and she became pregnant. When she became aware of her pregnancy, she looked on her mistress with disdain. ⁵ So Sarai said to Abram: "You are responsible for this outrage against me. I myself gave my maid to your embrace; but ever since she became aware of her pregnancy, she has been looking on me with disdain. May the LORD decide between you and me!" ⁶ Abram told Sarai: "Your maid is in your power. Do to her whatever you please." Sarai then abused her so much that Hagar ran away from her.

⁷ The LORD's messenger found her by a spring in the wilderness, the spring on the road to Shur, ⁸and he asked, "Hagar, maid of Sarai, where have you come from and where are you going?" She answered, "I am running away from my mistress, Sarai." ⁹But the LORD's messenger told her: "Go back to your mistress and submit to her abusive treatment. ¹⁰I will make your descendants so numerous," added the LORD's messenger, "that they will be too many to count. ¹¹ Besides," the LORD's messenger said to her:

"You are now pregnant and shall bear a
    son;
  you shall name him Ishmael,
For the LORD has heard you,
  God has answered you.

¹² This one shall be a wild ass of a man,
  his hand against everyone,
  and everyone's hand against him;
In opposition to all his kin
  shall he encamp."

¹⁵Hagar bore Abram a son, and Abram named the son whom Hagar bore him Ishmael. ¹⁶Abram was eighty-six years old when Hagar bore him Ishmael.

Or Genesis 16:6B-12, 15-16

⁶Abram told Sarai: "Your maid is in your power. Do to her whatever you please." Sarai then abused her so much that Hagar ran away from her.

⁷The LORD's messenger found her by a spring in the wilderness, the spring on the road to Shur, ⁸and he asked, "Hagar, maid of Sarai, where have you come from and where are you going?" She answered, "I am running away from my mistress, Sarai." ⁹But the LORD's messenger told her: "Go back to your mistress and submit to her abusive treatment. ¹⁰I will make your descendants so numerous," added the LORD's messenger, "that they will be too many to count. ¹¹Besides," the LORD's messenger said to her:

"You are now pregnant and shall bear a
    son;
  you shall name him Ishmael,
For the LORD has heard you,
  God has answered you.

¹² This one shall be a wild ass of a man,
  his hand against everyone,
  and everyone's hand against him;
In opposition to all his kin
  shall he encamp."

¹⁵Hagar bore Abram a son, and Abram named the son whom Hagar bore him Ishmael. ¹⁶Abram was eighty-six years old when Hagar bore him Ishmael.

Responsorial Psalm: Psalms 106:1B-2, 3-4A, 4B-5
R. *⁽¹ᵇ⁾ Give thanks to the Lord, for he is good.* or: *R. Alleluia.*
¹ᴮ Give thanks to the LORD, for he is good,
    for his mercy endures forever.
² Who can tell the mighty deeds of the LORD,
    or proclaim all his praises?
R. Give thanks to the Lord, for he is good. or: ***R. Alleluia.***
³ Blessed are they who observe what is right,
    who do always what is just.
⁴ᴬ Remember us, O LORD, as you favor your
    people.
R. Give thanks to the Lord, for he is good. or: ***R. Alleluia.***
⁴ᴮ Visit me with your saving help,
⁵ that I may see the prosperity of your chosen
    ones,
  rejoice in the joy of your people,
  and glory with your inheritance.
R. Give thanks to the Lord, for he is good. or: ***R. Alleluia.***

Alleluia: John 14:23
R. Alleluia, alleluia.
²³ Whoever loves me will keep my word,
and my Father will love him
and we will come to him.
R. Alleluia, alleluia.

Gospel: Matthew 7:21-29
Jesus said to his disciples: ²¹"Not everyone who says to me, 'Lord, Lord,' will enter the Kingdom of heaven, but only the one who does the will of my Father in heaven. ²²Many will say to me on that day, 'Lord, Lord, did we not prophesy in your name? Did we not drive out demons in your name? Did we not do mighty deeds in your name?' ²³Then I will declare to them solemnly, 'I never knew you. Depart from me, you evildoers.'

    ²⁴ "Everyone who listens to these words of mine and acts on them will be like a wise man who built his house on rock. ²⁵The rain fell, the floods came, and the winds blew and buffeted the house. But it did not collapse; it had been set solidly on rock. ²⁶And everyone who listens to these words of mine but does not act on them will be like a fool who built his house on sand. ²⁷The rain fell, the floods came, and the winds blew and buffeted the house. And it collapsed and was completely ruined."

    ²⁸When Jesus finished these words, the crowds were astonished at his teaching, for he taught them as one having authority, and not as their scribes.

Friday June 27, 2025
Solemnity of the Most Sacred Heart of Jesus
First Reading: Ezekiel 34:11-16

¹¹Thus says the Lord GOD: I myself will look after and tend my sheep. ¹²As a shepherd tends his flock when he finds himself among his scattered sheep, so will I tend my sheep. I will rescue them from every place where they were scattered when it was cloudy and dark. ¹³I will lead them out from among the peoples and gather them from the foreign lands; I will bring them back to their own country and pasture them upon the mountains of Israel in the land's ravines and all its inhabited places. ¹⁴ In good pastures will I pasture them, and on the mountain heights of Israel shall be their grazing ground. There they shall lie down on good grazing ground, and in rich pastures shall they be pastured on the mountains of Israel. ¹⁵ I myself will pasture my sheep; I myself will give them rest, says the Lord GOD. ¹⁶ The lost I will seek out, the strayed I will bring back, the injured I will bind up, the sick I will heal, but the sleek and the strong I will destroy, shepherding them rightly.

Responsorial Psalm: Psalms 23:1-3A, 3B-4, 5, 6.

R. ⁽¹⁾ *The Lord is my shepherd; there is nothing I shall want.*

¹ The LORD is my shepherd; I shall not want.
   ² In verdant pastures he gives me repose;
beside restful waters he leads me;
   ³ᴬ he refreshes my soul.

R. *The Lord is my shepherd; there is nothing I shall want.*

³ᴮ He guides me in right paths
   for his name's sake.
⁴ Even though I walk in the dark valley
   I fear no evil; for you are at my side
with your rod and your staff
   that give me courage.

R. *The Lord is my shepherd; there is nothing I shall want.*

⁵ You spread the table before me
   in the sight of my foes;
you anoint my head with oil;
   my cup overflows.

R. *The Lord is my shepherd; there is nothing I shall want.*

⁶ Only goodness and kindness follow me
   all the days of my life;
and I shall dwell in the house of the LORD
   for years to come.

R. *The Lord is my shepherd; there is nothing I shall want.*

Second Reading: Romans 5:5B-11

Brothers and sisters: [5B] The love of God has been poured out into our hearts through the Holy Spirit that has been given to us. [6] For Christ, while we were still helpless, died at the appointed time for the ungodly. [7] Indeed, only with difficulty does one die for a just person, though perhaps for a good person one might even find courage to die. [8] But God proves his love for us in that while we were still sinners Christ died for us. [9] How much more then, since we are now justified by his blood, will we be saved through him from the wrath. [10] Indeed, if, while we were enemies, we were reconciled to God through the death of his Son, how much more, once reconciled, will we be saved by his life. [11] Not only that, but we also boast of God through our Lord Jesus Christ, through whom we have now received reconciliation.

Alleluia: Matthew 11:29AB
R. Alleluia, alleluia.
[29] Take my yoke upon you, says the Lord,
and learn from me, for I am meek and
    humble of heart.
R. Alleluia, alleluia.

Or John 10:14
R. Alleluia, alleluia.
[14] I am the good shepherd, says the Lord,
I know my sheep, and mine know me.
R. Alleluia, alleluia.

Gospel: Luke 15:3-7

[3] Jesus addressed this parable to the Pharisees and scribes: [4] "What man among you having a hundred sheep and losing one of them would not leave the ninety-nine in the desert and go after the lost one until he finds it? [5] And when he does find it, he sets it on his shoulders with great joy [6] and, upon his arrival home, he calls together his friends and neighbors and says to them, 'Rejoice with me because I have found my lost sheep.' [7] I tell you, in just the same way there will be more joy in heaven over one sinner who repents than over ninety-nine righteous people who have no need of repentance."

Saturday June 28, 2025
Memorial of the Immaculate Heart of Mary
First Reading: Genesis 18:1-15

[1] The LORD appeared to Abraham by the Terebinth of Mamre, as Abraham sat in the entrance of his tent, while the day was growing hot. [2] Looking up, he saw three men standing nearby. When he saw them, he ran from the entrance of the tent to greet them; and bowing to the ground, [3] he said: "Sir, if I may ask you this favor,

please do not go on past your servant. ⁴Let some water be brought, that you may bathe your feet, and then rest yourselves under the tree. ⁵Now that you have come this close to your servant, let me bring you a little food, that you may refresh yourselves; and afterward you may go on your way." The men replied, "Very well, do as you have said."

⁶Abraham hastened into the tent and told Sarah, "Quick, three measures of fine flour! Knead it and make rolls." ⁷He ran to the herd, picked out a tender, choice steer, and gave it to a servant, who quickly prepared it. ⁸Then Abraham got some curds and milk, as well as the steer that had been prepared, and set these before them; and he waited on them under the tree while they ate.

⁹They asked him, "Where is your wife Sarah?" He replied, "There in the tent." ¹⁰One of them said, "I will surely return to you about this time next year, and Sarah will then have a son." Sarah was listening at the entrance of the tent, just behind him. ¹¹Now Abraham and Sarah were old, advanced in years, and Sarah had stopped having her womanly periods. ¹²So Sarah laughed to herself and said, "Now that I am so withered and my husband is so old, am I still to have sexual pleasure?" ¹³But the LORD said to Abraham: "Why did Sarah laugh and say, 'Shall I really bear a child, old as I am?' ¹⁴Is anything too marvelous for the LORD to do? At the appointed time, about this time next year, I will return to you, and Sarah will have a son." ¹⁵Because she was afraid, Sarah dissembled, saying, "I didn't laugh." But he replied, "Yes you did."

Responsorial Psalm: Luke 1:46-47, 48-49, 50 AND 53, 54-55

R. *(see 54b)* ***The Lord has remembered his mercy.***

⁴⁶ "My soul proclaims the greatness of the
        Lord,
    ⁴⁷ my spirit rejoices in God my Savior."

R. The Lord has remembered his mercy.

⁴⁸ "For he has looked with favor on his lowly
        servant.
From this day all generations will call me
        blessed:
    ⁴⁹ the Almighty has done great things for
        me,
    and holy is his Name."

R. The Lord has remembered his mercy.

⁵⁰ "He has mercy on those who fear him
    in every generation.
⁵³ He has filled the hungry with good things,
    and the rich he has sent away empty."

R. The Lord has remembered his mercy.

⁵⁴ "He has come to the help of his servant
        Israel
    for he has remembered his promise of
        mercy,
⁵⁵ The promise he made to our fathers,

to Abraham and his children for ever."
R. The Lord has remembered his mercy.

Alleluia: see Luke 2:19
R. Alleluia, alleluia.
Blessed is the Virgin Mary who kept the word of God
and pondered it in her heart.
R. Alleluia, alleluia.

Gospel: Luke 2:41-51
[41]Each year Jesus parents went to Jerusalem for the feast of Passover, [42]and when he was twelve years old, they went up according to festival custom. [43]After they had completed its days, as they were returning, the boy Jesus remained behind in Jerusalem, but his parents did not know it. [44]Thinking that he was in the caravan, they journeyed for a day and looked for him among their relatives and acquaintances, [45]but not finding him, they returned to Jerusalem to look for him. [46]After three days they found him in the temple, sitting in the midst of the teachers, listening to them and asking them questions, [47]and all who heard him were astounded at his understanding and his answers. [48]When his parents saw him, they were astonished, and his mother said to him, "Son, why have you done this to us? Your father and I have been looking for you with great anxiety." [49]And he said to them, "Why were you looking for me? Did you not know that I must be in my Father's house?" [50]But they did not understand what he said to them. [51]He went down with them and came to Nazareth, and was obedient to them; and his mother kept all these things in her heart.

Sunday June 29, 2025
Solemnity of Saints Peter and Paul, Apostles
First Reading: Acts 12:1-11

[1] In those days, King Herod laid hands upon some members of the Church to harm them. [2] He had James, the brother of John, killed by the sword, [3] and when he saw that this was pleasing to the Jews he proceeded to arrest Peter also. —It was the feast of Unleavened Bread.— [4] He had him taken into custody and put in prison under the guard of four squads of four soldiers each. He intended to bring him before the people after Passover. [5] Peter thus was being kept in prison, but prayer by the Church was fervently being made to God on his behalf.

[6] On the very night before Herod was to bring him to trial, Peter, secured by double chains, was sleeping between two soldiers, while outside the door guards kept watch on the prison. [7] Suddenly the angel of the Lord stood by him, and a light shone in the cell. He tapped Peter on the side and awakened him, saying, "Get up quickly." The chains fell from his wrists. [8] The angel said to him, "Put on your belt and your sandals." He did so. Then he said to him, "Put on your cloak and follow me." [9] So he followed him out, not realizing that what was happening through the angel was real; he thought he was seeing a vision. [10] They passed the first guard, then the second, and came to the iron gate leading out to the city, which opened for

them by itself. They emerged and made their way down an alley, and suddenly the angel left him. ¹¹ Then Peter recovered his senses and said, "Now I know for certain that the Lord sent his angel and rescued me from the hand of Herod and from all that the Jewish people had been expecting."

Responsorial Psalm: Psalms 34:2-3, 4-5, 6-7, 8-9

R. [5] *The angel of the Lord will rescue those who fear him.*

² I will bless the LORD at all times;
    his praise shall be ever in my mouth.
³ Let my soul glory in the LORD;
    the lowly will hear me and be glad.

R. The angel of the Lord will rescue those who fear him.

⁴ Glorify the LORD with me,
    let us together extol his name.
⁵ I sought the LORD, and he answered me
    and delivered me from all my fears.

R. The angel of the Lord will rescue those who fear him.

⁶ Look to him that you may be radiant with joy,
    and your faces may not blush with shame.
⁷ When the poor one called out, the LORD heard,
    and from all his distress he saved him.

R. The angel of the Lord will rescue those who fear him.

⁸ The angel of the LORD encamps
    around those who fear him, and delivers them.
⁹ Taste and see how good the LORD is;
    blessed the man who takes refuge in him.

R. The angel of the Lord will rescue those who fear him.

Second Reading: 2 Timothy 4:6-8, 17-18

⁶ I, Paul, am already being poured out like a libation, and the time of my departure is at hand. ⁷ I have competed well; I have finished the race; I have kept the faith. ⁸ From now on the crown of righteousness awaits me, which the Lord, the just judge, will award to me on that day, and not only to me, but to all who have longed for his appearance.

¹⁷ The Lord stood by me and gave me strength, so that through me the proclamation might be completed and all the Gentiles might hear it. And I was

rescued from the lion's mouth. ¹⁸ The Lord will rescue me from every evil threat and will bring me safe to his heavenly Kingdom. To him be glory forever and ever. Amen.

Alleluia: Matthew 16:18
R. Alleluia, alleluia.
¹⁸ You are Peter and upon this rock I will build
    my Church,
and the gates of the netherworld shall not
    prevail against it.
R. Alleluia, alleluia.

Gospel: Matthew 16:13-19
¹³ When Jesus went into the region of Caesarea Philippi he asked his disciples, "Who do people say that the Son of Man is?" ¹⁴ They replied, "Some say John the Baptist, others Elijah, still others Jeremiah or one of the prophets." ¹⁵ He said to them, "But who do you say that I am?" ¹⁶ Simon Peter said in reply, "You are the Christ, the Son of the living God." ¹⁷Jesus said to him in reply, "Blessed are you, Simon son of Jonah. For flesh and blood has not revealed this to you, but my heavenly Father. ¹⁸ And so I say to you, you are Peter, and upon this rock I will build my Church, and the gates of the netherworld shall not prevail against it. ¹⁹ I will give you the keys to the Kingdom of heaven. Whatever you bind on earth shall be bound in heaven; and whatever you loose on earth shall be loosed in heaven."

Monday June 30, 2025
Monday of the Thirteenth Week in Ordinary Time
First Reading: Genesis 18:16-33
Abraham and the men who had visited him by the Terebinth of Mamre set out from there and looked down toward Sodom; ¹⁶Abraham was walking with them, to see them on their way. ¹⁷The LORD reflected: "Shall I hide from Abraham what I am about to do, ¹⁸now that he is to become a great and populous nation, and all the nations of the earth are to find blessing in him? ¹⁹Indeed, I have singled him out that he may direct his children and his household after him to keep the way of the LORD by doing what is right and just, so that the LORD may carry into effect for Abraham the promises he made about him." ²⁰Then the LORD said: "The outcry against Sodom and Gomorrah is so great, and their sin so grave, ²¹that I must go down and see whether or not their actions fully correspond to the cry against them that comes to me.
I mean to find out."

²²While the two men walked on farther toward Sodom, the LORD remained standing before Abraham. ²³Then Abraham drew nearer to him and said: "Will you sweep away the innocent with the guilty? ²⁴Suppose there were fifty innocent people in the city; would you wipe out the place, rather than spare it for the sake of the fifty innocent people within it? ²⁵Far be it from you to do such a thing, to make the innocent die with the guilty, so that the innocent and the guilty would be treated

alike! Should not the judge of all the world act with justice?" ²⁶The LORD replied, "If I find fifty innocent people in the city of Sodom, I will spare the whole place for their sake." ²⁷Abraham spoke up again: "See how I am presuming to speak to my Lord, though I am but dust and ashes! ²⁸What if there are five less than fifty innocent people? Will you destroy the whole city because of those five?" He answered, "I will not destroy it if I find forty-five there." ²⁹But Abraham persisted, saying, "What if only forty are found there?" He replied, "I will forbear doing it for the sake of forty." ³⁰Then Abraham said, "Let not my Lord grow impatient if I go on. What if only thirty are found there?" He replied, "I will forbear doing it if I can find but thirty there." Still Abraham went on, ³¹"Since I have thus dared to speak to my Lord, what if there are no more than twenty?" He answered, "I will not destroy it for the sake of the twenty." ³²But he still persisted: "Please, let not my Lord grow angry if I speak up this last time. What if there are at least ten there?" He replied, "For the sake of those ten, I will not destroy it."

³³The LORD departed as soon as he had finished speaking with Abraham, and Abraham returned home.

Responsorial Psalm: Psalms 103:1b-2, 3-4, 8-9, 10-11

R. ⁽⁸ᵃ⁾ *The Lord is kind and merciful.*
¹ᴮ Bless the LORD, O my soul;
    and all my being, bless his holy name.
² Bless the LORD, O my soul,
    and forget not all his benefits.
R. The Lord is kind and merciful.
³ He pardons all your iniquities,
    he heals all your ills.
⁴ He redeems your life from destruction,
    he crowns you with kindness and
        compassion.
R. The Lord is kind and merciful.
⁸ Merciful and gracious is the LORD,
    slow to anger and abounding in kindness.
⁹ He will not always chide,
    nor does he keep his wrath forever.
R. The Lord is kind and merciful.
¹⁰ Not according to our sins does he deal with
        us,
    nor does he requite us according to our
        crimes.
¹¹ For as the heavens are high above the earth,
    so surpassing is his kindness toward
        those who fear him.
R. The Lord is kind and merciful.

Alleluia: Psalms 95:8
R. Alleluia, alleluia.
⁸ If today you hear his voice,
harden not your hearts.
R. Alleluia, alleluia.

Gospel: Matthew 8:18-22
¹⁸When Jesus saw a crowd around him, he gave orders to cross to the other shore. ¹⁹A scribe approached and said to him, "Teacher, I will follow you wherever you go." ²⁰Jesus answered him, "Foxes have dens and birds of the sky have nests, but the Son of Man has nowhere to rest his head." ²¹Another of his disciples said to him, "Lord, let me go first and bury my father." ²²But Jesus answered him, "Follow me, and let the dead bury their dead."

JULY 2025
Tuesday July 1, 2025
Tuesday of the Thirteenth Week in Ordinary Time

First Reading: Genesis 19:15-29
¹⁵As dawn was breaking, the angels urged Lot on, saying, "On your way! Take with you your wife and your two daughters who are here, or you will be swept away in the punishment of Sodom." ¹⁶ When he hesitated, the men, by the LORD's mercy, seized his hand and the hands of his wife and his two daughters and led them to safety outside the city. ¹⁷As soon as they had been brought outside, he was told: "Flee for your life! Don't look back or stop anywhere on the Plain. Get off to the hills at once, or you will be swept away." ¹⁸ "Oh, no, my lord!" Lot replied, ¹⁹ "You have already thought enough of your servant to do me the great kindness of intervening to save my life. But I cannot flee to the hills to keep the disaster from overtaking me, and so I shall die. ²⁰ Look, this town ahead is near enough to escape to. It's only a small place. Let me flee there –it's a small place, is it not?– that my life may be saved." ²¹"Well, then," he replied, "I will also grant you the favor you now ask. I will not overthrow the town you speak of. ²²Hurry, escape there! I cannot do anything until you arrive there." That is why the town is called Zoar.

²³The sun was just rising over the earth as Lot arrived in Zoar; ²⁴at the same time the LORD rained down sulphurous fire upon Sodom and Gomorrah from the LORD out of heaven. ²⁵He overthrew those cities and the whole Plain, together with the inhabitants of the cities and the produce of the soil. ²⁶But Lot's wife looked back, and she was turned into a pillar of salt.

²⁷Early the next morning Abraham went to the place where he had stood in the LORD's presence. ²⁸As he looked down toward Sodom and Gomorrah and the whole region of the Plain, he saw dense smoke over the land rising like fumes from a furnace.

Thus it came to pass: ²⁹when God destroyed the Cities of the Plain, he was mindful of Abraham by sending Lot away from the upheaval by which God overthrew the cities where Lot had been living.

Responsorial Psalm: Psalms 26:2-3,9-10, 11-12
R. ⁽³ᵃ⁾ *O Lord, your mercy is before my eyes.*

² Search me, O LORD, and try me;
   test my soul and my heart.
³ For your mercy is before my eyes,
   and I walk in your truth.
R. O Lord, your mercy is before my eyes.
⁹ Gather not my soul with those of sinners,
   nor with men of blood my life.
¹⁰ On their hands are crimes,
   and their right hands are full of bribes.
R. O Lord, your mercy is before my eyes.
¹¹ But I walk in integrity;
   redeem me, and have mercy on me.
¹² My foot stands on level ground;
   in the assemblies I will bless the LORD.
R. O Lord, your mercy is before my eyes.

Alleluia: Psalms 130:5
R. Alleluia, alleluia.
⁵ I trust in the LORD;
my soul trusts in his word.
R. Alleluia, alleluia.

Gospel: Matthew 8:23-27
²³ As Jesus got into a boat, his disciples followed him. ²⁴ Suddenly a violent storm came up on the sea, so that the boat was being swamped by waves; but he was asleep. ²⁵ They came and woke him, saying, "Lord, save us! We are perishing!" ²⁶ He said to them, "Why are you terrified, O you of little faith?" Then he got up, rebuked the winds and the sea, and there was great calm. ²⁷ The men were amazed and said, "What sort of man is this, whom even the winds and the sea obey?"

Wednesday July 2, 2025
Wednesday of the Thirteenth Week in Ordinary Time
First Reading: Genesis 21:5, 8-20A
⁵Abraham was a hundred years old when his son Isaac was born to him. ⁸Isaac grew, and on the day of the child's weaning Abraham held a great feast.

⁹Sarah noticed the son whom Hagar the Egyptian had borne to Abraham playing with her son Isaac; ¹⁰so she demanded of Abraham: "Drive out that slave and her son! No son of that slave is going to share the inheritance with my son Isaac!" ¹¹Abraham was greatly distressed, especially on account of his son Ishmael. ¹²But God said to Abraham: "Do not be distressed about the boy or about your slave woman. Heed the demands of Sarah, no matter what she is asking of you; for it is through Isaac that descendants shall bear your name. ¹³As for the son of the slave woman, I will make a great nation of him also, since he too is your offspring."

¹⁴Early the next morning Abraham got some bread and a skin of water and gave them to Hagar. Then, placing the child on her back, he sent her away. As she

roamed aimlessly in the wilderness of Beer-sheba, [15]the water in the skin was used up. So she put the child down under a shrub, [16]and then went and sat down opposite him, about a bowshot away; for she said to herself, "Let me not watch to see the child die." As she sat opposite Ishmael, he began to cry. [17]God heard the boy's cry, and God's messenger called to Hagar from heaven: "What is the matter, Hagar? Don't be afraid; God has heard the boy's cry in this plight of his. [18]Arise, lift up the boy and hold him by the hand; for I will make of him a great nation." [19]Then God opened her eyes, and she saw a well of water. She went and filled the skin with water, and then let the boy drink.

[20A]God was with the boy as he grew up.

Responsorial Psalm: Psalms 34:7-8, 10-11, 12-13
R. [(7a)] *The Lord hears the cry of the poor.*
[7] When the poor one called out, the LORD
      heard,
   and from all his distress he saved him.
[8] The angel of the LORD encamps
   around those who fear him, and delivers
      them.
R. *The Lord hears the cry of the poor.*
[10] Fear the LORD, you his holy ones,
   for nought is lacking to those who fear
      him.
[11] The great grow poor and hungry;
   but those who seek the LORD want for no
      good thing.
R. *The Lord hears the cry of the poor.*
[12] Come, children, hear me;
   I will teach you the fear of the LORD.
[13] Which of you desires life,
   and takes delight in prosperous days?
R. *The Lord hears the cry of the poor.*

Alleluia: James 1:18
R. Alleluia, alleluia.
[18]The Father willed to give us birth by the
      word of truth
that we may be a kind of firstfruits of his
      creatures.
R. Alleluia, alleluia.

Gospel: Matthew 8:28-34
[28]When Jesus came to the territory of the Gadarenes, two demoniacs who were coming from the tombs met him. They were so savage that no one could travel by

that road. ²⁹They cried out, "What have you to do with us, Son of God? Have you come here to torment us before the appointed time?" ³⁰Some distance away a herd of many swine was feeding. ³¹The demons pleaded with him, "If you drive us out, send us into the herd of swine." ³²And he said to them, "Go then!" They came out and entered the swine, and the whole herd rushed down the steep bank into the sea where they drowned. ³³The swineherds ran away, and when they came to the town they reported everything, including what had happened to the demoniacs. ³⁴Thereupon the whole town came out to meet Jesus, and when they saw him they begged him to leave their district.

Thursday July 3, 2025
Feast of Saint Thomas, Apostle

First Reading: Ephesians 2:19-22

Brothers and sisters: ¹⁹ You are no longer strangers and sojourners, but you are fellow citizens with the holy ones and members of the household of God, ²⁰ built upon the foundation of the Apostles and prophets, with Christ Jesus himself as the capstone. ²¹ Through him, the whole structure is held together and grows into a temple sacred in the Lord; ²² in him you also are being built together into a dwelling place of God in the Spirit.

Responsorial Psalm: Psalms 117:1BC, 2

R. *(Mark 16:15)* **Go out to all the world and tell the Good News.**

¹ᴮᶜ Praise the LORD, all you nations;
    glorify him, all you peoples!

R. Go out to all the world and tell the Good News.

² For steadfast is his kindness for us,
    and the fidelity of the LORD endures forever.

R. Go out to all the world and tell the Good News.

Alleluia: John 20:29

R. Alleluia, alleluia.
²⁹ You believe in me, Thomas, because you have seen me, says the Lord;
blessed are those who have not seen, but still believe!
R. Alleluia, alleluia.

Gospel: John 20:24-29

²⁴ Thomas, called Didymus, one of the Twelve, was not with them when Jesus came. ²⁵ So the other disciples said to him, "We have seen the Lord." But Thomas said to them, "Unless I see the mark of the nails in his hands and put my finger into the nailmarks and put my hand into his side, I will not believe." ²⁶ Now a week later his disciples were again inside and Thomas was with them. Jesus came, although the doors were locked, and stood in their midst and said, "Peace be with you." ²⁷ Then he said to Thomas, "Put your finger here and see my hands, and bring your hand and put it into my side, and do not be unbelieving, but believe." ²⁸ Thomas answered and said to him, "My Lord and my God!" ²⁹ Jesus said to him, "Have you come to believe because you have seen me? Blessed are those who have not seen and have believed."

Friday July 4, 2025
Friday of Thirteenth Week in Ordinary Time
First Reading: Genesis 23:1-4,19;24:1-8,62-67

¹The span of Sarah's life was one hundred and twenty-seven years. ²She died in Kiriatharba (that is, Hebron) in the land of Canaan, and Abraham performed the customary mourning rites for her. ³Then he left the side of his dead one and addressed the Hittites: ⁴"Although I am a resident alien among you, sell me from your holdings a piece of property for a burial ground, that I may bury my dead wife."

¹⁹After the transaction, Abraham buried his wife Sarah in the cave of the field of Machpelah, facing Mamre (that is, Hebron) in the land of Canaan.

¹Abraham had now reached a ripe old age, and the LORD had blessed him in every way. ²Abraham said to the senior servant of his household, who had charge of all his possessions: "Put your hand under my thigh, ³and I will make you swear by the LORD, the God of heaven and the God of earth, that you will not procure a wife for my son from the daughters of the Canaanites among whom I live, ⁴but that you will go to my own land and to my kindred to get a wife for my son Isaac." ⁵The servant asked him: "What if the woman is unwilling to follow me to this land? Should I then take your son back to the land from which you migrated?" ⁶"Never take my son back there for any reason," Abraham told him. ⁷"The LORD, the God of heaven, who took me from my father's house and the land of my kin, and who confirmed by oath the promise he then made to me, 'I will give this land to your descendants'– he will send his messenger before you, and you will obtain a wife for my son there. ⁸If the woman is unwilling to follow you, you will be released from this oath. But never take my son back there!"

⁶²A long time later, Isaac went to live in the region of the Negeb. ⁶³One day toward evening he went out . . . in the field, and as he looked around, he noticed that camels were approaching. ⁶⁴Rebekah, too, was looking about, and when she saw him, she alighted from her camel. ⁶⁵She asked the servant, "Who is the man out there, walking through the fields toward us?" "That is my master," replied the servant. Then she covered herself with her veil.

⁶⁶The servant recounted to Isaac all the things he had done. ⁶⁷Then Isaac took Rebekah into his tent; he married her, and thus she became his wife. In his love for her, Isaac found solace after the death of his mother Sarah.

Responsorial Psalm: Psalms 106:1B-2, 3-4A, 4B-5

R. (1b) *Give thanks to the Lord, for he is good.*

¹ᴮ Give thanks to the LORD, for he is good,
   for his mercy endures forever.
² Who can tell the mighty deeds of the LORD,
   or proclaim all his praises?

R. *Give thanks to the Lord, for he is good.*

³ Blessed are they who observe what is right,
   who do always what is just.
⁴ᴬ Remember us, O LORD, as you favor your people.

R. *Give thanks to the Lord, for he is good.*

⁴ᴮ Visit me with your saving help,
⁵ That I may see the prosperity of your chosen ones,
   rejoice in the joy of your people,
   and glory with your inheritance.

R. *Give thanks to the Lord, for he is good.*

Alleluia: Matthew 11:28

R. Alleluia, alleluia.
²⁸ Come to me, all you who labor and are burdened,
and I will give you rest, says the Lord.
R. Alleluia, alleluia.

Gospel: Matthew 9:9-13

⁹ As Jesus passed by, he saw a man named Matthew sitting at the customs post. He said to him, "Follow me." And he got up and followed him. ¹⁰ While he was at table in his house, many tax collectors and sinners came and sat with Jesus and his disciples. ¹¹ The Pharisees saw this and said to his disciples, "Why does your teacher eat with tax collectors and sinners?" ¹² He heard this and said, "Those who are well do not need a physician, but the sick do. ¹³ Go and learn the meaning of the words, *I desire mercy, not sacrifice*. I did not come to call the righteous but sinners."

Saturday July 5, 2025
Saturday of the Thirteenth Week in Ordinary Time

First Reading: Genesis 27:1-5, 15-29

¹When Isaac was so old that his eyesight had failed him, he called his older son Esau and said to him, "Son!" "Yes, father!" he replied. ²Isaac then said, "As you can see, I am so old that I may now die at any time. ³Take your gear, therefore–your quiver and bow–and go out into the country to hunt some game for me. ⁴With your catch prepare an appetizing dish for me, such as I like, and bring it to me to eat, so that I may give you my special blessing before I die."

⁵Rebekah had been listening while Isaac was speaking to his son Esau. So, when Esau went out into the country to hunt some game for his father, ¹⁵Rebekah

[then] took the best clothes of her older son Esau that she had in the house, and gave them to her younger son Jacob to wear; ¹⁶and with the skins of the kids she covered up his hands and the hairless parts of his neck. ¹⁷Then she handed her son Jacob the appetizing dish and the bread she had prepared.

¹⁸Bringing them to his father, Jacob said, "Father!" "Yes?" replied Isaac. "Which of my sons are you?" ¹⁹Jacob answered his father: "I am Esau, your firstborn. I did as you told me. Please sit up and eat some of my game, so that you may give me your special blessing." ²⁰But Isaac asked, "How did you succeed so quickly, son?" He answered, ²¹"The LORD, your God, let things turn out well with me." Isaac then said to Jacob, "Come closer, son, that I may feel you, to learn whether you really are my son Esau or not." ²²So Jacob moved up closer to his father. When Isaac felt him, he said, "Although the voice is Jacob's, the hands are Esau's." ²³(He failed to identify him because his hands were hairy, like those of his brother Esau; so in the end, he gave him his blessing.) ²⁴Again he asked Jacob, "Are you really my son Esau?" "Certainly," Jacob replied. ²⁵Then Isaac said, "Serve me your game, son, that I may eat of it and then give you my blessing." Jacob served it to him, and Isaac ate; he brought him wine, and he drank. ²⁶Finally his father Isaac said to Jacob, "Come closer, son, and kiss me." ²⁷As Jacob went up and kissed him, Isaac smelled the fragrance of his clothes. With that, he blessed him saying,

"Ah, the fragrance of my son
    is like the fragrance of a field
    that the LORD has blessed!

²⁸"May God give to you
    of the dew of the heavens
And of the fertility of the earth
    abundance of grain and wine.

²⁹"Let peoples serve you,
    and nations pay you homage;
Be master of your brothers,
    and may your mother's sons bow down to
        you.
Cursed be those who curse you,
    and blessed be those who bless you."

Responsorial Psalm: Psalms 135:1B-2, 3-4, 5-6
R. ⁽³ᵃ⁾ ***Praise the Lord for the Lord is good!*** or: ***R. Alleluia.***
¹ᴮ Praise the name of the LORD;
    Praise, you servants of the LORD
² Who stand in the house of the LORD,
    in the courts of the house of our God.
R. Praise the Lord for the Lord is good! or: ***R. Alleluia.***

³ Praise the LORD, for the LORD is good;
>   sing praise to his name, which we love;
⁴ For the LORD has chosen Jacob for himself,
>   Israel for his own possession.

R. Praise the Lord for the Lord is good! or: **R. Alleluia.**

⁵ For I know that the LORD is great;
>   our LORD is greater than all gods.
⁶ All that the LORD wills he does
>   in heaven and on earth,
>   in the seas and in all the deeps.

R. Praise the Lord for the Lord is good! or: **R. Alleluia.**

Alleluia: John 10:27
R. Alleluia, alleluia.
²⁷ My sheep hear my voice, says the Lord;
I know them, and they follow me.
R. Alleluia, alleluia.

Gospel: Matthew 9:14-17
¹⁴ The disciples of John approached Jesus and said, "Why do we and the Pharisees fast much, but your disciples do not fast?" ¹⁵ Jesus answered them, "Can the wedding guests mourn as long as the bridegroom is with them? The days will come when the bridegroom is taken away from them, and then they will fast. ¹⁶ No one patches an old cloak with a piece of unshrunken cloth, for its fullness pulls away from the cloak and the tear gets worse. ¹⁷ People do not put new wine into old wineskins. Otherwise the skins burst, the wine spills out, and the skins are ruined. Rather, they pour new wine into fresh wineskins, and both are preserved."

Sunday July 6, 2025
Fourteenth Sunday in Ordinary Time, Year C

First Reading: Isaiah 66:10-14C
Thus says the LORD:

¹⁰ Rejoice with Jerusalem and be glad because
>   of her,
>   all you who love her;
exult, exult with her,
>   all you who were mourning over her!
Oh, that you may suck fully
>   of the milk of her comfort,
¹¹that you may nurse with delight
>   at her abundant breasts!
>   ¹²For thus says the LORD:
Lo, I will spread prosperity over Jerusalem
>   like a river,

and the wealth of the nations like an
   overflowing torrent.
As nurslings, you shall be carried in her
   arms,
   and fondled in her lap;
13as a mother comforts her child,
   so will I comfort you;
   in Jerusalem, you shall find your comfort.

14c When you see this, your heart shall rejoice
   and your bodies flourish like the grass;
the LORD's power shall be known to his
   servants.

Responsorial Psalm: Psalms 66:1-3, 4-5, 6-7, 16, 20
R. [1] *Let all the earth cry out to God with joy.*
2 Shout joyfully to God, all the earth,
   sing praise to the glory of his name;
   proclaim his glorious praise.
3 Say to God, "How tremendous are your
   deeds!"
R. *Let all the earth cry out to God with joy.*
4 "Let all on earth worship and sing praise to
   you,
   sing praise to your name!"
5 Come and see the works of God,
   his tremendous deeds among the
   children of Adam.
R. *Let all the earth cry out to God with joy.*
6 He has changed the sea into dry land;
   through the river they passed on foot;
   therefore let us rejoice in him.
7 He rules by his might forever.
R. *Let all the earth cry out to God with joy.*
16 Hear now, all you who fear God,
   while I declare what he has done for me.
20 Blessed be God who refused me not
   my prayer or his kindness!
R. *Let all the earth cry out to God with joy.*

Second Reading: Galatians 6:14-18
Brothers and sisters: 14May I never boast except in the cross of our Lord Jesus Christ, through which the world has been crucified to me, and I to the world. 15For

neither does circumcision mean anything, nor does uncircumcision, but only a new creation. ¹⁶Peace and mercy be to all who follow this rule and to the Israel of God.

¹⁷From now on, let no one make troubles for me; for I bear the marks of Jesus on my body.

¹⁸The grace of our Lord Jesus Christ be with your spirit, brothers and sisters. Amen.

Alleluia: Colossians 3:15a, 16a
R. Alleluia, alleluia.
¹⁵ᴬ Let the peace of Christ control your hearts;
¹⁶ᴬ let the word of Christ dwell in you richly.
R. Alleluia, alleluia.

Gospel: Luke 10:1-12, 17-20
¹ At that time the Lord appointed seventy-two others whom he sent ahead of him in pairs to every town and place he intended to visit. ²He said to them, "The harvest is abundant but the laborers are few; so ask the master of the harvest to send out laborers for his harvest. ³Go on your way; behold, I am sending you like lambs among wolves. ⁴Carry no money bag, no sack, no sandals; and greet no one along the way. ⁵ Into whatever house you enter, first say, 'Peace to this household.' ⁶ If a peaceful person lives there, your peace will rest on him; but if not, it will return to you. ⁷Stay in the same house and eat and drink what is offered to you, for the laborer deserves his payment. Do not move about from one house to another. ⁸Whatever town you enter and they welcome you, eat what is set before you, ⁹cure the sick in it and say to them, 'The kingdom of God is at hand for you.' ¹⁰Whatever town you enter and they do not receive you, go out into the streets and say, ¹¹'The dust of your town that clings to our feet, even that we shake off against you.' Yet know this: the kingdom of God is at hand. ¹² I tell you, it will be more tolerable for Sodom on that day than for that town."

¹⁷The seventy-two returned rejoicing, and said, "Lord, even the demons are subject to us because of your name." ¹⁸Jesus said, "I have observed Satan fall like lightning from the sky. ¹⁹ Behold, I have given you the power to 'tread upon serpents' and scorpions and upon the full force of the enemy and nothing will harm you. ²⁰ Nevertheless, do not rejoice because the spirits are subject to you, but rejoice because your names are written in heaven."

Or Luke 10:1-9
¹At that time the Lord appointed seventy-two others whom he sent ahead of him in pairs to every town and place he intended to visit. ² He said to them, "The harvest is abundant but the laborers are few; so ask the master of the harvest to send out laborers for his harvest. ³ Go on your way; behold, I am sending you like lambs among wolves. ⁴Carry no money bag, no sack, no sandals; and greet no one along the way. ⁵ Into whatever house you enter, first say, 'Peace to this household.' ⁶ If a peaceful person lives there, your peace will rest on him; but if not, it will return to

you. ⁷Stay in the same house and eat and drink what is offered to you, for the laborer deserves his payment. Do not move about from one house to another. ⁸Whatever town you enter and they welcome you, eat what is set before you, ⁹cure the sick in it and say to them, 'The kingdom of God is at hand for you.'"

Monday July 7, 2025
Monday of Fourteenth Week in Ordinary Time
First Reading: Genesis 28:10-22A

¹⁰Jacob departed from Beer-sheba and proceeded toward Haran. ¹¹When he came upon a certain shrine, as the sun had already set, he stopped there for the night. Taking one of the stones at the shrine, he put it under his head and lay down to sleep at that spot. ¹²Then he had a dream: a stairway rested on the ground, with its top reaching to the heavens; and God's messengers were going up and down on it. ¹³And there was the LORD standing beside him and saying: "I, the LORD, am the God of your forefather Abraham and the God of Isaac; the land on which you are lying I will give to you and your descendants. ¹⁴These shall be as plentiful as the dust of the earth, and through them you shall spread out east and west, north and south. In you and your descendants all the nations of the earth shall find blessing. ¹⁵Know that I am with you; I will protect you wherever you go, and bring you back to this land. I will never leave you until I have done what I promised you."

¹⁶When Jacob awoke from his sleep, he exclaimed, "Truly, the LORD is in this spot, although I did not know it!" ¹⁷In solemn wonder he cried out: "How awesome is this shrine! This is nothing else but an abode of God, and that is the gateway to heaven!" ¹⁸Early the next morning Jacob took the stone that he had put under his head, set it up as a memorial stone, and poured oil on top of it. ¹⁹He called the site Bethel, whereas the former name of the town had been Luz.

²⁰Jacob then made this vow: "If God remains with me, to protect me on this journey I am making and to give me enough bread to eat and clothing to wear, ²¹and I come back safe to my father's house, the LORD shall be my God. ²²This stone that I have set up as a memorial stone shall be God's abode."

Responsorial Psalm: Psalms 91:1-2, 3-4, 14-15AB

R. (see 2b) **In you, my God, I place my trust.**
¹ You who dwell in the shelter of the Most
    High,
   who abide in the shadow of the Almighty,
² Say to the LORD, "My refuge and my fortress,
   my God, in whom I trust."
R. In you, my God, I place my trust.
³ For he will rescue you from the snare of the
    fowler,
   from the destroying pestilence.
⁴ With his pinions he will cover you,
   and under his wings you shall take
       refuge.

R. In you, my God, I place my trust.
14 Because he clings to me, I will deliver him;
> I will set him on high because he
>> acknowledges my name.

15AB He shall call upon me, and I will answer him;
> I will be with him in distress.

R. In you, my God, I place my trust.

Alleluia: cf. 2 Timothy 1:10
R. Alleluia, alleluia.
10 Our Savior Jesus Christ has destroyed death and brought life to light through the Gospel.
R. Alleluia, alleluia.

Gospel: Matthew 9:18-26

18 While Jesus was speaking, an official came forward, knelt down before him, and said, "My daughter has just died. But come, lay your hand on her, and she will live." 19 Jesus rose and followed him, and so did his disciples. 20 A woman suffering hemorrhages for twelve years came up behind him and touched the tassel on his cloak. 21 She said to herself, "If only I can touch his cloak, I shall be cured." 22 Jesus turned around and saw her, and said, "Courage, daughter! Your faith has saved you." And from that hour the woman was cured.

23 When Jesus arrived at the official's house and saw the flute players and the crowd who were making a commotion, 24 he said, "Go away! The girl is not dead but sleeping." And they ridiculed him. 25 When the crowd was put out, he came and took her by the hand, and the little girl arose. 26 And news of this spread throughout all that land.

Tuesday July 8, 2025
Tuesday of the Fourteenth Week in Ordinary Time
First Reading: Genesis 32:23-33

23 In the course of the night, Jacob arose, took his two wives, with the two maidservants and his eleven children, and crossed the ford of the Jabbok. 24 After he had taken them across the stream and had brought over all his possessions, 25 Jacob was left there alone. Then some man wrestled with him until the break of dawn. 26 When the man saw that he could not prevail over him, he struck Jacob's hip at its socket, so that the hip socket was wrenched as they wrestled. 27 The man then said, "Let me go, for it is daybreak." But Jacob said, "I will not let you go until you bless me." 28 The man asked, "What is your name?" He answered, "Jacob." 29 Then the man said, "You shall no longer be spoken of as Jacob, but as Israel, because you have contended with divine and human beings and have prevailed." 30 Jacob then asked him, "Do tell me your name, please." He answered, "Why should you want to know my name?" With that, he bade him farewell. 31 Jacob named the place Peniel, "Because I have seen God face to face," he said, "yet my life has been spared."

32 At sunrise, as he left Penuel, Jacob limped along because of his hip. 33 That is why, to this day, the children of Israel do not eat the sciatic muscle that is on the hip socket, inasmuch as Jacob's hip socket was struck at the sciatic muscle.

Responsorial Psalm: Psalms 17:1B, 2-3, 6-7AB, 8B AND 15
R. (15a) In justice, I shall behold your face, O Lord.

¹ᴮ Hear, O LORD, a just suit;
    attend to my outcry;
    hearken to my prayer from lips without
        deceit.

R. In justice, I shall behold your face, O Lord.

² From you let my judgment come;
    your eyes behold what is right.
³ Though you test my heart, searching it in the
        night,
    though you try me with fire, you shall
        find no malice in me.

R. In justice, I shall behold your face, O Lord.

⁶ I call upon you, for you will answer me, O
        God;
    incline your ear to me; hear my word.
⁷ᴬᴮ Show your wondrous mercies,
    O savior of those who flee from their foes.

R. In justice, I shall behold your face, O Lord.

⁸ᴮ Hide me in the shadow of your wings.
¹⁵ I in justice shall behold your face;
    on waking, I shall be content in your
        presence.

R. In justice, I shall behold your face, O Lord.

Alleluia: John 10:14
R. Alleluia, alleluia.
¹⁴ I am the good shepherd, says the Lord;
I know my sheep, and mine know me.
R. Alleluia, alleluia.

Gospel: Matthew 9:32-38
³² A demoniac who could not speak was brought to Jesus, ³³ and when the demon was driven out the mute man spoke. The crowds were amazed and said, "Nothing like this has ever been seen in Israel." ³⁴ But the Pharisees said, "He drives out demons by the prince of demons."

³⁵ Jesus went around to all the towns and villages, teaching in their synagogues, proclaiming the Gospel of the Kingdom, and curing every disease and illness. ³⁶ At the sight of the crowds, his heart was moved with pity for them because they were troubled and abandoned, like sheep without a shepherd. ³⁷ Then he said to his disciples, "The harvest is abundant but the laborers are few; ³⁸ so ask the master of the harvest to send out laborers for his harvest."

Wednesday July 9, 2025
Wednesday of the Fourteenth Week in Ordinary Time
First Reading: Genesis 41:55-57; 42:5-7A, 17-24A

⁵⁵When hunger came to be felt throughout the land of Egypt and the people cried to Pharaoh for bread, Pharaoh directed all the Egyptians to go to Joseph and do whatever he told them. ⁵⁶When the famine had spread throughout the land, Joseph opened all the cities that had grain and rationed it to the Egyptians, since the famine had gripped the land of Egypt. ⁵⁷In fact, all the world came to Joseph to obtain rations of grain, for famine had gripped the whole world.

⁵The sons of Israel were among those who came to procure rations.

⁶It was Joseph, as governor of the country, who dispensed the rations to all the people. When Joseph's brothers came and knelt down before him with their faces to the ground, ⁷ᴬhe recognized them as soon as he saw them. But Joseph concealed his own identity from them and spoke sternly to them.

¹⁷With that, he locked them up in the guardhouse for three days.

¹⁸On the third day Joseph said to his brothers: "Do this, and you shall live; for I am a God-fearing man. ¹⁹If you have been honest, only one of your brothers need be confined in this prison, while the rest of you may go and take home provisions for your starving families. ²⁰But you must come back to me with your youngest brother. Your words will thus be verified, and you will not die." To this they agreed. ²¹To one another, however, they said: "Alas, we are being punished because of our brother. We saw the anguish of his heart when he pleaded with us, yet we paid no heed; that is why this anguish has now come upon us." ²²Reuben broke in, "Did I not tell you not to do wrong to the boy? But you would not listen! Now comes the reckoning for his blood." ²³The brothers did not know, of course, that Joseph understood what they said, since he spoke with them through an interpreter. ²⁴ᴬBut turning away from them, he wept.

Responsorial Psalm: Psalms 33:2-3, 10-11, 18-19

R. ⁽²²⁾ **Lord, let your mercy be on us, as we place
  our trust in you.**

² Give thanks to the LORD on the harp;
  with the ten-stringed lyre chant his
    praises.
³ Sing to him a new song;
  pluck the strings skillfully, with shouts of
    gladness.

**R. Lord, let your mercy be on us, as we place
  our trust in you.**

¹⁰ The LORD brings to nought the plans of
    nations;
  he foils the designs of peoples.
¹¹ But the plan of the LORD stands forever;
  the design of his heart, through all
    generations.

R. Lord, let your mercy be on us, as we place our trust in you.

18 But see, the eyes of the LORD are upon those who fear him,
 upon those who hope for his kindness,
19 To deliver them from death
 and preserve them in spite of famine.

R. Lord, let your mercy be on us, as we place our trust in you.

Alleluia: Mark 1:15
R. Alleluia, alleluia.
15 The Kingdom of God is at hand:
repent and believe in the Gospel.
R. Alleluia, alleluia.

Gospel: Matthew 10:1-7
1 Jesus summoned his Twelve disciples and gave them authority over unclean spirits to drive them out and to cure every disease and every illness. 2 The names of the Twelve Apostles are these: first, Simon called Peter, and his brother Andrew; James, the son of Zebedee, and his brother John; 3 Philip and Bartholomew, Thomas and Matthew the tax collector; James, the son of Alphaeus, and Thaddeus; 4 Simon the Cananean, and Judas Iscariot who betrayed Jesus.

5 Jesus sent out these Twelve after instructing them thus, "Do not go into pagan territory or enter a Samaritan town. 6 Go rather to the lost sheep of the house of Israel. 7 As you go, make this proclamation: 'The Kingdom of heaven is at hand.'"

Thursday July 10, 2025
Thursday of the Fourteenth Week in Ordinary Time
First Reading: Genesis 44:18-21, 23B-29; 45:1-5

18 Judah approached Joseph and said: "I beg you, my lord, let your servant speak earnestly to my lord, and do not become angry with your servant, for you are the equal of Pharaoh. 19 My lord asked your servants, 'Have you a father, or another brother?' 20 So we said to my lord, 'We have an aged father, and a young brother, the child of his old age. This one's full brother is dead, and since he is the only one by that mother who is left, his father dotes on him.' 21 Then you told your servants, 'Bring him down to me that my eyes may look on him. 23B Unless your youngest brother comes back with you, you shall not come into my presence again.' 24 When we returned to your servant our father, we reported to him the words of my lord.

25 "Later, our father told us to come back and buy some food for the family. 26 So we reminded him, 'We cannot go down there; only if our youngest brother is with us can we go, for we may not see the man if our youngest brother is not with us.' 27 Then your servant our father said to us, 'As you know, my wife bore me two sons. 28 One of them, however, disappeared, and I had to conclude that he must

have been torn to pieces by wild beasts; I have not seen him since. ²⁹If you now take this one away from me, too, and some disaster befalls him, you will send my white head down to the nether world in grief.'"

¹Joseph could no longer control himself in the presence of all his attendants, so he cried out, "Have everyone withdraw from me!" Thus no one else was about when he made himself known to his brothers. ²But his sobs were so loud that the Egyptians heard him, and so the news reached Pharaoh's palace. ³"I am Joseph," he said to his brothers. "Is my father still in good health?" But his brothers could give him no answer, so dumbfounded were they at him.

⁴"Come closer to me," he told his brothers. When they had done so, he said: "I am your brother Joseph, whom you once sold into Egypt. ⁵But now do not be distressed, and do not reproach yourselves for having sold me here. It was really for the sake of saving lives that God sent me here ahead of you."

Responsorial Psalm: Psalms 105:16-17, 18-19, 20-21
R. ⁽⁵ᵃ⁾ Remember the marvels the Lord has done. or: *R. Alleluia.*
¹⁶When the LORD called down a famine on the
> land
> and ruined the crop that sustained them,

¹⁷ He sent a man before them,
> Joseph, sold as a slave.

R. Remember the marvels the Lord has done. or: *R. Alleluia.*
¹⁸ They had weighed him down with fetters,
> and he was bound with chains,

¹⁹ Till his prediction came to pass
> and the word of the LORD proved him
> true.

R. Remember the marvels the Lord has done. or: *R. Alleluia.*
²⁰ The king sent and released him,
> the ruler of the peoples set him free.

²¹ He made him lord of his house
> and ruler of all his possessions.

R. Remember the marvels the Lord has done. or: *R. Alleluia.*

Alleluia: Mark 1:15
R. Alleluia, alleluia.
¹⁵The Kingdom of God is at hand:
repent and believe in the Gospel.
R. Alleluia, alleluia.

Gospel: Matthew 10:7-15
⁷ Jesus said to his Apostles: "As you go, make this proclamation: 'The Kingdom of heaven is at hand.' ⁸ Cure the sick, raise the dead, cleanse the lepers, drive out demons. Without cost you have received; without cost you are to give. ⁹ Do not

take gold or silver or copper for your belts; ¹⁰ no sack for the journey, or a second tunic, or sandals, or walking stick. The laborer deserves his keep. ¹¹ Whatever town or village you enter, look for a worthy person in it, and stay there until you leave. ¹² As you enter a house, wish it peace. ¹³ If the house is worthy, let your peace come upon it; if not, let your peace return to you. ¹⁴ Whoever will not receive you or listen to your words— go outside that house or town and shake the dust from your feet. ¹⁵ Amen, I say to you, it will be more tolerable for the land of Sodom and Gomorrah on the day of judgment than for that town."

Friday July 11, 2025
Memorial of Saint Benedict, Abbot
First Reading: Genesis 46:1-7, 28-30

¹Israel set out with all that was his. When he arrived at Beer-sheba, he offered sacrifices to the God of his father Isaac. ²There God, speaking to Israel in a vision by night, called, "Jacob! Jacob!" He answered, "Here I am." ³Then he said: "I am God, the God of your father. Do not be afraid to go down to Egypt, for there I will make you a great nation. ⁴Not only will I go down to Egypt with you; I will also bring you back here, after Joseph has closed your eyes."

⁵So Jacob departed from Beer-sheba, and the sons of Israel put their father and their wives and children on the wagons that Pharaoh had sent for his transport. ⁶They took with them their livestock and the possessions they had acquired in the land of Canaan. Thus Jacob and all his descendants migrated to Egypt. ⁷His sons and his grandsons, his daughters and his granddaughters—all his descendants—he took with him to Egypt.

²⁸Israel had sent Judah ahead to Joseph, so that he might meet him in Goshen. On his arrival in the region of Goshen, ²⁹Joseph hitched the horses to his chariot and rode to meet his father Israel in Goshen. As soon as Joseph saw him, he flung himself on his neck and wept a long time in his arms. ³⁰And Israel said to Joseph, "At last I can die, now that I have seen for myself that Joseph is still alive."

Responsorial Psalm: Psalms 37:3-4, 18-19, 27-28, 39-40
R. *(39a)* ***The salvation of the just comes from the Lord.***
³ Trust in the LORD and do good,
    that you may dwell in the land and be fed
        in security.
⁴ Take delight in the LORD,
    and he will grant you your heart's
        requests.
R. *The salvation of the just comes from the Lord.*
¹⁸The LORD watches over the lives of the
        wholehearted;
    their inheritance lasts forever.
¹⁹ They are not put to shame in an evil time;
    in days of famine they have plenty.
R. *The salvation of the just comes from the Lord.*

²⁷ Turn from evil and do good,
   that you may abide forever;
²⁸ For the LORD loves what is right,
   and forsakes not his faithful ones.
R. The salvation of the just comes from the Lord.
³⁹ The salvation of the just is from the LORD;
   he is their refuge in time of distress.
⁴⁰ And the LORD helps them and delivers them;
   he delivers them from the wicked and
      saves them,
   because they take refuge in him.
R. The salvation of the just comes from the Lord.

Alleluia: John 16:13A; 14:26D
R. Alleluia, alleluia.
¹³ᴬ When the Spirit of truth comes,
he will guide you to all truth
²⁶ᴰ and remind you of all I told you.
R. Alleluia, alleluia.

Gospel: Matthew 10:16-23
¹⁶ Jesus said to his Apostles: "Behold, I am sending you like sheep in the midst of wolves; so be shrewd as serpents and simple as doves. ¹⁷ But beware of men, for they will hand you over to courts and scourge you in their synagogues, ¹⁸ and you will be led before governors and kings for my sake as a witness before them and the pagans. ¹⁹ When they hand you over, do not worry about how you are to speak or what you are to say. You will be given at that moment what you are to say. ²⁰ For it will not be you who speak but the Spirit of your Father speaking through you. ²¹ Brother will hand over brother to death, and the father his child; children will rise up against parents and have them put to death. ²² You will be hated by all because of my name, but whoever endures to the end will be saved. ²³ When they persecute you in one town, flee to another. Amen, I say to you, you will not finish the towns of Israel before the Son of Man comes."

Saturday July 12, 2025
Saturday of the Fourteenth Week in Ordinary Time
First Reading: Genesis 49:29-32; 50:15-26A
²⁹Jacob gave his sons this charge: "Since I am about to be taken to my people, bury me with my fathers in the cave that lies in the field of Ephron the Hittite, ³⁰the cave in the field of Machpelah, facing on Mamre, in the land of Canaan, the field that Abraham bought from Ephron the Hittite for a burial ground. ³¹There Abraham and his wife Sarah are buried, and so are Isaac and his wife Rebekah, and there, too, I buried Leah—³²the field and the cave in it that had been purchased from the Hittites."

¹⁵Now that their father was dead, Joseph's brothers became fearful and thought, "Suppose Joseph has been nursing a grudge against us and now plans to pay us back in full for all the wrong we did him!" ¹⁶So they approached Joseph and said: "Before your father died, he gave us these instructions: ¹⁷'You shall say to Joseph, Jacob begs you to forgive the criminal wrongdoing of your brothers, who treated you so cruelly.' Please, therefore, forgive the crime that we, the servants of your father's God, committed." When they spoke these words to him, Joseph broke into tears. ¹⁸Then his brothers proceeded to fling themselves down before him and said, "Let us be your slaves!" ¹⁹But Joseph replied to them: "Have no fear. Can I take the place of God? ²⁰Even though you meant harm to me, God meant it for good, to achieve his present end, the survival of many people. ²¹Therefore have no fear. I will provide for you and for your children." By thus speaking kindly to them, he reassured them.

²²Joseph remained in Egypt, together with his father's family. He lived a hundred and ten years. ²³He saw Ephraim's children to the third generation, and the children of Manasseh's son Machir were also born on Joseph's knees.

²⁴Joseph said to his brothers: "I am about to die. God will surely take care of you and lead you out of this land to the land that he promised on oath to Abraham, Isaac and Jacob." ²⁵Then, putting the sons of Israel under oath, he continued, "When God thus takes care of you, you must bring my bones up with you from this place." ²⁶ᴬJoseph died at the age of a hundred and ten.

Responsorial Psalm: Psalms 105:1-2, 3-4, 6-7
R. (see Psalm 69:33) **Be glad you lowly ones; may your hearts be glad!**

¹ Give thanks to the LORD, invoke his name;
   make known among the nations his deeds.
² Sing to him, sing his praise,
   proclaim all his wondrous deeds.

R. Be glad you lowly ones; may your hearts be glad!

³ Glory in his holy name;
   rejoice, O hearts that seek the LORD!
⁴ Look to the LORD in his strength;
   seek to serve him constantly.

R. Be glad you lowly ones; may your hearts be glad!

⁶ You descendants of Abraham, his servants,
   sons of Jacob, his chosen ones!
⁷ He, the LORD, is our God;
   throughout the earth his judgments prevail.

R. Be glad you lowly ones; may your hearts be glad!

Alleluia: 1 Peter 4:14
R. Alleluia, alleluia.
14 If you are insulted for the name of Christ,
> blessed are you,
for the Spirit of God rests upon you.
R. Alleluia, alleluia.

Gospel: Matthew 10:24-33
24 Jesus said to his Apostles: "No disciple is above his teacher, no slave above his master. 25 It is enough for the disciple that he become like his teacher, for the slave that he become like his master. If they have called the master of the house Beelzebul, how much more those of his household! 26 "Therefore do not be afraid of them. Nothing is concealed that will not be revealed, nor secret that will not be known. 27 What I say to you in the darkness, speak in the light; what you hear whispered, proclaim on the housetops. 28 And do not be afraid of those who kill the body but cannot kill the soul; rather, be afraid of the one who can destroy both soul and body in Gehenna. 29 Are not two sparrows sold for a small coin? Yet not one of them falls to the ground without your Father's knowledge. 30 Even all the hairs of your head are counted. 31 So do not be afraid; you are worth more than many sparrows. 32 Everyone who acknowledges me before others I will acknowledge before my heavenly Father. 33 But whoever denies me before others, I will deny before my heavenly Father."

Sunday July 13, 2025
Fifteenth Sunday in Ordinary Time, Year C

First Reading: Deuteronomy 30:10-14
Moses said to the people: 10"If only you would heed the voice of the LORD, your God, and keep his commandments and statutes that are written in this book of the law, when you return to the LORD, your God, with all your heart and all your soul.

11"For this command that I enjoin on you today is not too mysterious and remote for you. 12 It is not up in the sky, that you should say, 'Who will go up in the sky to get it for us and tell us of it, that we may carry it out?' 13 Nor is it across the sea, that you should say, 'Who will cross the sea to get it for us and tell us of it, that we may carry it out?' 14 No, it is something very near to you, already in your mouths and in your hearts; you have only to carry it out."

Responsorial Psalm: Psalms 69:14, 17, 30-31, 33-34, 36, 37
R. (cf. 33) ***Turn to the Lord in your need, and you will live.***
14 I pray to you, O LORD,
> for the time of your favor, O God!
In your great kindness answer me
> with your constant help.
17 Answer me, O LORD, for bounteous is
> your kindness:
in your great mercy turn toward me.

R. Turn to the Lord in your need, and you will live.

³⁰ I am afflicted and in pain;
> let your saving help, O God, protect me.

³¹ I will praise the name of God in song,
> and I will glorify him with thanksgiving.

R. Turn to the Lord in your need, and you will live.

³³ "See, you lowly ones, and be glad;
> you who seek God, may your hearts revive!

³⁴ For the LORD hears the poor,
> and his own who are in bonds he spurns not."

R. Turn to the Lord in your need, and you will live.

³⁶ For God will save Zion
> and rebuild the cities of Judah.

³⁷ The descendants of his servants shall inherit it,
> and those who love his name shall inhabit it.

R. Turn to the Lord in your need, and you will live.

Or Psalms 19:8, 9, 10, 11

R.⁽⁹ᵃ⁾ Your words, Lord, are Spirit and life.

⁸ The law of the LORD is perfect,
> refreshing the soul;

the decree of the LORD is trustworthy,
> giving wisdom to the simple.

R. Your words, Lord, are Spirit and life.

⁹ The precepts of the LORD are right,
> rejoicing the heart;

the command of the LORD is clear,
> enlightening the eye.

R. Your words, Lord, are Spirit and life.

¹⁰ The fear of the LORD is pure,
> enduring forever;

the ordinances of the LORD are true,
> all of them just.

R. Your words, Lord, are Spirit and life.

¹¹ They are more precious than gold,

    than a heap of purest gold;
sweeter also than syrup
    or honey from the comb.
R. Your words, Lord, are Spirit and life.

Second Reading: Colossians 1:15-20

^{15}Christ Jesus is the image of the invisible God, the firstborn of all creation. ^{16}For in him were created all things in heaven and on earth, the visible and the invisible, whether thrones or dominions or principalities or powers; all things were created through him and for him. ^{17}He is before all things, and in him, all things hold together. ^{18} He is the head of the body, the church. He is the beginning, the firstborn from the dead, that in all things he himself might be preeminent. ^{19} For in him all the fullness was pleased to dwell, ^{20}and through him to reconcile all things for him, making peace by the blood of his cross through him, whether those on earth or those in heaven.

Alleluia: cf. John 6:63C, 68C
R. Alleluia, alleluia.
^{63C} Your words, Lord, are Spirit and life;
^{68C} you have the words of everlasting life.
R. Alleluia, alleluia.

Gospel: Luke 10:25-37

^{25}There was a scholar of the law who stood up to test Jesus and said, "Teacher, what must I do to inherit eternal life?" ^{26}Jesus said to him, "What is written in the law? How do you read it?" ^{27} He said in reply, *You shall love the Lord, your God, with all your heart, with all your being, with all your strength,*
and with all your mind, and your neighbor as yourself." ^{28}He replied to him, "You have answered correctly; do this and you will live."

^{29}But because he wished to justify himself, he said to Jesus, "And who is my neighbor?" ^{30}Jesus replied, "A man fell victim to robbers as he went down from Jerusalem to Jericho. They stripped and beat him and went off leaving him half-dead. ^{31}A priest happened to be going down that road, but when he saw him, he passed by on the opposite side. ^{32}Likewise a Levite came to the place, and when he saw him, he passed by on the opposite side. ^{33}But a Samaritan traveler who came upon him was moved with compassion at the sight. ^{34}He approached the victim, poured oil and wine over his wounds and bandaged them. Then he lifted him up on his own animal, took him to an inn, and cared for him. ^{35}The next day he took out two silver coins and gave them to the innkeeper with the instruction, 'Take care of him. If you spend more than what I have given you, I shall repay you on my way back.' ^{36}Which of these three, in your opinion, was a neighbor to the robbers' victim?" ^{37}He answered, "The one who treated him with mercy." Jesus said to him, "Go and do likewise."

Monday July 14, 2025
Memorial of Saint Kateri Tekakwitha

First Reading: Exodus 1:8-14, 22

⁸A new king, who knew nothing of Joseph, came to power in Egypt. ⁹He said to his subjects, "Look how numerous and powerful the people of the children of Israel are growing, more so than we ourselves! ¹⁰Come, let us deal shrewdly with them to stop their increase; otherwise, in time of war they too may join our enemies to fight against us, and so leave our country."

¹¹Accordingly, taskmasters were set over the children of Israel to oppress them with forced labor. Thus they had to build for Pharaoh the supply cities of Pithom and Raamses. ¹²Yet the more they were oppressed, the more they multiplied and spread. ¹³The Egyptians, then, dreaded the children of Israel and reduced them to cruel slavery, ¹⁴making life bitter for them with hard work in mortar and brick and all kinds of field work – the whole cruel fate of slaves.

²²Pharaoh then commanded all his subjects, "Throw into the river every boy that is born to the Hebrews, but you may let all the girls live."

Responsorial Psalm: Psalms 124:1B-3, 4-6, 7-8

R. ⁽⁸ᵃ⁾ *Our help is in the name of the Lord.*

¹ᴮ Had not the LORD been with us –
    let Israel say, ² had not the LORD been with
        us–
When men rose up against us,
    ³ then would they have swallowed us alive,
When their fury was inflamed against us.

R. *Our help is in the name of the Lord.*

⁴ Then would the waters have overwhelmed
        us;
The torrent would have swept over us;
    ⁵ over us then would have swept
        the raging waters.
⁶ Blessed be the LORD, who did not leave us
        a prey to their teeth.

R. *Our help is in the name of the Lord.*

⁷ We were rescued like a bird
        from the fowlers' snare;
Broken was the snare,
        and we were freed.
⁸ Our help is in the name of the LORD,
        who made heaven and earth.

R. *Our help is in the name of the Lord.*

Alleluia: Matthew 5:10
R. Alleluia, alleluia.
¹⁰ Blessed are they who are persecuted for the
 sake of righteousness,
for theirs is the Kingdom of heaven.
R. Alleluia, alleluia.

Gospel: Matthew 10:34-11:1
³⁴ Jesus said to his Apostles: "Do not think that I have come to bring peace upon the earth. I have come to bring not peace but the sword. ³⁵ For I have come to set

a man against his father,
 a daughter against her mother,
and a daughter-in-law against her mother-
 in-law;
³⁶ and one's enemies will be those of his
 household.

³⁷ "Whoever loves father or mother more than me is not worthy of me, and whoever loves son or daughter more than me is not worthy of me; ³⁸ and whoever does not take up his cross and follow after me is not worthy of me. ³⁹ Whoever finds his life will lose it, and whoever loses his life for my sake will find it.
⁴⁰ "Whoever receives you receives me, and whoever receives me receives the one who sent me. ⁴¹ Whoever receives a prophet because he is a prophet will receive a prophet's reward, and whoever receives a righteous man because he is righteous will receive a righteous man's reward. ⁴² And whoever gives only a cup of cold water to one of these little ones to drink because he is a disciple— amen, I say to you, he will surely not lose his reward."
¹ When Jesus finished giving these commands to his Twelve disciples, he went away from that place to teach and to preach in their towns.

Tuesday July 15, 2025
Memorial of Saint Bonaventure, Bp & Doc
First Reading: Exodus 2:1-15A
¹A certain man of the house of Levi married a Levite woman, ²who conceived and bore a son. Seeing that he was a goodly child, she hid him for three months. ³When she could hide him no longer, she took a papyrus basket, daubed it with bitumen and pitch, and putting the child in it, placed it among the reeds on the river bank. ⁴His sister stationed herself at a distance to find out what would happen to him.
⁵Pharaoh's daughter came down to the river to bathe, while her maids walked along the river bank. Noticing the basket among the reeds, she sent her handmaid to fetch it. ⁶On opening it, she looked, and lo, there was a baby boy, crying! She was moved with pity for him and said, "It is one of the Hebrews' children." ⁷Then his sister asked Pharaoh's daughter, "Shall I go and call one of the

Hebrew women to nurse the child for you?" ⁸"Yes, do so," she answered. So the maiden went and called the child's own mother. ⁹Pharaoh's daughter said to her, "Take this child and nurse it for me, and I will repay you." The woman therefore took the child and nursed it. ¹⁰When the child grew, she brought him to Pharaoh's daughter, who adopted him as her son and called him Moses; for she said, "I drew him out of the water."

¹¹On one occasion, after Moses had grown up, when he visited his kinsmen and witnessed their forced labor, he saw an Egyptian striking a Hebrew, one of his own kinsmen. ¹²Looking about and seeing no one, he slew the Egyptian and hid him in the sand. ¹³The next day he went out again, and now two Hebrews were fighting! So he asked the culprit, "Why are you striking your fellow Hebrew?" ¹⁴But the culprit replied, "Who has appointed you ruler and judge over us? Are you thinking of killing me as you killed the Egyptian?" Then Moses became afraid and thought, "The affair must certainly be known."

¹⁵ᴬPharaoh, too, heard of the affair and sought to put Moses to death. But Moses fled from him and stayed in the land of Midian.

Responsorial Psalm: Psalms 69:3, 14, 30-31, 33-34

R. (see 33) *Turn to the Lord in your need, and you will live.*

³ I am sunk in the abysmal swamp
    where there is no foothold;
I have reached the watery depths;
    the flood overwhelms me.

R. Turn to the Lord in your need, and you will live.

¹⁴ But I pray to you, O LORD,
    for the time of your favor, O God!
In your great kindness answer me
    with your constant help.

R. Turn to the Lord in your need, and you will live.

³⁰ But I am afflicted and in pain;
    let your saving help, O God, protect me;
³¹ I will praise the name of God in song,
    and I will glorify him with thanksgiving.

R. Turn to the Lord in your need, and you will live.

³³ "See, you lowly ones, and be glad;
    you who seek God, may your hearts
        revive!
³⁴ For the LORD hears the poor,
    and his own who are in bonds he spurns
        not."

R. Turn to the Lord in your need, and you will

live.

Alleluia: Psalms 95:8
R. Alleluia, alleluia.
⁸ If today you hear his voice,
harden not your hearts.
R. Alleluia, alleluia.

Gospel: Matthew 11:20-24
²⁰ Jesus began to reproach the towns where most of his mighty deeds had been done, since they had not repented. ²² "Woe to you, Chorazin! Woe to you, Bethsaida! For if the mighty deeds done in your midst had been done in Tyre and Sidon, they would long ago have repented in sackcloth and ashes. But I tell you, it will be more tolerable for Tyre and Sidon on the day of judgment than for you. ²³ And as for you, Capernaum:

Will you be exalted to heaven?
You will go down to the netherworld.

For if the mighty deeds done in your midst had been done in Sodom, it would have remained until this day. ²⁴ But I tell you, it will be more tolerable for the land of Sodom on the day of judgment than for you."

Wednesday July 16, 2025
Wednesday of the Fifteenth Week in Ordinary Time
First Reading: Exodus 3:1-6, 9-12
¹Moses was tending the flock of his father-in-law Jethro, the priest of Midian. Leading the flock across the desert, he came to Horeb, the mountain of God. ²There an angel of the LORD appeared to him in fire flaming out of a bush. As he looked on, he was surprised to see that the bush, though on fire, was not consumed. ³So Moses decided, "I must go over to look at this remarkable sight, and see why the bush is not burned."

⁴When the LORD saw him coming over to look at it more closely, God called out to him from the bush, "Moses! Moses!" He answered, "Here I am." ⁵God said, "Come no nearer! Remove the sandals from your feet, for the place where you stand is holy ground. ⁶I am the God of your father," he continued, "the God of Abraham, the God of Isaac, the God of Jacob. ⁹The cry of the children of Israel has reached me, and I have truly noted that the Egyptians are oppressing them. ¹⁰Come, now! I will send you to Pharaoh to lead my people, the children of Israel, out of Egypt."

¹¹But Moses said to God, "Who am I that I should go to Pharaoh and lead the children of Israel out of Egypt?" ¹²He answered, "I will be with you; and this shall be your proof that it is I who have sent you: when you bring my people out of Egypt, you will worship God on this very mountain."

Responsorial Psalm: Psalms 103:1B-2, 3-4, 6-7
R. ⁽⁸ᵃ⁾ ***The Lord is kind and merciful.***

¹ᴮ Bless the LORD, O my soul;
   and all my being, bless his holy name.
² Bless the LORD, O my soul,
   and forget not all his benefits.
R. The Lord is kind and merciful.
³ He pardons all your iniquities,
   he heals all your ills.
⁴ He redeems your life from destruction,
   he crowns you with kindness and compassion.
R. The Lord is kind and merciful.
⁶ The LORD secures justice
   and the rights of all the oppressed.
⁷ He has made known his ways to Moses,
   and his deeds to the children of Israel.
R. The Lord is kind and merciful.

Alleluia: Matthew 11:25
R. Alleluia, alleluia.
²⁵ Blessed are you, Father, Lord of heaven and
      earth,
you have revealed to little ones the
      mysteries of the Kingdom.
R. Alleluia, alleluia.

Gospel: Matthew 11:25-27
²⁵ At that time Jesus exclaimed: "I give praise to you, Father, Lord of heaven and earth, for although you have hidden these things from the wise and the learned you have revealed them to the childlike. ²⁶ Yes, Father, such has been your gracious will. ²⁷ All things have been handed over to me by my Father. No one knows the Son except the Father, and no one knows the Father except the Son and anyone to whom the Son wishes to reveal him."

Thursday July 17, 2025
Thursday of Fifteenth Week in Ordinary Time
First Reading: Exodus 3:13-20
¹³Moses, hearing the voice of the LORD from the burning bush, said to him, "When I go to the children of Israel and say to them, 'The God of your fathers has sent me to you,' if they ask me, 'What is his name?' what am I to tell them?" ¹⁴God replied, "I am who am." Then he added, "This is what you shall tell the children of Israel: I AM sent me to you."

¹⁵God spoke further to Moses, "Thus shall you say to the children of Israel: The LORD, the God of your fathers, the God of Abraham, the God of Isaac, the God of Jacob, has sent me to you.

"This is my name forever;
   this my title for all generations.

[16]"Go and assemble the elders of Israel, and tell them: The LORD, the God of your fathers, the God of Abraham, Isaac, and Jacob, has appeared to me and said: I am concerned about you and about the way you are being treated in Egypt; [17]so I have decided to lead you up out of the misery of Egypt into the land of the Canaanites, Hittites, Amorites, Perizzites, Hivites, and Jebusites, a land flowing with milk and honey.

[18]"Thus they will heed your message. Then you and the elders of Israel shall go to the king of Egypt and say to him: "The LORD, the God of the Hebrews, has sent us word. Permit us, then, to go a three-days' journey in the desert, that we may offer sacrifice to the LORD, our God.

[19]"Yet I know that the king of Egypt will not allow you to go unless he is forced. [20]I will stretch out my hand, therefore, and smite Egypt by doing all kinds of wondrous deeds there. After that he will send you away."

Responsorial Psalm: Psalms 105:1 AND 5, 8-9, 24-25, 26-27

R. [8a] The Lord remembers his covenant for ever. or: *R. Alleluia.*

[1] Give thanks to the LORD, invoke his name;
    make known among the nations his
        deeds.
[5] Recall the wondrous deeds that he has
        wrought,
    his portents, and the judgments he has
        uttered.

R. The Lord remembers his covenant for ever. or: *R. Alleluia.*

[8] He remembers forever his covenant
    which he made binding for a thousand
        generations—
[9] Which he entered into with Abraham
    and by his oath to Isaac.

R. The Lord remembers his covenant for ever. or: *R. Alleluia.*

[24] He greatly increased his people
    and made them stronger than their foes,
[25] Whose hearts he changed, so that they hated
        his people,
    and dealt deceitfully with his servants.

R. The Lord remembers his covenant for ever. or: *R. Alleluia.*

[26] He sent Moses his servant;
    Aaron, whom he had chosen.
[27] They wrought his signs among them,
    and wonders in the land of Ham.

R. The Lord remembers his covenant for ever. or: *R. Alleluia.*

Alleluia: Matthew 11:28

R. Alleluia, alleluia.
[28]Come to me, all you who labor and are

burdened,
and I will give you rest, says the Lord.
R. Alleluia, alleluia.

Gospel: Matthew 11:28-30

[28] Jesus said: "Come to me, all you who labor and are burdened, and I will give you rest. [29] Take my yoke upon you and learn from me, for I am meek and humble of heart; and you will find rest for yourselves. [30] For my yoke is easy, and my burden light."

Friday July 18, 2025
Friday of Fifteenth Week in Ordinary Time
First Reading: Exodus 11:10-12:14

[10]Although Moses and Aaron performed various wonders in Pharaoh's presence, the LORD made Pharaoh obstinate, and he would not let the children of Israel leave his land.

[1]The LORD said to Moses and Aaron in the land of Egypt, [2]"This month shall stand at the head of your calendar; you shall reckon it the first month of the year. [3]Tell the whole community of Israel: On the tenth of this month every one of your families must procure for itself a lamb, one apiece for each household. [4]If a family is too small for a whole lamb, it shall join the nearest household in procuring one and shall share in the lamb in proportion to the number of persons who partake of it. [5]The lamb must be a year-old male and without blemish. You may take it from either the sheep or the goats. [6]You shall keep it until the fourteenth day of this month, and then, with the whole assembly of Israel present, it shall be slaughtered during the evening twilight. [7]They shall take some of its blood and apply it to the two doorposts and the lintel of every house in which they partake of the lamb. [8]That same night they shall eat its roasted flesh with unleavened bread and bitter herbs. [9]It shall not be eaten raw or boiled, but roasted whole, with its head and shanks and inner organs. [10]None of it must be kept beyond the next morning; whatever is left over in the morning shall be burned up.

[11]"This is how you are to eat it: with your loins girt, sandals on your feet and your staff in hand, you shall eat like those who are in flight. It is the Passover of the LORD. [12]For on this same night I will go through Egypt, striking down every first born of the land, both man and beast, and executing judgment on all the gods of Egypt – I, the LORD! [13]But the blood will mark the houses where you are. Seeing the blood, I will pass over you; thus, when I strike the land of Egypt, no destructive blow will come upon you.

[14]"This day shall be a memorial feast for you, which all your generations shall celebrate with pilgrimage to the LORD, as a perpetual institution."

Responsorial Psalm: Psalms 116:12-13, 15 AND 16BC, 17-18

**R. [13] I will take the cup of salvation, and call on
the name of the Lord.**

[12] How shall I make a return to the LORD
   for all the good he has done for me?
[13] The cup of salvation I will take up,
   and I will call upon the name of the LORD.
R. I will take the cup of salvation, and call on the

name of the Lord.

¹⁵ Precious in the eyes of the LORD
   is the death of his faithful ones.
^{16B} I am your servant, the son of your handmaid;
   you have loosed my bonds.

R. I will take the cup of salvation, and call on the name of the Lord.

¹⁷ To you will I offer sacrifice of thanksgiving,
   and I will call upon the name of the LORD.
¹⁸ My vows to the LORD I will pay
   in the presence of all his people.

R. I will take the cup of salvation, and call on the name of the Lord.

Alleluia: John 10:27

R. Alleluia, alleluia.
²⁷ My sheep hear my voice, says the Lord,
I know them, and they follow me.
R. Alleluia, alleluia.

Gospel: Matthew 12:1-8

¹ Jesus was going through a field of grain on the sabbath. His disciples were hungry and began to pick the heads of grain and eat them. ² When the Pharisees saw this, they said to him, "See, your disciples are doing what is unlawful to do on the sabbath." ³ He said to the them, "Have you not read what David did when he and his companions were hungry, ⁴ how he went into the house of God and ate the bread of offering, which neither he nor his companions but only the priests could lawfully eat? ⁵ Or have you not read in the law that on the sabbath the priests serving in the temple violate the sabbath and are innocent? ⁶ I say to you, something greater than the temple is here. ⁷ If you knew what this meant, *I desire mercy, not sacrifice*, you would not have condemned these innocent men. ⁸ For the Son of Man is Lord of the sabbath."

Saturday July 19, 2025
Saturday of Fifteenth Week in Ordinary Time

First Reading: Exodus 12:37-42

³⁷The children of Israel set out from Rameses for Succoth, about six hundred thousand men on foot, not counting the little ones. ³⁸A crowd of mixed ancestry also went up with them, besides their livestock, very numerous flocks and herds. ³⁹Since the dough they had brought out of Egypt was not leavened, they baked it into unleavened loaves. They had rushed out of Egypt and had no opportunity even to prepare food for the journey.

⁴⁰The time the children of Israel had stayed in Egypt was four hundred and thirty years. ⁴¹At the end of four hundred and thirty years, all the hosts of the LORD left the land of Egypt on this very date. ⁴²This was a night of vigil for the LORD, as

he led them out of the land of Egypt; so on this same night all the children of Israel must keep a vigil for the LORD throughout their generations.

Responsorial Psalm: Psalms 136:1 AND 23-24, 10-12, 13-15
R. His mercy endures forever. or: *R. Alleluia.*
[1] Give thanks to the LORD, for he is good,
>   for his mercy endures forever;

[23] Who remembered us in our abjection,
>   for his mercy endures forever;

[24] And freed us from our foes,
>   for his mercy endures forever.

R. His mercy endures forever. or: *R. Alleluia.*
[10] Who smote the Egyptians in their first-born,
>   for his mercy endures forever;

[11] And brought out Israel from their midst,
>   for his mercy endures forever;

[12] With a mighty hand and an outstretched
>   arm,
>   for his mercy endures forever.

R. His mercy endures forever. or: *R. Alleluia.*
[13] Who split the Red Sea in twain,
>   for his mercy endures forever;

[14] And led Israel through its midst,
>   for his mercy endures forever;

[15] But swept Pharaoh and his army into the
>   Red Sea,
>   for his mercy endures forever.

R. His mercy endures forever. or: *R. Alleluia.*

Alleluia: 2 Corinthians 5:19
R. Alleluia, alleluia.
[19] God was reconciling the world to himself in
>   Christ,
and entrusting to us the message of
>   reconciliation.
R. Alleluia, alleluia.

Gospel: Matthew 12:14-21
[14] The Pharisees went out and took counsel against Jesus to put him to death. [15] When Jesus realized this, he withdrew from that place. Many people followed him, and he cured them all, [16] but he warned them not to make him known. [17] This was to fulfill what had been spoken through Isaiah the prophet:

[18] *Behold, my servant whom I have chosen,*

my beloved in whom I delight;
I shall place my Spirit upon him,
and he will proclaim justice to the Gentiles.
[19] *He will not contend or cry out,*
nor will anyone hear his voice in the streets.
[20] *A bruised reed he will not break,*
a smoldering wick he will not quench,
until he brings justice to victory.
[21] *And in his name the Gentiles will hope.*

Sunday July 20, 2025
Sixteenth Sunday in Ordinary Time, Year C

First Reading: Genesis 18:1-10A

[1] The LORD appeared to Abraham by the terebinth of Mamre, as he sat in the entrance of his tent, while the day was growing hot. [2] Looking up, Abraham saw three men standing nearby. When he saw them, he ran from the entrance of the tent to greet them; and bowing to the ground, he said: [3] "Sir, if I may ask you this favor, please do not go on past your servant. [4] Let some water be brought, that you may bathe your feet, and then rest yourselves under the tree. [5] Now that you have come this close to your servant, let me bring you a little food, that you may refresh yourselves; and afterward you may go on your way." The men replied, "Very well, do as you have said."

[6] Abraham hastened into the tent and told Sarah, "Quick, three measures of fine flour! Knead it and make rolls." [7] He ran to the herd, picked out a tender, choice steer, and gave it to a servant, who quickly prepared it. [8] Then Abraham got some curds and milk, as well as the steer that had been prepared, and set these before the three men; and he waited on them under the tree while they ate.

[9] They asked Abraham, "Where is your wife Sarah?" He replied, "There in the tent." [10A] One of them said, "I will surely return to you about this time next year, and Sarah will then have a son."

Responsorial Psalm: Psalms 15:2-3A, 3BC-4AB, 5

R. [1a] **He who does justice will live in the presence of the Lord.**

[2] One who walks blamelessly and does justice;
who thinks the truth in his heart
[3A] and slanders not with his tongue.

R. **He who does justice will live in the presence of the Lord.**

[3BC] Who harms not his fellow man,
nor takes up a reproach against his neighbor;
[4AB] by whom the reprobate is despised,
while he honors those who fear the LORD.

***R. He who does justice will live in the presence
of the Lord.***
⁵ Who lends not his money at usury
    and accepts no bribe against the
        innocent.
One who does these things
    shall never be disturbed.
***R. He who does justice will live in the presence
of the Lord.***

Second Reading: Colossians 1:24-28
Brothers and sisters: ⁴Now I rejoice in my sufferings for your sake, and in my flesh I am filling up what is lacking in the afflictions of Christ on behalf of his body, which is the church, ²⁵of which I am a minister in accordance with God's stewardship given to me to bring to completion for you the word of God, ²⁶the mystery hidden from ages and from generations past. But now it has been manifested to his holy ones, ²⁷to whom God chose to make known the riches of the glory of this mystery among the Gentiles; it is Christ in you, the hope for glory. ²⁸It is he whom we proclaim, admonishing everyone and teaching everyone with all wisdom, that we may present everyone perfect in Christ.

Alleluia: cf. Luke 8:15
R. Alleluia, alleluia.
¹⁵Blessed are they who have kept the word
    with a generous heart
and yield a harvest through perseverance.
R. Alleluia, alleluia.

Gospel: Luke 10:38-42
³⁸Jesus entered a village where a woman whose name was Martha welcomed him. ³⁹She had a sister named Mary who sat beside the Lord at his feet listening to him speak. ⁴⁰Martha, burdened with much serving, came to him and said, "Lord, do you not care that my sister has left me by myself to do the serving? Tell her to help me." ⁴¹The Lord said to her in reply, "Martha, Martha, you are anxious and worried about many things. ⁴²There is need of only one thing. Mary has chosen the better part and it will not be taken from her."

Monday July 21, 2025
Monday of Sixteenth Week in Ordinary Time
First Reading: Exodus 14:5-18
⁵When it was reported to the king of Egypt that the people had fled, Pharaoh and his servants changed their minds about them. They exclaimed, "What have we done! Why, we have released Israel from our service!" ⁶So Pharaoh made his chariots ready and mustered his soldiers— ⁷six hundred first-class chariots and all

the other chariots of Egypt, with warriors on them all. ⁸So obstinate had the LORD made Pharaoh that he pursued the children of Israel even while they were marching away in triumph. ⁹The Egyptians, then, pursued them; Pharaoh's whole army, his horses, chariots and charioteers, caught up with them as they lay encamped by the sea, at Pi-hahiroth, in front of Baal-zephon.

¹⁰Pharaoh was already near when the children of Israel looked up and saw that the Egyptians were on the march in pursuit of them. In great fright they cried out to the LORD. ¹¹And they complained to Moses, "Were there no burial places in Egypt that you had to bring us out here to die in the desert? Why did you do this to us? Why did you bring us out of Egypt? ¹²Did we not tell you this in Egypt, when we said, 'Leave us alone. Let us serve the Egyptians'? Far better for us to be the slaves of the Egyptians than to die in the desert." ¹³But Moses answered the people, "Fear not! Stand your ground, and you will see the victory the LORD will win for you today. These Egyptians whom you see today you will never see again. ¹⁴The LORD himself will fight for you; you have only to keep still."

¹⁵Then the LORD said to Moses, "Why are you crying out to me? Tell the children of Israel to go forward. ¹⁶And you, lift up your staff and, with hand outstretched over the sea, split the sea in two, that the children of Israel may pass through it on dry land. ¹⁷But I will make the Egyptians so obstinate that they will go in after them. Then I will receive glory through Pharaoh and all his army, his chariots and charioteers. ¹⁸The Egyptians shall know that I am the LORD, when I receive glory through Pharaoh and his chariots and charioteers."

Responsorial Psalm: Exodus 15:1BC-2, 3-4, 5-6

R. *(1b)* Let us sing to the Lord; he has covered himself in glory.

¹ᴮᶜ I will sing to the LORD, for he is gloriously triumphant;
    horse and chariot he has cast into the sea.
² My strength and my courage is the LORD,
    and he has been my savior.
He is my God, I praise him;
    the God of my father, I extol him.

R. Let us sing to the Lord; he has covered himself in glory.

³ The LORD is a warrior,
    LORD is his name!
⁴ Pharaoh's chariots and army he hurled into the sea;
    the elite of his officers were submerged in the Red Sea.

R. Let us sing to the Lord; he has covered himself in glory.

⁵ The flood waters covered them,
    they sank into the depths like a stone.

[6] Your right hand, O LORD, magnificent in
power,
your right hand, O LORD, has shattered the
enemy.
R. Let us sing to the Lord; he has covered himself in glory.

Alleluia: Psalms 95:8
R. Alleluia, alleluia.
[8] If today you hear his voice,
harden not your hearts.
R. Alleluia, alleluia.

Gospel: Matthew 12:38-42
[38]Some of the scribes and Pharisees said to Jesus, "Teacher, we wish to see a sign from you." [39]He said to them in reply, "An evil and unfaithful generation seeks a sign, but no sign will be given it except the sign of Jonah the prophet. [40]Just as Jonah was in the belly of the whale three days and three nights, so will the Son of Man be in the heart of the earth three days and three nights. [41]At the judgment, the men of Nineveh will arise with this generation and condemn it, because they repented at the preaching of Jonah; and there is something greater than Jonah here. [42]At the judgment the queen of the south will arise with this generation and condemn it, because she came from the ends of the earth to hear the wisdom of Solomon; and there is something greater than Solomon here."

Tuesday July 22, 2025
Feast of Saint Mary Magdalene
First Reading: Songs of Solomon 3:1-4B
The Bride says:

[1] On my bed at night I sought him
whom my heart loves—
I sought him but I did not find him.
[2] I will rise then and go about the city;
in the streets and crossings I will seek
Him whom my heart loves.
I sought him but I did not find him.
[3] The watchmen came upon me,
as they made their rounds of the city:
Have you seen him whom my heart
loves?
[4] I had hardly left them
when I found him whom my heart
loves.

OR 2 Corinthians 5:14-17

Brothers and sisters: [14] The love of Christ impels us, once we have come to the conviction that one died for all; therefore, all have died. [15] He indeed died for all, so that those who live might no longer live for themselves but for him who for their sake died and was raised.

[16] Consequently, from now on we regard no one according to the flesh; even if we once knew Christ according to the flesh, yet now we know him so no longer. [17] So whoever is in Christ is a new creation: the old things have passed away; behold, new things have come.

Responsorial Psalm: Psalms 63:2,3-4,5-6, 8-9

R. [2] My soul is thirsting for you, O Lord my God.
[2] O God, you are my God whom I seek;
>   for you my flesh pines and my soul thirsts
>   like the earth, parched, lifeless and
>   without water.

R. My soul is thirsting for you, O Lord my God.
[3] Thus have I gazed toward you in the
>   sanctuary
>   to see your power and your glory,
[4] For your kindness is a greater good than life;
>   my lips shall glorify you.

R. My soul is thirsting for you, O Lord my God.
[5] Thus will I bless you while I live;
>   lifting up my hands, I will call upon your
>   name.
[6] As with the riches of a banquet shall my soul
>   be satisfied,
>   and with exultant lips my mouth shall
>   praise you.

R. My soul is thirsting for you, O Lord my God.
[8] You are my help,
>   and in the shadow of your wings I shout
>   for joy.
[9] My soul clings fast to you;
>   your right hand upholds me.

R. My soul is thirsting for you, O Lord my God.

Alleluia

R. Alleluia, alleluia.
Tell us, Mary, what did you see on the way?
I saw the glory of the risen Christ, I saw his
>   empty tomb.
R. Alleluia, alleluia.

Gospel: John 20:1-2, 11-18

¹ On the first day of the week, Mary Magdalene came to the tomb early in the morning, while it was still dark, and saw the stone removed from the tomb. ² So she ran and went to Simon Peter and to the other disciple whom Jesus loved, and told them, "They have taken the Lord from the tomb, and we don't know where they put him."

¹¹ Mary stayed outside the tomb weeping. And as she wept, she bent over into the tomb ¹² and saw two angels in white sitting there, one at the head and one at the feet where the Body of Jesus had been. ¹³ And they said to her, "Woman, why are you weeping?" She said to them, "They have taken my Lord, and I don't know where they laid him." ¹⁴ When she had said this, she turned around and saw Jesus there, but did not know it was Jesus. ¹⁵ Jesus said to her, "Woman, why are you weeping? Whom are you looking for?" She thought it was the gardener and said to him, "Sir, if you carried him away, tell me where you laid him, and I will take him." ¹⁶ Jesus said to her, "Mary!" She turned and said to him in Hebrew, "*Rabbouni*," which means Teacher. ¹⁷ Jesus said to her, "Stop holding on to me, for I have not yet ascended to the Father. But go to my brothers and tell them, 'I am going to my Father and your Father, to my God and your God.'" ¹⁸ Mary Magdalene went and announced to the disciples, "I have seen the Lord," and then reported what he told her.

Wednesday July 23, 2025
Wednesday of the Sixteenth Week in Ordinary Time
First Reading: Exodus 16:1-5, 9-15

¹The children of Israel set out from Elim, and came into the desert of Sin, which is between Elim and Sinai, on the fifteenth day of the second month after their departure from the land of Egypt. ²Here in the desert the whole assembly of the children of Israel grumbled against Moses and Aaron. ³The children of Israel said to them, "Would that we had died at the LORD's hand in the land of Egypt, as we sat by our fleshpots and ate our fill of bread! But you had to lead us into this desert to make the whole community die of famine!"

⁴Then the LORD said to Moses, "I will now rain down bread from heaven for you. Each day the people are to go out and gather their daily portion; thus will I test them, to see whether they follow my instructions or not. ⁵On the sixth day, however, when they prepare what they bring in, let it be twice as much as they gather on the other days."

⁹Then Moses said to Aaron, "Tell the whole congregation of the children of Israel: Present yourselves before the LORD, for he has heard your grumbling." ¹⁰When Aaron announced this to the whole assembly of the children of Israel, they turned toward the desert, and lo, the glory of the LORD appeared in the cloud! ¹¹The LORD spoke to Moses and said, ¹²"I have heard the grumbling of the children of Israel. Tell them: In the evening twilight you shall eat flesh, and in the morning you shall have your fill of bread, so that you may know that I, the LORD, am your God."

¹³In the evening quail came up and covered the camp. In the morning a dew lay all about the camp, ¹⁴and when the dew evaporated, there on the surface of the desert were fine flakes like hoarfrost on the ground. ¹⁵On seeing it, the children of Israel asked one another, "What is this?" for they did not know what it was. But Moses told them, "This is the bread which the LORD has given you to eat."

Responsorial Psalm: Psalms 78:18-19, 23-24, 25-26, 27-28

R. *(24b)* ***The Lord gave them bread from heaven.***

[18] They tempted God in their hearts
  by demanding the food they craved.
[19] Yes, they spoke against God, saying,
  "Can God spread a table in the desert?"

R. The Lord gave them bread from heaven.

[23] Yet he commanded the skies above
  and the doors of heaven he opened;
[24] He rained manna upon them for food
  and gave them heavenly bread.

R. The Lord gave them bread from heaven.

[25] Man ate the bread of angels,
  food he sent them in abundance.
[26] He stirred up the east wind in the heavens,
  and by his power brought on the south wind.

R. The Lord gave them bread from heaven.

[27] And he rained meat upon them like dust,
  and, like the sand of the sea, winged fowl,
[28] Which fell in the midst of their camp
  round about their tents.

R. The Lord gave them bread from heaven.

Alleluia

R. Alleluia, alleluia.
The seed is the word of God, Christ is the
  sower;
all who come to him will live for ever.
R. Alleluia, alleluia.

Gospel: Matthew 13:1-9

[1] On that day, Jesus went out of the house and sat down by the sea. [2] Such large crowds gathered around him that he got into a boat and sat down, and the whole crowd stood along the shore. [3] And he spoke to them at length in parables, saying: "A sower went out to sow. [4] And as he sowed, some seed fell on the path, and birds came and ate it up. [5] Some fell on rocky ground, where it had little soil. It sprang up at once because the soil was not deep, [6] and when the sun rose it was scorched, and it withered for lack of roots. [7] Some seed fell among thorns, and the thorns grew up and choked it. [8] But some seed fell on rich soil, and produced fruit, a hundred or sixty or thirtyfold. [9] Whoever has ears ought to hear."

Thursday July 24, 2025
Thursday of Sixteenth Week I Ordinary Time
First Reading: Exodus 19:1-2, 9-11, 16-20B

[1] In the third month after their departure from the land of Egypt, on its first day, the children of Israel came to the desert of Sinai. [2] After the journey from Rephidim to the desert of Sinai, they pitched camp.

While Israel was encamped here in front of the mountain, [9] the LORD told Moses, "I am coming to you in a dense cloud, so that when the people hear me speaking with you, they may always have faith in you also." When Moses, then, had reported to the LORD the response of the people, [10] the LORD added, "Go to the people and have them sanctify themselves today and tomorrow. Make them wash their garments [11] and be ready for the third day; for on the third day the LORD will come down on Mount Sinai before the eyes of all the people."

[16] On the morning of the third day there were peals of thunder and lightning, and a heavy cloud over the mountain, and a very loud trumpet blast, so that all the people in the camp trembled. [17] But Moses led the people out of the camp to meet God, and they stationed themselves at the foot of the mountain. [18] Mount Sinai was all wrapped in smoke, for the LORD came down upon it in fire. The smoke rose from it as though from a furnace, and the whole mountain trembled violently. [19] The trumpet blast grew louder and louder, while Moses was speaking and God answering him with thunder.

[20AB] When the LORD came down to the top of Mount Sinai, he summoned Moses to the top of the mountain.

Responsorial Psalm: Daniel 3:52, 53, 54, 55, 56
R. (52b) Glory and praise for ever!
[52] "Blessed are you, O Lord, the God of our
> fathers,
>> praiseworthy and exalted above all
>>> forever;
And blessed is your holy and glorious name,
> praiseworthy and exalted above all for all
>> ages."

R. Glory and praise for ever!
[53] "Blessed are you in the temple of your holy
> glory,
>> praiseworthy and glorious above all
>>> forever."

R. Glory and praise for ever!
[54] "Blessed are you on the throne of your
> Kingdom,
>> praiseworthy and exalted above all
>>> forever."

R. Glory and praise for ever!
[55] "Blessed are you who look into the depths

from your throne upon the cherubim,
> praiseworthy and exalted above all
> forever."

R. Glory and praise for ever!

⁵⁶ "Blessed are you in the firmament of heaven,
> praiseworthy and glorious forever."

R. Glory and praise for ever!

Alleluia: Matthew 11:25

R. Alleluia, alleluia.
²⁵Blessed are you, Father, Lord of heaven and earth;
you have revealed to little ones the mysteries of the Kingdom.
R. Alleluia, alleluia.

Gospel: Matthew 13:10-17

¹⁰The disciples approached Jesus and said, "Why do you speak to the crowd in parables?" ¹¹He said to them in reply, "Because knowledge of the mysteries of the Kingdom of heaven has been granted to you, but to them it has not been granted. ¹²To anyone who has, more will be given and he will grow rich; from anyone who has not, even what he has will be taken away. ¹³This is why I speak to them in parables, because *they look but do not see and hear but do not listen or understand.* ¹⁴Isaiah's prophecy is fulfilled in them, which says:

*You shall indeed hear but not understand,
> you shall indeed look but never see.*
¹⁵*Gross is the heart of this people,
> they will hardly hear with their ears,
they have closed their eyes,
> lest they see with their eyes
> and hear with their ears
and understand with their hearts and be
> converted
> and I heal them.*

¹⁶"But blessed are your eyes, because they see, and your ears, because they hear. ¹⁷Amen, I say to you, many prophets and righteous people longed to see what you see but did not see it, and to hear what you hear but did not hear it."

Friday July 25, 2025
Feast of Saint James, Apostle

First Reading: 2 Corinthians 4:7-15

Brothers and sisters: ⁷ We hold this treasure in earthen vessels, that the surpassing power may be of God and not from us. ⁸ We are afflicted in every way, but not constrained; perplexed, but not driven to despair; ⁹ persecuted, but not abandoned; struck down, but not destroyed; ¹⁰ always carrying about in the body the dying of Jesus, so that the life of Jesus may also be manifested in our body. ¹¹ For we who live are constantly being given up to death for the sake of Jesus, so that the life of Jesus may be manifested in our mortal flesh.

¹² So death is at work in us, but life in you. ¹³ Since, then, we have the same spirit of faith, according to what is written, *I believed, therefore I spoke*, we too believe and therefore speak, ¹⁴ knowing that the one who raised the Lord Jesus will raise us also with Jesus and place us with you in his presence. ¹⁵ Everything indeed is for you, so that the grace bestowed in abundance on more and more people may cause the thanksgiving to overflow for the glory of God.

Responsorial Psalm: Psalms 126:1BC-2AB, 2CD-3, 4-5, 6
R. ⁽⁵⁾ Those who sow in tears shall reap rejoicing.
¹ᴮᶜ When the LORD brought back the captives of
       Zion,
    we were like men dreaming.
²ᴬᴮ Then our mouth was filled with laughter,
    and our tongue with rejoicing.
R. Those who sow in tears shall reap rejoicing.
²ᶜᴰ Then they said among the nations,
      "The LORD has done great things for
        them."
³ The LORD has done great things for us;
    we are glad indeed.
R. Those who sow in tears shall reap rejoicing.
⁴ Restore our fortunes, O LORD,
    like the torrents in the southern desert.
⁵ Those that sow in tears
    shall reap rejoicing.
R. Those who sow in tears shall reap rejoicing.
⁶ Although they go forth weeping,
    carrying the seed to be sown,
They shall come back rejoicing,
    carrying their sheaves.
R. Those who sow in tears shall reap rejoicing.

Alleluia: cf. John 15:16
R. Alleluia, alleluia.
¹⁶ I chose you from the world,
to go and bear fruit that will last, says the
    Lord.
R. Alleluia, alleluia.

Gospel: Matthew 20:20-28

20 The mother of the sons of Zebedee approached Jesus with her sons and did him homage, wishing to ask him for something. 21 He said to her, "What do you wish?" She answered him, "Command that these two sons of mine sit, one at your right and the other at your left, in your Kingdom." 22 Jesus said in reply, "You do not know what you are asking. Can you drink the chalice that I am going to drink?" They said to him, "We can." 23 He replied, "My chalice you will indeed drink, but to sit at my right and at my left, this is not mine to give but is for those for whom it has been prepared by my Father." 24 When the ten heard this, they became indignant at the two brothers. 25 But Jesus summoned them and said, "You know that the rulers of the Gentiles lord it over them, and the great ones make their authority over them felt. 26 But it shall not be so among you. Rather, whoever wishes to be great among you shall be your servant; 27 whoever wishes to be first among you shall be your slave. 28 Just so, the Son of Man did not come to be served but to serve and to give his life as a ransom for many."

Saturday July 26, 2025
Memorial of Saints Joachim and Anne

First Reading: Exodus 24:3-8

3 When Moses came to the people and related all the words and ordinances of the LORD, they all answered with one voice, "We will do everything that the LORD has told us." 4 Moses then wrote down all the words of the LORD and, rising early the next day, he erected at the foot of the mountain an altar and twelve pillars for the twelve tribes of Israel. 5 Then, having sent certain young men of the children of Israel to offer burnt offerings and sacrifice young bulls as peace offerings to the LORD, 6 Moses took half of the blood and put it in large bowls; the other half he splashed on the altar. 7 Taking the book of the covenant, he read it aloud to the people, who answered, "All that the LORD has said, we will heed and do." 8 Then he took the blood and sprinkled it on the people, saying, "This is the blood of the covenant that the LORD has made with you in accordance with all these words of his."

Responsorial Psalm: Psalms 50:1B-2, 5-6, 14-15

R. (14a) *Offer to God a sacrifice of praise.*
1B God the LORD has spoken and summoned the
    earth,
  from the rising of the sun to its setting.
2 From Zion, perfect in beauty,
  God shines forth.
R. *Offer to God a sacrifice of praise.*
5 "Gather my faithful ones before me,
  those who have made a covenant with
    me by sacrifice."
6 And the heavens proclaim his justice;
  for God himself is the judge.
R. *Offer to God a sacrifice of praise.*
14 "Offer to God praise as your sacrifice
  and fulfill your vows to the Most High;

¹⁵ Then call upon me in time of distress;
> I will rescue you, and you shall glorify me."

R. Offer to God a sacrifice of praise.

Alleluia: James 1:21BC
R. Alleluia, alleluia.
²¹ᴮᶜ Humbly welcome the word that has been planted in you
and is able to save your souls.
R. Alleluia, alleluia.

Gospel: Matthew 13:24-30
²⁴ Jesus proposed a parable to the crowds. "The Kingdom of heaven may be likened to a man who sowed good seed in his field. ²⁵ While everyone was asleep his enemy came and sowed weeds all through the wheat, and then went off. ²⁶ When the crop grew and bore fruit, the weeds appeared as well. ²⁷ The slaves of the householder came to him and said, 'Master, did you not sow good seed in your field? Where have the weeds come from?' ²⁸ He answered, 'An enemy has done this.' His slaves said to him, 'Do you want us to go and pull them up?' ²⁹ He replied, 'No, if you pull up the weeds you might uproot the wheat along with them. ³⁰ Let them grow together until harvest; then at harvest time I will say to the harvesters, "First collect the weeds and tie them in bundles for burning; but gather the wheat into my barn."'"

Sunday July 27, 2025
Seventeenth Sunday in Ordinary Time Year C
First Reading: Genesis 18:20-32
²⁰In those days, the LORD said: "The outcry against Sodom and Gomorrah is so great, and their sin so grave, ²¹that I must go down and see whether or not their actions fully correspond to the cry against them that comes to me. I mean to find out."

²²While Abraham's visitors walked on farther toward Sodom, the LORD remained standing before Abraham. ²³Then Abraham drew nearer and said: "Will you sweep away the innocent with the guilty? ²⁴Suppose there were fifty innocent people in the city; would you wipe out the place, rather than spare it for the sake of the fifty innocent people within it?

²⁵ Far be it from you to do such a thing, to make the innocent die with the guilty so that the innocent and the guilty would be treated alike! Should not the judge of all the world act with justice?" ²⁶The LORD replied, "If I find fifty innocent people in the city of Sodom, I will spare the whole place for their sake." ²⁷Abraham spoke up again: "See how I am presuming to speak to my Lord, though I am but dust and ashes! ²⁸What if there are five less than fifty innocent people? Will you destroy the whole city because of those five?" He answered, "I will not destroy it, if I find forty-five there." ²⁹But Abraham persisted, saying "What if only forty are found there?"

He replied, "I will forbear doing it for the sake of the forty." ³⁰Then Abraham said, "Let not my Lord grow impatient if I go on. What if only thirty are found there?" He replied, "I will forbear doing it if I can find but thirty there." ³¹Still Abraham went on, "Since I have thus dared to speak to my Lord, what if there are no more than twenty?" The LORD answered, "I will not destroy it, for the sake of the twenty." ³²But he still persisted: "Please, let not my Lord grow angry if I speak up this last time. What if there are at least ten there?" He replied, "For the sake of those ten, I will not destroy it."

Responsorial Psalm: Psalms 138:1-2, 2-3, 6-7, 7-8

R. ⁽³ᵃ⁾ *Lord, on the day I called for help, you answered me.*

¹I will give thanks to you, O LORD, with all my heart,
 for you have heard the words of my mouth;
 in the presence of the angels I will sing your praise;
²ᴬᴮ I will worship at your holy temple
 and give thanks to your name.

R. *Lord, on the day I called for help, you answered me.*

²ᴮᶜ Because of your kindness and your truth;
 for you have made great above all things
 your name and your promise.
³ When I called you answered me;
 you built up strength within me.

R. *Lord, on the day I called for help, you answered me.*

⁶ The LORD is exalted, yet the lowly he sees,
 and the proud he knows from afar.
⁷ᴬᴮᶜ Though I walk amid distress, you preserve me;
 against the anger of my enemies you raise your hand.

R. *Lord, on the day I called for help, you answered me.*

⁷ᶜ Your right hand saves me.
 ⁸The LORD will complete what he has done for me;
your kindness, O LORD, endures forever;
 forsake not the work of your hands.

R. *Lord, on the day I called for help, you answered me.*

Second Reading: Colossians 2:12-14

Brothers and sisters: ¹²You were buried with him in baptism, in which you were also raised with him through faith in the power of God, who raised him from the dead. ¹³And even when you were dead in transgressions and the uncircumcision of your flesh, he brought you to life along with him, having forgiven us all our transgressions; ¹⁴obliterating the bond against us, with its legal claims, which was opposed to us, he also removed it from our midst, nailing it to the cross.

Alleluia: Romans 8:15BC

R. Alleluia, alleluia.
¹⁵ᴮᶜ You have received a Spirit of adoption,
through which we cry, Abba, Father.
R. Alleluia, alleluia.

Gospel: Luke 11:1-13

¹Jesus was praying in a certain place, and when he had finished, one of his disciples said to him, "Lord, teach us to pray just as John taught his disciples." ²He said to them, "When you pray, say:

Father, hallowed be your name,
> your kingdom come.
> ³Give us each day our daily bread
> ⁴and forgive us our sins
> for we ourselves forgive everyone in debt
> > to us,
> and do not subject us to the final test."

⁵And he said to them, "Suppose one of you has a friend to whom he goes at midnight and says, 'Friend, lend me three loaves of bread, ⁶for a friend of mine has arrived at my house from a journey and I have nothing to offer him,' ⁷and he says in reply from within, 'Do not bother me; the door has already been locked and my children and I are already in bed. I cannot get up to give you anything.' ⁸I tell you, if he does not get up to give the visitor the loaves because of their friendship, he will get up to give him whatever he needs because of his persistence.

⁹"And I tell you, ask and you will receive; seek and you will find; knock and the door will be opened to you. ¹⁰ For everyone who asks, receives; and the one who seeks, finds; and to the one who knocks, the door will be opened. ¹¹What father among you would hand his son a snake when he asks for a fish? ¹² Or hand him a scorpion when he asks for an egg? ¹³ If you then, who are wicked, know how to give good gifts to your children, how much more will the Father in heaven give the Holy Spirit to those who ask him?"

Monday July 28, 2025
Monday of the Seventeenth Week in Ordinary Time
First Reading: Exodus 32:15-24, 30-34

[15]Moses turned and came down the mountain with the two tablets of the commandments in his hands, tablets that were written on both sides, front and back; [16]tablets that were made by God, having inscriptions on them that were engraved by God himself. [17]Now, when Joshua heard the noise of the people shouting, he said to Moses, "That sounds like a battle in the camp." [18]But Moses answered, "It does not sound like cries of victory, nor does it sound like cries of defeat; the sounds that I hear are cries of revelry." [19]As he drew near the camp, he saw the calf and the dancing. With that, Moses' wrath flared up, so that he threw the tablets down and broke them on the base of the mountain. [20]Taking the calf they had made, he fused it in the fire and then ground it down to powder, which he scattered on the water and made the children of Israel drink.

[21]Moses asked Aaron, "What did this people ever do to you that you should lead them into so grave a sin?" [22]Aaron replied, "Let not my lord be angry. You know well enough how prone the people are to evil. [23]They said to me, 'Make us a god to be our leader; as for the man Moses who brought us out of the land of Egypt, we do not know what has happened to him.' [24]So I told them, 'Let anyone who has gold jewelry take it off.' They gave it to me, and I threw it into the fire, and this calf came out."

[30]On the next day Moses said to the people, "You have committed a grave sin. I will go up to the LORD, then; perhaps I may be able to make atonement for your sin." [31]So Moses went back to the LORD and said, "Ah, this people has indeed committed a grave sin in making a god of gold for themselves! [32]If you would only forgive their sin! If you will not, then strike me out of the book that you have written." [33]The LORD answered, "Him only who has sinned against me will I strike out of my book. [34]Now, go and lead the people to the place I have told you. My angel will go before you. When it is time for me to punish, I will punish them for their sin."

Responsorial Psalm: Psalms 106:19-20, 21-22, 23

R. [(1a)] *Give thanks to the Lord, for he is good.*
[19] Our fathers made a calf in Horeb
    and adored a molten image;
[20] They exchanged their glory
    for the image of a grass-eating bullock.
R. Give thanks to the Lord, for he is good.
[21] They forgot the God who had saved them,
    who had done great deeds in Egypt,
[22] Wondrous deeds in the land of Ham,
    terrible things at the Red Sea.
R. Give thanks to the Lord, for he is good.
[23] Then he spoke of exterminating them,
    but Moses, his chosen one,
Withstood him in the breach
    to turn back his destructive wrath.

R. Give thanks to the Lord, for he is good.

Alleluia: James 1:18
R. Alleluia, alleluia.
[18] The Father willed to give us birth by the
    word of truth
that we may be a kind of firstfruits of his
    creatures.
R. Alleluia, alleluia.

Gospel: Matthew 13:31-35
[31] Jesus proposed a parable to the crowds. "The Kingdom of heaven is like a mustard seed that a person took and sowed in a field. [32] It is the smallest of all the seeds, yet when full-grown it is the largest of plants. It becomes a large bush, and the *birds of the sky come and dwell in its branches.*"

[33] He spoke to them another parable. "The Kingdom of heaven is like yeast that a woman took and mixed with three measures of wheat flour until the whole batch was leavened."

[34] All these things Jesus spoke to the crowds in parables. He spoke to them only in parables, [35] to fulfill what had been said through the prophet:

*I will open my mouth in parables,
    I will announce what has lain hidden from
        the foundation of the world.*

Tuesday July 29, 2025
Memorial of Saints Martha, Mary, and Lazarus
First Reading: Exodus 33: 7-11; 34: 5b-9, 28
[7] The tent, which was called the meeting tent, Moses used to pitch at some distance away, outside the camp. Anyone who wished to consult the LORD would go to this meeting tent outside the camp. [8] Whenever Moses went out to the tent, the people would all rise and stand at the entrance of their own tents, watching Moses until he entered the tent. [9] As Moses entered the tent, the column of cloud would come down and stand at its entrance while the LORD spoke with Moses. [10] On seeing the column of cloud stand at the entrance of the tent, all the people would rise and worship at the entrance of their own tents. [11] The LORD used to speak to Moses face to face, as one person speaks to another. Moses would then return to the camp, but his young assistant, Joshua, son of Nun, would not move out of the tent.

[5] Moses stood there with the LORD and proclaimed his name, "LORD." [6] Thus the LORD passed before him and cried out, "The LORD, the LORD, a merciful and gracious God, slow to anger and rich in kindness and fidelity, [7] continuing his kindness for a thousand generations, and forgiving wickedness and crime and sin; yet not declaring the guilty guiltless, but punishing children and grandchildren to the third and fourth generation for their fathers' wickedness!"

⁸ Moses at once bowed down to the ground in worship. Then he said, "If I find favor with you, O LORD, do come along in our company. This is indeed a stiff-necked people; yet pardon our wickedness and sins, and receive us as you own."
²⁸So Moses was there with the LORD for forty days and forty nights, without eating any food or drinking any water, and he wrote on the tablets the words of the covenant, the ten commandments.

Responsorial Psalm: Psalms 103: 6-7, 8-9, 10-11, 12-13
R. ⁽⁸ᵃ⁾ The Lord is kind and merciful.
⁶ The LORD secures justice
    and the rights of all the oppressed.
⁷ He has made known his ways to Moses,
    and his deeds to the children of Israel.
R. The Lord is kind and merciful.
⁸ Merciful and gracious is the LORD,
    slow to anger and abounding in kindness.
⁹ He will not always chide,
    nor does he keep his wrath forever.
R. The Lord is kind and merciful.
¹⁰ Not according to our sins does he deal with us,
    nor does he requite us according to our crimes.
¹¹ For as the heavens are high above the earth,
    so surpassing is his kindness toward those who fear him.
R. The Lord is kind and merciful.
¹² As far as the east is from the west,
    so far has he put our transgressions from
        us.
¹³ As a father has compassion on his children,
    so the LORD has compassion on those who
        fear him.
R. The Lord is kind and merciful.

Alleluia
R. Alleluia, alleluia.
I am the light of the world, says the Lord;
whoever follows me will have the light of life.
R. Alleluia, alleluia.

Gospel: John 11:19-27
¹⁹Many of the Jews had come to Martha and Mary to comfort them about their brother [Lazarus, who had died]. ²⁰When Martha heard that Jesus was coming, she went to meet him; but Mary sat at home. ²¹Martha said to Jesus, "Lord, if you had been here, my brother would not have died. ²²[But] even now I know that whatever you ask of God, God will give you." ²³Jesus said to her, "Your brother will

rise." ²⁴Martha said to him, "I know he will rise, in the resurrection on the last day." ²⁵Jesus told her, "I am the resurrection and the life; whoever believes in me, even if he dies, will live, ²⁶and everyone who lives and believes in me will never die. Do you believe this?" ²⁷She said to him, "Yes, Lord. I have come to believe that you are the Messiah, the Son of God, the one who is coming into the world."

Or Luke 10:38-42
³⁸Jesus entered a village where a woman whose name was Martha welcomed him. ³⁹She had a sister named Mary [who] sat beside the Lord at his feet listening to him speak. ⁴⁰ Martha, burdened with much serving, came to him and said, "Lord, do you not care that my sister has left me by myself to do the serving? Tell her to help me." ⁴¹The Lord said to her in reply, "Martha, Martha, you are anxious and worried about many things. ⁴²There is need of only one thing. Mary has chosen the better part and it will not be taken from her."

Wednesday July 30, 2025
Wednesday of Seventeenth Week in Ordinary Time
First Reading: Exodus 34:29-35
²⁹As Moses came down from Mount Sinai with the two tablets of the commandments in his hands, he did not know that the skin of his face had become radiant while he conversed with the LORD. ³⁰When Aaron, then, and the other children of Israel saw Moses and noticed how radiant the skin of his face had become, they were afraid to come near him. ³¹Only after Moses called to them did Aaron and all the rulers of the community come back to him. Moses then spoke to them. ³²Later on, all the children of Israel came up to him, and he enjoined on them all that the LORD had told him on Mount Sinai. ³³When he finished speaking with them, he put a veil over his face. ³⁴Whenever Moses entered the presence of the LORD to converse with him, he removed the veil until he came out again. On coming out, he would tell the children of Israel all that had been commanded. ³⁵Then the children of Israel would see that the skin of Moses' face was radiant; so he would again put the veil over his face until he went in to converse with the LORD.

Responsorial Psalm: Psalms 99:5, 6, 7, 9
R. *(see 9c)* **Holy is the Lord our God.**
⁵ Extol the LORD, our God,
    and worship at his footstool;
    holy is he!
R. Holy is the Lord our God.
⁶ Moses and Aaron were among his priests,
    and Samuel, among those who called
        upon his name;
    they called upon the LORD, and he
        answered them.
R. Holy is the Lord our God.

⁷ From the pillar of cloud he spoke to them;
  they heard his decrees and the law he
    gave them.
R. Holy is the Lord our God.
⁹ Extol the LORD, our God,
  and worship at his holy mountain;
  for holy is the LORD, our God.
R. Holy is the Lord our God.

Alleluia: John 15:15B
R. Alleluia, alleluia.
¹⁵ᴮ I call you my friends, says the Lord,
for I have made known to you all that the
    Father has told me.
R. Alleluia, alleluia.

Gospel: Matthew 13:44-46
Jesus said to his disciples: ⁴⁴ "The Kingdom of heaven is like a treasure buried in a field, which a person finds and hides again, and out of joy goes and sells all that he has and buys that field. ⁴⁵ Again, the Kingdom of heaven is like a merchant searching for fine pearls. ⁴⁶ When he finds a pearl of great price, he goes and sells all that he has and buys it."

Thursday July 31, 2025
Memorial of Saint Ignatius Loyola, Priest
First Reading: Exodus 40:16-21, 34-38
¹⁶Moses did exactly as the LORD had commanded him. ¹⁷On the first day of the first month of the second year the Dwelling was erected. ¹⁸It was Moses who erected the Dwelling. He placed its pedestals, set up its boards, put in its bars, and set up its columns. ¹⁹He spread the tent over the Dwelling and put the covering on top of the tent, as the LORD had commanded him. ²⁰He took the commandments and put them in the ark; he placed poles alongside the ark and set the propitiatory upon it. ²¹He brought the ark into the Dwelling and hung the curtain veil, thus screening off the ark of the commandments, as the LORD had commanded him.

³⁴Then the cloud covered the meeting tent, and the glory of the LORD filled the Dwelling. ³⁵Moses could not enter the meeting tent, because the cloud settled down upon it and the glory of the LORD filled the Dwelling. ³⁶Whenever the cloud rose from the Dwelling, the children of Israel would set out on their journey. ³⁷But if the cloud did not lift, they would not go forward; only when it lifted did they go forward. ³⁸In the daytime the cloud of the LORD was seen over the Dwelling; whereas at night, fire was seen in the cloud by the whole house of Israel in all the stages of their journey.

Responsorial Psalm: Psalms 84:3, 4, 5-6A AND 8A, 11
R. ⁽²⁾ *How lovely is your dwelling place, O Lord,*
        mighty God!

[3] My soul yearns and pines
   for the courts of the LORD.
My heart and my flesh
   cry out for the living God.
**R. How lovely is your dwelling place, O Lord,
   mighty God!**

[4] Even the sparrow finds a home,
   and the swallow a nest
   in which she puts her young–
Your altars, O LORD of hosts,
   my king and my God!
**R. How lovely is your dwelling place, O Lord,
   mighty God!**

[5] Blessed they who dwell in your house!
   continually they praise you.
[6A] Blessed the men whose strength you are!
[8A] They go from strength to strength.
**R. How lovely is your dwelling place, O Lord,
   mighty God!**

[11] I had rather one day in your courts
   than a thousand elsewhere;
I had rather lie at the threshold of the house
      of my God
   than dwell in the tents of the wicked.
**R. How lovely is your dwelling place, O Lord,
   mighty God!**

Alleluia: cf. Acts 16:14B
R. Alleluia, alleluia.
[14B] Open our heart, O Lord,
to listen to the words of your Son.
R. Alleluia, alleluia.

Gospel: Matthew 13:47-53

Jesus said to the disciples: [47] "The Kingdom of heaven is like a net thrown into the sea, which collects fish of every kind. [48] When it is full they haul it ashore and sit down to put what is good into buckets. What is bad they throw away. [49] Thus it will be at the end of the age. The angels will go out and separate the wicked from the righteous [50] and throw them into the fiery furnace, where there will be wailing and grinding of teeth."

[51] "Do you understand all these things?" They answered, "Yes." [52] And he replied, "Then every scribe who has been instructed in the Kingdom of heaven is like the head of a household who brings from his storeroom both the new and the old." [53] When Jesus finished these parables, he went away from there.

AUGUST 2025
Friday August 1, 2025
Memorial of Saint Alphonsus Mary de Liguori, Bishop & Doctor
First Reading: Leviticus 23:1, 4-11, 15-16, 27, 34B-37

¹The LORD said to Moses, ⁴"These are the festivals of the LORD which you shall celebrate at their proper time with a sacred assembly. ⁵The Passover of the LORD falls on the fourteenth day of the first month, at the evening twilight. ⁶The fifteenth day of this month is the LORD's feast of Unleavened Bread. For seven days you shall eat unleavened bread. ⁷On the first of these days you shall hold a sacred assembly and do no sort of work. ⁸On each of the seven days you shall offer an oblation to the LORD. Then on the seventh day you shall again hold a sacred assembly and do no sort of work."

⁹The LORD said to Moses, ¹⁰"Speak to the children of Israel and tell them: When you come into the land which I am giving you, and reap your harvest, you shall bring a sheaf of the first fruits of your harvest to the priest, ¹¹who shall wave the sheaf before the LORD that it may be acceptable for you. On the day after the sabbath the priest shall do this.

¹⁵"Beginning with the day after the sabbath, the day on which you bring the wave-offering sheaf, ¹⁶you shall count seven full weeks, and then on the day after the seventh week, the fiftieth day, you shall present the new cereal offering to the LORD.

²⁷"The tenth of this seventh month is the Day of Atonement, when you shall hold a sacred assembly and mortify yourselves and offer an oblation to the LORD.

³⁴ᴮ"The fifteenth day of this seventh month is the LORD's feast of Booths, which shall continue for seven days. ³⁵On the first day there shall be a sacred assembly, and you shall do no sort of work. ³⁶For seven days you shall offer an oblation to the LORD, and on the eighth day you shall again hold a sacred assembly and offer an oblation to the LORD. On that solemn closing you shall do no sort of work.

³⁷"These, therefore, are the festivals of the LORD on which you shall proclaim a sacred assembly, and offer as an oblation to the LORD burnt offerings and cereal offerings, sacrifices and libations, as prescribed for each day."

Responsorial Psalm: Psalms 81:3-4, 5-6, 10-11AB
R. ⁽²ᵃ⁾ *Sing with joy to God our help.*
³ Take up a melody, and sound the timbrel,
    the pleasant harp and the lyre.
⁴ Blow the trumpet at the new moon,
    at the full moon, on our solemn feast.
R. *Sing with joy to God our help.*
⁵ For it is a statute in Israel,
    an ordinance of the God of Jacob,
⁶ Who made it a decree for Joseph
    when he came forth from the land of
       Egypt.
R. *Sing with joy to God our help.*

¹⁰ There shall be no strange god among you
    nor shall you worship any alien god.
¹¹ᴬᴮ I, the LORD, am your God
    who led you forth from the land of Egypt.
R. Sing with joy to God our help.

Alleluia: 1 Peter 1:25
R. Alleluia, alleluia.
²⁵ The word of the Lord remains forever;
this is the word that has been proclaimed to
    you.
R. Alleluia, alleluia.

Gospel: Matthew 13:54-58
⁵⁴ Jesus came to his native place and taught the people in their synagogue. They were astonished and said, "Where did this man get such wisdom and mighty deeds? ⁵⁵ Is he not the carpenter's son? Is not his mother named Mary and his brothers James, Joseph, Simon, and Judas? ⁵⁶ Are not his sisters all with us? Where did this man get all this?" ⁵⁷ And they took offense at him. But Jesus said to them, "A prophet is not without honor except in his native place and in his own house." ⁵⁸ And he did not work many mighty deeds there because of their lack of faith.

Saturday August 2, 2025
Saturday of the Seventeenth Week in Ordinary Time
First Reading: Leviticus 25:1, 8-17
¹The LORD said to Moses on Mount Sinai, ⁸"Seven weeks of years shall you count– seven times seven years– so that the seven cycles amount to forty-nine years. ⁹Then, on the tenth day of the seventh month, let the trumpet resound; on this, the Day of Atonement, the trumpet blast shall re-echo throughout your land. ¹⁰This fiftieth year you shall make sacred by proclaiming liberty in the land for all its inhabitants. It shall be a jubilee for you, when every one of you shall return to his own property, every one to his own family estate. ¹¹In this fiftieth year, your year of jubilee, you shall not sow, nor shall you reap the after growth or pick the grapes from the untrimmed vines. ¹²Since this is the jubilee, which shall be sacred for you, you may not eat of its produce, except as taken directly from the field.

¹³"In this year of jubilee, then, every one of you shall return to his own property. ¹⁴Therefore, when you sell any land to your neighbor or buy any from him, do not deal unfairly. ¹⁵On the basis of the number of years since the last jubilee shall you purchase the land from your neighbor; and so also, on the basis of the number of years for crops, shall he sell it to you. ¹⁶When the years are many, the price shall be so much the more; when the years are few, the price shall be so much the less. For it is really the number of crops that he sells you.¹⁷Do not deal unfairly, then; but stand in fear of your God. I, the LORD, am your God."

Responsorial Psalm: Psalms 67:2-3, 5, 7-8
R. (4) *O God, let all the nations praise you!*
² May God have pity on us and bless us;
    may he let his face shine upon us.
³ So may your way be known upon earth;
    among all nations, your salvation.
R. *O God, let all the nations praise you!*
⁵ May the nations be glad and exult
    because you rule the peoples in equity;
    the nations on the earth you guide.
R. *O God, let all the nations praise you!*
⁷ The earth has yielded its fruits;
    God, our God, has blessed us.
⁸ May God bless us,
    and may all the ends of the earth fear him!
R. *O God, let all the nations praise you!*

Alleluia: Matthew 5:10
R. Alleluia, alleluia.
¹⁰ Blessed are they who are persecuted for the sake of righteousness
for theirs is the Kingdom of heaven.
R. Alleluia, alleluia.

Gospel: Matthew 14:1-12
¹ Herod the tetrarch heard of the reputation of Jesus ² and said to his servants, "This man is John the Baptist. He has been raised from the dead; that is why mighty powers are at work in him." ³ Now Herod had arrested John, bound him, and put him in prison on account of Herodias, the wife of his brother Philip, ⁴ for John had said to him, "It is not lawful for you to have her." ⁵ Although he wanted to kill him, he feared the people, for they regarded him as a prophet. ⁶ But at a birthday celebration for Herod, the daughter of Herodias performed a dance before the guests and delighted Herod ⁷ so much that he swore to give her whatever she might ask for. ⁸ Prompted by her mother, she said, "Give me here on a platter the head of John the Baptist." ⁹ The king was distressed, but because of his oaths and the guests who were present, he ordered that it be given, ¹⁰ and he had John beheaded in the prison. ¹¹ His head was brought in on a platter and given to the girl, who took it to her mother. ¹² His disciples came and took away the corpse and buried him; and they went and told Jesus.

Sunday August 3, 2025
Eighteenth Sunday in Ordinary Time, Year C
First Reading: Ecclesiastes 1:2; 2:21-23
²Vanity of vanities, says Qoheleth,

vanity of vanities! All things are vanity!

²¹Here is one who has labored with wisdom and knowledge and skill, and yet to another who has not labored over it, he must leave property. This also is vanity and a great misfortune.
²²For what profit comes to man from all the toil and anxiety of heart with which he has labored under the sun? ²³All his days sorrow and grief are his occupation; even at night his mind is not at rest. This also is vanity.

Responsorial Psalm: Psalms 90:3-4, 5-6, 12-13, 14 AND 17

R. ⁽¹⁾ *If today you hear his voice, harden not your hearts.*

³ You turn man back to dust,
    saying, "Return, O children of men."
⁴ For a thousand years in your sight
    are as yesterday, now that it is past,
    or as a watch of the night.

R. *If today you hear his voice, harden not your hearts.*

⁵ You make an end of them in their sleep;
    the next morning they are like the changing grass,
⁶ Which at dawn springs up anew,
    but by evening wilts and fades.

R. *If today you hear his voice, harden not your hearts.*

¹² Teach us to number our days aright,
    that we may gain wisdom of heart.
¹³ Return, O LORD! How long?
    Have pity on your servants!

R. *If today you hear his voice, harden not your hearts.*

¹⁴ Fill us at daybreak with your kindness,
    that we may shout for joy and gladness
    all our days.
¹⁷ And may the gracious care of the LORD our God be ours;
    prosper the work of our hands for us!
    Prosper the work of our hands!

R. *If today you hear his voice, harden not your hearts.*

Second Reading: Colossians 3:1-5, 9-11

Brothers and sisters: ¹If you were raised with Christ, seek what is above, where Christ is seated at the right hand of God. ²Think of what is above, not of what is on earth. ³For you have died, and your life is hidden with Christ in God. ⁴When Christ your life appears, then you too will appear with him in glory.

⁵Put to death, then, the parts of you that are earthly: immorality, impurity, passion, evil desire, and the greed that is idolatry. ⁹Stop lying to one another, since you have taken off the old self with its practices ¹⁰and have put on the new self, which is being renewed, for knowledge, in the image of its creator. ¹¹Here there is not Greek and Jew, circumcision and uncircumcision, barbarian, Scythian, slave, free; but Christ is all and in all.

Alleluia: Matthew 5:3

R. Alleluia, alleluia.
³ Blessed are the poor in spirit,
for theirs is the kingdom of heaven.
R. Alleluia, alleluia.

Gospel: Luke 12:13-21

¹³Someone in the crowd said to Jesus, "Teacher, tell my brother to share the inheritance with me." ¹⁴He replied to him, "Friend, who appointed me as your judge and arbitrator?" ¹⁵Then he said to the crowd, "Take care to guard against all greed, for though one may be rich, one's life does not consist of possessions."

¹⁶Then he told them a parable. "There was a rich man whose land produced a bountiful harvest. ¹⁷He asked himself, 'What shall I do, for I do not have space to store my harvest?' ¹⁸And he said, 'This is what I shall do: I shall tear down my barns and build larger ones. There I shall store all my grain and other goods ¹⁹and I shall say to myself, "Now as for you, you have so many good things stored up for many years, rest, eat, drink, be merry!"' ²⁰But God said to him, 'You fool, this night your life will be demanded of you; and the things you have prepared, to whom will they belong?' ²¹Thus will it be for all who store up treasure for themselves but are not rich in what matters to God."

Monday August 4, 2025
Memorial of Saint John Mary Vianney, Priest

First Reading: Numbers 11:4B-15

The children of Israel lamented, ⁴ᴮ"Would that we had meat for food! ⁵We remember the fish we used to eat without cost in Egypt, and the cucumbers, the melons, the leeks, the onions, and the garlic. ⁶But now we are famished; we see nothing before us but this manna."

⁷Manna was like coriander seed and had the color of resin. ⁸When they had gone about and gathered it up, the people would grind it between millstones or pound it in a mortar, then cook it in a pot and make it into loaves, which tasted like cakes made with oil. ⁹At night, when the dew fell upon the camp, the manna also fell.

¹⁰When Moses heard the people, family after family, crying at the entrance of their tents, so that the LORD became very angry, he was grieved. ¹¹"Why do you treat your servant so badly?" Moses asked the LORD. "Why are you so

displeased with me that you burden me with all this people? ¹²Was it I who conceived all this people? Or was it I who gave them birth, that you tell me to carry them at my bosom, like a foster father carrying an infant, to the land you have promised under oath to their fathers? ¹³Where can I get meat to give to all this people? For they are crying to me, 'Give us meat for our food.' ¹⁴I cannot carry all this people by myself, for they are too heavy for me. ¹⁵If this is the way you will deal with me, then please do me the favor of killing me at once, so that I need no longer face this distress."

Responsorial Psalm: Psalms 81:12-13, 14-15, 16-17
R. ⁽²ᵃ⁾ Sing with joy to God our help.
¹² "My people heard not my voice,
    and Israel obeyed me not;
¹³ So I gave them up to the hardness of their
    hearts;
    they walked according to their own
    counsels."
R. Sing with joy to God our help.
¹⁴ "If only my people would hear me,
    and Israel walk in my ways,
¹⁵ Quickly would I humble their enemies;
    against their foes I would turn my hand."
R. Sing with joy to God our help.
¹⁶ "Those who hated the LORD would seek to
    flatter me,
    but their fate would endure forever,
¹⁷ While Israel I would feed with the best of
    wheat,
    and with honey from the rock I would fill
    them."
R. Sing with joy to God our help.

Alleluia: Matthew 4:4
R. Alleluia, alleluia.
⁴ One does not live on bread alone,
But on every word that comes forth from the
    mouth of God.
R. Alleluia, alleluia.

Gospel: Matthew 14:13-21
¹³ When Jesus heard of the death of John the Baptist, he withdrew in a boat to a deserted place by himself. The crowds heard of this and followed him on foot from their towns.¹⁴ When he disembarked and saw the vast crowd, his heart was moved with pity for them, and he cured their sick.¹⁵ When it was evening, the disciples

approached him and said, "This is a deserted place and it is already late; dismiss the crowds so that they can go to the villages and buy food for themselves." [16] He said to them, "There is no need for them to go away; give them some food yourselves." [17] But they said to him, "Five loaves and two fish are all we have here." [18] Then he said, "Bring them here to me," [19] and he ordered the crowds to sit down on the grass. Taking the five loaves and the two fish, and looking up to heaven, he said the blessing, broke the loaves, and gave them to the disciples, who in turn gave them to the crowds. [20] They all ate and were satisfied, and they picked up the fragments left over–twelve wicker baskets full. [21] Those who ate were about five thousand men, not counting women and children.

Tuesday August 5, 2025
Tuesday of Eighteenth Week in Ordinary Time

First Reading: Numbers 12:1-13

[1]Miriam and Aaron spoke against Moses on the pretext of the marriage he had contracted with a Cushite woman. [2]They complained, "Is it through Moses alone that the LORD speaks? Does he not speak through us also?" And the LORD heard this. [3]Now, Moses himself was by far the meekest man on the face of the earth. [4]So at once the LORD said to Moses and Aaron and Miriam, "Come out, you three, to the meeting tent." And the three of them went. [5]Then the LORD came down in the column of cloud, and standing at the entrance of the tent, called Aaron and Miriam. When both came forward, [6]he said, "Now listen to the words of the LORD:

Should there be a prophet among you,
    in visions will I reveal myself to him,
    in dreams will I speak to him;
[7]not so with my servant Moses!
Throughout my house he bears my trust:
    [8]face to face I speak to him;
    plainly and not in riddles.
The presence of the LORD he beholds.

Why, then, did you not fear to speak against my servant Moses?"
[9]So angry was the LORD against them that when he departed, [10]and the cloud withdrew from the tent, there was Miriam, a snow-white leper! When Aaron turned and saw her a leper, [11]he said to Moses, "Ah, my lord! Please do not charge us with the sin that we have foolishly committed! [12]Let her not thus be like the stillborn babe that comes forth from its mother's womb with its flesh half consumed." [13]Then Moses cried to the LORD, "Please, not this! Pray, heal her!"

Responsorial Psalm: Psalms 51:3-4, 5-6AB, 6CD-7, 12-13
R. (see 3a) **Be merciful, O Lord, for we have sinned.**
[3] Have mercy on me, O God, in your goodness;
    in the greatness of your compassion wipe
        out my offense.

⁴ Thoroughly wash me from my guilt
    and of my sin cleanse me.
R. Be merciful, O Lord, for we have sinned.
⁵ For I acknowledge my offense;
    and my sin is before me always:
⁶ᴬᴮ "Against you only have I sinned;
    and done what is evil in your sight."
R. Be merciful, O Lord, for we have sinned.
⁶ᶜᴰ That you may be justified in your sentence,
    vindicated when you condemn.
⁷ Indeed, in guilt was I born,
    and in sin my mother conceived me.
R. Be merciful, O Lord, for we have sinned.
¹² A clean heart create for me, O God,
    and a steadfast spirit renew within me.
¹³ Cast me not off from your presence,
    and your Holy Spirit take not from me.
R. Be merciful, O Lord, for we have sinned.

Alleluia: John 1:49B
R. Alleluia, alleluia.
⁴⁹ᴮ Rabbi, you are the Son of God;
you are the King of Israel.
R. Alleluia, alleluia.

Gospel: Matthew 15:1-2, 10-14
¹Some Pharisees and scribes came to Jesus from Jerusalem and said, ²"Why do your disciples break the tradition of the elders? They do not wash their hands when they eat a meal." ¹⁰He summoned the crowd and said to them, "Hear and understand. ¹¹It is not what enters one's mouth that defiles the man; but what comes out of the mouth is what defiles one." ¹²Then his disciples approached and said to him, "Do you know that the Pharisees took offense when they heard what you said?" ¹³He said in reply, "Every plant that my heavenly Father has not planted will be uprooted. ¹⁴Let them alone; they are blind guides of the blind. If a blind man leads a blind man, both will fall into a pit."

Or Matthew 14:22-36
²²Jesus made the disciples get into a boat and precede him to the other side of the sea, while he dismissed the crowds. ²³After doing so, he went up on the mountain by himself to pray. When it was evening he was there alone. ²⁴Meanwhile the boat, already a few miles offshore, was being tossed about by the waves, for the wind was against it. ²⁵During the fourth watch of the night, he came toward them, walking on the sea. ²⁶When the disciples saw him walking on the sea they were terrified. "It is a ghost," they said, and they cried out in fear. ²⁷At once Jesus spoke

to them, "Take courage, it is I; do not be afraid." ²⁸Peter said to him in reply, "Lord, if it is you, command me to come to you on the water." ²⁹He said, "Come." Peter got out of the boat and began to walk on the water toward Jesus. ³⁰But when he saw how strong the wind was he became frightened; and, beginning to sink, he cried out, "Lord, save me!" ³¹Immediately Jesus stretched out his hand and caught him, and said to him, "O you of little faith, why did you doubt?" ³²After they got into the boat, the wind died down. ³³Those who were in the boat did him homage, saying, "Truly, you are the Son of God."

³⁴After making the crossing, they came to land at Gennesaret. ³⁵When the men of that place recognized him, they sent word to all the surrounding country. People brought to him all those who were sick ³⁶and begged him that they might touch only the tassel on his cloak, and as many as touched it were healed.

Wednesday August 6, 2025
Feast of the Transfiguration of the Lord
First Reading: Daniel 7:9-10, 13-14

As I watched:

⁹ Thrones were set up
    and the Ancient One took his throne.
His clothing was bright as snow,
    and the hair on his head as white as
        wool;
his throne was flames of fire,
    with wheels of burning fire.
¹⁰ A surging stream of fire
    flowed out from where he sat;
thousands upon thousands were ministering
        to him,
    and myriads upon myriads attended him.

The court was convened and the books were opened.
¹³ As the visions during the night continued,
I saw:

One like a Son of man coming,
    on the clouds of heaven;
when he reached the Ancient One
    and was presented before him,
¹⁴ the one like a Son of man received dominion,
        glory, and kingship;
    all peoples, nations, and languages serve
        him.
His dominion is an everlasting dominion

that shall not be taken away,
his kingship shall not be destroyed.

Responsorial Psalm: Psalms 97:1-2, 5-6, 9
R. (1a and 9a) **The Lord is king, the Most High over all the earth.**
[1] The LORD is king; let the earth rejoice;
let the many islands be glad.
[2] Clouds and darkness are round about him,
justice and judgment are the foundation
of his throne.
R. The Lord is king, the Most High over all the earth.
[5] The mountains melt like wax before the LORD,
before the LORD of all the earth.
[6] The heavens proclaim his justice,
and all peoples see his glory.
R. The Lord is king, the Most High over all the earth.
[9] Because you, O LORD, are the Most High over all the earth,
exalted far above all gods.
R. The Lord is king, the Most High over all the earth.

Second Reading: 2 Peter 1:16-19
Beloved: [16] We did not follow cleverly devised myths when we made known to you the power and coming of our Lord Jesus Christ, but we had been eyewitnesses of his majesty. [17] For he received honor and glory from God the Father when that unique declaration came to him from the majestic glory, "This is my Son, my beloved, with whom I am well pleased." [18] We ourselves heard this voice come from heaven while we were with him on the holy mountain. [19] Moreover, we possess the prophetic message that is altogether reliable. You will do well to be attentive to it, as to a lamp shining in a dark place, until day dawns and the morning star rises in your hearts.

Alleluia: Matthew 17:5C
R. Alleluia, alleluia.
[5C] This is my beloved Son, with whom I am well pleased;
listen to him.
R. Alleluia, alleluia.

Gospel: Luke 9:28b-36

[28]Jesus took Peter, John, and James and went up the mountain to pray. [29]While he was praying his face changed in appearance and his clothing became dazzling white. [30]And behold, two men were conversing with him, Moses and Elijah, [31]who appeared in glory and spoke of his exodus that he was going to accomplish in Jerusalem. [32] Peter and his companions had been overcome by sleep, but becoming fully awake, they saw his glory and the two men standing with him. [33] As they were about to part from him, Peter said to Jesus, "Master, it is good that we are here; let us make three tents, one for you, one for Moses, and one for Elijah." But he did not know what he was saying. [34]While he was still speaking, a cloud came and cast a shadow over them, and they became frightened when they entered the cloud. [35]Then from the cloud came a voice that said, "This is my chosen Son; listen to him." [36] After the voice had spoken, Jesus was found alone. They fell silent and did not at that time tell anyone what they had seen.

Thursday August 7, 2025
Thursday of Eighteenth Week in Ordinary Time

First Reading: Numbers 20:1-13

[1]The whole congregation of the children of Israel arrived in the desert of Zin in the first month, and the people settled at Kadesh. It was here that Miriam died, and here that she was buried.

[2]As the community had no water, they held a council against Moses and Aaron. [3]The people contended with Moses, exclaiming, "Would that we too had perished with our kinsmen in the LORD's presence! [4]Why have you brought the LORD's assembly into this desert where we and our livestock are dying? [5]Why did you lead us out of Egypt, only to bring us to this wretched place
which has neither grain nor figs nor vines nor pomegranates? Here there is not even water to drink!" [6]But Moses and Aaron went away from the assembly to the entrance of the meeting tent, where they fell prostrate.

Then the glory of the LORD appeared to them, [7]and the LORD said to Moses, [8]"Take your staff and assemble the community, you and your brother Aaron, and in their presence order the rock to yield its waters. From the rock you shall bring forth water for the congregation and their livestock to drink." [9]So Moses took his staff from its place before the LORD, as he was ordered. [10]He and Aaron assembled the community in front of the rock, where he said to them, "Listen to me, you rebels! Are we to bring water for you out of this rock?" [11]Then, raising his hand, Moses struck the rock twice with his staff, and water gushed out in abundance for the people and their livestock to drink. [12]But the LORD said to Moses and Aaron, "Because you were not faithful to me in showing forth my sanctity before the children of Israel, you shall not lead this community into the land I will give them."

[13]These are the waters of Meribah, where the children of Israel contended against the LORD, and where the LORD revealed his sanctity among them.

Responsorial Psalm: Psalms 95:1-2, 6-7, 8-9

R. [(8)] *If today you hear his voice, harden not your hearts.*

[1] Come, let us sing joyfully to the LORD;

let us acclaim the Rock of our salvation.
² Let us come into his presence with
     thanksgiving;
   let us joyfully sing psalms to him.
R. If today you hear his voice, harden not your hearts.
⁶ Come, let us bow down in worship;
   let us kneel before the LORD who made us.
⁷ For he is our God,
   and we are the people he shepherds, the
     flock he guides.
R. If today you hear his voice, harden not your hearts.
⁸ Oh, that today you would hear his voice:
   "Harden not your hearts as at Meribah,
   as in the day of Massah in the desert,
⁹ Where your fathers tested me;
   they tested me though they had seen my
     works."
R. If today you hear his voice, harden not your hearts.

Alleluia: Matthew 16:18
R. Alleluia, alleluia.
¹⁸ You are Peter, and upon this rock I will build
     my Church,
and the gates of the netherworld shall not
     prevail against it.
R. Alleluia, alleluia.

Gospel: Matthew 16:13-23
¹³ Jesus went into the region of Caesarea Philippi and he asked his disciples, "Who do people say that the Son of Man is?" ¹⁴ They replied, "Some say John the Baptist, others Elijah, still others Jeremiah or one of the prophets." ¹⁵ He said to them, "But who do you say that I am?" ¹⁶ Simon Peter said in reply, "You are the Christ, the Son of the living God." ¹⁷ Jesus said to him in reply, "Blessed are you, Simon son of Jonah. For flesh and blood has not revealed this to you, but my heavenly Father. ¹⁸ And so I say to you, you are Peter, and upon this rock I will build my Church, and the gates of the netherworld shall not prevail against it. ¹⁹ I will give you the keys to the Kingdom of heaven. Whatever you bind on earth shall be bound in heaven; and whatever you loose on earth shall be loosed in heaven." ²⁰ Then he strictly ordered his disciples to tell no one that he was the Christ.

²¹ From that time on, Jesus began to show his disciples that he must go to Jerusalem and suffer greatly from the elders, the chief priests, and the scribes, and be killed and on the third day be raised. ²² Then Peter took Jesus aside and began to rebuke him, "God forbid, Lord! No such thing shall ever happen to you." ²³ He turned and said to Peter, "Get behind me, Satan! You are an obstacle to me. You are thinking not as God does, but as human beings do."

Friday August 8, 2025
Memorial of Saint Dominic, Priest

First Reading: Deuteronomy 4:32-40

Moses said to the people: ³²"Ask now of the days of old, before your time, ever since God created man upon the earth; ask from one end of the sky to the other: Did anything so great ever happen before? Was it ever heard of? ³³Did a people ever hear the voice of God speaking from the midst of fire, as you did, and live? ³⁴Or did any god venture to go and take a nation for himself from the midst of another nation, by testings, by signs and wonders, by war, with his strong hand and outstretched arm, and by great terrors, all of which the LORD, your God, did for you in Egypt before your very eyes? ³⁵All this you were allowed to see that you might know the LORD is God and there is no other. ³⁶Out of the heavens he let you hear his voice to discipline you; on earth he let you see his great fire, and you heard him speaking out of the fire. ³⁷For love of your fathers he chose their descendants and personally led you out of Egypt by his great power, ³⁸driving out of your way nations greater and mightier than you, so as to bring you in and to make their land your heritage, as it is today. ³⁹This is why you must now know, and fix in your heart, that the LORD is God in the heavens above and on earth below, and that there is no other. ⁴⁰You must keep his statutes and commandments which I enjoin on you today, that you and your children after you may prosper, and that you may have long life on the land which the LORD, your God, is giving you forever."

Responsorial Psalm: Psalms 77:12-13, 14-15, 16 AND 21

R. *⁽¹²ᵃ⁾ I remember the deeds of the Lord.*
¹² I remember the deeds of the LORD;
    yes, I remember your wonders of old.
¹³ And I meditate on your works;
    your exploits I ponder.
R. *I remember the deeds of the Lord.*
¹⁴ O God, your way is holy;
    what great god is there like our God?
¹⁵ You are the God who works wonders;
    among the peoples you have made
        known your power.
R. *I remember the deeds of the Lord.*
¹⁶ With your strong arm you redeemed your
    people,
    the sons of Jacob and Joseph.
²¹ You led your people like a flock

under the care of Moses and Aaron.
R. I remember the deeds of the Lord.

Alleluia: Matthew 16:18
R. Alleluia, alleluia.
18 Blessed are they who are persecuted for the
  sake of righteousness;
for theirs is the Kingdom of heaven.
R. Alleluia, alleluia.

Gospel: Matthew 16:24-28
24 Jesus said to his disciples, "Whoever wishes to come after me must deny himself, take up his cross, and follow me. 25 For whoever wishes to save his life will lose it, but whoever loses his life for my sake will find it. 26 What profit would there be for one to gain the whole world and forfeit his life? Or what can one give in exchange for his life? 27 For the Son of Man will come with his angels in his Father's glory, and then he will repay each according to his conduct. 28 Amen, I say to you, there are some standing here who will not taste death until they see the Son of Man coming in his Kingdom."

Saturday August 9, 2025
Saturday of Eighteenth Week in Ordinary Time
First Reading: Deuteronomy 6:4-13
Moses said to the people: 4"Hear, O Israel! The LORD is our God, the LORD alone! 5Therefore, you shall love the LORD, your God, with all your heart, and with all your soul, and with all your strength. 6Take to heart these words which I enjoin on you today. 7Drill them into your children. Speak of them at home and abroad, whether you are busy or at rest. 8Bind them at your wrist as a sign and let them be as a pendant on your forehead. 9Write them on the doorposts of your houses and on your gates.

10"When the LORD, your God, brings you into the land which he swore to your fathers: Abraham, Isaac and Jacob, that he would give you, a land with fine, large cities that you did not build, 11with houses full of goods of all sorts that you did not garner, with cisterns that you did not dig, with vineyards and olive groves that you did not plant; and when, therefore, you eat your fill, 12take care not to forget the LORD, who brought you out of the land of Egypt, that place of slavery. 13The LORD, your God, shall you fear; him shall you serve, and by his name shall you swear."

Responsorial Psalm: Psalms 18:2-3A, 3BC-4, 47 AND 51
R. (2) I love you, Lord, my strength.
2 I love you, O LORD, my strength,
  3A O LORD, my rock, my fortress, my
    deliverer.
R. I love you, Lord, my strength.
3BC My God, my rock of refuge,
  my shield, the horn of my salvation, my

stronghold!
⁴ Praised be the LORD, I exclaim!
    And I am safe from my enemies.
R. I love you, Lord, my strength.
⁴⁷ The LORD live! And blessed be my Rock!
    Extolled be God my savior!
⁵¹ You who gave great victories to your king,
    and showed kindness to your anointed,
    to David and his posterity forever.
R. I love you, Lord, my strength.

Alleluia: 2 Timothy 1:10
R. Alleluia, alleluia.
¹⁰ Our Savior Jesus Christ has destroyed death and brought life to light through the Gospel.
R. Alleluia, alleluia.

Gospel: Matthew 17:14-20
¹⁴A man came up to Jesus, knelt down before him, ¹⁵and said, "Lord, have pity on my son, who is a lunatic and suffers severely; often he falls into fire, and often into water. ¹⁶I brought him to your disciples, but they could not cure him." ¹⁷Jesus said in reply, "O faithless and perverse generation, how long will I be with you? How long will I endure you? Bring the boy here to me." ¹⁸Jesus rebuked him and the demon came out of him, and from that hour the boy was cured. ¹⁹Then the disciples approached Jesus in private and said, "Why could we not drive it out?" ²⁰He said to them, "Because of your little faith. Amen, I say to you, if you have faith the size of a mustard seed, you will say to this mountain, 'Move from here to there,' and it will move. Nothing will be impossible for you."

Sunday August 10, 2025
Nineteenth Sunday in Ordinary Time, Year C

First Reading: Wisdom 18:6-9
⁶The night of the passover was known
        beforehand to our fathers,
    that, with sure knowledge of the oaths in
        which they put their faith,
    they might have courage.
⁷Your people awaited the salvation of the just
    and the destruction of their foes.
⁸For when you punished our adversaries,
    in this you glorified us whom you had
        summoned.
⁹For in secret the holy children of the good
        were offering sacrifice
    and putting into effect with one accord
        the divine institution.

Responsorial Psalm: Psalms 33:1, 12, 18-19, 20-22

*R. (12b) Blessed the people the Lord has chosen
    to be his own.*

¹ Exult, you just, in the LORD;
    praise from the upright is fitting.
¹² Blessed the nation whose God is the LORD,
    the people he has chosen for his own
        inheritance.

*R. Blessed the people the Lord has chosen to be
    his own.*

¹⁸ See, the eyes of the LORD are upon those who
        fear him,
    upon those who hope for his kindness,
¹⁹ To deliver them from death
    and preserve them in spite of famine.

*R. Blessed the people the Lord has chosen to be
    his own.*

²⁰ Our soul waits for the LORD,
    who is our help and our shield.
²² May your kindness, O LORD, be upon us
    who have put our hope in you.

*R. Blessed the people the Lord has chosen to be
    his own.*

Second Reading: Hebrews 11:1-2, 8-19

Brothers and sisters: ¹Faith is the realization of what is hoped for and evidence of things not seen. ²Because of it the ancients were well attested.

⁸By faith Abraham obeyed when he was called to go out to a place that he was to receive as an inheritance; he went out, not knowing where he was to go. ⁹By faith he sojourned in the promised land as in a foreign country, dwelling in tents with Isaac and Jacob, heirs of the same promise; ¹⁰for he was looking forward to the city with foundations, whose architect and maker is God. ¹¹By faith he received power to generate, even though he was past the normal age —and Sarah herself was sterile— for he thought that the one who had made the promise was trustworthy. ¹²So it was that there came forth from one man, himself as good as dead, descendants as numerous as the stars in the sky and as countless as the sands on the seashore.

¹³All these died in faith. They did not receive what had been promised but saw it and greeted it from afar and acknowledged themselves to be strangers and aliens on earth, ¹⁴for those who speak thus show that they are seeking a homeland. ¹⁵If they had been thinking of the land from which they had come, they would have had opportunity to return. ¹⁶But now they desire a better homeland, a heavenly one. Therefore, God is not ashamed to be called their God, for he has prepared a city for them.

¹⁷By faith Abraham, when put to the test, offered up Isaac, and he who had received the promises was ready to offer his only son, ¹⁸of whom it was said, "Through Isaac descendants shall bear your name." He reasoned that God was able to raise even from the dead, and he received Isaac back as a symbol.

Or Hebrews 11:1-2, 8-12

Brothers and sisters: ¹Faith is the realization of what is hoped for and evidence of things not seen. ²Because of it the ancients were well attested.

⁸By faith Abraham obeyed when he was called to go out to a place that he was to receive as an inheritance; he went out, not knowing where he was to go. ⁹By faith he sojourned in the promised land as in a foreign country, dwelling in tents with Isaac and Jacob, heirs of the same promise; ¹⁰for he was looking forward to the city with foundations, whose architect and maker is God. ¹¹By faith he received power to generate, even though he was past the normal age —and Sarah herself was sterile— for he thought that the one who had made the promise was trustworthy. ¹²So it was that there came forth from one man, himself as good as dead, descendants as numerous as the stars in the sky and as countless as the sands on the seashore.

Alleluia: Matthew 24;42A, 44

R. Alleluia, alleluia.
⁴²ᴬ Stay awake and be ready!
⁴⁴ For you do not know on what day your
    Lord will come.
R. Alleluia, alleluia.

Gospel: Luke 12:32-48

Jesus said to his disciples: ³²"Do not be afraid any longer, little flock, for your Father is pleased to give you the kingdom. ³³Sell your belongings and give alms. Provide money bags for yourselves that do not wear out, an inexhaustible treasure in heaven that no thief can reach nor moth destroy. ³⁴For where your treasure is, there also will your heart be.

³⁵"Gird your loins and light your lamps ³⁶and be like servants who await their master's return from a wedding, ready to open immediately when he comes and knocks. ³⁷Blessed are those servants whom the master finds vigilant on his arrival. Amen, I say to you, he will gird himself, have them recline at table, and proceed to wait on them. ³⁸And should he come in the second or third watch and find them prepared in this way, blessed are those servants. ³⁹Be sure of this: if the master of the house had known the hour when the thief was coming, he would not have let his house be broken into. ⁴⁰You also must be prepared, for at an hour you do not expect, the Son of Man will come." ⁴¹Then Peter said, "Lord, is this parable meant for us or for everyone?" ⁴²And the Lord replied, "Who, then, is the faithful and prudent steward whom the master will put in charge of his servants to distribute the food allowance at the proper time? ⁴³Blessed is that servant whom his master on arrival finds doing so. ⁴⁴Truly, I say to you, the master will put the

servant in charge of all his property. ⁴⁵But if that servant says to himself, 'My master is delayed in coming,' and begins to beat the menservants and the maidservants, to eat and drink and get drunk, ⁴⁶then that servant's master will come on an unexpected day and at an unknown hour and will punish the servant severely and assign him a place with the unfaithful. ⁴⁷That servant who knew his master's will but did not make preparations nor act in accord with his will shall be beaten severely; ⁴⁸and the servant who was ignorant of his master's will but acted in a way deserving of a severe beating shall be beaten only lightly. Much will be required of the person entrusted with much, and still more will be demanded of the person entrusted with more."

Or Luke 12:35-40
Jesus said to his disciples: ³⁵"Gird your loins and light your lamps ³⁶and be like servants who await their master's return from a wedding, ready to open immediately when he comes and knocks. ³⁷Blessed are those servants whom the master finds vigilant on his arrival. Amen, I say to you, he will gird himself, have them recline at table, and proceed to wait on them. ³⁸And should he come in the second or third watch and find them prepared in this way, blessed are those servants. ³⁹Be sure of this: if the master of the house had known the hour when the thief was coming, he would not have let his house be broken into. ⁴⁰You also must be prepared, for at an hour you do not expect, the Son of Man will come."

Monday August 11, 2025
Memorial of Saint Clare, Virgin
First Reading: Deuteronomy 10:12-22
Moses said to the people: ¹²"And now, Israel, what does the LORD, your God, ask of you but to fear the LORD, your God, and follow his ways exactly, to love and serve the LORD, your God, with all your heart and all your soul,¹³to keep the commandments and statutes of the LORD which I enjoin on you today for your own good? ¹⁴Think! The heavens, even the highest heavens, belong to the LORD, your God, as well as the earth and everything on it. ¹⁵Yet in his love for your fathers the LORD was so attached to them as to choose you, their descendants, in preference to all other peoples, as indeed he has now done. ¹⁶Circumcise your hearts, therefore, and be no longer stiff-necked. ¹⁷For the LORD, your God, is the God of gods, the LORD of lords, the great God, mighty and awesome, who has no favorites, accepts no bribes; ¹⁸who executes justice for the orphan and the widow, and befriends the alien, feeding and clothing him. ¹⁹So you too must befriend the alien, for you were once aliens yourselves in the land of Egypt. ²⁰The LORD, your God, shall you fear, and him shall you serve; hold fast to him and swear by his name. ²¹He is your glory, he, your God, who has done for you those great and terrible things which your own eyes have seen. ²²Your ancestors went down to Egypt seventy strong, and now the LORD, your God, has made you as numerous as the stars of the sky."

Responsorial Psalm: Psalms 147:12-13, 14-15, 19-20
R. (12a) *Praise the Lord, Jerusalem.*
¹² Glorify the LORD, O Jerusalem;
    praise your God, O Zion.
¹³ For he has strengthened the bars of your
        gates;
    he has blessed your children within you.
R. Praise the Lord, Jerusalem.
¹⁴ He has granted peace in your borders;
    with the best of wheat he fills you.
¹⁵ He sends forth his command to the earth;
    swiftly runs his word!
R. Praise the Lord, Jerusalem.
¹⁹ He has proclaimed his word to Jacob,
    his statutes and his ordinances to Israel.
²⁰ He has not done thus for any other nation;
    his ordinances he has not made known to
        them. Alleluia.
R. Praise the Lord, Jerusalem.

Alleluia: cf. 2 Thessalonians 2:14
R. Alleluia, alleluia.
¹⁴ God has called you through the Gospel
to possess the glory of our Lord Jesus Christ.
R. Alleluia, alleluia.

Gospel: Matthew 17:22-27
²² As Jesus and his disciples were gathering in Galilee, Jesus said to them, "The Son of Man is to be handed over to men, ²³ and they will kill him, and he will be raised on the third day." And they were overwhelmed with grief.

²⁴ When they came to Capernaum, the collectors of the temple tax approached Peter and said, "Does not your teacher pay the temple tax?" ²⁵ "Yes," he said. When he came into the house, before he had time to speak, Jesus asked him, "What is your opinion, Simon? From whom do the kings of the earth take tolls or census tax? From their subjects or from foreigners?" ²⁶ When he said, "From foreigners," Jesus said to him, "Then the subjects are exempt. ²⁷ But that we may not offend them, go to the sea, drop in a hook, and take the first fish that comes up. Open its mouth and you will find a coin worth twice the temple tax. Give that to them for me and for you."

Tuesday August 12, 2025
Tuesday of the Nineteenth Week in Ordinary Time
First Reading: Deuteronomy 31:1-8
¹When Moses had finished speaking to all Israel, ²he said to them, "I am now one hundred and twenty years old and am no longer able to move about freely;

besides, the LORD has told me that I shall not cross this Jordan. ³It is the LORD, your God, who will cross before you; he will destroy these nations before you, that you may supplant them. It is Joshua who will cross before you, as the LORD promised. ⁴The LORD will deal with them just as he dealt with Sihon and Og, the kings of the Amorites whom he destroyed, and with their country. ⁵When, therefore, the LORD delivers them up to you, you must deal with them exactly as I have ordered you. ⁶Be brave and steadfast; have no fear or dread of them, for it is the LORD, your God, who marches with you; he will never fail you or forsake you."

⁷Then Moses summoned Joshua and in the presence of all Israel said to him, "Be brave and steadfast, for you must bring this people into the land which the LORD swore to their fathers he would give them; you must put them in possession of their heritage. ⁸It is the LORD who marches before you; he will be with you and will never fail you or forsake you. So do not fear or be dismayed."

Responsorial Psalm: Deuteronomy 32:3-4AB, 7, 8, 9 AND 12

R.⁽⁹ᵃ⁾ *The portion of the Lord is his people.*
² For I will sing the LORD's renown.
   Oh, proclaim the greatness of our God!
⁴ᴬᴮ The Rock—how faultless are his deeds,
   how right all his ways!
R. *The portion of the Lord is his people.*
⁷ Think back on the days of old,
   reflect on the years of age upon age.
Ask your father and he will inform you,
   ask your elders and they will tell you.
R. *The portion of the Lord is his people.*
⁸When the Most High assigned the nations
      their heritage,
   when he parceled out the descendants of
      Adam,
He set up the boundaries of the peoples
   after the number of the sons of Israel.
R. *The portion of the Lord is his people.*
⁹ While the LORD's own portion was Jacob,
   his hereditary share was Israel.
¹² The LORD alone was their leader,
   no strange god was with him.
R. *The portion of the Lord is his people.*

Alleluia: Matthew 11:29AB

R. Alleluia, alleluia.
²⁹ᴬᴮ Take my yoke upon you and learn from me,
for I am meek and humble of heart.
R. Alleluia, alleluia.

Gospel: Matthew 18:1-5, 10, 12-14

¹ The disciples approached Jesus and said, "Who is the greatest in the Kingdom of heaven?" ² He called a child over, placed it in their midst, ³ and said, "Amen, I say to you, unless you turn and become like children, you will not enter the Kingdom of heaven. ⁴ Whoever becomes humble like this child is the greatest in the Kingdom of heaven. ⁵ And whoever receives one child such as this in my name receives me.

¹⁰ "See that you do not despise one of these little ones, for I say to you that their angels in heaven always look upon the face of my heavenly Father. ¹² What is your opinion? If a man has a hundred sheep and one of them goes astray, will he not leave the ninety-nine in the hills and go in search of the stray? ¹³ And if he finds it, amen, I say to you, he rejoices more over it than over the ninety-nine that did not stray. ¹⁴ In just the same way, it is not the will of your heavenly Father that one of these little ones be lost."

Wednesday August 13, 2025
Wednesday of the Nineteenth Week in Ordinary Time
First Reading: Deuteronomy 34:1-12

¹Moses went up from the plains of Moab to Mount Nebo, the headland of Pisgah which faces Jericho, and the LORD showed him all the land— Gilead, and as far as Dan, ²all Naphtali, the land of Ephraim and Manasseh, all the land of Judah as far as the Western Sea, ³the Negeb, the circuit of the Jordan with the lowlands at Jericho, city of palms, and as far as Zoar. ⁴The LORD then said to him, "This is the land which I swore to Abraham, Isaac, and Jacob that I would give to their descendants. I have let you feast your eyes upon it, but you shall not cross over." ⁵So there, in the land of Moab, Moses, the servant of the LORD, died as the LORD had said; ⁶and he was buried in the ravine opposite Beth-peor in the land of Moab, but to this day no one knows the place of his burial. ⁷Moses was one hundred and twenty years old when he died, yet his eyes were undimmed and his vigor unabated. ⁸For thirty days the children of Israel wept for Moses in the plains of Moab, till they had completed the period of grief and mourning for Moses.

⁹Now Joshua, son of Nun, was filled with the spirit of wisdom, since Moses had laid his hands upon him; and so the children of Israel gave him their obedience, thus carrying out the LORD's command to Moses.

¹⁰Since then no prophet has arisen in Israel like Moses, whom the LORD knew face to face. ¹¹He had no equal in all the signs and wonders the LORD sent him to perform in the land of Egypt against Pharaoh and all his servants and against all his land, ¹²and for the might and the terrifying power that Moses exhibited in the sight of all Israel.

Responsorial Psalm: Psalms 66:1-3A, 5 AND 8, 16-17

R. (see 20a and 10b) **Blessed be God who filled my soul with fire!**
² Shout joyfully to God, all the earth;
    sing praise to the glory of his name;
    proclaim his glorious praise.
³ᴬ Say to God: "How tremendous are your
    deeds!"
R. Blessed be God who filled my soul with fire!
⁵ Come and see the works of God,

his tremendous deeds among the
> children of Adam.

⁸ Bless our God, you peoples;
> loudly sound his praise.

R. Blessed be God who filled my soul with fire!

¹⁶ Hear now, all you who fear God, while I declare
> what he has done for me.

¹⁷ When I appealed to him in words,
> praise was on the tip of my tongue.

R. Blessed be God who filled my soul with fire!

Alleluia: 2 Corinthians 5:19
R. Alleluia, alleluia.
¹⁹ God was reconciling the world to himself in
> Christ,
and entrusting to us the message of
> reconciliation.
R. Alleluia, alleluia.

Gospel: Matthew 18:15-20
Jesus said to his disciples: ¹⁵ "If your brother sins against you, go and tell him his fault between you and him alone. If he listens to you, you have won over your brother. ¹⁶ If he does not listen, take one or two others along with you, so that every fact may be established on the testimony of two or three witnesses. ¹⁷ If he refuses to listen to them, tell the Church. If he refuses to listen even to the Church, then treat him as you would a Gentile or a tax collector. ¹⁸ Amen, I say to you, whatever you bind on earth shall be bound in heaven, and whatever you loose on earth shall be loosed in heaven. ¹⁹ Again, amen, I say to you, if two of you agree on earth about anything for which they are to pray, it shall be granted to them by my heavenly Father. ²⁰ For where two or three are gathered together in my name, there am I in the midst of them."

Thursday August 14, 2025
Memorial of Saint Maximilian Kolbe, Priest & Martyr
First Reading: Joshua 3:7-10A, 11, 13-17
⁷The LORD said to Joshua, "Today I will begin to exalt you in the sight of all Israel, that they may know I am with you, as I was with Moses. ⁸Now command the priests carrying the ark of the covenant to come to a halt in the Jordan when you reach the edge of the waters."

⁹So Joshua said to the children of Israel, "Come here and listen to the words of the LORD, your God. ¹⁰ᴬThis is how you will know that there is a living God in your midst, who at your approach will dispossess the Canaanites. ¹¹The ark of the covenant of the LORD of the whole earth will precede you into the Jordan. ¹³When the soles of the feet of the priests carrying the ark of the LORD, the Lord of the

whole earth, touch the water of the Jordan, it will cease to flow; for the water flowing down from upstream will halt in a solid bank."

¹⁴The people struck their tents to cross the Jordan, with the priests carrying the ark of the covenant ahead of them. ¹⁵No sooner had these priestly bearers of the ark waded into the waters at the edge of the Jordan, which overflows all its banks during the entire season of the harvest, ¹⁶than the waters flowing from upstream halted, backing up in a solid mass for a very great distance indeed, from Adam, a city in the direction of Zarethan; while those flowing downstream toward the Salt Sea of the Arabah disappeared entirely. Thus the people crossed over opposite Jericho. ¹⁷While all Israel crossed over on dry ground, the priests carrying the ark of the covenant of the LORD remained motionless on dry ground in the bed of the Jordan until the whole nation had completed the passage.

Responsorial Psalm: Psalms 114:1-2, 3-4, 5-6
R. Alleluia!
¹When Israel came forth from Egypt,
    the house of Jacob from a people of alien
        tongue,
² Judah became his sanctuary,
    Israel his domain.
R. Alleluia!
³ The sea beheld and fled;
    Jordan turned back.
⁴ The mountains skipped like rams,
    the hills like the lambs of the flock.
R. Alleluia!
⁵ Why is it, O sea, that you flee?
    O Jordan, that you turn back?
⁶ You mountains, that you skip like rams?
    You hills, like the lambs of the flock?
R. Alleluia!

Alleluia: Psalms 119:135
R. Alleluia, alleluia.
¹³⁵Let your countenance shine upon your
        servant
and teach me your statutes.
R. Alleluia, alleluia.

Gospel: Matthew 18:21-19:1
²¹Peter approached Jesus and asked him, "Lord, if my brother sins against me, how often must I forgive him? As many as seven times?" ²²Jesus answered, "I say to you, not seven times but seventy-seven times. ²³That is why the Kingdom of heaven may be likened to a king who decided to settle accounts with his servants.

[24] When he began the accounting, a debtor was brought before him who owed him a huge amount. [25] Since he had no way of paying it back, his master ordered him to be sold, along with his wife, his children, and all his property, in payment of the debt. [26] At that, the servant fell down, did him homage, and said, 'Be patient with me, and I will pay you back in full.' [27] Moved with compassion the master of that servant let him go and forgave him the loan. [28] When that servant had left, he found one of his fellow servants who owed him a much smaller amount. He seized him and started to choke him, demanding, 'Pay back what you owe.' [29] Falling to his knees, his fellow servant begged him, 'Be patient with me, and I will pay you back.' [30] But he refused. Instead, he had the fellow servant put in prison until he paid back the debt. [31] Now when his fellow servants saw what had happened, they were deeply disturbed, and went to their master and reported the whole affair. [32] His master summoned him and said to him, 'You wicked servant! I forgave you your entire debt because you begged me to. [33] Should you not have had pity on your fellow servant, as I had pity on you?' [34] Then in anger his master handed him over to the torturers until he should pay back the whole debt. [35] So will my heavenly Father do to you, unless each of you forgives his brother from his heart."

[1] When Jesus finished these words, he left Galilee and went to the district of Judea across the Jordan.

Thursday August 14, 2025
Assumption of the Blessed Virgin Mary – Vigil Mass
First Reading: 1 Chronicles 15:3-4, 15-16; 16:1-2

[3] David assembled all Israel in Jerusalem to bring the ark of the LORD to the place which he had prepared for it. [4] David also called together the sons of Aaron and the Levites.

[15] The Levites bore the ark of God on their shoulders with poles, as Moses had ordained according to the word of the LORD.

[16] David commanded the chiefs of the Levites to appoint their kinsmen as chanters, to play on musical instruments, harps, lyres, and cymbals, to make a loud sound of rejoicing.

[1] They brought in the ark of God and set it within the tent which David had pitched for it. Then they offered up burnt offerings and peace offerings to God. [2] When David had finished offering up the burnt offerings and peace offerings, he blessed the people in the name of the LORD.

Responsorial Psalm: Psalms 132:6-7, 9-10, 13-14
R. [8] *Lord, go up to the place of your rest, you and the ark of your holiness.*

[6] Behold, we heard of it in Ephrathah;
  we found it in the fields of Jaar.
[7] Let us enter his dwelling,
  let us worship at his footstool.
R. *Lord, go up to the place of your rest, you and the ark of your holiness.*

⁹ May your priests be clothed with justice;
>   let your faithful ones shout merrily for
>   joy.
¹⁰ For the sake of David your servant,
>   reject not the plea of your anointed.

***R. Lord, go up to the place of your rest, you and
the ark of your holiness.***

¹³ For the LORD has chosen Zion;
>   he prefers her for his dwelling.
¹⁴ "Zion is my resting place forever;
>   in her will I dwell, for I prefer her."

***R. Lord, go up to the place of your rest, you and
the ark of your holiness.***

Second Reading: 1 Corinthians 15:54B-57

Brothers and sisters: ⁵⁴ᴮ When that which is mortal clothes itself with immortality, then the word that is written shall come about:

*⁵⁵ Death is swallowed up in victory.
Where, O death, is your victory?
Where, O death, is your sting?*

⁵⁶ The sting of death is sin, and the power of sin is the law. ⁵⁷ But thanks be to God who gives us the victory through our Lord Jesus Christ.

Alleluia: Luke 11:28
R. Alleluia, alleluia.
²⁸ Blessed are they who hear the word of God
and observe it.
R. Alleluia, alleluia.

Gospel: Luke 11:27-28
²⁷ While Jesus was speaking, a woman from the crowd called out and said to him, "Blessed is the womb that carried you and the breasts at which you nursed." ²⁸ He replied, "Rather, blessed are those who hear the word of God and observe it."

Friday August 15, 2025
Solemnity of the Assumption of the Blessed Virgin Mary (Mass during the Day)
First Reading: Revelation 11:19A; 12:1-6A, 10AB

¹⁹ᴬ God's temple in heaven was opened, and the ark of his covenant could be seen in the temple.
    ¹A great sign appeared in the sky, a woman clothed with the sun, with the moon under her feet, and on her head a crown of twelve stars. ² She was with child

and wailed aloud in pain as she labored to give birth. ³ Then another sign appeared in the sky; it was a huge red dragon, with seven heads and ten horns, and on its heads were seven diadems. ⁴ Its tail swept away a third of the stars in the sky and hurled them down to the earth. Then the dragon stood before the woman about to give birth, to devour her child when she gave birth. ⁵ She gave birth to a son, a male child, destined to rule all the nations with an iron rod. Her child was caught up to God and his throne. ⁶ᴬ The woman herself fled into the desert where she had a place prepared by God.

¹⁰ᴬᴮ Then I heard a loud voice in heaven say: "Now have salvation and power come, and the Kingdom of our God and the authority of his Anointed One."

Responsorial Psalm: Psalms 45:10, 11, 12, 16

R. ⁽¹⁰ᵇᶜ⁾ The queen stands at your right hand, arrayed in gold.

¹⁰ The queen takes her place at your right hand
   in gold of Ophir.

R. The queen stands at your right hand, arrayed in gold.

¹¹ Hear, O daughter, and see; turn your ear,
   forget your people and your father's
      house.

R. The queen stands at your right hand, arrayed in gold.

¹² So shall the king desire your beauty;
   for he is your lord.

R. The queen stands at your right hand, arrayed in gold.

¹⁶ They are borne in with gladness and joy;
   they enter the palace of the king.

R. The queen stands at your right hand, arrayed in gold.

Second Reading: 1 Corinthians 15:20-27

Brothers and sisters: ²⁰ Christ has been raised from the dead, the firstfruits of those who have fallen asleep. ²¹ For since death came through man, the resurrection of the dead came also through man. ²² For just as in Adam all die, so too in Christ shall all be brought to life, ²³ but each one in proper order: Christ the firstfruits; then, at his coming, those who belong to Christ; ²⁴ then comes the end, when he hands over the Kingdom to his God and Father, when he has destroyed every sovereignty and every authority and power. ²⁵ For he must reign until he has put all his enemies under his feet. ²⁶ The last enemy to be destroyed is death, ²⁷ for "he subjected everything under his feet."

Alleluia
R. Alleluia, alleluia.
Mary is taken up to heaven;
a chorus of angels exults.
R. Alleluia, alleluia.

Gospel: Luke 1:39-56

39 Mary set out and traveled to the hill country in haste to a town of Judah, 40 where she entered the house of Zechariah and greeted Elizabeth. 41 When Elizabeth heard Mary's greeting, the infant leaped in her womb, and Elizabeth, filled with the Holy Spirit, 42 cried out in a loud voice and said, "Blessed are you among women, and blessed is the fruit of your womb. 43 And how does this happen to me that the mother of my Lord should come to me? 44 For at the moment the sound of your greeting reached my ears, the infant in my womb leaped for joy. 45 Blessed are you who believed that what was spoken to you by the Lord would be fulfilled."

46 And Mary said:

"My soul proclaims the greatness of the
> Lord;
47 my spirit rejoices in God my Savior
48 for he has looked upon his lowly servant.
From this day all generations will call me
> blessed:
49 the Almighty has done great things for
> me
and holy is his Name.
50 He has mercy on those who fear him
in every generation.
51 He has shown the strength of his arm,
and has scattered the proud in their
> conceit.
52 He has cast down the mighty from their
> thrones,
and has lifted up the lowly.
53 He has filled the hungry with good things,
and the rich he has sent away empty.
54 He has come to the help of his servant Israel
for he has remembered his promise of mercy,
55 the promise he made to our fathers,
to Abraham and his children forever."

56 Mary remained with her about three months and then returned to her home.

Saturday August 16, 2025
Saturday of the Nineteenth Week in Ordinary Time
First Reading: Joshua 24:14-29

Joshua gathered together all the tribes of Israel at Shechem, and addressed them, saying: ¹⁴"Fear the LORD and serve him completely and sincerely. Cast out the gods your fathers served beyond the River and in Egypt, and serve the LORD. ¹⁵If it does not please you to serve the LORD, decide today whom you will serve, the gods your fathers served beyond the River or the gods of the Amorites in whose country you are dwelling. As for me and my household, we will serve the LORD."

¹⁶But the people answered, "Far be it from us to forsake the LORD for the service of other gods. ¹⁷For it was the LORD, our God, who brought us and our fathers up out of the land of Egypt, out of a state of slavery. He performed those great miracles before our very eyes and protected us along our entire journey and among all the peoples through whom we passed. ¹⁸At our approach the LORD drove out all the peoples, including the Amorites who dwelt in the land. Therefore we also will serve the LORD, for he is our God."

¹⁹Joshua in turn said to the people, "You may not be able to serve the LORD, for he is a holy God; he is a jealous God who will not forgive your transgressions or your sins. ²⁰If, after the good he has done for you, you forsake the LORD and serve strange gods, he will do evil to you and destroy you."

²¹But the people answered Joshua, "We will still serve the LORD." ²²Joshua therefore said to the people, "You are your own witnesses that you have chosen to serve the LORD." They replied, "We are, indeed!" Joshua continued: ²³"Now, therefore, put away the strange gods that are among you and turn your hearts to the LORD, the God of Israel." ²⁴Then the people promised Joshua, "We will serve the LORD, our God, and obey his voice."

²⁵So Joshua made a covenant with the people that day and made statutes and ordinances for them at Shechem, ²⁶which he recorded in the book of the law of God. Then he took a large stone and set it up there under the oak that was in the sanctuary of the LORD. ²⁷And Joshua said to all the people, "This stone shall be our witness, for it has heard all the words which the LORD spoke to us. It shall be a witness against you, should you wish to deny your God." ²⁸Then Joshua dismissed the people, each to his own heritage.

²⁹After these events, Joshua, son of Nun, servant of the LORD, died at the age of a hundred and ten.

Responsorial Psalm: Psalms 16:1-2A AND 5, 7-8, 11

R. (see 5a) **You are my inheritance, O Lord.**
¹Keep me, O God, for in you I take refuge;
 ²ᴬI say to the LORD, "My Lord are you."
⁵O LORD, my allotted portion and my cup,
 you it is who hold fast my lot.
R. You are my inheritance, O Lord.
⁷I bless the LORD who counsels me;

even in the night my heart exhorts me.
⁸I set the LORD ever before me;
   with him at my right hand I shall not be
      disturbed.
R. You are my inheritance, O Lord.
¹¹ You will show me the path to life,
   fullness of joys in your presence,
   the delights at your right hand forever.
R. You are my inheritance, O Lord.

Alleluia: cf. Matthew 11:25
R. Alleluia, alleluia.
²⁵ Blessed are you, Father, Lord of heaven and
      earth;
you have revealed to little ones the
      mysteries of the Kingdom.
R. Alleluia, alleluia.

Gospel: Matthew 19:13-15
¹³ Children were brought to Jesus that he might lay his hands on them and pray. The disciples rebuked them, ¹⁴ but Jesus said, "Let the children come to me, and do not prevent them; for the Kingdom of heaven belongs to such as these." ¹⁵ After he placed his hands on them, he went away.

Sunday August 17, 2025
Twentieth Sunday in Ordinary Time, Year C

First Reading: Jeremiah 38:4-6, 8-10
⁴In those days, the princes said to the king: "Jeremiah ought to be put to death; he is demoralizing the soldiers who are left in this city, and all the people, by speaking such things to them; he is not interested in the welfare of our people, but in their ruin." ⁵King Zedekiah answered: "He is in your power"; for the king could do nothing with them. ⁶And so they took Jeremiah and threw him into the cistern of Prince Malchiah, which was in the quarters of the guard, letting him down with ropes. There was no water in the cistern, only mud, and Jeremiah sank into the mud.

⁸Ebed-melech, a court official, went there from the palace and said to him: ⁹"My lord king, these men have been at fault in all they have done to the prophet Jeremiah, casting him into the cistern. He will die of famine on the spot, for there is no more food in the city." ¹⁰Then the king ordered Ebed-melech the Cushite to take three men along with him, and draw the prophet Jeremiah out of the cistern before he should die.

Responsorial Psalm: Psalms 40:2, 3, 4, 18
R. ⁽¹⁴ᵇ⁾ Lord, come to my aid!
²I have waited, waited for the LORD,
   and he stooped toward me.
R. Lord, come to my aid!

³The LORD heard my cry.
He drew me out of the pit of destruction,
    out of the mud of the swamp;
he set my feet upon a crag;
    he made firm my steps.
R. Lord, come to my aid!
⁴And he put a new song into my mouth,
    a hymn to our God.
Many shall look on in awe
    and trust in the LORD.
R. Lord, come to my aid!
¹⁸ Though I am afflicted and poor,
    yet the LORD thinks of me.
You are my help and my deliverer;
    O my God, hold not back!
R. Lord, come to my aid!

Second Reading: Hebrews 12:1-4

Brothers and sisters: ¹Since we are surrounded by so great a cloud of witnesses, let us rid ourselves of every burden and sin that clings to us and persevere in running the race that lies before us ²while keeping our eyes fixed on Jesus, the leader and perfecter of faith. For the sake of the joy that lay before him he endured the cross, despising its shame, and has taken his seat at the right of the throne of God. ³Consider how he endured such opposition from sinners, in order that you may not grow weary and lose heart. ⁴In your struggle against sin you have not yet resisted to the point of shedding blood.

Alleluia: John 10:27
R. Alleluia, alleluia.
²⁷My sheep hear my voice, says the Lord;
I know them, and they follow me.
R. Alleluia, alleluia.

Gospel: Luke 12:49-53

Jesus said to his disciples: ⁴⁹"I have come to set the earth on fire, and how I wish it were already blazing!
⁵⁰There is a baptism with which I must be baptized, and how great is my anguish until it is accomplished! ⁵¹Do you think that I have come to establish peace on the earth? No, I tell you, but rather division. ⁵²From now on a household of five will be divided, three against two and two against three; ⁵³a father will be divided against his son and a son against his father, a mother against her daughter and a daughter against her mother, a mother-in-law against her daughter-in-law and a daughter-in-law against her mother-in-law."

Monday August 18, 2025
Monday of Twentieth Week in Ordinary Time

First Reading: Judges 2:11-19

[11] The children of Israel offended the LORD by serving the Baals. [12] Abandoning the LORD, the God of their fathers, who led them out of the land of Egypt, they followed the other gods of the various nations around them, and by their worship of these gods provoked the LORD.

[13] Because they had thus abandoned him and served Baal and the Ashtaroth, [14] the anger of the LORD flared up against Israel, and he delivered them over to plunderers who despoiled them. He allowed them to fall into the power of their enemies round about whom they were no longer able to withstand. [15] Whatever they undertook, the LORD turned into disaster for them, as in his warning he had sworn he would do, till they were in great distress. [16] Even when the LORD raised up judges to deliver them from the power of their despoilers, [17] they did not listen to their judges, but abandoned themselves to the worship of other gods. They were quick to stray from the way their fathers had taken, and did not follow their example of obedience to the commandments of the LORD. [18] Whenever the LORD raised up judges for them, he would be with the judge and save them from the power of their enemies as long as the judge lived; it was thus the LORD took pity on their distressful cries of affliction under their oppressors. [19] But when the judge died, they would relapse and do worse than their ancestors, following other gods in service and worship, relinquishing none of their evil practices or stubborn conduct.

Responsorial Psalm: Psalms 106:34-35, 36-37, 39-40, 43AB AND 44

R. [4a] *Remember us, O Lord, as you favor your people.*

[34] They did not exterminate the peoples,
   as the LORD had commanded them,
[35] But mingled with the nations
   and learned their works.

R. *Remember us, O Lord, as you favor your people.*

[36] They served their idols,
   which became a snare for them.
[37] They sacrificed their sons
   and their daughters to demons.

R. *Remember us, O Lord, as you favor your people.*

[39] They became defiled by their works,
   and wanton in their crimes.
[40] And the LORD grew angry with his people,
   and abhorred his inheritance.

R. *Remember us, O Lord, as you favor your people.*

[43AB] Many times did he rescue them,

but they embittered him with their
  counsels.
⁴⁴ Yet he had regard for their affliction
  when he heard their cry.
R. Remember us, O Lord, as you favor your people.

Alleluia: Matthew 5:3
R. Alleluia, alleluia.
³ Blessed are the poor in spirit;
for theirs is the Kingdom of heaven.
R. Alleluia, alleluia.

Gospel: Matthew 19:16-22
¹⁶A young man approached Jesus and said, "Teacher, what good must I do to gain eternal life?" ¹⁷ He answered him, "Why do you ask me about the good? There is only One who is good. If you wish to enter into life, keep the commandments." ¹⁸He asked him, "Which ones?" And Jesus replied, *"You shall not kill; you shall not commit adultery; you shall not steal; you shall not bear false witness;* ¹⁹ *honor your father and your mother;* and *you shall love your neighbor as yourself."* ²⁰ The young man said to him, "All of these I have observed. What do I still lack?" ²¹Jesus said to him, "If you wish to be perfect, go, sell what you have and give to the poor, and you will have treasure in heaven. Then come, follow me." ²² When the young man heard this statement, he went away sad, for he had many possessions.

Tuesday August 19, 2025
Tuesday of Twentieth Week in Ordinary Time
First Reading: Judges 6:11-24A
¹¹The angel of the LORD came and sat under the terebinth in Ophrah that belonged to Joash the Abiezrite. While his son Gideon was beating out wheat in the wine press to save it from the Midianites, ¹²the angel of the LORD appeared to him and said, "The LORD is with you, O champion!" ¹³Gideon said to him, "My Lord, if the LORD is with us, why has all this happened to us? Where are his wondrous deeds of which our fathers told us when they said, 'Did not the LORD bring us up from Egypt?' For now the LORD has abandoned us and has delivered us into the power of Midian." ¹⁴The LORD turned to him and said, "Go with the strength you have and save Israel from the power of Midian. It is I who send you." ¹⁵But Gideon answered him, "Please, my lord, how can I save Israel? My family is the lowliest in Manasseh, and I am the most insignificant in my father's house." ¹⁶"I shall be with you," the LORD said to him, "and you will cut down Midian to the last man." ¹⁷Gideon answered him, "If I find favor with you, give me a sign that you are speaking with me. ¹⁸Do not depart from here, I pray you, until I come back to you and bring out my offering and set it before you." He answered, "I will await your return."

¹⁹So Gideon went off and prepared a kid and a measure of flour in the form of unleavened cakes. Putting the meat in a basket and the broth in a pot, he brought them out to him under the terebinth and presented them. ²⁰The angel of God said to him, "Take the meat and unleavened cakes and lay them on this rock; then pour out the broth." When he had done so, ²¹the angel of the LORD stretched out the tip of the staff he held, and touched the meat and unleavened cakes. Thereupon a fire came up from the rock that consumed the meat and unleavened cakes, and the angel of the LORD disappeared from sight. ²²Gideon, now aware that it had been the angel of the LORD, said, "Alas, Lord GOD, that I have seen the angel of the LORD face to face!" ²³The LORD answered him, "Be calm, do not fear. You shall not die." ²⁴ᴬSo Gideon built there an altar to the LORD and called it Yahweh-shalom.

Responsorial Psalm: Psalms 85:9, 11-12, 13-14
R. *(see 9b)* **The Lord speaks of peace to his people.**
⁹ I will hear what God proclaims;
   the LORD–for he proclaims peace
To his people, and to his faithful ones,
   and to those who put in him their hope.
R. The Lord speaks of peace to his people.
¹¹ Kindness and truth shall meet;
   justice and peace shall kiss.
¹² Truth shall spring out of the earth,
   and justice shall look down from heaven.
R. The Lord speaks of peace to his people.
¹³ The LORD himself will give his benefits;
   our land shall yield its increase.
¹⁴ Justice shall walk before him,
   and salvation, along the way of his steps.
R. The Lord speaks of peace to his people.

Alleluia: 2 Corinthians 8:9
R. Alleluia, alleluia.
⁹ Jesus Christ became poor although he was
      rich
so that by his poverty you might become
      rich.
R. Alleluia, alleluia.

Gospel: Matthew 19:23-30
²³ Jesus said to his disciples: "Amen, I say to you, it will be hard for one who is rich to enter the Kingdom of heaven. ²⁴ Again I say to you, it is easier for a camel to pass through the eye of a needle than for one who is rich to enter the Kingdom of God." ²⁵ When the disciples heard this, they were greatly astonished and said, "Who then can be saved?" ²⁶ Jesus looked at them and said, "For men this is

impossible, but for God all things are possible." ²⁷ Then Peter said to him in reply, "We have given up everything and followed you. What will there be for us?" ²⁸Jesus said to them, "Amen, I say to you that you who have followed me, in the new age, when the Son of Man is seated on his throne of glory, will yourselves sit on twelve thrones, judging the twelve tribes of Israel. ²⁹ And everyone who has given up houses or brothers or sisters or father or mother or children or lands for the sake of my name will receive a hundred times more, and will inherit eternal life. ³⁰ But many who are first will be last, and the last will be first."

Wednesday August 20, 2025
Memorial of Saint Bernard, Abbot & Doctor

First Reading: Judges 9:6-15

⁶All the citizens of Shechem and all Beth-millo came together and proceeded to make Abimelech king by the terebinth at the memorial pillar in Shechem.

⁷When this was reported to him, Jotham went to the top of Mount Gerizim and, standing there, cried out to them in a loud voice: "Hear me, citizens of Shechem, that God may then hear you! ⁸Once the trees went to anoint a king over themselves. So they said to the olive tree, 'Reign over us.' ⁹But the olive tree answered them, 'Must I give up my rich oil, whereby men and gods are honored, and go to wave over the trees?' ¹⁰Then the trees said to the fig tree, 'Come; you reign over us!' ¹¹But the fig tree answered them, 'Must I give up my sweetness and my good fruit, and go to wave over the trees?' ¹²Then the trees said to the vine, 'Come you, and reign over us.' ¹³But the vine answered them, 'Must I give up my wine that cheers gods and men, and go to wave over the trees?' ¹⁴Then all the trees said to the buckthorn, 'Come; you reign over us!' ¹⁵But the buckthorn replied to the trees, 'If you wish to anoint me king over you in good faith, come and take refuge in my shadow. Otherwise, let fire come from the buckthorn and devour the cedars of Lebanon.'"

Responsorial Psalm: Psalms 21:2-3, 4-5, 6-7

R.⁽²ᵃ⁾ *Lord, in your strength the king is glad.*
²O LORD, in your strength the king is glad;
    in your victory how greatly he rejoices!
³ You have granted him his heart's desire;
    you refused not the wish of his lips.
R. Lord, in your strength the king is glad.
⁴ For you welcomed him with goodly
        blessings,
    you placed on his head a crown of pure
        gold.
⁵ He asked life of you: you gave him
    length of days forever and ever.
R. Lord, in your strength the king is glad.
⁶ Great is his glory in your victory;
    majesty and splendor you conferred

> upon him.
> 7 You made him a blessing forever,
> > you gladdened him with the joy of your face.

R. Lord, in your strength the king is glad.

Alleluia: Hebrews 4:12
R. Alleluia, alleluia.
12 The word of God is living and effective,
able to discern the reflections and thoughts
of the heart.
R. Alleluia, alleluia.

Gospel: Matthew 20:1-16
Jesus told his disciples this parable: 1 "The Kingdom of heaven is like a landowner who went out at dawn to hire laborers for his vineyard. 2 After agreeing with them for the usual daily wage, he sent them into his vineyard. 3 Going out about nine o'clock, he saw others standing idle in the marketplace, 4 and he said to them, 'You too go into my vineyard, and I will give you what is just.' 5 So they went off. And he went out again around noon, and around three o'clock, and did likewise. 6 Going out about five o'clock, he found others standing around, and said to them, 'Why do you stand here idle all day?' 7 They answered, 'Because no one has hired us.' He said to them, 'You too go into my vineyard.' 8 When it was evening the owner of the vineyard said to his foreman, 'Summon the laborers and give them their pay, beginning with the last and ending with the first.' 9 When those who had started about five o'clock came, each received the usual daily wage. 10 So when the first came, they thought that they would receive more, but each of them also got the usual wage. 11 And on receiving it they grumbled against the landowner, 12 saying, 'These last ones worked only one hour, and you have made them equal to us, who bore the day's burden and the heat.' 13 He said to one of them in reply, 'My friend, I am not cheating you. Did you not agree with me for the usual daily wage? 14 Take what is yours and go. What if I wish to give this last one the same as you? 15 Or am I not free to do as I wish with my own money? Are you envious because I am generous?' 16 Thus, the last will be first, and the first will be last."

Thursday August 21, 2025
Memorial of Saint Pius X, Pope

First Reading: Judges 11:29-39A
29 The Spirit of the LORD came upon Jephthah. He passed through Gilead and Manasseh, and through Mizpah-Gilead as well, and from there he went on to the Ammonites. 30 Jephthah made a vow to the LORD. "If you deliver the Ammonites into my power," he said, 31 "whoever comes out of the doors of my house to meet me when I return in triumph from the Ammonites shall belong to the LORD. I shall offer him up as a burnt offering."

32 Jephthah then went on to the Ammonites to fight against them, and the LORD delivered them into his power, 33 so that he inflicted a severe defeat on

them, from Aroer to the approach of Minnith (twenty cities in all) and as far as Abel-keramim. Thus were the Ammonites brought into subjection by the children of Israel. ³⁴When Jephthah returned to his house in Mizpah, it was his daughter who came forth, playing the tambourines and dancing. She was an only child: he had neither son nor daughter besides her. ³⁵When he saw her, he rent his garments and said, "Alas, daughter, you have struck me down and brought calamity upon me. For I have made a vow to the LORD and I cannot retract." ³⁶She replied, "Father, you have made a vow to the LORD. Do with me as you have vowed, because the LORD has wrought vengeance for you on your enemies the Ammonites." ³⁷Then she said to her father, "Let me have this favor. Spare me for two months, that I may go off down the mountains to mourn my virginity with my companions." ³⁸"Go," he replied, and sent her away for two months. So she departed with her companions and mourned her virginity on the mountains. ³⁹ᴬAt the end of the two months she returned to her father,
who did to her as he had vowed.

Responsorial Psalm: Psalms 40:5, 7-8A, 8B-9, 10
R. ⁽⁸ᵃ ᵃⁿᵈ ⁹ᵃ⁾ *Here I am, Lord; I come to do your will.*
⁵ Blessed the man who makes the LORD his
            trust;
        who turns not to idolatry
        or to those who stray after falsehood.
R. Here I am, Lord; I come to do your will.
⁷ Sacrifice or oblation you wished not,
        but ears open to obedience you gave me.
⁸ᴬ Burnt offerings or sin-offerings you sought
            not;
        then said I, "Behold I come."
R. Here I am, Lord; I come to do your will.
⁸ᴮ "In the written scroll it is prescribed for me.
⁹To do your will, O my God, is my delight,
        and your law is within my heart!"
R. Here I am, Lord; I come to do your will.
¹⁰I announced your justice in the vast
            assembly;
        I did not restrain my lips, as you, O LORD,
            know.
R. Here I am, Lord; I come to do your will.

Alleluia: Psalms 95:8
R. Alleluia, alleluia.
⁸ If today you hear his voice,
harden not your hearts.
R. Alleluia, alleluia.

Gospel: Matthew 22:1-14

¹ Jesus again in reply spoke to the chief priests and the elders of the people in parables saying, ² "The Kingdom of heaven may be likened to a king who gave a wedding feast for his son. ³ He dispatched his servants to summon the invited guests to the feast, but they refused to come. ⁴ A second time he sent other servants, saying, 'Tell those invited: "Behold, I have prepared my banquet, my calves and fattened cattle are killed, and everything is ready; come to the feast."' ⁵ Some ignored the invitation and went away, one to his farm, another to his business. ⁶ The rest laid hold of his servants, mistreated them, and killed them. ⁷ The king was enraged and sent his troops, destroyed those murderers, and burned their city. ⁸ Then the king said to his servants, 'The feast is ready, but those who were invited were not worthy to come. ⁹ Go out, therefore, into the main roads and invite to the feast whomever you find.' ¹⁰ The servants went out into the streets and gathered all they found, bad and good alike, and the hall was filled with guests. ¹¹ But when the king came in to meet the guests he saw a man there not dressed in a wedding garment. ¹² He said to him, 'My friend, how is it that you came in here without a wedding garment?' But he was reduced to silence. ¹³ Then the king said to his attendants, 'Bind his hands and feet, and cast him into the darkness outside, where there will be wailing and grinding of teeth.' ¹⁴ Many are invited, but few are chosen."

Friday August 22, 2025
Memorial of Our Lady, Mother and Queen

First Reading: Ruth 1:1, 3-6, 14B-16, 22

¹Once in the time of the judges there was a famine in the land; so a man from Bethlehem of Judah departed with his wife and two sons to reside on the plateau of Moab. ³Elimelech, the husband of Naomi, died, and she was left with her two sons, ⁴who married Moabite women, one named Orpah, the other Ruth. When they had lived there about ten years, ⁵both Mahlon and Chilion died also, and the woman was left with neither her two sons nor her husband. ⁶She then made ready to go back from the plateau of Moab because word reached her there that the LORD had visited his people and given them food.

¹⁴ᴮOrpah kissed her mother-in-law good-bye, but Ruth stayed with her.

¹⁵Naomi said, "See now! Your sister-in-law has gone back to her people and her god. Go back after your sister-in-law!" ¹⁶But Ruth said, "Do not ask me to abandon or forsake you! For wherever you go, I will go, wherever you lodge I will lodge, your people shall be my people, and your God my God."

²²Thus it was that Naomi returned with the Moabite daughter-in-law, Ruth, who accompanied her back from the plateau of Moab. They arrived in Bethlehem at the beginning of the barley harvest.

Responsorial Psalm: Psalms 146:5-6AB, 6C-7, 8-9A, 9BC-10

R. *(1b) Praise the Lord, my soul!*
⁵Blessed is he whose help is the God of Jacob,
　　whose hope is in the LORD, his God,
⁶ᴬᴮ Who made heaven and earth,
　　the sea and all that is in them.
R. Praise the Lord, my soul!

⁶ᶜ The LORD keeps faith forever,
⁷ secures justice for the oppressed,
gives food to the hungry.
The LORD sets captives free.
R. Praise the Lord, my soul!
⁸ The LORD gives sight to the blind.
The LORD raises up those who were bowed
down;
The LORD loves the just.
⁹ᴬ The LORD protects strangers.
R. Praise the Lord, my soul!
⁹ᴮᶜ The fatherless and the widow he sustains,
but the way of the wicked he thwarts.
¹⁰ The LORD shall reign forever;
your God, O Zion, through all
generations. Alleluia.
R. Praise the Lord, my soul!

Alleluia: Psalms 25:4B, 5A
R. Alleluia, alleluia.
⁴ᴮ Teach me your paths, my God,
⁵ᴬ guide me in your truth.
R. Alleluia, alleluia.

Gospel: Matthew 22:34-40
³⁴ When the Pharisees heard that Jesus had silenced the Sadducees, they gathered together, ³⁵ and one of them, a scholar of the law, tested him by asking, ³⁶ "Teacher, which commandment in the law is the greatest?" ³⁷ He said to him, "You shall love the Lord, your God, with all your heart, with all your soul, and with all your mind. ³⁸ This is the greatest and the first commandment. ³⁹ The second is like it: You shall love your neighbor as yourself. ⁴⁰ The whole law and the prophets depend on these two commandments."

Saturday August 23, 2025
Saturday of the Twentieth Week in Ordinary Time
First Reading: Ruth 2:1-3, 8-11; 4:13-17
¹Naomi had a prominent kinsman named Boaz, of the clan of her husband Elimelech. ²Ruth the Moabite said to Naomi, "Let me go and glean ears of grain in the field of anyone who will allow me that favor." Naomi said to her, "Go, my daughter," and she went. ³The field she entered to glean after the harvesters happened to be the section belonging to Boaz of the clan of Elimelech.

⁸Boaz said to Ruth, "Listen, my daughter! Do not go to glean in anyone else's field; you are not to leave here. Stay here with my women servants. ⁹Watch to see which field is to be harvested, and follow them; I have commanded the young men to do you no harm. When you are thirsty, you may go and drink from

the vessels the young men have filled." ¹⁰Casting herself prostrate upon the ground, Ruth said to him, "Why should I, a foreigner, be favored with your notice?" ¹¹Boaz answered her: "I have had a complete account of what you have done for your mother-in-law after your husband's death; you have left your father and your mother and the land of your birth, and have come to a people whom you did not know previously."

¹³Boaz took Ruth. When they came together as man and wife, the LORD enabled her to conceive and she bore a son. ¹⁴Then the women said to Naomi, "Blessed is the LORD who has not failed to provide you today with an heir! May he become famous in Israel! ¹⁵He will be your comfort and the support of your old age, for his mother is the daughter-in-law who loves you. She is worth more to you than seven sons!" ¹⁶Naomi took the child, placed him on her lap, and became his nurse. ¹⁷And the neighbor women gave him his name, at the news that a grandson had been born to Naomi. They called him Obed. He was the father of Jesse, the father of David.

Responsorial Psalm: Psalms 128:1B-2, 3, 4, 5
R. ⁽⁴⁾ See how the Lord blesses those who fear him.
¹ᴮ Blessed are you who fear the LORD,
    who walk in his ways!
² For you shall eat the fruit of your
      handiwork;
    blessed shall you be, and favored.
R. See how the Lord blesses those who fear him.
³ You wife shall be like a fruitful vine
    in the recesses of your home;
Your children like olive plants
    around your table.
R. See how the Lord blesses those who fear him.
⁴ Behold, thus is the man blessed
    who fears the LORD.
R. See how the Lord blesses those who fear him.
⁵ The LORD bless you from Zion:
    may you see the prosperity of Jerusalem
      all the days of your life.
R. See how the Lord blesses those who fear him.

Alleluia: Matthew 23:9B, 10B
R. Alleluia, alleluia.
⁹ᴮ You have but one Father in heaven;
¹⁰ᴮ you have but one master, the Christ.
R. Alleluia, alleluia.

Gospel: Matthew 23:1-12

¹Jesus spoke to the crowds and to his disciples, ²saying, "The scribes and the Pharisees have taken their seat on the chair of Moses. ³Therefore, do and observe all things whatsoever they tell you, but do not follow their example. For they preach but they do not practice. ⁴They tie up heavy burdens hard to carry and lay them on people's shoulders, but they will not lift a finger to move them. ⁵All their works are performed to be seen. They widen their phylacteries and lengthen their tassels. ⁶They love places of honor at banquets, seats of honor in synagogues, ⁷greetings in marketplaces, and the salutation 'Rabbi.' ⁸As for you, do not be called 'Rabbi.' You have but one teacher, and you are all brothers. ⁹Call no one on earth your father; you have but one Father in heaven. ¹⁰Do not be called 'Master'; you have but one master, the Christ. ¹¹The greatest among you must be your servant. ¹²Whoever exalts himself will be humbled; but whoever humbles himself will be exalted."

Sunday August 24, 2025
Twenty-first Sunday in Ordinary Time Year C
First Reading: Isaiah 66:18-21

¹⁸ Thus says the LORD:

I know their works and their thoughts,
and I come to gather nations of every
  language;
 they shall come and see my glory.
¹⁹I will set a sign among them;
  from them I will send fugitives to the
   nations:
  to Tarshish, Put and Lud, Mosoch, Tubal
   and Javan,
  to the distant coastlands
  that have never heard of my fame, or
   seen my glory;
  and they shall proclaim my glory among
   the nations.
²⁰ They shall bring all your brothers and sisters
   from all the nations
  as an offering to the LORD,
  on horses and in chariots, in carts, upon
   mules and dromedaries,
  to Jerusalem, my holy mountain, says the
   LORD,
  just as the Israelites bring their offering
  to the house of the LORD in clean vessels.
²¹ Some of these I will take as priests and
   Levites, says the LORD.

Responsorial Psalm: Psalms 117:1, 2
R. (Mk 16:15) ***Go out to all the world and tell the Good News.*** or: ***R. Alleluia***.

¹ Praise the LORD all you nations;
    glorify him, all you peoples!

R. Go out to all the world and tell the Good News. or: ***R. Alleluia***.

² For steadfast is his kindness toward us,
    and the fidelity of the LORD endures forever.

R. Go out to all the world and tell the Good News. or: ***R. Alleluia***.

Second Reading: Hebrews 12:5-7, 11-13
Brothers and sisters, ⁵You have forgotten the exhortation addressed to you as children:

"My son, do not disdain the discipline of the Lord
    or lose heart when reproved by him;
⁶for whom the Lord loves, he disciplines;
    he scourges every son he acknowledges."

⁷Endure your trials as "discipline"; God treats you as sons. For what "son" is there whom his father does not discipline? ¹¹At the time, all discipline seems a cause not for joy but for pain, yet later it brings the peaceful fruit of righteousness to those who are trained by it.

¹²So strengthen your drooping hands and your weak knees. ¹³Make straight paths for your feet, that what is lame may not be disjointed but healed.

Alleluia: John 14:6
R. Alleluia, alleluia.

⁶ I am the way, the truth and the life, says the Lord;
no one comes to the Father, except through me.

R. Alleluia, alleluia.

Gospel: Luke 13:22-30
²²Jesus passed through towns and villages, teaching as he went and making his way to Jerusalem. ²³Someone asked him, "Lord, will only a few people be saved?" He answered them, ²⁴"Strive to enter through the narrow gate, for many, I tell you, will attempt to enter but will not be strong enough. ²⁵After the master of the house has arisen and locked the door, then will you stand outside knocking and saying, 'Lord, open the door for us.' He will say to you in reply, 'I do not know where you are from. ²⁶And you will say, 'We ate and drank in your company and you taught in

our streets.' ²⁷Then he will say to you, 'I do not know where you are from. Depart from me, all you evildoers!' ²⁸And there will be wailing and grinding of teeth when you see Abraham, Isaac, and Jacob and all the prophets in the kingdom of God and you yourselves cast out. ²⁹And people will come from the east and the west and from the north and the south and will recline at table in the kingdom of God. ³⁰For behold, some are last who will be first, and some are first who will be last."

Monday August 25, 2025
Monday of the Twenty-first Week in Ordinary Time
First Reading: 1 Thessalonians 1:1-5, 8B-10

¹Paul, Silvanus, and Timothy to the Church of the Thessalonians in God the Father and the Lord Jesus Christ: grace to you and peace.

²We give thanks to God always for all of you, remembering you in our prayers, ³unceasingly calling to mind your work of faith and labor of love and endurance in hope of our Lord Jesus Christ, before our God and Father, ⁴knowing, brothers and sisters loved by God, how you were chosen. ⁵For our Gospel did not come to you in word alone, but also in power and in the Holy Spirit and with much conviction. You know what sort of people we were among you for your sake. ⁸ᴮIn every place your faith in God has gone forth, so that we have no need to say anything. ⁹For they themselves openly declare about us what sort of reception we had among you, and how you turned to God from idols to serve the living and true God and ¹⁰to await his Son from heaven, whom he raised from the dead, Jesus, who delivers us from the coming wrath.

Responsorial Psalm: Psalms 149:1B-2, 3-4, 5-6A AND 9B

*R. (see 4a) **The Lord takes delight in his people.** or: **R. Alleluia.***

¹ᴮSing to the LORD a new song
   of praise in the assembly of the faithful.
² Let Israel be glad in their maker,
   let the children of Zion rejoice in their
      king.

*R. **The Lord takes delight in his people.** or: **R. Alleluia.***

³ Let them praise his name in the festive
      dance,
   let them sing praise to him with timbrel
      and harp.
⁴ For the LORD loves his people,
   and he adorns the lowly with victory.

*R. **The Lord takes delight in his people.** or: **R. Alleluia.***

⁵ Let the faithful exult in glory;
   let them sing for joy upon their couches;
⁶ᴬ Let the high praises of God be in their
      throats.
      ⁹ᴮ This is the glory of all his faithful.
         Alleluia!

R. *The Lord takes delight in his people.* or: **R.** *Alleluia.*

Alleluia: John 10:27
R. Alleluia, alleluia.
27 My sheep hear my voice, says the Lord;
I know them, and they follow me.
R. Alleluia, alleluia.

Gospel: Matthew 23:13-22
Jesus said to the crowds and to his disciples: 13 "Woe to you, scribes and Pharisees, you hypocrites. You lock the Kingdom of heaven before men. You do not enter yourselves, nor do you allow entrance to those trying to enter.

15 "Woe to you, scribes and Pharisees, you hypocrites. You traverse sea and land to make one convert, and when that happens you make him a child of Gehenna twice as much as yourselves.

16 "Woe to you, blind guides, who say, 'If one swears by the temple, it means nothing, but if one swears by the gold of the temple, one is obligated.' 17 Blind fools, which is greater, the gold, or the temple that made the gold sacred? 18 And you say, 'If one swears by the altar, it means nothing, but if one swears by the gift on the altar, one is obligated.' 19 You blind ones, which is greater, the gift, or the altar that makes the gift sacred? 20 One who swears by the altar swears by it and all that is upon it; 21 one who swears by the temple swears by it and by him who dwells in it; 22 one who swears by heaven swears by the throne of God and by him who is seated on it."

Tuesday August 26, 2025
Tuesday of Twenty-first Week in Ordinary Time
First Reading: 1 Thessalonians 2:1-8

1You yourselves know, brothers and sisters, that our reception among you was not without effect. 2 Rather, after we had suffered and been insolently treated, as you know, in Philippi, we drew courage through our God to speak to you the Gospel of God with much struggle. 3Our exhortation was not from delusion or impure motives, nor did it work through deception. 4But as we were judged worthy by God to be entrusted with the Gospel, that is how we speak, not as trying to please men, but rather God, who judges our hearts. 5Nor, indeed, did we ever appear with flattering speech, as you know, or with a pretext for greed —God is witness— 6nor did we seek praise from men, either from you or from others, 7although we were able to impose our weight as Apostles of Christ. Rather, we were gentle among you, as a nursing mother cares for her children. 8With such affection for you, we were determined to share with you not only the Gospel of God, but our very selves as well, so dearly beloved had you become to us.

Responsorial Psalm: Psalms 139:1-3, 4-6
R. (1) *You have searched me and you know me, Lord.*
1O LORD, you have probed me and you know

me;
²you know when I sit and when I stand;
you understand my thoughts from afar.
³ My journeys and my rest you scrutinize,
with all my ways you are familiar.
R. You have searched me and you know me, Lord.
⁴ Even before a word is on my tongue,
behold, O LORD, you know the whole of it.
⁵ Behind me and before, you hem me in
and rest your hand upon me.
⁶ Such knowledge is too wonderful for me;
too lofty for me to attain.
R. You have searched me and you know me, Lord.

Alleluia: Hebrews 4:12
R. Alleluia, alleluia.
¹² The word of God is living and effective,
able to discern reflections and thoughts of
the heart.
R. Alleluia, alleluia.

Gospel: Matthew 23:23-26
Jesus said: ²³ "Woe to you, scribes and Pharisees, you hypocrites. You pay tithes of mint and dill and cummin, and have neglected the weightier things of the law: judgment and mercy and fidelity. But these you should have done, without neglecting the others. ²⁴ Blind guides, who strain out the gnat and swallow the camel!

²⁵ "Woe to you, scribes and Pharisees, you hypocrites. You cleanse the outside of cup and dish, but inside they are full of plunder and self-indulgence. ²⁶ Blind Pharisee, cleanse first the inside of the cup, so that the outside also may be clean."

Wednesday August 27, 2025
Memorial of Saint Monica

First Reading: 1 Thessalonians 2:9-13
⁹You recall, brothers and sisters, our toil and drudgery. Working night and day in order not to burden any of you, we proclaimed to you the Gospel of God. ¹⁰You are witnesses, and so is God, how devoutly and justly and blamelessly we behaved toward you believers. ¹¹As you know, we treated each one of you as a father treats his children, ¹²exhorting and encouraging you and insisting that you walk in a manner worthy of the God who calls you into his Kingdom and glory.

¹³And for this reason we too give thanks to God unceasingly, that, in receiving the word of God from hearing us, you received it not as the word of men, but as it truly is, the word of God, which is now at work in you who believe.

Responsorial Psalm: Psalms 139:7-8, 9-10, 11-12AB

R. (1) **You have searched me and you know me, Lord.**

7 Where can I go from your spirit?
　　From your presence where can I flee?
8 If I go up to the heavens, you are there;
　　if I sink to the nether world, you are
　　　　present there.

R. You have searched me and you know me, Lord.

9 If I take the wings of the dawn,
　　if I settle at the farthest limits of the sea,
10 Even there your hand shall guide me,
　　and your right hand hold me fast.

R. You have searched me and you know me, Lord.

11 If I say, "Surely the darkness shall hide me,
　　and night shall be my light"–
12A For you darkness itself is not dark,
　　and night shines as the day.

R. You have searched me and you know me, Lord.

Alleluia: 1 John 2:5

R. Alleluia, alleluia.
5 Whoever keeps the word of Christ,
the love of God is truly perfected in him.
R. Alleluia, alleluia.

Gospel: Matthew 23:27-32

Jesus said, 27 "Woe to you, scribes and Pharisees, you hypocrites. You are like whitewashed tombs, which appear beautiful on the outside, but inside are full of dead men's bones and every kind of filth. 28 Even so, on the outside you appear righteous, but inside you are filled with hypocrisy and evildoing.

29 "Woe to you, scribes and Pharisees, you hypocrites. You build the tombs of the prophets and adorn the memorials of the righteous, 30 and you say, 'If we had lived in the days of our ancestors, we would not have joined them in shedding the prophets' blood.' 31 Thus you bear witness against yourselves that you are the children of those who murdered the prophets; 32 now fill up what your ancestors measured out!"

Thursday August 28, 2025
Memorial of Saint Augustine, Bishop & Doctor

First Reading: 1 Thessalonians 3:7-13

7 We have been reassured about you, brothers and sisters, in our every distress and affliction, through your faith. 8 For we now live, if you stand firm in the Lord.

⁹What thanksgiving, then, can we render to God for you, for all the joy we feel on your account before our God? ¹⁰Night and day we pray beyond measure to see you in person and to remedy the deficiencies of your faith. ¹¹Now may God himself, our Father, and our Lord Jesus direct our way to you, ¹²and may the Lord make you increase and abound in love for one another and for all, just as we have for you, ¹³so as to strengthen your hearts, to be blameless in holiness before our God and Father at the coming of our Lord Jesus with all his holy ones. Amen.

Responsorial Psalm: Psalms 90:3-5A, 12-13, 14 AND 17

R. ⁽¹⁴⁾ *Fill us with your love, O Lord, and we will sing for joy!*

³ You turn man back to dust,
    saying, "Return, O children of men."
⁴ For a thousand years in your sight
    are as yesterday, now that it is past,
    ⁵ᴬ or as a watch of the night.

R. *Fill us with your love, O Lord, and we will sing for joy!*

¹² Teach us to number our days aright,
    that we may gain wisdom of heart.
¹³ Return, O LORD! How long?
    Have pity on your servants!

R. *Fill us with your love, O Lord, and we will sing for joy!*

¹⁴ Fill us at daybreak with your kindness,
    that we may shout for joy and gladness
      all our days.
¹⁷ And may the gracious care of the LORD our
    God be ours;
    prosper the work of our hands for us!
    Prosper the work of our hands!

R. *Fill us with your love, O Lord, and we will sing for joy!*

Alleluia: Matthew 24:42A, 44

R. Alleluia, alleluia.
⁴²ᴬStay awake!
⁴⁴For you do not know when the Son of Man will come.
R. Alleluia, alleluia.

Gospel: Matthew 24:42-51

Jesus said to his disciples: ⁴²"Stay awake! For you do not know on which day your Lord will come. ⁴³Be sure of this: if the master of the house had known the hour of night when the thief was coming, he would have stayed awake and not let his house be broken into. ⁴⁴So too, you also must be prepared, for at an hour you do not expect, the Son of Man will come.

⁴⁵"Who, then, is the faithful and prudent servant, whom the master has put in charge of his household to distribute to them their food at the proper time? ⁴⁶Blessed is that servant whom his master on his arrival finds doing so. ⁴⁷Amen, I say to you, he will put him in charge of all his property. ⁴⁸But if that wicked servant says to himself, 'My master is long delayed,' ⁴⁹and begins to beat his fellow servants, and eat and drink with drunkards, ⁵⁰the servant's master will come on an unexpected day and at an unknown hour ⁵¹and will punish him severely and assign him a place with the hypocrites, where there will be wailing and grinding of teeth."

Friday August 29, 2025
Memorial of the Beheading of Saint John the Baptist

First Reading: 1 Thessalonians 4:1-8

Brothers and sisters, ¹we earnestly ask and exhort you in the Lord Jesus that, as you received from us how you should conduct yourselves to please God – and as you are conducting yourselves – you do so even more. ²For you know what instructions we gave you through the Lord Jesus.

³This is the will of God, your holiness: that you refrain from immorality, ⁴that each of you know how to acquire a wife for himself in holiness and honor, ⁵not in lustful passion as do the Gentiles who do not know God; ⁶not to take advantage of or exploit a brother or sister in this matter, for the Lord is an avenger in all these things, as we told you before and solemnly affirmed. ⁷For God did not call us to impurity but to holiness. ⁸Therefore, whoever disregards this, disregards not a human being but God, who also gives his Holy Spirit to you.

Responsorial Psalm: Psalms 97:1 AND 2B, 5-6, 10, 11-12

R. *(12a)* *Rejoice in the Lord, you just!*
¹The LORD is king; let the earth rejoice;
   let the many isles be glad.
      ²ᴮJustice and judgment are the foundation
         of his throne.
R. *Rejoice in the Lord, you just!*
⁵The mountains melt like wax before the
         LORD,
   before the LORD of all the earth.
⁶The heavens proclaim his justice,
   and all peoples see his glory.
R. *Rejoice in the Lord, you just!*
¹⁰The LORD loves those who hate evil;
   he guards the lives of his faithful ones;
   from the hand of the wicked he delivers
         them.
R. *Rejoice in the Lord, you just!*

¹¹Light dawns for the just;
    and gladness, for the upright of heart.
¹²Be glad in the LORD, you just,
    and give thanks to his holy name.
R. Rejoice in the Lord, you just!

Alleluia: Luke 21:36
R. Alleluia, alleluia.
³⁶ Be vigilant at all times and pray,
that you may have the strength to stand
    before the Son of Man.
R. Alleluia, alleluia.

Gospel: Matthew 25:1-13
Jesus told his disciples this parable: ¹ "The Kingdom of heaven will be like ten virgins who took their lamps and went out to meet the bridegroom. ² Five of them were foolish and five were wise. ³ The foolish ones, when taking their lamps, brought no oil with them, ⁴ but the wise brought flasks of oil with their lamps. ⁵ Since the bridegroom was long delayed, they all became drowsy and fell asleep. ⁶ At midnight, there was a cry, 'Behold, the bridegroom! Come out to meet him!' ⁷ Then all those virgins got up and trimmed their lamps. ⁸ The foolish ones said to the wise, 'Give us some of your oil, for our lamps are going out.' ⁹ But the wise ones replied, 'No, for there may not be enough for us and you. Go instead to the merchants and buy some for yourselves.' ¹⁰ While they went off to buy it, the bridegroom came and those who were ready went into the wedding feast with him. Then the door was locked. ¹¹ Afterwards the other virgins came and said, 'Lord, Lord, open the door for us!' ¹² But he said in reply, 'Amen, I say to you, I do not know you.' ¹³ Therefore, stay awake, for you know neither the day nor the hour."

Saturday August 30, 2025
Saturday of the Twenty-first Week in Ordinary Time
First Reading: 1 Thessalonians 4:9-11
Brothers and sisters: ⁹On the subject of fraternal charity you have no need for anyone to write you, for you yourselves have been taught by God to love one another. ¹⁰Indeed, you do this for all the brothers throughout Macedonia. Nevertheless we urge you, brothers and sisters, to progress even more, ¹¹and to aspire to live a tranquil life, to mind your own affairs, and to work with your own hands, as we instructed you.

Responsorial Psalm: Psalms 98:1, 7-8, 9
R. ⁽⁹⁾ The Lord comes to rule the earth with justice.
¹Sing to the LORD a new song,
    for he has done wondrous deeds;
His right hand has won victory for him,
    his holy arm.
R. The Lord comes to rule the earth with justice.

⁷Let the sea and what fills it resound,
    the world and those who dwell in it;
⁸Let the rivers clap their hands,
    the mountains shout with them for joy.
R. The Lord comes to rule the earth with justice.
⁹Before the LORD, for he comes,
    for he comes to rule the earth;
He will rule the world with justice
    and the peoples with equity.
R. The Lord comes to rule the earth with justice.

Alleluia: John 13:34
R. Alleluia, alleluia.
³⁴ I give you a new commandment:
love one another as I have loved you.
R. Alleluia, alleluia.

Gospel: Matthew 25:14-30
Jesus told his disciples this parable: ¹⁴ "A man going on a journey called in his servants and entrusted his possessions to them. ¹⁵ To one he gave five talents; to another, two; to a third, one — to each according to his ability. Then he went away. ¹⁶ Immediately the one who received five talents went and traded with them, and made another five. ¹⁷ Likewise, the one who received two made another two. ¹⁸ But the man who received one went off and dug a hole in the ground and buried his master's money. ¹⁹ After a long time the master of those servants came back and settled accounts with them. ²⁰ The one who had received five talents came forward bringing the additional five. He said, 'Master, you gave me five talents. See, I have made five more.' ²¹ His master said to him, 'Well done, my good and faithful servant. Since you were faithful in small matters, I will give you great responsibilities. Come, share your master's joy.' ²² Then the one who had received two talents also came forward and said, 'Master, you gave me two talents. See, I have made two more.' ²³ His master said to him, 'Well done, my good and faithful servant. Since you were faithful in small matters, I will give you great responsibilities. Come, share your master's joy.' ²⁴ Then the one who had received the one talent came forward and said, 'Master, I knew you were a demanding person, harvesting where you did not plant and gathering where you did not scatter; ²⁵ so out of fear I went off and buried your talent in the ground. Here it is back.' ²⁶ His master said to him in reply, 'You wicked, lazy servant! So you knew that I harvest where I did not plant and gather where I did not scatter? ²⁷ Should you not then have put my money in the bank so that I could have got it back with interest on my return? ²⁸ Now then! Take the talent from him and give it to the one with ten. ²⁹ For to everyone who has, more will be given and he will grow rich; but from the one who has not, even what he has will be taken away. ³⁰ And throw this useless servant into the darkness outside, where there will be wailing and grinding of teeth.'"

Sunday August 31, 2025
Twenty-second Sunday in ordinary Time, Year C

First Reading: Sirach 3:17-18, 21, 29-30

¹⁷My child, conduct your affairs with humility,
> and you will be loved more than a giver
>> of gifts.

¹⁸Humble yourself the more, the greater you
> are,
> and you will find favor with God.

²¹What is too sublime for you, seek not,
> into things beyond your strength search
>> not.

²⁹ The mind of a sage appreciates proverbs,
> and an attentive ear is the joy of the wise.

³⁰ Water quenches a flaming fire,
> and alms atone for sins.

Responsorial Psalm: Psalms 68:4-5, 6-7, 10-11

R. (cf. 11b) *God, in your goodness, you have made a home for the poor.*

⁴The just rejoice and exult before God;
> they are glad and rejoice.

⁵Sing to God, chant praise to his name,
> whose name is the LORD.

R. God, in your goodness, you have made a home for the poor.

⁶ The father of orphans and the defender of
> widows
> is God in his holy dwelling.

⁷ God gives a home to the forsaken;
> he leads forth prisoners to prosperity.

R. God, in your goodness, you have made a home for the poor.

¹⁰ A bountiful rain you showered down, O God,
> upon your inheritance;
> you restored the land when it languished;

¹¹ your flock settled in it;
> in your goodness, O God, you provided it
>> for the needy.

R. God, in your goodness, you have made a home for the poor.

Second Reading: Hebrews 12:18-19, 22-24A

Brothers and sisters: [18]You have not approached that which could be touched and a blazing fire and gloomy darkness [19]and storm and a trumpet blast and a voice speaking words such that those who heard begged that no message be further addressed to them. [22]No, you have approached Mount Zion and the city of the living God, the heavenly Jerusalem, and countless angels in festal gathering, [23]and the assembly of the firstborn enrolled in heaven, and God the judge of all, and the spirits of the just made perfect, [24]and Jesus, the mediator of a new covenant, and the sprinkled blood that speaks more eloquently than that of Abel.

Alleluia: Matthew 11:29AB

R. Alleluia, alleluia.
[29]Take my yoke upon you, says the Lord,
and learn from me, for I am meek and
　　humble of heart.
R. Alleluia, alleluia.

Gospel: Luke 14:1, 7-14

[1]On a sabbath Jesus went to dine at the home of one of the leading Pharisees, and the people there were observing him carefully.

[7]He told a parable to those who had been invited, noticing how they were choosing the places of honor at the table. [8]"When you are invited by someone to a wedding banquet, do not recline at table in the place of honor. A more distinguished guest than you may have been invited by him, [9]and the host who invited both of you may approach you and say, 'Give your place to this man,' and then you would proceed with embarrassment to take the lowest place. [10]Rather, when you are invited, go and take the lowest place so that when the host comes to you he may say, 'My friend, move up to a higher position.' Then you will enjoy the esteem of your companions at the table. [11]For everyone who exalts himself will be humbled, but the one who humbles himself will be exalted." [12]Then he said to the host who invited him, "When you hold a lunch or a dinner, do not invite your friends or your brothers or your relatives or your wealthy neighbors, in case they may invite you back and you have repayment.
[13] Rather, when you hold a banquet, invite the poor, the crippled, the lame, the blind; [14]Blessed indeed will you be because of their inability to repay you. For you will be repaid at the resurrection of the righteous."

SEPTEMBER 2025

Monday September 1, 2025
Monday of the Twenty-second Week in Ordinary Time

First Reading: 1 Thessalonians 4:13-18

[13]We do not want you to be unaware, brothers and sisters, about those who have fallen asleep, so that you may not grieve like the rest, who have no hope. [14]For if we believe that Jesus died and rose, so too will God, through Jesus, bring with him those who have fallen asleep. [15]Indeed, we tell you this, on the word of the Lord,

that we who are alive, who are left until the coming of the Lord, will surely not precede those who have fallen asleep. ¹⁶For the Lord himself, with a word of command, with the voice of an archangel and with the trumpet of God, will come down from heaven, and the dead in Christ will rise first. ¹⁷Then we who are alive, who are left, will be caught up together with them in the clouds to meet the Lord in the air. Thus we shall always be with the Lord. ¹⁸Therefore, console one another with these words.

Responsorial Psalm: Psalms 96:1 AND 3, 4-5, 11-12, 13
R. ⁽¹³ᵇ⁾ The Lord comes to judge the earth.
¹ Sing to the LORD a new song;
    sing to the LORD, all you lands.
³ Tell his glory among the nations;
    among all peoples, his wondrous deeds.
R. The Lord comes to judge the earth.
⁴ For great is the LORD and highly to be praised;
    awesome is he, beyond all gods.
⁵For all the gods of the nations are things of nought,
    but the LORD made the heavens.
R. The Lord comes to judge the earth.
¹¹Let the heavens be glad and the earth rejoice;
    let the sea and what fills it resound;
¹² let the plains be joyful and all that is in them!
Then shall all the trees of the forest exult.
R. The Lord comes to judge the earth.
¹³ Before the LORD, for he comes;
    for he comes to rule the earth.
He shall rule the world with justice
    and the peoples with his constancy.
R. The Lord comes to judge the earth.

Alleluia: cf. Luke 4:18
R. Alleluia, alleluia.
¹⁹ The Spirit of the Lord is upon me;
he has sent me to bring glad tidings to the poor.
R. Alleluia, alleluia.

Gospel: Luke 4:16-30

[16] Jesus came to Nazareth, where he had grown up, and went according to his custom into the synagogue on the sabbath day. He stood up to read [17] and was handed a scroll of the prophet Isaiah. He unrolled the scroll and found the passage where it was written:

[18] *The Spirit of the Lord is upon me,*
because he has anointed me
to bring glad tidings to the poor.
He has sent me to proclaim liberty to captives
and recovery of sight to the blind,
to let the oppressed go free,
[19] *and to proclaim a year acceptable to the Lord.*

[20] Rolling up the scroll, he handed it back to the attendant and sat down, and the eyes of all in the synagogue looked intently at him. [21] He said to them, "Today this Scripture passage is fulfilled in your hearing." [22] And all spoke highly of him and were amazed at the gracious words that came from his mouth. They also asked, "Is this not the son of Joseph?" [23] He said to them, "Surely you will quote me this proverb, 'Physician, cure yourself,' and say, 'Do here in your native place the things that we heard were done in Capernaum.'" [24] And he said, "Amen, I say to you, no prophet is accepted in his own native place. [25] Indeed, I tell you, there were many widows in Israel in the days of Elijah when the sky was closed for three and a half years and a severe famine spread over the entire land. [26] It was to none of these that Elijah was sent, but only to a widow in Zarephath in the land of Sidon. [27] Again, there were many lepers in Israel during the time of Elisha the prophet; yet not one of them was cleansed, but only Naaman the Syrian." [28] When the people in the synagogue heard this, they were all filled with fury. [29] They rose up, drove him out of the town, and led him to the brow of the hill on which their town had been built, to hurl him down headlong. [30] But he passed through the midst of them and went away.

Tuesday September 2, 2025
Tuesday of the Twenty-second Week in Ordinary Time
First Reading: 1 Thessalonians 5:1-6, 9-11

[1] Concerning times and seasons, brothers and sisters, you have no need for anything to be written to you. [2] For you yourselves know very well that the day of the Lord will come like a thief at night. [3] When people are saying, "Peace and security," then sudden disaster comes upon them, like labor pains upon a pregnant woman, and they will not escape.

[4] But you, brothers and sisters, are not in darkness, for that day to overtake you like a thief. [5] For all of you are children of the light and children of the day. We are not of the night or of darkness. [6] Therefore, let us not sleep as the rest do, but let us stay alert and sober. [9] For God did not destine us for wrath, but to gain salvation through our Lord Jesus Christ, [10] who died for us, so that whether we are awake or asleep we may live together with him. [11] Therefore, encourage one another and build one another up, as indeed you do.

Responsorial Psalm: Psalms 27:1, 4, 13-14
R. (13) I believe that I shall see the good things of the Lord in the land of the living.

¹ The LORD is my light and my salvation;
   whom should I fear?
The LORD is my life's refuge;
   of whom should I be afraid?
R. I believe that I shall see the good things of the Lord in the land of the living.

⁴ One thing I ask of the LORD;
   this I seek:
To dwell in the house of the LORD
   all the days of my life,
That I may gaze on the loveliness of the LORD
   and contemplate his temple.
R. I believe that I shall see the good things of the Lord in the land of the living.

¹³ I believe that I shall see the bounty of the LORD
   in the land of the living.
¹⁴ Wait for the LORD with courage;
   be stouthearted, and wait for the LORD.
R. I believe that I shall see the good things of the Lord in the land of the living.

Alleluia: Luke 7:16
R. Alleluia, alleluia.
¹⁶ A great prophet has arisen in our midst
and God has visited his people.
R. Alleluia, alleluia.

Gospel: Luke 4:31-37
³¹ Jesus went down to Capernaum, a town of Galilee. He taught them on the sabbath, ³² and they were astonished at his teaching because he spoke with authority. ³³ In the synagogue there was a man with the spirit of an unclean demon, and he cried out in a loud voice, ³⁴ "What have you to do with us, Jesus of Nazareth? Have you come to destroy us? I know who you are — the Holy One of God!" ³⁵ Jesus rebuked him and said, "Be quiet! Come out of him!" Then the demon threw the man down in front of them and came out of him without doing him any harm. ³⁶ They were all amazed and said to one another, "What is there about his word? For with authority and power he commands the unclean spirits, and they come out." ³⁷ And news of him spread everywhere in the surrounding region.

Wednesday September 3, 2025
Memorial of Saint Gregory the Great, Pope & Doctor

First Reading: Colossians 1:1-8

¹Paul, an Apostle of Christ Jesus by the will of God, and Timothy our brother, ²to the holy ones and faithful brothers and sisters in Christ in Colossae: grace to you and peace from God our Father.

³We always give thanks to God, the Father of our Lord Jesus Christ, when we pray for you, ⁴for we have heard of your faith in Christ Jesus and the love that you have for all the holy ones ⁵because of the hope reserved for you in heaven. Of this you have already heard through the word of truth, the Gospel, ⁶that has come to you. Just as in the whole world it is bearing fruit and growing, so also among you, from the day you heard it and came to know the grace of God in truth, ⁷as you learned it from Epaphras our beloved fellow slave, who is a trustworthy minister of Christ on your behalf ⁸ and who also told us of your love in the Spirit.

Responsorial Psalm: Psalms 52:10, 11

R. ⁽¹⁰⁾ *I trust in the mercy of God for ever.*

¹⁰ I, like a green olive tree
    in the house of God,
Trust in the mercy of God
    forever and ever.

R. *I trust in the mercy of God for ever.*

¹¹ I will thank you always for what you have
    done,
    and proclaim the goodness of your name
    before your faithful ones.

R. *I trust in the mercy of God for ever.*

Alleluia: Luke 4:18

R. Alleluia, alleluia.
¹⁸ The Lord sent me to bring glad tidings to the
    poor
and to proclaim liberty to captives.
R. Alleluia, alleluia.

Gospel: Luke 4:38-44

³⁸ After Jesus left the synagogue, he entered the house of Simon. Simon's mother-in-law was afflicted with a severe fever, and they interceded with him about her. ³⁹ He stood over her, rebuked the fever, and it left her. She got up immediately and waited on them.

⁴⁰ At sunset, all who had people sick with various diseases brought them to him. He laid his hands on each of them and cured them. ⁴¹ And demons also came

out from many, shouting, "You are the Son of God." But he rebuked them and did not allow them to speak because they knew that he was the Christ.

⁴² At daybreak, Jesus left and went to a deserted place. The crowds went looking for him, and when they came to him, they tried to prevent him from leaving them. ⁴³ But he said to them, "To the other towns also I must proclaim the good news of the Kingdom of God, because for this purpose I have been sent." ⁴⁴ And he was preaching in the synagogues of Judea.

Thursday September 4, 2025
Thursday of the Twenty-second Week in Ordinary Time
First Reading: Colossians 1:9-14

Brothers and sisters: ⁹From the day we heard about you, we do not cease praying for you and asking that you may be filled with the knowledge of God's will through all spiritual wisdom and understanding ¹⁰to walk in a manner worthy of the Lord, so as to be fully pleasing, in every good work bearing fruit and growing in the knowledge of God,¹¹strengthened with every power, in accord with his glorious might, for all endurance and patience, ¹²with joy giving thanks to the Father, who has made you fit to share in the inheritance of the holy ones in light. ¹³He delivered us from the power of darkness and transferred us to the Kingdom of his beloved Son, ¹⁴in whom we have redemption, the forgiveness of sins.

Responsorial Psalm: Psalms 98:2-3AB, 3CD-4, 5-6
R. ⁽²⁾ *The Lord has made known his salvation.*
² The LORD has made his salvation known:
>   in the sight of the nations he has revealed
>   his justice.
³ᴬᴮHe has remembered his kindness and his
>   faithfulness
>   toward the house of Israel.
R. The Lord has made known his salvation.
³ᶜᴰAll the ends of the earth have seen
>   the salvation by our God.
⁴ Sing joyfully to the LORD, all you lands;
>   break into song; sing praise.
R. The Lord has made known his salvation.
⁵ Sing praise to the LORD with the harp,
>   with the harp and melodious song.
⁶ With trumpets and the sound of the horn
>   sing joyfully before the King, the LORD.
R. The Lord has made known his salvation.

Alleluia: Matthew 4:19
R. Alleluia, alleluia.
¹⁹ Come after me, says the Lord,
and I will make you fishers of men.

R. Alleluia, alleluia.

Gospel: Luke 5:1-11

[1] While the crowd was pressing in on Jesus and listening to the word of God, he was standing by the Lake of Gennesaret. [2] He saw two boats there alongside the lake; the fishermen had disembarked and were washing their nets. [3] Getting into one of the boats, the one belonging to Simon, he asked him to put out a short distance from the shore. Then he sat down and taught the crowds from the boat. [4] After he had finished speaking, he said to Simon, "Put out into deep water and lower your nets for a catch." [5] Simon said in reply, "Master, we have worked hard all night and have caught nothing, but at your command I will lower the nets." [6] When they had done this, they caught a great number of fish and their nets were tearing. [7] They signaled to their partners in the other boat to come to help them. They came and filled both boats so that the boats were in danger of sinking. [8] When Simon Peter saw this, he fell at the knees of Jesus and said, "Depart from me, Lord, for I am a sinful man." [9] For astonishment at the catch of fish they had made seized him and all those with him, [10] and likewise James and John, the sons of Zebedee, who were partners of Simon. Jesus said to Simon, "Do not be afraid; from now on you will be catching men." [11] When they brought their boats to the shore, they left everything and followed him.

Friday September 5, 2025
Friday of the Twenty-second Week in Ordinary Time

First Reading: Colossians 1:15-20

Brothers and sisters: [15] Christ Jesus is the image of the invisible God, the firstborn of all creation. [16] For in him were created all things in heaven and on earth, the visible and the invisible, whether thrones or dominions or principalities or powers; all things were created through him and for him. [17] He is before all things, and in him all things hold together. [18] He is the head of the Body, the Church. He is the beginning, the firstborn from the dead, that in all things he himself might be preeminent. [19] For in him all the fullness was pleased to dwell, [20] and through him to reconcile all things for him, making peace by the Blood of his cross through him, whether those on earth or those in heaven.

Responsorial Psalm: Psalms 100:1B-2, 3, 4, 5

R. [(2b)] *Come with joy into the presence of the Lord.*
[1B] Sing joyfully to the LORD, all you lands;
   [2] serve the LORD with gladness;
   come before him with joyful song.
R. Come with joy into the presence of the Lord.
[3] Know that the LORD is God;
   he made us, his we are;
   his people, the flock he tends.
R. Come with joy into the presence of the Lord.
[4] Enter his gates with thanksgiving,
   his courts with praise;
Give thanks to him; bless his name.
R. Come with joy into the presence of the Lord.

⁵ For he is good,
>   the LORD, whose kindness endures
>   forever,
>   and his faithfulness, to all generations.

R. Come with joy into the presence of the Lord.

Alleluia: John 8:12
R. Alleluia, alleluia.
¹² I am the light of the world, says the Lord;
whoever follows me will have the light of
life.
R. Alleluia, alleluia.

Gospel: Luke 5:33-39
³³ The scribes and Pharisees said to Jesus, "The disciples of John the Baptist fast often and offer prayers, and the disciples of the Pharisees do the same; but yours eat and drink." ³⁴ Jesus answered them, "Can you make the wedding guests fast while the bridegroom is with them? ³⁵ But the days will come, and when the bridegroom is taken away from them, then they will fast in those days." ³⁶ And he also told them a parable. "No one tears a piece from a new cloak to patch an old one. Otherwise, he will tear the new and the piece from it will not match the old cloak. ³⁷ Likewise, no one pours new wine into old wineskins. Otherwise, the new wine will burst the skins, and it will be spilled, and the skins will be ruined. ³⁸ Rather, new wine must be poured into fresh wineskins. ³⁹ And no one who has been drinking old wine desires new, for he says, 'The old is good.'"

Saturday September 6, 2025
Saturday of the Twenty-second Week in Ordinary Time
First Reading: Colossians 1:21-23
Brothers and sisters: ²¹You once were alienated and hostile in mind because of evil deeds; ²²God has now reconciled you in the fleshly Body of Christ through his death, to present you holy, without blemish, and irreproachable before him, ²³provided that you persevere in the faith, firmly grounded, stable, and not shifting from the hope of the Gospel that you heard, which has been preached to every creature under heaven, of which I, Paul, am a minister.

Responsorial Psalm: Psalms 54:3-4, 6 AND 8
R. ⁽⁶⁾ God himself is my help.
³ O God, by your name save me,
>   and by your might defend my cause.
⁴ O God, hear my prayer;
>   hearken to the words of my mouth.

R. God himself is my help.
⁶ Behold, God is my helper;
>   the Lord sustains my life.

⁸ Freely will I offer you sacrifice;
> I will praise your name, O LORD, for its goodness.

R. God himself is my help.

Alleluia: John 14:6
R. Alleluia, alleluia.
⁶ I am the way and the truth and the life, says the Lord;
no one comes to the Father except through me.
R. Alleluia, alleluia.

Gospel: Luke 6:1-5
¹ While Jesus was going through a field of grain on a sabbath, his disciples were picking the heads of grain, rubbing them in their hands, and eating them. ² Some Pharisees said, "Why are you doing what is unlawful on the sabbath?" ³ Jesus said to them in reply, "Have you not read what David did when he and those who were with him were hungry? ⁴ How he went into the house of God, took the bread of offering, which only the priests could lawfully eat, ate of it, and shared it with his companions?" ⁵ Then he said to them, "The Son of Man is lord of the sabbath."

Sunday September 7, 2025
Twenty-third Sunday in Ordinary Time, Year C

First Reading: Wisdom 9:13-18B
¹³Who can know God's counsel,
> or who can conceive what the LORD intends?

¹⁴For the deliberations of mortals are timid,
> and unsure are our plans.

¹⁵For the corruptible body burdens the soul
> and the earthen shelter weighs down the mind that has many concerns.

¹⁶ And scarce do we guess the things on earth,
> and what is within our grasp we find with difficulty;
> but when things are in heaven, who can search them out?

¹⁷ Or who ever knew your counsel, except you had given wisdom
> and sent your holy spirit from on high?

¹⁸ᴮ And thus were the paths of those on earth made straight.

Responsorial Psalm: Psalms 90:3-4, 5-6, 12-13, 14 AND 17

R. (1) In every age, O Lord, you have been our refuge.

³ You turn man back to dust,
    saying, "Return, O children of men."
⁴ For a thousand years in your sight
    are as yesterday, now that it is past,
    or as a watch of the night.

R. In every age, O Lord, you have been our refuge.

⁵ You make an end of them in their sleep;
    the next morning they are like the changing grass,
⁶ Which at dawn springs up anew,
    but by evening wilts and fades.

R. In every age, O Lord, you have been our refuge.

¹² Teach us to number our days aright,
    that we may gain wisdom of heart.
¹³ Return, O LORD! How long?
    Have pity on your servants!

R. In every age, O Lord, you have been our refuge.

¹⁴ Fill us at daybreak with your kindness,
    that we may shout for joy and gladness
    all our days.
¹⁷ And may the gracious care of the LORD our God be ours;
    prosper the work of our hands for us!
    Prosper the work of our hands!

R. In every age, O Lord, you have been our refuge.

Second Reading: Philemon 9-10, 12-17

⁹I, Paul, an old man, and now also a prisoner for Christ Jesus, ¹⁰urge you on behalf of my child Onesimus, whose father I have become in my imprisonment; ¹²I am sending him, that is, my own heart, back to you. ¹³I should have liked to retain him for myself, so that he might serve me on your behalf in my imprisonment for the gospel, ¹⁴but I did not want to do anything without your consent, so that the good you do might not be forced but voluntary. ¹⁵Perhaps this is why he was away from you for a while, that you might have him back forever, ¹⁶no longer as a slave but more than a slave, a brother, beloved especially to me, but even more so to you, as a man and in the Lord. ¹⁷So if you regard me as a partner, welcome him as you would me.

Alleluia: Psalms 119:135
R. Alleluia, alleluia.
¹³⁵ Let your face shine upon your servant;
and teach me your laws.
R. Alleluia, alleluia.

Gospel: Luke 14:25-33
²⁵Great crowds were traveling with Jesus, and he turned and addressed them, ²⁶"If anyone comes to me without hating his father and mother, wife and children, brothers and sisters, and even his own life, he cannot be my disciple. ²⁷Whoever does not carry his own cross and come after me cannot be my disciple. ²⁸Which of you wishing to construct a tower does not first sit down and calculate the cost to see if there is enough for its completion? ²⁹Otherwise, after laying the foundation and finding himself unable to finish the work the onlookers should laugh at him ³⁰and say, 'This one began to build but did not have the resources to finish.' ³¹Or what king marching into battle would not first sit down and decide whether with ten thousand troops he can successfully oppose another king advancing upon him with twenty thousand troops? ³²But if not, while he is still far away, he will send a delegation to ask for peace terms. ³³In the same way, anyone of you who does not renounce all his possessions cannot be my disciple."

Monday September 8, 2025
Feast of Nativity of the Blessed Virgin Mary
First Reading: Micah 5:1-4A
The LORD says:

¹You, Bethlehem-Ephrathah,
    too small to be among the clans of
        Judah,
From you shall come forth for me
    one who is to be ruler in Israel;
Whose origin is from of old,
    from ancient times.
²(Therefore the Lord will give them up,
        until the time
    when she who is to give birth has
        borne,
And the rest of his brethren shall return
    to the children of Israel.)
³He shall stand firm and shepherd his
        flock
    by the strength of the LORD,
    in the majestic name of the LORD, his
        God;
And they shall remain, for now his
        greatness

shall reach to the ends of the earth;
⁴ᴬ he shall be peace.

Or Romans 8:28-30

Brothers and sisters: ²⁸We know that all things work for good for those who love God, who are called according to his purpose. ²⁹For those he foreknew he also predestined to be conformed to the image of his Son, so that he might be the firstborn among many brothers. ³⁰And those he predestined he also called; and those he called he also justified; and those he justified he also glorified.

Responsorial Psalm: Psalms 13:6AB, 6C

R. *(Isaiah 61:10)* **With delight I rejoice in the Lord.**
⁶ᴬᴮThough I trusted in your mercy,
    let my heart rejoice in your salvation.
R. With delight I rejoice in the Lord.
⁶ᶜLet me sing of the LORD, "He has been good to
    me."
R. With delight I rejoice in the Lord.

Alleluia

R. Alleluia, alleluia.
Blessed are you, holy Virgin Mary, deserving
    of all praise;
from you rose the sun of justice, Christ our
    God.
R. Alleluia, alleluia.

Gospel: Matthew 1:1-16, 18-23

¹The book of the genealogy of Jesus Christ, the son of David, the son of Abraham.

²Abraham became the father of Isaac, Isaac the father of Jacob, Jacob the father of Judah and his brothers. ³Judah became the father of Perez and Zerah, whose mother was Tamar. Perez became the father of Hezron, Hezron the father of Ram, ⁴Ram the father of Amminadab. Amminadab became the father of Nahshon, Nahshon the father of Salmon, ⁵Salmon the father of Boaz, whose mother was Rahab. Boaz became the father of Obed, whose mother was Ruth. Obed became the father of Jesse, ⁶Jesse the father of David the king.

David became the father of Solomon, whose mother had been the wife of Uriah. ⁷Solomon became the father of Rehoboam, Rehoboam the father of Abijah, Abijah the father of Asaph. ⁸Asaph became the father of Jehoshaphat, Jehoshaphat the father of Joram, Joram the father of Uzziah. ⁹Uzziah became the father of Jotham, Jotham the father of Ahaz, Ahaz the father of Hezekiah. ¹⁰Hezekiah became the father of Manasseh, Manasseh the father of Amos, Amos the father of Josiah. ¹¹Josiah became the father of Jechoniah and his brothers at the time of the Babylonian exile.

¹²After the Babylonian exile, Jechoniah became the father of Shealtiel, Shealtiel the father of Zerubbabel, ¹³Zerubbabel the father of Abiud. Abiud became the father of Eliakim, Eliakim the father of Azor, ¹⁴Azor the father of Zadok. Zadok became the father of Achim, Achim the father of Eliud, ¹⁵Eliud the father of Eleazar. Eleazar became the father of Matthan, Matthan the father of Jacob, ¹⁶ Jacob the father of Joseph, the husband of Mary. Of her was born Jesus who is called the Christ.

¹⁸Now this is how the birth of Jesus Christ came about. When his mother Mary was betrothed to Joseph, but before they lived together, she was found with child through the Holy Spirit. ¹⁹Joseph her husband, since he was a righteous man, yet unwilling to expose her to shame, decided to divorce her quietly. ²⁰Such was his intention when, behold, the angel of the Lord appeared to him in a dream and said, "Joseph, son of David, do not be afraid to take Mary your wife into your home. For it is through the Holy Spirit that this child has been conceived in her. ²¹She will bear a son and you are to name him Jesus, because he will save his people from their sins." ²²All this took place to fulfill what the Lord had said through the prophet:

²³*Behold, the virgin shall conceive and bear*
   a son,
and they shall name him Emmanuel,

which means "God is with us."

Or Matthew 1:18-23

¹⁸Now this is how the birth of Jesus Christ came about. When his mother Mary was betrothed to Joseph, but before they lived together, she was found with child through the Holy Spirit. ¹⁹Joseph her husband, since he was a righteous man, yet unwilling to expose her to shame, decided to divorce her quietly. ²⁰Such was his intention when, behold, the angel of the Lord appeared to him in a dream and said, "Joseph, son of David, do not be afraid to take Mary your wife into your home. For it is through the Holy Spirit that this child has been conceived in her. ²¹She will bear a son and you are to name him Jesus, because he will save his people from their sins." ²²All this took place to fulfill what the Lord had said through the prophet:

²³*Behold, the virgin shall conceive and bear*
   a son,
and they shall name him Emmanuel,

which means "God is with us."

Tuesday September 9, 2025
Memorial of Saint Peter Claver, Priest
First Reading: Colossians 2:6-15

Brothers and sisters: ⁶As you received Christ Jesus the Lord, walk in him, ⁷rooted in him and built upon him and established in the faith as you were taught, abounding in thanksgiving. ⁸See to it that no one captivate you with an empty, seductive philosophy according to the tradition of men, according to the elemental powers of the world and not according to Christ.

⁹For in him dwells the whole fullness of the deity bodily, ¹⁰and you share in this fullness in him, who is the head of every principality and power. ¹¹In him you were also circumcised with a circumcision not administered by hand, by stripping off the carnal body, with the circumcision of Christ. ¹²You were buried with him in baptism, in which you were also raised with him through faith in the power of God, who raised him from the dead. ¹³And even when you were dead in transgressions and the uncircumcision of your flesh, he brought you to life along with him, having forgiven us all our transgressions; ¹⁴obliterating the bond against us, with its legal claims, which was opposed to us, he also removed it from our midst, nailing it to the cross; ¹⁵despoiling the principalities and the powers, he made a public spectacle of them, leading them away in triumph by it.

Responsorial Psalm: Psalms 145:1B-2, 8-9, 10-11
R. ⁽⁹⁾ *The Lord is compassionate toward all his works.*

¹ᴮ I will extol you, O my God and King,
and I will bless your name forever and ever.
² Every day will I bless you,
and I will praise your name forever and ever.

R. *The Lord is compassionate toward all his works.*

⁸ The LORD is gracious and merciful,
slow to anger and of great kindness.
⁹ The LORD is good to all
and compassionate toward all his works.

R. *The Lord is compassionate toward all his works.*

¹⁰ Let all your works give you thanks, O LORD,
and let your faithful ones bless you.
¹¹ Let them discourse of the glory of your Kingdom
and speak of your might.

R. *The Lord is compassionate toward all his works.*

Alleluia: cf. John 15:16
R. Alleluia, alleluia.
¹⁶ I chose you from the world,
That you may go and bear fruit that will last,
says the Lord.

R. Alleluia, alleluia.

Gospel: Luke 6:12-19

12 Jesus departed to the mountain to pray, and he spent the night in prayer to God. 13 When day came, he called his disciples to himself, and from them he chose Twelve, whom he also named Apostles: 14 Simon, whom he named Peter, and his brother Andrew, James, John, Philip, Bartholomew, 15 Matthew, Thomas, James the son of Alphaeus, Simon who was called a Zealot, 16 and Judas the son of James, and Judas Iscariot, who became a traitor.

17 And he came down with them and stood on a stretch of level ground. A great crowd of his disciples and a large number of the people from all Judea and Jerusalem and the coastal region of Tyre and Sidon 18 came to hear him and to be healed of their diseases; and even those who were tormented by unclean spirits were cured. 19 Everyone in the crowd sought to touch him because power came forth from him and healed them all.

Wednesday September 10, 2025
Wednesday of Twenty-third Week in Ordinary Time

First Reading: Colossians 3:1-11

Brothers and sisters: ¹If you were raised with Christ, seek what is above, where Christ is seated at the right hand of God. ²Think of what is above, not of what is on earth. ³For you have died, and your life is hidden with Christ in God. ⁴When Christ your life appears, then you too will appear with him in glory.

⁵Put to death, then, the parts of you that are earthly: immorality, impurity, passion, evil desire, and the greed that is idolatry. ⁶Because of these the wrath of God is coming upon the disobedient. ⁷By these you too once conducted yourselves, when you lived in that way. ⁸But now you must put them all away: anger, fury, malice, slander, and obscene language out of your mouths. ⁹Stop lying to one another, since you have taken off the old self with its practices ¹⁰and have put on the new self, which is being renewed, for knowledge, in the image of its creator. ¹¹Here there is not Greek and Jew, circumcision and uncircumcision, barbarian, Scythian, slave, free; but Christ is all and in all.

Responsorial Psalm: Psalms 145:2-3, 10-11, 12-13AB

R. ⁽⁹⁾ **The Lord is compassionate toward all his works.**

² Every day will I bless you,
  and I will praise your name forever and ever.
³ Great is the LORD and highly to be praised;
  his greatness is unsearchable.

R. **The Lord is compassionate toward all his works.**

¹⁰ Let all your works give you thanks, O LORD,
  and let your faithful ones bless you.
¹¹ Let them discourse of the glory of your Kingdom

and speak of your might.
R. The Lord is compassionate toward all his works.
¹² Making known to men your might
and the glorious splendor of your Kingdom.
¹³ᴬᴮ Your Kingdom is a Kingdom for all ages,
and your dominion endures through all generations.
R. The Lord is compassionate toward all his works.

Alleluia: Luke 6:23AB
R. Alleluia, alleluia.
²³ᴬᴮ Rejoice and leap for joy!
Your reward will be great in heaven.
R. Alleluia, alleluia.

Gospel: Luke 6:20-26
²⁰ Raising his eyes toward his disciples Jesus said:

"Blessed are you who are poor,
for the Kingdom of God is yours.
²¹ Blessed are you who are now hungry,
for you will be satisfied.
Blessed are you who are now weeping,
for you will laugh.
²² Blessed are you when people hate you,
and when they exclude and insult you,
and denounce your name as evil
on account of the Son of Man.

²³ Rejoice and leap for joy on that day! Behold, your reward will be great in heaven. For their ancestors treated the prophets in the same way.

²⁴ But woe to you who are rich,
for you have received your consolation.
²⁵ But woe to you who are filled now,
for you will be hungry.
Woe to you who laugh now,
for you will grieve and weep.
²⁶ Woe to you when all speak well of you,
for their ancestors treated the false prophets in this way."

Thursday September 11, 2025
Thursday of Twenty-third Week in Ordinary Time

First Reading: Colossians 3:12-17

Brothers and sisters: [12]Put on, as God's chosen ones, holy and beloved, heartfelt compassion, kindness, humility, gentleness, and patience, [13]bearing with one another and forgiving one another, if one has a grievance against another; as the Lord has forgiven you, so must you also do. [14]And over all these put on love, that is, the bond of perfection. [15]And let the peace of Christ control your hearts, the peace into which you were also called in one Body. And be thankful. [16]Let the word of Christ dwell in you richly, as in all wisdom you teach and admonish one another, singing psalms, hymns, and spiritual songs with gratitude in your hearts to God. [17]And whatever you do, in word or in deed, do everything in the name of the Lord Jesus, giving thanks to God the Father through him.

Responsorial Psalm: Psalms 150:1B-2, 3-4, 5-6

R. [6] Let everything that breathes praise the Lord!

[1B] Praise the LORD in his sanctuary,
    praise him in the firmament of his
        strength.
[2] Praise him for his mighty deeds,
    praise him for his sovereign majesty.

R. Let everything that breathes praise the Lord!

[3] Praise him with the blast of the trumpet,
    praise him with lyre and harp,
[4] Praise him with timbrel and dance,
    praise him with strings and pipe.

R. Let everything that breathes praise the Lord!

[5] Praise him with sounding cymbals,
    praise him with clanging cymbals.
[6] Let everything that has breath
    praise the LORD! Alleluia.

R. Let everything that breathes praise the Lord!

Alleluia: 1 John 4:12

R. Alleluia, alleluia.
[12] If we love one another,
God remains in us,
and his love is brought to perfection in us.
R. Alleluia, alleluia.

Gospel: Luke 6:27-38

Jesus said to his disciples: [27] "To you who hear I say, love your enemies, do good to those who hate you, [28] bless those who curse you, pray for those who mistreat you. [29] To the person who strikes you on one cheek, offer the other one as well, and from the person who takes your cloak, do not withhold even your tunic. ³⁰ Give to everyone who asks of you, and from the one who takes what is yours do not demand it back. ³¹ Do to others as you would have them do to you. ³² For if you love those who love you, what credit is that to you? Even sinners love those who love them. ³³ And if you do good to those who do good to you, what credit is that to you? Even sinners do the same. ³⁴ If you lend money to those from whom you expect repayment, what credit is that to you? Even sinners lend to sinners, and get back the same amount. ³⁵ But rather, love your enemies and do good to them, and lend expecting nothing back; then your reward will be great and you will be children of the Most High, for he himself is kind to the ungrateful and the wicked. ³⁶ Be merciful, just as also your Father is merciful.

³⁷ "Stop judging and you will not be judged. Stop condemning and you will not be condemned. Forgive and you will be forgiven. ³⁸ Give and gifts will be given to you; a good measure, packed together, shaken down, and overflowing, will be poured into your lap. For the measure with which you measure will in return be measured out to you."

Friday September 12, 2025
Friday of the Twenty-third Week in Ordinary Time
First Reading: 1 Timothy 1:1-2, 12-14

¹Paul, an Apostle of Christ Jesus by command of God our savior and of Christ Jesus our hope, ²to Timothy, my true child in faith: grace, mercy, and peace from God the Father and Christ Jesus our Lord.

¹²I am grateful to him who has strengthened me, Christ Jesus our Lord, because he considered me trustworthy in appointing me to the ministry. ¹³I was once a blasphemer and a persecutor and an arrogant man, but I have been mercifully treated because I acted out of ignorance in my unbelief. ¹⁴Indeed, the grace of our Lord has been abundant, along with the faith and love that are in Christ Jesus.

Responsorial Psalm: Psalms 16:1B-2A AND 5, 7-8, 11
R. (see 5) **You are my inheritance, O Lord.**
¹ᴮ Keep me, O God, for in you I take refuge;
    ²ᴬ I say to the LORD, "My Lord are you."
⁵ O LORD, my allotted portion and my cup,
    you it is who hold fast my lot.
R. **You are my inheritance, O Lord.**
⁷ I bless the LORD who counsels me;
    even in the night my heart exhorts me.
⁸ I set the LORD ever before me;
    with him at my right hand I shall not be
        disturbed.
R. **You are my inheritance, O Lord.**
¹¹ You will show me the path to life,
    fullness of joys in your presence,

the delights at your right hand forever.
R. You are my inheritance, O Lord.

Alleluia: 1 John 17:17B, 17A
R. Alleluia, alleluia.
[17B] Your word, O Lord, is truth;
[17A] consecrate us in the truth.
R. Alleluia, alleluia.

Gospel: Luke 6:39-42
[39] Jesus told his disciples a parable: "Can a blind person guide a blind person? Will not both fall into a pit? [40] No disciple is superior to the teacher; but when fully trained, every disciple will be like his teacher. [41] Why do you notice the splinter in your brother's eye, but do not perceive the wooden beam in your own? [42] How can you say to your brother, 'Brother, let me remove that splinter in your eye,' when you do not even notice the wooden beam in your own eye? You hypocrite! Remove the wooden beam from your eye first; then you will see clearly to remove the splinter in your brother's eye."

Saturday September 13, 2025
Memorial of Saint John Chrysostom, Bishop and Doctor

First Reading: 1 Timothy 1:15-17
Beloved: [15] This saying is trustworthy and deserves full acceptance: Christ Jesus came into the world to save sinners. Of these I am the foremost. [16] But for that reason I was mercifully treated, so that in me, as the foremost, Christ Jesus might display all his patience as an example for those who would come to believe in him for everlasting life. [17] To the king of ages, incorruptible, invisible, the only God, honor and glory forever and ever. Amen.

Responsorial Psalm: Psalms 113:1B-2, 3-4, 5 AND 6-7
R. (2) Blessed be the name of the Lord for ever.
[1B] Praise, you servants of the LORD,
   praise the name of the LORD.
[2] Blessed be the name of the LORD
   both now and forever.
R. Blessed be the name of the Lord for ever.
[3] From the rising to the setting of the sun
   is the name of the LORD to be praised.
[4] High above all nations is the LORD;
   above the heavens is his glory.
R. Blessed be the name of the Lord for ever.
[5] Who is like the LORD, our God,
   [6] and looks upon the heavens and the earth
      below?
[7] He raises up the lowly from the dust;
   from the dunghill he lifts up the poor.

R. Blessed be the name of the Lord for ever.

Alleluia: John 14:23
R. Alleluia, alleluia.
[23]Whoever loves me will keep my word,
and my Father will love him,
and we will come to him.
R. Alleluia, alleluia.

Gospel: Luke 6:43-49
Jesus said to his disciples: [43]"A good tree does not bear rotten fruit, nor does a rotten tree bear good fruit. [44]For every tree is known by its own fruit. For people do not pick figs from thornbushes, nor do they gather grapes from brambles. [45]A good person out of the store of goodness in his heart produces good, but an evil person out of a store of evil produces evil; for from the fullness of the heart the mouth speaks.

[46]"Why do you call me, 'Lord, Lord,' but not do what I command? [47]I will show you what someone is like who comes to me, listens to my words, and acts on them. [48]That one is like a man building a house, who dug deeply and laid the foundation on rock; when the flood came, the river burst against that house but could not shake it because it had been well built. [49]But the one who listens and does not act is like a person who built a house on the ground without a foundation. When the river burst against it, it collapsed at once and was completely destroyed."

Sunday September 14, 2025
Feast of the Exaltation of the Holy Cross
First Reading: Numbers 21:4B-9
[4B] With their patience worn out by the journey, [5] the people complained against God and Moses, "Why have you brought us up from Egypt to die in this desert, where there is no food or water? We are disgusted with this wretched food!"

[6] In punishment the LORD sent among the people saraph serpents, which bit the people so that many of them died. [7] Then the people came to Moses and said, "We have sinned in complaining against the LORD and you. Pray the LORD to take the serpents from us." So Moses prayed for the people, [8] and the LORD said to Moses, "Make a saraph and mount it on a pole, and if any who have been bitten look at it, they will live." [9] Moses accordingly made a bronze serpent and mounted it on a pole, and whenever anyone who had been bitten by a serpent looked at the bronze serpent, he lived.

Responsorial Psalm: Psalms 78:1BC-2, 34-35, 36-37, 38
R. [See 7b] **Do not forget the works of the Lord!**
[1BC] Hearken, my people, to my teaching;
    incline your ears to the words of my
        mouth.
[2] I will open my mouth in a parable,
    I will utter mysteries from of old.

R. Do not forget the works of the Lord!
³⁴ While he slew them they sought him
    and inquired after God again,
³⁵ Remembering that God was their rock
    and the Most High God, their redeemer.
R. Do not forget the works of the Lord!
³⁶ But they flattered him with their mouths
    and lied to him with their tongues,
³⁷ Though their hearts were not steadfast
      toward him,
    nor were they faithful to his covenant.
R. Do not forget the works of the Lord!
³⁸ But he, being merciful, forgave their sin
    and destroyed them not;
Often he turned back his anger
    and let none of his wrath be roused.
R. Do not forget the works of the Lord!

Second Reading: Philippians 2:6-11

Brothers and sisters:

⁶ Christ Jesus, though he was in the form of
      God,
    did not regard equality with God
    something to be grasped.
⁷ Rather, he emptied himself,
    taking the form of a slave,
    coming in human likeness;
    and found human in appearance,
⁸ he humbled himself,
    becoming obedient to death,
    even death on a cross.
⁹ Because of this, God greatly exalted him
    and bestowed on him the name
    that is above every name,
¹⁰ that at the name of Jesus
    every knee should bend,
    of those in heaven and on earth and
      under the earth,
¹¹ and every tongue confess that
    Jesus Christ is Lord,
    to the glory of God the Father.

Alleluia
R. Alleluia, alleluia.
We adore you, O Christ, and we bless you,
because by your Cross you have redeemed
>the world.
R. Alleluia, alleluia.

Gospel: John 3:13-17
Jesus said to Nicodemus: 13 "No one has gone up to heaven except the one who has come down from heaven, the Son of Man. 14 And just as Moses lifted up the serpent in the desert, so must the Son of Man be lifted up, 15 so that everyone who believes in him may have eternal life."

16 For God so loved the world that he gave his only Son, so that everyone who believes in him might not perish but might have eternal life. 17 For God did not send his Son into the world to condemn the world, but that the world might be saved through him.

Monday September 15, 2025
Memorial of Our Lady of Sorrows

First Reading: 1 Timothy 2:1-8
Beloved: ¹First of all, I ask that supplications, prayers, petitions, and thanksgivings be offered for everyone, ²for kings and for all in authority, that we may lead a quiet and tranquil life in all devotion and dignity. ³This is good and pleasing to God our savior, ⁴who wills everyone to be saved and to come to knowledge of the truth.

⁵For there is one God.
>There is also one mediator between God
>>and men,
the man Christ Jesus,
>⁶who gave himself as ransom for all.

This was the testimony at the proper time. ⁷For this I was appointed preacher and Apostle (I am speaking the truth, I am not lying), teacher of the Gentiles in faith and truth.
>⁸It is my wish, then, that in every place the men should pray, lifting up holy hands, without anger or argument.

Responsorial Psalm: Psalms 28:2, 7, 8-9
**R. ⁽⁶⁾ Blessed be the Lord, for he has heard my
>prayer.**
² Hear the sound of my pleading, when I cry to
>you,
>>lifting up my hands toward your holy
>>>shrine.
**R. Blessed be the Lord, for he has heard my
>prayer.**
⁷ The LORD is my strength and my shield.

In him my heart trusts, and I find help;
> then my heart exults, and with my song I
>> give him thanks.

R. Blessed be the Lord, for he has heard my prayer.

[8] The LORD is the strength of his people,
> the saving refuge of his anointed.

[9] Save your people, and bless your inheritance;
> feed them, and carry them forever!

R. Blessed be the Lord, for he has heard my prayer.

Alleluia: John 3:16

R. Alleluia, alleluia.
[16] God so loved the world that he gave his only-begotten Son,
so that everyone who believes in him might have eternal life.
R. Alleluia, alleluia.

Gospel: Luke 7:1-10

[1] When Jesus had finished all his words to the people, he entered Capernaum. [2] A centurion there had a slave who was ill and about to die, and he was valuable to him. [3] When he heard about Jesus, he sent elders of the Jews to him, asking him to come and save the life of his slave. [4] They approached Jesus and strongly urged him to come, saying, "He deserves to have you do this for him, [5] for he loves our nation and he built the synagogue for us." [6] And Jesus went with them, but when he was only a short distance from the house, the centurion sent friends to tell him, "Lord, do not trouble yourself, for I am not worthy to have you enter under my roof. [7] Therefore, I did not consider myself worthy to come to you; but say the word and let my servant be healed. [8] For I too am a person subject to authority, with soldiers subject to me. And I say to one, 'Go,' and he goes; and to another, 'Come here,' and he comes; and to my slave, 'Do this,' and he does it." [9] When Jesus heard this he was amazed at him and, turning, said to the crowd following him, "I tell you, not even in Israel have I found such faith." [10] When the messengers returned to the house, they found the slave in good health.

Tuesday September 16, 2025

Memorial of Saints Cornelius, Pope, and Cyprian, Bishop & Martyr

First Reading: 1 Timothy 3:1-13

[1] Beloved, this saying is trustworthy: whoever aspires to the office of bishop desires a noble task. [2] Therefore, a bishop must be irreproachable, married only once, temperate, self-controlled, decent, hospitable, able to teach, [3] not a drunkard, not aggressive, but gentle, not contentious, not a lover of money. [4] He must manage his own household well, keeping his children under control with perfect dignity; [5] for

if a man does not know how to manage his own household, how can he take care of the Church of God? ⁶He should not be a recent convert, so that he may not become conceited and thus incur the Devil's punishment. ⁷He must also have a good reputation among outsiders, so that he may not fall into disgrace, the Devil's trap.

⁸Similarly, deacons must be dignified, not deceitful, not addicted to drink, not greedy for sordid gain, ⁹holding fast to the mystery of the faith with a clear conscience. ¹⁰Moreover, they should be tested first; then, if there is nothing against them, let them serve as deacons. ¹¹Women, similarly, should be dignified, not slanderers, but temperate and faithful in everything. ¹²Deacons may be married only once and must manage their children and their households well. ¹³Thus those who serve well as deacons gain good standing and much confidence in their faith in Christ Jesus.

Responsorial Psalm: Psalms 101:1B-2AB, 2CD-3AB, 5, 6
R. ⁽²⁾ I will walk with blameless heart.
¹ᴮ Of mercy and judgment I will sing;
    to you, O LORD, I will sing praise.
²ᴬᴮ I will persevere in the way of integrity;
    when will you come to me?
R. I will walk with blameless heart.
²ᶜᴰ I will walk with blameless heart,
    within my house;
³ᴬᴮ I will not set before my eyes
    any base thing.
R. I will walk with blameless heart.
⁵ Whoever slanders his neighbor in secret,
    him will I destroy.
The man of haughty eyes and puffed-up
        heart
    I will not endure.
R. I will walk with blameless heart.
⁶ My eyes are upon the faithful of the land,
    that they may dwell with me.
He who walks in the way of integrity
    shall be in my service.
R. I will walk with blameless heart.

Alleluia: Luke 7:16
R. Alleluia, alleluia.
¹⁶ A great prophet has arisen in our midst and God has visited his people.
R. Alleluia, alleluia.

Gospel: Luke 7:11-17

[11] Jesus journeyed to a city called Nain, and his disciples and a large crowd accompanied him. [12] As he drew near to the gate of the city, a man who had died was being carried out, the only son of his mother, and she was a widow. A large crowd from the city was with her. [13] When the Lord saw her, he was moved with pity for her and said to her, "Do not weep." [14] He stepped forward and touched the coffin; at this the bearers halted, and he said, "Young man, I tell you, arise!" [15] The dead man sat up and began to speak, and Jesus gave him to his mother. [16] Fear seized them all, and they glorified God, exclaiming, "A great prophet has arisen in our midst," and "God has visited his people." [17] This report about him spread through the whole of Judea and in all the surrounding region.

Wednesday September 17, 2025
Wednesday of Twenty-fourth Week in Ordinary Time

First Reading: 1 Timothy 3:14-16

Beloved: [14]I am writing you, although I hope to visit you soon. [15]But if I should be delayed, you should know how to behave in the household of God, which is the Church of the living God, the pillar and foundation of truth. [16]Undeniably great is the mystery of devotion,

Who was manifested in the flesh,
    vindicated in the spirit,
    seen by angels,
    proclaimed to the Gentiles,
    believed in throughout the world,
    taken up in glory.

Responsorial Psalm: Psalms 111:1-2, 3-4, 5-6

R. (2) How great are the works of the Lord!

[1] I will give thanks to the LORD with all my
      heart
   in the company and assembly of the just.
[2] Great are the works of the LORD,
   exquisite in all their delights.

R. How great are the works of the Lord!

[3] Majesty and glory are his work,
   and his justice endures forever.
[4] He has won renown for his wondrous deeds;
   gracious and merciful is the LORD.

R. How great are the works of the Lord!

[5] He has given food to those who fear him;
   he will forever be mindful of his
      covenant.
[6] He has made known to his people the power
      of his works,
   giving them the inheritance of the
      nations.

R. How great are the works of the Lord!

Alleluia: John 6:63C, 68C
R. Alleluia, alleluia.
[63C] Your words, Lord, are Spirit and life,
[68C] you have the words of everlasting life.
R. Alleluia, alleluia.

Gospel: Luke 7:31-35
Jesus said to the crowds: [31] "To what shall I compare the people of this generation? What are they like? [32] They are like children who sit in the marketplace and call to one another,

'We played the flute for you, but you did not
>dance.
>We sang a dirge, but you did not weep.'

[33] For John the Baptist came neither eating food nor drinking wine, and you said, 'He is possessed by a demon.' [34] The Son of Man came eating and drinking and you said, 'Look, he is a glutton and a drunkard, a friend of tax collectors and sinners.' [35] But wisdom is vindicated by all her children."

Thursday September 18, 2025
Thursday of Twenty-fourth Week in Ordinary Time
First Reading: 1 Timothy 4:12-16
Beloved: [12]Let no one have contempt for your youth, but set an example for those who believe in speech, conduct, love, faith, and purity. [13]Until I arrive, attend to the reading, exhortation, and teaching. [14]Do not neglect the gift you have, which was conferred on you through the prophetic word with the imposition of hands by the presbyterate. [15]Be diligent in these matters, be absorbed in them, so that your progress may be evident to everyone. [16]Attend to yourself and to your teaching; persevere in both tasks, for by doing so you will save both yourself and those who listen to you.

Responsorial Psalm: Psalms 111:7-8, 9, 10
R. [(2)] **How great are the works of the Lord!**
[7] The works of his hands are faithful and just;
>sure are all his precepts,
[8] Reliable forever and ever,
>wrought in truth and equity.
R. How great are the works of the Lord!
[9] He has sent deliverance to his people;
>he has ratified his covenant forever;
>holy and awesome is his name.
R. How great are the works of the Lord!
[10] The fear of the LORD is the beginning of

wisdom;
  prudent are all who live by it.
  His praise endures forever.
R. How great are the works of the Lord!

Alleluia: Matthew 11:28
R. Alleluia, alleluia.
²⁸ Come to me, all you who labor and are burdened,
and I will give you rest, says the Lord.
R. Alleluia, alleluia.

Gospel: Luke 7:36-50
³⁶A certain Pharisee invited Jesus to dine with him, and he entered the Pharisee's house and reclined at table. ³⁷Now there was a sinful woman in the city who learned that he was at table in the house of the Pharisee. Bringing an alabaster flask of ointment, ³⁸she stood behind him at his feet weeping and began to bathe his feet with her tears. Then she wiped them with her hair, kissed them, and anointed them with the ointment. ³⁹When the Pharisee who had invited him saw this he said to himself, "If this man were a prophet, he would know who and what sort of woman this is who is touching him, that she is a sinner." ⁴⁰Jesus said to him in reply, "Simon, I have something to say to you." "Tell me, teacher," he said. ⁴¹"Two people were in debt to a certain creditor; one owed five hundred days' wages and the other owed fifty. ⁴²Since they were unable to repay the debt, he forgave it for both. Which of them will love him more?" ⁴³Simon said in reply, "The one, I suppose, whose larger debt was forgiven." He said to him, "You have judged rightly." ⁴⁴Then he turned to the woman and said to Simon, "Do you see this woman? When I entered your house, you did not give me water for my feet, but she has bathed them with her tears and wiped them with her hair. ⁴⁵You did not give me a kiss, but she has not ceased kissing my feet since the time I entered. ⁴⁶You did not anoint my head with oil, but she anointed my feet with ointment. ⁴⁷So I tell you, her many sins have been forgiven; hence, she has shown great love. But the one to whom little is forgiven, loves little." ⁴⁸He said to her, "Your sins are forgiven." ⁴⁹The others at the table said to themselves, "Who is this who even forgives sins?" ⁵⁰But he said to the woman, "Your faith has saved you; go in peace."

Friday September 19, 2025
Friday of Twenty-fourth Week in Ordinary Time
First Reading: 1 Timothy 6:2C-12
Beloved: ²ᶜTeach and urge these things. ³Whoever teaches something different and does not agree with the sound words of our Lord Jesus Christ and the religious teaching ⁴is conceited, understanding nothing, and has a morbid disposition for arguments and verbal disputes. From these come envy, rivalry, insults, evil suspicions, ⁵and mutual friction among people with corrupted minds, who are deprived of the truth, supposing religion to be a means of gain. ⁶Indeed, religion with contentment is a great gain. ⁷For we brought nothing into the world, just as we shall not be able to take anything out of it. ⁸If we have food and clothing,

we shall be content with that. ⁹Those who want to be rich are falling into temptation and into a trap and into many foolish and harmful desires, which plunge them into ruin and destruction. ¹⁰For the love of money is the root of all evils, and some people in their desire for it have strayed from the faith and have pierced themselves with many pains.

¹¹But you, man of God, avoid all this. Instead, pursue righteousness, devotion, faith, love, patience, and gentleness. ¹²Compete well for the faith. Lay hold of eternal life, to which you were called when you made the noble confession in the presence of many witnesses.

Responsorial Psalm: Psalms 49:6-7, 8-10, 17-18, 19-20

R. Blessed the poor in spirit; the Kingdom of heaven is theirs!

⁶ Why should I fear in evil days
   when my wicked ensnarers ring me round?
⁷ They trust in their wealth;
   the abundance of their riches is their boast.

R. Blessed the poor in spirit; the Kingdom of heaven is theirs!

⁸ Yet in no way can a man redeem himself,
   or pay his own ransom to God;
⁹ Too high is the price to redeem one's life; ¹⁰ he would never have enough
   to remain alive always and not see destruction.

R. Blessed the poor in spirit; the Kingdom of heaven is theirs!

¹⁷ Fear not when a man grows rich,
   when the wealth of his house becomes great,
¹⁸ For when he dies, he shall take none of it;
   his wealth shall not follow him down.

R. Blessed the poor in spirit; the Kingdom of heaven is theirs!

¹⁹ Though in his lifetime he counted himself blessed,
   "They will praise you for doing well for yourself,"
²⁰ He shall join the circle of his forebears
   who shall never more see light.

R. Blessed the poor in spirit; the Kingdom of heaven is theirs!

Alleluia: cf. Matthew 11:25
R. Alleluia, alleluia.
²⁵ Blessed are you, Father, Lord of heaven and
　　　　earth;
you have revealed to little ones the
　　　　mysteries of the Kingdom.
R. Alleluia, alleluia.

Gospel: Luke 8:1-3
¹ Jesus journeyed from one town and village to another, preaching and proclaiming the good news of the Kingdom of God. Accompanying him were the Twelve ² and some women who had been cured of evil spirits and infirmities, Mary, called Magdalene, from whom seven demons had gone out, ³ Joanna, the wife of Herod's steward Chuza, Susanna, and many others who provided for them out of their resources.

Saturday September 20, 2025
Memorial of Saint Andrew Kim Taegon, Priest, and Paul Chong Hasang, and their Companions, Martyrs
First Reading: 1 Timothy 6:13-16
Beloved: ¹³I charge you before God, who gives life to all things, and before Christ Jesus, who gave testimony under Pontius Pilate for the noble confession, ¹⁴to keep the commandment without stain or reproach until the appearance of our Lord Jesus Christ ¹⁵that the blessed and only ruler will make manifest at the proper time, the King of kings and Lord of lords, ¹⁶who alone has immortality, who dwells in unapproachable light, and whom no human being has seen or can see. To him be honor and eternal power. Amen.

Responsorial Psalm: Psalms 100:1B-2, 3, 4, 5
R. ⁽²⁾ *Come with joy into the presence of the Lord.*
¹ᴮ Sing joyfully to the LORD, all you lands;
　　　²serve the LORD with gladness;
　　　come before him with joyful song.
R. *Come with joy into the presence of the Lord.*
³ Know that the LORD is God;
　　　he made us, his we are;
　　　his people, the flock he tends.
R. *Come with joy into the presence of the Lord.*
⁴ Enter his gates with thanksgiving,
　　　his courts with praise;
Give thanks to him; bless his name.
R. *Come with joy into the presence of the Lord.*
⁵ For he is good:
　　　the LORD, whose kindness endures
　　　　　forever,
　　　and his faithfulness, to all generations.

R. Come with joy into the presence of the Lord.

Alleluia: Luke 8:15
R. Alleluia, alleluia.
[15]Blessed are they who have kept the word
　　with a generous heart
and yield a harvest through perseverance.
R. Alleluia, alleluia.

Gospel: Luke 8:4-15
[4]When a large crowd gathered, with people from one town after another journeying to Jesus, he spoke in a parable. [5]"A sower went out to sow his seed. And as he sowed, some seed fell on the path and was trampled, and the birds of the sky ate it up. [6]Some seed fell on rocky ground, and when it grew, it withered for lack of moisture. [7]Some seed fell among thorns, and the thorns grew with it and choked it. [8]And some seed fell on good soil, and when it grew, it produced fruit a hundredfold." After saying this, he called out, "Whoever has ears to hear ought to hear."

[9]Then his disciples asked him what the meaning of this parable might be. [10]He answered, "Knowledge of the mysteries of the Kingdom of God has been granted to you; but to the rest, they are made known through parables so that *they may look but not see, and hear but not understand*.

[11]"This is the meaning of the parable. The seed is the word of God. [12]Those on the path are the ones who have heard, but the Devil comes and takes away the word from their hearts that they may not believe and be saved. [13]Those on rocky ground are the ones who, when they hear, receive the word with joy, but they have no root; they believe only for a time and fall away in time of temptation. [14]As for the seed that fell among thorns, they are the ones who have heard, but as they go along, they are choked by the anxieties and riches and pleasures of life, and they fail to produce mature fruit. [15]But as for the seed that fell on rich soil, they are the ones who, when they have heard the word, embrace it with a generous and good heart, and bear fruit through perseverance."

Sunday September 21, 2025
Twenty-fifth Sunday in Ordinary Time, Year C

First Reading: Amos 8:4-7
[4]Hear this, you who trample upon the needy
　　and destroy the poor of the land!
[5]"When will the new moon be over," you ask,
　　"that we may sell our grain,
　　and the sabbath, that we may display the
　　　　wheat?
We will diminish the ephah,
　　add to the shekel,
　　and fix our scales for cheating!
[6]We will buy the lowly for silver,
　　and the poor for a pair of sandals;

even the refuse of the wheat we will sell!"
⁷The LORD has sworn by the pride of Jacob:
> Never will I forget a thing they have done!

Responsorial Psalm: Psalms 113:1-2, 4-6, 7-8

R. (cf. 1a, 7b) **Praise the Lord who lifts up the poor.** or: *R. Alleluia.*

¹ Praise, you servants of the LORD,
> praise the name of the LORD.

² Blessed be the name of the LORD
> both now and forever.

***R. Praise the Lord who lifts up the poor.** or: R. Alleluia.*

⁴High above all nations is the LORD;
> above the heavens is his glory.

⁶ Who is like the LORD, our God, who is
>> enthroned on high
> and looks upon the heavens and the earth
>> below?

***R. Praise the Lord who lifts up the poor.** or: R. Alleluia.*

⁷ He raises up the lowly from the dust;
> from the dunghill he lifts up the poor

⁸ to seat them with princes,
> with the princes of his own people.

***R. Praise the Lord who lifts up the poor.** or: R. Alleluia.*

Second Reading: 1 Timothy 2:1-8

Beloved: ¹First of all, I ask that supplications, prayers, petitions, and thanksgivings be offered for everyone, ²for kings and for all in authority, that we may lead a quiet and tranquil life in all devotion and dignity. ³This is good and pleasing to God our savior, ⁴who wills everyone to be saved and to come to knowledge of the truth.

⁵For there is one God.
> There is also one mediator between God
>> and men,

the man Christ Jesus,
> ⁶who gave himself as ransom for all.

This was the testimony at the proper time. ⁷For this I was appointed preacher and apostle —I am speaking the truth, I am not lying—, teacher of the Gentiles in faith and truth.

⁸It is my wish, then, that in every place the men should pray, lifting up holy hands, without anger or argument.

Alleluia: cf. 2 Corinthians 8:9
R. Alleluia, alleluia.
⁹Though our Lord Jesus Christ was rich, he
  became poor,
so that by his poverty you might become
  rich.
R. Alleluia, alleluia.

Gospel: Luke 16:1-13
¹Jesus said to his disciples, "A rich man had a steward who was reported to him for squandering his property. ²He summoned him and said, 'What is this I hear about you? Prepare a full account of your stewardship, because you can no longer be my steward.' ³The steward said to himself, 'What shall I do, now that my master is taking the position of steward away from me? I am not strong enough to dig and I am ashamed to beg. ⁴I know what I shall do so that, when I am removed from the stewardship, they may welcome me into their homes.' ⁵He called in his master's debtors one by one. To the first he said, 'How much do you owe my master?' ⁶He replied, 'One hundred measures of olive oil.' He said to him, 'Here is your promissory note. Sit down and quickly write one for fifty.' ⁷Then to another the steward said, 'And you, how much do you owe?' He replied, 'One hundred kors of wheat.' The steward said to him, 'Here is your promissory note; write one for eighty.' ⁸And the master commended that dishonest steward for acting prudently.

"For the children of this world are more prudent in dealing with their own generation than are the children of light. ⁹I tell you, make friends for yourselves with dishonest wealth, so that when it fails, you will be welcomed into eternal dwellings. ¹⁰The person who is trustworthy in very small matters is also trustworthy in great ones; and the person who is dishonest in very small matters is also dishonest in great ones. ¹¹If, therefore, you are not trustworthy with dishonest wealth, who will trust you with true wealth? ¹²If you are not trustworthy with what belongs to another, who will give you what is yours? ¹³No servant can serve two masters. He will either hate one and love the other, or be devoted to one and despise the other. You cannot serve both God and mammon."

Or Luke 16:10-13
Jesus said to his disciples: ¹⁰The person who is trustworthy in very small matters is also trustworthy in great ones; and the person who is dishonest in very small matters is also dishonest in great ones. ¹¹If, therefore, you are not trustworthy with dishonest wealth, who will trust you with true wealth? ¹²If you are not trustworthy with what belongs to another, who will give you what is yours? ¹³No servant can serve two masters. He will either hate one and love the other, or be devoted to one and despise the other. You cannot serve both God and mammon."

Monday September 22, 2025
Monday of the Twenty-fifth Week in Ordinary Time

First Reading: Ezra 1:1-6

¹In the first year of Cyrus, king of Persia, in order to fulfill the word of the LORD spoken by Jeremiah, the LORD inspired King Cyrus of Persia to issue this proclamation throughout his kingdom, both by word of mouth and in writing: ²"Thus says Cyrus, king of Persia: 'All the kingdoms of the earth the LORD, the God of heaven, has given to me, and he has also charged me to build him a house in Jerusalem, which is in Judah. ³Therefore, whoever among you belongs to any part of his people, let him go up, and may his God be with him! ⁴Let everyone who has survived, in whatever place he may have dwelt, be assisted by the people of that place with silver, gold, goods, and cattle, together with free-will offerings for the house of God in Jerusalem.'"

⁵Then the family heads of Judah and Benjamin and the priests and Levites– everyone, that is, whom God had inspired to do so– prepared to go up to build the house of the LORD in Jerusalem. ⁶All their neighbors gave them help in every way, with silver, gold, goods, and cattle, and with many precious gifts besides all their free-will offerings.

Responsorial Psalm: Psalms 126:1B-2AB, 2CD-3, 4-5, 6

R. (3) *The Lord has done marvels for us.*
¹ᴮWhen the LORD brought back the captives of
>   Zion,
> we were like men dreaming.
²ᴬᴮThen our mouth was filled with laughter,
> and our tongue with rejoicing.
R. *The Lord has done marvels for us.*
²ᶜᴰThen they said among the nations,
>   ³"The LORD has done great things for
>   them."
The LORD has done great things for us;
> we are glad indeed.
R. *The Lord has done marvels for us.*
⁴Restore our fortunes, O LORD,
> like the torrents in the southern desert.
⁵ Those that sow in tears
> shall reap rejoicing.
R. *The Lord has done marvels for us.*
⁶ Although they go forth weeping,
> carrying the seed to be sown,
They shall come back rejoicing,
> carrying their sheaves.
R. *The Lord has done marvels for us.*

Alleluia: Matthew 5:16
R. Alleluia, alleluia.
16 Let your light shine before others,
that they may see your good deeds and
　　glorify your heavenly Father.
R. Alleluia, alleluia.

Gospel: Luke 8:16-18
Jesus said to the crowd: 16 "No one who lights a lamp conceals it with a vessel or sets it under a bed; rather, he places it on a lampstand so that those who enter may see the light. 17 For there is nothing hidden that will not become visible, and nothing secret that will not be known and come to light. 18 Take care, then, how you hear. To anyone who has, more will be given, and from the one who has not, even what he seems to have will be taken away."

Tuesday September 23, 2025
Memorial of Saint Pius of Pietrelcina

First Reading: Ezra 6:7-8, 12B, 14-20
King Darius issued an order to the officials of West-of-Euphrates: 7"Let the governor and the elders of the Jews continue the work on that house of God; they are to rebuild it on its former site. 8I also issue this decree concerning your dealing with these elders of the Jews in the rebuilding of that house of God: From the royal revenue, the taxes of West-of-Euphrates, let these men be repaid for their expenses, in full and without delay. 12BI, Darius, have issued this decree; let it be carefully executed."

14The elders of the Jews continued to make progress in the building, supported by the message of the prophets, Haggai and Zechariah, son of Iddo. They finished the building according to the command of the God of Israel and the decrees of Cyrus and Darius and of Artaxerxes, king of Persia. 15They completed this house on the third day of the month Adar, in the sixth year of the reign of King Darius. 16The children of Israel– priests, Levites, and the other returned exiles– celebrated the dedication of this house of God with joy. 17For the dedication of this house of God, they offered one hundred bulls, two hundred rams, and four hundred lambs, together with twelve he-goats as a sin-offering for all Israel, in keeping with the number of the tribes of Israel. 18Finally, they set up the priests in their classes and the Levites in their divisions for the service of God in Jerusalem, as is prescribed in the book of Moses.

19The exiles kept the Passover on the fourteenth day of the first month. 20The Levites, every one of whom had purified himself for the occasion, sacrificed the Passover for the rest of the exiles, for their brethren the priests, and for themselves.

Responsorial Psalm: Psalms 122:1-2, 3-4AB, 4CD-5
R. (1) Let us go rejoicing to the house of the Lord.
1I rejoiced because they said to me,
　　"We will go up to the house of the LORD."
2And now we have set foot

within your gates, O Jerusalem.
R. *Let us go rejoicing to the house of the Lord.*
³Jerusalem, built as a city
   with compact unity.
⁴ᴬᴮ To it the tribes go up,
   the tribes of the LORD.
R. *Let us go rejoicing to the house of the Lord.*
⁴ᶜᴰ According to the decree for Israel,
   to give thanks to the name of the LORD.
⁵ In it are set up judgment seats,
   seats for the house of David.
R. *Let us go rejoicing to the house of the Lord.*

Alleluia: Luke 11:28
R. Alleluia, alleluia.
²⁸ Blessed are those who hear the word of God and observe it.
R. Alleluia, alleluia.

Gospel: Luke 8:19-21
¹⁹ The mother of Jesus and his brothers came to him but were unable to join him because of the crowd. ²⁰ He was told, "Your mother and your brothers are standing outside and they wish to see you." ²¹ He said to them in reply, "My mother and my brothers are those who hear the word of God and act on it."

Wednesday September 24, 2025
Wednesday of Twenty-fifth Week in Ordinary Time
First Reading: Ezra 9:5-9
⁵At the time of the evening sacrifice, I, Ezra, rose in my wretchedness, and with cloak and mantle torn I fell on my knees, stretching out my hands to the LORD, my God.

⁶I said: "My God, I am too ashamed and confounded to raise my face to you, O my God, for our wicked deeds are heaped up above our heads and our guilt reaches up to heaven. ⁷From the time of our fathers even to this day great has been our guilt, and for our wicked deeds we have been delivered up, we and our kings and our priests, to the will of the kings of foreign lands, to the sword, to captivity, to pillage, and to disgrace, as is the case today.

⁸"And now, but a short time ago, mercy came to us from the LORD, our God, who left us a remnant and gave us a stake in his holy place; thus our God has brightened our eyes and given us relief in our servitude. ⁹For slaves we are, but in our servitude our God has not abandoned us; rather, he has turned the good will of the kings of Persia toward us. Thus he has given us new life to raise again the house of our God and restore its ruins, and has granted us a fence in Judah and Jerusalem."

Responsorial Psalm: Tobit 13:2, 3-4A, 4BEFGHN, 7-8
R. *(1b)* *Blessed be God, who lives for ever.*
²He scourges and then has mercy;
> he casts down to the depths of the nether world,
> and he brings up from the great abyss.

No one can escape his hand.
R. Blessed be God, who lives for ever.
³ Praise him, you children of Israel, before the Gentiles,
> for though he has scattered you among them,

⁴ᴬhe has shown you his greatness even there.
R. Blessed be God, who lives for ever.
⁴ᴮ So now consider what he has done for you,
> and praise him with full voice.

Bless the Lord of righteousness,
> and exalt the King of ages.

R. Blessed be God, who lives for ever.
⁶ In the land of my exile I praise him
> and show his power and majesty to a sinful nation.

R. Blessed be God, who lives for ever.
⁷ Bless the Lord, all you his chosen ones,
> and may all of you praise his majesty.

⁸ Celebrate days of gladness, and give him praise.
R. Blessed be God, who lives for ever.

Alleluia: Mark 1:15
R. Alleluia, alleluia.
¹⁵ The Kingdom of God is at hand;
repent and believe in the Gospel.
R. Alleluia, alleluia.

Gospel: Luke 9:1-6
¹ Jesus summoned the Twelve and gave them power and authority over all demons and to cure diseases, ² and he sent them to proclaim the Kingdom of God and to heal the sick. ³ He said to them, "Take nothing for the journey, neither walking stick, nor sack, nor food, nor money, and let no one take a second tunic. ⁴ Whatever house you enter, stay there and leave from there. ⁵ And as for those who do not welcome you, when you leave that town, shake the dust from your feet in testimony against them." ⁶ Then they set out and went from village to village proclaiming the good news and curing diseases everywhere.

Thursday September 25, 2025
Thursday of Twenty-fifth Week in Ordinary Time

First Reading: Haggai 1:1-8

¹On the first day of the sixth month in the second year of King Darius, the word of the LORD came through the prophet Haggai to the governor of Judah, Zerubbabel, son of Shealtiel, and to the high priest Joshua, son of Jehozadak:

²Thus says the LORD of hosts: This people says: "The time has not yet come to rebuild the house of the LORD." ³(Then this word of the LORD came through Haggai, the prophet:) ⁴Is it time for you to dwell in your own paneled houses, while this house lies in ruins?

⁵Now thus says the LORD of hosts:
    Consider your ways!
⁶You have sown much, but have brought in
       little;
    you have eaten, but have not been
       satisfied;
You have drunk, but have not been
       exhilarated;
    have clothed yourselves, but not been
       warmed;
And whoever earned wages
    earned them for a bag with holes in it.
⁷Thus says the LORD of hosts:
Consider your ways!
    ⁸Go up into the hill country;
    bring timber, and build the house
That I may take pleasure in it
    and receive my glory, says the LORD.

Responsorial Psalm: Psalms 149:1B-2, 3-4, 5-6A AND 9B

R. (see 4a) **The Lord takes delight in his people.**

¹ᴮ Sing to the LORD a new song
    of praise in the assembly of the faithful.
² Let Israel be glad in their maker,
    let the children of Zion rejoice in their king.

R. The Lord takes delight in his people.

³ Let them praise his name in the festive
       dance,
    let them sing praise to him with timbrel
       and harp.
⁴For the LORD loves his people,
    and he adorns the lowly with victory.

R. The Lord takes delight in his people.

⁵ Let the faithful exult in glory;
> let them sing for joy upon their couches;

⁶ᴬ Let the high praises of God be in their
> throats.

⁹ᴮ This is the glory of all his faithful.
> Alleluia.

R. The Lord takes delight in his people.

Alleluia: John 14:6
R. Alleluia, alleluia.
⁶ I am the way and the truth and the life, says
> the Lord;
no one comes to the Father except through
> me.
R. Alleluia, alleluia.

Gospel: Luke 9:7-9
⁷ Herod the tetrarch heard about all that was happening, and he was greatly perplexed because some were saying, "John has been raised from the dead"; ⁸ others were saying, "Elijah has appeared"; still others, "One of the ancient prophets has arisen." ⁹ But Herod said, "John I beheaded. Who then is this about whom I hear such things?" And he kept trying to see him.

Friday September 26, 2025
Friday of Twenty-fifth Week in Ordinary Time
First Reading: Haggai 2:1-9

¹In the second year of King Darius, on the twenty-first day of the seventh month, the word of the LORD came through the prophet Haggai: ²Tell this to the governor of Judah, Zerubbabel, son of Shealtiel, and to the high priest Joshua, son of Jehozadak, and to the remnant of the people:

³Who is left among you
> that saw this house in its former glory?
And how do you see it now?
> Does it not seem like nothing in your
> > eyes?
⁴But now take courage, Zerubbabel, says the
> LORD,
> and take courage, Joshua, high priest, son
> > of Jehozadak,
And take courage, all you people of the land,
> says the LORD, and work!
> For I am with you, says the LORD of hosts.
⁵This is the pact that I made with you
> when you came out of Egypt,

And my spirit continues in your midst;
> do not fear!
> ⁶For thus says the LORD of hosts:
One moment yet, a little while,
> and I will shake the heavens and the earth,
> the sea and the dry land.
⁷I will shake all the nations,
> and the treasures of all the nations will come in,
And I will fill this house with glory,
> says the LORD of hosts.
⁸Mine is the silver and mine the gold,
> says the LORD of hosts.
⁹Greater will be the future glory of this house
> than the former, says the LORD of hosts;
And in this place I will give you peace,
> says the LORD of hosts!

Responsorial Psalm: Psalms 43:1, 2, 3, 4

R. ⁽⁵⁾ Hope in God; I will praise him, my savior and my God.

¹ Do me justice, O God, and fight my fight
> against a faithless people;
> > from the deceitful and impious man
> > > rescue me.

R. Hope in God; I will praise him, my savior and my God.

² For you, O God, are my strength.
> Why do you keep me so far away?
Why must I go about in mourning,
> with the enemy oppressing me?

R. Hope in God; I will praise him, my savior and my God.

³ Send forth your light and your fidelity;
> they shall lead me on
And bring me to your holy mountain,
> to your dwelling-place.

R. Hope in God; I will praise him, my savior and my God.

⁴ Then will I go in to the altar of God,
> the God of my gladness and joy;
Then will I give you thanks upon the harp,
> O God, my God!

R. Hope in God; I will praise him, my savior and

my God.

Alleluia: Mark 10:45
R. Alleluia, alleluia.
⁴⁵The Son of Man came to serve
and to give his life as a ransom for many.
R. Alleluia, alleluia.

Gospel: Luke 9:18-22
¹⁸Once when Jesus was praying in solitude, and the disciples were with him, he asked them, "Who do the crowds say that I am?" ¹⁹They said in reply, "John the Baptist; others, Elijah; still others, 'One of the ancient prophets has arisen.'" ²⁰Then he said to them, "But who do you say that I am?" Peter said in reply, "The Christ of God." ²¹He rebuked them and directed them not to tell this to anyone.

²²He said, "The Son of Man must suffer greatly and be rejected by the elders, the chief priests, and the scribes, and be killed and on the third day be raised."

Saturday September 27, 2025
Memorial of Saint Vincent de Paul, Priest

First Reading: Zechariah 2:5-9, 14-15A
⁵I, Zechariah, raised my eyes and looked: there was a man with a measuring line in his hand. ⁶I asked, "Where are you going?" He answered, "To measure Jerusalem, to see how great is its width and how great its length."

⁷Then the angel who spoke with me advanced, and another angel came out to meet him ⁸and said to him, "Run, tell this to that young man: People will live in Jerusalem as though in open country, because of the multitude of men and beasts in her midst. ⁹But I will be for her an encircling wall of fire, says the LORD, and I will be the glory in her midst."

¹⁴Sing and rejoice, O daughter Zion! See, I am coming to dwell among you, says the LORD. ¹⁵ᴬMany nations shall join themselves to the LORD on that day, and they shall be his people and he will dwell among you.

Responsorial Psalm: Jeremiah 31:10, 11-12AB, 13
**R. *(see 10d)* The Lord will guard us as a shepherd
     guards his flock.**
¹⁰Hear the word of the LORD, O nations,
    proclaim it on distant isles, and say:
He who scattered Israel, now gathers them
        together,
    he guards them as a shepherd guards his
        flock.
**R. The Lord will guard us as a shepherd guards
     his flock.**
¹¹ The LORD shall ransom Jacob,

    he shall redeem him from the hand of his
        conqueror.
12AB Shouting, they shall mount the heights of
        Zion,
    they shall come streaming to the LORD's
        blessings.

R. The Lord will guard us as a shepherd guards his flock.

13 Then the virgins shall make merry and
        dance,
    and young men and old as well.
I will turn their mourning into joy,
    I will console and gladden them after
        their sorrows.

R. The Lord will guard us as a shepherd guards his flock.

Alleluia: 2 Timothy 1:10
R. Alleluia, alleluia.
10 Our Savior Christ Jesus destroyed death
and brought life to light through the Gospel.
R. Alleluia, alleluia.

Gospel: Luke 9:43B-45
43B While they were all amazed at his every deed, Jesus said to his disciples, 44 "Pay attention to what I am telling you. The Son of Man is to be handed over to men." 45 But they did not understand this saying; its meaning was hidden from them so that they should not understand it, and they were afraid to ask him about this saying.

Sunday September 28, 2025
Twenty-sixth Sunday in Ordinary Time, Year C

First Reading: Amos 6:1A, 4-7
Thus says the LORD, the God of hosts:

1A Woe to the complacent in Zion!
4 Lying upon beds of ivory,
    stretched comfortably on their couches,
they eat lambs taken from the flock,
    and calves from the stall!
5 Improvising to the music of the harp,
    like David, they devise their own
        accompaniment.
6 They drink wine from bowls
    and anoint themselves with the best oils;
    yet they are not made ill by the collapse

of Joseph!
⁷Therefore, now they shall be the first to go
    into exile,
and their wanton revelry shall be done
    away with.

Responsorial Psalm: Psalms 146:7, 8-9, 9-10
R. ⁽¹ᵇ⁾ Praise the Lord, my soul! or: *R. Alleluia.*
⁷Blessed he who keeps faith forever,
    secures justice for the oppressed,
    gives food to the hungry.
The LORD sets captives free.
R. Praise the Lord, my soul! or: *R. Alleluia.*
⁸The LORD gives sight to the blind;
    the LORD raises up those who were bowed
        down.
The LORD loves the just;
    ⁹ᴬ the LORD protects strangers.
R. Praise the Lord, my soul! or: *R. Alleluia.*
⁹ᴮ The fatherless and the widow he sustains,
    but the way of the wicked he thwarts.
¹⁰ The LORD shall reign forever;
    your God, O Zion, through all
        generations. Alleluia.
R. Praise the Lord, my soul! or: *R. Alleluia.*

Second Reading: 1 Timothy 6:11-16
¹¹But you, man of God, pursue righteousness, devotion, faith, love, patience, and gentleness. ¹²Compete well for the faith. Lay hold of eternal life, to which you were called when you made the noble confession in the presence of many witnesses. ¹³I charge you before God, who gives life to all things, and before Christ Jesus, who gave testimony under Pontius Pilate for the noble confession, ¹⁴to keep the commandment without stain or reproach until the appearance of our Lord Jesus Christ ¹⁵that the blessed and only ruler will make manifest at the proper time, the King of kings and Lord of lords, ¹⁶who alone has immortality, who dwells in unapproachable light, and whom no human being has seen or can see. To him be honor and eternal power. Amen.

Alleluia: 2 Corinthians 8:9
R. Alleluia, alleluia.
⁹Though our Lord Jesus Christ was rich, he
    became poor,
so that by his poverty you might become
    rich.
R. Alleluia, alleluia.

Gospel: Luke 16:19-31

Jesus said to the Pharisees: [19]"There was a rich man who dressed in purple garments and fine linen and dined sumptuously each day. [20]And lying at his door was a poor man named Lazarus, covered with sores, [21]who would gladly have eaten his fill of the scraps that fell from the rich man's table. Dogs even used to come and lick his sores. [22]When the poor man died, he was carried away by angels to the bosom of Abraham. The rich man also died and was buried, [23]and from the netherworld, where he was in torment, he raised his eyes and saw Abraham far off and Lazarus at his side. [24]And he cried out, 'Father Abraham, have pity on me. Send Lazarus to dip the tip of his finger in water and cool my tongue, for I am suffering torment in these flames.' [25]Abraham replied, 'My child, remember that you received what was good during your lifetime while Lazarus likewise received what was bad; but now he is comforted here, whereas you are tormented. [26]Moreover, between us and you a great chasm is established to prevent anyone from crossing who might wish to go from our side to yours or from your side to ours.' [27]He said, 'Then I beg you, father, send him to my father's house, [28]for I have five brothers, so that he may warn them, lest they too come to this place of torment.' [29]But Abraham replied, 'They have Moses and the prophets. Let them listen to them.' [30]He said, 'Oh no, father Abraham, but if someone from the dead goes to them, they will repent.' [31]Then Abraham said, 'If they will not listen to Moses and the prophets, neither will they be persuaded if someone should rise from the dead.'"

Monday September 29, 2025
Feast of Saints Michael. Gabriel, and Raphael, Archangels
First Reading: Daniel 7:9-10, 13-14

[9]As I watched:

Thrones were set up
    and the Ancient One took his throne.
His clothing was bright as snow,
    and the hair on his head as white as
        wool;
His throne was flames of fire,
    with wheels of burning fire.
[10]A surging stream of fire
    flowed out from where he sat;
Thousands upon thousands were
        ministering to him,
    and myriads upon myriads attended
        him.

The court was convened, and the books were opened.
    [13]As the visions during the night continued, I saw

One like a son of man coming,
>> on the clouds of heaven;
When he reached the Ancient One
>> and was presented before him,
¹⁴He received dominion, glory, and
>> kingship;
>> nations and peoples of every
>> >> language serve him.
His dominion is an everlasting dominion
>> that shall not be taken away,
>> his kingship shall not be destroyed.

Or Revelation 12:7-12AB

⁷War broke out in heaven; Michael and his angels battled against the dragon. The dragon and its angels fought back, ⁸but they did not prevail and there was no longer any place for them in heaven. ⁹The huge dragon, the ancient serpent, who is called the Devil and Satan, who deceived the whole world, was thrown down to earth, and its angels were thrown down with it.
>> ¹⁰Then I heard a loud voice in heaven say:

"Now have salvation and power come,
>> and the Kingdom of our God
>> and the authority of his Anointed.
For the accuser of our brothers is cast
>> out,
>> who accuses them before our God
>> >> day and night.
¹¹They conquered him by the Blood of the
>> Lamb
>> and by the word of their testimony;
>> love for life did not deter them from
>> >> death.
¹²ᴬᴮTherefore, rejoice, you heavens,
>> and you who dwell in them."

Responsorial Psalm: Psalms 138:1-2AB, 2CDE-3, 4-5
R. ⁽¹⁾ *In the sight of the angels I will sing your praises, Lord.*

¹I will give thanks to you, O LORD, with all my
>> heart,
>> for you have heard the words of my
>> >> mouth;
>> in the presence of the angels I will sing
>> >> your praise;

²ᴬᴮI will worship at your holy temple
and give thanks to your name.
R. In the sight of the angels I will sing your praises, Lord.
²ᶜᴰᴱ Because of your kindness and your truth;
for you have made great above all things
your name and your promise.
³When I called, you answered me;
you built up strength within me.
R. In the sight of the angels I will sing your praises, Lord.
⁴All the kings of the earth shall give thanks to you, O LORD,
when they hear the words of your mouth;
⁵And they shall sing of the ways of the LORD:
"Great is the glory of the LORD."
R. In the sight of the angels I will sing your praises, Lord.

Alleluia: Psalms 103:21
R. Alleluia, alleluia.
²¹Bless the LORD, all you angels,
you ministers, who do his will.
R. Alleluia, alleluia.

Gospel: John 1:47-51
⁴⁷Jesus saw Nathanael coming toward him and said of him, "Here is a true child of Israel. There is no duplicity in him." ⁴⁸Nathanael said to him, "How do you know me?" Jesus answered and said to him, "Before Philip called you, I saw you under the fig tree." ⁴⁹Nathanael answered him, "Rabbi, you are the Son of God; you are the King of Israel." ⁵⁰Jesus answered and said to him, "Do you believe because I told you that I saw you under the fig tree? You will see greater things than this." ⁵¹And he said to him, "Amen, amen, I say to you, you will see heaven opened and the angels of God ascending and descending on the Son of Man."

Tuesday September 30, 2025
Memorial of Saint Jerome, Priest & Doctor
First Reading: Zechariah 8:20-23
²⁰Thus says the LORD of hosts: There shall yet come peoples, the inhabitants of many cities; ²¹and the inhabitants of one city shall approach those of another, and say, "Come! let us go to implore the favor of the LORD"; and, "I too will go to seek the LORD." ²²Many peoples and strong nations shall come to seek the LORD of hosts in Jerusalem and to implore the favor of the LORD. ²³Thus says the LORD of hosts: In those days ten men of every nationality, speaking different tongues, shall take hold, yes, take hold of every Jew by the edge of his garment and say,

"Let us go with you, for we have heard that God is with you."

Responsorial Psalm: Psalms 87:1B-3,4-5, 6-7
R. *(Zechariah 8:23)* **God is with us.**
¹ᴮHis foundation upon the holy mountains
 the LORD loves:
²The gates of Zion,
 more than any dwelling of Jacob.
³ Glorious things are said of you,
 O city of God!
R. God is with us.
⁴ I tell of Egypt and Babylon
 among those that know the LORD;
Of Philistia, Tyre, Ethiopia:
 "This man was born there."
⁵ And of Zion they shall say:
 "One and all were born in her;
And he who has established her
 is the Most High LORD."
R. God is with us.
⁶ They shall note, when the peoples are
 enrolled:
 "This man was born there."
⁷ And all shall sing, in their festive dance:
 "My home is within you."
R. God is with us.

Alleluia: Mark 10:45
R. Alleluia, alleluia.
⁴⁵ The Son of Man came to serve
and to give his life as a ransom for many.
R. Alleluia, alleluia.

Gospel: Luke 9:51-56
⁵¹ When the days for Jesus to be taken up were fulfilled, he resolutely determined to journey to Jerusalem, ⁵² and he sent messengers ahead of him. On the way they entered a Samaritan village to prepare for his reception there, ⁵³ but they would not welcome him because the destination of his journey was Jerusalem. ⁵⁴ When the disciples James and John saw this they asked, "Lord, do you want us to call down fire from heaven to consume them?" ⁵⁵ Jesus turned and rebuked them, and they journeyed to another village.

OCTOBER 2025
Wednesday October 1, 2025
Memorial of Saint Therese of the Child Jesus, Virgin & Doctor

First Reading: Nehemiah 2:1-8

¹In the month Nisan of the twentieth year of King Artaxerxes, when the wine was in my charge, I took some and offered it to the king. As I had never before been sad in his presence, ²the king asked me, "Why do you look sad? If you are not sick, you must be sad at heart." Though I was seized with great fear, ³I answered the king: "May the king live forever! How could I not look sad when the city where my ancestors are buried lies in ruins, and its gates have been eaten out by fire?" ⁴The king asked me, "What is it, then, that you wish?" I prayed to the God of heaven ⁵and then answered the king: "If it please the king, and if your servant is deserving of your favor, send me to Judah, to the city of my ancestors' graves, to rebuild it." ⁶Then the king, and the queen seated beside him, asked me how long my journey would take and when I would return. I set a date that was acceptable to him, and the king agreed that I might go.

⁷I asked the king further: "If it please the king, let letters be given to me for the governors of West-of-Euphrates, that they may afford me safe-conduct until I arrive in Judah; ⁸also a letter for Asaph, the keeper of the royal park, that he may give me wood for timbering the gates of the temple-citadel and for the city wall and the house that I shall occupy." The king granted my requests, for the favoring hand of my God was upon me.

Responsorial Psalm: Psalms 137:1-2,3, 4-5, 6

R. *(6ab)* ***Let my tongue be silenced if I ever forget you!***

¹ By the streams of Babylon
   we sat and wept
   when we remembered Zion.
² On the aspens of that land
   we hung up our harps.

R. *Let my tongue be silenced if I ever forget you!*

³ Though there our captors asked of us
   the lyrics of our songs,
And our despoilers urged us to be joyous:
   "Sing for us the songs of Zion!"

R. *Let my tongue be silenced if I ever forget you!*

⁴ How could we sing a song of the LORD
   in a foreign land?
⁵ If I forget you, Jerusalem,
   may my right hand be forgotten!

R. *Let my tongue be silenced if I ever forget you!*

⁶ May my tongue cleave to my palate
   if I remember you not,
If I place not Jerusalem
   ahead of my joy.

R. *Let my tongue be silenced if I ever forget you!*

Alleluia: Philippians 3:8-9
R. Alleluia, alleluia.
⁸I consider all things so much rubbish
⁹that I may gain Christ and be found in him.
R. Alleluia, alleluia.

Gospel: Luke 9:57-62
⁵⁷As Jesus and his disciples were proceeding on their journey, someone said to him, "I will follow you wherever you go." ⁵⁸Jesus answered him, "Foxes have dens and birds of the sky have nests, but the Son of Man has nowhere to rest his head." ⁵⁹And to another he said, "Follow me." But he replied, "Lord, let me go first and bury my father." ⁶⁰But he answered him, "Let the dead bury their dead. But you, go and proclaim the Kingdom of God." ⁶¹And another said, "I will follow you, Lord, but first let me say farewell to my family at home." ⁶²Jesus answered him, "No one who sets a hand to the plow and looks to what was left behind is fit for the Kingdom of God."

Thursday October 2, 2025
Memorial of the Holy Guardian Angels
First Reading: Nehemiah 8:1-4A, 5-6, 7B-12

¹The whole people gathered as one in the open space before the Water Gate, and they called upon Ezra the scribe to bring forth the book of the law of Moses which the LORD prescribed for Israel. ²On the first day of the seventh month, therefore, Ezra the priest brought the law before the assembly, which consisted of men, women, and those children old enough to understand. ³Standing at one end of the open place that was before the Water Gate, he read out of the book from daybreak until midday, in the presence of the men, the women, and those children old enough to understand; and all the people listened attentively to the book of the law. ⁴ᴬEzra the scribe stood on a wooden platform that had been made for the occasion. ⁵He opened the scroll so that all the people might see it (for he was standing higher up than any of the people); and, as he opened it, all the people rose. ⁶Ezra blessed the LORD, the great God, and all the people, their hands raised high, answered, "Amen, amen!" Then they bowed down and prostrated themselves before the LORD, their faces to the ground. ⁷ᴮAs the people remained in their places, ⁸Ezra read plainly from the book of the law of God, interpreting it so that all could understand what was read. ⁹Then Nehemiah, that is, His Excellency, and Ezra the priest-scribe and the Levites who were instructing the people said to all the people: "Today is holy to the LORD your God. Do not be sad, and do not weep"– for all the people were weeping as they heard the words of the law. ¹⁰He said further: "Go, eat rich foods and drink sweet drinks, and allot portions to those who had nothing prepared; for today is holy to our LORD. Do not be saddened this day, for rejoicing in the LORD must be your strength!" ¹¹And the Levites quieted all the people, saying, "Hush, for today is holy, and you must not be saddened." ¹²Then all the people went to eat and drink, to distribute portions, and to celebrate with great joy, for they understood the words that had been expounded to them.

Responsorial Psalm: Psalms 19:8, 9, 10, 11
R. (9ab) The precepts of the Lord give joy to the heart.
⁸ The law of the LORD is perfect,
    refreshing the soul;
The decree of the LORD is trustworthy,
    giving wisdom to the simple.
R. The precepts of the Lord give joy to the heart.
⁹ The precepts of the LORD are right,
    rejoicing the heart;
The command of the LORD is clear,
    enlightening the eye;
R. The precepts of the Lord give joy to the heart.
¹⁰ The fear of the LORD is pure,
    enduring forever;
The ordinances of the LORD are true,
    all of them just.
R. The precepts of the Lord give joy to the heart.
¹¹ They are more precious than gold,
    than a heap of purest gold;
Sweeter also than syrup
    or honey from the comb.
R. The precepts of the Lord give joy to the heart.

Alleluia: Mark 1:15
R. Alleluia, alleluia.
¹⁵ The Kingdom of God is at hand;
repent and believe in the Gospel.
R. Alleluia, alleluia.

Gospel: Luke 10:1-12
¹ Jesus appointed seventy-two other disciples whom he sent ahead of him in pairs to every town and place he intended to visit. ² He said to them, "The harvest is abundant but the laborers are few; so ask the master of the harvest to send out laborers for his harvest. ³ Go on your way; behold, I am sending you like lambs among wolves. ⁴ Carry no money bag, no sack, no sandals; and greet no one along the way. ⁵ Into whatever house you enter, first say, 'Peace to this household.' ⁶ If a peaceful person lives there, your peace will rest on him; but if not, it will return to you. ⁷ Stay in the same house and eat and drink what is offered to you, for the laborer deserves his payment. Do not move about from one house to another. ⁸ Whatever town you enter and they welcome you, eat what is set before you, ⁹ cure the sick in it and say to them, 'The Kingdom of God is at hand for you.' ¹⁰ Whatever town you enter and they do not receive you, go out into the streets and say, ¹¹ 'The dust of your town that clings to our feet, even that we shake off against you.' Yet know this: the Kingdom of God is at hand. ¹² I tell you, it will be more tolerable for Sodom on that day than for that town."

Friday October 3, 2025
Friday of the Twenty-sixth Week in Ordinary Time

First Reading: Baruch 1:15-22

During the Babylonian captivity, the exiles prayed: [15]"Justice is with the Lord, our God; and we today are flushed with shame, we men of Judah and citizens of Jerusalem,[16]that we, with our kings and rulers and priests and prophets, and with our ancestors, [17]have sinned in the Lord's sight [18]and disobeyed him. We have neither heeded the voice of the Lord, our God, nor followed the precepts which the Lord set before us. [19]From the time the Lord led our ancestors out of the land of Egypt until the present day, we have been disobedient to the Lord, our God, and only too ready to disregard his voice. [20]And the evils and the curse that the Lord enjoined upon Moses, his servant, at the time he led our ancestors forth from the land of Egypt to give us the land flowing with milk and honey, cling to us even today. [21]For we did not heed the voice of the Lord, our God, in all the words of the prophets whom he sent us, [22]but each one of us went off after the devices of his own wicked heart, served other gods, and did evil in the sight of the Lord, our God."

Responsorial Psalm: Psalms 79:1B-2,3-5, 8, 9

R. [9] *For the glory of your name, O Lord, deliver us.*

[1B]O God, the nations have come into your
  inheritance;
    they have defiled your holy temple,
    they have laid Jerusalem in ruins.
[2]They have given the corpses of your servants
    as food to the birds of heaven,
    the flesh of your faithful ones to the
      beasts of the earth.

R. For the glory of your name, O Lord, deliver us.

[3]They have poured out their blood like water
    round about Jerusalem,
    and there is no one to bury them.
[4] We have become the reproach of our
      neighbors,
    the scorn and derision of those around
      us.
[5] O LORD, how long? Will you be angry
      forever?
    Will your jealousy burn like fire?

R. For the glory of your name, O Lord, deliver us.

[8] Remember not against us the iniquities of
      the past;
    may your compassion quickly come to us,
    for we are brought very low.

R. For the glory of your name, O Lord, deliver us.

[9] Help us, O God our savior,

because of the glory of your name;
Deliver us and pardon our sins
>   for your name's sake.
R. For the glory of your name, O Lord, deliver us.

Alleluia: Psalms 95:8
R. Alleluia, alleluia.
8 If today you hear his voice,
harden not your hearts.
R. Alleluia, alleluia.

Gospel: Luke 10:13-16
Jesus said to them, 13 "Woe to you, Chorazin! Woe to you, Bethsaida! For if the mighty deeds done in your midst had been done in Tyre and Sidon, they would long ago have repented, sitting in sackcloth and ashes. 14 But it will be more tolerable for Tyre and Sidon at the judgment than for you. 15 And as for you, Capernaum, 'Will you be exalted to heaven? You will go down to the netherworld.' 16 Whoever listens to you listens to me. Whoever rejects you rejects me. And whoever rejects me rejects the one who sent me."

Saturday October 4, 2025
Memorial of Saint Francis of Assisi
First Reading: Baruch 4:5-12, 27-29
5 Fear not, my people!
>   Remember, Israel,
6 You were sold to the nations
>   not for your destruction;
It was because you angered God
>   that you were handed over to your foes.
7 For you provoked your Maker
>   with sacrifices to demons, to no-gods;
8 You forsook the Eternal God who nourished you,
>   and you grieved Jerusalem who fostered you.
9 She indeed saw coming upon you
>   the anger of God; and she said:

"Hear, you neighbors of Zion!
>   God has brought great mourning upon me,
10 For I have seen the captivity
>   that the Eternal God has brought
>   upon my sons and daughters.
11 With joy I fostered them;
>   but with mourning and lament I let them

go.
¹²Let no one gloat over me, a widow,
    bereft of many:
For the sins of my children I am left desolate,
    because they turned from the law of God.

²⁷"Fear not, my children; call out to God!
    He who brought this upon you will
        remember you.
²⁸As your hearts have been disposed to stray
        from God,
    turn now ten times the more to seek him;
²⁹For he who has brought disaster upon you
    will, in saving you, bring you back
        enduring joy."

Responsorial Psalm: Psalms 69:33-35, 36-37
R. ⁽³⁴⁾ The Lord listens to the poor.
³³ "See, you lowly ones, and be glad;
    you who seek God, may your hearts
        revive!
³⁴ For the LORD hears the poor,
    and his own who are in bonds he spurns
        not.
³⁵ Let the heavens and the earth praise him,
    the seas and whatever moves in them!"
R. The Lord listens to the poor.
³⁶ For God will save Zion
    and rebuild the cities of Judah.
³⁷ They shall dwell in the land and own it,
    and the descendants of his servants shall
        inherit it,
    and those who love his name shall
        inhabit it.
R. The Lord listens to the poor.

Alleluia: cf. Matthew 11:25
R. Alleluia, alleluia.
²⁵ Blessed are you, Father, Lord of heaven and
        earth,
you have revealed to little ones the
        mysteries of the Kingdom.
R. Alleluia, alleluia.

Gospel: Luke 10:17-24

[17] The seventy-two disciples returned rejoicing and said to Jesus, "Lord, even the demons are subject to us because of your name." [18] Jesus said, "I have observed Satan fall like lightning from the sky. [19] Behold, I have given you the power 'to tread upon serpents' and scorpions and upon the full force of the enemy and nothing will harm you. [20] Nevertheless, do not rejoice because the spirits are subject to you, but rejoice because your names are written in heaven."

[21] At that very moment he rejoiced in the Holy Spirit and said, "I give you praise, Father, Lord of heaven and earth, for although you have hidden these things from the wise and the learned you have revealed them to the childlike. Yes, Father, such has been your gracious will. [22] All things have been handed over to me by my Father. No one knows who the Son is except the Father, and who the Father is except the Son and anyone to whom the Son wishes to reveal him."

[23] Turning to the disciples in private he said, "Blessed are the eyes that see what you see. [24] For I say to you, many prophets and kings desired to see what you see, but did not see it, and to hear what you hear, but did not hear it."

Sunday October 5, 2025
Twenty-seventh Sunday in Ordinary Time, Year C

First Reading: Habakkuk 1:2-3; 2:2-4

[2] How long, O LORD? I cry for help
  but you do not listen!
I cry out to you, "Violence!"
  but you do not intervene.
[3] Why do you let me see ruin;
  why must I look at misery?
Destruction and violence are before me;
  there is strife, and clamorous discord.
[2] Then the LORD answered me and said:
  Write down the vision clearly upon the
    tablets,
  so that one can read it readily.
[3] For the vision still has its time,
  presses on to fulfillment, and will not
    disappoint;
if it delays, wait for it,
  it will surely come, it will not be late.
[4] The rash one has no integrity;
  but the just one, because of his faith, shall
    live.

Responsorial Psalm: Psalms 95:1-2, 6-7, 8-9

R. [(8)] *If today you hear his voice, harden not your hearts.*

[1] Come, let us sing joyfully to the LORD;

    let us acclaim the Rock of our salvation.
² Let us come into his presence with
        thanksgiving;
    let us joyfully sing psalms to him.
R. If today you hear his voice, harden not your hearts.
⁶ Come, let us bow down in worship;
    let us kneel before the LORD who made us.
⁷ For he is our God,
    and we are the people he shepherds, the
        flock he guides.
R. If today you hear his voice, harden not your hearts.
⁸ Oh, that today you would hear his voice:
    "Harden not your hearts as at Meribah,
    as in the day of Massah in the desert,
⁹ Where your fathers tempted me;
    they tested me though they had seen my
        works."
R. If today you hear his voice, harden not your hearts.

Second Reading: 2 Timothy 1:6-8, 13-14
Beloved: ⁶I remind you, to stir into flame the gift of God that you have through the imposition of my hands. ⁷For God did not give us a spirit of cowardice but rather of power and love and self-control. ⁸So do not be ashamed of your testimony to our Lord, nor of me, a prisoner for his sake; but bear your share of hardship for the gospel with the strength that comes from God.
    ¹³Take as your norm the sound words that you heard from me, in the faith and love that are in Christ Jesus. ¹⁴Guard this rich trust with the help of the Holy Spirit that dwells within us.

Alleluia: 1 Peter 1:25
R. Alleluia, alleluia.
²⁵The word of the Lord remains for ever.
This is the word that has been proclaimed to you.
R. Alleluia, alleluia.

Gospel: Luke 17:5-10
⁵The apostles said to the Lord, "Increase our faith." ⁶The Lord replied, "If you have faith the size of a mustard seed, you would say to this mulberry tree, 'Be uprooted and planted in the sea,' and it would obey you.
    ⁷"Who among you would say to your servant who has just come in from plowing or tending sheep in the field, 'Come here immediately and take your place

at table'? ⁸Would he not rather say to him, 'Prepare something for me to eat. Put on your apron and wait on me while I eat and drink. You may eat and drink when I am finished'? ⁹Is he grateful to that servant because he did what was commanded? ¹⁰So should it be with you. When you have done all you have been commanded, say, 'We are unprofitable servants; we have done what we were obliged to do.'"

Monday October 6, 2025
Monday of Twenty-seventh Week in Ordinary Time
First Reading: Jonah 1:1-2:1-2, 11

¹This is the word of the LORD that came to Jonah, son of Amittai:

²"Set out for the great city of Nineveh, and preach against it; their wickedness has come up before me." ³But Jonah made ready to flee to Tarshish away from the LORD. He went down to Joppa, found a ship going to Tarshish, paid the fare, and went aboard to journey with them to Tarshish, away from the LORD.

⁴The LORD, however, hurled a violent wind upon the sea, and in the furious tempest that arose the ship was on the point of breaking up. ⁵Then the mariners became frightened and each one cried to his god. To lighten the ship for themselves, they threw its cargo into the sea. Meanwhile, Jonah had gone down into the hold of the ship, and lay there fast asleep. ⁶The captain came to him and said, "What are you doing asleep? Rise up, call upon your God! Perhaps God will be mindful of us so that we may not perish."

⁷Then they said to one another, "Come, let us cast lots to find out on whose account we have met with this misfortune." So they cast lots, and thus singled out Jonah. ⁸"Tell us," they said, "what is your business? Where do you come from? What is your country, and to what people do you belong?" ⁹Jonah answered them, "I am a Hebrew, I worship the LORD, the God of heaven, who made the sea and the dry land."

¹⁰Now the men were seized with great fear and said to him, "How could you do such a thing!— They knew that he was fleeing from the LORD, because he had told them.— ¹¹They asked, "What shall we do with you, that the sea may quiet down for us?" For the sea was growing more and more turbulent. ¹²Jonah said to them, "Pick me up and throw me into the sea, that it may quiet down for you; since I know it is because of me that this violent storm has come upon you."

¹³Still the men rowed hard to regain the land, but they could not, for the sea grew ever more turbulent. ¹⁴Then they cried to the LORD: "We beseech you, O LORD, let us not perish for taking this man's life; do not charge us with shedding innocent blood, for you, LORD, have done as you saw fit." ¹⁵Then they took Jonah and threw him into the sea, and the sea's raging abated. Struck with great fear of the LORD, the men offered sacrifice and made vows to him.

¹But the LORD sent a large fish, that swallowed Jonah; and Jonah remained in the belly of the fish three days and three nights. ²From the belly of the fish Jonah prayed to the LORD, his God. ¹¹Then the LORD commanded the fish to spew Jonah upon the shore.

Responsorial Psalm: Jonah 2:3, 4, 5, 8
R. (cf. 7) **You will rescue my life from the pit, O Lord.**
³ Out of my distress I called to the LORD,

and he answered me;
From the midst of the nether world I cried
for help,
and you heard my voice.
R. You will rescue my life from the pit, O Lord.
⁴ For you cast me into the deep, into the heart
of the sea,
and the flood enveloped me;
All your breakers and your billows
passed over me.
R. You will rescue my life from the pit, O Lord.
⁵ Then I said, "I am banished from your sight!
yet would I again look upon your holy
temple."
R. You will rescue my life from the pit, O Lord.
⁸ When my soul fainted within me,
I remembered the LORD;
My prayer reached you
in your holy temple.
R. You will rescue my life from the pit, O Lord.

Alleluia: John 13:34
R. Alleluia, alleluia.
³⁴ I give you a new commandment:
love one another as I have loved you.
R. Alleluia, alleluia.

Gospel: Luke 10:25-37
²⁵ There was a scholar of the law who stood up to test Jesus and said, "Teacher, what must I do to inherit eternal life?" ²⁶ Jesus said to him, "What is written in the law? How do you read it?" ²⁷ He said in reply, "You shall love the Lord, your God, with all your heart, with all your being, with all your strength, and with all your mind, and your neighbor as yourself." ²⁸ He replied to him, "You have answered correctly; do this and you will live."

²⁹ But because he wished to justify himself, he said to Jesus, "And who is my neighbor?" ³⁰ Jesus replied, "A man fell victim to robbers as he went down from Jerusalem to Jericho. They stripped and beat him and went off leaving him half-dead. ³¹ A priest happened to be going down that road, but when he saw him, he passed by on the opposite side. ³² Likewise a Levite came to the place, and when he saw him, he passed by on the opposite side. ³³ But a Samaritan traveler who came upon him was moved with compassion at the sight. ³⁴ He approached the victim, poured oil and wine over his wounds and bandaged them. Then he lifted him up on his own animal, took him to an inn, and cared for him. ³⁵ The next day he took out two silver coins and gave them to the innkeeper with the instruction, 'Take

cáre of him. If you spend more than what I have given you, I shall repay you on my way back.' ³⁶ Which of these three, in your opinion, was neighbor to the robbers' victim?" ³⁷ He answered, "The one who treated him with mercy." Jesus said to him, "Go and do likewise."

Tuesday October 7, 2025
Memorial of Our Lady of the Rosary
First Reading: Jonah 3:1-10

¹The word of the LORD came to Jonah a second time: ²"Set out for the great city of Nineveh, and announce to it the message that I will tell you." ³So Jonah made ready and went to Nineveh, according to the LORD's bidding. Now Nineveh was an enormously large city; it took three days to go through it. ⁴Jonah began his journey through the city, and had gone but a single day's walk announcing, "Forty days more and Nineveh shall be destroyed," ⁵when the people of Nineveh believed God; they proclaimed a fast and all of them, great and small, put on sackcloth.

⁶When the news reached the king of Nineveh, he rose from his throne, laid aside his robe, covered himself with sackcloth, and sat in the ashes. ⁷Then he had this proclaimed throughout Nineveh, by decree of the king and his nobles: "Neither man nor beast, neither cattle nor sheep, shall taste anything; they shall not eat, nor shall they drink water. ⁸Man and beast shall be covered with sackcloth and call loudly to God; every man shall turn from his evil way and from the violence he has in hand. ⁹Who knows, God may relent and forgive, and withhold his blazing wrath, so that we shall not perish." ¹⁰When God saw by their actions how they turned from their evil way, he repented of the evil that he had threatened to do to them; he did not carry it out.

Responsorial Psalm: Psalms 130:1B-2, 3-4AB, 7-8

R. ⁽³⁾ If you, O Lord, mark iniquities, who can stand?

¹ᴮ Out of the depths I cry to you, O LORD;
   LORD, hear my voice!
² Let your ears be attentive
   to my voice in supplication.

R. If you, O Lord, mark iniquities, who can stand?

³ If you, O LORD, mark iniquities,
   LORD, who can stand?
⁴ᴬᴮ But with you is forgiveness,
   that you may be revered.

R. If you, O Lord, mark iniquities, who can stand?

⁷ Let Israel wait for the LORD,
For with the LORD is kindness
   and with him is plenteous redemption;
⁸ And he will redeem Israel
   from all their iniquities.

R. If you, O Lord, mark iniquities, who can stand?

Alleluia: Luke 11:28
R. Alleluia, alleluia.
28 Blessed are those who hear the word of God and observe it.
R. Alleluia, alleluia.

Gospel: Luke 10:38-42
38 Jesus entered a village where a woman whose name was Martha welcomed him. 39 She had a sister named Mary who sat beside the Lord at his feet listening to him speak. 40 Martha, burdened with much serving, came to him and said, "Lord, do you not care that my sister has left me by myself to do the serving? Tell her to help me." 41 The Lord said to her in reply, "Martha, Martha, you are anxious and worried about many things. 42 There is need of only one thing. Mary has chosen the better part and it will not be taken from her."

Wednesday October 8, 2025
Wednesday of the Twenty-seventh Week in Ordinary Time
First Reading: Jonah 4:1-11
1 Jonah was greatly displeased and became angry that God did not carry out the evil he threatened against Nineveh. 2 He prayed, "I beseech you, LORD, is not this what I said while I was still in my own country? This is why I fled at first to Tarshish. I knew that you are a gracious and merciful God, slow to anger, rich in clemency, loath to punish. 3 And now, LORD, please take my life from me; for it is better for me to die than to live." 4 But the LORD asked, "Have you reason to be angry?"

5 Jonah then left the city for a place to the east of it, where he built himself a hut and waited under it in the shade, to see what would happen to the city. 6 And when the LORD God provided a gourd plant that grew up over Jonah's head, giving shade that relieved him of any discomfort, Jonah was very happy over the plant. 7 But the next morning at dawn God sent a worm that attacked the plant, so that it withered. 8 And when the sun arose, God sent a burning east wind; and the sun beat upon Jonah's head till he became faint. Then Jonah asked for death, saying, "I would be better off dead than alive."

9 But God said to Jonah, "Have you reason to be angry over the plant?" "I have reason to be angry," Jonah answered, "angry enough to die." 10 Then the LORD said, "You are concerned over the plant which cost you no labor and which you did not raise; it came up in one night and in one night it perished. 11 And should I not be concerned over Nineveh, the great city, in which there are more than a hundred and twenty thousand persons who cannot distinguish their right hand from their left, not to mention the many cattle?"

Responsorial Psalm: Psalms 86:3-4, 5-6, 9-10
R. (15) Lord, you are merciful and gracious.
3 Have mercy on me, O Lord,

for to you I call all the day.
⁴ Gladden the soul of your servant,
for to you, O Lord, I lift up my soul.
R. Lord, you are merciful and gracious.
⁵ For you, O Lord, are good and forgiving,
abounding in kindness to all who call
upon you.
⁶ Hearken, O LORD, to my prayer
and attend to the sound of my pleading.
R. Lord, you are merciful and gracious.
⁹ All the nations you have made shall come
and worship you, O Lord,
and glorify your name.
¹⁰ For you are great, and you do wondrous
deeds;
you alone are God.
R. Lord, you are merciful and gracious.

Alleluia: Romans 8:15BC
R. Alleluia, alleluia.
¹⁵ᴮᶜ You have received a spirit of adoption as
sons
through which we cry: Abba! Father!
R. Alleluia, alleluia.

Gospel: Luke 11:1-4
¹ Jesus was praying in a certain place, and when he had finished, one of his disciples said to him, "Lord, teach us to pray just as John taught his disciples." ² He said to them, "When you pray, say:

Father, hallowed be your name,
your Kingdom come.
³ Give us each day our daily bread
⁴ and forgive us our sins
for we ourselves forgive everyone in debt
to us,
and do not subject us to the final test."

Thursday October 9, 2025
Thursday of the Twenty-seventh Week in Ordinary Time
First Reading: Malachi 3:13-20B
¹³You have defied me in word, says the LORD,
yet you ask, "What have we spoken
against you?"
¹⁴You have said, "It is vain to serve God,

and what do we profit by keeping his command,
And going about in penitential dress
in awe of the LORD of hosts?
¹⁵Rather must we call the proud blessed;
for indeed evildoers prosper,
and even tempt God with impunity."
¹⁶Then they who fear the LORD spoke with one another,
and the LORD listened attentively;
And a record book was written before him
of those who fear the LORD and trust in his name.
¹⁷And they shall be mine, says the LORD of hosts,
my own special possession, on the day I take action.
And I will have compassion on them,
as a man has compassion on his son who serves him.
¹⁸Then you will again see the distinction
between the just and the wicked;
Between the one who serves God,
and the one who does not serve him.
¹⁹For lo, the day is coming, blazing like an oven,
when all the proud and all evildoers will be stubble,
And the day that is coming will set them on fire,
leaving them neither root nor branch,
says the LORD of hosts.
²⁰ᴬᴮBut for you who fear my name, there will arise
the sun of justice with its healing rays.

Responsorial Psalm: Psalms 1:1-2,3, 4 AND 6
R. *(Ps 40:5a)* ***Blessed are they who hope in the Lord.***
¹ Blessed the man who follows not
the counsel of the wicked
Nor walks in the way of sinners,
nor sits in the company of the insolent,
² But delights in the law of the LORD
and meditates on his law day and night.
R. Blessed are they who hope in the Lord.

³ He is like a tree
>   planted near running water,
That yields its fruit in due season,
>   and whose leaves never fade.
>   Whatever he does, prospers.

R. Blessed are they who hope in the Lord.

⁴ Not so the wicked, not so;
>   they are like chaff which the wind drives
>   away.

⁶ For the LORD watches over the way of the
>   just,
>   but the way of the wicked vanishes.

R. Blessed are they who hope in the Lord.

Alleluia: cf. Acts 16:14B
R. Alleluia, alleluia.
¹⁴ᴮ Open our hearts, O Lord,
to listen to the words of your Son.
R. Alleluia, alleluia.

Gospel: Luke 11:5-13

Jesus said to his disciples: ⁵ "Suppose one of you has a friend to whom he goes at midnight and says, 'Friend, lend me three loaves of bread, ⁶ for a friend of mine has arrived at my house from a journey and I have nothing to offer him,' ⁷ and he says in reply from within, 'Do not bother me; the door has already been locked and my children and I are already in bed. I cannot get up to give you anything.' ⁸ I tell you, if he does not get up to give him the loaves because of their friendship, he will get up to give him whatever he needs because of his persistence.

⁹ "And I tell you, ask and you will receive; seek and you will find; knock and the door will be opened to you. ¹⁰ For everyone who asks, receives; and the one who seeks, finds; and to the one who knocks, the door will be opened. ¹¹ What father among you would hand his son a snake when he asks for a fish? ¹² Or hand him a scorpion when he asks for an egg? ¹³ If you then, who are wicked, know how to give good gifts to your children, how much more will the Father in heaven give the Holy Spirit to those who ask him?"

Friday October 10, 2025
Friday of the Twenty-seventh Week in Ordinary Time

First Reading: Joel 1:13-15; 2:1-2

¹³Gird yourselves and weep, O priests!
>   wail, O ministers of the altar!
Come, spend the night in sackcloth,
>   O ministers of my God!
The house of your God is deprived
>   of offering and libation.
¹⁴Proclaim a fast,

        call an assembly;
Gather the elders,
        all who dwell in the land,
Into the house of the LORD, your God,
        and cry to the LORD!

15Alas, the day!
        for near is the day of the LORD,
        and it comes as ruin from the Almighty.

1Blow the trumpet in Zion,
        sound the alarm on my holy mountain!
Let all who dwell in the land tremble,
        for the day of the LORD is coming;
Yes, it is near, a day of darkness and of
            gloom,
    2a day of clouds and somberness!
Like dawn spreading over the mountains,
        a people numerous and mighty!
Their like has not been from of old,
        nor will it be after them,
        even to the years of distant generations.

Responsorial Psalm: Psalms 9:2-3, 6 AND 16, 8-9
R. (9) The Lord will judge the world with justice.
2 I will give thanks to you, O LORD, with all my
        heart;
        I will declare all your wondrous deeds.
3 I will be glad and exult in you;
        I will sing praise to your name, Most
        High.
R. The Lord will judge the world with justice.
6 You rebuked the nations and destroyed the
        wicked;
        their name you blotted out forever and
        ever.
16 The nations are sunk in the pit they have
        made;
        in the snare they set, their foot is caught.
R. The Lord will judge the world with justice.
8 But the LORD sits enthroned forever;
        he has set up his throne for judgment.
9 He judges the world with justice;
        he governs the peoples with equity.
R. The Lord will judge the world with justice.

Alleluia: John 12:31B-32
R. Alleluia, alleluia.
³¹ᴮ The prince of this world will now be cast out,
³² and when I am lifted up from the earth
I will draw all to myself, says the Lord.
R. Alleluia, alleluia.

Gospel: Luke 11:15-26
¹⁵ When Jesus had driven out a demon, some of the crowd said: "By the power of Beelzebul, the prince of demons, he drives out demons." ¹⁶ Others, to test him, asked him for a sign from heaven. ¹⁷ But he knew their thoughts and said to them, "Every kingdom divided against itself will be laid waste and house will fall against house. ¹⁸ And if Satan is divided against himself, how will his kingdom stand? For you say that it is by Beelzebul that I drive out demons. ¹⁹ If I, then, drive out demons by Beelzebul, by whom do your own people drive them out? Therefore they will be your judges. ²⁰ But if it is by the finger of God that I drive out demons, then the Kingdom of God has come upon you. ²¹ When a strong man fully armed guards his palace, his possessions are safe. ²² But when one stronger than he attacks and overcomes him, he takes away the armor on which he relied and distributes the spoils. ²³ Whoever is not with me is against me, and whoever does not gather with me scatters.

²⁴ "When an unclean spirit goes out of someone, it roams through arid regions searching for rest but, finding none, it says, 'I shall return to my home from which I came.' ²⁵ But upon returning, it finds it swept clean and put in order. ²⁶ Then it goes and brings back seven other spirits more wicked than itself who move in and dwell there, and the last condition of that man is worse than the first."

Saturday October 11, 2025
Saturday of the Twenty-seventh Week in Ordinary Time
First Reading: Joel 4:12-21
Thus says the LORD:

¹²Let the nations bestir themselves and come
    up
        to the Valley of Jehoshaphat;
For there will I sit in judgment
    upon all the neighboring nations.

¹³Apply the sickle,
    for the harvest is ripe;
Come and tread,
    for the wine press is full;
The vats overflow,
    for great is their malice.
¹⁴Crowd upon crowd
    in the valley of decision;

For near is the day of the LORD
> in the valley of decision.
15Sun and moon are darkened,
> and the stars withhold their brightness.
16The LORD roars from Zion,
> and from Jerusalem raises his voice;
The heavens and the earth quake,
>> but the LORD is a refuge to his people,
>> a stronghold to the children of Israel.

17Then shall you know that I, the LORD, am your God,
> dwelling on Zion, my holy mountain;
Jerusalem shall be holy,
> and strangers shall pass through her no more.
18And then, on that day,
> the mountains shall drip new wine,
> and the hills shall flow with milk;
And the channels of Judah
> shall flow with water:
A fountain shall issue from the house of the LORD,
> to water the Valley of Shittim.
19Egypt shall be a waste,
> and Edom a desert waste,
Because of violence done to the people of Judah,
> because they shed innocent blood in their land.
20But Judah shall abide forever,
> and Jerusalem for all generations.
21I will avenge their blood,
> and not leave it unpunished.
> The LORD dwells in Zion.

Responsorial Psalm: Psalms 97:1-2,5-6,11-12
R. (12a) Rejoice in the Lord, you just!
1 The LORD is king; let the earth rejoice;
> let the many isles be glad.
2 Clouds and darkness are round about him,
>> justice and judgment are the foundation of his throne.
R. Rejoice in the Lord, you just!
5 The mountains melt like wax before the

LORD,
> before the LORD of all the earth.
⁶ The heavens proclaim his justice,
> and all peoples see his glory.

R. Rejoice in the Lord, you just!

¹¹ Light dawns for the just;
> and gladness, for the upright of heart.

¹² Be glad in the LORD, you just,
> and give thanks to his holy name.

R. Rejoice in the Lord, you just!

Alleluia: Luke 11:28
R. Alleluia, alleluia.
²⁸ Blessed are those who hear the word of God and observe it.
R. Alleluia, alleluia.

Gospel: Luke 11:27-28
²⁷ While Jesus was speaking, a woman from the crowd called out and said to him, "Blessed is the womb that carried you and the breasts at which you nursed." ²⁸ He replied, "Rather, blessed are those who hear the word of God and observe it."

Sunday October 12, 2025
Twenty-eighth Sunday in Ordinary Time, Year C

First Reading: 2 Kings 5:14-17
¹⁴Naaman went down and plunged into the Jordan seven times at the word of Elisha, the man of God. His flesh became again like the flesh of a little child, and he was clean of his leprosy.

¹⁵Naaman returned with his whole retinue to the man of God. On his arrival he stood before Elisha and said, "Now I know that there is no God in all the earth, except in Israel. Please accept a gift from your servant."

¹⁶Elisha replied, "As the LORD lives whom I serve, I will not take it;" and despite Naaman's urging, he still refused. ¹⁷Naaman said: "If you will not accept, please let me, your servant, have two mule-loads of earth, for I will no longer offer holocaust or sacrifice to any other god except to the LORD."

Responsorial Psalm: Psalms 98:1, 2-3, 3-4
R. (cf. 2b) The Lord has revealed to the nations his saving power.

¹Sing to the LORD a new song,
> for he has done wondrous deeds;
his right hand has won victory for him,
> his holy arm.

R. The Lord has revealed to the nations his saving power.

² The LORD has made his salvation known:

> in the sight of the nations he has revealed
>> his justice.
> ³ᴬᴮ He has remembered his kindness and his
>> faithfulness
> toward the house of Israel.

R. The Lord has revealed to the nations his saving power.

> ³ᶜᴰ All the ends of the earth have seen
>> the salvation by our God.
> ⁴ Sing joyfully to the LORD, all you lands:
>> break into song; sing praise.

R. The Lord has revealed to the nations his saving power.

Second Reading: 2 Timothy 2:8-13

Beloved: ⁸Remember Jesus Christ, raised from the dead, a descendant of David: such is my gospel, ⁹for which I am suffering, even to the point of chains, like a criminal. But the word of God is not chained. ¹⁰Therefore, I bear with everything for the sake of those who are chosen, so that they too may obtain the salvation that is in Christ Jesus, together with eternal glory. ¹¹This saying is trustworthy:

If we have died with him
> we shall also live with him;
¹²if we persevere
> we shall also reign with him.
But if we deny him
> he will deny us.
¹³If we are unfaithful
> he remains faithful,
> for he cannot deny himself.

Alleluia: 1 Thessalonians 5:18

R. Alleluia, alleluia.
¹⁸ In all circumstances, give thanks,
for this is the will of God for you in Christ
> Jesus.
R. Alleluia, alleluia.

Gospel: Luke 17:11-19

¹¹As Jesus continued his journey to Jerusalem, he traveled through Samaria and Galilee. ¹²As he was entering a village, ten lepers met him. They stood at a distance from him ¹³and raised their voices, saying, "Jesus, Master! Have pity on us!" ¹⁴And when he saw them, he said, "Go show yourselves to the priests." As they were going they were cleansed. ¹⁵And one of them, realizing he had been

healed, returned, glorifying God in a loud voice; ¹⁶and he fell at the feet of Jesus and thanked him. He was a Samaritan.¹⁷Jesus said in reply, "Ten were cleansed, were they not? Where are the other nine? ¹⁸Has none but this foreigner returned to give thanks to God?" ¹⁹Then he said to him, "Stand up and go; your faith has saved you."

Monday October 13, 2025
Monday of the Twenty-eighth Week in Ordinary Time

First Reading: Romans 1:1-7
¹Paul, a slave of Christ Jesus, called to be an Apostle and set apart for the Gospel of God, ²which he promised previously through his prophets in the holy Scriptures, ³the Gospel about his Son, descended from David according to the flesh, ⁴but established as Son of God in power according to the Spirit of holiness through resurrection from the dead, Jesus Christ our Lord. ⁵Through him we have received the grace of apostleship, to bring about the obedience of faith, for the sake of his name, among all the Gentiles, ⁶among whom are you also, who are called to belong to Jesus Christ; ⁷to all the beloved of God in Rome, called to be holy. Grace to you and peace from God our Father and the Lord Jesus Christ.

Responsorial Psalm: Psalms 98:1BCDE, 2-3AB, 3CD-4
R. ⁽²ᵃ⁾ *The Lord has made known his salvation.*
¹ᴮᶜᴰᴱ Sing to the LORD a new song,
    for he has done wondrous deeds;
His right hand has won victory for him,
    his holy arm.
R. *The Lord has made known his salvation.*
² The LORD has made his salvation known:
    in the sight of the nations he has revealed
        his justice.
³ᴬᴮ He has remembered his kindness and his
    faithfulness
    toward the house of Israel.
R. *The Lord has made known his salvation.*
³ᶜᴮ All the ends of the earth have seen
    the salvation by our God.
⁴ Sing joyfully to the LORD, all you lands;
    break into song; sing praise.
R. *The Lord has made known his salvation.*

Alleluia: Psalms 95:8
R. Alleluia, alleluia.
⁸ If today you hear his voice,
harden not your hearts.
R. Alleluia, alleluia.

Gospel: Luke 11:29-32

²⁹ While still more people gathered in the crowd, Jesus said to them, "This generation is an evil generation; it seeks a sign, but no sign will be given it, except the sign of Jonah. ³⁰ Just as Jonah became a sign to the Ninevites, so will the Son of Man be to this generation. ³¹ At the judgment the queen of the south will rise with the men of this generation and she will condemn them, because she came from the ends of the earth to hear the wisdom of Solomon, and there is something greater than Solomon here. ³² At the judgment the men of Nineveh will arise with this generation and condemn it, because at the preaching of Jonah they repented, and there is something greater than Jonah here."

Tuesday October 14, 2025
Tuesday of the Twenty-eighth Week in Ordinary Time
First Reading: Romans 1:16-25

Brothers and sisters: ¹⁶I am not ashamed of the Gospel. It is the power of God for the salvation of everyone who believes: for Jew first, and then Greek. ¹⁷For in it is revealed the righteousness of God from faith to faith; as it is written, "The one who is righteous by faith will live."

¹⁸The wrath of God is indeed being revealed from heaven against every impiety and wickedness of those who suppress the truth by their wickedness. ¹⁹For what can be known about God is evident to them, because God made it evident to them. ²⁰Ever since the creation of the world, his invisible attributes of eternal power and divinity have been able to be understood and perceived in what he has made. As a result, they have no excuse; ²¹for although they knew God they did not accord him glory as God or give him thanks. Instead, they became vain in their reasoning, and their senseless minds were darkened. ²²While claiming to be wise, they became fools ²³and exchanged the glory of the immortal God for the likeness of an image of mortal man or of birds or of four-legged animals or of snakes.

²⁴Therefore, God handed them over to impurity through the lusts of their hearts for the mutual degradation of their bodies. ²⁵They exchanged the truth of God for a lie and revered and worshiped the creature rather than the creator, who is blessed forever. Amen.

Responsorial Psalm: Psalms 19:2-3, 4-5

R. ⁽²ᵃ⁾ *The heavens proclaim the glory of God.*
² The heavens declare the glory of God,
    and the firmament proclaims his
        handiwork.
³ Day pours out the word to day,
    and night to night imparts knowledge.
R. *The heavens proclaim the glory of God.*
⁴ Not a word nor a discourse
    whose voice is not heard;
⁵ Through all the earth their voice resounds,
    and to the ends of the world, their
        message.

R. The heavens proclaim the glory of God.

Alleluia: Hebrews 4:12
R. Alleluia, alleluia.
¹² The word of God is living and effective,
able to discern reflections and thoughts of
    the heart.
R. Alleluia, alleluia.

Gospel: Luke 11:37-41
³⁷ After Jesus had spoken, a Pharisee invited him to dine at his home. He entered and reclined at table to eat. ³⁸ The Pharisee was amazed to see that he did not observe the prescribed washing before the meal. ³⁹ The Lord said to him, "Oh you Pharisees! Although you cleanse the outside of the cup and the dish, inside you are filled with plunder and evil. ⁴⁰ You fools! Did not the maker of the outside also make the inside? ⁴¹ But as to what is within, give alms, and behold, everything will be clean for you."

Wednesday October 15, 2025
Memorial of Saint Teresa of Avila, Virgin and Doctor

First Reading: Romans 2:1-11
¹You, O man, are without excuse, every one of you who passes judgment. For by the standard by which you judge another you condemn yourself, since you, the judge, do the very same things. ²We know that the judgment of God on those who do such things is true. ³Do you suppose, then, you who judge those who engage in such things and yet do them yourself, that you will escape the judgment of God? ⁴Or do you hold his priceless kindness, forbearance, and patience in low esteem, unaware that the kindness of God would lead you to repentance? ⁵By your stubbornness and impenitent heart, you are storing up wrath for yourself for the day of wrath and revelation of the just judgment of God, ⁶who will repay everyone according to his works, ⁷eternal life to those who seek glory, honor, and immortality through perseverance in good works, ⁸but wrath and fury to those who selfishly disobey the truth and obey wickedness. ⁹Yes, affliction and distress will come upon everyone who does evil, Jew first and then Greek. ¹⁰But there will be glory, honor, and peace for everyone who does good, Jew first and then Greek. ¹¹There is no partiality with God.

Responsorial Psalm: Psalms 62:2-3, 6-7, 9
*R. ⁽¹³ᵇ⁾ **Lord, you give back to everyone
    according to his works.***
² Only in God is my soul at rest;
    from him comes my salvation.
³ He only is my rock and my salvation,
    my stronghold; I shall not be disturbed at
        all.
R. Lord, you give back to everyone according to

> *his works.*

⁶ Only in God be at rest, my soul,
    for from him comes my hope.
⁷ He only is my rock and my salvation,
    my stronghold; I shall not be disturbed.
R. Lord, you give back to everyone according to his works.

⁹ Trust in him at all times, O my people!
    Pour out your hearts before him;
    God is our refuge!
R. Lord, you give back to everyone according to his works.

Alleluia: John 10:27
R. Alleluia, alleluia.
²⁷ My sheep hear my voice, says the Lord;
I know them, and they follow me.
R. Alleluia, alleluia.

Gospel: Luke 11:42-46
The Lord said: ⁴²"Woe to you Pharisees! You pay tithes of mint and of rue and of every garden herb, but you pay no attention to judgment and to love for God. These you should have done, without overlooking the others. ⁴³Woe to you Pharisees! You love the seat of honor in synagogues and greetings in marketplaces. ⁴⁴Woe to you! You are like unseen graves over which people unknowingly walk."

⁴⁵Then one of the scholars of the law said to him in reply, "Teacher, by saying this you are insulting us too." ⁴⁶And he said, "Woe also to you scholars of the law! You impose on people burdens hard to carry, but you yourselves do not lift one finger to touch them."

Thursday October 16, 2025
Thursday of the Twenty-eighth Week in Ordinary Time
First Reading: Romans 3:21-30
Brothers and sisters: ²¹Now the righteousness of God has been manifested apart from the law, though testified to by the law and the prophets, ²²the righteousness of God through faith in Jesus Christ for all who believe. For there is no distinction; ²³all have sinned and are deprived of the glory of God. ²⁴They are justified freely by his grace through the redemption in Christ Jesus, ²⁵whom God set forth as an expiation, through faith, by his Blood, to prove his righteousness because of the forgiveness of sins previously committed, ²⁶through the forbearance of God– to prove his righteousness in the present time, that he might be righteous and justify the one who has faith in Jesus.

²⁷What occasion is there then for boasting? It is ruled out. On what principle, that of works? No, rather on the principle of faith. ²⁸For we consider that a person

is justified by faith apart from works of the law. ²⁹Does God belong to Jews alone? Does he not belong to Gentiles, too? Yes, also to Gentiles, ³⁰for God is one and will justify the circumcised on the basis of faith and the uncircumcised through faith.

Responsorial Psalm: Psalms 130:1B-2, 3-4, 5-6AB

R. ⁽⁷⁾ *With the Lord there is mercy, and fullness of redemption.*

¹ᴮ Out of the depths I cry to you, O LORD;
  ² LORD, hear my voice!
Let your ears be attentive
  to my voice in supplication.

R. *With the Lord there is mercy, and fullness of redemption.*

³ If you, O LORD, mark iniquities,
  LORD, who can stand?
⁴ But with you is forgiveness,
  that you may be revered.

R. *With the Lord there is mercy, and fullness of redemption.*

⁵ I trust in the LORD;
  my soul trusts in his word.
⁶ᴬᴮ My soul waits for the LORD
  more than sentinels wait for the dawn.

R. *With the Lord there is mercy, and fullness of redemption.*

Alleluia: John 14:6

R. Alleluia, alleluia.
⁶ I am the way and the truth and the life, says
    the Lord;
no one comes to the Father except through
    me.
R. Alleluia, alleluia.

Gospel: Luke 11:47-54

The Lord said: ⁴⁷ "Woe to you who build the memorials of the prophets whom your fathers killed. ⁴⁸ Consequently, you bear witness and give consent to the deeds of your ancestors, for they killed them and you do the building. ⁴⁹ Therefore, the wisdom of God said, 'I will send to them prophets and Apostles; some of them they will kill and persecute' ⁵⁰ in order that this generation might be charged with the blood of all the prophets shed since the foundation of the world, ⁵¹ from the blood of Abel to the blood of Zechariah who died between the altar and the temple building. Yes, I tell you, this generation will be charged with their blood! ⁵² Woe to you, scholars of the law! You have taken away the key of knowledge. You yourselves did not enter and you stopped those trying to enter." ⁵³ When Jesus left, the scribes and Pharisees began to act with hostility toward him and to interrogate him about many things, ⁵⁴ for they were plotting to catch him at something he might say.

Friday October 17, 2025
Memorial of Saint Ignatius of Antioch, Bishop and Martyr
First Reading: Romans 4:1-8

Brothers and sisters: ¹What can we say that Abraham found, our ancestor according to the flesh? ²Indeed, if Abraham was justified on the basis of his works, he has reason to boast; but this was not so in the sight of God. ³For what does the Scripture say? *Abraham believed God, and it was credited to him as righteousness.* ⁴A worker's wage is credited not as a gift, but as something due. ⁵But when one does not work, yet believes in the one who justifies the ungodly, his faith is credited as righteousness. ⁶So also David declares the blessedness of the person to whom God credits righteousness apart from works:

⁷*Blessed are they whose iniquities are forgiven
    and whose sins are covered.*
⁸*Blessed is the man whose sin the Lord does
    not record.*

Responsorial Psalm: Psalms 32:1B-2, 5, 11
R. (see 7) *I turn to you, Lord, in time of trouble, and
    you fill me with the joy of salvation.*
¹ᴮ Blessed is he whose fault is taken away,
    whose sin is covered.
² Blessed the man to whom the LORD imputes
        not guilt,
    in whose spirit there is no guile.
**R. I turn to you, Lord, in time of trouble, and you
    fill me with the joy of salvation.**
⁵ Then I acknowledged my sin to you,
    my guilt I covered not.
I said, "I confess my faults to the LORD,"
    and you took away the guilt of my sin.
**R. I turn to you, Lord, in time of trouble, and you
    fill me with the joy of salvation.**
¹¹ Be glad in the LORD and rejoice, you just;
    exult, all you upright of heart.
**R. I turn to you, Lord, in time of trouble, and you
    fill me with the joy of salvation.**

Alleluia: Psalms 33:22
R. Alleluia, alleluia.
²²May your kindness, O LORD, be upon us;
who have put our hope in you.
R. Alleluia, alleluia.

Gospel: Luke 12:1-7
¹At that time: So many people were crowding together that they were trampling one another underfoot. Jesus began to speak, first to his disciples, "Beware of the leaven–that is, the hypocrisy–of the Pharisees.

²"There is nothing concealed that will not be revealed, nor secret that will not be known. ³Therefore whatever you have said in the darkness will be heard in the light, and what you have whispered behind closed doors will be proclaimed on the housetops. ⁴I tell you, my friends, do not be afraid of those who kill the body but after that can do no more. ⁵I shall show you whom to fear. Be afraid of the one who after killing has the power to cast into Gehenna; yes, I tell you, be afraid of that one. ⁶Are not five sparrows sold for two small coins? Yet not one of them has escaped the notice of God. ⁷Even the hairs of your head have all been counted. Do not be afraid. You are worth more than many sparrows."

Saturday October 18, 2025
Feast of Saint Luke, Evangelist

First Reading: 2 Timothy 4:10-17B
Beloved: ¹⁰ Demas, enamoured of the present world, deserted me and went to Thessalonica, Crescens to Galatia, and Titus to Dalmatia. ¹¹ Luke is the only one with me. Get Mark and bring him with you, for he is helpful to me in the ministry. ¹² I have sent Tychicus to Ephesus. ¹³ When you come, bring the cloak I left with Carpus in Troas, the papyrus rolls, and especially the parchments.

¹⁴ Alexander the coppersmith did me a great deal of harm; the Lord will repay him according to his deeds. ¹⁵ You too be on guard against him, for he has strongly resisted our preaching.

¹⁶ At my first defence no one appeared on my behalf, but everyone deserted me. May it not be held against them! ¹⁷ But the Lord stood by me and gave me strength so that through me the proclamation might be completed and all the Gentiles might hear it.

Responsorial Psalm: Psalms 145:10-11, 12-13, 17-18
R. *(12) Your friends make known, O Lord, the
    glorious splendor of your Kingdom.*
¹⁰ Let all your works give you thanks, O LORD,
    and let your faithful ones bless you.
¹¹Let them discourse of the glory of your
    Kingdom
    and speak of your might.
R. *Your friends make known, O Lord, the
    glorious splendor of your Kingdom.*
¹² Making known to men your might

and the glorious splendor of your Kingdom.
¹³ Your Kingdom is a Kingdom for all ages,
and your dominion endures through all generations.

R. Your friends make known, O Lord, the glorious splendor of your Kingdom.

¹⁷ The LORD is just in all his ways
and holy in all his works.
¹⁸ The LORD is near to all who call upon him,
to all who call upon him in truth.

R. Your friends make known, O Lord, the glorious splendor of your Kingdom.

Alleluia: cf. John 15:16
R. Alleluia, alleluia.
¹⁶ I chose you from the world,
to go and bear fruit that will last, says the Lord.
R. Alleluia, alleluia.

Gospel: Luke 10:1-9
¹ The Lord Jesus appointed seventy-two disciples whom he sent ahead of him in pairs to every town and place he intended to visit. ² He said to them, "The harvest is abundant but the laborers are few; so ask the master of the harvest to send out laborers for his harvest. ³ Go on your way; behold, I am sending you like lambs among wolves. ⁴ Carry no money bag, no sack, no sandals; and greet no one along the way. ⁵ Into whatever house you enter, first say, 'Peace to this household.' ⁶ If a peaceful person lives there, your peace will rest on him; but if not, it will return to you. ⁷ Stay in the same house and eat and drink what is offered to you, for the laborer deserves payment. Do not move about from one house to another. ⁸ Whatever town you enter and they welcome you, eat what is set before you, ⁹ cure the sick in it and say to them, 'The Kingdom of God is at hand for you.'"

Sunday October 19, 2025
Twenty-ninth Week Sunday in Ordinary Time, Year C
First Reading: Exodus 17:8-13
⁸In those days, Amalek came and waged war against Israel. ⁹ Moses, therefore, said to Joshua, "Pick out certain men, and tomorrow go out and engage Amalek in battle. I will be standing on top of the hill with the staff of God in my hand." ¹⁰So Joshua did as Moses told him: he engaged Amalek in battle after Moses had climbed to the top of the hill with Aaron and Hur. ¹¹As long as Moses kept his hands raised up, Israel had the better of the fight, but when he let his hands rest, Amalek had the better of the fight. ¹²Moses' hands, however, grew tired; so they put a rock in place for him to sit on. Meanwhile Aaron and Hur supported his hands, one on one side and one on the other, so that his hands remained steady till sunset. ¹³And Joshua mowed down Amalek and his people with the edge of the sword.

Responsorial Psalm: Psalms 121:1-2, 3-4, 5-6, 7-8

R. (cf. 2) *Our help is from the Lord, who made heaven and earth.*

¹ I lift up my eyes toward the mountains;
   whence shall help come to me?
² My help is from the LORD,
   who made heaven and earth.

R. *Our help is from the Lord, who made heaven and earth.*

³ May he not suffer your foot to slip;
   may he slumber not who guards you:
⁴ indeed he neither slumbers nor sleeps,
   the guardian of Israel.

R. *Our help is from the Lord, who made heaven and earth.*

⁵ The LORD is your guardian; the LORD is your shade;
   he is beside you at your right hand.
⁶ The sun shall not harm you by day,
   nor the moon by night.

R. *Our help is from the Lord, who made heaven and earth.*

⁷ The LORD will guard you from all evil;
   he will guard your life.
⁸ The LORD will guard your coming and your going,
   both now and forever.

R. *Our help is from the Lord, who made heaven and earth.*

Second Reading: 2 Timothy 3:14-4:2

Beloved: [14]Remain faithful to what you have learned and believed, because you know from whom you learned it, [15]and that from infancy you have known the sacred Scriptures, which are capable of giving you wisdom for salvation through faith in Christ Jesus. [16]All Scripture is inspired by God and is useful for teaching, for refutation, for correction, and for training in righteousness, [17]so that one who belongs to God may be competent, equipped for every good work.

[1]I charge you in the presence of God and of Christ Jesus, who will judge the living and the dead, and by his appearing and his kingly power: [2]proclaim the word; be persistent whether it is convenient or inconvenient; convince, reprimand, encourage through all patience and teaching.

Alleluia: Hebrews 4:12
R. Alleluia, alleluia.
[12]The word of God is living and effective,
discerning reflections and thoughts of the
heart.
R. Alleluia, alleluia.

Gospel: Luke 18:1-8
[1]Jesus told his disciples a parable about the necessity for them to pray always without becoming weary. [2] He said, "There was a judge in a certain town who neither feared God nor respected any human being. [3]And a widow in that town used to come to him and say, 'Render a just decision for me against my adversary.' [4]For a long time, the judge was unwilling, but eventually, he thought, 'While it is true that I neither fear God nor respect any human being, [5]because this widow keeps bothering me I shall deliver a just decision for her lest she finally come and strike me.'" [6]The Lord said, "Pay attention to what the dishonest judge says. [7]Will not God then secure the rights of his chosen ones who call out to him day and night? Will he be slow to answer them? [8]I tell you, he will see to it that justice is done for them speedily. But when the Son of Man comes, will he find faith on earth?"

Monday October 20, 2025
Monday of Twenty-ninth Week in Ordinary Time
First Reading: Romans 4:20-25
Brothers and sisters: [20]Abraham did not doubt God's promise in unbelief; rather, he was empowered by faith and gave glory to God [21]and was fully convinced that what God had promised he was also able to do. [22]That is why *it was credited to him as righteousness.* [23]But it was not for him alone that it was written that *it was credited to him*; [24]it was also for us, to whom it will be credited, who believe in the one who raised Jesus our Lord from the dead, [25]who was handed over for our transgressions and was raised for our justification.

Responsorial Psalm: Luke 1:69-70,71-72,73-75
**R. (see 68) Blessed be the Lord, the God of Israel;
he has come to his people.**

[69] He has come to his people and set them free.
[70] He has raised up for us a mighty savior,
born of the house of his servant David.

**R. Blessed be the Lord, the God of Israel; he has
come to his people.**

[71] Through his holy prophets he promised of
old
that he would save us from our enemies,
from the hands of all who hate us.
[72] He promised to show mercy to our fathers
and to remember his holy covenant.

R. Blessed be the Lord, the God of Israel; he has come to his people.

⁷³ This was the oath he swore to our father Abraham:
⁷⁴to set us free from the hands of our enemies,
free to worship him without fear,
⁷⁵holy and righteous in his sight all the days of our life.

R. Blessed be the Lord, the God of Israel; he has come to his people.

Alleluia: Matthew 5:3
R. Alleluia, alleluia.
³ Blessed are the poor in spirit;
for theirs is the Kingdom of heaven.
R. Alleluia, alleluia.

Gospel: Luke 12:13-21

¹³ Someone in the crowd said to Jesus, "Teacher, tell my brother to share the inheritance with me." ¹⁴ He replied to him, "Friend, who appointed me as your judge and arbitrator?" ¹⁵ Then he said to the crowd, "Take care to guard against all greed, for though one may be rich, one's life does not consist of possessions."

¹⁶ Then he told them a parable. "There was a rich man whose land produced a bountiful harvest. ¹⁷ He asked himself, 'What shall I do, for I do not have space to store my harvest?' ¹⁸ And he said, 'This is what I shall do: I shall tear down my barns and build larger ones. There I shall store all my grain and other goods ¹⁹ and I shall say to myself, "Now as for you, you have so many good things stored up for many years, rest, eat, drink, be merry!"' ²⁰ But God said to him, 'You fool, this night your life will be demanded of you; and the things you have prepared, to whom will they belong?' ²¹ Thus will it be for the one who stores up treasure for himself but is not rich in what matters to God."

Tuesday October 21, 2025
Tuesday of Twenty-ninth Week in Ordinary Time
First Reading: Romans 5:12, 15B, 17-19, 20B-21

Brothers and sisters: ¹²Through one man sin entered the world, and through sin, death, and thus death came to all men, inasmuch as all sinned.

¹⁵ᴮIf by that one person's transgression the many died, how much more did the grace of God and the gracious gift of the one man Jesus Christ overflow for the many. ¹⁷For if, by the transgression of the one, death came to reign through that one, how much more will those who receive the abundance of grace and the gift of justification come to reign in life through the one Jesus Christ. ¹⁸In conclusion, just as through one transgression condemnation came upon all, so, through one righteous act acquittal and life came to all. ¹⁹For just as through the disobedience of one man the many were made sinners, so, through the obedience of the one the

many will be made righteous. [20B]Where sin increased, grace overflowed all the more, [21]so that, as sin reigned in death, grace also might reign through justification for eternal life through Jesus Christ our Lord.

Responsorial Psalm: Psalms 40:7-8A, 8B-9, 10, 17
R. [8a and 9a] *Here I am, Lord; I come to do your will.*
[7]Sacrifice or oblation you wished not,
    but ears open to obedience you gave me.
[8A] Burnt offerings or sin-offerings you sought
       not;
    then said I, "Behold I come."
R. Here I am, Lord; I come to do your will.
[8B] "In the written scroll it is prescribed for me,
[9]To do your will, O my God, is my delight,
    and your law is within my heart!"
R. Here I am, Lord; I come to do yo```ur will.
[10]I announced your justice in the vast
       assembly;
    I did not restrain my lips, as you, O LORD,
       know.
R. Here I am, Lord; I come to do your will.
[17]May all who seek you
    exult and be glad in you,
And may those who love your salvation
    say ever, "The LORD be glorified."
R. Here I am, Lord; I come to do your will.

Alleluia: Luke 21:36
R. Alleluia, alleluia.
[36] Be vigilant at all times and pray
that you may have the strength to stand
       before the Son of Man.
R. Alleluia, alleluia.

Gospel: Luke 12:35-38
Jesus said to his disciples: [35] "Gird your loins and light your lamps [36] and be like servants who await their master's return from a wedding, ready to open immediately when he comes and knocks.[37] Blessed are those servants whom the master finds vigilant on his arrival. Amen, I say to you, he will gird himself, have them recline at table, and proceed to wait on them. [38] And should he come in the second or third watch and find them prepared in this way, blessed are those servants."

Wednesday October 22, 2025
Wednesday of Twenty-ninth Week in Ordinary Time

First Reading: Romans 6:12-18

Brothers and sisters: ¹²Sin must not reign over your mortal bodies so that you obey their desires. ¹³And do not present the parts of your bodies to sin as weapons for wickedness, but present yourselves to God as raised from the dead to life and the parts of your bodies to God as weapons for righteousness. ¹⁴For sin is not to have any power over you, since you are not under the law but under grace.

¹⁵What then? Shall we sin because we are not under the law but under grace? Of course not! ¹⁶Do you not know that if you present yourselves to someone as obedient slaves, you are slaves of the one you obey, either of sin, which leads to death, or of obedience, which leads to righteousness? ¹⁷But thanks be to God that, although you were once slaves of sin, you have become obedient from the heart to the pattern of teaching to which you were entrusted. ¹⁸Freed from sin, you have become slaves of righteousness.

Responsorial Psalm: Psalms 124:1B-3, 4-6, 7-8

R. ⁽⁸ᵃ⁾ *Our help is in the name of the Lord.*

¹ᴮ Had not the LORD been with us,
    let Israel say, had not the LORD been with
        us–
² When men rose up against us,
    then would they have swallowed us alive;
³ When their fury was inflamed against us.

R. *Our help is in the name of the Lord.*

⁴ Then would the waters have overwhelmed
    us;
⁵ The torrent would have swept over us;
    over us then would have swept the raging
        waters.
⁶ Blessed be the LORD, who did not leave us
    a prey to their teeth.

R. *Our help is in the name of the Lord.*

⁷ We were rescued like a bird
    from the fowlers' snare;
Broken was the snare,
    and we were freed.
⁸ Our help is in the name of the LORD,
    who made heaven and earth.

R. *Our help is in the name of the Lord.*

Alleluia: Matthew 24:42A, 44

R. **Alleluia, alleluia.**
⁴²ᴬ Stay awake!
⁴⁴ For you do not know when the Son of Man

will come.
R. Alleluia, alleluia.

Gospel: Luke 12:39-48

Jesus said to his disciples: ³⁹ "Be sure of this: if the master of the house had known the hour when the thief was coming, he would not have let his house be broken into. ⁴⁰ You also must be prepared, for at an hour you do not expect, the Son of Man will come."

⁴¹ Then Peter said, "Lord, is this parable meant for us or for everyone?" ⁴² And the Lord replied, "Who, then, is the faithful and prudent steward whom the master will put in charge of his servants to distribute the food allowance at the proper time? ⁴³ Blessed is that servant whom his master on arrival finds doing so. ⁴⁴ Truly, I say to you, he will put him in charge of all his property. ⁴⁵ But if that servant says to himself, 'My master is delayed in coming,' and begins to beat the menservants and the maidservants, to eat and drink and get drunk, ⁴⁶ then that servant's master will come on an unexpected day and at an unknown hour and will punish the servant severely and assign him a place with the unfaithful. ⁴⁷ That servant who knew his master's will but did not make preparations nor act in accord with his will shall be beaten severely; ⁴⁸ and the servant who was ignorant of his master's will but acted in a way deserving of a severe beating shall be beaten only lightly. Much will be required of the person entrusted with much, and still more will be demanded of the person entrusted with more."

Thursday October 23, 2025
Thursday of Twenty-ninth Week in Ordinary Time

First Reading: Romans 6:19-23

Brothers and sisters: ¹⁹I am speaking in human terms because of the weakness of your nature. For just as you presented the parts of your bodies as slaves to impurity and to lawlessness for lawlessness, so now present them as slaves to righteousness for sanctification. ²⁰For when you were slaves of sin, you were free from righteousness. ²¹But what profit did you get then from the things of which you are now ashamed? For the end of those things is death. ²²But now that you have been freed from sin and have become slaves of God, the benefit that you have leads to sanctification, and its end is eternal life. ²³For the wages of sin is death, but the gift of God is eternal life in Christ Jesus our Lord.

Responsorial Psalm: Psalms 1:1-2, 3,4 AND 6
R. *(Ps 40:5)* ***Blessed are they who hope in the Lord.***
¹ Blessed the man who follows not
    the counsel of the wicked
Nor walks in the way of sinners,
    nor sits in the company of the insolent,
² But delights in the law of the LORD
    and meditates on his law day and night.
R. Blessed are they who hope in the Lord.
³ He is like a tree
    planted near running water,
That yields its fruit in due season,

and whose leaves never fade.
Whatever he does, prospers.
R. Blessed are they who hope in the Lord.
⁴ Not so the wicked, not so;
they are like chaff which the wind drives away.
⁶ For the LORD watches over the way of the just,
but the way of the wicked vanishes.
R. Blessed are they who hope in the Lord.

Alleluia: Philippians 3:8-9
R. Alleluia, alleluia.
⁸ I consider all things so much rubbish
⁹ that I may gain Christ and be found in him.
R. Alleluia, alleluia.

Gospel: Luke 12:49-53
Jesus said to his disciples: ⁴⁹ "I have come to set the earth on fire, and how I wish it were already blazing! ⁵⁰ There is a baptism with which I must be baptized, and how great is my anguish until it is accomplished! ⁵¹ Do you think that I have come to establish peace on the earth? No, I tell you, but rather division. ⁵² From now on a household of five will be divided, three against two and two against three; ⁵³ a father will be divided against his son and a son against his father, a mother against her daughter and a daughter against her mother, a mother-in-law against her daughter-in-law and a daughter-in-law against her mother-in-law."

Friday October 24, 2025
Friday of Twenty-ninth Week in Ordinary Time
First Reading: Romans 7:18-25A
Brothers and sisters: ¹⁸I know that good does not dwell in me, that is, in my flesh. The willing is ready at hand, but doing the good is not. ¹⁹For I do not do the good I want, but I do the evil I do not want. ²⁰Now if I do what I do not want, it is no longer I who do it, but sin that dwells in me. ²¹So, then, I discover the principle that when I want to do right, evil is at hand. ²²For I take delight in the law of God, in my inner self, ²³but I see in my members another principle at war with the law of my mind, taking me captive to the law of sin that dwells in my members. ²⁴Miserable one that I am! Who will deliver me from this mortal body? ²⁵AThanks be to God through Jesus Christ our Lord.

Responsorial Psalm: Psalms 119:66, 68, 76, 77, 93, 94
R. ⁽⁶⁸ᵇ⁾ ***Lord, teach me your statutes.***
⁶⁶ Teach me wisdom and knowledge,
for in your commands I trust.
R. Lord, teach me your statutes.

⁶⁸ You are good and bountiful;
    teach me your statutes.
R. Lord, teach me your statutes.
⁷⁶ Let your kindness comfort me
    according to your promise to your servants.
R. Lord, teach me your statutes.
⁷⁷ Let your compassion come to me that I may live,
    for your law is my delight.
R. Lord, teach me your statutes.
⁹³ Never will I forget your precepts,
    for through them you give me life.
R. Lord, teach me your statutes.
⁹⁴ I am yours; save me,
    for I have sought your precepts.
R. Lord, teach me your statutes.

Alleluia: cf. Matthew 11:25
R. Alleluia, alleluia.
²⁵ Blessed are you, Father, Lord of heaven and earth;
you have revealed to little ones the mysteries of the Kingdom.
R. Alleluia, alleluia.

Gospel: Luke 12:54-59
⁵⁴ Jesus said to the crowds, "When you see a cloud rising in the west you say immediately that it is going to rain — and so it does; ⁵⁵ and when you notice that the wind is blowing from the south you say that it is going to be hot — and so it is. ⁵⁶ You hypocrites! You know how to interpret the appearance of the earth and the sky; why do you not know how to interpret the present time?

⁵⁷ "Why do you not judge for yourselves what is right? ⁵⁸ If you are to go with your opponent before a magistrate, make an effort to settle the matter on the way; otherwise your opponent will turn you over to the judge, and the judge hand you over to the constable, and the constable throw you into prison. ⁵⁹ I say to you, you will not be released until you have paid the last penny."

Saturday October 25, 2025
Saturday of Twenty-ninth Week in Ordinary Time
First Reading: Romans 8:1-11
Brothers and sisters: ¹Now there is no condemnation for those who are in Christ Jesus. ²For the law of the spirit of life in Christ Jesus has freed you from the law of sin and death. ³For what the law, weakened by the flesh, was powerless to do, this God has done: by sending his own Son in the likeness of sinful flesh and for the

sake of sin, he condemned sin in the flesh, ⁴so that the righteous decree of the law might be fulfilled in us, who live not according to the flesh but according to the spirit. ⁵For those who live according to the flesh are concerned with the things of the flesh, but those who live according to the spirit with the things of the spirit. ⁶The concern of the flesh is death, but the concern of the spirit is life and peace. ⁷For the concern of the flesh is hostility toward God; it does not submit to the law of God, nor can it; ⁸and those who are in the flesh cannot please God. ⁹But you are not in the flesh; on the contrary, you are in the spirit, if only the Spirit of God dwells in you. Whoever does not have the Spirit of Christ does not belong to him. ¹⁰But if Christ is in you, although the body is dead because of sin, the spirit is alive because of righteousness. ¹¹If the Spirit of the one who raised Jesus from the dead dwells in you, the one who raised Christ from the dead will give life to your mortal bodies also, through his Spirit that dwells in you.

Responsorial Psalm: Psalms 24:1B-2, 3-4AB, 5-6
R. (see 6) **Lord, this is the people that longs to see your face.**
¹ᴮ The LORD's are the earth and its fullness;
    the world and those who dwell in it.
² For he founded it upon the seas
    and established it upon the rivers.
R. Lord, this is the people that longs to see your face.
³ Who can ascend the mountain of the LORD?
    or who may stand in his holy place?
⁴ᴬᴮHe whose hands are sinless, whose heart is clean,
    who desires not what is vain.
R. Lord, this is the people that longs to see your face.
⁵ He shall receive a blessing from the LORD,
    a reward from God his savior.
⁶ Such is the race that seeks for him,
    that seeks the face of the God of Jacob.
R. Lord, this is the people that longs to see your face.

Alleluia: Ezekiel 33:11
R. Alleluia, alleluia.
¹¹ I take no pleasure in the death of the wicked man, says the Lord,
but rather in his conversion that he may live.
R. Alleluia, alleluia.

Gospel: Luke 13:1-9

[1]Some people told Jesus about the Galileans whose blood Pilate had mingled with the blood of their sacrifices. [2]He said to them in reply, "Do you think that because these Galileans suffered in this way they were greater sinners than all other Galileans? [3]By no means! But I tell you, if you do not repent, you will all perish as they did! [4]Or those eighteen people who were killed when the tower at Siloam fell on them— do you think they were more guilty than everyone else who lived in Jerusalem? [5]By no means! But I tell you, if you do not repent, you will all perish as they did!"

[6]And he told them this parable: "There once was a person who had a fig tree planted in his orchard, and when he came in search of fruit on it but found none, [7]he said to the gardener, 'For three years now I have come in search of fruit on this fig tree but have found none. So cut it down. Why should it exhaust the soil?' [8]He said to him in reply, 'Sir, leave it for this year also, and I shall cultivate the ground around it and fertilize it; [9]it may bear fruit in the future. If not you can cut it down.'"

Sunday October 26, 2025
Thirtieth Sunday in Ordinary Time, Year C

First Reading: Sirach 35:15BC-17, 20-22AB

[15BC]The LORD is a God of justice,
  who knows no favorites.
[16]Though not unduly partial toward the weak,
  yet he hears the cry of the oppressed.
[17]The Lord is not deaf to the wail of the
      orphan,
  nor to the widow when she pours out her
      complaint.
[20]The one who serves God willingly is heard;
  his petition reaches the heavens.
[21]The prayer of the lowly pierces the clouds;
  it does not rest till it reaches its goal,
nor will it withdraw till the Most High
      responds,
  [22AB]judges justly and affirms the right,
and the Lord will not delay.

Responsorial Psalm: Psalms 34:2-3, 17-18, 19, 23

R. [7a] **The Lord hears the cry of the poor.**
[2] I will bless the LORD at all times;
  his praise shall be ever in my mouth.
[3] Let my soul glory in the LORD;
  the lowly will hear me and be glad.
R. The Lord hears the cry of the poor.
[17] The LORD confronts the evildoers,
  to destroy remembrance of them from
      the earth.

¹⁸ When the just cry out, the LORD hears them,
and from all their distress he rescues
them.
R. The Lord hears the cry of the poor.
¹⁹The LORD is close to the brokenhearted;
and those who are crushed in spirit he
saves.
²³The LORD redeems the lives of his servants;
no one incurs guilt who takes refuge in
him.
R. The Lord hears the cry of the poor.

Second Reading: 2 Timothy 4:6-8, 16-18

Beloved: ⁶I am already being poured out like a libation, and the time of my departure is at hand. ⁷I have competed well; I have finished the race; I have kept the faith. ⁸From now on the crown of righteousness awaits me, which the Lord, the just judge, will award to me on that day, and not only to me, but to all who have longed for his appearance.

¹⁶At my first defense no one appeared on my behalf, but everyone deserted me. May it not be held against them! ¹⁷But the Lord stood by me and gave me strength, so that through me the proclamation might be completed and all the Gentiles might hear it. And I was rescued from the lion's mouth. ⁸The Lord will rescue me from every evil threat and will bring me safe to his heavenly kingdom. To him be glory forever and ever. Amen.

Alleluia: 2 Corinthians 5:19

R. Alleluia, alleluia.
¹⁹God was reconciling the world to himself in
Christ,
and entrusting to us the message of
salvation.
R. Alleluia, alleluia.

Gospel: Luke 18:9-14

⁹Jesus addressed this parable to those who were convinced of their own righteousness and despised everyone else. ¹⁰"Two people went up to the temple area to pray; one was a Pharisee and the other was a tax collector. ¹¹The Pharisee took up his position and spoke this prayer to himself, 'O God, I thank you that I am not like the rest of humanity— greedy, dishonest, adulterous— or even like this tax collector. ¹²I fast twice a week, and I pay tithes on my whole income.' ¹³But the tax collector stood off at a distance and would not even raise his eyes to heaven but beat his breast and prayed, 'O God, be merciful to me a sinner.' ¹⁴I tell you, the latter went home justified, not the former; for whoever exalts himself will be humbled, and the one who humbles himself will be exalted."

Monday October 27, 2025
Monday of the Thirtieth Week in Ordinary Time

First Reading: Romans 8:12-17

[12]Brothers and sisters, we are not debtors to the flesh, to live according to the flesh. [13]For if you live according to the flesh, you will die, but if by the spirit you put to death the deeds of the body, you will live.

[14]For those who are led by the Spirit of God are sons of God. [15]For you did not receive a spirit of slavery to fall back into fear, but you received a spirit of adoption, through which we cry, "*Abba*, Father!" [16]The Spirit himself bears witness with our spirit that we are children of God, [17]and if children, then heirs, heirs of God and joint heirs with Christ, if only we suffer with him so that we may also be glorified with him.

Responsorial Psalm: Psalms 68:2 AND 4, 6-7AB, 20-21

R. [21a] *Our God is the God of salvation.*
[2]God arises; his enemies are scattered,
    and those who hate him flee before him.
[4] But the just rejoice and exult before God;
    they are glad and rejoice.
R. *Our God is the God of salvation.*
[6] The father of orphans and the defender of widows
    is God in his holy dwelling.
[7AB] God gives a home to the forsaken;
    he leads forth prisoners to prosperity.
R. *Our God is the God of salvation.*
[20] Blessed day by day be the Lord,
    who bears our burdens; God, who is our salvation.
[21] God is a saving God for us;
    the LORD, my Lord, controls the passageways of death.
R. *Our God is the God of salvation.*

Alleluia: John 17:17B, 17A

R. **Alleluia, alleluia.**
[17B]Your word, O Lord, is truth;
[17A]consecrate us in the truth.
R. **Alleluia, alleluia.**

Gospel: Luke 13:10-17

[10]Jesus was teaching in a synagogue on the Sabbath. [11]And a woman was there who for eighteen years had been crippled by a spirit; she was bent over,

completely incapable of standing erect. [12] When Jesus saw her, he called to her and said, "Woman, you are set free of your infirmity." [13] He laid his hands on her, and she at once stood up straight and glorified God. [14] But the leader of the synagogue, indignant that Jesus had cured on the sabbath, said to the crowd in reply, "There are six days when work should be done. Come on those days to be cured, not on the sabbath day." [15] The Lord said to him in reply, "Hypocrites! Does not each one of you on the sabbath untie his ox or his ass from the manger and lead it out for watering? [16] This daughter of Abraham, whom Satan has bound for eighteen years now, ought she not to have been set free on the sabbath day from this bondage?" [17] When he said this, all his adversaries were humiliated; and the whole crowd rejoiced at all the splendid deeds done by him.

Tuesday October 28, 2025
Feast of Saints Simon and Jude, Apostles

First Reading: Ephesians 2:19-22

Brothers and sisters: [19] You are no longer strangers and sojourners, but you are fellow citizens with the holy ones and members of the household of God, [20] built upon the foundation of the Apostles and prophets, with Christ Jesus himself as the capstone. [21] Through him the whole structure is held together and grows into a temple sacred in the Lord; [22] in him you also are being built together into a dwelling place of God in the Spirit.

Responsorial Psalm: Psalms 19:2-3, 4-5

R. [5a] *Their message goes out through all the earth.*
[2] The heavens declare the glory of God,
    and the firmament proclaims his
        handiwork.
[3] Day pours out the word to day,
    and night to night imparts knowledge.
R. Their message goes out through all the earth.
[4] Not a word nor a discourse
    whose voice is not heard;
[5] Through all the earth their voice resounds,
    and to the ends of the world, their
        message.
R. Their message goes out through all the earth.

Alleluia: cf. Te Deum

R. Alleluia, alleluia.
We praise you, O God,
we acclaim you as Lord;
the glorious company of Apostles praise you.
R. Alleluia, alleluia.

Gospel: Luke 6:12-16

¹² Jesus went up to the mountain to pray, and he spent the night in prayer to God. ¹³ When day came, he called his disciples to himself, and from them he chose Twelve, whom he also named Apostles: ¹⁴ Simon, whom he named Peter, and his brother Andrew, James, John, Philip, Bartholomew, ¹⁵ Matthew, Thomas, James the son of Alphaeus, Simon who was called a Zealot,¹⁶ and Judas the son of James, and Judas Iscariot, who became a traitor.

Wednesday October 29, 2025
Wednesday of Thirtieth Week in Ordinary Time

First Reading: Romans 8:26-30

Brothers and sisters: ²⁶The Spirit comes to the aid of our weakness; for we do not know how to pray as we ought, but the Spirit himself intercedes with inexpressible groanings. ²⁷And the one who searches hearts knows what is the intention of the Spirit, because he intercedes for the holy ones according to God's will.

²⁸We know that all things work for good for those who love God, who are called according to his purpose. ²⁹For those he foreknew he also predestined to be conformed to the image of his Son, so that he might be the firstborn among many brothers. ³⁰And those he predestined he also called; and those he called he also justified; and those he justified he also glorified.

Responsorial Psalm: Psalms 13:4-5, 6

R. ⁽⁶ᵃ⁾ **My hope, O Lord, is in your mercy.**
⁴ Look, answer me, O LORD, my God!
⁵ Give light to my eyes that I may not sleep in
  death
    lest my enemy say, "I have overcome
      him";
    lest my foes rejoice at my downfall.
R. My hope, O Lord, is in your mercy.
⁶ Though I trusted in your mercy,
Let my heart rejoice in your salvation;
    let me sing of the LORD, "He has been good
      to me."
R. My hope, O Lord, is in your mercy.

Alleluia: cf. 2 Thessalonians 2:14

R. Alleluia, alleluia.
¹⁴ God has called us through the Gospel
to possess the glory of our Lord Jesus Christ.
R. Alleluia, alleluia.

Gospel: Luke 13:22-30

22 Jesus passed through towns and villages, teaching as he went and making his way to Jerusalem. 23 Someone asked him, "Lord, will only a few people be saved?" He answered them, 24 "Strive to enter through the narrow gate, for many, I tell you, will attempt to enter but will not be strong enough. 25 After the master of the house has arisen and locked the door, then will you stand outside knocking and saying, 'Lord, open the door for us.' He will say to you in reply, 'I do not know where you are from.' 26 And you will say, 'We ate and drank in your company and you taught in our streets.' 27 Then he will say to you, 'I do not know where you are from. Depart from me, all you evildoers!' 28 And there will be wailing and grinding of teeth when you see Abraham, Isaac, and Jacob and all the prophets in the Kingdom of God and you yourselves cast out. 29 And people will come from the east and the west and from the north and the south and will recline at table in the Kingdom of God. 30 For behold, some are last who will be first, and some are first who will be last."

Thursday October 30, 2025
Thursday of Thirtieth Week in Ordinary Time

First Reading: Romans 8:31B-39

Brothers and sisters: 31B If God is for us, who can be against us? 32 He did not spare his own Son but handed him over for us all, how will he not also give us everything else along with him? 33 Who will bring a charge against God's chosen ones? It is God who acquits us. 34 Who will condemn? It is Christ Jesus who died, rather, was raised, who also is at the right hand of God, who indeed intercedes for us. 35 What will separate us from the love of Christ? Will anguish, or distress, or persecution, or famine, or nakedness, or peril, or the sword? 36 As it is written:

For your sake we are being slain all the day;
we are looked upon as sheep to be
slaughtered.

37 No, in all these things we conquer overwhelmingly through him who loved us. 38 For I am convinced that neither death, nor life, nor angels, nor principalities, nor present things, nor future things, nor powers, 39 nor height, nor depth, nor any other creature will be able to separate us from the love of God in Christ Jesus our Lord.

Responsorial Psalm: Psalms 109:21-22, 26-27, 30-31

R. (26b) **Save me, O Lord, in your mercy.**
21 Do you, O GOD, my Lord, deal kindly with me
    for your name's sake;
  in your generous mercy rescue me;
22 For I am wretched and poor,
  and my heart is pierced within me.
R. **Save me, O Lord, in your mercy.**
26 Help me, O LORD, my God;
  save me, in your mercy,
27 And let them know that this is your hand;

that you, O LORD, have done this.
R. Save me, O Lord, in your mercy.
³⁰I will speak my thanks earnestly to the LORD,
    and in the midst of the throng I will
        praise him,
³¹For he stood at the right hand of the poor man,
    to save him from those who would
        condemn his soul.
R. Save me, O Lord, in your kindness.

Alleluia: cf. Luke 19:38; 2:14
R. Alleluia, alleluia.
³⁸ Blessed is the king who comes in the name of the Lord.
¹⁴ Glory to God in the highest and on earth peace to those on whom his favor rests.
R. Alleluia, alleluia.

Gospel: Luke 13:31-35
³¹ Some Pharisees came to Jesus and said, "Go away, leave this area because Herod wants to kill you." ³² He replied, "Go and tell that fox, 'Behold, I cast out demons and I perform healings today and tomorrow, and on the third day I accomplish my purpose. ³³ Yet I must continue on my way today, tomorrow, and the following day, for it is impossible that a prophet should die outside of Jerusalem.'
    ³⁴ "Jerusalem, Jerusalem, you who kill the prophets and stone those sent to you, how many times I yearned to gather your children together as a hen gathers her brood under her wings, but you were unwilling! ³⁵ Behold, your house will be abandoned. But I tell you, you will not see me until the time comes when you say, *Blessed is he who comes in the name of the Lord.*"

Friday October 31, 2025
Friday of Thirtieth Week in Ordinary Time
First Reading: Romans 9:1-5
Brothers and sisters:¹I speak the truth in Christ, I do not lie; my conscience joins with the Holy Spirit in bearing me witness ²that I have great sorrow and constant anguish in my heart. ³For I could wish that I myself were accursed and cut off from Christ for the sake of my own people, my kindred according to the flesh. ⁴They are children of Israel; theirs the adoption, the glory, the covenants, the giving of the law, the worship, and the promises; ⁵theirs the patriarchs, and from them, according to the flesh, is the Christ, who is over all, God blessed forever. Amen.

Responsorial Psalm: Psalms 147:12-13, 14-15, 19-20
R. Praise the Lord, Jerusalem.
¹²Glorify the LORD, O Jerusalem;
 praise your God, O Zion.
¹³ For he has strengthened the bars of your gates;
 he has blessed your children within you.
R. Praise the Lord, Jerusalem.
¹⁴He has granted peace in your borders;
 with the best of wheat he fills you.
¹⁵ He sends forth his command to the earth;
 swiftly runs his word!
R. Praise the Lord, Jerusalem.
¹⁹ He has proclaimed his word to Jacob,
 his statutes and his ordinances to Israel.
²⁰ He has not done thus for any other nation;
 his ordinances he has not made known to them. Alleluia.
R. Praise the Lord, Jerusalem.

Alleluia: John 10:27
R. Alleluia, alleluia.
²⁷My sheep hear my voice, says the Lord;
I know them, and they follow me.
R. Alleluia, alleluia.

Gospel: Luke 14:1-6
¹On a sabbath Jesus went to dine at the home of one of the leading Pharisees, and the people there were observing him carefully.²In front of him there was a man suffering from dropsy.³Jesus spoke to the scholars of the law and Pharisees in reply, asking, "Is it lawful to cure on the Sabbath or not?"⁴But they kept silent; so he took the man and, after he had healed him, dismissed him.⁵Then he said to them "Who among you, if your son or ox falls into a cistern, would not immediately pull him out on the sabbath day?" ⁶But they were unable to answer his question.

NOVEMBER 2025
Saturday November 1, 2025
Solemnity of All Saints (All Saints Day)
First Reading: Revelation 7:2-4, 9-14
² I, John, saw another angel come up from the East, holding the seal of the living God. He cried out in a loud voice to the four angels who were given power to damage the land and the sea, ³ "Do not damage the land or the sea or the trees until we put the seal on the foreheads of the servants of our God." ⁴ I heard the

number of those who had been marked with the seal, one hundred and forty-four thousand marked from every tribe of the children of Israel.

⁹ After this I had a vision of a great multitude, which no one could count, from every nation, race, people, and tongue. They stood before the throne and before the Lamb, wearing white robes and holding palm branches in their hands. ¹⁰ They cried out in a loud voice:

"Salvation comes from our God, who is
      seated on the throne,
   and from the Lamb."

¹¹ All the angels stood around the throne and around the elders and the four living creatures. They prostrated themselves before the throne, worshiped God, ¹² and exclaimed:

"Amen. Blessing and glory, wisdom and
      thanksgiving,
  honor, power, and might
  be to our God forever and ever. Amen."

¹³ Then one of the elders spoke up and said to me, "Who are these wearing white robes, and where did they come from?" ¹⁴ I said to him, "My lord, you are the one who knows." He said to me, "These are the ones who have survived the time of great distress; they have washed their robes and made them white in the Blood of the Lamb."

Responsorial Psalm: Psalms 24:1BC-2, 3-4AB, 5-6

*R. (see 6) **Lord, this is the people that longs to see your face.***

¹ᴮᶜ The LORD's are the earth and its fullness;
    the world and those who dwell in it.
² For he founded it upon the seas
    and established it upon the rivers.

R. Lord, this is the people that longs to see your face.

³ Who can ascend the mountain of the LORD?
    or who may stand in his holy place?
⁴ᴬᴮ One whose hands are sinless, whose heart is clean,
    who desires not what is vain.

R. Lord, this is the people that longs to see your face.

⁵ He shall receive a blessing from the LORD,
    a reward from God his savior.
⁶ Such is the race that seeks him,

that seeks the face of the God of Jacob.
R. Lord, this is the people that longs to see your face.

Second Reading: 1 John 3:1-3

Beloved: [1] See what love the Father has bestowed on us that we may be called the children of God. Yet so we are. The reason the world does not know us is that it did not know him. [2] Beloved, we are God's children now; what we shall be has not yet been revealed. We do know that when it is revealed we shall be like him, for we shall see him as he is. [3] Everyone who has this hope based on him makes himself pure, as he is pure.

Alleluia: Matthew 11:28
R. Alleluia, alleluia.
[28] Come to me, all you who labor and are burdened,
And I will give you rest, says the Lord.
R. Alleluia, alleluia.

Gospel: Matthew 5:1-12A

[1] When Jesus saw the crowds, he went up the mountain, and after he had sat down, his disciples came to him. [2] He began to teach them, saying:

[3] "Blessed are the poor in spirit,
    for theirs is the Kingdom of heaven.
[4] Blessed are they who mourn,
    for they will be comforted.
[5] Blessed are the meek,
    for they will inherit the land.
[6] Blessed are they who hunger and thirst for righteousness,
    for they will be satisfied.
[7] Blessed are the merciful,
    for they will be shown mercy.
[8] Blessed are the clean of heart,
    for they will see God.
[9] Blessed are the peacemakers,
    for they will be called children of God.
[10] Blessed are they who are persecuted for the sake of righteousness,
    for theirs is the Kingdom of heaven.
[11] Blessed are you when they insult you and persecute you
    and utter every kind of evil against you falsely because of me.

12A Rejoice and be glad,
> for your reward will be great in heaven."

Sunday November 2, 2025
Commemoration of All the Faithful Departed – All Souls Day

(The following are a selection of the readings that may be chosen for this day. Other alternative readings are: Wisdom 4:7-15, Psalm 25, Philippians 3:20-21, and John 11:25a, 26 or Isaiah 25:6-9, Psalm 27:1, 4, 7, 8b, 13-14, 2 Corinthians 4:14-5:1, and John 14:1-6)

First Reading: Wisdom 3:1-9

1 The souls of the just are in the hand of God,
> and no torment shall touch them.

2 They seemed, in the view of the foolish, to be dead;
> and their passing away was thought an affliction

3 and their going forth from us, utter destruction.

But they are in peace.

4 For if before men, indeed, they be punished,
> yet is their hope full of immortality;

5 chastised a little, they shall be greatly blessed,
> because God tried them
> and found them worthy of himself.

6 As gold in the furnace, he proved them,
> and as sacrificial offerings he took them to himself.

7 In the time of their visitation they shall shine,
> and shall dart about as sparks through stubble;

8 they shall judge nations and rule over peoples,
> and the LORD shall be their King forever.

9 Those who trust in him shall understand truth,
> and the faithful shall abide with him in love:

because grace and mercy are with his holy ones,
> and his care is with his elect.

Responsorial Psalm: Psalms 23:1-3A, 3B-4, 5, 6

R. (1) *The Lord is my shepherd; there is nothing I shall want.*

or:

Though I walk in the valley of darkness, I fear no evil, for you are with me.

[1] The LORD is my shepherd; I shall not want.
[2] In verdant pastures he gives me repose;
beside restful waters he leads me;
[3A] he refreshes my soul.

R. *The Lord is my shepherd; there is nothing I shall want.*

or:

Though I walk in the valley of darkness, I fear no evil, for you are with me.

[3B] He guides me in right paths
for his name's sake.
[4] Even though I walk in the dark valley
I fear no evil; for you are at my side
with your rod and your staff
that give me courage.

R. *The Lord is my shepherd; there is nothing I shall want.*

or:

Though I walk in the valley of darkness, I fear no evil, for you are with me.

[5] You spread the table before me
in the sight of my foes;
You anoint my head with oil;
my cup overflows.

R. *The Lord is my shepherd; there is nothing I shall want.*

or:

Though I walk in the valley of darkness, I fear no evil, for you are with me.

[6] Only goodness and kindness follow me
all the days of my life;
and I shall dwell in the house of the LORD
for years to come.

R. *The Lord is my shepherd; there is nothing*

> *I shall want.*

or:
> *Though I walk in the valley of darkness, I fear no evil, for you are with me.*

Second Reading: Romans 5:5-11

Brothers and sisters: ⁵ Hope does not disappoint, because the love of God has been poured out into our hearts through the Holy Spirit that has been given to us. ⁶ For Christ, while we were still helpless, died at the appointed time for the ungodly. ⁷ Indeed, only with difficulty does one die for a just person, though perhaps for a good person one might even find courage to die. ⁸ But God proves his love for us in that while we were still sinners Christ died for us. ⁹ How much more then, since we are now justified by his Blood, will we be saved through him from the wrath. ¹⁰ Indeed, if, while we were enemies, we were reconciled to God through the death of his Son, how much more, once reconciled, will we be saved by his life. ¹¹ Not only that, but we also boast of God through our Lord Jesus Christ, through whom we have now received reconciliation.

Or Romans 6:3-9

Brothers and sisters: ³ Are you unaware that we who were baptized into Christ Jesus were baptized into his death? ⁴ We were indeed buried with him through baptism into death, so that, just as Christ was raised from the dead by the glory of the Father, we too might live in newness of life.

⁵ For if we have grown into union with him through a death like his, we shall also be united with him in the resurrection. ⁶ We know that our old self was crucified with him, so that our sinful body might be done away with, that we might no longer be in slavery to sin. ⁷ For a dead person has been absolved from sin. ⁸ If, then, we have died with Christ, we believe that we shall also live with him. ⁹ We know that Christ, raised from the dead, dies no more; death no longer has power over him.

Alleluia: Matthew 25:34
R. Alleluia, alleluia.
³⁴ Come, you who are blessed by
>   my Father;
inherit the kingdom prepared
for you from the foundation of
>   the world.

R. Alleluia, alleluia.

Gospel: John 6:37-40

Jesus said to the crowds: ³⁷ "Everything that the Father gives me will come to me, and I will not reject anyone who comes to me, ³⁸ because I came down from heaven not to do my own will but the will of the one who sent me. ³⁹ And this is the will of the one who sent me, that I should not lose anything of what he gave me, but that I should raise it on the last day. ⁴⁰ For this is the will of my Father, that everyone who sees the Son and believes in him may have eternal life, and I shall raise him on the last day."

Monday November 3, 2025
Monday of the Thirty-first Week in Ordinary Time
First Reading: Romans 11:29-36

Brothers and sisters: ²⁹The gifts and the call of God are irrevocable.
³⁰Just as you once disobeyed God but have now received mercy because of their disobedience, ³¹so they have now disobeyed in order that, by virtue of the mercy shown to you, they too may now receive mercy. ³²For God delivered all to disobedience, that he might have mercy upon all. ³³Oh, the depth of the riches and wisdom and knowledge of God! How inscrutable are his judgments and how unsearchable his ways!

³⁴For who has known the mind of the Lord
 or who has been his counselor?
³⁵Or who has given him anything
 that he may be repaid?
³⁶For from him and through him and for him are all things. To God be glory forever. Amen.

Responsorial Psalm: Psalms 69:30-31, 33-34, 36
R. (14c) Lord, in your great love, answer me.
³⁰ But I am afflicted and in pain;
 let your saving help, O God, protect me.
³¹ I will praise the name of God in song,
 and I will glorify him with thanksgiving.
R. Lord, in your great love, answer me.
³³ "See, you lowly ones, and be glad;
 you who seek God, may your hearts
  revive!
³⁴ For the LORD hears the poor,
 and his own who are in bonds he spurns
  not."
R. Lord, in your great love, answer me.
³⁶ For God will save Zion
 and rebuild the cities of Judah.
They shall dwell in the land and own it,
 and the descendants of his servants shall
  inherit it,
 and those who love his name shall
  inhabit it.
R. Lord, in your great love, answer me.

Alleluia: John 8:31B-32
R. Alleluia, alleluia.
31B If you remain in my word, you will truly be
   my disciples,
32 and you will know the truth, says the Lord.
R. Alleluia, alleluia.

Gospel: Luke 14:12-14
On a sabbath Jesus went to dine at the home of one of the leading Pharisees. 12 He said to the host who invited him, "When you hold a lunch or a dinner, do not invite your friends or your brothers or sisters or your relatives or your wealthy neighbors, in case they may invite you back and you have repayment. 13 Rather, when you hold a banquet, invite the poor, the crippled, the lame, the blind; 14 blessed indeed will you be because of their inability to repay you. For you will be repaid at the resurrection of the righteous."

Tuesday November 4, 2025
Memorial of Saint Charles Borromeo, Bishop

First Reading: Romans 12:5-16AB
Brothers and sisters: 5We, though many, are one Body in Christ and individually parts of one another. 6Since we have gifts that differ according to the grace given to us, let us exercise them: if prophecy, in proportion to the faith; 7if ministry, in ministering; if one is a teacher, in teaching; 8if one exhorts, in exhortation; if one contributes, in generosity; if one is over others, with diligence; if one does acts of mercy, with cheerfulness.

9Let love be sincere; hate what is evil, hold on to what is good; 10love one another with mutual affection; anticipate one another in showing honor. 11Do not grow slack in zeal, be fervent in spirit, serve the Lord. 12Rejoice in hope, endure in affliction, persevere in prayer. 13Contribute to the needs of the holy ones, exercise hospitality. 14Bless those who persecute you, bless and do not curse them. 15Rejoice with those who rejoice, weep with those who weep. 16ABHave the same regard for one another; do not be haughty but associate with the lowly.

Responsorial Psalm: Psalms 131:1BCDE,2, 3
R. In you, O Lord, I have found my peace.
1O LORD, my heart is not proud,
   nor are my eyes haughty;
I busy not myself with great things,
   nor with things too sublime for me.
R. In you, O Lord, I have found my peace.
2Nay rather, I have stilled and quieted
   my soul like a weaned child.
Like a weaned child on its mother's lap,
   so is my soul within me.
R. In you, O Lord, I have found my peace.
3O Israel, hope in the LORD,
   both now and forever.

R. In you, O Lord, I have found my peace.

Alleluia: Matthew 11:28
R. Alleluia, alleluia.
²⁸ Come to me, all you who labor and are burdened,
and I will give you rest, says the Lord.
R. Alleluia, alleluia.

Gospel: Luke 14:15-24
¹⁵ One of those at table with Jesus said to him, "Blessed is the one who will dine in the Kingdom of God." ¹⁶ He replied to him, "A man gave a great dinner to which he invited many. ¹⁷ When the time for the dinner came, he dispatched his servant to say to those invited, 'Come, everything is now ready.' ¹⁸ But one by one, they all began to excuse themselves. The first said to him, 'I have purchased a field and must go to examine it; I ask you, consider me excused.' ¹⁹ And another said, 'I have purchased five yoke of oxen and am on my way to evaluate them; I ask you, consider me excused.' ²⁰ And another said, 'I have just married a woman, and therefore I cannot come.' ²¹ The servant went and reported this to his master. Then the master of the house in a rage commanded his servant, 'Go out quickly into the streets and alleys of the town and bring in here the poor and the crippled, the blind and the lame.' ²² The servant reported, 'Sir, your orders have been carried out and still there is room.' ²³ The master then ordered the servant, 'Go out to the highways and hedgerows and make people come in that my home may be filled. ²⁴ For, I tell you, none of those men who were invited will taste my dinner.'"

Wednesday November 5, 2025
Wednesday of Thirty-first Week in Ordinary Time
First Reading: Romans 13:8-10
Brothers and sisters: ⁸Owe nothing to anyone, except to love one another; for the one who loves another has fulfilled the law. ⁹The commandments, *You shall not commit adultery; you shall not kill; you shall not steal; you shall not covet*, and whatever other commandment there may be, are summed up in this saying, namely, *You shall love your neighbor as yourself*. ¹⁰Love does no evil to the neighbor; hence, love is the fulfillment of the law.

Responsorial Psalm: Psalms 112:1B-2, 4-5, 9
R. ⁽⁵ᵃ⁾ Blessed the man who is gracious and lends to those in need. or: *R. Alleluia.*
¹ᴮ Blessed the man who fears the LORD,
   who greatly delights in his commands.
² His posterity shall be mighty upon the earth;
   the upright generation shall be blessed.
R. Blessed the man who is gracious and lends to those in need. or: *R. Alleluia.*
⁴He dawns through the darkness, a light for
   the upright;

    he is gracious and merciful and just.
⁵ Well for the man who is gracious and lends,
    who conducts his affairs with justice.
**R. Blessed the man who is gracious and lends
to those in need.** or: **R. Alleluia.**
⁹ Lavishly he gives to the poor;
    his generosity shall endure forever;
    his horn shall be exalted in glory.
**R. Blessed the man who is gracious and lends
to those in need.** or: **R. Alleluia.**

Alleluia: 1 Peter 4:14
R. Alleluia, alleluia.
¹⁴ If you are insulted for the name of Christ,
    blessed are you,
for the Spirit of God rests upon you.
R. Alleluia, alleluia.

Gospel: Luke 14:25-33
²⁵ Great crowds were traveling with Jesus, and he turned and addressed them, ²⁶ "If anyone comes to me without hating his father and mother, wife and children, brothers and sisters, and even his own life, he cannot be my disciple. ²⁷ Whoever does not carry his own cross and come after me cannot be my disciple. ²⁸ Which of you wishing to construct a tower does not first sit down and calculate the cost to see if there is enough for its completion? ²⁹ Otherwise, after laying the foundation and finding himself unable to finish the work the onlookers should laugh at him ³⁰ and say, 'This one began to build but did not have the resources to finish.' ³¹Or what king marching into battle would not first sit down and decide whether with ten thousand troops he can successfully oppose another king advancing upon him with twenty thousand troops? ³² But if not, while he is still far away, he will send a delegation to ask for peace terms. ³³ In the same way, everyone of you who does not renounce all his possessions cannot be my disciple."

Thursday November 6, 2025
Thursday of Thirty-first Week in Ordinary Time
First Reading: Romans 14:7-12
Brothers and sisters: ⁷None of us lives for oneself, and no one dies for oneself. ⁸For if we live, we live for the Lord, and if we die, we die for the Lord; so then, whether we live or die, we are the Lord's. ⁹For this is why Christ died and came to life, that he might be Lord of both the dead and the living. ¹⁰Why then do you judge your brother or sister? Or you, why do you look down on your brother or sister? For we shall all stand before the judgment seat of God; ¹¹for it is written:

*As I live, says the Lord, every knee shall bend
    before me,
    and every tongue shall give praise to God.*

[12] So then each of us shall give an account of himself to God.

Responsorial Psalm: Psalms 27:1BCDE, 4, 13-14

R. (13) I believe that I shall see the good things of
the Lord in the land of the living.

[1] The LORD is my light and my salvation;
   whom should I fear?
The LORD is my life's refuge;
   of whom should I be afraid?

R. I believe that I shall see the good things of the
Lord in the land of the living.

[4] One thing I ask of the LORD;
   this I seek:
To dwell in the house of the LORD
   all the days of my life,
That I may gaze on the loveliness of the LORD
   and contemplate his temple.

R. I believe that I shall see the good things of the
Lord in the land of the living.

[13] I believe that I shall see the bounty of the
      LORD
   in the land of the living.
[14] Wait for the LORD with courage;
   be stouthearted, and wait for the LORD.

R. I believe that I shall see the good things of the
Lord in the land of the living.

Alleluia: Matthew 11:28

R. Alleluia, alleluia.
[28] Come to me, all you who labor and are
      burdened,
and I will give you rest, says the Lord.
R. Alleluia, alleluia.

Gospel: Luke 15:1-10

[1] The tax collectors and sinners were all drawing near to listen to Jesus, [2] but the Pharisees and scribes began to complain, saying, "This man welcomes sinners and eats with them." [3] So Jesus addressed this parable to them. [4] "What man among you having a hundred sheep and losing one of them would not leave the ninety-nine in the desert and go after the lost one until he finds it? [5] And when he does find it, he sets it on his shoulders with great joy [6] and, upon his arrival home, he calls together his friends and neighbors and says to them, 'Rejoice with me because I have found my lost sheep.' [7] I tell you, in just the same way there will be more joy in heaven over one sinner who repents than over ninety-nine righteous people who have no need of repentance.

⁸ "Or what woman having ten coins and losing one would not light a lamp and sweep the house, searching carefully until she finds it? ⁹ And when she does find it, she calls together her friends and neighbors and says to them, 'Rejoice with me because I have found the coin that I lost.' ¹⁰ In just the same way, I tell you, there will be rejoicing among the angels of God over one sinner who repents."

Friday November 7, 2025
Friday of Thirty-first Week in Ordinary Time
First Reading: Romans 15:14-21

¹⁴I myself am convinced about you, my brothers and sisters, that you yourselves are full of goodness, filled with all knowledge, and able to admonish one another. ¹⁵But I have written to you rather boldly in some respects to remind you, because of the grace given me by God ¹⁶to be a minister of Christ Jesus to the Gentiles in performing the priestly service of the Gospel of God, so that the offering up of the Gentiles may be acceptable, sanctified by the Holy Spirit.¹⁷In Christ Jesus, then, I have reason to boast in what pertains to God.¹⁸For I will not dare to speak of anything except what Christ has accomplished through me to lead the Gentiles to obedience by word and deed,¹⁹by the power of signs and wonders, by the power of the Spirit of God, so that from Jerusalem all the way around to Illyricum I have finished preaching the Gospel of Christ.²⁰Thus I aspire to proclaim the Gospel not where Christ has already been named, so that I do not build on another's foundation,²¹but as it is written:

Those who have never been told of him shall
   see,
   and those who have never heard of him
      shall understand.

Responsorial Psalm: Psalms 98:1, 2-3AB, 3CD-4
R. (see 2b) **The Lord has revealed to the nations his saving power.**

¹ Sing to the LORD a new song,
   for he has done wondrous deeds;
His right hand has won victory for him,
   his holy arm.
R. **The Lord has revealed to the nations his saving power.**

² The LORD has made his salvation known:
   in the sight of the nations he has revealed
      his justice.
³ᴬᴮ He has remembered his kindness and his
      faithfulness
   toward the house of Israel.
R. **The Lord has revealed to the nations his saving power.**

³ᶜᴰ All the ends of the earth have seen

the salvation by our God.
⁴ Sing joyfully to the LORD, all you lands;
    break into song; sing praise.
R. The Lord has revealed to the nations his saving power.

Alleluia: 1 John 2:5
R. Alleluia, alleluia.
⁵ Whoever keeps the word of Christ,
the love of God is truly perfected in him.
R. Alleluia, alleluia.

Gospel: Luke 16:1-8
¹ Jesus said to his disciples, "A rich man had a steward who was reported to him for squandering his property. ² He summoned him and said, 'What is this I hear about you? Prepare a full account of your stewardship, because you can no longer be my steward.' ³ The steward said to himself, 'What shall I do, now that my master is taking the position of steward away from me? I am not strong enough to dig and I am ashamed to beg. ⁴ I know what I shall do so that, when I am removed from the stewardship, they may welcome me into their homes.' ⁵ He called in his master's debtors one by one. To the first he said, 'How much do you owe my master?' ⁶ He replied, 'One hundred measures of olive oil.' He said to him, 'Here is your promissory note. Sit down and quickly write one for fifty.' ⁷ Then to another he said, 'And you, how much do you owe?' He replied, 'One hundred measures of wheat.' He said to him, 'Here is your promissory note; write one for eighty.' ⁸ And the master commended that dishonest steward for acting prudently. For the children of this world are more prudent in dealing with their own generation than the children of light."

Saturday November 8, 2025
Saturday of Thirty-first Week in Ordinary Time
First Reading: Romans 16:3-9, 16, 22-27
Brothers and sisters: ³Greet Prisca and Aquila, my co-workers in Christ Jesus,⁴who risked their necks for my life, to whom not only I am grateful but also all the churches of the Gentiles; ⁵greet also the Church at their house. Greet my beloved Epaenetus, who was the first fruits in Asia for Christ. ⁶Greet Mary, who has worked hard for you. ⁷Greet Andronicus and Junia, my relatives and my fellow prisoners; they are prominent among the Apostles and they were in Christ before me. ⁸Greet Ampliatus, my beloved in the Lord. ⁹Greet Urbanus, our co-worker in Christ, and my beloved Stachys.¹⁶Greet one another with a holy kiss. All the churches of Christ greet you.

²²I, Tertius, the writer of this letter, greet you in the Lord. ²³Gaius, who is host to me and to the whole Church, greets you. Erastus, the city treasurer, and our brother Quartus greet you.

²⁵Now to him who can strengthen you, according to my Gospel and the proclamation of Jesus Christ, according to the revelation of the mystery kept secret for long ages ²⁶but now manifested through the prophetic writings and, according

to the command of the eternal God, made known to all nations to bring about the obedience of faith, ²⁷to the only wise God, through Jesus Christ be glory forever and ever. Amen.

Responsorial Psalm: Psalms 145:2-3, 4-5, 10-11
R. ⁽¹ᵇ⁾ *I will praise your name for ever, Lord.*
² Every day will I bless you,
    and I will praise your name forever and ever.
³ Great is the LORD and highly to be praised;
    his greatness is unsearchable.
R. *I will praise your name for ever, Lord.*
⁴ Generation after generation praises your works
    and proclaims your might.
⁵ They speak of the splendor of your glorious majesty
    and tell of your wondrous works.
R. *I will praise your name for ever, Lord.*
¹⁰ Let all your works give you thanks, O LORD,
    and let your faithful ones bless you.
¹¹ Let them discourse of the glory of your Kingdom
    and speak of your might.
R. *I will praise your name for ever, Lord.*

Alleluia: 2 Corinthians 8:9
R. Alleluia, alleluia.
⁹ Jesus Christ became poor although he was rich,
so that by his poverty you might become rich.
R. Alleluia, alleluia.

Gospel: Luke 16:9-15
Jesus said to his disciples: ⁹"I tell you, make friends for yourselves with dishonest wealth, so that when it fails, you will be welcomed into eternal dwellings. ¹⁰The person who is trustworthy in very small matters is also trustworthy in great ones; and the person who is dishonest in very small matters is also dishonest in great ones. ¹¹If, therefore, you are not trustworthy with dishonest wealth, who will trust you with true wealth? ¹²If you are not trustworthy with what belongs to another, who will give you what is yours? ¹³No servant can serve two masters. He will either hate one and love the other, or be devoted to one and despise the other. You cannot serve God and mammon."

[14] The Pharisees, who loved money, heard all these things and sneered at him. [15] And he said to them, "You justify yourselves in the sight of others, but God knows your hearts; for what is of human esteem is an abomination in the sight of God."

Sunday November 9, 2025
Feast of Dedication of the Lateran Basilica in Rome
First Reading: Ezekiel 47:1-2, 8-9, 12

[1] The angel brought me back to the entrance of the temple, and I saw water flowing out from beneath the threshold of the temple toward the east, for the façade of the temple was toward the east; the water flowed down from the southern side of the temple, south of the altar. [2] He led me outside by the north gate, and around to the outer gate facing the east, where I saw water trickling from the southern side. [8] He said to me, "This water flows into the eastern district down upon the Arabah, and empties into the sea, the salt waters, which it makes fresh. [9] Wherever the river flows, every sort of living creature that can multiply shall live, and there shall be abundant fish, for wherever this water comes the sea shall be made fresh. [12] Along both banks of the river, fruit trees of every kind shall grow; their leaves shall not fade, nor their fruit fail. Every month they shall bear fresh fruit, for they shall be watered by the flow from the sanctuary. Their fruit shall serve for food, and their leaves for medicine."

Responsorial Psalm: Psalms 46:2-3, 5-6, 8-9

R. [5] *The waters of the river gladden the city of God, the holy dwelling of the Most High!*

[2] God is our refuge and our strength,
   an ever-present help in distress.
[3] Therefore, we fear not, though the earth be shaken
   and mountains plunge into the depths of the sea.

R. *The waters of the river gladden the city of God, the holy dwelling of the Most High!*

[5] There is a stream whose runlets gladden the city of God,
   the holy dwelling of the Most High.
[6] God is in its midst; it shall not be disturbed;
   God will help it at the break of dawn.

R. *The waters of the river gladden the city of God, the holy dwelling of the Most High!*

[8] The LORD of hosts is with us;
   our stronghold is the God of Jacob.
[9] Come! behold the deeds of the LORD,
   the astounding things he has wrought on

earth.
R. The waters of the river gladden the city of God, the holy dwelling of the Most High!

Second Reading: 1 Corinthians 3:9C-11, 16-17

Brothers and sisters: 9C You are God's building. 10 According to the grace of God given to me, like a wise master builder I laid a foundation, and another is building upon it. But each one must be careful how he builds upon it, 11 for no one can lay a foundation other than the one that is there, namely, Jesus Christ. 16 Do you not know that you are the temple of God, and that the Spirit of God dwells in you? 17 If anyone destroys God's temple, God will destroy that person; for the temple of God, which you are, is holy.

Alleluia: 2 Chronicles 7:16
R. Alleluia, alleluia.
16 I have chosen and consecrated this house,
　　says the Lord,
that my name may be there forever.
R. Alleluia, alleluia.

Gospel: John 2:13-22

13 Since the Passover of the Jews was near, Jesus went up to Jerusalem. 14 He found in the temple area those who sold oxen, sheep, and doves, as well as the money-changers seated there. 15 He made a whip out of cords and drove them all out of the temple area, with the sheep and oxen, and spilled the coins of the money-changers and overturned their tables, 16 and to those who sold doves he said, "Take these out of here, and stop making my Father's house a marketplace." 17 His disciples recalled the words of Scripture, *Zeal for your house will consume me.* 18 At this the Jews answered and said to him, "What sign can you show us for doing this?" 19 Jesus answered and said to them, "Destroy this temple and in three days I will raise it up." 20 The Jews said, "This temple has been under construction for forty-six years, and you will raise it up in three days?" 21 But he was speaking about the temple of his Body. 22 Therefore, when he was raised from the dead, his disciples remembered that he had said this, and they came to believe the Scripture and the word Jesus had spoken.

Monday November 10, 2025
Memorial of Saint Leo the Great, Pope & Doctor
First Reading: Wisdom 1:1-7
1 Love justice, you who judge the earth;
　　think of the Lord in goodness,
　　and seek him in integrity of heart;
2 Because he is found by those who test him
　　not,

  and he manifests himself to those who do
    not disbelieve him.
³For perverse counsels separate a man from
    God,
  and his power, put to the proof, rebukes
    the foolhardy;
⁴Because into a soul that plots evil, wisdom
    enters not,
   nor dwells she in a body under debt of
    sin.
⁵For the holy Spirit of discipline flees deceit
   and withdraws from senseless counsels;
   and when injustice occurs it is rebuked.
⁶For wisdom is a kindly spirit,
    yet she acquits not the blasphemer of his
      guilty lips;
Because God is the witness of his inmost self
    and the sure observer of his heart
    and the listener to his tongue.
⁷For the Spirit of the Lord fills the world,
    is all-embracing, and knows what man
      says.

Responsorial Psalm: Psalms 139:1B-3, 4-6, 7-8, 9-10

R. *(24b)* ***Guide me, Lord, along the everlasting way.***
¹ᴮ O LORD, you have probed me and you know
    me;
  ²you know when I sit and when I stand;
  you understand my thoughts from afar.
³My journeys and my rest you scrutinize,
  with all my ways you are familiar.
R. Guide me, Lord, along the everlasting way.
⁴ Even before a word is on my tongue,
  behold, O LORD, you know the whole of it.
⁵ Behind me and before, you hem me in
  and rest your hand upon me.
⁶ Such knowledge is too wonderful for me;
  too lofty for me to attain.
R. Guide me, Lord, along the everlasting way.
⁷ Where can I go from your spirit?
  From your presence where can I flee?
⁸ If I go up to the heavens, you are there;
  if I sink to the nether world, you are
    present there.
R. Guide me, Lord, along the everlasting way.

⁹ If I take the wings of the dawn,
    if I settle at the farthest limits of the sea,
¹⁰ Even there your hand shall guide me,
    and your right hand hold me fast.
R. Guide me, Lord, along the everlasting way.

Alleluia: Philippians 2:15D, 16A
R. Alleluia, alleluia.
¹⁵ᴰ Shine like lights in the world,
¹⁶ᴬ as you hold on to the word of life.
R. Alleluia, alleluia.

Gospel: Luke 17:1-6
¹ Jesus said to his disciples, "Things that cause sin will inevitably occur, but woe to the one through whom they occur. ² It would be better for him if a millstone were put around his neck and he be thrown into the sea than for him to cause one of these little ones to sin. ³ Be on your guard! If your brother sins, rebuke him; and if he repents, forgive him. ⁴ And if he wrongs you seven times in one day and returns to you seven times saying, 'I am sorry,' you should forgive him."

⁵ And the Apostles said to the Lord, "Increase our faith." ⁶ The Lord replied, "If you have faith the size of a mustard seed, you would say to this mulberry tree, 'Be uprooted and planted in the sea,' and it would obey you."

Tuesday November 11, 2025
Memorial Saint Martin of Tours, Bishop

First Reading: Wisdom 2:23-3:9
²³God formed man to be imperishable;
    the image of his own nature he made
        them.
²⁴But by the envy of the Devil, death entered
    the world,
    and they who are in his possession
        experience it.

¹But the souls of the just are in the hand of
    God,
    and no torment shall touch them.
²They seemed, in the view of the foolish, to be
    dead;
    and their passing away was thought an
        affliction
       ³and their going forth from us, utter
        destruction.
But they are in peace.
⁴For if before men, indeed, they be punished,

> yet is their hope full of immortality;
> ⁵Chastised a little, they shall be greatly blessed,
> > because God tried them
> > and found them worthy of himself.
> ⁶As gold in the furnace, he proved them,
> > and as sacrificial offerings he took them to himself.
> ⁷In the time of their visitation they shall shine,
> > and shall dart about as sparks through stubble;
> ⁸They shall judge nations and rule over peoples,
> > and the Lord shall be their King forever.
> ⁹Those who trust in him shall understand truth,
> > and the faithful shall abide with him in love:
> Because grace and mercy are with his holy ones,
> > and his care is with his elect.

Responsorial Psalm: Psalms 34:2-3, 16-17, 18-19

R.⁽²ᵃ⁾ I will bless the Lord at all times.
² I will bless the LORD at all times;
> his praise shall be ever in my mouth.
³ Let my soul glory in the LORD;
> the lowly will hear me and be glad.

R. I will bless the Lord at all times.

¹⁶ The LORD has eyes for the just,
> and ears for their cry.
¹⁷ The LORD confronts the evildoers,
> to destroy remembrance of them from the earth.

R. I will bless the Lord at all times.

¹⁸ When the just cry out, the LORD hears them,
> and from all their distress he rescues them.
¹⁹ The LORD is close to the brokenhearted;
> and those who are crushed in spirit he saves.

R. I will bless the Lord at all times.

Alleluia: John 14:23
R. Alleluia, alleluia.
²³ Whoever loves me will keep my word,
and my Father will love him,
and we will come to him.
R. Alleluia, alleluia.

Gospel: Luke 17:7-10
Jesus said to the Apostles: ⁷ "Who among you would say to your servant who has just come in from plowing or tending sheep in the field, 'Come here immediately and take your place at table'? ⁸ Would he not rather say to him, 'Prepare something for me to eat. Put on your apron and wait on me while I eat and drink. You may eat and drink when I am finished'? ⁹ Is he grateful to that servant because he did what was commanded? ¹⁰ So should it be with you. When you have done all you have been commanded, say, 'We are unprofitable servants; we have done what we were obliged to do.'"

Wednesday November 12, 2025
Memorial of Saint Josaphat, Bishop & Martyr

First Reading: Wisdom 6:1-11
¹Hear, O kings, and understand;
    learn, you magistrates of the earth's
        expanse!
²Hearken, you who are in power over the
        multitude
    and lord it over throngs of peoples!
³Because authority was given you by the Lord
    and sovereignty by the Most High,
    who shall probe your works and
        scrutinize your counsels.
⁴Because, though you were ministers of his
        kingdom, you judged not rightly,
    and did not keep the law,
    nor walk according to the will of God,
⁵Terribly and swiftly shall he come against
        you,
    because judgment is stern for the
        exalted–
⁶For the lowly may be pardoned out of mercy
    but the mighty shall be mightily put to
        the test.
⁷For the Lord of all shows no partiality,
    nor does he fear greatness,
Because he himself made the great as well as
        the small,
    and he provides for all alike;

⁸but for those in power a rigorous scrutiny
   impends.
⁹To you, therefore, O princes, are my words
   addressed
   that you may learn wisdom and that you
   may not sin.
¹⁰For those who keep the holy precepts
   hallowed shall be found holy,
   and those learned in them will have
   ready a response.
¹¹Desire therefore my words;
   long for them and you shall be instructed.

Responsorial Psalm: Psalms 82:3-4, 6-7
R. *(8a)* **Rise up, O God, bring judgment to the earth.**
³ Defend the lowly and the fatherless;
   render justice to the afflicted and the
      destitute.
⁴ Rescue the lowly and the poor;
   from the hand of the wicked deliver
      them.
R. Rise up, O God, bring judgment to the earth.
⁶ I said: "You are gods,
   all of you sons of the Most High;
⁷ yet like men you shall die,
   and fall like any prince."
R. Rise up, O God, bring judgment to the earth.

Alleluia: 1 Thessalonians 5:18
R. Alleluia, alleluia.
¹⁸ In all circumstances, give thanks,
for this is the will of God for you in Christ
      Jesus.
R. Alleluia, alleluia.

Gospel: Luke 17:11-19
¹¹ As Jesus continued his journey to Jerusalem, he traveled through Samaria and Galilee. ¹² As he was entering a village, ten lepers met him. They stood at a distance from him ¹³ and raised their voice, saying, "Jesus, Master! Have pity on us!" ¹⁴ And when he saw them, he said, "Go show yourselves to the priests." As they were going they were cleansed. ¹⁵ And one of them, realizing he had been healed, returned, glorifying God in a loud voice; ¹⁶ and he fell at the feet of Jesus and thanked him. He was a Samaritan. ¹⁷ Jesus said in reply, "Ten were cleansed, were they not? Where are the other nine? ¹⁸ Has none but this foreigner returned

to give thanks to God?" ¹⁹ Then he said to him, "Stand up and go; your faith has saved you."

Thursday November 13, 2025
Memorial of Saint Frances Xavier Cabrini

First Reading: Wisdom 7:22B-8:1

²²In Wisdom is a spirit
    intelligent, holy, unique,
Manifold, subtle, agile,
    clear, unstained, certain,
Not baneful, loving the good, keen,
    ²³unhampered, beneficent, kindly,
Firm, secure, tranquil,
    all-powerful, all-seeing,
And pervading all spirits,
    though they be intelligent, pure and very subtle.
²⁴For Wisdom is mobile beyond all motion,
    and she penetrates and pervades all things by reason of her purity.
²⁵For she is an aura of the might of God
    and a pure effusion of the glory of the Almighty;
    therefore nought that is sullied enters into her.
²⁶For she is the refulgence of eternal light,
    the spotless mirror of the power of God,
    the image of his goodness.
²⁷And she, who is one, can do all things,
    and renews everything while herself perduring;
And passing into holy souls from age to age,
    she produces friends of God and prophets.
²⁸For there is nought God loves, be it not one who dwells with Wisdom.
²⁹For she is fairer than the sun
    and surpasses every constellation of the stars.
Compared to light, she takes precedence;
    ³⁰for that, indeed, night supplants,
    but wickedness prevails not over Wisdom.

¹Indeed, she reaches from end to end

mightily
and governs all things well.

Responsorial Psalm: Psalms 119:89, 90, 91, 130, 135, 175

R. (89a) *Your word is for ever, O Lord.*
[89] Your word, O LORD, endures forever;
  it is firm as the heavens.
R. *Your word is for ever, O Lord.*
[90] Through all generations your truth endures;
  you have established the earth, and it stands firm.
R. *Your word is for ever, O Lord.*
[91] According to your ordinances they still stand firm:
  all things serve you.
R. *Your word is for ever, O Lord.*
[130] The revelation of your words sheds light,
  giving understanding to the simple.
R. *Your word is for ever, O Lord.*
[135] Let your countenance shine upon your servant,
  and teach me your statutes.
R. *Your word is for ever, O Lord.*
[175] Let my soul live to praise you,
  and may your ordinances help me.
R. *Your word is for ever, O Lord.*

Alleluia: John 15:5

R. Alleluia, alleluia.
[5] I am the vine, you are the branches, says the Lord:
whoever remains in me and I in him will bear much fruit.
R. Alleluia, alleluia.

Gospel: Luke 17:20-25

[20] Asked by the Pharisees when the Kingdom of God would come, Jesus said in reply, "The coming of the Kingdom of God cannot be observed, [21] and no one will announce, 'Look, here it is,' or, 'There it is.' For behold, the Kingdom of God is among you."

[22] Then he said to his disciples, "The days will come when you will long to see one of the days of the Son of Man, but you will not see it. [23] There will be those who will say to you, 'Look, there he is,' or 'Look, here he is.' Do not go off, do not run in pursuit. [24] For just as lightning flashes and lights up the sky from one side to the other, so will the Son of Man be in his day. [25] But first he must suffer greatly and be rejected by this generation."

Friday November 14, 2025
Friday of Thirty-second Week in Ordinary Time

First Reading: Wisdom 13:1-9

[1] All men were by nature foolish who were in ignorance of God,
and who from the good things seen did not succeed in knowing him who is,
and from studying the works did not discern the artisan;
[2] But either fire, or wind, or the swift air,
or the circuit of the stars, or the mighty water,
or the luminaries of heaven, the governors of the world, they considered gods.
[3] Now if out of joy in their beauty they thought them gods,
let them know how far more excellent is the Lord than these;
for the original source of beauty fashioned them.
[4] Or if they were struck by their might and energy,
let them from these things realize how much more powerful is he who made them.
[5] For from the greatness and the beauty of created things
their original author, by analogy, is seen.
[6] But yet, for these the blame is less;
For they indeed have gone astray perhaps,
though they seek God and wish to find him.
[7] For they search busily among his works,
but are distracted by what they see, because the things seen are fair.
[8] But again, not even these are pardonable.
[9] For if they so far succeeded in knowledge that they could speculate about the world,
how did they not more quickly find its Lord?

Responsorial Psalm: Psalms 19:2-3, 4-5AB
R. (2a) *The heavens proclaim the glory of God.*
² The heavens declare the glory of God,
   and the firmament proclaims his
      handiwork.
³ Day pours out the word to day,
   and night to night imparts knowledge.
R. *The heavens proclaim the glory of God.*
⁴ Not a word nor a discourse
   whose voice is not heard;
⁵ᴬᴮ Through all the earth their voice resounds,
   and to the ends of the world, their
      message.
R. *The heavens proclaim the glory of God.*

Alleluia: Luke 21:28
R. Alleluia, alleluia.
²⁸ Stand erect and raise your heads
because your redemption is at hand.
R. Alleluia, alleluia.

Gospel: Luke 17:26-37
Jesus said to his disciples: ²⁶ "As it was in the days of Noah, so it will be in the days of the Son of Man; ²⁷ they were eating and drinking, marrying and giving in marriage up to the day that Noah entered the ark, and the flood came and destroyed them all. ²⁸ Similarly, as it was in the days of Lot: they were eating, drinking, buying, selling, planting, building; ²⁹ on the day when Lot left Sodom, fire and brimstone rained from the sky to destroy them all. ³⁰ So it will be on the day the Son of Man is revealed. ³¹ On that day, someone who is on the housetop and whose belongings are in the house must not go down to get them, and likewise one in the field must not return to what was left behind. ³² Remember the wife of Lot. ³³ Whoever seeks to preserve his life will lose it, but whoever loses it will save it. ³⁴ I tell you, on that night there will be two people in one bed; one will be taken, the other left. ³⁵ And there will be two women grinding meal together; one will be taken, the other left." ³⁷ They said to him in reply, "Where, Lord?" He said to them, "Where the body is, there also the vultures will gather."

Saturday November 15, 2025
Saturday of Thirty-second Week in Ordinary Time
First Reading: Wisdom 18:14-16; 19:6-9
¹⁴When peaceful stillness compassed
      everything
   and the night in its swift course was half
      spent,
¹⁵Your all-powerful word, from heaven's royal
      throne

bounded, [16]a fierce warrior, into the
    doomed land,
  bearing the sharp sword of your
    inexorable decree.
And as he alighted, he filled every place with
    death;
  he still reached to heaven, while he stood
    upon the earth.

[6]For all creation, in its several kinds, was
    being made over anew,
  serving its natural laws,
    that your children might be preserved
      unharmed.
[7]The cloud overshadowed their camp;
  and out of what had before been water,
    dry land was seen emerging:
Out of the Red Sea an unimpeded road,
  and a grassy plain out of the mighty
    flood.
[8]Over this crossed the whole nation sheltered
    by your hand,
  after they beheld stupendous wonders.
[9]For they ranged about like horses,
  and bounded about like lambs,
    praising you, O Lord! their deliverer.

Responsorial Psalm: Psalms 105:2-3, 36-37, 42-43
R. [(5a)] *Remember the marvels the Lord has done!* or: *R. Alleluia*.
[2] Sing to him, sing his praise,
  proclaim all his wondrous deeds.
[3] Glory in his holy name;
  rejoice, O hearts that seek the LORD!
R. Remember the marvels the Lord has done! or: *R. Alleluia.*
[36] Then he struck every first-born throughout
    their land,
  the first fruits of all their manhood.
[37] And he led them forth laden with silver and
    gold,
  with not a weakling among their tribes.
R. Remember the marvels the Lord has done! or: *R. Alleluia.*
[42] For he remembered his holy word
  to his servant Abraham.
[43] And he led forth his people with joy;
  with shouts of joy, his chosen ones.

R. Remember the marvels the Lord has done! or: *R. Alleluia.*

Alleluia: cf. 2 Thessalonians 2:14
R. Alleluia, alleluia.
14 God has called us through the Gospel,
to possess the glory of our Lord Jesus Christ.
R. Alleluia, alleluia.

Gospel: Luke 18:1-8
1 Jesus told his disciples a parable about the necessity for them to pray always without becoming weary. He said, 2 "There was a judge in a certain town who neither feared God nor respected any human being. 3 And a widow in that town used to come to him and say, 'Render a just decision for me against my adversary.' 4 For a long time the judge was unwilling, but eventually he thought, 'While it is true that I neither fear God nor respect any human being, 5 because this widow keeps bothering me I shall deliver a just decision for her lest she finally come and strike me.'" 6 The Lord said, "Pay attention to what the dishonest judge says. 7 Will not God then secure the rights of his chosen ones who call out to him day and night? Will he be slow to answer them? 8 I tell you, he will see to it that justice is done for them speedily. But when the Son of Man comes, will he find faith on earth?"

Sunday November 16, 2025
Thirty-third Sunday in Ordinary Time, Year C

First Reading: Malachi 3:19-20A
19 Lo, the day is coming, blazing like an oven,
  when all the proud and all evildoers will
    be stubble,
and the day that is coming will set them on
    fire,
  leaving them neither root nor branch,
  says the LORD of hosts.
20A But for you who fear my name, there will
    arise
  the sun of justice with its healing rays.

Responsorial Psalm: Psalms 98:5-6, 7-8, 9
R. (cf. 9) The Lord comes to rule the earth with justice.
5 Sing praise to the LORD with the harp,
  with the harp and melodious song.
6 With trumpets and the sound of the horn
  sing joyfully before the King, the LORD.
R. The Lord comes to rule the earth with justice.
7 Let the sea and what fills it resound,
  the world and those who dwell in it;

⁸ let the rivers clap their hands,
>   the mountains shout with them for joy.

R. The Lord comes to rule the earth with justice.

⁹ Before the LORD, for he comes,
>   for he comes to rule the earth;
> he will rule the world with justice
>   and the peoples with equity.

R. The Lord comes to rule the earth with justice.

Second Reading: 2 Thessalonians 3:7-12

Brothers and sisters: ⁷You know how one must imitate us. For we did not act in a disorderly way among you, ⁸nor did we eat food received free from anyone. On the contrary, in toil and drudgery, night and day we worked, so as not to burden any of you. ⁹Not that we do not have the right. Rather, we wanted to present ourselves as a model for you, so that you might imitate us. ¹⁰In fact, when we were with you, we instructed you that if anyone was unwilling to work, neither should that one eat. ¹¹We hear that some are conducting themselves among you in a disorderly way, by not keeping busy but minding the business of others. ¹²Such people we instruct and urge in the Lord Jesus Christ to work quietly and to eat their own food.

Alleluia: Luke 21:28

R. Alleluia, alleluia.
²⁸ Stand erect and raise your heads
because your redemption is at hand.
R. Alleluia, alleluia.

Gospel: Luke 21:5-19

⁵While some people were speaking about how the temple was adorned with costly stones and votive offerings, Jesus said, ⁶"All that you see here— the days will come when there will not be left a stone upon another stone that will not be thrown down."

⁷Then they asked him, "Teacher, when will this happen? And what sign will there be when all these things are about to happen?" ⁸He answered, "See that you not be deceived, for many will come in my name, saying, 'I am he,' and 'The time has come.' Do not follow them! ⁹When you hear of wars and insurrections, do not be terrified; for such things must happen first, but it will not immediately be the end." ¹⁰Then he said to them, "Nation will rise against nation, and kingdom against kingdom. ¹¹There will be powerful earthquakes, famines, and plagues from place to place; and awesome sights and mighty signs will come from the sky.

¹²"Before all this happens, however, they will seize and persecute you, they will hand you over to the synagogues and to prisons, and they will have you led before kings and governors because of my name. ¹³It will lead to your giving testimony. ¹⁴Remember, you are not to prepare your defense beforehand, ¹⁵for I myself shall give you a wisdom in speaking that all your adversaries will be

powerless to resist or refute. ¹⁶You will even be handed over by parents, brothers, relatives, and friends, and they will put some of you to death. ¹⁷You will be hated by all because of my name, ¹⁸but not a hair on your head will be destroyed. ¹⁹By your perseverance you will secure your lives."

Monday November 17, 2025
Memorial of Saint Elizabeth of Hungary, Religious
First Reading: 1 Maccabees 1:10-15, 41-43, 54-57, 62-63

[From the descendants of Alexander's officers] ¹⁰there sprang a sinful offshoot, Antiochus Epiphanes, son of King Antiochus, once a hostage at Rome. He became king in the year one hundred and thirty-seven of the kingdom of the Greeks.

¹¹In those days there appeared in Israel men who were breakers of the law, and they seduced many people, saying: "Let us go and make an alliance with the Gentiles all around us; since we separated from them, many evils have come upon us." ¹²The proposal was agreeable; ¹³some from among the people promptly went to the king, and he authorized them to introduce the way of living of the Gentiles. ¹⁴Thereupon they built a gymnasium in Jerusalem according to the Gentile custom. ¹⁵They covered over the mark of their circumcision and abandoned the holy covenant; they allied themselves with the Gentiles and sold themselves to wrongdoing.

⁴¹Then the king wrote to his whole kingdom that all should be one people, ⁴²each abandoning his particular customs. All the Gentiles conformed to the command of the king, ⁴³and many children of Israel were in favor of his religion; they sacrificed to idols and profaned the sabbath.

⁵⁴On the fifteenth day of the month Chislev, in the year one hundred and forty-five, the king erected the horrible abomination upon the altar of burnt offerings and in the surrounding cities of Judah they built pagan altars. ⁵⁵They also burned incense at the doors of the houses and in the streets. ⁵⁶Any scrolls of the law which they found they tore up and burnt. ⁵⁷Whoever was found with a scroll of the covenant, and whoever observed the law, was condemned to death by royal decree. ⁶²But many in Israel were determined and resolved in their hearts not to eat anything unclean; ⁶³they preferred to die rather than to be defiled with unclean food or to profane the holy covenant; and they did die. ⁶⁴Terrible affliction was upon Israel.

Responsorial Psalm: Psalms 119:53, 61, 134, 150, 155, 158

R. *(see 88)* *Give me life, O Lord, and I will do your commands.*

⁵³Indignation seizes me because of the wicked
 who forsake your law.

R. *Give me life, O Lord, and I will do your commands.*

⁶¹ Though the snares of the wicked are twined about me,
 your law I have not forgotten.

R. *Give me life, O Lord, and I will do your commands.*

¹³⁴ Redeem me from the oppression of men,
  that I may keep your precepts.
R. Give me life, O Lord, and I will do your commands.
¹⁵⁰ I am attacked by malicious persecutors
  who are far from your law.
R. Give me life, O Lord, and I will do your commands.
¹⁵⁵ Far from sinners is salvation,
  because they seek not your statutes.
R. Give me life, O Lord, and I will do your commands.
¹⁵⁸ I beheld the apostates with loathing,
  because they kept not to your promise.
R. Give me life, O Lord, and I will do your commands.

Alleluia: John 8:12
R. Alleluia, alleluia.
¹² I am the light of the world, says the Lord;
whoever follows me will have the light of
  life.
R. Alleluia, alleluia.

Gospel: Luke 18:35-43
³⁵As Jesus approached Jericho a blind man was sitting by the roadside begging, ³⁶ and hearing a crowd going by, he inquired what was happening. ³⁷ They told him, "Jesus of Nazareth is passing by." ³⁸ He shouted, "Jesus, Son of David, have pity on me!" ³⁹ The people walking in front rebuked him, telling him to be silent, but he kept calling out all the more, "Son of David, have pity on me!" ⁴⁰ Then Jesus stopped and ordered that he be brought to him; and when he came near, Jesus asked him, ⁴¹ "What do you want me to do for you?" He replied, "Lord, please let me see." ⁴² Jesus told him, "Have sight; your faith has saved you." ⁴³ He immediately received his sight and followed him, giving glory to God. When they saw this, all the people gave praise to God.

Tuesday November 18, 2025
Tuesday of Thirty-third Week in Ordinary Time
First Reading: 2 Maccabees 6:18-31
¹⁸Eleazar, one of the foremost scribes, a man of advanced age and noble appearance, was being forced to open his mouth to eat pork. ¹⁹But preferring a glorious death to a life of defilement, ²⁰he spat out the meat, and went forward of his own accord to the instrument of torture, as people ought to do who have the courage to reject the food which it is unlawful to taste even for love of life. ²¹Those in charge of that unlawful ritual meal took the man aside privately, because of their

long acquaintance with him, and urged him to bring meat of his own providing, such as he could legitimately eat, and to pretend to be eating some of the meat of the sacrifice prescribed by the king; ²²in this way he would escape the death penalty, and be treated kindly because of their old friendship with him. ²³But Eleazar made up his mind in a noble manner, worthy of his years, the dignity of his advanced age, the merited distinction of his gray hair, and of the admirable life he had lived from childhood; and so he declared that above all he would be loyal to the holy laws given by God.

He told them to send him at once to the abode of the dead, explaining: ²⁴"At our age it would be unbecoming to make such a pretense; many young people would think the ninety-year-old Eleazar had gone over to an alien religion. ²⁵Should I thus pretend for the sake of a brief moment of life, they would be led astray by me, while I would bring shame and dishonor on my old age. ²⁶Even if, for the time being, I avoid the punishment of men, I shall never, whether alive or dead, escape the hands of the Almighty. ²⁷Therefore, by manfully giving up my life now, I will prove myself worthy of my old age, ²⁸and I will leave to the young a noble example of how to die willingly and generously for the revered and holy laws."

Eleazar spoke thus, and went immediately to the instrument of torture. ²⁹Those who shortly before had been kindly disposed, now became hostile toward him because what he had said seemed to them utter madness. ³⁰When he was about to die under the blows, he groaned and said: "The Lord in his holy knowledge knows full well that, although I could have escaped death, I am not only enduring terrible pain in my body from this scourging, but also suffering it with joy in my soul because of my devotion to him." ³¹This is how he died, leaving in his death a model of courage and an unforgettable example of virtue not only for the young but for the whole nation.

Responsorial Psalm: Psalms 3:2-3, 4-5, 6-7

R. *(6b)* ***The Lord upholds me.***
² O LORD, how many are my adversaries!
    Many rise up against me!
³ Many are saying of me,
    "There is no salvation for him in God."
R. *The Lord upholds me.*
⁴ But you, O LORD, are my shield;
    my glory, you lift up my head!
⁵ When I call out to the LORD,
    he answers me from his holy mountain.
R. *The Lord upholds me.*
⁶ When I lie down in sleep,
    I wake again, for the LORD sustains me.
⁷ I fear not the myriads of people
    arrayed against me on every side.
R. *The Lord upholds me.*

Alleluia: 1 John 4:10B
R. Alleluia, alleluia.
[10B] God loved us, and send his Son
as expiation for our sins.
R. Alleluia, alleluia.

Gospel: Luke 19:1-10
[1] At that time Jesus came to Jericho and intended to pass through the town. [2] Now a man there named Zacchaeus, who was a chief tax collector and also a wealthy man, [3] was seeking to see who Jesus was; but he could not see him because of the crowd, for he was short in stature. [4] So he ran ahead and climbed a sycamore tree in order to see Jesus, who was about to pass that way. [5] When he reached the place, Jesus looked up and said, "Zacchaeus, come down quickly, for today I must stay at your house." [6] And he came down quickly and received him with joy. [7] When they saw this, they began to grumble, saying, "He has gone to stay at the house of a sinner." [8] But Zacchaeus stood there and said to the Lord, "Behold, half of my possessions, Lord, I shall give to the poor, and if I have extorted anything from anyone I shall repay it four times over." [9] And Jesus said to him, "Today salvation has come to this house because this man too is a descendant of Abraham. [10] For the Son of Man has come to seek and to save what was lost."

Wednesday November 19, 2025
Wednesday of Thirty-third Week in Ordinary Time
First Reading: 2 Maccabees 7:1, 20-31
[1] It happened that seven brothers with their mother were arrested and tortured with whips and scourges by the king, to force them to eat pork in violation of God's law.

[20] Most admirable and worthy of everlasting remembrance was the mother, who saw her seven sons perish in a single day, yet bore it courageously because of her hope in the Lord. [21] Filled with a noble spirit that stirred her womanly heart with manly courage, she exhorted each of them in the language of their ancestors with these words: [22] "I do not know how you came into existence in my womb; it was not I who gave you the breath of life, nor was it I who set in order the elements of which each of you is composed. [23] Therefore, since it is the Creator of the universe who shapes each man's beginning, as he brings about the origin of everything, he, in his mercy, will give you back both breath and life, because you now disregard yourselves for the sake of his law."

[24] Antiochus, suspecting insult in her words, thought he was being ridiculed. As the youngest brother was still alive, the king appealed to him, not with mere words, but with promises on oath, to make him rich and happy if he would abandon his ancestral customs: he would make him his Friend and entrust him with high office. [25] When the youth paid no attention to him at all, the king appealed to the mother, urging her to advise her boy to save his life. [26] After he had urged her for a long time, she went through the motions of persuading her son. In derision of the cruel tyrant, [27] she leaned over close to her son and said in their native language: "Son, have pity on me, who carried you in my womb for nine months, nursed you

for three years, brought you up, educated and supported you to your present age. ²⁸I beg you, child, to look at the heavens and the earth and see all that is in them; then you will know that God did not make them out of existing things; and in the same way the human race came into existence. ²⁹Do not be afraid of this executioner, but be worthy of your brothers and accept death, so that in the time of mercy I may receive you again with them."

³⁰She had scarcely finished speaking when the youth said: "What are you waiting for? I will not obey the king's command. I obey the command of the law given to our fathers through Moses. ³¹But you, who have contrived every kind of affliction for the Hebrews, will not escape the hands of God."

Responsorial Psalm: Psalms 17:1BCD, 5-6, 8B AND 15

R. ⁽¹⁵ᵇ⁾ **Lord, when your glory appears, my joy will be full.**

¹ᴮᶜᴰ Hear, O LORD, a just suit;
   attend to my outcry;
   hearken to my prayer from lips without
      deceit.

R. **Lord, when your glory appears, my joy will be full.**

⁵ My steps have been steadfast in your paths,
   my feet have not faltered.
⁶ I call upon you, for you will answer me, O
      God;
   incline your ear to me; hear my word.

R. **Lord, when your glory appears, my joy will be full.**

⁸ᴮ Keep me as the apple of your eye;
   hide me in the shadow of your wings.
¹⁵ But I in justice shall behold your face;
   on waking, I shall be content in your
      presence.

R. **Lord, when your glory appears, my joy will be full.**

Alleluia: cf. John 15:16

R. **Alleluia, alleluia.**
¹⁶ I chose you from the world,
to go and bear fruit that will last, says the
      Lord.
R. **Alleluia, alleluia.**

Gospel: Luke 19:11-28

[11] While people were listening to Jesus speak, he proceeded to tell a parable because he was near Jerusalem and they thought that the Kingdom of God would appear there immediately. [12] So he said, "A nobleman went off to a distant country to obtain the kingship for himself and then to return. [13] He called ten of his servants and gave them ten gold coins and told them, 'Engage in trade with these until I return.' [14] His fellow citizens, however, despised him and sent a delegation after him to announce, 'We do not want this man to be our king.' [15] But when he returned after obtaining the kingship, he had the servants called, to whom he had given the money, to learn what they had gained by trading. [16] The first came forward and said, 'Sir, your gold coin has earned ten additional ones.' [17] He replied, 'Well done, good servant! You have been faithful in this very small matter; take charge of ten cities.' [18] Then the second came and reported, 'Your gold coin, sir, has earned five more.' [19] And to this servant too he said, 'You, take charge of five cities.' [20] Then the other servant came and said, 'Sir, here is your gold coin; I kept it stored away in a handkerchief, [21] for I was afraid of you, because you are a demanding man; you take up what you did not lay down and you harvest what you did not plant.' [22] He said to him, 'With your own words I shall condemn you, you wicked servant. You knew I was a demanding man, taking up what I did not lay down and harvesting what I did not plant; [23] why did you not put my money in a bank? Then on my return I would have collected it with interest.' [24] And to those standing by he said, 'Take the gold coin from him and give it to the servant who has ten.' [25] But they said to him, 'Sir, he has ten gold coins.' [26] He replied, 'I tell you, to everyone who has, more will be given, but from the one who has not, even what he has will be taken away. [27] Now as for those enemies of mine who did not want me as their king, bring them here and slay them before me.'"

[28] After he had said this, he proceeded on his journey up to Jerusalem.

Thursday November 20, 2025
Thursday of Thirty-third Week in Ordinary Time
First Reading: 1 Maccabees 2:15-29

[15] The officers of the king in charge of enforcing the apostasy came to the city of Modein to organize the sacrifices. [16] Many of Israel joined them, but Mattathias and his sons gathered in a group apart. [17] Then the officers of the king addressed Mattathias: "You are a leader, an honorable and great man in this city, supported by sons and kin. [18] Come now, be the first to obey the king's command, as all the Gentiles and the men of Judah and those who are left in Jerusalem have done. Then you and your sons shall be numbered among the King's Friends, and shall be enriched with silver and gold and many gifts." [19] But Mattathias answered in a loud voice: "Although all the Gentiles in the king's realm obey him, so that each forsakes the religion of his fathers and consents to the king's orders, [20] yet I and my sons and my kin will keep to the covenant of our fathers. [21] God forbid that we should forsake the law and the commandments. [22] We will not obey the words of the king nor depart from our religion in the slightest degree."

²³As he finished saying these words, a certain Jew came forward in the sight of all to offer sacrifice on the altar in Modein according to the king's order. ²⁴When Mattathias saw him, he was filled with zeal; his heart was moved and his just fury was aroused; he sprang forward and killed him upon the altar. ²⁵At the same time, he also killed the messenger of the king who was forcing them to sacrifice, and he tore down the altar. ²⁶Thus he showed his zeal for the law, just as Phinehas did with Zimri, son of Salu.

²⁷Then Mattathias went through the city shouting, "Let everyone who is zealous for the law and who stands by the covenant follow after me!" ²⁸Thereupon he fled to the mountains with his sons, leaving behind in the city all their possessions. ²⁹Many who sought to live according to righteousness and religious custom went out into the desert to settle there.

Responsorial Psalm: Psalms 50:1B-2, 5-6, 14-15
R. *⁽²³ᵇ⁾* **To the upright I will show the saving power of God.**

¹ᴮGod the LORD has spoken and summoned the earth,
> from the rising of the sun to its setting.

² From Zion, perfect in beauty,
> God shines forth.

R. To the upright I will show the saving power of God.

⁵ "Gather my faithful ones before me,
> those who have made a covenant with me by sacrifice."

⁶ And the heavens proclaim his justice;
> for God himself is the judge.

R. To the upright I will show the saving power of God.

¹⁴ "Offer to God praise as your sacrifice
> and fulfill your vows to the Most High;

¹⁵ Then call upon me in time of distress;
> I will rescue you, and you shall glorify me."

R. To the upright I will show the saving power of God.

Alleluia: Psalms 95:8
R. Alleluia, alleluia.
⁸ If today you hear his voice,
harden not your hearts.
R. Alleluia, alleluia.

Gospel: Luke 19:41-44

41 As Jesus drew near Jerusalem, he saw the city and wept over it, 42 saying, "If this day you only knew what makes for peace— but now it is hidden from your eyes. 43 For the days are coming upon you when your enemies will raise a palisade against you; they will encircle you and hem you in on all sides. 44 They will smash you to the ground and your children within you, and they will not leave one stone upon another within you because you did not recognize the time of your visitation."

Friday November 21, 2025
The Presentation of the Blessed Virgin Mary
First Reading: 1 Maccabees 4:36-37, 52-59

36 Judas and his brothers said, "Now that our enemies have been crushed, let us go up to purify the sanctuary and rededicate it." 37 So the whole army assembled, and went up to Mount Zion.

52 Early in the morning on the twenty-fifth day of the ninth month, that is, the month of Chislev, in the year one hundred and forty-eight, they arose 53 and offered sacrifice according to the law on the new altar of burnt offerings that they had made. 54 On the anniversary of the day on which the Gentiles had defiled it, on that very day it was reconsecrated with songs, harps, flutes, and cymbals. 55 All the people prostrated themselves and adored and praised Heaven, who had given them success.

56 For eight days they celebrated the dedication of the altar and joyfully offered burnt offerings and sacrifices of deliverance and praise. 57 They ornamented the facade of the temple with gold crowns and shields; they repaired the gates and the priests' chambers and furnished them with doors. 58 There was great joy among the people now that the disgrace of the Gentiles was removed. 59 Then Judas and his brothers and the entire congregation of Israel decreed that the days of the dedication of the altar should be observed with joy and gladness on the anniversary every year for eight days, from the twenty-fifth day of the month Chislev.

Responsorial Psalm: 1 Chronicles 29:10BCD, 11ABC, 11D-12A, 12BCD

R. (13b) *We praise your glorious name, O mighty God.*
10BCD "Blessed may you be, O LORD,
   God of Israel our father,
   from eternity to eternity."
R. *We praise your glorious name, O mighty God.*
11ABC "Yours, O LORD, are grandeur and power,
   majesty, splendor, and glory.
For all in heaven and on earth is yours."
R. *We praise your glorious name, O mighty God.*
11D "Yours, O LORD, is the sovereignty;
   you are exalted as head over all.
12A Riches and honor are from you."
R. *We praise your glorious name, O mighty God.*
12BCD "You have dominion over all,
In your hand are power and might;

it is yours to give grandeur and strength
   to all."
R. We praise your glorious name, O mighty God.

Alleluia: John 10:27
R. Alleluia, alleluia.
27 My sheep hear my voice, says the Lord;
I know them, and they follow me.
R. Alleluia, alleluia.

Gospel: Luke 19:45-48
45 Jesus entered the temple area and proceeded to drive out those who were selling things, 46 saying to them, "It is written, *My house shall be a house of prayer, but you have made it a den of thieves.*" 47 And every day he was teaching in the temple area. The chief priests, the scribes, and the leaders of the people, meanwhile, were seeking to put him to death, 48 but they could find no way to accomplish their purpose because all the people were hanging on his words.

Saturday November 22, 2025
Memorial of Saint Cecilia, Virgin & Martyr
First Reading: 1 Maccabees 6:1-13
1 As King Antiochus was traversing the inland provinces, he heard that in Persia there was a city called Elymais, famous for its wealth in silver and gold, 2 and that its temple was very rich, containing gold helmets, breastplates, and weapons left there by Alexander, son of Philip, king of Macedon, the first king of the Greeks. 3 He went therefore and tried to capture and pillage the city. But he could not do so, because his plan became known to the people of the city 4 who rose up in battle against him. So he retreated and in great dismay withdrew from there to return to Babylon.

5 While he was in Persia, a messenger brought him news that the armies sent into the land of Judah had been put to flight; 6 that Lysias had gone at first with a strong army and been driven back by the children of Israel; that they had grown strong by reason of the arms, men, and abundant possessions taken from the armies they had destroyed; 7 that they had pulled down the Abomination which he had built upon the altar in Jerusalem; and that they had surrounded with high walls both the sanctuary, as it had been before, and his city of Beth-zur.

8 When the king heard this news, he was struck with fear and very much shaken. Sick with grief because his designs had failed, he took to his bed. 9 There he remained many days, overwhelmed with sorrow, for he knew he was going to die.

10 So he called in all his Friends and said to them: "Sleep has departed from my eyes, for my heart is sinking with anxiety. 11 I said to myself: 'Into what tribulation have I come, and in what floods of sorrow am I now! Yet I was kindly and beloved in my rule.' 12 But I now recall the evils I did in Jerusalem, when I carried away all the vessels of gold and silver that were in it, and for no cause gave orders that the inhabitants of Judah be destroyed. 13 I know that this is why these evils have overtaken me; and now I am dying, in bitter grief, in a foreign land."

Responsorial Psalm: Psalms 9:2-3, 4 AND 6, 16 AND 19

R. (see 16a) *I will rejoice in your salvation, O Lord.*

²I will give thanks to you, O LORD, with all my heart;
  I will declare all your wondrous deeds.
³I will be glad and exult in you;
  I will sing praise to your name, Most High.

R. I will rejoice in your salvation, O Lord.

⁴Because my enemies are turned back,
  overthrown and destroyed before you.
⁶You rebuked the nations and destroyed the wicked;
  their name you blotted out forever and ever.

R. I will rejoice in your salvation, O Lord.

¹⁶ The nations are sunk in the pit they have made;
  in the snare they set, their foot is caught.
¹⁹ For the needy shall not always be forgotten,
  nor shall the hope of the afflicted forever perish.

R. I will rejoice in your salvation, O Lord.

Alleluia: cf. 2 Timothy 1:10

R. Alleluia, alleluia.
¹⁰ Our Savior Jesus Christ has destroyed death
and brought life to light through the Gospel.
R. Alleluia, alleluia.

Gospel: Luke 20:27-40

²⁷ Some Sadducees, those who deny that there is a resurrection, came forward and put this question to Jesus, ²⁸ saying, "Teacher, Moses wrote for us, *If someone's brother dies leaving a wife but no child, his brother must take the wife and raise up descendants for his brother.* ²⁹ Now there were seven brothers; the first married a woman but died childless. ³⁰ Then the second ³¹ and the third married her, and likewise all the seven died childless. ³² Finally the woman also died. ³³ Now at the resurrection whose wife will that woman be? For all seven had been married to her." ³⁴ Jesus said to them, "The children of this age marry and remarry; ³⁵ but those who are deemed worthy to attain to the coming age and to the resurrection of the dead neither marry nor are given in marriage. ³⁶ They can no longer die, for they are like angels; and they are the children of God because they are the ones who will rise. ³⁷ That the dead will rise even Moses made known in the passage about the bush, when he called 'Lord' the God of Abraham, the God

of Isaac, and the God of Jacob; ³⁸ and he is not God of the dead, but of the living, for to him all are alive." ³⁹ Some of the scribes said in reply, "Teacher, you have answered well." ⁴⁰ And they no longer dared to ask him anything.

Sunday November 23, 2025
Feast of Christ the Universal King, Year C

First Reading: 2 Samuel 5:1-3

¹In those days, all the tribes of Israel came to David in Hebron and said: "Here we are, your bone and your flesh. ²In days past, when Saul was our king, it was you who led the Israelites out and brought them back. And the LORD said to you, 'You shall shepherd my people Israel and shall be commander of Israel.'" ³When all the elders of Israel came to David in Hebron, King David made an agreement with them there before the LORD, and they anointed him king of Israel.

Responsorial Psalm: Psalms 122:1-2, 3-4, 4-5

R. (cf. 1) Let us go rejoicing to the house of the Lord.

¹I rejoiced because they said to me,
 "We will go up to the house of the LORD."
² And now we have set foot
 within your gates, O Jerusalem.

R. Let us go rejoicing to the house of the Lord.

³Jerusalem, built as a city
 with compact unity.
⁴ᴬᴮTo it the tribes go up,
 the tribes of the LORD.

R. Let us go rejoicing to the house of the Lord.

⁴ᶜᴰAccording to the decree for Israel,
 to give thanks to the name of the LORD.
⁵In it are set up judgment seats,
 seats for the house of David.

R. Let us go rejoicing to the house of the Lord.

Second Reading: Colossians 1:12-20

Brothers and sisters: ¹²Let us give thanks to the Father, who has made you fit to share in the inheritance of the holy ones in light. ¹³He delivered us from the power of darkness and transferred us to the kingdom of his beloved Son, ¹⁴in whom we have redemption, the forgiveness of sins.

¹⁵He is the image of the invisible God,
 the firstborn of all creation.
¹⁶For in him were created all things in heaven
  and on earth,
 the visible and the invisible,
 whether thrones or dominions or
  principalities or powers;

all things were created through him and
> for him.
¹⁷He is before all things,
> and in him all things hold together.
¹⁸He is the head of the body, the church.
He is the beginning, the firstborn from the
> dead,
> that in all things he himself might be
> preeminent.
¹⁹For in him all the fullness was pleased to
> dwell,
> ²⁰and through him to reconcile all things
> for him,
> making peace by the blood of his cross
> through him, whether those on earth or
> those in heaven.

Alleluia: Mark 11:9, 10
R. Alleluia, alleluia.
⁹ Blessed is he who comes in the name of the
> Lord!
¹⁰ Blessed is the kingdom of our father David
> that is to come!
R. Alleluia, alleluia.

Gospel: Luke 23:35-43
³⁵The rulers sneered at Jesus and said, "He saved others, let him save himself if he is the chosen one, the Christ of God." ³⁶Even the soldiers jeered at him. As they approached to offer him wine ³⁷they called out, "If you are King of the Jews, save yourself." ³⁸Above him there was an inscription that read, "This is the King of the Jews."

³⁹Now one of the criminals hanging there reviled Jesus, saying, "Are you not the Christ? Save yourself and us." ⁴⁰The other, however, rebuking him, said in reply, "Have you no fear of God, for you are subject to the same condemnation? ⁴¹And indeed, we have been condemned justly, for the sentence we received corresponds to our crimes, but this man has done nothing criminal." ⁴²Then he said, "Jesus, remember me when you come into your kingdom." ⁴³He replied to him, "Amen, I say to you, today you will be with me in Paradise."

Monday November 24, 2025
Memorial of Saint Andrew Dung-Lac and his Companions, Martyrs
First Reading: Daniel 1:1-6, 8-20
¹In the third year of the reign of Jehoiakim, king of Judah, King Nebuchadnezzar of Babylon came and laid siege to Jerusalem. ²The Lord handed over to him Jehoiakim, king of Judah, and some of the vessels of the temple of God; he carried them off to the land of Shinar, and placed the vessels in the temple treasury of his god.

³The king told Ashpenaz, his chief chamberlain, to bring in some of the children of Israel of royal blood and of the nobility, ⁴young men without any defect, handsome, intelligent and wise, quick to learn, and prudent in judgment, such as could take their place in the king's palace; they were to be taught the language and literature of the Chaldeans; after three years' training they were to enter the king's service. ⁵The king allotted them a daily portion of food and wine from the royal table. ⁶Among these were men of Judah: Daniel, Hananiah, Mishael, and Azariah.

⁸But Daniel was resolved not to defile himself with the king's food or wine; so he begged the chief chamberlain to spare him this defilement. ⁹Though God had given Daniel the favor and sympathy of the chief chamberlain, ¹⁰he nevertheless said to Daniel, "I am afraid of my lord the king; it is he who allotted your food and drink. If he sees that you look wretched by comparison with the other young men of your age, you will endanger my life with the king." ¹¹Then Daniel said to the steward whom the chief chamberlain had put in charge of Daniel, Hananiah, Mishael, and Azariah, ¹²"Please test your servants for ten days. Give us vegetables to eat and water to drink.¹³Then see how we look in comparison with the other young men who eat from the royal table, and treat your servants according to what you see." ¹⁴He acceded to this request, and tested them for ten days; ¹⁵after ten days they looked healthier and better fed than any of the young men who ate from the royal table. ¹⁶So the steward continued to take away the food and wine they were to receive, and gave them vegetables. ¹⁷To these four young men God gave knowledge and proficiency in all literature and science, and to Daniel the understanding of all visions and dreams. ¹⁸At the end of the time the king had specified for their preparation, the chief chamberlain brought them before Nebuchadnezzar. ¹⁹When the king had spoken with all of them, none was found equal to Daniel, Hananiah, Mishael, and Azariah; and so they entered the king's service. ²⁰In any question of wisdom or prudence which the king put to them, he found them ten times better than all the magicians and enchanters in his kingdom.

Responsorial Psalm: Daniel 3:52, 53, 54, 55, 56

R. (52b) Glory and praise for ever!
⁵²"Blessed are you, O Lord, the God of our
    fathers,
  praiseworthy and exalted above all
    forever;
And blessed is your holy and glorious name,
  praiseworthy and exalted above all for all
    ages."
R. Glory and praise for ever!
⁵³"Blessed are you in the temple of your holy
    glory,
  praiseworthy and glorious above all
    forever."
R. Glory and praise for ever!
⁵⁴"Blessed are you on the throne of your
    Kingdom,
  praiseworthy and exalted above all

forever."
R. Glory and praise for ever!
⁵⁵"Blessed are you who look into the depths
from your throne upon the cherubim,
praiseworthy and exalted above all
forever."
R. Glory and praise for ever!
⁵⁶"Blessed are you in the firmament of heaven,
praiseworthy and glorious forever."
R. Glory and praise for ever!

Alleluia: Matthew 24:42A, 44
R. Alleluia, alleluia.
⁴²ᴬ Stay awake!
⁴⁴ For you do not know when the Son of Man
will come.
R. Alleluia, alleluia.

Gospel: Luke 21:1-4
¹ When Jesus looked up he saw some wealthy people putting their offerings into the treasury ² and he noticed a poor widow putting in two small coins. ³ He said, "I tell you truly, this poor widow put in more than all the rest; ⁴ for those others have all made offerings from their surplus wealth, but she, from her poverty, has offered her whole livelihood."

Tuesday November 25, 2025
Tuesday of Thirty-fourth Week in Ordinary Time
First Reading: Daniel 2:31-45
Daniel said to Nebuchadnezzar: ³¹"In your vision, O king, you saw a statue, very large and exceedingly bright, terrifying in appearance as it stood before you. ³²The head of the statue was pure gold, its chest and arms were silver, its belly and thighs bronze, ³³the legs iron, its feet partly iron and partly tile. ³⁴While you looked at the statue, a stone which was hewn from a mountain without a hand being put to it, struck its iron and tile feet, breaking them in pieces. ³⁵The iron, tile, bronze, silver, and gold all crumbled at once, fine as the chaff on the threshing floor in summer, and the wind blew them away without leaving a trace. But the stone that struck the statue became a great mountain and filled the whole earth.

³⁶"This was the dream; the interpretation we shall also give in the king's presence. ³⁷You, O king, are the king of kings; to you the God of heaven has given dominion and strength, power and glory; ³⁸men, wild beasts, and birds of the air, wherever they may dwell, he has handed over to you, making you ruler over them all; you are the head of gold. ³⁹Another kingdom shall take your place, inferior to yours, then a third kingdom, of bronze, which shall rule over the whole earth. ⁴⁰There shall be a fourth kingdom, strong as iron; it shall break in pieces and subdue all these others, just as iron breaks in pieces and crushes everything else.

⁴¹The feet and toes you saw, partly of potter's tile and partly of iron, mean that it shall be a divided kingdom, but yet have some of the hardness of iron. As you saw the iron mixed with clay tile, ⁴²and the toes partly iron and partly tile, the kingdom shall be partly strong and partly fragile. ⁴³The iron mixed with clay tile means that they shall seal their alliances by intermarriage, but they shall not stay united, any more than iron mixes with clay. ⁴⁴In the lifetime of those kings the God of heaven will set up a kingdom that shall never be destroyed or delivered up to another people; rather, it shall break in pieces all these kingdoms and put an end to them, and it shall stand forever. ⁴⁵That is the meaning of the stone you saw hewn from the mountain without a hand being put to it, which broke in pieces the tile, iron, bronze, silver, and gold. The great God has revealed to the king what shall be in the future; this is exactly what you dreamed, and its meaning is sure."

Responsorial Psalm: Daniel 3:57, 58, 59, 60, 61
R. ⁽⁵⁹ᵇ⁾ Give glory and eternal praise to him.
⁵⁷"Bless the Lord, all you works of the Lord,
    praise and exalt him above all forever."
R. Give glory and eternal praise to him.
⁵⁸"Angels of the Lord, bless the Lord,
    praise and exalt him above all forever."
R. Give glory and eternal praise to him.
⁵⁹ "You heavens, bless the Lord,
    praise and exalt him above all forever."
R. Give glory and eternal praise to him.
⁶⁰"All you waters above the heavens, bless the
        Lord,
    praise and exalt him above all forever."
R. Give glory and eternal praise to him.
⁶¹"All you hosts of the Lord, bless the Lord;
    praise and exalt him above all forever."
R. Give glory and eternal praise to him.

Alleluia: Revelation 2:10C
R. Alleluia, alleluia.
¹⁰ᶜ Remain faithful until death,
and I will give you the crown of life.
R. Alleluia, alleluia.

Gospel: Luke 21:5-11
⁵ While some people were speaking about how the temple was adorned with costly stones and votive offerings, Jesus said, ⁶ "All that you see here— the days will come when there will not be left a stone upon another stone that will not be thrown down."
⁷ Then they asked him, "Teacher, when will this happen? And what sign will there be when all these things are about to happen?" ⁸ He answered, "See that you

not be deceived, for many will come in my name, saying, 'I am he,' and 'The time has come.' Do not follow them! ⁹ When you hear of wars and insurrections, do not be terrified; for such things must happen first, but it will not immediately be the end." ¹⁰ Then he said to them, "Nation will rise against nation, and kingdom against kingdom. ¹¹ There will be powerful earthquakes, famines, and plagues from place to place; and awesome sights and mighty signs will come from the sky."

Wednesday November 26, 2025
Wednesday of Thirty-fourth Week in Ordinary Time
First Reading: Daniel 5:1-6,13-14,16-17, 23-28

¹King Belshazzar gave a great banquet for a thousand of his lords, with whom he drank. ²Under the influence of the wine, he ordered the gold and silver vessels which Nebuchadnezzar, his father, had taken from the temple in Jerusalem, to be brought in so that the king, his lords, his wives and his entertainers might drink from them. ³When the gold and silver vessels taken from the house of God in Jerusalem had been brought in, and while the king, his lords, his wives and his entertainers were drinking ⁴wine from them, they praised their gods of gold and silver, bronze and iron, wood and stone.

⁵Suddenly, opposite the lampstand, the fingers of a human hand appeared, writing on the plaster of the wall in the king's palace. When the king saw the wrist and hand that wrote, ⁶his face blanched; his thoughts terrified him, his hip joints shook, and his knees knocked.

¹³Then Daniel was brought into the presence of the king. The king asked him, "Are you the Daniel, the Jewish exile, whom my father, the king, brought from Judah? ¹⁴I have heard that the Spirit of God is in you, that you possess brilliant knowledge and extraordinary wisdom. ¹⁶I have heard that you can interpret dreams and solve difficulties; if you are able to read the writing and tell me what it means, you shall be clothed in purple, wear a gold collar about your neck, and be third in the government of the kingdom."

¹⁷Daniel answered the king: "You may keep your gifts, or give your presents to someone else; but the writing I will read for you, O king, and tell you what it means. ²³You have rebelled against the Lord of heaven. You had the vessels of his temple brought before you, so that you and your nobles, your wives and your entertainers, might drink wine from them; and you praised the gods of silver and gold, bronze and iron, wood and stone, that neither see nor hear nor have intelligence. But the God in whose hand is your life breath and the whole course of your life, you did not glorify. ²⁴By him were the wrist and hand sent, and the writing set down.

²⁵"This is the writing that was inscribed: MENE, TEKEL, and PERES. These words mean: ²⁶MENE, God has numbered your kingdom and put an end to it; ²⁷TEKEL, you have been weighed on the scales and found wanting; ²⁸PERES, your kingdom has been divided and given to the Medes and Persians."

Responsorial Psalm: Daniel 3:62, 63, 64, 65, 66, 67
R. ⁽⁵⁹ᵇ⁾ *Give glory and eternal praise to him.*

⁶²"Sun and moon, bless the Lord;
   praise and exalt him above all forever."
R. Give glory and eternal praise to him.
⁶³"Stars of heaven, bless the Lord;
   praise and exalt him above all forever."
R. Give glory and eternal praise to him.
⁶⁴"Every shower and dew, bless the Lord;
   praise and exalt him above all forever."
R. Give glory and eternal praise to him.

⁶⁵"All you winds, bless the Lord;
   praise and exalt him above all forever."
R. Give glory and eternal praise to him.
⁶⁶"Fire and heat, bless the Lord;
   praise and exalt him above all forever."
R. Give glory and eternal praise to him.
⁶⁷"Cold and chill, bless the Lord;
   praise and exalt him above all forever."
R. Give glory and eternal praise to him.

Alleluia: Revelation 2:10C
R. Alleluia, alleluia.
¹⁰ᶜ Remain faithful until death,
and I will give you the crown of life.
R. Alleluia, alleluia.

Gospel: Luke 21:12-19
Jesus said to the crowd: ¹² "They will seize and persecute you, they will hand you over to the synagogues and to prisons, and they will have you led before kings and governors because of my name. ¹³ It will lead to your giving testimony. ¹⁴ Remember, you are not to prepare your defense beforehand, ¹⁵ for I myself shall give you a wisdom in speaking that all your adversaries will be powerless to resist or refute. ¹⁶ You will even be handed over by parents, brothers, relatives, and friends, and they will put some of you to death. ¹⁷ You will be hated by all because of my name, ¹⁸ but not a hair on your head will be destroyed. ¹⁹ By your perseverance you will secure your lives."

Thursday November 27, 2025
Thursday of the Thirty-fourth Week in Ordinary Time
First Reading: Daniel 6:12-28
¹²Some men rushed into the upper chamber of Daniel's home and found him praying and pleading before his God. ¹³Then they went to remind the king about the prohibition: "Did you not decree, O king, that no one is to address a petition to god or man for thirty days, except to you, O king; otherwise he shall be cast into a den of lions?" The king answered them, "The decree is absolute, irrevocable under the Mede and Persian law." ¹⁴To this they replied, "Daniel, the Jewish exile, has

paid no attention to you, O king, or to the decree you issued; three times a day he offers his prayer." ¹⁵The king was deeply grieved at this news and he made up his mind to save Daniel; he worked till sunset to rescue him. ¹⁶But these men insisted. They said, "Keep in mind, O king, that under the Mede and Persian law every royal prohibition or decree is irrevocable." ¹⁷So the king ordered Daniel to be brought and cast into the lions' den. To Daniel he said, "May your God, whom you serve so constantly, save you."

¹⁸ To forestall any tampering, the king sealed with his own ring and the rings of the lords the stone that had been brought to block the opening of the den.

¹⁹Then the king returned to his palace for the night; he refused to eat and he dismissed the entertainers. Since sleep was impossible for him, ²⁰the king rose very early the next morning and hastened to the lions' den. ²¹As he drew near, he cried out to Daniel sorrowfully, "O Daniel, servant of the living God, has the God whom you serve so constantly been able to save you from the lions?" ²²Daniel answered the king: "O king, live forever! ²³My God has sent his angel and closed the lions' mouths so that they have not hurt me. For I have been found innocent before him; neither to you have I done any harm, O king!" ²⁴This gave the king great joy. At his order Daniel was removed from the den, unhurt because he trusted in his God. ²⁵The king then ordered the men who had accused Daniel, along with their children and their wives, to be cast into the lions' den. Before they reached the bottom of the den, the lions overpowered them and crushed all their bones.

²⁶Then King Darius wrote to the nations and peoples of every language, wherever they dwell on the earth: "All peace to you! ²⁷I decree that throughout my royal domain the God of Daniel is to be reverenced and feared:

"For he is the living God, enduring forever;
> his Kingdom shall not be destroyed,
> and his dominion shall be without end.

²⁸ He is a deliverer and savior,
> working signs and wonders in heaven
>> and on earth,
> and he delivered Daniel from the lions'
>> power."

Responsorial Psalm: Daniel 3:68, 69, 70, 71, 72, 73, 74
R. (59b) Give glory and eternal praise to him.
⁶⁸"Dew and rain, bless the Lord;
> praise and exalt him above all forever."
R. Give glory and eternal praise to him.
⁶⁹"Frost and chill, bless the Lord;
> praise and exalt him above all forever."
R. Give glory and eternal praise to him.
⁷⁰"Ice and snow, bless the Lord;
> praise and exalt him above all forever."

R. Give glory and eternal praise to him.
[71]"Nights and days, bless the Lord;
> praise and exalt him above all forever."
R. Give glory and eternal praise to him.
[72]"Light and darkness, bless the Lord;
> praise and exalt him above all forever."
R. Give glory and eternal praise to him.
[73] "Lightnings and clouds, bless the Lord;
> praise and exalt him above all forever."
R. Give glory and eternal praise to him.
[74] "Let the earth bless the Lord,
> praise and exalt him above all forever."
R. Give glory and eternal praise to him.

Alleluia: Luke 21:28
R. Alleluia, alleluia.
[28] Stand erect and raise your heads
because your redemption is at hand.
R. Alleluia, alleluia.

Gospel: Luke 21:20-28
Jesus said to his disciples: [20] "When you see Jerusalem surrounded by armies, know that its desolation is at hand. [21] Then those in Judea must flee to the mountains. Let those within the city escape from it, and let those in the countryside not enter the city, [22] for these days are the time of punishment when all the Scriptures are fulfilled. [23] Woe to pregnant women and nursing mothers in those days, for a terrible calamity will come upon the earth and a wrathful judgment upon this people. [24] They will fall by the edge of the sword and be taken as captives to all the Gentiles; and Jerusalem will be trampled underfoot by the Gentiles until the times of the Gentiles are fulfilled.

[25] "There will be signs in the sun, the moon, and the stars, and on earth nations will be in dismay, perplexed by the roaring of the sea and the waves. [26] People will die of fright in anticipation of what is coming upon the world, for the powers of the heavens will be shaken. [27] And then they will see the Son of Man coming in a cloud with power and great glory. [28] But when these signs begin to happen, stand erect and raise your heads because your redemption is at hand."

Friday November 28, 2025
Friday of Thirty-fourth Week in Ordinary Time
First Reading: Daniel 7:2-14
[2] In a vision I, Daniel, saw during the night, the four winds of heaven stirred up the great sea, [3] from which emerged four immense beasts, each different from the others. [4] The first was like a lion, but with eagle's wings. While I watched, the wings were plucked; it was raised from the ground to stand on two feet like a man, and given a human mind. [5] The second was like a bear; it was raised up on one side, and among the teeth in its mouth were three tusks. It was given the order, "Up,

devour much flesh." ⁶After this I looked and saw another beast, like a leopard; on its back were four wings like those of a bird, and it had four heads. To this beast dominion was given. ⁷After this, in the visions of the night I saw the fourth beast, different from all the others, terrifying, horrible, and of extraordinary strength; it had great iron teeth with which it devoured and crushed, and what was left it trampled with its feet. ⁸I was considering the ten horns it had, when suddenly another, a little horn, sprang out of their midst, and three of the previous horns were torn away to make room for it. This horn had eyes like a man, and a mouth that spoke arrogantly. ⁹As I watched,

Thrones were set up
    and the Ancient One took his throne.
His clothing was snow bright,
    and the hair on his head as white as
        wool;
His throne was flames of fire,
    with wheels of burning fire.
¹⁰A surging stream of fire
    flowed out from where he sat;
Thousands upon thousands were
    ministering to him,
    and myriads upon myriads attended him.

The court was convened, and the books were opened. ¹¹I watched, then, from the first of the arrogant words which the horn spoke, until the beast was slain and its body thrown into the fire to be burnt up. ¹²The other beasts, which also lost their dominion, were granted a prolongation of life for a time and a season. ¹³As the visions during the night continued, I saw

One like a son of man coming,
    on the clouds of heaven;
When he reached the Ancient One
    and was presented before him,
¹⁴He received dominion, glory, and kingship;
    nations and peoples of every language
        serve him.
His dominion is an everlasting dominion
    that shall not be taken away,
    his kingship shall not be destroyed.

Responsorial Psalm: Daniel 3:75, 76, 77, 78, 79, 80, 81
R. Give glory and eternal praise to him!
⁷⁵ "Mountains and hills, bless the Lord;
    praise and exalt him above all forever."

R. Give glory and eternal praise to him!
76 "Everything growing from the earth, bless the Lord;
    praise and exalt him above all forever.
R. Give glory and eternal praise to him!"
77 "You springs, bless the Lord;
    praise and exalt him above all forever."
R. Give glory and eternal praise to him!
78 "Seas and rivers, bless the Lord;
    praise and exalt him above all forever."
R. Give glory and eternal praise to him!
79 "You dolphins and all water creatures, bless the Lord;
    praise and exalt him above all forever."
R. Give glory and eternal praise to him!
80 "All you birds of the air, bless the Lord;
    praise and exalt him above all forever."
R. Give glory and eternal praise to him!
81 "All you beasts, wild and tame, bless the Lord;
    praise and exalt him above all forever."
R. Give glory and eternal praise to him!

Alleluia: Luke 21:28
R. Alleluia, alleluia.
28 Stand erect and raise your heads
because your redemption is at hand.
R. Alleluia, alleluia.

Gospel: Luke 21:29-33
29 Jesus told his disciples a parable. "Consider the fig tree and all the other trees. 30 When their buds burst open, you see for yourselves and know that summer is now near; 31 in the same way, when you see these things happening, know that the Kingdom of God is near. 32 Amen, I say to you, this generation will not pass away until all these things have taken place. 33 Heaven and earth will pass away, but my words will not pass away."

Saturday November 29, 2025
Saturday of Thirty-fourth Week in Ordinary Time
First Reading: Daniel 7:15-27
15 I, Daniel, found my spirit anguished within its covering of flesh, and I was terrified by the visions of my mind. 16 I approached one of those present and asked him what all this meant in truth; in answer, he made known to me the meaning of the things: 17 "These four great beasts stand for four kingdoms which shall arise on the earth. 18 But the holy ones of the Most High shall receive the kingship, to possess it forever and ever."

[19] But I wished to make certain about the fourth beast, so very terrible and different from the others, devouring and crushing with its iron teeth and bronze claws, and trampling with its feet what was left; [20] about the ten horns on its head, and the other one that sprang up, before which three horns fell; about the horn with the eyes and the mouth that spoke arrogantly, which appeared greater than its fellows. [21] For, as I watched, that horn made war against the holy ones and was victorious [22] until the Ancient One arrived; judgment was pronounced in favor of the holy ones of the Most High, and the time came when the holy ones possessed the kingdom.

[23] He answered me thus:

"The fourth beast shall be a fourth kingdom on earth
different from all the others;
It shall devour the whole earth,
beat it down, and crush it.
[24] The ten horns shall be ten kings
rising out of that kingdom;
another shall rise up after them,
Different from those before him,
who shall lay low three kings.
[25] He shall speak against the Most High
and oppress the holy ones of the Most High,
thinking to change the feast days and the law.
They shall be handed over to him
for a year, two years, and a half-year.
[26] But when the court is convened,
and his power is taken away
by final and absolute destruction,
[27] Then the kingship and dominion and majesty
of all the kingdoms under the heavens
shall be given to the holy people of the Most High,
Whose Kingdom shall be everlasting:
all dominions shall serve and obey him."

Responsorial Psalm: Daniel 3:82, 83, 84, 85, 86, 87
R. Give glory and eternal praise to him.
[82] "You sons of men, bless the Lord;
praise and exalt him above all forever."
R. Give glory and eternal praise to him.
[83] "O Israel, bless the Lord;
praise and exalt him above all forever."

R. Give glory and eternal praise to him.
84"Priests of the Lord, bless the Lord;
    praise and exalt him above all forever."
R. Give glory and eternal praise to him.
85"Servants of the Lord, bless the Lord;
    praise and exalt him above all forever."
R. Give glory and eternal praise to him.
86"Spirits and souls of the just, bless the Lord;
    praise and exalt him above all forever."
R. Give glory and eternal praise to him.
87"Holy men of humble heart, bless the Lord;
    praise and exalt him above all forever."
R. Give glory and eternal praise to him.

Alleluia: Luke 21:36
R. Alleluia, alleluia.
36Be vigilant at all times and pray
That you may have the strength to stand
    before the Son of Man.
R. Alleluia, alleluia.

Gospel: Luke 21:34-36
34Jesus said to his disciples: "Beware that your hearts do not become drowsy from carousing and drunkenness and the anxieties of daily life, and that day catch you by surprise 35 like a trap. For that day will assault everyone who lives on the face of the earth. 36Be vigilant at all times and pray that you have the strength to escape the tribulations that are imminent and to stand before the Son of Man."

Sunday November 30, 2025
First Sunday of Advent, Year A

First Reading: Isaiah 2:1-5
1This is what Isaiah, son of Amoz, saw concerning Judah and Jerusalem.

    2In days to come,
the mountain of the LORD's house
    shall be established as the highest
        mountain
    and raised above the hills.
All nations shall stream toward it;
    3many peoples shall come and say:
"Come, let us climb the LORD's mountain,
    to the house of the God of Jacob,
that he may instruct us in his ways,
    and we may walk in his paths."
For from Zion shall go forth instruction,

and the word of the LORD from Jerusalem.
⁴He shall judge between the nations,
> and impose terms on many peoples.
They shall beat their swords into plowshares
> and their spears into pruning hooks;
one nation shall not raise the sword against another,
> nor shall they train for war again.
⁵O house of Jacob, come,
> let us walk in the light of the LORD!

Responsorial Psalm: Psalms 122: 1-2, 3-4, 4-5, 6-7, 8-9
R. Let us go rejoicing to the house of the Lord.
¹ I rejoiced because they said to me,
> "We will go up to the house of the LORD."
² And now we have set foot
> within your gates, O Jerusalem.

R. Let us go rejoicing to the house of the Lord.
³ Jerusalem, built as a city
> with compact unity.
⁴ To it the tribes go up,
> the tribes of the LORD.

R. Let us go rejoicing to the house of the Lord.
⁴ According to the decree for Israel,
> to give thanks to the name of the LORD.
⁵ In it are set up judgment seats,
> seats for the house of David.

R. Let us go rejoicing to the house of the Lord.
⁶ Pray for the peace of Jerusalem!
> May those who love you prosper!
⁷ May peace be within your walls,
> prosperity in your buildings.

R. Let us go rejoicing to the house of the Lord.
⁸ Because of my brothers and friends
> I will say, "Peace be within you!"
⁹ Because of the house of the LORD, our God,
> I will pray for your good.

R. Let us go rejoicing to the house of the Lord.

Second Reading: Romans 13:11-14
Brothers and sisters: ¹¹You know the time; it is the hour now for you to awake from sleep. For our salvation is nearer now than when we first believed; ¹²the night is advanced, the day is at hand. Let us then throw off the works of darkness and put on the armor of light; ¹³let us conduct ourselves properly as in the day, not in

orgies and drunkenness, not in promiscuity and lust, not in rivalry and jealousy. ¹⁴But put on the Lord Jesus Christ, and make no provision for the desires of the flesh.

Alleluia: cf. Psalms 85:8
R. Alleluia, alleluia.
⁸ Show us, Lord, your love;
and grant us your salvation.
R. Alleluia, alleluia.

Gospel: Matthew 24:37-44
³⁷Jesus said to his disciples: "As it was in the days of Noah, so it will be at the coming of the Son of Man. ³⁸In those days before the flood, they were eating and drinking, marrying and giving in marriage, up to the day that Noah entered the ark. ³⁹They did not know until the flood came and carried them all away. So will it be also at the coming of the Son of Man. ⁴⁰Two men will be out in the field; one will be taken, and one will be left. ⁴¹Two women will be grinding at the mill; one will be taken, and one will be left. ⁴²Therefore, stay awake! For you do not know on which day your Lord will come. ⁴³Be sure of this: if the master of the house had known the hour of night when the thief was coming, he would have stayed awake and not let his house be broken into. ⁴⁴So too, you also must be prepared, for at an hour you do not expect, the Son of Man will come."

DECEMBER 2025
Monday December 1, 2025
Monday of the First Week of Advent

First Reading: Isaiah 4:2-6
²On that day,
The branch of the LORD will be luster and glory,
  and the fruit of the earth will be honor and splendor
  for the survivors of Israel.
³ He who remains in Zion
  and he who is left in Jerusalem
Will be called holy:
  every one marked down for life in Jerusalem.
⁴ When the LORD washes away
  the filth of the daughters of Zion,
And purges Jerusalem's blood from her midst
  with a blast of searing judgment,
⁵Then will the LORD create,
  over the whole site of Mount Zion
  and over her place of assembly,
A smoking cloud by day
  and a light of flaming fire by night.
⁶ For over all, the LORD's glory will be shelter and protection:

shade from the parching heat of day,
refuge and cover from storm and rain.

Responsorial Psalm: Psalms 122:1-2, 3-4B, 4CD-5, 6-7, 8-9
R. Let us go rejoicing to the house of the Lord.
[1] I rejoiced because they said to me,
"We will go up to the house of the LORD."
[2] And now we have set foot
within your gates, O Jerusalem.
R. Let us go rejoicing to the house of the Lord.
[3] Jerusalem, built as a city
with compact unity.
[4AB] To it the tribes go up,
the tribes of the LORD.
R. Let us go rejoicing to the house of the Lord.
[4CD] According to the decree for Israel,
to give thanks to the name of the LORD.
[5] In it are set up judgment seats,
seats for the house of David.
R. Let us go rejoicing to the house of the Lord.
[6] Pray for the peace of Jerusalem!
May those who love you prosper!
[7] May peace be within your walls,
prosperity in your buildings.
R. Let us go rejoicing to the house of the Lord.
[8] Because of my relatives and friends
I will say, "Peace be within you!"
[9] Because of the house of the LORD, our God,
I will pray for your good.
R. Let us go rejoicing to the house of the Lord.

Alleluia: cf. Psalms 80:4
R. Alleluia, alleluia.
[4] Come and save us, Lord our God;
let your face shine upon us, that we may be
saved.
R. Alleluia, alleluia.

Gospel: Matthew 8:5-11
[5] When Jesus entered Capernaum, a centurion approached him and appealed to him, [6] saying, "Lord, my servant is lying at home paralyzed, suffering dreadfully." [7] He said to him, "I will come and cure him." [8] The centurion said in reply, "Lord, I am not worthy to have you enter under my roof; only say the word and my servant will be healed. [9] For I too am a man subject to authority, with soldiers subject to me.

And I say to one, 'Go,' and he goes; and to another, 'Come here,' and he comes; and to my slave, 'Do this,' and he does it." ¹⁰ When Jesus heard this, he was amazed and said to those following him, "Amen, I say to you, in no one in Israel have I found such faith. ¹¹ I say to you, many will come from the east and the west, and will recline with Abraham, Isaac, and Jacob at the banquet in the Kingdom of heaven."

Tuesday December 2, 2025
Tuesday of the First Week of Advent

First Reading: Isaiah 11:1-10

¹ On that day,
A shoot shall sprout from the stump of Jesse,
    and from his roots a bud shall blossom.
² The Spirit of the LORD shall rest upon him:
    a Spirit of wisdom and of understanding,
A Spirit of counsel and of strength,
    a Spirit of knowledge and of fear of the
        LORD,
³ and his delight shall be the fear of the
        LORD.
Not by appearance shall he judge,
    nor by hearsay shall he decide,
⁴ But he shall judge the poor with justice,
    and decide aright for the land's afflicted.
He shall strike the ruthless with the rod of
        his mouth,
    and with the breath of his lips he shall
        slay the wicked.
⁵ Justice shall be the band around his waist,
    and faithfulness a belt upon his hips.

⁶ Then the wolf shall be a guest of the lamb,
    and the leopard shall lie down with the
        kid;
The calf and the young lion shall browse
        together,
    with a little child to guide them.
⁷ The cow and the bear shall be neighbors,
    together their young shall rest;
    the lion shall eat hay like the ox.
⁸ The baby shall play by the cobra's den,
    and the child lay his hand on the adder's
        lair.
⁹ There shall be no harm or ruin on all my
        holy mountain;

for the earth shall be filled with
>knowledge of the LORD,
as water covers the sea.

¹⁰ On that day,
The root of Jesse,
>set up as a signal for the nations,
The Gentiles shall seek out,
>for his dwelling shall be glorious.

Responsorial Psalm: Psalms 72:1-2, 7-8, 12-13, 17

R. (see 7) ***Justice shall flourish in his time, and fullness of peace for ever.***

¹ O God, with your judgment endow the king,
>and with your justice, the king's son;
² He shall govern your people with justice
>and your afflicted ones with judgment.

R. *Justice shall flourish in his time, and fullness of peace for ever.*

⁷ Justice shall flower in his days,
>and profound peace, till the moon be no more.
⁸ May he rule from sea to sea,
>and from the River to the ends of the earth.

R. *Justice shall flourish in his time, and fullness of peace for ever.*

¹² He shall rescue the poor when he cries out,
>and the afflicted when he has no one to help him.
¹³ He shall have pity for the lowly and the poor;
>the lives of the poor he shall save.

R. *Justice shall flourish in his time, and fullness of peace for ever.*

¹⁷ May his name be blessed forever;
>as long as the sun his name shall remain.
In him shall all the tribes of the earth be blessed;
>all the nations shall proclaim his happiness.

R. *Justice shall flourish in his time, and fullness of peace for ever.*

Alleluia
R. Alleluia, alleluia.
Behold, our Lord shall come with power;
he will enlighten the eyes of his servants.
R. Alleluia, alleluia.

Gospel: Luke 10:21-24
21 Jesus rejoiced in the Holy Spirit and said, "I give you praise, Father, Lord of heaven and earth, for although you have hidden these things from the wise and the learned you have revealed them to the childlike. Yes, Father, such has been your gracious will. 22 All things have been handed over to me by my Father. No one knows who the Son is except the Father, and who the Father is except the Son and anyone to whom the Son wishes to reveal him."

23 Turning to the disciples in private he said, "Blessed are the eyes that see what you see. 24 For I say to you, many prophets and kings desired to see what you see, but did not see it, and to hear what you hear, but did not hear it."

Wednesday December 3, 2025
Memorial of Saint Francis Xavier, Priest

First Reading: Isaiah 25:6-10A
6 On this mountain the LORD of hosts
    will provide for all peoples
A feast of rich food and choice wines,
    juicy, rich food and pure, choice wines.
7 On this mountain he will destroy
    the veil that veils all peoples,
The web that is woven over all nations;
    8 he will destroy death forever.
The Lord GOD will wipe away
    the tears from all faces;
The reproach of his people he will remove
    from the whole earth; for the LORD has
        spoken.

    9 On that day it will be said:
"Behold our God, to whom we looked to save
        us!
    This is the LORD for whom we looked;
    let us rejoice and be glad that he has
        saved us!"
10A For the hand of the LORD will rest on this
    mountain.

Responsorial Psalm: Psalms 23:1-3A, 3B-4, 5, 6

R. *(6cd)* **I shall live in the house of the Lord all the days of my life.**

¹ The LORD is my shepherd; I shall not want.
² In verdant pastures he gives me repose;
Beside restful waters he leads me;
³ᴬ he refreshes my soul.

R. I shall live in the house of the Lord all the days of my life.

³ᴮ He guides me in right paths
for his name's sake.
⁴ Even though I walk in the dark valley
I fear no evil; for you are at my side
With your rod and your staff
that give me courage.

R. I shall live in the house of the Lord all the days of my life.

⁵ You spread the table before me
in the sight of my foes;
You anoint my head with oil;
my cup overflows.

R. I shall live in the house of the Lord all the days of my life.

⁶ Only goodness and kindness follow me
all the days of my life;
And I shall dwell in the house of the LORD
for years to come.

R. I shall live in the house of the Lord all the days of my life.

Alleluia

R. Alleluia, alleluia.
Behold, the Lord comes to save his people;
blessed are those prepared to meet him.
R. Alleluia, alleluia.

Gospel: Matthew 15:29-37

At that time: ²⁹ Jesus walked by the Sea of Galilee, went up on the mountain, and sat down there. ³⁰ Great crowds came to him, having with them the lame, the blind, the deformed, the mute, and many others. They placed them at his feet, and he cured them. ³¹ The crowds were amazed when they saw the mute speaking, the deformed made whole, the lame walking, and the blind able to see, and they glorified the God of Israel.

32 Jesus summoned his disciples and said, "My heart is moved with pity for the crowd, for they have been with me now for three days and have nothing to eat. I do not want to send them away hungry, for fear they may collapse on the way." 33 The disciples said to him, "Where could we ever get enough bread in this deserted place to satisfy such a crowd?" 34 Jesus said to them, "How many loaves do you have?" "Seven," they replied, "and a few fish." 35 He ordered the crowd to sit down on the ground. 36 Then he took the seven loaves and the fish, gave thanks, broke the loaves, and gave them to the disciples, who in turn gave them to the crowds. 37 They all ate and were satisfied. They picked up the fragments left over—seven baskets full.

Thursday December 4, 2025
Thursday of the First Week of Advent

First Reading: Isaiah 26:1-6

1 On that day they will sing this song in the land of Judah:

"A strong city have we;
    he sets up walls and ramparts to protect
        us.
2 Open up the gates
    to let in a nation that is just,
    one that keeps faith.
3 A nation of firm purpose you keep in peace;
    in peace, for its trust in you."

4 Trust in the LORD forever!
    For the LORD is an eternal Rock.
5 He humbles those in high places,
    and the lofty city he brings down;
He tumbles it to the ground,
    levels it with the dust.
6 It is trampled underfoot by the needy,
    by the footsteps of the poor.

Responsorial Psalm: Psalms 118:1 and 8-9, 19-21, 25-27A

R. (26a) *Blessed is he who comes in the name of the Lord.* or: *Alleluia.*
1 Give thanks to the LORD, for he is good,
    for his mercy endures forever.
8 It is better to take refuge in the LORD
    than to trust in man.
9 It is better to take refuge in the LORD
    than to trust in princes.
R. *Blessed is he who comes in the name of the
    Lord.* or: *Alleluia.*
19 Open to me the gates of justice;
    I will enter them and give thanks to the

       LORD.
²⁰ This gate is the LORD's;
    the just shall enter it.
²¹ I will give thanks to you, for you have
       answered me
    and have been my savior.
R. Blessed is he who comes in the name of the Lord.* or: *Alleluia.
²⁵ O LORD, grant salvation!
    O LORD, grant prosperity!
²⁶ Blessed is he who comes in the name of the
       LORD;
    we bless you from the house of the LORD.
    ²⁷ᴬ The LORD is God, and he has given us
       light.
R. Blessed is he who comes in the name of the Lord.* or: *Alleluia.

Alleluia: Isaiah 55:6
R. Alleluia, alleluia.
⁶ Seek the LORD while he may be found;
call him while he is near.
R. Alleluia, alleluia.

Gospel: Matthew 7:21, 24-27
Jesus said to his disciples: ²¹ "Not everyone who says to me, 'Lord, Lord,' will enter the Kingdom of heaven, but only the one who does the will of my Father in heaven.

    ²⁴ "Everyone who listens to these words of mine and acts on them will be like a wise man who built his house on rock. ²⁵ The rain fell, the floods came, and the winds blew and buffeted the house. But it did not collapse; it had been set solidly on rock. ²⁶ And everyone who listens to these words of mine but does not act on them will be like a fool who built his house on sand. ²⁷ The rain fell, the floods came, and the winds blew and buffeted the house. And it collapsed and was completely ruined."

Friday December 5, 2025
Friday of the First Week of Advent

First Reading: Isaiah 29:17-24
Thus says the Lord GOD:

¹⁷ But a very little while,
       and Lebanon shall be changed into an
          orchard,
       and the orchard be regarded as a forest!
¹⁸ On that day the deaf shall hear
       the words of a book;

And out of gloom and darkness,
> the eyes of the blind shall see.

¹⁹ The lowly will ever find joy in the LORD,
> and the poor rejoice in the Holy One of Israel.

²⁰ For the tyrant will be no more
> and the arrogant will have gone;

All who are alert to do evil will be cut off,
> ²¹ those whose mere word condemns a man,

Who ensnare his defender at the gate,
> and leave the just man with an empty claim.

²² Therefore thus says the LORD,
> the God of the house of Jacob,
> who redeemed Abraham:

Now Jacob shall have nothing to be ashamed of,
> nor shall his face grow pale.

²³ When his children see
> the work of my hands in his midst,

They shall keep my name holy;
> they shall reverence the Holy One of Jacob,
> and be in awe of the God of Israel.

²⁴ Those who err in spirit shall acquire understanding,
> and those who find fault shall receive instruction.

Responsorial Psalm: Psalms 27:1, 4, 13-14

R. ⁽¹ᵃ⁾ The Lord is my light and my salvation.

¹ The LORD is my light and my salvation;
> whom should I fear?

The LORD is my life's refuge;
> of whom should I be afraid?

R. The Lord is my light and my salvation.

¹ One thing I ask of the LORD;
> this I seek:

To dwell in the house of the LORD
> all the days of my life,

That I may gaze on the loveliness of the LORD
> and contemplate his temple.

R. The Lord is my light and my salvation.

¹³ I believe that I shall see the bounty of the

LORD
in the land of the living.
¹⁴ Wait for the LORD with courage;
be stouthearted, and wait for the LORD.
R. The Lord is my light and my salvation.

Alleluia
R. Alleluia, alleluia.
Behold, our Lord shall come with power;
he will enlighten the eyes of his servants.
R. Alleluia, alleluia.

Gospel: Matthew 9:27-31
²⁷ As Jesus passed by, two blind men followed him, crying out, "Son of David, have pity on us!" ²⁸ When he entered the house, the blind men approached him and Jesus said to them, "Do you believe that I can do this?" "Yes, Lord," they said to him. ²⁹ Then he touched their eyes and said, "Let it be done for you according to your faith." ³⁰ And their eyes were opened. Jesus warned them sternly, "See that no one knows about this." ³¹ But they went out and spread word of him through all that land.

Saturday December 6, 2025
Saturday of the First Week of Advent
First Reading: Isaiah 30:19-21, 23-26
Thus says the Lord GOD,
¹⁹ the Holy One of Israel:
O people of Zion, who dwell in Jerusalem,
no more will you weep;
He will be gracious to you when you cry out,
as soon as he hears he will answer you.
²⁰ The Lord will give you the bread you need
and the water for which you thirst.
No longer will your Teacher hide himself,
but with your own eyes you shall see
your Teacher,
²¹ While from behind, a voice shall sound in
your ears:
"This is the way; walk in it,"
when you would turn to the right or to
the left.

²³ He will give rain for the seed
that you sow in the ground,
And the wheat that the soil produces
will be rich and abundant.
On that day your flock will be given pasture

and the lamb will graze in spacious
>meadows;
24 The oxen and the asses that till the ground
>will eat silage tossed to them
>with shovel and pitchfork.
25 Upon every high mountain and lofty hill
>there will be streams of running water.
On the day of the great slaughter,
>when the towers fall,
26 The light of the moon will be like that of the
>sun
>>and the light of the sun will be seven
>>>times greater
>>like the light of seven days.
On the day the LORD binds up the wounds of
>his people,
>>he will heal the bruises left by his blows.

Responsorial Psalm: Psalms 147:1-2,3-4, 5-6

*R. (See Isaiah 30:18d) **Blessed are all who wait for the Lord.***
1 Praise the LORD, for he is good;
>sing praise to our God, for he is gracious;
>>it is fitting to praise him.
2 The LORD rebuilds Jerusalem;
>the dispersed of Israel he gathers.

R. Blessed are all who wait for the Lord.

3 He heals the brokenhearted
>and binds up their wounds.
4 He tells the number of the stars;
>he calls each by name.

R. Blessed are all who wait for the Lord.

5 Great is our LORD and mighty in power:
>to his wisdom there is no limit.
6 The LORD sustains the lowly;
>the wicked he casts to the ground.

R. Blessed are all who wait for the Lord.

Alleluia: Isaiah 33:22

R. Alleluia, alleluia.
22 The LORD is our Judge, our Lawgiver, our
>King;
he it is who will save us.
R. Alleluia, alleluia.

Gospel: Matthew 9:35-10:1, 5A, 6-8

35 Jesus went around to all the towns and villages, teaching in their synagogues, proclaiming the Gospel of the Kingdom, and curing every disease and illness. 36 At the sight of the crowds, his heart was moved with pity for them because they were troubled and abandoned, like sheep without a shepherd. 37 Then he said to his disciples, "The harvest is abundant but the laborers are few; 38 so ask the master of the harvest to send out laborers for his harvest."

1 Then he summoned his Twelve disciples and gave them authority over unclean spirits to drive them out and to cure every disease and every illness.

5A Jesus sent out these Twelve after instructing them thus, 6 "Go to the lost sheep of the house of Israel. 7 As you go, make this proclamation: 'The Kingdom of heaven is at hand.' 8 Cure the sick, raise the dead, cleanse lepers, drive out demons. Without cost you have received; without cost you are to give."

Sunday December 7, 2025
Second Sunday of Advent, Year A

First Reading: Isaiah 11:1-10

1 On that day, a shoot shall sprout from the stump of Jesse,
and from his roots a bud shall blossom.
2 The spirit of the LORD shall rest upon him:
a spirit of wisdom and of understanding,
a spirit of counsel and of strength,
a spirit of knowledge and of fear of the LORD,
3 and his delight shall be the fear of the LORD.
Not by appearance shall he judge,
nor by hearsay shall he decide,
4 but he shall judge the poor with justice,
and decide aright for the land's afflicted.
He shall strike the ruthless with the rod of his mouth,
and with the breath of his lips he shall slay the wicked.
5 Justice shall be the band around his waist,
and faithfulness a belt upon his hips.
6 Then the wolf shall be a guest of the lamb,
and the leopard shall lie down with the kid;
the calf and the young lion shall browse together,
with a little child to guide them.
7 The cow and the bear shall be neighbors,

together their young shall rest;
the lion shall eat hay like the ox.
⁸The baby shall play by the cobra's den,
and the child lay his hand on the adder's lair.
⁹There shall be no harm or ruin on all my holy mountain;
for the earth shall be filled with knowledge of the LORD,
as water covers the sea.
¹⁰On that day, the root of Jesse,
set up as a signal for the nations,
the Gentiles shall seek out,
for his dwelling shall be glorious.

Responsorial Psalm: Psalms 72:1-2, 7-8, 12-13, 17

R. (cf. 7) Justice shall flourish in his time, and fullness of peace for ever.

¹O God, with your judgment endow the king,
and with your justice, the king's son;
² he shall govern your people with justice
and your afflicted ones with judgment.

R. Justice shall flourish in his time, and fullness of peace for ever.

⁷Justice shall flower in his days,
and profound peace, till the moon be no more.
⁸May he rule from sea to sea,
and from the River to the ends of the earth.

R. Justice shall flourish in his time, and fullness of peace for ever.

¹²For he shall rescue the poor when he cries out,
and the afflicted when he has no one to help him.
¹³He shall have pity for the lowly and the poor;
the lives of the poor he shall save.

R. Justice shall flourish in his time, and fullness of peace for ever.

¹⁷May his name be blessed forever;
as long as the sun his name shall remain.
In him shall all the tribes of the earth be blessed;

> all the nations shall proclaim his
> > happiness.
>
> **R. Justice shall flourish in his time, and fullness
> of peace for ever.**

Second Reading: Romans 15:4-9

Brothers and sisters: [4]Whatever was written previously was written for our instruction, that by endurance and by the encouragement of the Scriptures we might have hope. [5]May the God of endurance and encouragement grant you to think in harmony with one another, in keeping with Christ Jesus, [6]that with one accord you may with one voice glorify the God and Father of our Lord Jesus Christ.

[7]Welcome one another, then, as Christ welcomed you, for the glory of God. [8]For I say that Christ became a minister of the circumcised to show God's truthfulness, to confirm the promises to the patriarchs, [9]but so that the Gentiles might glorify God for his mercy. As it is written:

Therefore, I will praise you among the
> *Gentiles*
> *and sing praises to your name.*

Alleluia: Luke 3:4, 6

R. Alleluia, alleluia.
[4]Prepare the way of the Lord, make straight
> his paths:
[6]all flesh shall see the salvation of God.
R. Alleluia, alleluia.

Gospel: Matthew 3:1-12

[1]John the Baptist appeared, preaching in the desert of Judea [2]and saying, "Repent, for the kingdom of heaven is at hand!" [3]It was of him that the prophet Isaiah had spoken when he said:

A voice of one crying out in the desert,
Prepare the way of the Lord,
> *make straight his paths.*

[4]John wore clothing made of camel's hair and had a leather belt around his waist. His food was locusts and wild honey. [5]At that time Jerusalem, all Judea, and the whole region around the Jordan were going out to him [6]and were being baptized by him in the Jordan River as they acknowledged their sins.

[7]When he saw many of the Pharisees and Sadducees coming to his baptism, he said to them, "You brood of vipers! Who warned you to flee from the coming wrath? [8]Produce good fruit as evidence of your repentance. [9]And do not presume to say to yourselves, 'We have Abraham as our father.' For I tell you, God

can raise up children to Abraham from these stones. ¹⁰Even now the ax lies at the root of the trees. Therefore every tree that does not bear good fruit will be cut down and thrown into the fire. ¹¹I am baptizing you with water, for repentance, but the one who is coming after me is mightier than I. I am not worthy to carry his sandals. He will baptize you with the Holy Spirit and fire. ¹²His winnowing fan is in his hand. He will clear his threshing floor and gather his wheat into his barn, but the chaff he will burn with unquenchable fire."

Monday December 8, 2025

Solemnity of the Immaculate Conception of the Blessed Virgin Mary
First Reading: Genesis 3:9-15, 20

⁹ After the man, Adam, had eaten of the tree, the LORD God called to the man and asked him, "Where are you?" ¹⁰ He answered, "I heard you in the garden; but I was afraid, because I was naked, so I hid myself." ¹¹ Then he asked, "Who told you that you were naked? You have eaten, then, from the tree of which I had forbidden you to eat!" ¹² The man replied, "The woman whom you put here with me — she gave me fruit from the tree, and so I ate it." ¹³ The LORD God then asked the woman, "Why did you do such a thing?" The woman answered, "The serpent tricked me into it, so I ate it."

¹⁴ Then the LORD God said to the serpent:

"Because you have done this, you shall be
    banned
  from all the animals
  and from all the wild creatures;
on your belly shall you crawl,
  and dirt shall you eat
  all the days of your life.
¹⁵ I will put enmity between you and the
    woman,
  and between your offspring and hers;
he will strike at your head,
  while you strike at his heel."

²⁰ The man called his wife Eve, because she became the mother of all the living.

Responsorial Psalm: Psalms 98:1, 2-3AB, 3CD-4

R. ⁽¹⁾ *Sing to the Lord a new song, for he has done marvelous deeds.*

¹ Sing to the LORD a new song,
  for he has done wondrous deeds;
His right hand has won victory for him,
  his holy arm.

R. Sing to the Lord a new song, for he has done marvelous deeds.

² The LORD has made his salvation known:

in the sight of the nations he has revealed
> his justice.
³ᴬᴮ He has remembered his kindness and his
> faithfulness
toward the house of Israel.
R. Sing to the Lord a new song, for he has done
> ***marvelous deeds.***

³ᶜᴰ All the ends of the earth have seen
> the salvation by our God.
⁴ Sing joyfully to the LORD, all you lands;
> break into song; sing praise.
R. Sing to the Lord a new song, for he has done
> ***marvelous deeds.***

Second Reading: Ephesians 1:3-6, 11-12

Brothers and sisters: ³ Blessed be the God and Father of our Lord Jesus Christ, who has blessed us in Christ with every spiritual blessing in the heavens, ⁴ as he chose us in him, before the foundation of the world, to be holy and without blemish before him. In love ⁵ he destined us for adoption to himself through Jesus Christ, in accord with the favor of his will, ⁶ for the praise of the glory of his grace that he granted us in the beloved.

¹¹ In him we were also chosen, destined in accord with the purpose of the One who accomplishes all things according to the intention of his will, ¹² so that we might exist for the praise of his glory, we who first hoped in Christ.

Alleluia: cf. Luke 1:28
R. Alleluia, alleluia.
²⁸ Hail, Mary, full of grace, the Lord is with you;
blessed are you among women.
R. Alleluia, alleluia.

Gospel: Luke 1:26-38

²⁶ The angel Gabriel was sent from God to a town of Galilee called Nazareth, ²⁷ to a virgin betrothed to a man named Joseph, of the house of David, and the virgin's name was Mary. ²⁸ And coming to her, he said, "Hail, full of grace! The Lord is with you." ²⁹ But she was greatly troubled at what was said and pondered what sort of greeting this might be. ³⁰ Then the angel said to her, "Do not be afraid, Mary, for you have found favor with God. ³¹ Behold, you will conceive in your womb and bear a son, and you shall name him Jesus. ³² He will be great and will be called Son of the Most High, and the Lord God will give him the throne of David his father, ³³ and he will rule over the house of Jacob forever, and of his Kingdom there will be no end." ³⁴ But Mary said to the angel, "How can this be, since I have no relations with a man?" ³⁵ And the angel said to her in reply, "The Holy Spirit will come upon you, and the power of the Most High will overshadow you. Therefore the child to be

born will be called holy, the Son of God. ³⁶ And behold, Elizabeth, your relative, has also conceived a son in her old age, and this is the sixth month for her who was called barren; ³⁷ for nothing will be impossible for God." ³⁸ Mary said, "Behold, I am the handmaid of the Lord. May it be done to me according to your word." Then the angel departed from her.

Tuesday December 9, 2025
Tuesday of the Second Week of Advent
First Reading: Isaiah 40:1-11

¹ Comfort, give comfort to my people,
  says your God.
² Speak tenderly to Jerusalem, and proclaim to her
  that her service is at an end,
  her guilt is expiated;
Indeed, she has received from the hand of the LORD
  double for all her sins.

³ A voice cries out:
In the desert prepare the way of the LORD!
  Make straight in the wasteland a highway
    for our God!
⁴ Every valley shall be filled in,
  every mountain and hill shall be made low;
The rugged land shall be made a plain,
  the rough country, a broad valley.
⁵ Then the glory of the LORD shall be revealed,
  and all people shall see it together;
  for the mouth of the LORD has spoken.

⁶ A voice says, "Cry out!"
  I answer, "What shall I cry out?"
"All flesh is grass,
  and all their glory like the flower of the field.
⁷ The grass withers, the flower wilts,
  when the breath of the LORD blows upon it.
  So then, the people is the grass.
⁸ Though the grass withers and the flower wilts,
  the word of our God stands forever."

⁹ Go up onto a high mountain,
    Zion, herald of glad tidings;
Cry out at the top of your voice,
    Jerusalem, herald of good news!
Fear not to cry out
    and say to the cities of Judah:
    Here is your God!
¹⁰ Here comes with power
    the Lord GOD,
    who rules by his strong arm;
Here is his reward with him,
    his recompense before him.
¹¹ Like a shepherd he feeds his flock;
    in his arms he gathers the lambs,
Carrying them in his bosom,
    and leading the ewes with care.

Responsorial Psalm: Psalms 96:1-2, 3 AND 10AC, 11-12, 13

R. *(see Isaiah 40:10)* **The Lord our God comes with power.**

¹ Sing to the LORD a new song;
    sing to the LORD, all you lands.
² Sing to the LORD; bless his name;
    announce his salvation, day after day.

R. The Lord our God comes with power.

³ Tell his glory among the nations;
    among all peoples, his wondrous deeds.
¹⁰ᴬᶜ Say among the nations: The LORD is king;
    he governs the peoples with equity.

R. The Lord our God comes with power.

¹¹ Let the heavens be glad and the earth rejoice;
    let the sea and what fills it resound;
¹² let the plains be joyful and all that is in them!
Then let all the trees of the forest rejoice.

R. The Lord our God comes with power.

¹³ They shall exult before the LORD, for he comes;
    for he comes to rule the earth.
He shall rule the world with justice
    and the peoples with his constancy.

R. The Lord our God comes with power.

Alleluia
R. Alleluia, alleluia.
The day of the Lord is near;
Behold, he comes to save us.
R. Alleluia, alleluia.

Gospel: Matthew 18:12-14
Jesus said to his disciples: [12] "What is your opinion? If a man has a hundred sheep and one of them goes astray, will he not leave the ninety-nine in the hills and go in search of the stray? [13] And if he finds it, amen, I say to you, he rejoices more over it than over the ninety-nine that did not stray. [14] In just the same way, it is not the will of your heavenly Father that one of these little ones be lost."

Wednesday December 10, 2025
Wednesday of the Second Week of Advent

First Reading: Isaiah 40:25-31

[25] To whom can you liken me as an equal?
> says the Holy One.

[26] Lift up your eyes on high
> and see who has created these things:

He leads out their army and numbers them,
> calling them all by name.

By his great might and the strength of his power
> not one of them is missing!

[27] Why, O Jacob, do you say,
> and declare, O Israel,

"My way is hidden from the LORD,
> and my right is disregarded by my God"?

[28] Do you not know
> or have you not heard?

The LORD is the eternal God,
> creator of the ends of the earth.

He does not faint nor grow weary,
> and his knowledge is beyond scrutiny.

[29] He gives strength to the fainting;
> for the weak he makes vigor abound.

[30] Though young men faint and grow weary,
> and youths stagger and fall,

[31] They that hope in the LORD will renew their strength,
> they will soar as with eagles' wings;

They will run and not grow weary,
> walk and not grow faint.

Responsorial Psalm: Psalms 103:1-2, 3-4, 8 and 10
R. (1) *O bless the Lord, my soul!*
¹ Bless the LORD, O my soul;
> and all my being, bless his holy name.
² Bless the LORD, O my soul,
> and forget not all his benefits.

R. O bless the Lord, my soul!
³ He pardons all your iniquities,
> he heals all your ills.
⁴ He redeems your life from destruction,
> he crowns you with kindness and
>> compassion.

R. O bless the Lord, my soul!
⁸ Merciful and gracious is the LORD,
> slow to anger and abounding in kindness.
¹⁰ Not according to our sins does he deal with
> us,
> nor does he requite us according to our
>> crimes.

R. O bless the Lord, my soul!

Alleluia
R. Alleluia, alleluia.
Behold, the Lord comes to save his people;
blessed are those prepared to meet him.
R. Alleluia, alleluia.

Gospel: Matthew 11:28-30
Jesus said to the crowds: ²⁸ "Come to me, all you who labor and are burdened, and I will give you rest. ²⁹ Take my yoke upon you and learn from me, for I am meek and humble of heart; and you will find rest for yourselves. ³⁰ For my yoke is easy, and my burden light."

Thursday December 11, 2025
Thursday of the Second Week of Advent

First Reading: Isaiah 41:13-20
¹³I am the LORD, your God,
> who grasp your right hand;
It is I who say to you, "Fear not,
> I will help you."
¹⁴Fear not, O worm Jacob,
> O maggot Israel;
I will help you, says the LORD;
> your redeemer is the Holy One of Israel.
¹⁵I will make of you a threshing sledge,
> sharp, new, and double-edged,

To thresh the mountains and crush them,
> to make the hills like chaff.
¹⁶When you winnow them, the wind shall
> carry them off
> and the storm shall scatter them.
But you shall rejoice in the LORD,
> and glory in the Holy One of Israel.

¹⁷The afflicted and the needy seek water in
> vain,
> their tongues are parched with thirst.
I, the LORD, will answer them;
> I, the God of Israel, will not forsake them.
¹⁸I will open up rivers on the bare heights,
> and fountains in the broad valleys;
I will turn the desert into a marshland,
> and the dry ground into springs of water.
¹⁹I will plant in the desert the cedar,
> acacia, myrtle, and olive;
I will set in the wasteland the cypress,
> together with the plane tree and the pine,
²⁰That all may see and know,
> observe and understand,
That the hand of the LORD has done this,
> the Holy One of Israel has created it.

Responsorial Psalm: Psalms 145:1 AND 9, 10-11, 12-13AB

R. (8) The Lord is gracious and merciful; slow to anger, and of great kindness.

¹ I will extol you, O my God and King,
> and I will bless your name forever and
> ever.
⁹ The LORD is good to all
> and compassionate toward all his works.

R. The Lord is gracious and merciful; slow to anger, and of great kindness.

¹⁰ Let all your works give you thanks, O LORD,
> and let your faithful ones bless you.
¹¹ Let them discourse of the glory of your
> Kingdom
> and speak of your might.

R. The Lord is gracious and merciful; slow to anger, and of great kindness.

¹² Let them make known to men your might
> and the glorious splendor of your

Kingdom.
13AB Your Kingdom is a Kingdom for all ages,
and your dominion endures through all generations.
R. The Lord is gracious and merciful; slow to anger, and of great kindness.

Alleluia: Isaiah 45:8
R. Alleluia, alleluia.
⁸Let the clouds rain down the Just One,
and the earth bring forth a Savior.
R. Alleluia, alleluia.

Gospel: Matthew 11:11-15
Jesus said to the crowds: ¹¹"Amen, I say to you, among those born of women there has been none greater than John the Baptist; yet the least in the Kingdom of heaven is greater than he. ¹²From the days of John the Baptist until now, the Kingdom of heaven suffers violence, and the violent are taking it by force. ¹³All the prophets and the law prophesied up to the time of John. And if you are willing to accept it, he is Elijah, the one who is to come. Whoever has ears ought to hear."

Friday December 12, 2025
Feast of Our Lady of Guadalupe

First Reading: Zechariah 2:14-17
¹⁴ Sing and rejoice, O daughter Zion!
See, I am coming to dwell among you,
    says the LORD.
¹⁵ Many nations shall join themselves to
    the LORD on that day,
and they shall be his people,
and he will dwell among you,
and you shall know that the LORD of
    hosts has sent me to you.
¹⁶ The LORD will possess Judah as his
    portion in the holy land,
and he will again choose Jerusalem.
¹⁷ Silence, all mankind, in the presence of
    the LORD!
For he stirs forth from his holy
    dwelling.

Or Revelation 11:19A; 12:1-6A, 10AB
¹⁹ᴬ God's temple in heaven was opened, and the ark of his covenant could be seen in the temple.

[1] A great sign appeared in the sky, a woman clothed with the sun, with the moon under her feet, and on her head a crown of twelve stars. [2] She was with child and wailed aloud in pain as she labored to give birth. [3] Then another sign appeared in the sky; it was a huge red dragon, with seven heads and ten horns, and on its heads were seven diadems. [4] Its tail swept away a third of the stars in the sky and hurled them down to the earth. Then the dragon stood before the woman about to give birth, to devour her child when she gave birth. [5] She gave birth to a son, a male child, destined to rule all the nations with an iron rod. Her child was caught up to God and his throne. [6A] The woman herself fled into the desert where she had a place prepared by God.

[10AB] Then I heard a loud voice in heaven say: "Now have salvation and power come, and the Kingdom of our God and the authority of his Anointed."

Responsorial Psalm: Judith 13:18BCDE, 19

R. [15:9d] **You are the highest honor of our race.**
[18BCDE] Blessed are you, daughter, by the Most High
    God,
  above all the women on earth;
  and blessed be the LORD God,
  the creator of heaven and earth.
R. You are the highest honor of our race.
[19] Your deed of hope will never be forgotten
    by those who tell of the might of God.
R. You are the highest honor of our race.

Alleluia
R. Alleluia, alleluia.
Blessed are you, holy Virgin Mary, deserving
    of all praise;
From you rose the sun of justice, Christ our God.
R. Alleluia, alleluia.

Gospel: Luke 1:26-38
[26] The angel Gabriel was sent from God to a town of Galilee called Nazareth, [27] to a virgin betrothed to a man named Joseph, of the house of David, and the virgin's name was Mary. [28] And coming to her, he said, "Hail, full of grace! The Lord is with you." [29] But she was greatly troubled at what was said and pondered what sort of greeting this might be. [30] Then the angel said to her, "Do not be afraid, Mary, for you have found favor with God. [31] Behold, you will conceive in your womb and bear a son, and you shall name him Jesus. [32] He will be great and will be called Son of the Most High, and the Lord God will give him the throne of David his father, [33] and he will rule over the house of Jacob forever, and of his Kingdom there will be no end." [34] But Mary said to the angel, "How can this be, since I have no relations with a man?" [35] And the angel said to her in reply, "The Holy Spirit will come upon you, and the power of the Most High will overshadow you. Therefore the child to be born will

be called holy, the Son of God. ³⁶ And behold, Elizabeth, your relative, has also conceived a son in her old age, and this is the sixth month for her who was called barren; ³⁷ for nothing will be impossible for God." ³⁸ Mary said, "Behold, I am the handmaid of the Lord. May it be done to me according to your word." Then the angel departed from her.

Or Luke 1:39-47

³⁹ Mary set out and traveled to the hill country in haste to a town of Judah, ⁴⁰ where she entered the house of Zechariah and greeted Elizabeth. ⁴¹ When Elizabeth heard Mary's greeting, the infant leaped in her womb, and Elizabeth, filled with the Holy Spirit, ⁴² cried out in a loud voice and said, "Most blessed are you among women, and blessed is the fruit of your womb. ⁴³ And how does this happen to me, that the mother of my Lord should come to me? ⁴⁴ For at the moment the sound of your greeting reached my ears, the infant in my womb leaped for joy. ⁴⁵ Blessed are you who believed that what was spoken to you by the Lord would be fulfilled."

⁴⁶ And Mary said:

"My soul proclaims the greatness of the
    Lord;
⁴⁷ my spirit rejoices in God my savior."

Saturday December 13, 2025
Memorial of Saint Lucy, Virgin & Martyr
First Reading: Sirach 48:1-4, 9-11

¹ In those days,
like a fire there appeared the prophet Elijah
    whose words were as a flaming furnace.
² Their staff of bread he shattered,
    in his zeal he reduced them to straits;
³ By the Lord's word he shut up the heavens
    and three times brought down fire.
⁴ How awesome are you, Elijah, in your
       wondrous deeds!
    Whose glory is equal to yours?
⁹ You were taken aloft in a whirlwind of fire,
    in a chariot with fiery horses.
¹⁰ You were destined, it is written, in time to
       come
    to put an end to wrath before the day of
       the LORD,
To turn back the hearts of fathers toward
       their sons,
    and to re-establish the tribes of Jacob.
¹¹ Blessed is he who shall have seen you
    and who falls asleep in your friendship.

Responsorial Psalm: Psalms 80:2AC AND 3B, 15-16, 18-19

R. (4) *Lord, make us turn to you; let us see your face and we shall be saved.*

2AC O shepherd of Israel, hearken,
From your throne upon the cherubim, shine forth.
3B Rouse your power.

R. *Lord, make us turn to you; let us see your face and we shall be saved.*

15 Once again, O LORD of hosts,
look down from heaven, and see;
16 Take care of this vine,
and protect what your right hand has planted,
the son of man whom you yourself made strong.

R. *Lord, make us turn to you; let us see your face and we shall be saved.*

18 May your help be with the man of your right hand,
with the son of man whom you yourself made strong.
19 Then we will no more withdraw from you;
give us new life, and we will call upon your name.

R. *Lord, make us turn to you; let us see your face and we shall be saved.*

Alleluia: Luke 3:4, 6

R. Alleluia, alleluia.
4 Prepare the way of the Lord, make straight his paths:
6 All flesh shall see the salvation of God.
R. Alleluia, alleluia.

Gospel: Matthew 17:9A, 10-13

9A As they were coming down from the mountain, 10 the disciples asked Jesus, "Why do the scribes say that Elijah must come first?" 11 He said in reply, "Elijah will indeed come and restore all things; 12 but I tell you that Elijah has already come, and they did not recognize him but did to him whatever they pleased. So also will the Son of Man suffer at their hands." 13 Then the disciples understood that he was speaking to them of John the Baptist.

Sunday December 14, 2025
Third Sunday of Advent, Year A

First Reading: Isaiah 35:1-6A, 10

[1] The desert and the parched land will exult;
    the steppe will rejoice and bloom.
[2] They will bloom with abundant flowers,
    and rejoice with joyful song.
The glory of Lebanon will be given to them,
    the splendor of Carmel and Sharon;
they will see the glory of the LORD,
    the splendor of our God.
[3] Strengthen the hands that are feeble,
    make firm the knees that are weak,
[4] say to those whose hearts are frightened:
    Be strong, fear not!
Here is your God,
    he comes with vindication;
with divine recompense
    he comes to save you.
[5] Then will the eyes of the blind be opened,
    the ears of the deaf be cleared;
[6] then will the lame leap like a stag,
    then the tongue of the mute will sing.

[10] Those whom the LORD has ransomed will return
    and enter Zion singing,
    crowned with everlasting joy;
they will meet with joy and gladness,
    sorrow and mourning will flee.

Responsorial Psalm: Psalms 146:6-7,8-9,9-10

R. (cf. Is 35:4) **Lord, come and save us.** or: **R. Alleluia.**

[6] The LORD God keeps faith forever,
    [7] secures justice for the oppressed,
    gives food to the hungry.
The LORD sets captives free.

R. Lord, come and save us. or: **R. Alleluia.**

[8] The LORD gives sight to the blind;
    the LORD raises up those who were bowed down.
The LORD loves the just;
    [9A] the LORD protects strangers.

R. Lord, come and save us. or: **R. Alleluia.**

9BC The fatherless and the widow he sustains,
   but the way of the wicked he thwarts.
10 The LORD shall reign forever;
   your God, O Zion, through all
      generations.
R. Lord, come and save us. or: **R. Alleluia.**

Second Reading: James 5:7-10

7 Be patient, brothers and sisters, until the coming of the Lord. See how the farmer waits for the precious fruit of the earth, being patient with it until it receives the early and the late rains. 8 You too must be patient. Make your hearts firm, because the coming of the Lord is at hand. 9 Do not complain, brothers and sisters, about one another, that you may not be judged. Behold, the Judge is standing before the gates. 10 Take as an example of hardship and patience, brothers and sisters, the prophets who spoke in the name of the Lord.

Alleluia: Isaiah 61:1 (cited in Luke 4:18)

R. Alleluia, alleluia.
18 The Spirit of the Lord is upon me,
because he has anointed me
to bring glad tidings to the poor.
R. Alleluia, alleluia.

Gospel: Matthew 11:2-11

2 When John the Baptist heard in prison of the works of the Christ, he sent his disciples to Jesus 3 with this question, "Are you the one who is to come, or should we look for another?" 4 Jesus said to them in reply, "Go and tell John what you hear and see: 5 the blind regain their sight, the lame walk, lepers are cleansed, the deaf hear, the dead are raised, and the poor have the good news proclaimed to them. 6 And blessed is the one who takes no offense at me."

7 As they were going off, Jesus began to speak to the crowds about John, "What did you go out to the desert to see? A reed swayed by the wind? 8 Then what did you go out to see? Someone dressed in fine clothing? Those who wear fine clothing are in royal palaces. 9 Then why did you go out? To see a prophet? Yes, I tell you, and more than a prophet. 10 This is the one about whom it is written:

Behold, I am sending my messenger ahead of
   you;
   he will prepare your way before you.

11 Amen, I say to you, among those born of women there has been none greater than John the Baptist; yet the least in the kingdom of heaven is greater than he."

Monday December 15, 2025
Monday of the Third Week of Advent

First Reading: Numbers 24:2-7, 15-17A

[2] When Balaam raised his eyes and saw Israel encamped, tribe by tribe, the spirit of God came upon him, [3] and he gave voice to his oracle:

The utterance of Balaam, son of Beor,
    the utterance of a man whose eye is true,
[4] The utterance of one who hears what God says,
    and knows what the Most High knows,
Of one who sees what the Almighty sees,
    enraptured, and with eyes unveiled:
[5] How goodly are your tents, O Jacob;
    your encampments, O Israel!
[6] They are like gardens beside a stream,
    like the cedars planted by the LORD.
[7] His wells shall yield free-flowing waters,
    he shall have the sea within reach;
His king shall rise higher,
    and his royalty shall be exalted.

[15] Then Balaam gave voice to his oracle:

The utterance of Balaam, son of Beor,
    the utterance of the man whose eye is true,
[16] The utterance of one who hears what God says,
    and knows what the Most High knows,
Of one who sees what the Almighty sees,
    enraptured, and with eyes unveiled.
[17A] I see him, though not now;
    I behold him, though not near:
A star shall advance from Jacob,
    and a staff shall rise from Israel.

Responsorial Psalm: Psalms 25:4-5AB, 6 and 7BC, 8-9

R. (4) *Teach me your ways, O Lord.*
[4] Your ways, O LORD, make known to me;
    teach me your paths,
[5AB] Guide me in your truth and teach me,
    for you are God my savior.
R. Teach me your ways, O Lord.

⁶ Remember that your compassion, O LORD,
　　and your kindness are from of old.
⁷BC In your kindness remember me,
　　because of your goodness, O LORD.
R. Teach me your ways, O Lord.
⁸ Good and upright is the LORD;
　　thus he shows sinners the way.
⁹ He guides the humble to justice,
　　he teaches the humble his way.
R. Teach me your ways, O Lord.

Alleluia: Psalms 85:8
R. Alleluia, alleluia.
⁸ Show us, LORD, your love,
and grant us your salvation.
R. Alleluia, alleluia.

Gospel: Matthew 21:23-27
²³ When Jesus had come into the temple area, the chief priests and the elders of the people approached him as he was teaching and said, "By what authority are you doing these things? And who gave you this authority?" ²⁴ Jesus said to them in reply, "I shall ask you one question, and if you answer it for me, then I shall tell you by what authority I do these things. ²⁵ Where was John's baptism from? Was it of heavenly or of human origin?" They discussed this among themselves and said, "If we say 'Of heavenly origin,' he will say to us, 'Then why did you not believe him?' ²⁶ But if we say, 'Of human origin,' we fear the crowd, for they all regard John as a prophet." ²⁷ So they said to Jesus in reply, "We do not know." He himself said to them, "Neither shall I tell you by what authority I do these things."

Tuesday December 16, 2025
Tuesday of the Third Week of Advent
First Reading: Zephaniah 3:1-2, 9-13
Thus says the LORD:

¹Woe to the city, rebellious and polluted,
　　to the tyrannical city!
²She hears no voice,
　　accepts no correction;
In the LORD she has not trusted,
　　to her God she has not drawn near.

⁹For then I will change and purify
　　the lips of the peoples,
That they all may call upon the name of the
　　　LORD,
　　to serve him with one accord;

¹⁰From beyond the rivers of Ethiopia
    and as far as the recesses of the North,
        they shall bring me offerings.

    ¹¹On that day
You need not be ashamed
    of all your deeds,
        your rebellious actions against me;
For then will I remove from your midst
    the proud braggarts,
And you shall no longer exalt yourself
    on my holy mountain.
¹²But I will leave as a remnant in your midst
    a people humble and lowly,
Who shall take refuge in the name of the
    LORD:
    ¹³the remnant of Israel.
They shall do no wrong
    and speak no lies;
Nor shall there be found in their mouths
    a deceitful tongue;
They shall pasture and couch their flocks
    with none to disturb them.

Responsorial Psalm: Psalms 34:2-3, 6-7, 17-18, 19, 23

*R. ⁽⁷ᵃ⁾ **The Lord hears the cry of the poor.***
²I will bless the LORD at all times;
    his praise shall be ever in my mouth.
³Let my soul glory in the LORD;
    the lowly will hear me and be glad.
R. The Lord hears the cry of the poor.
⁶Look to him that you may be radiant with
    joy,
    and your faces may not blush with
    shame.
⁷When the poor one called out, the LORD
    heard,
    and from all his distress he saved him.
R. The Lord hears the cry of the poor.
¹⁷The LORD confronts the evildoers,
    to destroy remembrance of them from
    the earth.
¹⁸When the just cry out, the LORD hears them,
    and from all their distress he rescues
    them.

R. The Lord hears the cry of the poor.
[19] The LORD is close to the brokenhearted;
 and those who are crushed in spirit he saves.
[23] The LORD redeems the lives of his servants;
 no one incurs guilt who takes refuge in him.
R. The Lord hears the cry of the poor.

Alleluia
R. Alleluia, alleluia.
Come, O Lord, do not delay;
forgive the sins of your people.
R. Alleluia, alleluia.

Gospel: Matthew 21:28-32
Jesus said to the chief priests and the elders of the people: [28]"What is your opinion? A man had two sons. He came to the first and said, 'Son, go out and work in the vineyard today.' [29]The son said in reply, 'I will not,' but afterwards he changed his mind and went. [30]The man came to the other son and gave the same order. He said in reply, 'Yes, sir,' but did not go. [31]Which of the two did his father's will?" They answered, "The first." Jesus said to them, "Amen, I say to you, tax collectors and prostitutes are entering the Kingdom of God before you. [32]When John came to you in the way of righteousness, you did not believe him; but tax collectors and prostitutes did. Yet even when you saw that, you did not later change your minds and believe him."

Wednesday December 17, 2025

First Reading: Genesis 49:2, 8-10
[2] Jacob called his sons and said to them:

"Assemble and listen, sons of Jacob,
 listen to Israel, your father.

[8] "You, Judah, shall your brothers praise
 –your hand on the neck of your enemies;
 the sons of your father shall bow down to you.
[9] Judah, like a lion's whelp,
 you have grown up on prey, my son.
He crouches like a lion recumbent,
 the king of beasts–who would dare rouse him?
[10] The scepter shall never depart from Judah,
 or the mace from between his legs,
While tribute is brought to him,

and he receives the people's homage."

Responsorial Psalm: Psalms 72:1-2, 3-4AB, 7-8, 17

R. *(see 7)* *Justice shall flourish in his time, and fullness of peace for ever.*

¹ O God, with your judgment endow the king,
and with your justice, the king's son;
² He shall govern your people with justice
and your afflicted ones with judgment.

R. Justice shall flourish in his time, and fullness of peace for ever.

³ The mountains shall yield peace for the people,
and the hills justice.
⁴ᴬᴮ He shall defend the afflicted among the people,
save the children of the poor.

R. Justice shall flourish in his time, and fullness of peace for ever.

⁷ Justice shall flower in his days,
and profound peace, till the moon be no more.
⁸ May he rule from sea to sea,
and from the River to the ends of the earth.

R. Justice shall flourish in his time, and fullness of peace for ever.

¹⁷ May his name be blessed forever;
as long as the sun his name shall remain.
In him shall all the tribes of the earth be blessed;
all the nations shall proclaim his happiness.

R. Justice shall flourish in his time, and fullness of peace for ever.

Alleluia

R. Alleluia, alleluia.
O Wisdom of our God Most High,
guiding creation with power and love:
come to teach us the path of knowledge!
R. Alleluia, alleluia.

Gospel: Matthew 1:1-17

¹ The book of the genealogy of Jesus Christ, the son of David, the son of Abraham.

² Abraham became the father of Isaac, Isaac the father of Jacob, Jacob the father of Judah and his brothers. ³ Judah became the father of Perez and Zerah, whose mother was Tamar. Perez became the father of Hezron, Hezron the father of Ram, ⁴ Ram the father of Amminadab. Amminadab became the father of Nahshon, Nahshon the father of Salmon, ⁵ Salmon the father of Boaz, whose mother was Rahab. Boaz became the father of Obed, whose mother was Ruth. Obed became the father of Jesse, ⁶ Jesse the father of David the king.

David became the father of Solomon, whose mother had been the wife of Uriah. ⁷ Solomon became the father of Rehoboam, Rehoboam the father of Abijah, Abijah the father of Asaph. ⁸ Asaph became the father of Jehoshaphat, Jehoshaphat the father of Joram, Joram the father of Uzziah. ⁹ Uzziah became the father of Jotham, Jotham the father of Ahaz, Ahaz the father of Hezekiah. ¹⁰ Hezekiah became the father of Manasseh, Manasseh the father of Amos, Amos the father of Josiah. ¹¹ Josiah became the father of Jechoniah and his brothers at the time of the Babylonian exile.

¹² After the Babylonian exile, Jechoniah became the father of Shealtiel, Shealtiel the father of Zerubbabel, ¹³ Zerubbabel the father of Abiud. Abiud became the father of Eliakim, Eliakim the father of Azor, ¹⁴ Azor the father of Zadok. Zadok became the father of Achim, Achim the father of Eliud, ¹⁵ Eliud the father of Eleazar. Eleazar became the father of Matthan, Matthan the father of Jacob, ¹⁶ Jacob the father of Joseph, the husband of Mary. Of her was born Jesus who is called the Christ.

¹⁷ Thus the total number of generations from Abraham to David is fourteen generations; from David to the Babylonian exile, fourteen generations; from the Babylonian exile to the Christ, fourteen generations.

Thursday December 18, 2025

First Reading: Jeremiah 23:5-8

⁵ Behold, the days are coming, says the LORD,
    when I will raise up a righteous shoot to
        David;
As king he shall reign and govern wisely,
    he shall do what is just and right in the
        land.
⁶ In his days Judah shall be saved,
    Israel shall dwell in security.
This is the name they give him:
    "The LORD our justice."

⁷ Therefore, the days will come, says the LORD,
    when they shall no longer say, "As the
        LORD lives,
who brought the children of Israel out of
    the land of Egypt";
⁸ but rather, "As the LORD lives,

who brought the descendants of the
    house of Israel
up from the land of the north"–
and from all the lands to which I
    banished them;
they shall again live on their own land.

Responsorial Psalm: Psalms 72:1-2, 12-13, 18-19

R. (see 7) *Justice shall flourish in his time, and fullness of peace for ever.*

[1] O God, with your judgment endow the king,
    and with your justice, the king's son;
[2] He shall govern your people with justice
    and your afflicted ones with judgment.

R. Justice shall flourish in his time, and fullness of peace for ever.

[12] For he shall rescue the poor when he cries out,
    and the afflicted when he has no one to help him.
[12] He shall have pity for the lowly and the poor;
    the lives of the poor he shall save.

R. Justice shall flourish in his time, and fullness of peace for ever.

[18] Blessed be the LORD, the God of Israel,
    who alone does wondrous deeds.
[19] And blessed forever be his glorious name;
    may the whole earth be filled with his glory.

R. Justice shall flourish in his time, and fullness of peace for ever.

Alleluia

R. Alleluia, alleluia.
O Leader of the House of Israel,
giver of the Law to Moses on Sinai:
come to rescue us with your mighty power!
R. Alleluia, alleluia.

Gospel: Matthew 1:18-25

[18] This is how the birth of Jesus Christ came about. When his mother Mary was betrothed to Joseph, but before they lived together, she was found with child through the Holy Spirit. [19] Joseph her husband, since he was a righteous man, yet

unwilling to expose her to shame, decided to divorce her quietly. ²⁰ Such was his intention when, behold, the angel of the Lord appeared to him in a dream and said, "Joseph, son of David, do not be afraid to take Mary your wife into your home. For it is through the Holy Spirit that this child has been conceived in her. ²¹ She will bear a son and you are to name him Jesus, because he will save his people from their sins." ²² All this took place to fulfill what the Lord had said through the prophet:

²³ *Behold, the virgin shall be with child and bear*
  a son,
and they shall name him Emmanuel,

which means "God is with us." ²⁴ When Joseph awoke, he did as the angel of the Lord had commanded him and took his wife into his home. ²⁵ He had no relations with her until she bore a son, and he named him Jesus.

Friday December 19, 2025

First Reading: Judges 13:2-7, 24-25A

² There was a certain man from Zorah, of the clan of the Danites, whose name was Manoah. His wife was barren and had borne no children. ³ An angel of the LORD appeared to the woman and said to her, "Though you are barren and have had no children, yet you will conceive and bear a son. ⁴ Now, then, be careful to take no wine or strong drink and to eat nothing unclean. ⁵ As for the son you will conceive and bear, no razor shall touch his head, for this boy is to be consecrated to God from the womb. It is he who will begin the deliverance of Israel from the power of the Philistines."

⁶ The woman went and told her husband, "A man of God came to me; he had the appearance of an angel of God, terrible indeed. I did not ask him where he came from, nor did he tell me his name. ⁷ But he said to me, 'You will be with child and will bear a son. So take neither wine nor strong drink, and eat nothing unclean. For the boy shall be consecrated to God from the womb, until the day of his death.'"

²⁴ The woman bore a son and named him Samson. The boy grew up and the LORD blessed him; ²⁵ᴬ the Spirit of the LORD stirred him.

Responsorial Psalm: Psalms 71:3-4A, 5-6AB, 16-17

R. *(See 8)* **My mouth shall be filled with your praise,**
  and I will sing your glory!
³ Be my rock of refuge,
  a stronghold to give me safety,
  for you are my rock and my fortress.
⁴ᴬ O my God, rescue me from the hand of the
  wicked.
R. My mouth shall be filled with your praise, and
  I will sing your glory!
⁵ For you are my hope, O LORD;
  my trust, O God, from my youth.
⁶ᴬᴮ On you I depend from birth;

from my mother's womb you are my
    strength.
***R. My mouth shall be filled with your praise, and
I will sing your glory!***
[16] I will treat of the mighty works of the LORD;
    O God, I will tell of your singular justice.
[17] O God, you have taught me from my youth,
    and till the present I proclaim your
        wondrous deeds.
***R. My mouth shall be filled with your praise, and
I will sing your glory!***

Alleluia
R. Alleluia, alleluia.
O Root of Jesse's stem,
sign of God's love for all his people:
come to save us without delay!
R. Alleluia, alleluia.

Gospel: Luke 1:5-25
[5] In the days of Herod, King of Judea, there was a priest named Zechariah of the priestly division of Abijah; his wife was from the daughters of Aaron, and her name was Elizabeth. [6] Both were righteous in the eyes of God, observing all the commandments and ordinances of the Lord blamelessly. [7] But they had no child, because Elizabeth was barren and both were advanced in years.

[8] Once when he was serving as priest in his division's turn before God, [9] according to the practice of the priestly service, he was chosen by lot to enter the sanctuary of the Lord to burn incense. [10] Then, when the whole assembly of the people was praying outside at the hour of the incense offering, [11] the angel of the Lord appeared to him, standing at the right of the altar of incense. [12] Zechariah was troubled by what he saw, and fear came upon him.

[13] But the angel said to him, "Do not be afraid, Zechariah, because your prayer has been heard. Your wife Elizabeth will bear you a son, and you shall name him John. [14] And you will have joy and gladness, and many will rejoice at his birth, [15] for he will be great in the sight of the Lord. He will drink neither wine nor strong drink. He will be filled with the Holy Spirit even from his mother's womb, [16] and he will turn many of the children of Israel to the Lord their God. [17] He will go before him in the spirit and power of Elijah to turn the hearts of fathers toward children and the disobedient to the understanding of the righteous, to prepare a people fit for the Lord."

[18] Then Zechariah said to the angel, "How shall I know this? For I am an old man, and my wife is advanced in years." [19] And the angel said to him in reply, "I am Gabriel, who stand before God. I was sent to speak to you and to announce to you this good news. [20] But now you will be speechless and unable to talk until the day

these things take place, because you did not believe my words, which will be fulfilled at their proper time." ²¹ Meanwhile the people were waiting for Zechariah and were amazed that he stayed so long in the sanctuary. ²² But when he came out, he was unable to speak to them, and they realized that he had seen a vision in the sanctuary. He was gesturing to them but remained mute.

²³ Then, when his days of ministry were completed, he went home.

²⁴ After this time his wife Elizabeth conceived, and she went into seclusion for five months, saying, ²⁵ "So has the Lord done for me at a time when he has seen fit to take away my disgrace before others."

Saturday December 20, 2025

First Reading: Isaiah 7:10-14

¹⁰ The LORD spoke to Ahaz: ¹¹ Ask for a sign from the LORD, your God; let it be deep as the nether world, or high as the sky! ¹² But Ahaz answered, "I will not ask! I will not tempt the LORD!" ¹³ Then Isaiah said: Listen, O house of David! Is it not enough for you to weary men, must you also weary my God? ¹⁴ Therefore the Lord himself will give you this sign: the virgin shall conceive and bear a son, and shall name him Emmanuel.

Responsorial Psalm: Psalms 24:1-2, 3-4AB, 5-6

R. *(See 7c and 10b)* **Let the Lord enter; he is the king of glory.**

¹ The LORD's are the earth and its fullness;
    the world and those who dwell in it.
² For he founded it upon the seas
    and established it upon the rivers.

R. Let the Lord enter; he is the king of glory.

³ Who can ascend the mountain of the LORD?
    or who may stand in his holy place?
⁴ᴬᴮ He whose hands are sinless, whose heart is
        clean,
    who desires not what is vain.

R. Let the Lord enter; he is the king of glory.

⁵ He shall receive a blessing from the LORD,
    a reward from God his savior.
⁶ Such is the race that seeks for him,
    that seeks the face of the God of Jacob.

R. Let the Lord enter; he is the king of glory.

Alleluia

R. Alleluia, alleluia.
O Key of David,
opening the gates of God's eternal Kingdom:
come and free the prisoners of darkness!
R. Alleluia, alleluia.

Gospel: Luke 1:26-38

26 In the sixth month, the angel Gabriel was sent from God to a town of Galilee called Nazareth, 27 to a virgin betrothed to a man named Joseph, of the house of David, and the virgin's name was Mary. 28 And coming to her, he said, "Hail, full of grace! The Lord is with you." 29 But she was greatly troubled at what was said and pondered what sort of greeting this might be. 30 Then the angel said to her, "Do not be afraid, Mary, for you have found favor with God. 31 Behold, you will conceive in your womb and bear a son, and you shall name him Jesus. 32 He will be great and will be called Son of the Most High, and the Lord God will give him the throne of David his father, 33 and he will rule over the house of Jacob forever, and of his Kingdom there will be no end."

34 But Mary said to the angel, "How can this be, since I have no relations with a man?" 35 And the angel said to her in reply, "The Holy Spirit will come upon you, and the power of the Most High will overshadow you. Therefore the child to be born will be called holy, the Son of God. 36 And behold, Elizabeth, your relative, has also conceived a son in her old age, and this is the sixth month for her who was called barren; 37 for nothing will be impossible for God."

38 Mary said, "Behold, I am the handmaid of the Lord. May it be done to me according to your word." Then the angel departed from her.

Sunday December 21, 2025
Fourth Sunday of Advent, Year A

First Reading: Isaiah 7:10-14

10 The LORD spoke to Ahaz, saying: 11 Ask for a sign from the LORD, your God; let it be deep as the netherworld, or high as the sky! 12 But Ahaz answered, "I will not ask! I will not tempt the LORD!" 13 Then Isaiah said: Listen, O house of David! Is it not enough for you to weary people, must you also weary my God? 14 Therefore the Lord himself will give you this sign: the virgin shall conceive, and bear a son, and shall name him Emmanuel.

Responsorial Psalm: Psalms 24:1-2, 3-4, 5-6

R. *(7c and 10b)* **Let the Lord enter; he is king of glory.**

1 The LORD's are the earth and its fullness;
   the world and those who dwell in it.
2 For he founded it upon the seas
   and established it upon the rivers.

R. Let the Lord enter; he is king of glory.

3 Who can ascend the mountain of the LORD?
   or who may stand in his holy place?
4 One whose hands are sinless, whose heart is clean,
   who desires not what is vain.

R. Let the Lord enter; he is king of glory.

5 He shall receive a blessing from the LORD,
   a reward from God his savior.
6 Such is the race that seeks for him,
   that seeks the face of the God of Jacob.

R. Let the Lord enter; he is king of glory.

Second Reading: Romans 1:1-7
[1]Paul, a slave of Christ Jesus, called to be an apostle and set apart for the gospel of God, [2]which he promised previously through his prophets in the holy Scriptures, [3]the gospel about his Son, descended from David according to the flesh, [4]but established as Son of God in power according to the Spirit of holiness through resurrection from the dead, Jesus Christ our Lord. [5]Through him we have received the grace of apostleship, to bring about the obedience of faith, for the sake of his name, among all the Gentiles, [6]among whom are you also, who are called to belong to Jesus Christ; [7]to all the beloved of God in Rome, called to be holy. Grace to you and peace from God our Father and the Lord Jesus Christ.

Alleluia: Matthew 1:23
R. Alleluia, alleluia.
[23]The virgin shall conceive, and bear a son,
and they shall name him Emmanuel.
R. Alleluia, alleluia.

Gospel: Matthew 1:18-24
[18]This is how the birth of Jesus Christ came about. When his mother Mary was betrothed to Joseph, but before they lived together, she was found with child through the Holy Spirit. [19]Joseph her husband, since he was a righteous man, yet unwilling to expose her to shame, decided to divorce her quietly. [20]Such was his intention when, behold, the angel of the Lord appeared to him in a dream and said, "Joseph, son of David, do not be afraid to take Mary your wife into your home. For it is through the Holy Spirit that this child has been conceived in her. [21]She will bear a son and you are to name him Jesus, because he will save his people from their sins." [22]All this took place to fulfill what the Lord had said through the prophet:

[23]*Behold, the virgin shall conceive and bear a*
    son,
  and they shall name him Emmanuel,

which means "God is with us." [24]When Joseph awoke, he did as the angel of the Lord had commanded him and took his wife into his home.

Monday December 22, 2025

First Reading: 1 Samuel 1:24-28
In those days, [24]Hannah brought Samuel with her, along with a three-year-old bull, an ephah of flour, and a skin of wine, and presented him at the temple of the LORD in Shiloh. [25]After the boy's father had sacrificed the young bull, [26]Hannah, his mother, approached Eli and said: "Pardon, my lord! As you live, my lord, I am the woman who stood near you here, praying to the LORD. [27]I prayed for this child, and the LORD granted my request. [28]Now I, in turn, give him to the LORD; as long as he lives, he shall be dedicated to the LORD." She left Samuel there.

Responsorial Psalm: 1 Samuel 2:1, 4-5, 6-7, 8ABCD

R. (see 1a) *My heart exults in the Lord, my Savior.*

¹"My heart exults in the LORD,
    my horn is exalted in my God.
I have swallowed up my enemies;
    I rejoice in my victory."

R. *My heart exults in the Lord, my Savior.*

⁴"The bows of the mighty are broken,
    while the tottering gird on strength.
⁵The well-fed hire themselves out for bread,
    while the hungry batten on spoil.
The barren wife bears seven sons,
    while the mother of many languishes."

R. *My heart exults in the Lord, my Savior.*

⁶"The LORD puts to death and gives life;
    he casts down to the nether world;
    he raises up again.
⁷The LORD makes poor and makes rich,
    he humbles, he also exalts."

R. *My heart exults in the Lord, my Savior.*

8ABCD "He raises the needy from the dust;
    from the dung heap he lifts up the poor,
To seat them with nobles
    and make a glorious throne their
        heritage."

R. *My heart exults in the Lord, my Savior.*

Alleluia

R. Alleluia, alleluia.
O King of all nations and keystone of the
        Church:
come and save man, whom you formed from
        the dust!
R. Alleluia, alleluia.

Gospel: Luke 1:46-56

⁴⁶Mary said:

"My soul proclaims the greatness of the
        Lord;
    ⁴⁷my spirit rejoices in God my savior,
    ⁴⁸for he has looked upon his lowly servant.
From this day all generations will call me
        blessed:

⁴⁹the Almighty has done great things for
   me,
   and holy is his Name.
⁵⁰He has mercy on those who fear him
   in every generation.
⁵¹He has shown the strength of his arm,
   and has scattered the proud in their
      conceit.
⁵²He has cast down the mighty from their
      thrones
   and has lifted up the lowly.
⁵³He has filled the hungry with good things,
   and the rich he has sent away empty.
⁵⁴He has come to the help of his servant Israel
   for he remembered his promise of mercy,
⁵⁵the promise he made to our fathers,
   to Abraham and his children for ever.

⁵⁶Mary remained with Elizabeth about three months and then returned to her home.

Tuesday December 23, 2025
First Reading: Malachi 3:1-4, 23-24

¹ Thus says the Lord GOD:
Lo, I am sending my messenger
   to prepare the way before me;
And suddenly there will come to the temple
   the LORD whom you seek,
And the messenger of the covenant whom
      you desire.
   Yes, he is coming, says the LORD of hosts.
² But who will endure the day of his coming?
   And who can stand when he appears?
For he is like the refiner's fire,
   or like the fuller's lye.
³ He will sit refining and purifying silver,
   and he will purify the sons of Levi,
Refining them like gold or like silver
   that they may offer due sacrifice to the
      LORD.
⁴ Then the sacrifice of Judah and Jerusalem
   will please the LORD,
   as in the days of old, as in years gone by.

²³ Lo, I will send you
   Elijah, the prophet,

Before the day of the LORD comes,
> the great and terrible day,

²⁴ To turn the hearts of the fathers to their
> children,
> and the hearts of the children to their
> fathers,

Lest I come and strike
> the land with doom.

Responsorial Psalm: Psalms 25:4-5AB, 8-9, 10 AND 14

R. (see Luke 21:28) ***Lift up your heads and see; your redemption is near at hand.***

⁴ Your ways, O LORD, make known to me;
> teach me your paths,

⁵ᴬᴮ Guide me in your truth and teach me,
> for you are God my savior.

R. Lift up your heads and see; your redemption is near at hand.

⁸ Good and upright is the LORD;
> thus he shows sinners the way.

⁹ He guides the humble to justice,
> he teaches the humble his way.

R. Lift up your heads and see; your redemption is near at hand.

¹⁰ All the paths of the LORD are kindness and
> constancy
> toward those who keep his covenant and
> his decrees.

¹⁴ The friendship of the LORD is with those who
> fear him,
> and his covenant, for their instruction.

R. Lift up your heads and see; your redemption is near at hand.

Alleluia

R. Alleluia, alleluia.
O King of all nations and keystone of the
> Church:
come and save man, whom you formed from
> the dust!
R. Alleluia, alleluia.

Gospel: Luke 1:57-66

57 When the time arrived for Elizabeth to have her child she gave birth to a son. 58 Her neighbors and relatives heard that the Lord had shown his great mercy toward her, and they rejoiced with her. 59 When they came on the eighth day to circumcise the child, they were going to call him Zechariah after his father, 60 but his mother said in reply, "No. He will be called John." 61 But they answered her, "There is no one among your relatives who has this name." 62 So they made signs, asking his father what he wished him to be called. 63 He asked for a tablet and wrote, "John is his name," and all were amazed. 64 Immediately his mouth was opened, his tongue freed, and he spoke blessing God. 65 Then fear came upon all their neighbors, and all these matters were discussed throughout the hill country of Judea. 66 All who heard these things took them to heart, saying, "What, then, will this child be?" For surely the hand of the Lord was with him.

Wednesday December 24, 2025

First Reading: 2 Samuel 7:1-5,8B-12, 14A, 16

1 When King David was settled in his palace, and the LORD had given him rest from his enemies on every side, 2 he said to Nathan the prophet, "Here I am living in a house of cedar, while the ark of God dwells in a tent!" 3 Nathan answered the king, "Go, do whatever you have in mind, for the LORD is with you." 4 But that night the LORD spoke to Nathan and said: 5 "Go, tell my servant David, 'Thus says the LORD: Should you build me a house to dwell in?

8B "'It was I who took you from the pasture and from the care of the flock to be commander of my people Israel. 9 I have been with you wherever you went, and I have destroyed all your enemies before you. And I will make you famous like the great ones of the earth. 10 I will fix a place for my people Israel; I will plant them so that they may dwell in their place without further disturbance. Neither shall the wicked continue to afflict them as they did of old, 11 since the time I first appointed judges over my people Israel. I will give you rest from all your enemies. The LORD also reveals to you that he will establish a house for you. 12 And when your time comes and you rest with your ancestors, I will raise up your heir after you, sprung from your loins, and I will make his Kingdom firm. 14A I will be a father to him, and he shall be a son to me. 16 Your house and your Kingdom shall endure forever before me; your throne shall stand firm forever.'"

Responsorial Psalm: Psalms 89:2-3, 4-5, 27 AND 29

R. (2) *For ever I will sing the goodness of the Lord.*
2 The favors of the LORD I will sing forever;
　　through all generations my mouth shall
　　　　proclaim your faithfulness.
3 For you have said, "My kindness is
　　established forever";
　　in heaven you have confirmed your
　　　　faithfulness.
R. *For ever I will sing the goodness of the Lord.*
4 "I have made a covenant with my chosen
　　one,

I have sworn to David my servant:
⁵ Forever will I confirm your posterity
and establish your throne for all generations."
R. For ever I will sing the goodness of the Lord.
²⁷ "He shall say of me, 'You are my father,
my God, the rock, my savior.'
²⁹ Forever I will maintain my kindness toward him,
and my covenant with him stands firm."
R. For ever I will sing the goodness of the Lord.

Alleluia
R. Alleluia, alleluia.
O Radiant Dawn,
splendor of eternal light, sun of justice:
come and shine on those who dwell in
darkness and in the shadow of death.
R. Alleluia, alleluia.

Gospel: Luke 1:67-79
⁶⁷ Zechariah his father, filled with the Holy Spirit, prophesied, saying:

⁶⁸ "Blessed be the Lord, the God of Israel;
for he has come to his people and set them free.
⁶⁹ He has raised up for us a mighty Savior,
born of the house of his servant David.
⁷⁰ Through his prophets he promised of old
⁷¹ that he would save us from our enemies,
from the hands of all who hate us.
⁷² He promised to show mercy to our fathers
and to remember his holy covenant.
⁷³ This was the oath he swore to our father Abraham:
⁷⁴ to set us free from the hand of our enemies,
free to worship him without fear,
⁷⁵ holy and righteous in his sight
all the days of our life.
⁷⁶ You, my child, shall be called the prophet of the Most High,
for you will go before the Lord to prepare his way,

⁷⁷ to give his people knowledge of salvation
    by the forgiveness of their sins.
⁷⁸ In the tender compassion of our God
    the dawn from on high shall break upon us,
⁷⁹ to shine on those who dwell in darkness
    and the shadow of death,
and to guide our feet into the way of peace."

Wednesday December 24, 2025
The Nativity of the Lord – Vigil Mass

First Reading: Isaiah 62:1-5

¹ For Zion's sake I will not be silent,
    for Jerusalem's sake I will not be quiet,
until her vindication shines forth like the dawn
    and her victory like a burning torch.

² Nations shall behold your vindication,
    and all the kings your glory;
you shall be called by a new name
    pronounced by the mouth of the LORD.
³ You shall be a glorious crown in the hand of the LORD,
    a royal diadem held by your God.
⁴ No more shall people call you "Forsaken,"
    or your land "Desolate,"
but you shall be called "My Delight,"
    and your land "Espoused."
For the LORD delights in you
    and makes your land his spouse.
⁵ As a young man marries a virgin,
    your Builder shall marry you;
and as a bridegroom rejoices in his bride
    so shall your God rejoice in you.

Responsorial Psalm: Psalms 89:4-5, 16-17, 27, 29

R. *(2a)* **For ever I will sing the goodness of the Lord.**

⁴ I have made a covenant with my chosen one,
    I have sworn to David my servant:
⁵ Forever will I confirm your posterity
    and establish your throne for all generations.

R. For ever I will sing the goodness of the Lord.

¹⁶ Blessed the people who know the joyful
>   shout;
>   in the light of your countenance, O LORD,
>   they walk.

¹⁷ At your name they rejoice all the day,
>   and through your justice they are exalted.

R. For ever I will sing the goodness of the Lord.

²⁷ He shall say of me, "You are my father,
>   my God, the rock, my savior."

²⁹ Forever I will maintain my kindness toward
>   him,
>   and my covenant with him stands firm.

R. For ever I will sing the goodness of the Lord.

Second Reading: Acts 13:16-17, 22-25

¹⁶ When Paul reached Antioch in Pisidia and entered the synagogue, he stood up, motioned with his hand, and said, "Fellow Israelites and you others who are God-fearing, listen. ¹⁷ The God of this people Israel chose our ancestors and exalted the people during their sojourn in the land of Egypt. With uplifted arm he led them out of it. ²² Then he removed Saul and raised up David as king; of him he testified, 'I have found David, son of Jesse, a man after my own heart; he will carry out my every wish.' ²³ From this man's descendants God, according to his promise, has brought to Israel a savior, Jesus. ²⁴ John heralded his coming by proclaiming a baptism of repentance to all the people of Israel; ²⁵ and as John was completing his course, he would say, 'What do you suppose that I am? I am not he. Behold, one is coming after me; I am not worthy to unfasten the sandals of his feet.'"

Alleluia

R. Alleluia, alleluia.
Tomorrow the wickedness of the earth will
>   be destroyed:
the Savior of the world will reign over us.
R. Alleluia, alleluia.

Gospel: Matthew 1:1-25

¹ The book of the genealogy of Jesus Christ, the son of David, the son of Abraham.
² Abraham became the father of Isaac, Isaac the father of Jacob, Jacob the father of Judah and his brothers. ³ Judah became the father of Perez and Zerah, whose mother was Tamar. Perez became the father of Hezron, Hezron the father of Ram, ⁴ Ram the father of Amminadab. Amminadab became the father of Nahshon, Nahshon the father of Salmon, ⁵ Salmon the father of Boaz, whose mother was Rahab. Boaz became the father of Obed, whose mother was Ruth. Obed became the father of Jesse, ⁶ Jesse the father of David the king.

David became the father of Solomon, whose mother had been the wife of Uriah. [7] Solomon became the father of Rehoboam, Rehoboam the father of Abijah, Abijah the father of Asaph. [8] Asaph became the father of Jehoshaphat, Jehoshaphat the father of Joram, Joram the father of Uzziah. [9] Uzziah became the father of Jotham, Jotham the father of Ahaz, Ahaz the father of Hezekiah. [10] Hezekiah became the father of Manasseh, Manasseh the father of Amos, Amos the father of Josiah. [11] Josiah became the father of Jechoniah and his brothers at the time of the Babylonian exile.

[12] After the Babylonian exile, Jechoniah became the father of Shealtiel, Shealtiel the father of Zerubbabel, [13] Zerubbabel the father of Abiud. Abiud became the father of Eliakim, Eliakim the father of Azor, [14] Azor the father of Zadok. Zadok became the father of Achim, Achim the father of Eliud, [15] Eliud the father of Eleazar. Eleazar became the father of Matthan, Matthan the father of Jacob, [16] Jacob the father of Joseph, the husband of Mary. Of her was born Jesus who is called the Christ.

[17] Thus the total number of generations from Abraham to David is fourteen generations; from David to the Babylonian exile, fourteen generations; from the Babylonian exile to the Christ, fourteen generations.

[18] Now this is how the birth of Jesus Christ came about. When his mother Mary was betrothed to Joseph, but before they lived together, she was found with child through the Holy Spirit. [19] Joseph her husband, since he was a righteous man, yet unwilling to expose her to shame, decided to divorce her quietly. [20] Such was his intention when, behold, the angel of the Lord appeared to him in a dream and said, "Joseph, son of David, do not be afraid to take Mary your wife into your home. For it is through the Holy Spirit that this child has been conceived in her. [21] She will bear a son and you are to name him Jesus, because he will save his people from their sins." [22] All this took place to fulfill what the Lord had said through the prophet:

[23] *Behold, the virgin shall conceive and bear*
    a son,
and they shall name him Emmanuel,

which means "God is with us." [24] When Joseph awoke, he did as the angel of the Lord had commanded him and took his wife into his home. [25] He had no relations with her until she bore a son, and he named him Jesus.

Or Matthew 1:18-25

[18] Now this is how the birth of Jesus Christ came about. When his mother Mary was betrothed to Joseph, but before they lived together, she was found with child through the Holy Spirit. [19] Joseph her husband, since he was a righteous man, yet unwilling to expose her to shame, decided to divorce her quietly. [20] Such was his intention when, behold, the angel of the Lord appeared to him in a dream and said, "Joseph, son of David, do not be afraid to take Mary your wife into your home. For it is through the Holy Spirit that this child has been conceived in her. [21] She will bear a son and you are to name him Jesus, because he will save his people from their sins." [22] All this took place to fulfill what the Lord had said through the prophet:

²³ *Behold, the virgin shall conceive and bear*
a son,
and they shall name him Emmanuel,

which means "God is with us." ²⁴ When Joseph awoke, he did as the angel of the Lord had commanded him and took his wife into his home. ²⁵ He had no relations with her until she bore a son, and he named him Jesus.

Wednesday December 24, 2025
The Nativity of the Lord – Mid Night Vigil Mass

First Reading: Isaiah 9:1-6
¹ The people who walked in darkness
   have seen a great light;
upon those who dwelt in the land of gloom
   a light has shone.
² You have brought them abundant joy
   and great rejoicing,
as they rejoice before you as at the harvest,
   as people make merry when dividing
      spoils.
³ For the yoke that burdened them,
   the pole on their shoulder,
and the rod of their taskmaster
   you have smashed, as on the day of
      Midian.
⁴ For every boot that tramped in battle,
   every cloak rolled in blood,
   will be burned as fuel for flames.
⁵ For a child is born to us, a son is given us;
   upon his shoulder dominion rests.
They name him Wonder-Counselor, God-
      Hero,
   Father-Forever, Prince of Peace.
⁶ His dominion is vast
   and forever peaceful,
from David's throne, and over his kingdom,
   which he confirms and sustains
by judgment and justice,
   both now and forever.
The zeal of the LORD of hosts will do this!

Responsorial Psalm: Psalms 96: 1-2, 2-3, 11-12, 13
R. *(Luke 2:11)* **Today is born our Savior, Christ the Lord.**
¹ Sing to the LORD a new song;
   sing to the LORD, all you lands.

²ᴬ Sing to the LORD; bless his name.
R. Today is born our Savior, Christ the Lord.
²ᴮ Announce his salvation, day after day.
> ³ Tell his glory among the nations;
> among all peoples, his wondrous deeds.

R. Today is born our Savior, Christ the Lord.
¹¹ Let the heavens be glad and the earth
> rejoice;
> let the sea and what fills it resound;
> ¹² let the plains be joyful and all that is in them!

Then shall all the trees of the forest exult.
R. Today is born our Savior, Christ the Lord.
¹³ They shall exult before the LORD, for he
> comes;
> for he comes to rule the earth.

He shall rule the world with justice
> and the peoples with his constancy.

R. Today is born our Savior, Christ the Lord.

Second Reading: Titus 2:11-14
Beloved: ¹¹ The grace of God has appeared, saving all ¹² and training us to reject godless ways and worldly desires and to live temperately, justly, and devoutly in this age, ¹³ as we await the blessed hope, the appearance of the glory of our great God and savior Jesus Christ, ¹⁴ who gave himself for us to deliver us from all lawlessness and to cleanse for himself a people as his own, eager to do what is good.

Alleluia: Luke 2:10-11
R. Alleluia, alleluia.
¹⁰ I proclaim to you good news of great joy:
¹¹ today a Savior is born for us,
Christ the Lord.
R. Alleluia, alleluia.

Gospel: Luke 2:1-14
¹ In those days a decree went out from Caesar Augustus that the whole world should be enrolled. ² This was the first enrollment, when Quirinius was governor of Syria. ³ So all went to be enrolled, each to his own town. ⁴ And Joseph too went up from Galilee from the town of Nazareth to Judea, to the city of David that is called Bethlehem, because he was of the house and family of David, ⁵ to be enrolled with Mary, his betrothed, who was with child. ⁶ While they were there, the time came for her to have her child, ⁷ and she gave birth to her firstborn son. She wrapped him in swaddling clothes and laid him in a manger, because there was no room for them in the inn.

⁸ Now there were shepherds in that region living in the fields and keeping the night watch over their flock. ⁹ The angel of the Lord appeared to them and the glory of the Lord shone around them, and they were struck with great fear. ¹⁰ The angel said to them, "Do not be afraid; for behold, I proclaim to you good news of great joy that will be for all the people. ¹¹For today in the city of David a savior has been born for you who is Christ and Lord. ¹² And this will be a sign for you: you will find an infant wrapped in swaddling clothes and lying in a manger." ¹³ And suddenly there was a multitude of the heavenly host with the angel, praising God and saying:

¹⁴ "Glory to God in the highest
    and on earth peace to those on whom his
        favor rests."

Thursday December 25, 2025
The Nativity of the Lord – Mass at Dawn

First Reading: Isaiah 62:11-12

¹¹ See, the LORD proclaims
    to the ends of the earth:
say to daughter Zion,
    your savior comes!
Here is his reward with him,
    his recompense before him.
    ¹² They shall be called the holy people,
    the redeemed of the LORD,
and you shall be called "Frequented,"
    a city that is not forsaken.

Responsorial Psalm: Psalms 97:1, 6, 11-12

R. *A light will shine on us this day: the Lord is born for us.*

¹ The LORD is king; let the earth rejoice;
    let the many isles be glad.
⁶ The heavens proclaim his justice,
    and all peoples see his glory.

R. *A light will shine on us this day: the Lord is born for us.*

¹¹ Light dawns for the just;
    and gladness, for the upright of heart.
¹² Be glad in the LORD, you just,
    and give thanks to his holy name.

R. *A light will shine on us this day: the Lord is born for us.*

Second Reading: Titus 3:4-7

Beloved: [4] When the kindness and generous love of God our savior appeared, [5] not because of any righteous deeds we had done but because of his mercy, He saved us through the bath of rebirth and renewal by the Holy Spirit, [6] whom he richly poured out on us through Jesus Christ our savior, [7] so that we might be justified by his grace and become heirs in hope of eternal life.

Alleluia: Luke 2:14

R. Alleluia, alleluia.
[14] Glory to God in the highest,
and on earth peace to those
on whom his favor rests.
R. Alleluia, alleluia.

Gospel: Luke 2:15-20

[15] When the angels went away from them to heaven, the shepherds said to one another, "Let us go, then, to Bethlehem to see this thing that has taken place, which the Lord has made known to us." [16] So they went in haste and found Mary and Joseph, and the infant lying in the manger. [17] When they saw this, they made known the message that had been told them about this child. [18] All who heard it were amazed by what had been told them by the shepherds. [19] And Mary kept all these things, reflecting on them in her heart. [20] Then the shepherds returned, glorifying and praising God for all they had heard and seen, just as it had been told to them.

Thursday December 25, 2025
The Nativity of the Lord – Mass During the Day

First Reading: Isaiah 52:7-10

[7] How beautiful upon the mountains
    are the feet of him who brings glad
        tidings,
announcing peace, bearing good news,
    announcing salvation, and saying to Zion,
    "Your God is King!"

[8] Hark! Your sentinels raise a cry,
    together they shout for joy,
for they see directly, before their eyes,
    the LORD restoring Zion.
[9] Break out together in song,
    O ruins of Jerusalem!
For the LORD comforts his people,
    he redeems Jerusalem.
[10] The LORD has bared his holy arm
    in the sight of all the nations;
all the ends of the earth will behold

the salvation of our God.

Responsorial Psalm: Psalms 98:1,2-3, 3-4,5-6
R. *(3c)* ***All the ends of the earth have seen the saving power of God.***
¹ Sing to the LORD a new song,
    for he has done wondrous deeds;
his right hand has won victory for him,
    his holy arm.
R. All the ends of the earth have seen the saving power of God.
² The LORD has made his salvation known:
    in the sight of the nations he has revealed
        his justice.
³ He has remembered his kindness and his
        faithfulness
    toward the house of Israel.
R. All the ends of the earth have seen the saving power of God.
³ All the ends of the earth have seen
    the salvation by our God.
⁴ Sing joyfully to the LORD, all you lands;
    break into song; sing praise.
R. All the ends of the earth have seen the saving power of God.
⁵ Sing praise to the LORD with the harp,
    with the harp and melodious song.
⁶ With trumpets and the sound of the horn
    sing joyfully before the King, the LORD.
R. All the ends of the earth have seen the saving power of God.

Second Reading: Hebrews 1:1-6
Brothers and sisters: ¹ In times past, God spoke in partial and various ways to our ancestors through the prophets; ² in these last days, he has spoken to us through the Son, whom he made heir of all things and through whom he created the universe,

³ who is the refulgence of his glory,
    the very imprint of his being,
    and who sustains all things by his mighty
        word.
When he had accomplished purification
        from sins,
    he took his seat at the right hand of the

> Majesty on high,
> ⁴ as far superior to the angels
> as the name he has inherited is more
> excellent than theirs.

⁵ For to which of the angels did God ever say:

*You are my son; this day I have begotten
you*?
Or again:

*I will be a father to him, and he shall be a
son to me*?

⁶ And again, when he leads the firstborn into the world, he says:

Let all the angels of God worship him.

Alleluia
R. Alleluia, alleluia.
A holy day has dawned upon us.
Come, you nations, and adore the Lord.
For today a great light has come upon the
earth.
R. Alleluia, alleluia.

Gospel: John 1:1-18
¹ In the beginning was the Word,
and the Word was with God,
and the Word was God.
² He was in the beginning with God.
³ All things came to be through him,
and without him nothing came to be.
What came to be ⁴ through him was life,
and this life was the light of the
human race;
⁵ the light shines in the darkness,
and the darkness has not overcome
it.

⁶ A man named John was sent from God. ⁷ He came for testimony, to testify to the light, so that all might believe through him. ⁸ He was not the light, but came to testify to the light. ⁹ The true light, which enlightens everyone, was coming into the world.

¹⁰ He was in the world,
> and the world came to be through him,
> but the world did not know him.

¹¹ He came to what was his own,
> but his own people did not accept him.

¹² But to those who did accept him he gave power to become children of God, to those who believe in his name, ¹³ who were born not by natural generation nor by human choice nor by a man's decision but of God.

¹⁴ And the Word became flesh
> and made his dwelling among us,
> and we saw his glory,
> the glory as of the Father's only Son,
> full of grace and truth.

¹⁵ John testified to him and cried out, saying, "This was he of whom I said, 'The one who is coming after me ranks ahead of me because he existed before me.'" ¹⁶ From his fullness we have all received, grace in place of grace, ¹⁷ because while the law was given through Moses, grace and truth came through Jesus Christ. ¹⁸ No one has ever seen God. The only Son, God, who is at the Father's side, has revealed him.

Or John 1:1-5, 9-14

¹ In the beginning was the Word,
> and the Word was with God,
> and the Word was God.

² He was in the beginning with God.

³ All things came to be through him,
> and without him nothing came to be.

What came to be ⁴ through him was life,
> and this life was the light of the human race;

⁵ the light shines in the darkness,
> and the darkness has not overcome it.

⁹ The true light, which enlightens everyone,
> was coming into the world.

¹⁰ He was in the world,
> and the world came to be through him,
> but the world did not know him.

¹¹ He came to what was his own,
>   but his own people did not accept him.

¹² But to those who did accept him he gave power to become children of God, to those who believe in his name, ¹³ who were born not by natural generation nor by human choice nor by a man's decision but of God.

¹⁴ And the Word became flesh
>   and made his dwelling among us,
>   and we saw his glory,
>   the glory as of the Father's only Son,
>   full of grace and truth.

Friday December 26, 2025
Feast of Saint Stephen, First Martyr

First Reading: Acts 6:8-10; 7:54-59

⁸ Stephen, filled with grace and power, was working great wonders and signs among the people. ⁹ Certain members of the so-called Synagogue of Freedmen, Cyrenians, and Alexandrians, and people from Cilicia and Asia, came forward and debated with Stephen, ¹⁰ but they could not withstand the wisdom and the spirit with which he spoke.

⁵⁴ When they heard this, they were infuriated, and they ground their teeth at him. ⁵⁵ But he, filled with the Holy Spirit, looked up intently to heaven and saw the glory of God and Jesus standing at the right hand of God, ⁵⁶ and he said, "Behold, I see the heavens opened and the Son of Man standing at the right hand of God." ⁵⁷ But they cried out in a loud voice, covered their ears, and rushed upon him together. ⁵⁸ They threw him out of the city, and began to stone him. The witnesses laid down their cloaks at the feet of a young man named Saul. ⁵⁹ As they were stoning Stephen, he called out, "Lord Jesus, receive my spirit."

Responsorial Psalm: Psalms 31:3CD-4, 6 AND 8AB, 16BC AND 17

R. ⁽⁶⁾ *Into your hands, O Lord, I commend my spirit.*

³ᶜᴰ Be my rock of refuge,
>   a stronghold to give me safety.
⁴ You are my rock and my fortress;
>   for your name's sake you will lead and guide me.

R. *Into your hands, O Lord, I commend my spirit.*

⁶ Into your hands I commend my spirit;
>   you will redeem me, O LORD, O faithful God.
⁸ᴬᴮ I will rejoice and be glad because of your mercy.

R. *Into your hands, O Lord, I commend my spirit.*

¹⁶ᴮᶜ Rescue me from the clutches of my enemies
>   and my persecutors.

[17] Let your face shine upon your servant;
> save me in your kindness.

R. Into your hands, O Lord, I commend my spirit.

Alleluia: Psalms 118:26A, 27A
R. Alleluia, alleluia.
[26A] Blessed is he who comes in the name of the LORD;
[27A] the LORD is God and has given us light.
R. Alleluia, alleluia.

Gospel: Matthew 10:17-22
Jesus said to his disciples: [17] "Beware of men, for they will hand you over to courts and scourge you in their synagogues, [18] and you will be led before governors and kings for my sake as a witness before them and the pagans. [19] When they hand you over, do not worry about how you are to speak or what you are to say. You will be given at that moment what you are to say. [20] For it will not be you who speak but the Spirit of your Father speaking through you. [21] Brother will hand over brother to death, and the father his child; children will rise up against parents and have them put to death. [22] You will be hated by all because of my name, but whoever endures to the end will be saved."

Saturday December 27, 2025
Feast of Saint John, Apostle and Evangelist
First Reading: 1 John 1:1-4
Beloved:

[1] What was from the beginning,
> what we have heard,
> what we have seen with our eyes,
> what we looked upon
> and touched with our hands
> concerns the Word of life —
[2] for the life was made visible;
> we have seen it and testify to it
> and proclaim to you the eternal life
> that was with the Father and was made
>> visible to us —
[3] what we have seen and heard
> we proclaim now to you,
> so that you too may have fellowship with
>> us;
> for our fellowship is with the Father
> and with his Son, Jesus Christ.

[4] We are writing this so that our joy may be complete.

Responsorial Psalm: Psalms 97:1-2,5-6,11-12
R. *(12) Rejoice in the Lord, you just!*
¹ The LORD is king; let the earth rejoice;
    let the many isles be glad.
² Clouds and darkness are around him,
    justice and judgment are the foundation
        of his throne.
R. Rejoice in the Lord, you just!
⁵ The mountains melt like wax before the
    LORD,
    before the LORD of all the earth.
⁶ The heavens proclaim his justice,
    and all peoples see his glory.
R. Rejoice in the Lord, you just!
¹¹ Light dawns for the just;
    and gladness, for the upright of heart.
¹² Be glad in the LORD, you just,
    and give thanks to his holy name.
R. Rejoice in the Lord, you just!

Alleluia: *Te Deum*
R. Alleluia, alleluia.
We praise you, O God,
we acclaim you as Lord;
the glorious company of Apostles praise you.
R. Alleluia, alleluia.

Gospel: John 20:1A AND 2-8
¹ᴬ On the first day of the week, ² Mary Magdalene ran and went to Simon Peter and to the other disciple whom Jesus loved, and told them, "They have taken the Lord from the tomb, and we do not know where they put him." ³ So Peter and the other disciple went out and came to the tomb. ⁴ They both ran, but the other disciple ran faster than Peter and arrived at the tomb first; ⁵ he bent down and saw the burial cloths there, but did not go in. ⁶ When Simon Peter arrived after him, he went into the tomb and saw the burial cloths there, ⁷ and the cloth that had covered his head, not with the burial cloths but rolled up in a separate place. ⁸ Then the other disciple also went in, the one who had arrived at the tomb first, and he saw and believed.

Sunday December 28, 2025
Feast of the Holy Family of Jesus, Mary and Joseph
First Reading: Sirach 3:2-6, 12-14
² God sets a father in honor over his
    children;
    a mother's authority he confirms

over her sons.
³ Whoever honors his father atones for
sins,
and preserves himself from them.
When he prays, he is heard;
⁴ he stores up riches who reveres his
mother.
⁵ Whoever honors his father is gladdened
by children,
and, when he prays, is heard.
⁶ Whoever reveres his father will live a
long life;
he who obeys his father brings
comfort to his mother.

¹² My son, take care of your father when
he is old;
grieve him not as long as he lives.
¹³ Even if his mind fail, be considerate of
him;
revile him not all the days of his life;
¹⁴ kindness to a father will not be
forgotten,
firmly planted against the debt of
your sins
—a house raised in justice to you.

Responsorial Psalm: Psalms 128:1-2, 3, 4-5.
R. ^(cf. 1) ***Blessed are those who fear the Lord and walk in his ways.***
¹ Blessed is everyone who fears the LORD,
who walks in his ways!
² For you shall eat the fruit of your handiwork;
blessed shall you be, and favored.
R. Blessed are those who fear the Lord and walk in his ways.
³ Your wife shall be like a fruitful vine
in the recesses of your home;
your children like olive plants
around your table.
R. Blessed are those who fear the Lord and walk in his ways.
⁴ Behold, thus is the man blessed
who fears the LORD.
⁵ The LORD bless you from Zion:

may you see the prosperity of Jerusalem
all the days of your life.
R. Blessed are those who fear the Lord and walk in his ways.

Second Reading: Colossians 3:12-21
Brothers and sisters: ¹² Put on, as God's chosen ones, holy and beloved, heartfelt compassion, kindness, humility, gentleness, and patience, ¹³ bearing with one another and forgiving one another, if one has a grievance against another; as the Lord has forgiven you, so must you also do. ¹⁴ And over all these put on love, that is, the bond of perfection. ¹⁵ And let the peace of Christ control your hearts, the peace into which you were also called in one body. And be thankful. ¹⁶ Let the word of Christ dwell in you richly, as in all wisdom you teach and admonish one another, singing psalms, hymns, and spiritual songs with gratitude in your hearts to God. ¹⁷ And whatever you do, in word or in deed, do everything in the name of the Lord Jesus, giving thanks to God the Father through him.

¹⁸ Wives, be subordinate to your husbands, as is proper in the Lord. ¹⁹ Husbands, love your wives, and avoid any bitterness toward them. ²⁰ Children, obey your parents in everything, for this is pleasing to the Lord. ²¹ Fathers, do not provoke your children, so they may not become discouraged.

Or Colossians 3:12-17
Brothers and sisters: ¹² Put on, as God's chosen ones, holy and beloved, heartfelt compassion, kindness, humility, gentleness, and patience, ¹³ bearing with one another and forgiving one another, if one has a grievance against another; as the Lord has forgiven you, so must you also do. ¹⁴ And over all these put on love, that is, the bond of perfection. ¹⁵ And let the peace of Christ control your hearts, the peace into which you were also called in one body. And be thankful. ¹⁶ Let the word of Christ dwell in you richly, as in all wisdom you teach and admonish one another, singing psalms, hymns, and spiritual songs with gratitude in your hearts to God. ¹⁷ And whatever you do, in word or in deed, do everything in the name of the Lord Jesus, giving thanks to God the Father through him.

Alleluia: Colossians 3:15A, 16A
R. Alleluia, alleluia.
¹⁵ᴬ Let the peace of Christ control your hearts;
¹⁶ᴬ let the word of Christ dwell in you richly.
R. Alleluia, alleluia.

Gospel: Matthew 2:13-15; 19-23
¹³When the magi had departed, behold, the angel of the Lord appeared to Joseph in a dream and said, "Rise, take the child and his mother, flee to Egypt, and stay there until I tell you. Herod is going to search for the child to destroy him." ¹⁴ Joseph rose and took the child and his mother by night and departed for Egypt. ¹⁵ He stayed there until the death of Herod, that what the Lord had said through the prophet might be fulfilled, *Out of Egypt I called my son.*

[19] When Herod had died, behold, the angel of the Lord appeared in a dream to Joseph in Egypt [20] and said, "Rise, take the child and his mother and go to the land of Israel, for those who sought the child's life are dead." [21] He rose, took the child and his mother, and went to the land of Israel. [22] But when he heard that Archelaus was ruling over Judea in place of his father Herod, he was afraid to go back there. And because he had been warned in a dream, he departed for the region of Galilee. [23] He went and dwelt in a town called Nazareth, so that what had been spoken through the prophets might be fulfilled, *He shall be called a Nazorean.*

Monday December 29, 2025
Fifth Day in the Octave of Christmas

First Reading: 1 John 2:3-11

Beloved: [3] The way we may be sure that we know Jesus is to keep his commandments. [4] Whoever says, "I know him," but does not keep his commandments is a liar, and the truth is not in him. [5] But whoever keeps his word, the love of God is truly perfected in him. This is the way we may know that we are in union with him: [6] whoever claims to abide in him ought to walk just as he walked.

[7] Beloved, I am writing no new commandment to you but an old commandment that you had from the beginning. The old commandment is the word that you have heard. [8] And yet I do write a new commandment to you, which holds true in him and among you, for the darkness is passing away, and the true light is already shining. [9] Whoever says he is in the light, yet hates his brother, is still in the darkness. [10] Whoever loves his brother remains in the light, and there is nothing in him to cause a fall. [11] Whoever hates his brother is in darkness; he walks in darkness and does not know where he is going because the darkness has blinded his eyes.

Responsorial Psalm: Psalms 96:1-2A, 2B-3, 5B-6

R. (11a) Let the heavens be glad and the earth rejoice!
[1] Sing to the LORD a new song;
　　sing to the LORD, all you lands.
[2A] Sing to the LORD; bless his name.
R. Let the heavens be glad and the earth rejoice!
[2B] Announce his salvation, day after day.
[3] Tell his glory among the nations;
　　among all peoples, his wondrous deeds.
R. Let the heavens be glad and the earth rejoice!
[5B] The LORD made the heavens.
[6] Splendor and majesty go before him;
　　praise and grandeur are in his sanctuary.
R. Let the heavens be glad and the earth rejoice!

Alleluia: Luke 2:32

R. Alleluia, alleluia.
[32] A light of revelation to the Gentiles
and glory for your people Israel.

R. Alleluia, alleluia.

Gospel: Luke 2:22-35

22 When the days were completed for their purification according to the law of Moses, They took him up to Jerusalem to present him to the Lord, 23 just as it is written in the law of the Lord, *Every male that opens the womb shall be consecrated to the Lord,* 24 and to offer the sacrifice of *a pair of turtledoves or two young pigeons,* in accordance with the dictate in the law of the Lord.

25 Now there was a man in Jerusalem whose name was Simeon. This man was righteous and devout, awaiting the consolation of Israel, and the Holy Spirit was upon him. 26 It had been revealed to him by the Holy Spirit that he should not see death before he had seen the Christ of the Lord. 27 He came in the Spirit into the temple; and when the parents brought in the child Jesus to perform the custom of the law in regard to him, 28 he took him into his arms and blessed God, saying:

29 "Lord, now let your servant go in peace;
   your word has been fulfilled:
30 my own eyes have seen the salvation
   31 which you prepared in the sight of every people,
32 a light to reveal you to the nations
   and the glory of your people Israel."

33 The child's father and mother were amazed at what was said about him; 34 and Simeon blessed them and said to Mary his mother, "Behold, this child is destined for the fall and rise of many in Israel, and to be a sign that will be contradicted (35 and you yourself a sword will pierce) so that the thoughts of many hearts may be revealed."

Tuesday December 30, 2025
Sixth Day in the Octave of Christmas

First Reading: 1 John 2:12-17

12 I am writing to you, children, because your sins have been forgiven for his name's sake.

13 I am writing to you, fathers, because you know him who is from the beginning.

I am writing to you, young men, because you have conquered the Evil One.

14 I write to you, children, because you know the Father.

I write to you, fathers, because you know him who is from the beginning.

I write to you, young men, because you are strong and the word of God remains in you, and you have conquered the Evil One.

15 Do not love the world or the things of the world. If anyone loves the world, the love of the Father is not in him. 16 For all that is in the world, sensual lust, enticement for the eyes, and a pretentious life, is not from the Father but is from the world. 17 Yet the world and its enticement are passing away. But whoever does the will of God remains forever.

Responsorial Psalm: Psalms 96:7-8A, 8B-9, 10

R. (11a) *Let the heavens be glad and the earth rejoice!*
7 Give to the LORD, you families of nations,

give to the LORD glory and praise;
⁸ᴬ give to the LORD the glory due his name!
R. Let the heavens be glad and the earth rejoice!
⁸ᴮ Bring gifts, and enter his courts;
⁹ worship the LORD in holy attire.
Tremble before him, all the earth.
R. Let the heavens be glad and the earth rejoice!
¹⁰ Say among the nations: The LORD is king.
He has made the world firm, not to be
   moved;
   he governs the peoples with equity.
R. Let the heavens be glad and the earth rejoice!

Alleluia
R. Alleluia, alleluia.
A holy day has dawned upon us.
Come, you nations, and adore the Lord.
Today a great light has come upon the earth.
R. Alleluia, alleluia.

Gospel: Luke 2:36-40
³⁶ There was a prophetess, Anna, the daughter of Phanuel, of the tribe of Asher. She was advanced in years, having lived seven years with her husband after her marriage, ³⁷ and then as a widow until she was eighty-four. She never left the temple, but worshiped night and day with fasting and prayer. ³⁸ And coming forward at that very time, she gave thanks to God and spoke about the child to all who were awaiting the redemption of Jerusalem. ³⁹ When they had fulfilled all the prescriptions of the law of the Lord, they returned to Galilee, to their own town of Nazareth. ⁴⁰ The child grew and became strong, filled with wisdom; and the favor of God was upon him.

Wednesday December 31, 2025
The Seventh Day in the Octave of Christmas
First Reading: 1 John 2:18-21
¹⁸ Children, it is the last hour; and just as you heard that the antichrist was coming, so now many antichrists have appeared. Thus we know this is the last hour. ¹⁹ They went out from us, but they were not really of our number; if they had been, they would have remained with us. Their desertion shows that none of them was of our number. ²⁰ But you have the anointing that comes from the Holy One, and you all have knowledge. ²¹ I write to you not because you do not know the truth but because you do, and because every lie is alien to the truth.

Responsorial Psalm: Psalms 96:1-2,11-12,13
R. ⁽¹¹ᵃ⁾ Let the heavens be glad and the earth rejoice!
¹ Sing to the LORD a new song;

sing to the LORD, all you lands.
² Sing to the LORD; bless his name;
> announce his salvation, day after day.

R. Let the heavens be glad and the earth rejoice!

¹¹ Let the heavens be glad and the earth rejoice;
> let the sea and what fills it resound;
>> ¹² let the plains be joyful and all that is in them!

Then shall all the trees of the forest exult
> before the LORD.

R. Let the heavens be glad and the earth rejoice!

¹³ The LORD comes,
> he comes to rule the earth.

He shall rule the world with justice
> and the peoples with his constancy.

R. Let the heavens be glad and the earth rejoice!

Alleluia: John 1:14A, 12A

R. Alleluia, alleluia.

¹⁴ᴬ The Word of God became flesh and dwelt among us.
¹²ᴬ To those who accepted him
he gave power to become the children of God.

R. Alleluia, alleluia.

Gospel: John 1:1-18

¹ In the beginning was the Word,
> and the Word was with God,
> and the Word was God.

² He was in the beginning with God.
³ All things came to be through him,
> and without him nothing came to be.

What came to be ⁴ through him was life,
> and this life was the light of the human race;
>> ⁵ the light shines in the darkness,
>> and the darkness has not overcome it.

⁶ A man named John was sent from God. ⁷ He came for testimony, to testify to the light, so that all might believe through him. ⁸ He was not the light, but came to testify to the light. ⁹ The true light, which enlightens everyone, was coming into the world.

¹⁰ He was in the world,
    and the world came to be through him,
    but the world did not know him.
¹¹ He came to what was his own,
    but his own people did not accept him.

¹² But to those who did accept him he gave power to become children of God, to those who believe in his name, ¹³ who were born not by natural generation nor by human choice nor by a man's decision but of God.

¹⁴ And the Word became flesh
    and made his dwelling among us,
    and we saw his glory,
    the glory as of the Father's only-begotten
        Son,
    full of grace and truth.

¹⁵ John testified to him and cried out, saying, "This was he of whom I said, 'The one who is coming after me ranks ahead of me because he existed before me.'" ¹⁶ From his fullness we have all received, grace in place of grace, ¹⁷because while the law was given through Moses, grace and truth came through Jesus Christ. ¹⁸ No one has ever seen God. The only-begotten Son, God, who is at the Father's side, has revealed him.

For comments, suggestions, support, requests, and other pieces of information that might make our publication serve its audience better, kindly contact the director of Catholic Lectionary Publishers through email: okoraforinnocent977@gmail.com.

Made in the USA
Columbia, SC
12 June 2025